Praise for  ire

"Eric Bergerud has res‑ ‑‑ ‑‑‑ campaign to its rightful place of in‑
—Kennith Haga‑ ‑ *New York Times Book Review*

"Grippingly told . . . shows vividly the effect of war on the human spirit."
—*The Cleveland Plain Dealer*

"Quite possibly the most important book written to date on the Pacific War. Bergerud sees beyond the general's war and looks directly at the dynamics that shaped the brutal killing grounds of the South Pacific."
—Dominic J. Caraccilo, Department of History, West Point

"One of the best books about WWII, capturing both the powerful if narrow view of the combat soldier and the panoramic vantage point of the military historian."
—*Kirkus Reviews*

"A definitive presentation of the dynamics of jungle war . . . Bergerud makes a major contribution here to our understanding not only of a specific campaign but of the nature of war itself."
—*Publishers Weekly*

"A splendid effort."
—*St. Louis Post-Dispatch*

PENGUIN BOOKS

TOUCHED WITH FIRE

Eric Bergerud is a professor of military and American
history at Lincoln University in San Francisco. He is
the author of two highly regarded works on the Vietnam War, *Red Thunder*, *Tropic Lightning* (available from
Penguin) and *The Dynamics of Defeat*. He lives in Albany,
California.

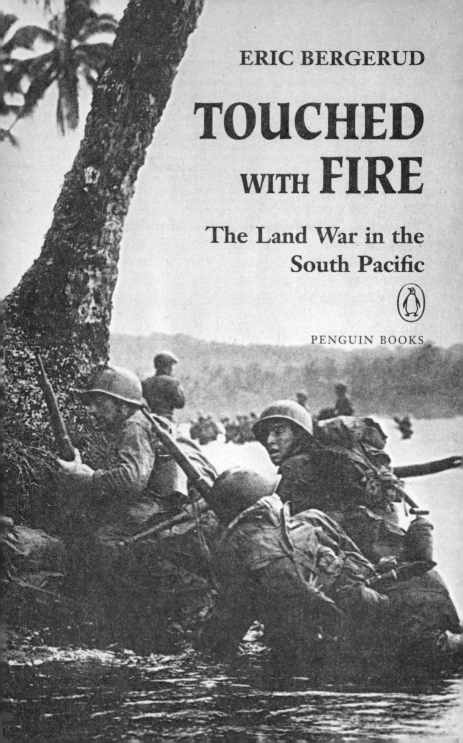

ERIC BERGERUD

TOUCHED
WITH FIRE

The Land War in the
South Pacific

PENGUIN BOOKS

PENGUIN BOOKS

Published by the Penguin Group
Penguin Group (USA) Inc., 375 Hudson Street, New York, New York 10014, U.S.A.
Penguin Group (Canada), 10 Alcorn Avenue, Toronto,
Ontario, Canada M4V 3B2 (a division of Pearson Penguin Canada Inc.)
Penguin Books Ltd, 80 Strand, London WC2R 0RL, England
Penguin Ireland, 25 St Stephen's Green, Dublin 2, Ireland (a division of Penguin Books Ltd)
Penguin Group (Australia), 250 Camberwell Road, Camberwell,
Victoria 3124, Australia (a division of Pearson Australia Group Pty Ltd)
Penguin Books India Pvt Ltd, 11 Community Centre, Panchsheel Park, New Delhi – 110 017, India
Penguin Group (NZ), cnr Airborne and Rosedale Roads, Albany,
Auckland 1310, New Zealand (a division of Pearson New Zealand Ltd)
Penguin Books (South Africa) (Pty) Ltd, 24 Sturdee Avenue,
Rosebank, Johannesburg 2196, South Africa

Penguin Books Ltd, Registered Offices: 80 Strand, London WC2R 0RL, England

First published in the United States of America by Viking Penguin,
a division of Penguin Books USA Inc. 1996
Published in Penguin Books 1997

10

Copyright © Eric Bergerud, 1996
All rights reserved

Maps by the author

Photograph on pages iv–v: During a rainstorm American troops
land on Rendova, a small island a few hundred yards
from New Georgia. (*National Archives*)

THE LIBRARY OF CONGRESS HAS CATALOGUED THE HARDCOVER AS FOLLOWS:
Bergerud, Eric M.
Touched with fire: the land war in the South
Pacific/Eric M. Bergerud.
p.   cm.
Includes bibliographical references and index.
ISBN 0-670-86158-8 (hc.)
ISBN 0 14 02.4696 7 (pbk.)
1. World War, 1939–1945—Campaigns—Oceania.
2. Oceania—History, Military.   I. Title.
D767.9.B47   1996
940.54´26—dc20   95–34149

Printed in the United States of America
Set in Janson Text
Designed by Francesca Belanger

To Bonnie and David Lee

We have shared the incommunicable experience of war.
In our youths, our hearts were touched with fire.

OLIVER WENDELL HOLMES
Memorial Day Address, 1884

Preface

This book deals with the long and brutal ground war fought between Japan and the Allies in the South Pacific. The struggle took place on a huge battlefield that included New Guinea, New Britain, and the Solomon Islands. The period I examine begins in the summer of 1942 when both sides, almost simultaneously, started serious military operations in the area. The first move took place on July 21, 1942, when the Japanese landed an elite infantry strike force on the coast of New Guinea and launched an audacious offensive over the rugged Owen Stanley Mountains toward the strategically vital Allied base at Port Moresby. The second move followed on August 7, 1942, when U.S. Marines took a beachhead on Guadalcanal, opening the struggle for the Solomon Islands. Initially, both operations were relatively small. However, together these actions triggered a conflict that quickly grew very large, very important, and very violent. I end my account in early 1944 when the Allies, triumphant in the South Pacific, broke out of the area and accelerated their drive toward the Japanese home islands.

I chose the time (mid-1942 until early 1944) and location (the Solomon Islands and New Guinea, both near Australia) for three reasons. First, because the Japanese wanted to isolate Australia, and the Allies wanted to defend it, the Pacific war was fought almost exclusively in this area for a year and a half after the Battle of Midway in June 1942. This simple fact is rarely appreciated in accounts of the war. Many authors have written in detail about Pearl Harbor, Bataan, and Midway early in the clash, and the bloody island encounters at places such as Saipan, Iwo Jima, and Okinawa later in the conflict.

However, except for the fight on Guadalcanal, only one part of a much larger drama, few outside the narrow field of military history have paid attention to the complex and vital events in New Guinea and the Solomons. Consequently, the general public has largely forgotten a long and crucial portion of the Pacific war.

Second, unlike the concluding year and a half of war when Allied material strength overwhelmed Japan, the two sides in the South Pacific fought much of the time on roughly equal terms. This factor is important because it allows me to illustrate the unique type of war fought by each side before the Allies were able to dictate events completely. Since the combatants began at approximately equal strength, I also can analyze the complex process that led to the unraveling of Japan's ability to wage land war effectively against the Allies. In July 1942 the Japanese Army was invincible. In the fall of 1943 both Australians and Americans ripped it to shreds in every encounter. My book deals with a campaign, not a single battle. The stage is large enough and the time frame long enough to illustrate and analyze the "turning of the tide" in the Pacific war. In itself, this is an interesting, important, and, I believe, poorly understood subject.

Third, the nature of ground combat in the South Pacific was unique in this century. Although the strategic dynamic of the campaign concentrated on seizing and holding air and naval bases, most of the fighting, as is usually the case in war, was done by infantry. The Japanese and Allied armies confronted each other on terrain that was incredibly hostile, primitive, and largely unknown. Because the dense jungle battlefield greatly lessened the tactical effectiveness of modern weapons, the war became a ferocious slugging match between light-infantry armies at extremely close quarters. Furthermore, the radical battle ethos of the Japanese initiated a vicious circle of violence where no mercy was asked or given, creating, in essence, a war of annihilation. It was war at its most basic and its most brutal.

This book is not a standard narrative history. Because the stakes were so high, and Japan's ultimate defeat in the theater so important, specialists in the field have written much about the subject in the past fifty years. Both the U.S. and Australian governments commissioned large, detailed, and very good multivolume official histories of the war. Controversies over the various plans made and policies followed by various leaders punctuated the war itself and have become a part of its historiography. In particular, I think it is safe to say, anything done by General Douglas MacArthur and his staff has become fair game for historical scrutiny.

Because the narrative groundwork has been done, I have not tried to create another account of the war in the South Pacific as viewed by important military commanders. Instead, aided by dozens of original interviews with American and Australian veterans of the conflict, I have tried to examine and explain the war's texture and tempo. War has a grim purpose and is extremely complex. Sophisticated planning and doctrine are present at every level. Yet at the point of fire, battle is the essence of chaos and violence. I have tried to find the point where the coherence of war meets the brutal experience that confronts those who fight it. In other words, rather than treating the struggle as a chess game between rival leaders, I have tried to reconstruct and cast light upon the flow of battle. Strategic matters enter into the story at a number of points, but the core of my book concerns the men who fought the war, the weapons they used, how they viewed events, and the nature of the battlefield where they tended to their forbidding task.

I have employed a topical, rather than chronological, structure in this book. Throughout the text, frequent mention is made of fierce battles in faraway places. Some of the names and places might be familiar to the modern reader. Most probably are not. Consequently, in the introduction I have presented a brief strategic narrative of the struggle in the South Pacific. Enthusiasts of military history will find nothing novel there. However, those new to the subject, I believe, may profit from the context provided. I have also included a brief chronology of important events for quick reference. Once acquainted with the basic course of the campaign, the reader can better see beyond the war of the generals, and look directly at the dynamics that shaped the long and fierce struggle in the South Pacific.

The core of the text is divided into two parts. In Part I, I examine the hideous battlefield men confronted in the South Pacific. It is a vital part of the story, as the harsh and dangerous nature of the land itself touched every facet of the war that took place there. I also introduce the participants in the violent encounter. The armies involved represented different cultures and differed greatly in character, level of training, and military technique. To illustrate how the combatants went about their tasks, and how they differed as combat forces, I examine an early battle fought by each.

In Part II, I describe and analyze the dynamics of combat in the South Pacific. I cover many topics, including weaponry, tactics, chaotic firefights, air attack, care for the wounded, the impact of stress, and life behind the lines. All of these subjects, and others, make up the mosaic of life in a battle zone. Also, in South Pacific combat it was rare for soldiers to surrender or take prisoners. I have tried to explain how this dreadful process developed. The last chapter deals with the surprisingly rapid collapse of the Japanese position in the South Pacific and the final tragic battle of the campaign.

I think my approach offers much to the general reader. Instead of presenting another recapitulation of operational maneuver, I attempt to show how the conflict took the form that it did and why. I hope my book will help people better understand some things of very great importance. Although my work deals with a particular time and place, the currents I describe run very deep. Many of the matters I have dealt with are central to the brutal core of battle and touch on the heart of war. It is an extraordinary story.

The story, however, is not complete. The encounter in the South Pacific included fierce fighting on the land, in the air, and at sea. I have dealt with the air and naval war when they influenced the ground struggle directly. However, I did not attempt to analyze either in depth. My approach is not a judgment on the relative importance of the one aspect of the struggle compared to another. On the contrary, both the air and naval wars were so complex, important, and interesting that I could not have done them justice here without allowing the book to grow to unmanageable size. I hope to return to these subjects in the future.

My book is written from the Allied point of view. Although the "Allies" in the South Pacific were a part of the massive coalition aligned against Germany and Japan during World War II, in practice the term refers to the United States and Australia. (Great Britain, the Netherlands, and the Free French played a small role in the air and naval war, but none was a factor in ground operations. New Zealand contributed valuable air and naval units to the conflict. New Zealand also fielded an infantry division in the South Pacific, but it saw almost no combat during the period I examine.) The many volumes of official histories from the United States and Australia, as well as the interviews I have conducted, provide a very solid base for my line of inquiry.

Naturally, I have dealt also with Japan. There are several fine secondary works concerning the Japanese war effort. In addition, the American government accumulated much information on all facets of the Japanese war effort for the *Strategic Bombing Survey* compiled immediately after the war. In addition, after the war General MacArthur's headquarters in Tokyo authorized a detailed account of Japanese operations written by former Japanese officers, which provides an indispensable view of the Pacific war from Tokyo's viewpoint. Unfortunately, there are formidable linguistic and practical barriers facing anyone wishing to interview Japanese veterans. Nevertheless, I believe that I have covered the Japanese war effort accurately and fairly. It will be obvious that I believe that the unique ferocity of the war in the Pacific stemmed primarily from Japanese policy. I think that it is self-evident that something went very wrong in Japan during the 1930s and that the war in Asia was due to Tokyo's aggressive policies. I also believe that the foul political atmosphere found in many countries in the decades between the world wars was unique to this period of history. Nothing that I have written detracts from the great respect that I hold for Japan and its people.

There is much interest today in historical issues that relate to race and gender. Indeed, many specialists in these fields are examining the experience of racial minorities and women during World War II. I do not join them. My book deals with war at the point of fire. Ground combat in the South Pacific was the domain of men. Because American combat units were racially segregated during the period I examine, black soldiers were not there. (Ironically, most American divisions had a contingent of Nisei soldiers working for intelligence.) Obviously, the contemporary military has changed fundamentally in this regard. Nevertheless, the contribution of blacks and women in the South Pacific theater of war took place for the most part in the rear areas and largely after the period I have examined. The issues involved are important and deserve a more detailed treatment than I can offer here.

I have kept the number of footnotes to a minimum. In the section on sources there is a list of all the veterans who have helped me on this volume and a select bibliography. I have also included a short glossary of military terms. Some details, however, need explanation or definition. I have handled them with brief comments within the text, enclosed by brackets, followed by my initials.

I have also created several maps to guide the reader through an unfamiliar part of the world. However, at this juncture it is appropriate to explain some basic geographical terms. The vast Pacific Ocean has no obvious dividing lines separating one zone from another than the equator itself. A standard world map will show the North Pacific and South Pacific oceans. During the war, the American military subdivided the Pacific into various theaters. As luck would have it, the dividing line between two areas that Washington designated the "South Pacific Theater" and the "Southwest Pacific Theater" went north–south through the Solomon Islands. Therefore, in the administrative atlas of an American general, Guadalcanal was in the South Pacific and New Guinea in the Southwest Pacific. The Japanese called the same territory the Southeast Zone. For matters of simplicity I have followed the lead of the area's inhabitants and employed the term "South Pacific" to identify the entire region under consideration.

New Guinea and the surrounding islands also cause some problems in terminology. At the start of World War II, the massive island was divided into three sections. The western half was Dutch New Guinea, long controlled by the Netherlands. Within the eastern half of the island Northeast New Guinea and Papua were situated. Great Britain transferred Papua to Australian control early in the twentieth century. After World War I the League of Nations allocated the German-controlled territories in the South Pacific to Australia as a mandate. Northeast New Guinea was the largest portion. However, the mandate also included the Bismarck Archipelago, a group of islands off the coast of Northeast New Guinea. The largest island in the archipelago was New Britain, which possessed a fine harbor at the small settlement of Rabaul. To complicate things further, the Germans had also possessed Bougainville, which was geographically and ethnically a part of the British-controlled Solomon Islands. Bougainville too, therefore, was a part of the Australian mandate. At present, Indonesia controls the former Dutch holdings on New Guinea. All the areas formerly administered by Australia make up the independent country of Papua New Guinea. The Solomon Islands, minus Bougainville, are now an independent republic.

In practice, the simple term "New Guinea" was often used to describe any portion of the island. Most of the military activity on New Guinea described in this book took place in Papua. The difference between Papua and Northeast New Guinea was purely administrative and corresponded to no geographic feature. Most soldiers did not know, or care, which part of New Guinea they were in. Fortunately for the reader, the actual area contested was not large and the place-names few. A glance at one of the maps included should clarify things quickly.

Acknowledgments

I have many people to thank. Mark Stafford, Steve Flanders, and others affiliated with Penguin USA have helped from the first day. The administration at Lincoln University has given me important support. The fine staff at Air University at Maxwell Air Force Base performed "above and beyond" during my stay there. Ted Blahnik and others from the Guadalcanal Campaign Veterans Association were extremely generous with their time.

Most of all, I deeply appreciate the help given to me by dozens of World War II veterans from the American and Australian armed forces. I personally interviewed most of the veterans who contributed their time. Others sent me audio tapes or written accounts describing their experiences and reflections. I did edit the material to make context obvious. However, I tried my utmost to preserve the actual words used. If a phrase is emphasized in a quotation, it is because the contributor wanted it so. Although a half century has passed since the events the veterans eloquently describe, their accounts correspond extremely well with the official histories and other contemporary sources. More important, they provide details of larger events that have not been recorded. They lived through a hard but crucial time in history, and their thoughts and perspective have proved invaluable to every facet of my research. Any errors made are mine alone.

Contents

Illustrations follow page 166.

List of Maps

TOUCHED
WITH FIRE

Introduction

The Strategic Magnet: A Brief Narrative of the War in the South Pacific

G reat wars possess a powerful momentum that rarely can be controlled. Battle is so unpredictable, and the actions of one side so intimately connected with the actions taken on the other, that the duration and outcome of conflicts are often decided in places totally unforeseen at the beginning of hostilities. No one in 1939, for instance, could have foretold that World War II in Europe would turn on the outcome of an air battle over Great Britain. A clash between Nazi Germany and the Soviet Union was predictable enough, but no one could have anticipated that Adolf Hitler's dreams of empire would end at the minor city of Stalingrad at the same time a German armored column was approaching the Caspian Sea. The notion that the Allies and Germany would fight a major land campaign in North Africa would have been dismissed out of hand before hostilities.

So it was in the South Pacific. No commander on either side at the start of the war foresaw the great battles that ultimately raged in the Solomons and New Guinea. The battlefield itself possessed nothing desired by Japan or the Allies. There were no raw materials to gain or deny the enemy. There were no symbolic political issues at stake that could compromise the position of one side or the other. No new allies could be gained or lost. Nevertheless, the same fundamental impulse that drove Tokyo to gamble on war in the first place also propelled both sides to this remote corner of the globe. Although there was nothing tangible at stake directly, the struggle in the South Pacific had a powerful internal logic. The genesis of the showdown north of Australia lay in both Japan's essential war aims and the basic military assumptions developed by both sides before hostilities.

Simply put, Japan took the momentous gamble in December 1941 of simultaneously attacking the United States and the British Empire because Tokyo believed that Nazi Germany's triumphs provided a unique opportunity for Japan to become a great world power. In the decades before World War II, many leaders in Tokyo were preoccupied with the perception of Japan's weakness. The home islands, so the argument went, lacked most basic natural resources, were deficient in agricultural land, and suffered from overpopulation. Japan's only asset was the spirit of its people. In a world dominated by industrial might, however, many in Tokyo believed that spirit was not enough. In addition, the nightmare of a hostile coalition combining to humiliate Japan was always present. Japan would be secure, nationalists contended, only when it controlled directly a resource base adequate for full-scale industrial development. Because such thoughts were deeply and widely held, Japan was an eager player in Asian power politics beginning in the late nineteenth century. In the years before World War I, Tokyo seized Korea, joined European colonial powers in carving out a sphere of influence in China, and shocked the world by defeating Russia in a war. In 1914, Japan quickly joined the Western Allies and occupied Germany's possessions in China and the Central Pacific.

For a short period after World War I, Tokyo, already possessing a sizable empire, moved toward a more flexible policy. Like the United States, Japan's foreign trade boomed during World War I. Furthermore, the European nations and Russia were weakened by war and revolution and could pose no immediate threat. Although the Japanese military warned against any policy that made Japan dependent upon foreign trade and foreign markets, Tokyo renounced further territorial ambitions and concentrated on an export-driven economic expansion. However, the Great Depression, starting in 1929, hammered Japanese exports. Apparently proven right by events, Japanese militarists moved to impose their views on the government. Swiftly the Japanese Army seized the coal- and iron-rich Chinese province of Manchuria in 1931. A vicious circle soon developed. China would never accept the state of affairs in Manchuria. Japan's imperial position in Manchuria, however, would be secure only when China acquiesced on the matter. Consequently, in 1937 Japan attacked China itself. Although the Japanese Army advanced deep into China, soon Imperial forces were bogged down in a low-level but exhausting war of attrition. Japan lacked the strength to crush all Chinese resistance. It also lacked the foresight to retreat politically. Steadily, relations with the United States soured over the China problem. Tokyo's position seemed very difficult to many in the government. However, the European war that broke out in 1939 appeared to offer a fortuitous way out of Japan's dilemma.

Japan did not take the decision to go to war lightly. Nevertheless, as many in the Army and Navy argued strongly, an unprecedented situation existed due to European events. Like everyone else in the world, the Japanese were awed by the German blitzkrieg in France during May 1940. Indeed, months after France capitulated, Tokyo moved military forces into French Indochina. Events accelerated the following year. Assuming that Germany's attack on the Soviet Union in the summer of 1941 would succeed, Japanese militarists contended that Britain and the United States would be preoccupied by the German threat and would not dare allocate large military resources to Asia. France and the Netherlands already defeated by Hitler, were not factors. The American Pacific Fleet posed a serious strategic problem that required action. Nevertheless, the United States' Atlantic commitments would be sizable. Furthermore, Japanese hawks argued that the isolationist American public would not support a long war far from its shores. A slowly tightening American economic boycott of critical exports to Japan hastened the decision to act.

Japan's principal war aim was the conquest of European colonial empires in Asia. Once the British, French, and Dutch were cast aside, Tokyo would gain for itself control of the substantial natural resources present in the East Indies, an area the Japanese called the "Southern Resource Zone." When added to the industrial sectors of Japan and northern China, the oil, rubber, and rice of Southeast Asia would give Japan the geopolitical base required to create a great and modern industrial empire. At the same time, a crushing defeat of the West and an extension of Japanese power into Burma, Tokyo believed, would force the Chinese government to see reason and end the costly war in China on terms acceptable to Japan.

Japanese hawks viewed war with the United States as a necessary means to achieve these ends, not a desirable event on its own terms. The Roosevelt administration, Tokyo believed, would not allow a massive Japanese thrust into Southeast Asia. Consequently, the Japanese decided to attack the United States with the purpose of forcing its acquiescence to Tokyo's Asian political aims. The Japanese had no desire, for instance, to land forces on the American mainland. Tokyo ordered a move against the Philippines because it was the most important American advance base in Asia, not because it considered the area an important part of the Southern Resource Zone. The Imperial Navy planned the strike against the American fleet at Pearl Harbor to prevent it from interfering in the conquest of Southeast Asia.

The Japanese decided, consequently, to launch a lightning military campaign that would cripple American and British military forces and put Southeast Asia in Tokyo's hands before Japan's enemies could catch their breath. Once these objectives were met, Tokyo planned to create a massive defensive perimeter protecting the home islands and the Southern Resource Zone in Southeast Asia. In a short time, the Japanese hoped, the Americans and British would see the futility of fighting a prolonged war in Asia and yield to events. Once a peace was made recognizing Japan's preeminent position in Southeast Asia and Manchuria, Japan could begin the long-term task of building up its manufacturing base. All the nations "liberated" from colonial control would join a Japanese-led "Greater East Asian Co-Prosperity Sphere." Eventually, the Japanese Empire would equal and then surpass the industrial might of the West. The argument was compelling, and gave Japanese hawks the political ammunition required to gain support for their grandiose military solution to Japan's geopolitical problems.

Across the Pacific the American government watched developments in Japan with great concern. Soon after the fall of France, the American military began secret joint planning with the British for a future war. Because the possibility of a war with both Germany and Japan was obvious, the future Allies had to establish basic strategic priorities. One of the first decisions made, with the full backing of President Franklin Roosevelt and General George C. Marshall, head of the Joint Chiefs of Staff, was that the major Anglo-American effort would be made against Germany in case of a two-front war. Germany was the strongest potential enemy and, unlike Japan, posed a potential threat to the Western Hemisphere. Therefore, American prewar naval planners, operating, sometimes unwillingly, under Roosevelt's order to defeat Hitler first, prepared a Pacific war scenario that foresaw a long defensive stage during which the United States would build up its position in Hawaii and Australia. A string of fortified island air bases stretching across the South Pacific would link the two bastions. The U.S. Pacific Fleet would stand in reserve, alert to counter any Japanese attack on the Allied defensive line. When the United States mobilized its industrial strength, forces in the Pacific would commence selective attacks against the Japanese. After Germany was defeated, according to American plans, the United States and the British Empire would move overwhelming resources to the Pacific and crush Japan.

In line with the "Germany first" policy, the last set of pre–Pearl Harbor naval war plans reversed the long-standing policy of attempting to reinforce the Philippine Islands in case of Japanese attack. (This decision was bitterly resented and fiercely resisted by General Douglas MacArthur in Manila.) Wisely, the American Navy realized that America's possessions in Asia would have to be sacrificed temporarily to ensure a rational allocation of limited resources available for the Pacific. Although incapable of foreseeing the remarkable course of events between Pearl Harbor and Midway, the predictions of the prewar planners in Washington proved well thought out. They did not appreciate, however, how difficult it would be to separate a defensive posture from an offensive one. (It is worth noting that American planners were seriously hampered by a very reasonable fear that Germany would triumph completely in Europe. This uncertainty led them to assume that a sizable portion of the American surface fleet would remain in Atlantic waters. At the time of Pearl Harbor, consequently, Japan possessed a numerical superiority in every category of warship in the Pacific. Japanese air superiority in the Pacific was very substantial.)

Ironically, both sides on the eve of hostilities were anticipating, at some stage of the struggle, holding a maritime defense of air bases supported by a mobile fleet. Two opinions shared by military leaders of both nations largely explain the extraordinary symmetry of their plans for conflict. First, the exceptional importance of air and naval power in the Pacific was well recognized by both sides at the outset of hostilities. Navies and air forces are extremely expensive, and Japan was a relatively poor country. Nevertheless, the Japanese Army Air Force was large and possessed modern types of aircraft. The Army lacked the resources to develop a massive fleet of heavy bombers, but considering their presupposition that a war with the United States would be short, it made no sense to develop one. In addition, Tokyo spent staggering sums on the Imperial Navy considering the wealth of the nation. The Japanese Navy Air Force, as illustrated dramatically at Pearl Harbor, was a pioneer in the use and development of aircraft carriers. As American sailors learned in the waters off Guadalcanal, Imperial warships were also deadly opponents in surface combat.

In the United States, although official Army Air Force doctrine (an independent U.S. Air Force was founded immediately after the war) emphasized the importance of fighter aircraft and tactical bombers, virtually every aviation officer in the service by 1939 believed that bombers attacking targets behind the front lines would be the weapon of decision in any future conflict. When war began in Europe, and President Roosevelt himself ordered that aircraft be given top priority in production and employment, bomber advocates rapidly took over the Army Air Force. However, despite tight budgets during the Depression, the Army had been careful to develop modern versions of all types of land-based aircraft, creating the skeleton for a very well balanced air arm. Better prototypes were in development by the time of Pearl Harbor. Planes and pilots were scarce in December 1941, but the problem was short-term. The factories were already swinging into full-scale production and pilot training greatly expanded. The air supremacy enjoyed by the Japanese in the early months of the war would prove short-lived.

The U.S. fleet was the best equipped and most modern of the American armed forces in 1941. Because the fleet could either defend a "fortress America" or project American power abroad, it was the one service that received support during the interwar period from both isolationists and internationalists in Congress. Although defects in weaponry and doctrine appeared in combat, the Navy was sound at the base, possessing powerful ships and good men. In addition, the American Navy had its own air arm (as did the Marine Corps, under nominal Navy control). As it had in the Army, the importance of airpower in war planning had steadily increased during the interwar period. The old-fashioned battleship admiral was a thing of the past by 1941. Admiral Ernest King, commander in chief of the U.S. fleet, had commanded aircraft carriers and was deeply involved with naval aviation. America's fleet of eleven aircraft carriers in 1941 was equaled only by Japan's. The massive American military budgets adopted in 1940 and 1941 authorized the construction of dozens of aircraft carriers of all types. In addition, all American naval aircraft that saw substantial service in World War II were in development or production before Pearl Harbor.

Second, both Japanese and American military men concluded that land-based airpower was inherently superior to sea-based airpower. Both also believed that an enemy fleet could operate in a zone controlled by friendly land-based bombers only at huge risk. The combination of a strong air group based on land, supported when necessary by friendly naval forces, both sides accepted, would make an extremely strong defense. If either land-based or fleet-based airpower was powerful enough, an enemy attack would be doomed. As the Pacific war unfolded, the United States demonstrated that these ideas were sound if the forces and leadership were adequate and geography favored the defender. The Japanese experience, as we shall see, was the opposite.

Although Washington planned to stand on the defensive in the opening stage of a war with Japan, no one expected the staggering onslaught unleashed by Tokyo on December 7, 1941. The first three months of the war appeared to be a spectacular vindication of Japanese aspirations and methods. After the electrifying blow at Pearl Harbor, Imperial forces swept from one victory to another. The destruction of British-led forces in Malaya was the greatest land victory in Japanese history. Japan's military crushed Allied resistance in the East Indies and seized its much-coveted oil fields with little problem. Only on the Bataan Peninsula in the Philippines did the Japanese suffer a reverse, and it proved temporary.

While Imperial forces seized major objectives one after another, they also occupied smaller places that Tokyo planned to include in its defensive perimeter. This effort took them to distant spots, such as Tarawa and Wake. It also led the Japanese, for the first time, to the South Pacific. In late January 1942 a Japanese task force began a series of small invasions at selective points in areas controlled by Australia. Brushing aside the scanty resistance offered by the tiny Australian garrisons, in February and March Imperial forces seized the small settlements of Lae and Salamaua in Northeast New Guinea. They also occupied the Bismarck Archipelago, with its fine harbor and small airstrip at the village of Rabaul on the island of New Britain. In following weeks, small Japanese contingents landed on Bougainville and other places in the upper Solomon Islands.

The easy conquest of outposts on and near New Guinea whetted Tokyo's appetite for bigger game. Occupation of all the Solomon Islands could provide a springboard for further operations against the supply line between the United States and Australia. In addition, the small harbor town of Port Moresby, which served as the administrative capital of Papua, was an ideal base for air attacks against northern Australia. Furthermore, as highlighted by the Doolittle raid on Tokyo in April, the U.S. Pacific Fleet still had powerful aircraft carriers that had to be dealt with. Tokyo believed, correctly, that a serious threat to Australia would precipitate a naval battle with the United States. For all these reasons, in early May 1942 the Japanese Navy sent invasion convoys toward Tulagi, the tiny island near Guadalcanal that served as headquarters for the handful of British administrators working in the Solomons, and Port Moresby in Papua. The Imperial Navy, hoping for an American response, covered these convoys with two powerful task forces that included three aircraft carriers.

The result was the Battle of the Coral Sea. At this stage of the war the American cryptographers could read portions of the Japanese naval codes. Admiral Chester Nimitz at Pearl Harbor, therefore, knew in April the outline of the Japanese move. The Americans dispatched two of their precious carriers to the South Pacific where they joined a sizable group of American and Australian cruisers and destroyers. In a confused carrier battle that took place on May 7–8, the two sides traded air strikes. The Japanese sank the *Lexington* and damaged the *Yorktown*, both large carriers. In return, American planes sank the light carrier *Shoho* and damaged the *Shokaku*, Japan's newest large carrier.

Tokyo, overestimating the damage inflicted, counted the engagement as another in their string of victories. In a narrow tactical sense they were correct, as American naval losses surpassed their own. However, the American fleet had done its work. With one carrier destroyed and another damaged, the Japanese strike force had to withdraw. The small invasion convoy sent to Tulagi completed its mission. However, without air cover, the larger convoy steaming slowly toward Port Moresby was vulnerable to air attack from Australian bases and interception by Allied warships. Consequently, the Imperial Navy recalled the transports. Port Moresby and northern Australia, for the moment, were safe.

In retrospect we can see that the Battle of the Coral Sea was a great setback for Japan. This was not at all evident at the time. The failure of the Port Moresby operation, set against the stunning victories of the same period, appeared in Tokyo to be the sort of minor setback one would expect in war. After all, in six months Tokyo had seized all the territory it had desired before hostilities. The only goal not yet achieved was the annihilation of American naval airpower. Few in Tokyo doubted that Japan could bring the Americans to battle and few doubted the outcome. Before the Imperial fleet sailed to Midway, Japanese gains had been immense and the costs minuscule.

However, it is clear that Japan's imperial ambitions were founded on several defective political and military assumptions. One setback for Japan was obvious at the start. The fury in the United States following Pearl Harbor destroyed one of the suppositions behind Tokyo's plans. The Americans, it was all too evident, would not make peace quickly. Just as seriously, Hitler's defeat in front of Moscow the same week that Japanese aircraft attacked Pearl Harbor brought into question the crucial notion that Germany would triumph in Europe. Both events made it more imperative to strengthen the Empire's defensive barrier.

Unfortunately for Japan, we can also see in retrospect that Tokyo's plan to build a maritime Maginot Line in the Pacific was conceptually bankrupt. Japanese military leaders believed that a chain of powerful air and naval bases, backed by their powerful battle fleet, could create the kind of "defense in depth" generals desire in a land campaign. The Japanese analogy was a bad one, however. A defensive line in a land battle requires a secure position to serve as an anchor. In World War I, for instance, the twin strategic anchors for both sides on the Western Front were the English Channel and the Swiss Alps. Because it was impossible to outflank either barrier, the combatants had to face the miserable task of forcing their way through the line. In the huge expanse of the Pacific, however, there was no feasible place for the Japanese to anchor their defensive position. Consequently, the analogy with a defensive line on land broke down badly in a maritime war. Instead of creating a mutually supporting defensive system that would force an attacker to move against predictable points, the Japanese created a line of poorly linked redoubts that the Allies could penetrate or outflank from several different directions. The individual strong points, as events proved, were very vulnerable to piecemeal siege once the Allies gathered the required strength.

It is crucial to understand that although there were massive land campaigns on the Asian mainland during World War II, the war between the United States and Japan was an island war. Japan itself is an island nation. None of the Pacific islands, Japan included, was self-sufficient from a military point of view. This fact had immense military consequences. If an enemy attacker was able to sustain air and naval supremacy over an area, it would close the sea lanes needed to supply the defender's garrisons. Furthermore, it was not necessary for the attacker to have total superiority to do terrible damage. If the enemy air and naval forces were strong enough to watch the waters and attack merchant shipping, they could sever supply lines between an island bastion and rear areas. What ensued was an air and naval blockade, the maritime equivalent of a siege on land.

Implications of a blockade or siege in the Pacific were crucial to the course of operations, and the results physically hideous for those individuals on the receiving end. Open sea lanes allowed ships to bring military supplies necessary for armies and fleets to fight, and the food required to feed the people involved. When isolated, military assets wasted away rapidly with no hope of recovery. All too soon, shortages of rations caused increasingly severe malnutrition that debilitated or killed the people under siege. The Japanese garrisons that eventually withered in the South Pacific suffered through an early version of the "potato winter" that drove the Japanese civilian population into abject misery during 1945. As shown many times in the Pacific, an isolated garrison lost all military value because its men were forced into a harsh, semiagrarian existence to survive. World War II in the Pacific, therefore, was a war of strangulation. The fate of Japan's island bases, such as their great bastion at Rabaul, was ultimately the fate of Japan.

Lieutenant General George Kenney, commander of the U.S. Army Fifth Air Force in Australia, understood this. In October 1942 he wrote a letter to his superior, General Henry "Hap" Arnold, which included a keen appreciation of the unfolding campaign in the Pacific:

> The artillery in this theater flies. . . . In the Pacific we have a number of islands garrisoned by small forces. These islands are nothing more or less than aerodromes or aerodrome areas from which modern fire-power is launched. Sometimes they are true islands like Wake or Midway, sometimes they are localities on large land masses. Port Moresby, Lae and Buna are all on the island of New Guinea, but the only practical way to get from one

to the other is by air or by water: they are all islands as far as warfare is concerned. Each is garrisoned by a small force and each can be taken by a small force once local air control is secured. Every time one of these islands is taken, the rear is better secured and the emplacements for the flying artillery are advanced closer and closer to Japan itself.

Japan's ultimate demise was due to many factors. One of the most important was Tokyo's inability to find a secure anchor for its defensive chain. The Empire's island redoubts were not intended to withstand a sustained onslaught of land-based aerial attack. In land war, a break in a defensive line endangers the entire position; the break must be sealed through counterattack, or the army must retreat to a new line. Japan's position, based on a wall of island air bases, was very similar. A crack in the wall anywhere would jeopardize the entire structure. Both sides knew this. When American victory at the Battle of Midway in June 1942 forced Japan to reexamine the direction of the war, some harsh realities came into focus very quickly.

On the surface, Japan's position appeared very strong despite the air and naval losses at Midway. The Imperial Navy still possessed several aircraft carriers and a vast surface fleet. (The notion that Japan lost large numbers of irreplaceable fighter pilots at Midway is not true. Most Japanese fighters defended the carriers. After American aircraft sank the carriers, many of the pilots in the air were able to ditch near friendly vessels. Many aircraft were refueling when American bombs struck and many pilots survived. Several flights of bombers, however, attacking distant American carriers, were annihilated.) The Japanese Army had not tasted defeat. The Imperial Army air fleets were large, well trained, and growing. Furthermore, Tokyo had seized the basic military objectives it had started the war to obtain. Further attacks were not necessary to gain places of value. Japan's essential task was defensive, protecting what it had occupied. This fact made the allocation of resources, in theory, much more flexible.

Also, the Japanese possessed some important geographical advantages. In each part of the Pacific, Japan possessed bases that potentially could support substantial air and naval forces. Tokyo also profited from what military men call "interior lines." Shifting major naval or air forces from one portion of the Pacific to another entailed a far shorter movement for Japan than for the United States. The linchpin of Japan's naval defense was the great lagoon of Truk in the Caroline Islands in the Central Pacific. During much of the period covered in this book, Truk served as the operational headquarters of the Imperial Combined Fleet, commanded by Fleet Admiral Isoroku Yamamoto. Truk was 2,400 miles south of Japan. Within 1,000 miles of Truk lay the Central Pacific bastions of Tarawa and Kwajalein, and the large bases of Saipan and Guam to the northwest. Therefore, a fleet based at Truk was a few days' journey from most points of value in the Pacific. The Japanese could transfer aircraft through Truk faster yet. In contrast, if the United States wished to move resources from Hawaii to Australia, or vice versa, a 5,200-mile journey was required. In addition, Truk provided a perfect staging base to support Rabaul, 900 miles to the south. Ships based at Rabaul could strike quickly at any point in the Solomons or New Guinea. The Japanese built several air bases in the Rabaul area from which they could bomb targets as distant as Darwin, Australia. They protected Rabaul with a substantial garrison that later grew to over 80,000 men.

Yet Tokyo faced serious problems, some of which were not obvious. The most significant difficulty was the simple fact that Japan was not a rich country and could not, in the long run, compete with the United States in weapons production. As observed by many Imperial officers after hostilities, Japan prepared for a battle, not a war. Therefore, Japan could fight the United States successfully only if every bit of military potential was employed efficiently. Japan's relative economic weakness was widely recognized in Tokyo. After Midway, many realists in the Japanese government concluded that "victory" against the United States would entail some type of compromise peace that would fall far short of creating a Japanese-dominated new order in Asia.

However, the early victories hid the fact that the Japanese war effort was crippled from the inside by endless political struggle and personality conflicts that led to convoluted and often ineffective decision-making. At the center of the problem was the old rivalry between the Japanese Army and the Japanese Navy. The Imperial Army claimed to be the true inheritor of the samurai spirit. More important, it was the older and larger service and dominated the Japanese government in 1942. It is very difficult for historians to reconstruct how the Japanese military reached major decisions in the early stage of the Pacific war. Japanese deliberations were always oblique, and feuding cliques in Tokyo continually shifted in their alignments. Informal arrangements made in local theaters frequently had more importance than decisions made at the top in Tokyo. The reason was simple enough. Because every strategic issue had political ramifications at home, the Army and Navy rarely described their plans in detail when dealing with each other. Although the American Joint Chiefs of Staff experienced tremendous struggles over turf and resources, leaders in Washington knew where they stood. In Tokyo, on the other hand, much was left unsaid, and a cloud of uncertainty hindered purposeful action. For instance, in theory the Japanese Navy had primary responsibility for the maritime war against the United States. Nevertheless, the Army frequently vetoed Navy plans while suggesting nothing in their place. At the beginning of the war, the Navy argued for an invasion of Australia. The Army turned it down, claiming that the necessary shipping was unavailable. In truth, the Army wished to keep its forces along the Soviet frontier in Manchuria so they could profit from the anticipated collapse in Moscow. When the situation deteriorated in the South Pacific, and the Soviet Union stabilized its position, the Imperial Army found the means to transport at least 200,000 additional men to New Guinea and the Solomons. Lastly, coordination between the Japanese Seventeenth Army, based at Rabaul, and the Imperial Combined Fleet, based at Truk, was minimal.

Segregating plans and operations into spheres of influence was a very poor way to run a war. Japanese planning was frequently haphazard and based on flimsy assumptions. The sort of detailed and rigorous analysis that the Allies employed on a good day was very rare with the Japanese. Indeed, Japanese operations throughout the campaign in the South Pacific had an ad hoc nature that led over and over to insufficient measures undertaken a little too late. After the war, Japanese officers of the two services widely agreed that poor co-operation between the Army and Navy was a significant reason for Japan's defeat.

The muddle caused by poor command relationships was very evident after Midway. Although Japanese Army commanders claimed not to want another major campaign, they agreed with their naval counterparts that the Empire could not stand passively on the defensive and yield the military initiative to the Allies. Despite their losses at Midway, Tokyo considered launching an offensive into the Indian Ocean in case Germany broke through to Central Asia. The Indian Ocean drive was a contingency plan, however, and probably not very serious; it was dropped quickly without protest when serious fighting began in the South Pacific. Indeed, far more immediate problems faced Tokyo. Triumphant at Midway and quickly mobilizing for total war, the United States was very clearly in no mood to make peace. Instead, with every passing day, American men and supplies headed toward both Hawaii and Australia. A twin buildup of Allied resources in both the Central and South Pacific presented a strategic quandary for Japan. In time the advantage of interior lines would lose its meaning. If the Americans could strike both from Hawaii toward the center of the Empire's defenses and from Australia against the south, Imperial defenses would be stretched to the breaking point. Something had to be done.

After Midway, the Japanese ceased considering another assault on Hawaii. Australia was a different matter. The southern section of the Japanese maritime line, based at Rabaul in New Britain, was within range of Allied land-based air attack coming from Australia and New Guinea. Conversely, Allied positions in New Guinea and the Solomon islands east of Rabaul were within range of Japanese action. Defense and offense were intermingled from the start.

Australia was a serious threat to Japan's defense strategy. It posed problems that Japanese planners never adequately faced before or during the conflict. Australia was far more than another Pacific atoll with a good harbor. It was a continent-size, self-sufficient base area that could support an attack force of unlimited size. Australia was also a major source of military production and military manpower.

To make matters worse, it was closer to the East Indies than was Japan itself. Australia, and the islands linking Australia to the United States, provided excellent bases for Allied fleets. Washington dispatched sizable garrisons to several of these islands, including Fiji and Samoa. Two islands east of Australia, New Caledonia and Espiritu Santo, served for two years as primary advance bases for the U.S. Pacific Fleet operating in the Solomons. In June 1942, Australia still held the northeastern coast of Papua. Furthermore, Australian and American forces at Port Moresby could support a counteroffensive against the Japanese outposts in Northeast New Guinea. Air bases at Port Moresby and northern Australia put Allied bombers within range of Rabaul and other Japanese positions in the area. If the Allies could solidify their position in Papua, Rabaul was open to concentrated attack. As leaders in both Tokyo and Washington realized, if the Allies could move past Rabaul in strength, the door to the Philippines and the Southern Resource Zone itself was wide open. The stakes in the South Pacific were growing very high.

Therefore, unless the Japanese could make the South Pacific link of their overall defensive position immensely strong, the whole chain built for the defense of the Empire was in jeopardy. A war between two land-based air forces would be a war of attrition, exactly what Japan wanted to avoid. The Japanese, once cured at Midway of grandiose dreams of destroying the U.S. fleet at one blow, were drawn inevitably toward Port Moresby and the South Pacific. If this area could be taken, then the way was open to further advances toward the South Pacific islands that controlled the sea lanes between the United States and Australia. In addition, with the aid of Japanese land-based airpower, the American fleet possibly could be enticed into battle, defeated, and Midway avenged. The Japanese, despite many conquests, had to push on or perish. Advancing further, however, threatened to stretch Japan's resources. If spread too thin, weakened Japanese forces somewhere would be vulnerable to defeat. This is precisely what happened in the South Pacific. It was a quandary with no real answer.

Having little choice, the Japanese decided to move forward. The main thrust decided upon was an Army offensive against Port

Moresby starting in July. In the Army's eyes, the Navy had failed badly at both the Coral Sea and Midway. Still flushed from their stunning victory in Malaya, Japanese generals decided to take matters into their own hands in Papua. The Navy, in any case, was reorganizing after Midway and not prepared in July for a large fleet action. Consequently, the Seventeenth Army at Rabaul assembled an elite formation of shock troops designated the South Seas Detachment. Little help from the Navy was asked or wanted. The Combined Fleet agreed to provide a small number of warships required to protect landings at Buna, on the northeastern coast of Papua. The fleet assigned some naval engineers to the landing force to help establish a rudimentary supply system. Naval aircraft would help by continuing their heavy attacks against Port Moresby and Darwin. The Imperial fleet at Truk knew the outlines of the operation but little else. In the Army's eyes, there was no need for detailed joint planning. Once ashore at Buna, the Army intended to attack Port Moresby overland across the rugged Owen Stanley Mountains. Surprise, audacity, and Japanese spirit would succeed where naval operations had failed.

The Imperial Navy was not idle. Considering the blow suffered at Midway, naval planners remained very aggressive. As mentioned earlier, the Navy had landed a small contingent on the little island of Tulagi during the Coral Sea operation in May. Twenty miles from Tulagi is the large island of Guadalcanal. In May, Guadalcanal was not an objective. However, with the Germans preparing advances in the USSR and North Africa in the summer of 1942, the Imperial Navy wished to keep its options open. A great German victory might force the Americans to shift forces to Europe. In addition, after victory in New Guinea, another advance might be possible against the American supply lines to Australia. Some planners in the Navy argued forcefully that a victory in Papua would allow an invasion of northern Australia itself. If nothing else, Japanese intelligence knew that the Allies were conducting reconnaissance near Tulagi. Wishing, at the minimum, to forestall an Allied move in the Solomon Islands that could threaten Rabaul, Tokyo dispatched a small expedition of engineers and laborers to unoccupied Guadalcanal at the end of

June. On Tulagi the Japanese established a small seaplane base that hosted a number of Zero floatplane fighters. The Zeros were there to protect a construction brigade sent to Guadalcanal to build a true air base. Just as the Army was preparing for its bold move against Port Moresby, the Navy was slowly getting involved in the Solomons. The Japanese did not want a showdown in the Solomons until after operations in New Guinea were brought to a successful close. Yet they were making it very difficult to avoid one. The Japanese were paving the road to an eventuality they did not wish in the slightest: simultaneous large battles in Papua and the Solomons.

Although hugely relieved after Midway, American planners had no clear route to follow in the Pacific. The sting of Pearl Harbor was still very much felt. American losses at the battles of the Coral Sea and Midway had been serious. In addition, a potential threat to the line of communication between the United States and Australia was obvious. So was Allied weakness in New Guinea. In addition, even though the Allies waged a far more efficient war than did the Japanese, bickering and ego conflicts hampered things at every turn. Two lines of strategic conflict in Washington interacted with a serious clash of egos to complicate the matter. First, there was the ambiguous position of the Pacific theater. As previously mentioned, the United States and Britain had adopted a "Germany first" strategy. Washington, however, did not anticipate Pearl Harbor or the Japanese blitzkrieg that followed. Early in the war Washington faced the real possibility that Hawaii might be lost and communications with Australia cut completely. A disaster of this magnitude was not part of the plan. The Navy, realizing that it would have the job of keeping Japan at bay, had always wanted more resources allocated to the Pacific. With disaster looming in the Pacific, Washington made extra resources available. Favorable events on the European battlefield also allowed the Navy to shift many of the carriers, battleships, and cruisers based on the East Coast of the United States to the Pacific. Indeed, in the first year of war, more men and supplies went to the Pacific than were shipped to Europe. (In 1943 the flood of men and supplies to Europe began in earnest. However, in general, the Navy throughout the war was able to procure far more resources for the Pacific than Marshall planned. No doubt the American public's angry reaction to Pearl Harbor had much to do with this.)

The naval victories at the Coral Sea and Midway eased the immediate threat, but the bickering continued at full force. Ultimately Washington agreed to send several infantry divisions, support troops, and air groups to the Pacific. What to do with these resources ignited another squabble. Admiral King possessed a hatred for the Army and the British. No supporter of "Germany first," King argued for a rapid naval and Marine Corps buildup in the Pacific. The fleet and the Marines, King proposed, should launch an immediate offensive against the Japanese in the Solomons to put pressure on Rabaul and ward off any Japanese drive toward the supply line with Australia. When the ships and men were available, a larger drive would start through the Central Pacific, aimed directly at Japan. The Army, in King's scheme of things, would garrison positions taken by the Marines and offer air support where possible.

Admiral King was a cold man and had many enemies. General Marshall, as noted, did not want a large campaign in the Pacific at all early in the conflict. In the Pacific, King's major nemesis was General Douglas MacArthur. MacArthur turned King's arguments on their head. After escaping from the Philippines, MacArthur was given command of the Southwest Pacific Theater, which included all Australian forces. Using Australia and New Guinea as a base, MacArthur requested a sizable strike force of U.S. Army divisions and a powerful air force. The U.S. fleet and the Marines would coordinate their efforts with MacArthur's forces in a rapid move against Rabaul. MacArthur had geography on his side. Australia was a substantial base and, as MacArthur knew well, possessed formidable armed forces that could play a large role in an early move against Japan. Ultimately, MacArthur believed that a drive up the New Guinea coast and capture of Rabaul would allow a return to the Philippine Islands. Returning to the Philippines would vindicate MacArthur personally. It would also sever communications between the East Indies and Tokyo and serve, MacArthur believed, as the best possible springboard for an offensive against the Japanese home islands. Remarkably, MacArthur and his staff, fresh from humiliation in the

Philippines and facing possible catastrophe in New Guinea, were already developing the outline for the offensive that took MacArthur to Tokyo Bay. Contemptuous of King, MacArthur agreed with the admiral on only one issue. The United States should send more men and material to the Pacific.

In a wartime democracy, domestic politics undoubtedly influenced planning. The American public was outraged at Japan and more fearful of Tokyo's advance than the more dangerous German offensive into Russia. Pressured from several directions, Marshall worked out one of the many compromises that proved necessary to keep the war moving forward. After acrimonious argument with King, Marshall persuaded him to sign a joint directive outlining strategy for the initial stage of the Pacific war. American forces in the Pacific were ordered to undertake an offensive consisting of three tasks. The first task, under the control of Admiral Robert L. Ghormley, naval commander of the South Pacific Theater, called for the seizure of Tulagi and "adjacent islands" in the Solomons. Ironically, Guadalcanal, soon the scene of America's first large land battle of World War II, was not on the original list. The Navy anticipated that a move into the Solomons would put pressure on Rabaul and keep the Japanese off balance while the Allies built up forces. MacArthur agreed to support Ghormley with Australian aircraft and warships, which were theoretically under his command. Task two entailed the seizure of the rest of the Solomons and the conquest of the northwest coast of New Guinea. Task three called for the conquest of Rabaul. Tasks two and three would be under General MacArthur's overall strategic direction. King had advocated the Tulagi move early in the war and it had his full support. But tasks two and three, King believed, would divert precious strength from the buildup for an offensive in the Central Pacific. King accepted the directive, but reserved the authority to withdraw any naval units he saw fit if the need arose.

The American design for victory was a blueprint for organizational disaster. The personal hatreds ran deep, particularly on the parts of King and MacArthur, and the lines of command were fuzzy, to put it mildly. Fortunately for the Allies, Marshall and Roosevelt proved skilled at making convoluted command arrangements work. In the South Pacific events took a favorable turn for the Americans early in the game. Unsatisfied with events at Guadalcanal, King relieved Admiral Ghormley in November 1942 and replaced him with Admiral William Halsey. Whatever the two men felt toward each other personally, MacArthur and Halsey worked very smoothly when King was out of the picture. MacArthur did not aspire to manage military operations in the Solomons closely. Halsey and he exchanged suggestions, but Halsey was allowed to run the war in the Solomons. MacArthur ran the war in New Guinea.

Much ink has been spilled since the war over the strategic arguments that plagued the Allies in both the Pacific and Europe. The personalities involved were colorful, and the issues invite partisanship. However, it is important to put these quarrels in perspective. Whatever the level of bickering and conflict that took place, it did not approach the sort of massive deceit that plagued Japanese command relationships. Allied planning was more systematic, better thought out, and far better executed than was Japanese.

Events moved quickly in the South Pacific. The directive establishing command relationships and operational plans for the Pacific was signed by Marshall and King on July 2, 1942. The ink was barely dry when a major and urgent change of plans was necessary. On July 4, American reconnaissance discovered the Japanese construction brigade on Guadalcanal. This news confirmed the worst fears at Pearl Harbor and Washington. The Japanese, it appeared, were going to move against the American-Australian supply line. Guadalcanal was hastily made the main objective of the initial Marine Corps assault scheduled for August. American commanders decided to proceed with the Guadalcanal invasion, realizing now that the move would be contested. Furthermore, the Navy and Marines would go in blind. In the decades before the war, the Navy and Marines had collected detailed information about most of the island groups in the Pacific. The Solomons were not among them. Beyond possessing British Admiralty charts of the coastline, and some aerial reconnaissance photos, the Marines knew nothing about the target of their first large attack of World War II. At the same time the U.S. Navy was scurrying about trying to learn anything it could about Guadalcanal, MacArthur decided to move Australian forces to Buna on the coast of Papua and establish an air base. However, unknown to the Americans, the Japanese also had plans for the same place coveted by MacArthur.

The Japanese moved first by a matter of weeks, landing on the northeastern coast of New Guinea at Buna on July 21, 1942. The tiny village of Buna, and the nearby points of Sanananda and Gona, were to serve as a base to support a land attack across Papua to Port Moresby. Between Buna and Port Moresby, however, lay the rugged and poorly explored Owen Stanley Mountains. A crude trail passed through the Owen Stanleys starting at the settlement of Kokoda on a plateau not far from Buna. The Kokoda Trail gave its name to the extremely rugged route across the Owen Stanleys and an epic series of battles that took place between the Japanese and Australians. At Kokoda itself there was a small force of Australian Militia. Advancing with customary speed, the Japanese moved on Kokoda within hours of landing. Soon a race was under way. Outnumbered Australian defenders attempted to slow the Japanese spearhead, knowing that help was in the immediate area. Australia had followed Britain into war in 1939. After Pearl Harbor, the Australian government recalled two battle-hardened Australian divisions fighting the Axis in the Mideast, and ordered them to reorganize in northern Australia. Not anticipating the rash Japanese move, Australian forces had to deploy hurriedly to Port Moresby and move up the Kokoda Trail to stop the Japanese.

Fortunately for the Allies, the terrain proved far more formidable than the Japanese had anticipated. Allied aircraft attacked Japanese mountain supply routes. Japanese forces, which always traveled light in the jungle, suffered serious problems with basic supplies early in their advance. Consequently, the South Seas Detachment could not move forward as fast as desired. Yet the Japanese spearhead was made up of elite shock troops, and they possessed numerical superiority. Despite dogged Australian resistance, which depleted their strength, the Japanese continued to move over the Kokoda Trail toward Port Moresby.

While the South Seas Detachment moved forward, the Americans landed in the Solomons in early August. Although the Imperial Navy was alarmed, it misjudged the size of the American effort. The Imperial Army paid little attention, because the Solomons were a matter for the Navy. Instead, the Japanese Army could see a great victory and urged its men forward in New Guinea. In late August Tokyo stumbled for the first time in the Papua campaign. Although growing very concerned about Guadalcanal, the Japanese Navy proceeded with an already planned amphibious attack on Milne Bay, a small anchorage south of Port Moresby. Not realizing the extent of the Australian buildup in the area, Imperial naval assault forces suffered a stinging defeat after a week of fierce fighting. It was Japan's first defeat in New Guinea, but not its last.

While the struggle at Milne Bay was taking place, the first large battles between Australian regular forces and the Japanese spearhead took place. Not knowing the terrible conditions in the Owen Stanleys any better than their enemy, the Australians timed their advance poorly, and moved units into battle piecemeal. The fighting was bitter, but the Japanese continued to hold the upper hand and shoved the Australians aside. In early September the Japanese advance, badly in need of rest and resupply, came to a temporary halt along a ridgeline at Ioribaiwa. Japanese observers at night could see the searchlights at Port Moresby, forty miles away. Between the Japanese and Moresby, however, were the Australians. They had taken up a position on the Imita Ridge, the last piece of high ground left in front of Port Moresby. The Australians welcomed the respite and the opportunity to move up fresh troops and reorganize. The Japanese, just a few miles away, believed they were awaiting resupply and reinforcement for the final drive to victory. In late September, however, the South Seas Detachment received the shocking order to withdraw. The unwanted new battle in the Solomons had taken a serious turn for the worse. The South Seas Detachment would have to wait until Imperial forces destroyed the American Marines. On September 28, the Japanese began the trek back up the Kokoda Trail, with the Australians close behind.

While Tokyo concentrated on its audacious move across the Owen Stanleys, events in the Solomons took a dramatic turn. The

Japanese, transfixed by Port Moresby, prepared to reinforce their advance in New Guinea. The Marine landing at Guadalcanal on August 7, 1942, despite the chaos and near calamity at the outset, took the Japanese completely by surprise. Although Japanese intelligence underestimated the size of the Guadalcanal landing force, Admiral Yamamoto saw the potential danger immediately. In Japanese eyes, the American move was a threat to Rabaul, and thus a menace to all Japanese operations in the theater. The Americans, Yamamoto and his staff agreed, must be ejected from Guadalcanal. Yamamoto boarded his flagship, the great battleship *Mushashi*, and established his headquarters at Truk, better to control operations. Although not expected fully by either side, a major confrontation was brewing. With the struggle in New Guinea increasing in ferocity, the great battle for the Solomons also was under way.

In July 1863 a Confederate column made for the town of Gettysburg because, it was rumored, a large supply of shoes was there for the taking. This decision precipitated the greatest battle of the Civil War. Although this small, almost random act determined the location of the battle, the confrontation itself was inevitable. Lee had invaded the North seeking a fight, and the Army of the Potomac had no choice but to provide one. The contract was made, only the details had to be inserted.

Japan's small expedition to Guadalcanal was similar to the Confederate foray to Gettysburg. Like the Southern officers in Pennsylvania, no one in Japanese headquarters expected that their occupation of Guadalcanal would precipitate a massive response by the Americans in the Solomons. However, the internal logic of events in the South Pacific made a colossal showdown inevitable. Although the exact location where the battle would begin was largely due to happenstance, a great confrontation was inevitable in the summer and fall of 1942. The result was a ferocious campaign throughout the South Pacific lasting a year and a half that ultimately shattered Japan's ability to wage offensive war.

Although the Marines anticipated a fierce fight, they encountered little resistance during the initial landing on Guadalcanal. A short but rugged battle ensued on Tulagi where the Japanese, in a grim portent of coming events, fought to the last man. Japanese air attacks hurriedly organized at Rabaul did little damage because of cloudy weather and the fighter cover provided for the Marines from four American aircraft carriers. Larger Japanese strikes the next day likewise failed, and the Americans were on Guadalcanal in force. The crucial job of unloading combat supplies was poorly handled by all involved, however, and the Marines unknowingly were in for some lean times because of it. Nevertheless, casualties were light, and on the second day the Marines captured the Japanese airstrip. The Guadalcanal operation was a success, or so it seemed.

Vice Admiral Gunichi Mikawa, the brilliant commander of the Japanese Eighth Fleet at Rabaul, ordered a counterattack within hours of receiving news of the landing. Mikawa gathered a force of seven cruisers and one destroyer and headed toward Guadalcanal. Aware of the dangers posed by American carriers, Mikawa believed he could time his advance to arrive at night. The Japanese Navy was well trained in surface battle at night and possessed superior optics and excellent torpedoes. Mikawa's plan succeeded brilliantly, slipping through an American destroyer screen, the Japanese cruisers opened fire at 2:00 A.M. on August 9. Forty minutes later three American and one Australian cruiser were sinking. Fortunately for the Americans, Mikawa's force was disorganized. Understandably fearful of air attack in the morning, Mikawa withdrew instead of hunting down the transports off Guadalcanal and Tulagi.

We will never know what would have happened had Mikawa pressed his attack. Had the Japanese destroyed the American transports, the Marines would have been in dire straits. Yet the Allied fleet had large numbers of destroyers and three cruisers that were never committed. Unknown to Mikawa, the American carriers had withdrawn. However, one of them, the *Wasp*, might have turned back had Admiral Kelly Turner, commander of the invasion fleet, urgently requested it. It is possible that Mikawa's withdrawal was a very wise move. As it turned out, the catastrophe at what the Americans called the Battle of Savo Island encouraged Turner to leave the area quickly. When American ships departed the next day, they were still carrying men and supplies they were unable to unload on time. Left alone, the

Marines on Guadalcanal were in a precarious position. Major General Archer Vandegrift, the Marine commander, realized this and organized his 12,000 men in a defensive perimeter guarding the partially constructed airstrip that American engineers, using Japanese heavy equipment and eating captured rations, rushed to complete.

After the American carriers withdrew, Japanese air and naval power at Rabaul had no opposition at Guadalcanal for two weeks. The South Seas Detachment had stripped Rabaul itself of most immediately available troops. Consequently, a large Japanese assault on Guadalcanal would require assembling troops and scarce transports from scattered points in the East Indies. Rather than wait for the arrival of adequate transport and more infantry, the Japanese used their temporary superiority in the air and on the sea to dispatch a landing force of 1,000 elite assault troops at Truk to Guadalcanal. Hoping that a lightning assault would dislodge the Americans, on August 21 the Japanese attacked the Marine perimeter. It was the first of a series of desperate Japanese night assaults against the Americans guarding the airfield. Although outnumbered, the Japanese arrogantly attacked a strong position. The Marines slaughtered the attackers. On the same day, the first American aircraft arrived at the airstrip, which the Marines had named Henderson Field in honor of a hero of the Battle of Midway. In coming months pilots from the Marine Corps, Army Air Force, and U.S. Navy flew together as part of the famous "Cactus Air Force" on Guadalcanal.

The Marines' destruction of their first attack removed any Japanese doubts concerning the seriousness of the situation. Major air, land, and naval forces scattered throughout the general area moved toward Rabaul and Truk to join the struggle for Guadalcanal. Although the Imperial Navy was still confident of victory, every reverse at Guadalcanal upped the stakes of the game. The Japanese, far more interested in New Guinea, were drawn steadily into a battle of attrition at a place they did not choose. Tokyo, although it did not realize it at the moment, was facing exactly the same type of catastrophe that would strike the Nazis at Stalingrad in a matter of weeks.

Furthermore, the completion of Henderson Field changed the strategic equation radically. The Japanese could not count on absolute naval or air superiority. Surprise was also difficult to achieve. Although the Japanese Navy had changed its codes after Midway, American intelligence grew skilled at tracking Japanese fleet movements. More important, throughout New Guinea and the Solomons, Australian and British colonial officials took to the bush when the Japanese arrived. Supported by the goodwill of the native peoples, these famous "coast watchers" radioed news of Japanese air and naval movements to Allied intelligence.

In addition, the American airmen on Guadalcanal possessed many of the same advantages held by the Royal Air Force during the Battle of Britain. Complementing the coast watchers, Americans had radar for air defense. Japanese air units were more powerful, but their journey from Rabaul was long and dangerous. (Japanese losses due to accident and bad weather were very heavy.) When Japanese aircraft reached Guadalcanal, American aircraft were ready to greet them. Japanese fighters, operating at the extreme end of their range, could not engage in prolonged combat without running out of fuel on the return flight. Any Japanese aircraft lost was gone forever. In contrast, an American pilot who could bail out or ditch a stricken plane might be back in action within hours. The same American planes made Japanese naval deployments difficult. Moving transports within attack range of American aircraft was particularly risky. Conversely, air cover from Henderson allowed a trickle of American supply vessels to arrive at Guadalcanal, ending Japanese hopes of starving out the Marines. Henderson Field, it was obvious to both sides, was at the center of the battle. Whoever controlled Henderson controlled Guadalcanal. As was becoming obvious, whoever controlled Guadalcanal controlled the Solomons.

What ensued, therefore, was a fascinating but grim set of tactical improvisations by both sides. The Solomons chain is about 500 miles long. On the northwestern end is the large island of Bougainville. Guadalcanal is situated near the southeastern edge of the chain. Imagine an axis drawn directly between Bougainville and Guadalcanal. There are islands on both sides of this line, but nothing to interrupt it. The water between the various islands was called the "Slot" by the Americans. Day after day fast Japanese destroyers, carrying troops and supplies (dubbed the "Tokyo Express" by the Marines), moved through the Slot and deposited their men and cargo at night near Tassafaronga Point on Guadalcanal, approximately fifteen miles west of the Marine perimeter. Americans relied on close air support to cover their reinforcement by conventional transports at Lunga Point near Henderson during daylight. Periodically, an attempt to reinforce land forces led to a naval battle. The Battle of the Eastern Solomons, an indecisive carrier battle, took place on August 24. It slowed but did not stop the Japanese buildup of troops on Guadalcanal.

A race was on between the opposing navies to reinforce their respective land forces on Guadalcanal. Judging strictly by the numbers, the Japanese were winning the race to reinforce. In truth, however, they were losing it. Starting with the shattered remnants of their original construction brigade dispersed by the Americans on the first day of the battle, the Japanese by October reached numerical parity with the Marines with both sides fielding approximately 30,000 men. (Battle strength is much harder to compute. Disease weakened both sides seriously, and thousands of men were required for supply services. The Japanese had approximately 12,000 assault troops when they attacked Henderson Field in late October. Roughly 15,000 Americans were actually defending the perimeter.) The Japanese landed men and basic supplies but they were woefully short of artillery, medicine, and canned rations. They had no defense against marauding U.S. Army fighter-bombers flying from Henderson. Although the Americans fell prey to malaria and other tropical diseases, the Japanese suffered worse. Their buildup, consequently, always lacked depth and led to precipitate action. For example, the second attack on Henderson was a three-day slugfest that the Marines called the Battle of Bloody Ridge (September 12–14). Although the Japanese attack was brilliantly conceived and came closer then any other to taking Henderson, ultimately the Japanese did not have the firepower or "punch" to prevail. The 3,000 attackers retreated after a shattering defeat and began to wither in the face of malnutrition and disease.

Thrown back a second time, the Japanese built up a larger force for yet another try. This time they also committed powerful elements of the Combined Fleet at Truk. It was a perfect time to do so. In preceding weeks, Japanese submarines had dealt the U.S. fleet a heavy blow by sinking the carrier *Wasp* and seriously damaging the carrier *Saratoga* and the new battleship *North Carolina*. Further weakened by the losses at Savo Island and smaller engagements, the American fleet had lost the momentary advantage gained at Midway. In mid-October Japanese battleships bombarded Henderson and almost brought it to its knees. Covered by air and naval power, the Japanese attempted to bring in a troop convoy on conventional transports. Most of the men and supplies on these slow ships landed successfully, but the Marine pilots on Henderson scratched together a force large enough to devastate the last ships to unload.

Attempting unsuccessfully to coordinate naval, land, and air actions in their largest offensive, the Japanese attack in late October turned into a badly managed fiasco. Reinforced by more Marines and a U.S. Army regiment, Vandegrift's men knew what to expect. The Japanese assault was overly complex. Instead of dividing the Americans, as intended, the various Japanese units attacked piecemeal. The Marines and GIs demolished all these attacks between October 22 and 25. (Perhaps because the Japanese assault was spread across the American perimeter for three days, this crucial battle for Henderson Field never received a specific name.) Tokyo gained some revenge the next day when another carrier battle took place at the Battle of Santa Cruz. The Americans lost the *Hornet*, and the *Enterprise*, the only remaining carrier in operation, was badly damaged. In return the Japanese lost a light carrier and suffered serious damage to a large one. Japanese carrier air fleets, however, had lost more planes than the Americans. Both carrier fleets withdrew, not to meet again for over a year.

Pressed in New Guinea and defeated again in Guadalcanal, Yamamoto readied Japanese forces for a final attempt to gain victory. The Japanese Army, facing advancing Australians in New Guinea, was also beginning to understand how badly the situation was developing in the South Pacific. Army officers in the immediate area knew the situation was serious and made a series of "local agreements" with their comrades in the Navy to allocate troops to Guadalcanal. The Army high command in Tokyo, however, concentrating on their "sphere" in New Guinea, had been very slow to appreciate the magnitude of the threat posed by the Americans at Guadalcanal. After the failure of the October offensive, Tokyo became fully committed to triumph on Guadalcanal.

To achieve victory, the Japanese planned to commit another division of troops and the full force of the Combined Fleet. The Japanese Navy would protect another convoy of transports and launch a sustained naval and air bombardment that would destroy Henderson. With Henderson neutralized, the additional ground forces would go ashore and put the Americans under siege. Guadalcanal, a battle the Japanese did not want to start, had become one they could not lose.

Yamamoto's decision to make a final assault on Guadalcanal precipitated one of the largest and most violent naval battles in history. Throughout this period Japanese and American destroyers and cruisers had met in confused night engagements. With battleships not a major presence, and the carriers gone, the naval war became a fierce struggle between smaller warships, often fighting at point-blank range at night. American sailors gave the deep water just off the coast of Guadalcanal the ominous name of Ironbottom Sound because so many warships were sunk within sight of the island. In November 1942, as both the Japanese and Americans reinforced their land forces on Guadalcanal, the stage was set for a fearful showdown at sea. The Japanese excelled at the use of torpedoes, while the Americans possessed early types of radar and superior gunnery. Both sides' strengths came into play during the three-night Battle of Guadalcanal (November 12–15) on the waters of Ironbottom Sound. The Americans received welcome reinforcement from the wounded *Enterprise*, which dispatched its attack planes to Henderson. When the smoke had cleared, much of the prewar American fleet had been sunk or damaged. Japanese torpedoes and guns sank six American destroyers and two cruisers. Four destroyers, one cruiser, and one battleship received serious damage. Nearly 2,000 American sailors lost their lives, including 700 on the cruiser *Juneau* alone. In return, the Americans sank two Japanese destroyers, a cruiser, and two battleships.

More important, American aircraft flying from Henderson destroyed the Japanese troop convoy.

The Japanese fleet could not sustain the naval and air losses it was suffering at Guadalcanal. Furthermore, the same American planes that devastated the Japanese troop convoy on the shores of Guadalcanal protected American transports that brought substantial reinforcements to the island. Any chance of the Japanese launching another ground attack on Henderson evaporated as the Americans decisively won the race to reinforce Guadalcanal. In December the American force was over 50,000 men. It was large enough that Halsey felt free to relieve the exhausted 1st Marine Division and send it to Australia for a well-deserved rest.

As the 1st Marines left the island, the Japanese had fewer than 20,000 men left on Guadalcanal. Their Army was devastated by disease and acute malnutrition. Wise officers at Rabaul and Truk soon came to the conclusion that Japan could not continue to bleed itself to death at Guadalcanal and must break off the battle. Because so much prestige was at stake, Tokyo proved hard to convince. In December, however, the Americans brought matters to a head when they launched an offensive out of their perimeter aimed at sweeping the Japanese off the island. The American attack was cautious and designed to keep casualties low. Nevertheless, the advance was inexorable. Before the malnourished but still sizable Japanese force on Guadalcanal faced annihilation, the Japanese Navy successfully evacuated 13,000 men. Most of the survivors suffered so badly from disease and malnutrition that few fought again. Those Japanese who could not leave fought to the last man. This pattern repeated itself at the conclusion of every campaign in the South Pacific, and lent to the war an unusual savagery. Tragically, the refusal of Japanese units to surrender when facing certain annihilation became the norm for the entire Pacific war.

The Japanese suffered a catastrophe on Guadalcanal. Approximately 25,000 men lost their lives, 600 aircraft were lost, and twenty-four warships were sunk. But the significance of the battle went far beyond the physical losses. Tokyo had assumed before the war that American troops did not have the skill and courage necessary to stand against Japanese infantry. Guadalcanal had proven this conception to be fanciful, the product of self-delusion. The Americans did rely more heavily on firepower, but, as shown on Guadalcanal, firepower was very effective against Japanese ground forces that stressed massed nighttime assaults. This was very bad news for Tokyo. If American courage and American firepower could triumph over Japanese spirit on Guadalcanal, it could do so in other places as well. In addition, all the strategic considerations that had brought the Japanese to Guadalcanal in the first place took on an ominous new significance. Free to develop Guadalcanal at will, the Americans constructed a powerful air base that grew as large as Rabaul. American shipyards, by the beginning of 1943, were finally working at full speed. Despite the many ships sunk during the Guadalcanal campaign, the American fleet began to grow rapidly. With Guadalcanal lost, the Japanese position in the Solomons was in danger. If the Solomons fell, Allied aircraft could operate from Rabaul's doorstep. If the Allies could neutralize Rabaul, they could break out of the South Pacific and move toward the Southern Resource Zone.

The defeat at Guadalcanal also doomed the Japanese expedition to New Guinea. While the great land and naval battles raged in October and November on or near Guadalcanal, the struggle in Papua deteriorated seriously from Tokyo's point of view. Deprived of reinforcement because of fighting in the Solomons, the Japanese spearhead near Port Moresby had retreated back up the Kokoda Trail in October. Still assuming that the offensive would begin again, Major General Tomitaro Horii, personally commanding the South Seas Detachment in Papua, decided to make a stand near Kokoda instead of pulling back to the coast at Buna. The position Horii chose was an area along the trail between the two native settlements of Oivi and Gorari, a few miles east of Kokoda. Standing on the defensive, Horii was confident his crack troops could stop the Australians. By early November, however, the Australians had learned much about warfare in the jungle. At Oivi-Gorari the Australians fought a brilliant battle, outflanking the Japanese position and shoving Horii's men off the trail and into a river. Because the jungle terrain was so dense, many of the Japanese managed to slip through to the coast. (Horii was not among them; he drowned attempting to reach Buna.) The Japanese retreat turned into a rout. At Oivi-Gorari the Australians showed dramatically that their infantry had become the best in the Pacific.

The campaign in Papua, however, had a violent last act. The Japanese had brought engineers to Buna when they first landed, hoping to build a small road along the Kokoda Trail. Their road-building mission proved impossible, but the engineers found much to do fortifying the coastal area between Gona and Buna. When they had finished in November, the Japanese had a fortified zone that was approximately ten miles long and several miles deep, placed in some of the worst terrain on earth. In this hideous area 7,000 Japanese troops, of whom approximately half were survivors of the battles on the Kokoda Trail, awaited an inevitable Allied attack.

In late November the Australians approached Buna from Kokoda. In the meantime, the American 32d Division moved up the Papuan coastline in a motley convoy of fishing boats and coastal steamers. Because the waters were reef-invested, poorly charted, and close to Japanese air bases, the U.S. Navy refused to support the operation with transports and warships. (Sophisticated shallow-draft landing craft had not yet arrived in the Pacific.) The Navy's decision had important ramifications. It was not possible to haul artillery or heavy equipment over the Kokoda Trail. It was also impossible to bring in artillery on the tiny vessels used to haul men and food. Consequently, the 32d Division, which was unprepared for nightmarish combat in a Papuan swamp in any case, went into battle without artillery. Unfortunately for the poorly trained Americans, they were entering an area filled with nearly invisible and well-fortified Japanese machine-gun nests.

The American and Australian advance against the Buna-Gona fortified zone began on November 18, 1942. Progress forward could be measured in yards. Weakened by disease, Allied troops were frustrated by the dreadful swamp and invisible Japanese fire. Fortunately for the Allies, the Japanese received few supplies and were suffering from malnourishment and disease far worse than they were. Consequently, frequently more by luck than skill, American units found cracks in the Japanese position and exploited them. The Australians did better, but also found going very hard. Fighting near the coastal settlement of Sanananda was some of the worst encountered by the Australians in the war.

MacArthur was displeased with events in Buna. It was not the first time the general showed his wrath. Earlier in August, MacArthur had infuriated Australian officers by questioning the skill of Australian infantry then falling back toward Port Moresby. MacArthur's anxieties caused a large command shake-up in Australian forces that proved, in the long run, to be an improvement. Nevertheless, Australian pride was hurt and careers were damaged during the affair, and MacArthur gained enemies quickly inside the Australian Army. When MacArthur turned his ire toward the 32d Division, another ugly situation arose. The division's commander was relieved and replaced by a MacArthur protégé, Major General Robert Eichelberger. Eichelberger proved a good commander, but, like all officers in the Pacific, he treaded warily when dealing with MacArthur. Many men in the 32d Division felt that MacArthur did not understand the beastly situation at the front and had done little to support them. Bad blood existed on both matters throughout the war and after.

Slowly the Allies gained the upper hand at Buna. In early December American engineers opened a good air base at Dobodura near Buna. The supply situation, therefore, eased greatly. The Australians managed to bring in small numbers of artillery pieces by air, adding much-needed punch to their forces. Australian engineers also succeeded, despite American skepticism, in transporting a few light tanks to Buna on coastal barges. Although small in number, the tanks proved indispensable in the areas where they could operate. A series of tank attacks in early December started the destruction of the Japanese position at Buna. Yet the Allies required six more weeks of vicious close combat to finally prevail. On January 23, 1943, the last Japanese positions in the Buna area fell and the miserable campaign was over. Toward the end of the fighting, Japanese positions became unraveled. Rather than surrender, many Japanese soldiers committed suicide. Hundreds of exhausted Japanese troops wandered about, resisting feebly if at all. Yet they would not surrender, and Allied soldiers gunned them down.

Shocked by the unfolding disasters in both New Guinea and Guadalcanal, the Japanese Army began to see the full dimensions of the threat developing in the South Pacific. In late November it activated the new Eighteenth Army and assigned to it the defense of New Guinea. The Japanese Seventeenth Army was charged with defending the Solomons. After months of unusual lassitude toward the theater, the Army authorized a major buildup of forces. The Japanese already had bases at Lae and Salamaua, north up the coast from Buna. In December they seized several new bases in New Guinea, including Finschhafen and Wewak. Steadily Japanese reinforcements came in. In the next year, an additional 200,000 troops moved into New Guinea and the Solomons.

The Japanese Army Air Force also moved into the area, operating primarily out of the new base at Wewak. Previously, the Japanese naval air arm had carried the load in the South Pacific. Their losses were so severe that plans to rebuild the carrier air groups were scrapped so more aircraft could be sent to Rabaul. The Army's decision to move a major portion of its air force was intended to allow the Navy to concentrate on the Solomons while the Army contested the New Guinea skies. Both services faced arduous tasks. The Army's air units had gained much experience in China. Facing the Americans and Australians was a much tougher assignment. Furthermore, because of heavy losses during 1942, the naval air arm never regained the qualitative edge that made it so effective early in the war.

In 1943 the Americans started to deploy new models of fighter aircraft such as the P-38 Lightning and F-4U Corsair that were considerably better than the redoubtable Zero or any other fighter in the Japanese arsenal. The number of Allied aircraft was also going up, as was the quality of the pilots. The Allies were quick to put their growing air strength into action. The Japanese had no choice but to fight the growing Allied air armada. Throughout 1943 a ceaseless air war raged between land-based squadrons over both New Guinea and the Solomons. Steadily, the Allies gained air superiority throughout the South Pacific. In this period, the great American aces like Richard

Bong, Pappy Boyington, and Charles MacDonald accumulated large numbers of victories and became national heroes in the process. Japanese factories and training facilities kept the air fleets in operation, but the "kill ratio" grew so out of balance that fighter combat in the South Pacific took on the quality of a massacre. American bombers and transport aircraft also flooded into the area.

Although the air and naval war continued without letup, after Buna and Guadalcanal there were no Allied major land operations until the summer of 1943. Throughout the year, MacArthur and King jousted over allocation of resources and the direction of the Pacific war. MacArthur championed a concentration of effort in the South Pacific, leading to an advance toward the Philippines and the East Indies. King fought for a massive drive directly at Japan through the Central Pacific. The dispute was complicated and included Marshall and Roosevelt at a number of junctures. The details need not concern us here. In the end, the American war machine produced enough to support an offensive by both MacArthur through New Guinea and the Philippines and an amphibious drive through the Central Pacific. Historians have argued for fifty years whether two drives were necessary, and, if not, which should have been taken. As will be clear, I believe MacArthur had much the better argument. Nevertheless, it is the type of question that defies a final answer.

While the Japanese readied their defenses, and American military leaders feuded in Washington, Halsey and MacArthur, after much consultation, each prepared an attack for the summer on the Japanese position in the South Pacific. Although the operational details were left up to the respective commanders, the offensives were scheduled to support each other by preventing a concentration of Japanese strength in either New Guinea or the Solomons.

Both attacks began in the last days of June 1943. Halsey's first target was the island of New Georgia, 200 miles up the Slot from Guadalcanal, which he believed to be a necessary site for fighter bases to support air bombardment of Rabaul. As we shall see in more detail later, the New Georgia operation was, at best, a Pyrrhic victory for the Americans, with casualties almost as serious as those suffered on Guadalcanal. Fortunately for the Allies, Halsey redeemed much of the situation by seizing the almost-undefended small island of Vella Lavella fifty miles northwest of New Georgia. With the Americans between the remaining garrisons in the central Solomons and Rabaul, the Japanese were forced to evacuate their men quickly. On November 1, 1943, Halsey directed the newly formed 3d Marine Division to assault the large island of Bougainville, the last Japanese outpost before Rabaul. In sharp contrast to New Georgia, Halsey sent his troops ashore at a weakly held portion of the island. They quickly established a perimeter along the Torokina River and built an air base behind it. Four months later the Japanese attacked the Bougainville perimeter and were smashed.

MacArthur's portion of the advance went more smoothly. MacArthur was determined to never again assault a Japanese fortified zone as his men had done at Buna. Consequently, he and the Australians developed a brilliant plan of operations that shattered the Japanese position in New Guinea at very little cost. On June 30, American troops landed on the coast near the Japanese base of Salamaua. As they moved inland, they were met by an Australian column advancing from the interior. Fighting cautiously, the Allies suffered low casualties. The Japanese, however, reinforced Salamaua. When they did so they weakened their more important base at Lae. In early September, the Australian Imperial Force (AIF) landed at Lae and nearby Finschhafen and pushed back the Japanese further. An American landing at Saidor in January 1944 threatened to cut off all the Japanese defenders facing the Australians. The Japanese had no choice but to retreat headlong through some of the worst terrain in New Guinea.

Events in the South Pacific came to a close very rapidly in late 1943. (I shall analyze the Japanese collapse in more detail in the last chapter.) The easy victories at Vella Lavella and Lae showed how much stronger the Allies had become and how much more quickly they could move. In the fall MacArthur and Marshall decided that Rabaul did not require a direct land assault. Instead, late in the year, Allied air forces began a withering air offensive against both Rabaul and Wewak. In a matter of weeks, the proud and tenacious Japanese air arm in the South Pacific was crushed.

In November 1943 Admiral King's long-awaited offensive into
the Central Pacific began with the landing at Tarawa in the Gilbert
Islands. In February 1944, MacArthur broke out of the South Pacific
by landing on the Admiralty Islands, north of Rabaul. What little remained of the Japanese fleet and air arm in the South Pacific rede-
ployed to Truk. The large Japanese garrisons that remained on New
Guinea, Rabaul, and Bougainville were cut off from the Japanese
Empire. Although the Allies harassed some of these troops, no attempt was made to exterminate these garrisons. Some Japanese units
simply withered in the face of disease and malnutrition. Others reverted to a semiagrarian existence to stay alive, confined, in essence,
to the largest prisoner-of-war camp in the world.

The Pacific war continued for another harsh year and a half, and
the butcher bill grew very large. Yet, as a military struggle, the war
was over. Although the Japanese resisted every Allied advance fero-
ciously, the issue was never in doubt during any battle after late 1943.
The Japanese tactic of suicide air attack is grim testimony to the
quantitative and qualitative advantage the Allies enjoyed after 1944.

Given the defeat of Nazi Germany, the ultimate outcome of
World War II in the Pacific was inevitable. Yet it was in the South
Pacific, where the two sides fought tooth and nail in a position of relative equality, that the Japanese lost their ability to control the flow
of battle. It was in the South Pacific where thousands of their best
fighting men perished. It was in the South Pacific where both the
Japanese and Allies realized that the military and political assumptions upon which Japan had based its war effort were completely in
error. Finally, it was in the South Pacific where the conflict between
the Japanese and their enemies took on the undeniable character of
a war of annihilation. It is time to look deeply at the complex factors
that shaped this frightful conflict. In doing so, a half century distant
from events, we can also gaze at the heart of World War II.

MAPS

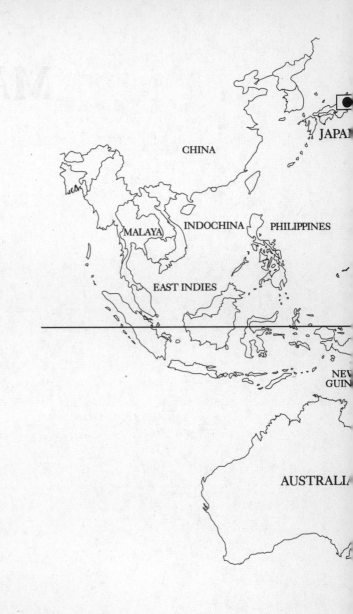

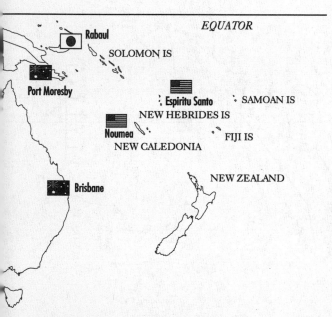

The Pacific
Summer, 1942

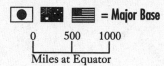 = Major Base

```
0        500     1000
├────────┼────────┤
   Miles at Equator
```

MARIANAS IS

◉ Saipan

Pearl Harbor

HAWAII

MARSHALL IS

CAROLINE IS   ◉ Truk

GILBERT IS

EQUATOR

◉ Rabaul

SOLOMON IS

Port Moresby

■ Espiritu Santo   SAMOAN IS

NEW HEBRIDES IS

Noumea

NEW CALEDONIA   FIJI IS

Brisbane   NEW ZEALAND

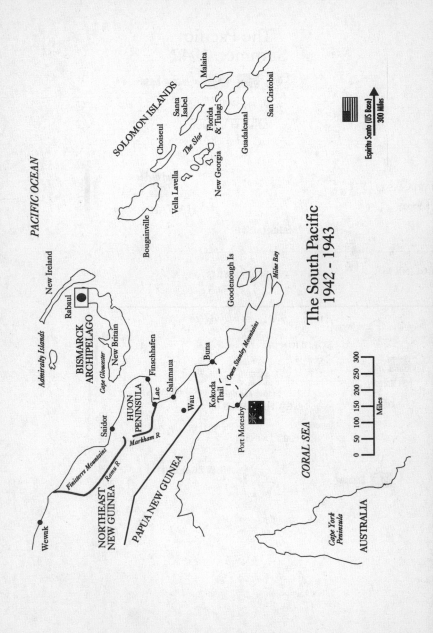

The South Pacific
1942 - 1943

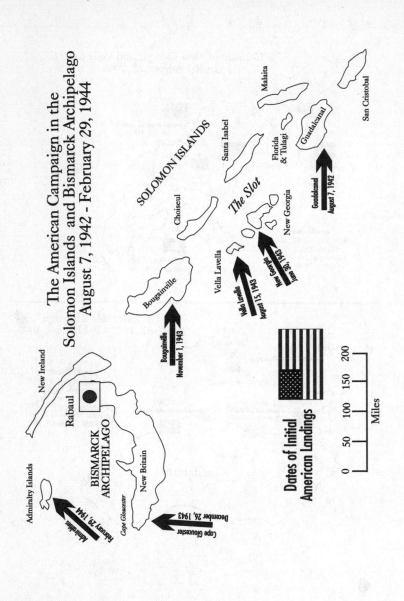

The American Campaign in the
Solomon Islands and Bismarck Archipelago
August 7, 1942 - February 29, 1944

New Ireland

Admiralty Islands

Rabaul

BISMARCK
ARCHIPELAGO

Cape Gloucester

New Britain

Admiralties
February 29, 1944

Cape Gloucester
December 26, 1943

Bougainville

Bougainville
November 1, 1943

SOLOMON ISLANDS

Choiseul

Santa Isabel

Malaita

The Slot

Vella Lavella

Vella Lavella
August 15, 1943

New Georgia
June 30, 1943

New Georgia

Florida
& Tulagi

Guadalcanal

Guadalcanal
August 7, 1942

San Cristobal

Dates of Initial
American Landings

| 0 | 50 | 100 | 150 | 200 |

Miles

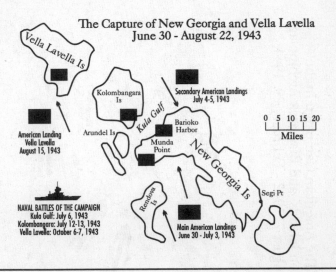

The Capture of New Georgia and Vella Lavella
June 30 - August 22, 1943

Vella Lavella Is

Kolombangara Is

Secondary American Landings
July 4-5, 1943

Kula Gulf

Barioko Harbor

American Landing
Vella Lavella
August 15, 1943

Arundel Is

Munda Point

New Georgia Is

0 5 10 15 20
Miles

Segi Pt

NAVAL BATTLES OF THE CAMPAIGN
Kula Gulf: July 6, 1943
Kolombangara: July 12-13, 1943
Vella Lavella: October 6-7, 1943

Rendova Is

Main American Landings
June 30 - July 3, 1943

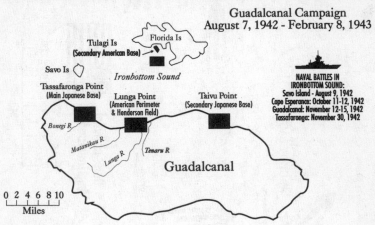

Guadalcanal Campaign
August 7, 1942 - February 8, 1943

Tulagi Is
(Secondary American Base)

Florida Is

Savo Is

Ironbottom Sound

NAVAL BATTLES IN
IRONBOTTOM SOUND:
Savo Island - August 9, 1942
Cape Esperanca: October 11-12, 1942
Guadalcanal: November 12-15, 1942
Tassafaronga: November 30, 1942

Tassafaronga Point
(Main Japanese Base)

Lunga Point
(American Perimeter
& Henderson Field)

Taivu Point
(Secondary Japanese Base)

Bonegi R.

Matanikau R.

Lunga R.

Tenaru R.

Guadalcanal

0 2 4 6 8 10
Miles

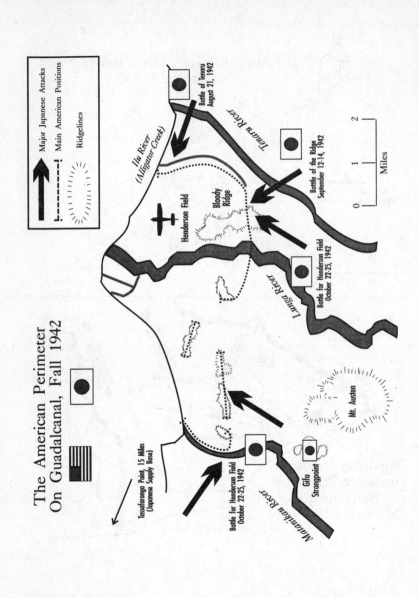

The American Perimeter
On Guadalcanal, Fall 1942

Major Japanese Attacks
Main American Positions
Ridgelines

Miles
0   1   2

Battle of Tenaru
August 21, 1942

*Ilu River
(Alligator Creek)*

Tenaru River

Henderson Field

Bloody Ridge

Battle of the Ridge
September 12-14, 1942

Battle for Henderson Field
October 22-25, 1942

Lunga River

Tassafaronga Point, 15 Miles
(Japanese Supply Base)

Battle for Henderson Field
October 22-25, 1942

Mt. Austen

Gifu Strongpoint

Matanikau River

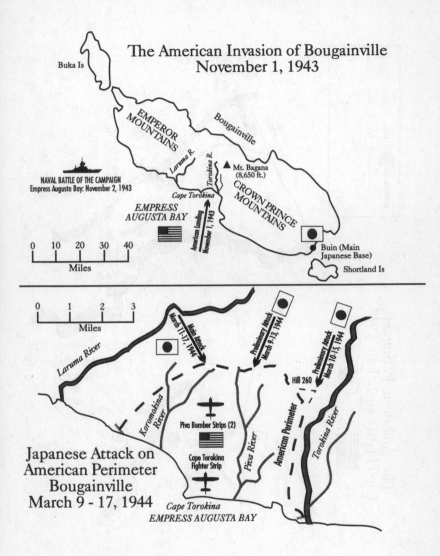

The American Invasion of Bougainville
November 1, 1943

Buka Is

EMPEROR MOUNTAINS

Bougainville

Laruma R.

Torokina R.

▲ Mt. Bagana
(8,650 ft.)

NAVAL BATTLE OF THE CAMPAIGN
Empress Augusta Bay: November 2, 1943

Cape Torokina

CROWN PRINCE MOUNTAINS

EMPRESS AUGUSTA BAY

American Landing
November 1, 1943

| 0 | 10 | 20 | 30 | 40 |

Miles

Buin (Main Japanese Base)

Shortland Is

| 0 | 1 | 2 | 3 |

Miles

Laruma River

March 11-17, 1944
Main Attack

Preliminary Attack
March 9-13, 1944

Preliminary Attack
March 10-15, 1944

Hill 260

Koromokina River

Piva Bomber Strips (2)

Piva River

American Perimeter

Torokina River

Cape Torokina Fighter Strip

Japanese Attack on American Perimeter Bougainville
March 9 - 17, 1944

Cape Torokina
EMPRESS AUGUSTA BAY

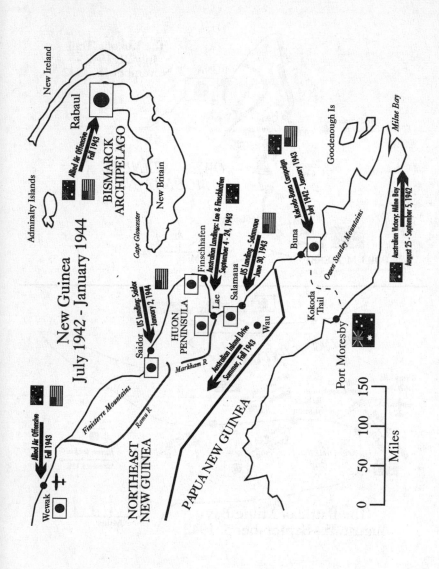

New Guinea
July 1942 - January 1944

New Ireland

Admiralty Islands

Rabaul

Allied Air Offensive
Fall 1943

BISMARCK ARCHIPELAGO

New Britain

Cape Gloucester

Goodenough Is

Milne Bay

Kokoda-Buna Campaign
July 1942 - January 1943

Australian Victory: Milne Bay
August 25 - September 5, 1942

Buna

Owen Stanley Mountains

Kokoda Trail

Port Moresby

Australian Landings: Lae & Finschhafen
September 4 - 24, 1943

Finschhafen

US Landing - Salamaua
June 30, 1943

Lae

Salamaua

Wau

HUON PENINSULA

US Landing: Saidor
January 2, 1944

Saidor

Markham R

Australian Island Drive
Summer, Fall 1943

Finisterre Mountains

Ramu R

NORTHEAST NEW GUINEA

PAPUA NEW GUINEA

Allied Air Offensive
Fall 1943

Wewak

Miles
0   50   100   150

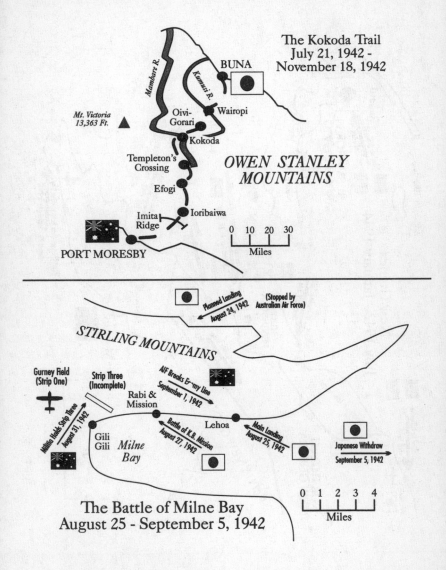

The Kokoda Trail
July 21, 1942 –
November 18, 1942

Mt. Victoria
13,363 Ft.

Mambare R.

Kumusi R.

BUNA

Wairopi

Oivi-
Gorari

Kokoda

Templeton's
Crossing

OWEN STANLEY
MOUNTAINS

Efogi

Imita
Ridge

Ioribaiwa

PORT MORESBY

0 10 20 30

Miles

Planned Landing
August 24, 1942

(Stopped by
Australian Air Force)

STIRLING MOUNTAINS

Gurney Field
(Strip One)

Strip Three
(Incomplete)

AIF Breaks Enemy Line
September 1, 1942

Rabi &
Mission

Militia Holds Strip Three
August 31, 1942

Lehoa

Battle of K.B. Mission
August 27, 1942

Main Landing
August 25, 1942

Japanese Withdraw
September 5, 1942

Gili
Gili

Milne
Bay

The Battle of Milne Bay
August 25 – September 5, 1942

0 1 2 3 4

Miles

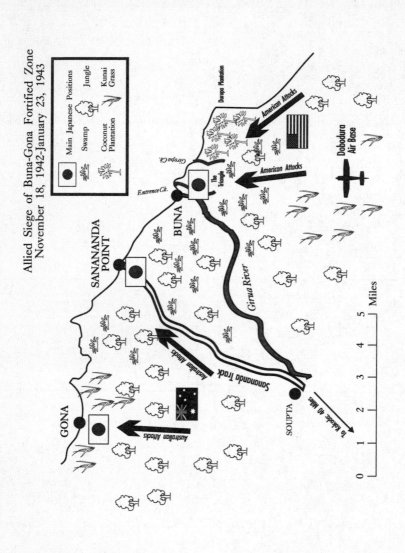

Allied Siege of Buna-Gona Fortified Zone
November 18, 1942–January 23, 1943

PART I

THE BATTLEFIELD AND THE ARMIES

The soldiers who fought the harsh war in the South Pacific lived at a time when their military commanders had a very firm grasp of the essentials of twentieth-century land warfare. Before 1941, land battles of all types and scales had occurred almost continuously throughout the world in the twentieth century. The Japanese were involved in some of the first during their violent war with Russia in 1904. Many Australian and American commanders personally confronted the twin killers of the modern battlefield, artillery and machine guns, during World War I. Their Japanese opponents had closely observed events in the European trenches and put what they learned and refined into action when they assaulted China first in 1931 and again in 1937. After 1939, several hundred Australian veterans of the Great War led a new generation of their countrymen against the relentlessly efficient German Wehrmacht in the Mideast. Although the United States proved woefully unprepared for World War II, many of its officers knew what was coming. They watched and examined events in Asia and Europe intently. During the wretched months after Pearl Harbor, American commanders gained bitter but valuable lessons concerning ground combat from their defeats in the Pacific. The basics of land war were no secret in Tokyo, Canberra, or Washington.

Nevertheless, as the Greek general and historian Thucydides observed 2,400 years ago, "War is a stern teacher." Despite the development and refinement of massive military forces and new weapons devoted to the struggle on land, unusual and unforeseen circumstances existed in the South Pacific. On one hand, the struggle was on the cutting edge of advanced combat technique. Infantrymen sent to fight under the Southern Cross entered a world where aircraft, the newest of the world's weapons, dominated the struggle at a strategic level. Their fate was likewise intimately linked to increasingly sophisticated sea battles that led to the birth of modern naval warfare.

In stark contrast, land combat in the South Pacific was harsh, crude, and, from a military viewpoint, technically primitive. The situation was unique in time and place. None of the combatants initially possessed the knowledge or equipment to overcome the challenges raised by the brutal and distant terrain with technology and appropriate weaponry. The secondary status given to the Pacific by the Allies slowed the introduction of more appropriate tools of war for American and Australian soldiers. Japan lacked the economic resources to equip its army with more complex weaponry and support services. In addition, ethnic arrogance and racism were common to all combatants. This, combined with a fanatical and wasteful battle ethos on the part of the Japanese, created a horrifying battle psychology that transformed what would have been a cruel struggle into a battle to the death.

However, more than any other factor, the savage physical environment shaped every facet of the land war in the South Pacific. The battlefield was a miserable, disease-infested place created by the forces of nature gone berserk. The influence played by the hostile terrain and vicious climate on military operations cannot be overstated or overemphasized. It was literally true that in order to fight each other, the armies involved first had to do battle with the land. Indeed, as the ruthless dynamics of fighting grew clear, intelligent commanders made tactical moves specifically designed to allow the jungle itself to do the killing. In consequence, although the struggle in the South Pacific contained elements of modern industrial warfare, its essence more closely resembled a knife fight out of the Stone Age.

Chapter 1

The War Against the Land

Major General Stanley Larsen, during a long and distinguished military career, fought in three Asian wars for the United States. He first experienced combat as a young officer in the U.S. 25th Infantry Division on Guadalcanal in late 1942. Years later he commented, "The war we confronted on Guadalcanal is, in my opinion, almost impossible to comprehend because the terrain, the climate, the physical nature of the battlefield is beyond the experience of people who were not there to see it." Larsen's point is well made. Every facet of war in the South Pacific was shaped or conditioned by a unique geography and savage terrain. To understand the essence of the war in this theater, we must first examine the battlefield itself.

Geography and terrain are vital subjects in military affairs. Although related, they are not the same. Military geography concerns the relationship of one place to another. Considerations include distance between points, the size and importance of objectives, and the lines of communication available. In this realm, strategic and logistic planning meld. In contrast, the nature of the terrain lies at the heart of military tactics. Every officer, noncommissioned officer, and soldier is trained at some level to understand and utilize terrain features to increase the power of a defensive position or, conversely, to choose the best possible line of attack. Understanding and exploiting terrain well is the mark of a superior combat leader at any level.

Both military geography and terrain were understood and handled in strikingly similar ways by the armies of World War II. Many officers on the huge staffs that accompanied all armed services concerned themselves with identifying points of importance and getting large forces to them. Some of the most brilliant officers of all armies analyzed operational options: what places had value, which were obtainable, how much effort was required to gain the object and sustain the required forces. Repeated staff exercises dealt with these matters. Studies by the hundreds existed, supported by reams of statistics allowing planners to anticipate, for instance, how much material would be required by so many men in operation for so many days. In addition, by 1942 most armies had much contemporary experience in these matters.

The same was true in the realm of tactics and terrain. Firepower, whether delivered by artillery, machine guns, tanks, or aircraft, was recognized as a central factor of modern battle. The power and reach of modern weapons and the ever-increasing size of land forces resulted in a massive leap in the size of the battle zone. The larger battle zone also emphasized the importance of proper use of terrain. The defense sought locations of concealment where it had unencumbered fields of fire. If it succeeded, assaulting troops would never see the defenders, but would discover their presence when unseen machine guns or mortars opened fire, killing attackers trying to move forward. The attackers learned to identify likely defensive strong points, probe them, and, once the defenders were found, bring artillery, mortars, and bombs down upon them. Direct infantry assault, although sometimes necessary, was always risky. Good World War II armies attempted to lessen the risk by using "fire and movement" tactics. Small infantry units would leap forward a short distance while being covered by the machine-gun and rifle fire from a cooperating unit. After moving forward, the original advancing unit "hit the dirt" and commenced fire intended to cover a leapfrog advance by the unit that originally supported them. Alternating advance and covering fire, the units moved forward. There was great urgency in managing attacks correctly because, as every officer knew, a badly conducted assault resulted in disaster.

At a certain point terrain and geography overlapped. The soldiers had to be supplied and protected from the elements. Military engineers increased in importance along with growth of wheeled transport. Armies could not supply large numbers of men and weapons without sophisticated lines of communication. On land, this meant railroads as close as possible to the front. Once at the railhead, men loaded their supplies on vehicles, either trucks or horse-drawn wagons, and moved them up. Armies had field kitchens, provided some type of shelter for men at the front, and maintained a medical apparatus that tended to the ill and wounded. To some degree, all armies attempted to provide small creature comforts to their soldiers. Every army had different uniforms suitable for various climates. Generals rotated combat units when possible between the front and the rear. In the rear, although conditions were frequently spartan, men found small comforts such as sleep, liquor, or hot food. If very lucky, soldiers might also be able to meet women in the rear.

It is worth noting that the physical worlds inhabited by the men of the warring nations were also very similar. The climate and terrain in Japan and China are very much like those found in much of Europe, the United States, or Australia. The officers serving Japan, the United States, or Australia could have "talked shop" with little difficulty before 1941. Training in the Australian "outback" proved a decent prelude for combat along the Mediterranean coast. Maneuvers in South Carolina would have been suitable preparation for a campaign in southern China.

The military forces of Japan, Australia, and the United States had something else in common: none was in the least prepared for a major war in the South Pacific, one of the world's most remote areas. Nor were they ready for a terrain that not only raised tactical problems of extraordinary difficulty but was often more dangerous than the weapons wielded by the enemy. In short, they were not ready for the viper pit they all encountered in New Guinea and the Solomon Islands.

The military geography of the South Pacific had extremely striking attributes. For example, in the very large area encompassing New Guinea and the Solomons Islands in 1942 there were no cities or towns. This was true even though European contact with the area went back centuries. The Portuguese first brought back news of New Guinea in the sixteenth century. The world's second-largest island received its European name, Neuve Guinea, because the leader of a Spanish expedition believed the dark-skinned inhabitants to be of the same stock as the people of the Guinea coast of Africa. (Papua comes from the Dutch term for "fuzzy" and refers to the bushy hair found on Melanesians.) After the Portuguese came the Dutch, who took control of the western half of New Guinea. In the nineteenth century the British and Germans came, followed in later decades by the Australians.

Yet after 400 years of European control, all that existed was a scattering of coconut plantations and a few sleepy trading outposts and small Christian missions. Although difficult to determine precisely, it is likely that in 1942 the German-founded outpost at Rabaul on New Britain, a part of the Bismarck Archipelago, was the largest settlement, with a population of perhaps 2,500. A few settlements on New Guinea, such as Lae, Finschhafen, and Port Moresby, were about the same size. The scale of what Europeans considered civilization in the South Pacific was smaller yet in the Solomons. Tulagi, the British administrative center for the Solomons, was little more than an anchorage, a couple of buildings, and a Union Jack.

The obvious question is why, after such a long period, so little had happened to disturb this primitive part of the world. Simple expanse is part of the answer. Men measure distances in the South Pacific with large numbers. For instance, it is 1,500 air miles between Port Moresby and Brisbane. It is 900 miles from Port Moresby to Rabaul. As thousands of Japanese pilots learned, it is approximately an 800-mile flight from Rabaul to Guadalcanal. (It takes no military talent to see why Rabaul, equidistant from Guadalcanal and Port Moresby, became the central point of the entire struggle.)

Yet "remote" is a relative term. The land that served as a battlefield in the South Pacific is wedged between great cultures. Directly to the west and northwest are Indonesia and the Philippines. Australia lies just a few miles south of New Guinea. Despite the relative proximity of Southeast Asia and Australia, a series of formidable defenses in the South Pacific, natural and human, kept the outside world at bay until well into the twentieth century.

Each of the major topographical features of the area created extraordinary military challenges, and we shall examine them all in greater detail. For the present, it is enough to note that both New Guinea and the Solomons are home to some of the most rugged mountain ranges and ridgelines on the globe. Precipitous ridges fan out, dissecting the landscape further. Near the coast are densely forested swamps and acres of tall, razor-sharp kunai grass. Many of the hundreds of indigenous cultures were intensely martial. Tribal warfare was very common and often extremely violent. Early Europeans found hostility in the area, and many early settlements were destroyed.

Slowly in the late nineteenth century, some missionaries and a few planters established isolated settlements along the coast of New Guinea and in the Solomons. Armed with quinine to keep malaria in check, they created a tiny society existing on the fringe of a larger world. The coconut plantations were the largest commercial enterprises in the South Pacific. Yet these settlements were minute in comparison to the huge cash-crop plantations found in the East Indies. The British and Australian governments sent out a handful of administrators who worked with tribal groups principally for an orderly supply of short-term contract labor.

The minimal European presence in the Solomons and New Guinea was confined to the coast. Westerners knew almost nothing about the inland areas of New Guinea or the larger islands in the Solomons. A handful of prospectors altered this situation slightly in New Guinea. In the 1930s, largely due to the discovery of gold in river valleys in the interior, Europeans came into contact for the first time with a large Stone Age culture, consisting of over 700 linguistic groups and a population of 1.5 million, living in the New Guinea highlands. As one might expect, the region became a haven for anthropologists, writers, and adventurers of all sorts. Yet the numbers of outsiders remained small. Only one inland settlement at Wau, a place we shall encounter again, proved worthy of development.

Because no large towns existed, much less cities, there were no roads that merited the name in New Guinea or the Solomons. In September 1942 Art Kessenich was one of the first Americans of the 32d Division to fly into Port Moresby, the most important town con-

trolled by the Allies in Papua. He found something less than a bus-
tling metropolis:

> Port Moresby was a town of about 2,000 people. It had a hotel,
> which was the advance Headquarters of the Fifth Air Force.
> There was a Catholic church. MacArthur's staff took over the
> government house. The Great Man himself, of course, was in
> Brisbane, but his forward staff was there. There were some stores
> and shops. But it was all very antique. A native village was a
> stone's throw away. Out in the marshlands that surrounded
> Moresby, some of our goofballs used to hunt crocodiles in native
> canoes. When I returned in 1981 I found a city of 40,000. It was
> unbelievable.

A few weeks earlier, Australian infantryman Norman Grinyer
had arrived at Port Moresby when the Japanese were still advancing
toward the town. During this period, Japanese aircraft attacked Port
Moresby frequently to prevent reinforcement. Grinyer describes the
situation:

> We berthed at Moresby, were unloaded at the town and trans-
> ported by truck to the air strip and barracks. The town was a
> shambles. Built of timber-framed, fabric-covered buildings, it
> was not demolished, but reduced by gaping holes caused by
> shrapnel. The barracks and strip were completely devastated.
> There were rows of shattered toilet bowls and concrete slabs ly-
> ing naked where ablutions and things had been. On the strip a
> wrecked plane was plowed in. There were bones laying about the
> wreckage, vertebrae and flying boots with the remains of a foot
> inside.
>   It rained twice a day, at 8:00 A.M. and 4:00 P.M. In between it
> was steam dry. At night we slept under a mosquito net, and in the
> morning it was covered with grubs. The trees were stunted and
> sparse. The water in the river was undrinkable. The water in our
> bottles was foul by morning. We lived on dehydrated mutton and
> vegetables that were stewed in such a way that there would be
> enough to go around. The cooks did their best with curries to
> disguise the flavor but it still tasted *dead*. In the field, we devel-

oped a unique type of field oven. We gouged out a hole in a three-or or four-foot-high termite mound. In it we inserted a flue vent, fired the entrance, and blocked it with something. We would then scrape the fire out, insert the food, and allow it to bake, just like an oven.

As is evident from the accounts above, the European presence was minimal. This situation had important consequences during the war. First, everything required to make war had to come from the outside. Nevertheless, when the Japanese forced the issue, the Allies responded. Both sides, consequently, used only the barest necessities for operations. Shipping was painfully short on both sides. Likewise the organizational apparatus required to manage a complex war far away was rudimentary and untested in Tokyo, Washington, or Canberra. Consequently, supplies of all sorts existed in minimal quantities. However, getting supplies, men, and weapons to the front was only part of the problem. Because the terrain was so difficult, and true roads extremely rare, armies faced serious problems distributing what was available to troops on the move. The major form of transport inland was native bearer or infantryman. Stripped of supply vehicles, armies moved at a snail's pace and carried very little firepower. Artillery and armor, so crucial elsewhere in World War II, played very restricted roles. Often infantrymen were thrown back upon their own weapons and ingenuity. In no theater of war during the twentieth century did infantry experience as much combat at point-blank range as they found in the South Pacific. Ultimately, the Allies' ability to come to grips with this supply nightmare, and Japan's failure to do so, proved crucial to the Allied triumph. Supplies allowed one to make war. They also kept armies alive. Armies without supplies faced the jungle alone, and, in the South Pacific, the jungle killed.

The geopolitical isolation of the South Pacific battlefields affected the minds of the combatants as well as their bodies. Infantry, as we shall see, normally fought blindly. Their commanders did likewise. So little was known about the area, and so little was known about the type of warfare required to prevail there, that both sides made many decisions based on erroneous information. Maps were initially extremely crude or nonexistent. Company commanders, if they were lucky, led their men using aerial photos or sketch maps. "Flying blind" was an invitation to military calamity. Sharp officers and their men realized this state of affairs rapidly. The South Pacific was war on a shoestring. It was a battle zone marked by extraordinary initiative on all levels. Everyone in the South Pacific was forced to write his own book. It was an environment where "smarts" were as important as courage.

Another geographical trait of the South Pacific had immense importance. New Guinea and the Solomons lay on or near the equator. They are surrounded by immense bodies of water. If a hot sun and much water are in constant contact, humidity and rain result. The weather patterns are in constant flux. Along the equator meteorologists have identified the intertropical convergence zone, a junction between air streams originating in the Northern and Southern hemispheres. Consequently rain comes and goes with extraordinary rapidity. The "wet season" runs typically from December through March. The "dry season" takes place from May through October. To those serving in the area, the difference was one of degree only. It rains daily during the dry season, although the amount is less. A pelting wall of water is common during wet periods. The highland areas receive 200 inches or more of rain annually. Areas along the coast will get well over 100 per year. The resulting weather created a battlefield loathed by infantrymen.

Heat, Humidity, Rain, and Mud

Rain, mist, and mud were the constant companions of the soldiers in the South Pacific. For the most part so was intense heat. The heat, combined with the moisture, made saturated air, creating what was in effect a giant sauna. Soldiers frequently believed the temperature was higher than it was because of this. Most men hated the combination. Robert Kennington, a 25th Division infantryman on Guadalcanal, describes the situation well:

I was raised in Florida and live in North Carolina, so I know a little about heat. Guadalcanal put both of them to shame. In the jungles the trees block any breeze. You don't get any air at all. You can cut the humidity with a knife. It felt like it was 127 degrees in the shade. Some of the guys in my regiment were felled by the heat before they got to our positions. They just passed out along the trail. I would never have made it except for the tough training I had in Hawaii.

Frank Hurray began his thirty-year military career in the U.S. Army commanding a squad in New Guinea in January 1944. He points out an obvious accompaniment to the heat:

When moving through the New Guinea jungle you had to watch weight you carried closely. You had a very tough problem with the heat. You can't bear a heavy pack. Everything in New Guinea was dirty, filthy, and muddy. Your clothes would stand up. You'd wear them so long, you could put them out and watch them walk. You were very unclean, which made you unhappy with yourself. It was degrading. I saw much combat, but the personal filth is one of my most unpleasant memories of the war.

Hurray and Kennington were, considering the situation, healthy. The ferocity of the heat was amplified when men were under physical stress, a common condition in the South Pacific. A dramatic example of this occurred in late September 1942 when the Australians were nearing the end of their retreat toward Port Moresby. Several wounded were left behind near the Kokoda Trail in the care of a pair of enlisted men, J. H. Burns and A. F. Zanker. The battalion promised to send native stretcher-bearers and rescue patrols as soon as possible. The Australian official history cites Burns's record of the two-week ordeal:

[September 21] The heat and flies were so bad that they almost drove us to the first degree of insanity. The heat was terrific and the flies—I think we had all that were in New Guinea . . . [September 23] Wednesday was one of our hardest days. The sun was fiercer than ever and it took a lot out of the lads. Corporal Williams spent a horrible night and we decided to put him on a new

stretcher and put the first fresh dressings on his wounds. It was
a terrific job. Both Zanker and I had a couple of blackouts doing
it. Friday dawns with a blazing hot sun and millions of flies.
Again I spent the night with Corporal Williams and at 0800
hours he had a drink and at 0810 we found him dead.

On October 2 a rescue patrol found the little group. Only one
more man had died. Nevertheless, the wounded faced another five
days borne on stretchers before they arrived at Port Moresby for
proper care. But I have left out a portion of this story. Burns and
Zanker were in the Owen Stanley Mountains. Although pounded by
heat during the day, at night they endured bitter cold caused by the
altitude. Worse still, just as the humidity amplified the impact of
heat, it likewise created a damp bone-chilling type of cold. It is worth
pointing out that infantrymen in the mountains were overburdened
with the bare essentials of war and could not carry the equipment to
ward off the elements. Australian infantryman Bill Crooks's unit
helped pursue the Japanese back up the Kokoda Trail in late 1942.
He describes night in the Owen Stanley Mountains:

High in the mountains we faced deep peasoup mists and cold at
night. Mind you, it was frequently pouring rain also. It was *bloody
freezing cold*. We were in shirt sleeves. We couldn't use our light
sweater or groundsheet because we wanted those dry for what
passed for sleep. We scavenged for airdropped food bags made of
jute. We would cut holes in them for head and arms. They were
odd-looking greatcoats, but better than nothing. Unfortunately,
these quickly disintegrated in the jungle and one would hope to
claim another.

Throughout history soldiers have despised rain and the mud that
results. Combine the two and the simplest activity becomes an ordeal. It is a rare campaign when the two do not cause problems or
wreak havoc. During World War II, it is likely that mud did more to
slow Hitler's assault on the Soviet Union than did the snow. GIs in
Italy or along the Siegfried Line learned to hate it. However, in the
South Pacific, rain and mud took on a different dimension. To begin

with, they were always present. There was no genuinely dry terrain in the theater. Volcanic soil, so common in the South Pacific, turns to an ugly slush when rained upon, creating some of the most noxious mud on the planet. Movement, consequently, was slowed. Engineers created roads of a sort near supply points, but paved them only at the most important points. In July 1943 Frank Chadwick was with the heavily armed Marine 9th Defense Battalion during the fierce struggle for the Japanese airstrip at Munda Point on the island of New Georgia. His unit was placed on nearby Rendova Island, close enough for their 155mm howitzers to shell Munda. Behind their position was Rendova Peak, the volcanic mountain that dominated the landscape. The Japanese Naval Air Force fought hard for Munda, sending in regular attacks from Rabaul. The planes attacking Chadwick's positions came over the cloud-enshrouded peak. An ugly combination of circumstances resulted:

> We had rain the first few days on Rendova; it was a field of mud. The guns and vehicles were up to their hubs in mud. We had tractors to pull the artillery, but in the sludge they weren't enough. So we hooked up the tractors and had forty guys help push the guns through the mud.
>
> It was so hot and steamy, that everything you had on in the morning was soaking wet whether it rained or not. Those clouds over the mountain that shielded the Jap Air Force when they approached also contained rain. Sometimes it rained so hard you couldn't see two or three feet in front of you. But it always stopped by 10:30 or 11:00 A.M. You could rest assured the planes had already left their bases and would be by promptly.

In November 1943 Chuck Ables was a young intelligence officer with the 3d Marine Division when it landed on the island of Bougainville. Bougainville, very near Rabaul, was heavily garrisoned by Japanese troops. To avoid a battle at the beachhead, Admiral Halsey ordered the Marines to go ashore at Empress Augusta Bay. The Japanese had only lightly garrisoned the area, believing that the wretched terrain would prevent American attack. Halsey's landing succeeded admirably, but the troops were deposited in a foul spot on a foul island in the middle of the rainy season. Ables did not enjoy the situation:

> They tell me that Bougainville is the rainiest place in the tropics. I know that they get over 200 inches a year. We must have got over 150 of it the first week we were there. We made friends with people in New Zealand and they insisted they make special boots for us. Tailor-made boots, really great, that came up about calf high. Little cleats on the bottom, hobnails, the whole bit. For the first few days we couldn't take our boots off. When we did, we couldn't believe what our feet looked like. They didn't look like they belonged to us they were so bad.
>
> The second place we moved to was wet with standing water. In the mornings, roads were pure mud: you couldn't get vehicles through. When the rains quit, the Seabees [a nickname based on the acronym "CB," which stood for Construction Battalion; the Seabees were the Navy's famous engineers—EB] started working again. They cut logs and laid them across the mud. The sun was so hot the mud would dry and there would be clouds of dust. In late afternoon, however, the rain clouds would build up over Mount Bagana, one of the highest mountains in the Solomons, and by about five o'clock in the afternoon it was absolutely pouring. The next day, the cycle repeated itself.

Like many soldiers, Ables found memories of the relentless assault from the elements more distasteful than those concerning the dangers of combat:

> The following campaigns we participated in on Guam and Iwo Jima were far more violent than Bougainville. I came a lot closer to being killed during both of those campaigns. But of all the twenty-eight months I spent overseas nothing compared to Bougainville for miserable living conditions we had to put up with. While our combat casualties were comparatively light, Bougainville had to be the closest thing to a living hell that I ever saw in my life.

Although patrols and probes were common during the day, American and Australian soldiers near the front dug in before sunset.

The age-old entrenching tool, outside of rations and weaponry, was the most important article carried by infantry in the South Pacific. Allied soldiers at night stayed in their foxholes. Infantry assumed that anyone they saw or heard moving about in the dark was Japanese and fired immediately. Therefore, the men sat in their holes throughout the night. If pinned down, they sat in their holes in the day. Louis Kidhardt, a lieutenant with the 25th Division on Guadalcanal in January 1943, describes the result:

> You had to dig a foxhole, you had no choice. You used your entrenching tool and went to work. Things were worst if it rained during the night where you stayed. There was more rain in the South Pacific than anywhere I've ever seen. Often we sat in our holes during torrential downpours. The constant rain turned everything to mud. That's how you got all that fungus: you sat in the mud all night. You would hope for daylight so you could see what was around you. Usually we had two men in a foxhole: alternate guard, and the other would sleep the best he could. As we said, you slept with "one eye open."

The Australians on Papua enjoyed similar accommodations at night. While pursuing the Japanese over the Owen Stanley Mountains, two Australian companies established a nighttime perimeter in the middle of the day's battlefield. The Australian official history cites an officer's impressions:

> As we dug a two-company perimeter for the night a desolate scene was presented; our own and enemy dead lying in grotesque positions, bullet-scarred trees with the peeled bark showing ghostlike, our own lads digging silently. And with the coming of darkness came the rain, persistent and cold, and in this atmosphere we settled in our weapon pits for the night. At night we could hear the Jap chattering and moving about.

The official history also cites the impressions of Captain J. W. Dunlop. Dunlop served during the violent siege of the Japanese fortifications at Sanananda on the New Guinea coast in December

1942–January 1943, and recalled that the nightmare endured in the pits might last weeks:

> The weather alternated between hot sun and heavy rain. Both phases were uncomfortable everywhere; they were hell for the forward troops who spent the three weeks either burning in hot sun (with no daylight shelter in forward pits) or in feet of water.

In short, the men who made war in the South Pacific in one way or another were never truly dry or clean. The wretched conditions are well summed up by Donald Fall, a member of the famous 1st Marine Division involved with the landing at Cape Gloucester on New Britain Island in December 1943. The landing at Cape Gloucester resembled the Bougainville operation in many ways. General MacArthur, like Halsey weeks before, intentionally picked a landing site possessing miserable terrain. As at Bougainville, MacArthur's move spared Fall's men a pitched battle with the Japanese. Fall, like many in his unit, was a veteran of the nightmare on Guadalcanal, but the wretched conditions on Cape Gloucester impressed those already familiar with hardship:

> The worst part of the New Britain operation was not the fighting, but the living conditions. The water was terrible, you were soaked all the time. This was rain forest. If you dug a foxhole, and it rained all night, you'd come out withered like a prune. That day you might have gone through a kunai field, or been stuck with thorns, and your body is sweating. At night you'd wrap yourself in your poncho and try to sleep. In the morning you were drenched with sweat. So even if you tried to keep the rain off you got wet.

The forbidding climate enveloped all the soldiers in the South Pacific. It would have made the theater difficult had the terrain been benign. However, that was not the case. On the contrary, the beastly climate either created or accentuated the impact of some of the harshest terrain ever faced by land armies in the history of war.

A Malignant World:
Battle Terrain in the South Pacific

The heat and rain that made life miserable for fighting men also created a world of remarkable fecundity in the South Pacific. The volcanic soil of the area is not rich to begin with, and the pounding rain leaches it of nutrients. Yet for species that can adapt, moisture brings with it an astonishing cycle of life, death, and decay creating new life. Naturally, heat and moisture accelerate the process of decay, just as they accelerate growth. The extraordinary pace of growth and decay creates in the South Pacific a biological cloud-cuckoo-land. It is the home of equatorial rain forest, or, in the words of an earlier generation, it is the jungle.

The jungle in the South Pacific varied in its particulars greatly. Yet the single distinguishing characteristic of jungle is a canopy created by the foliage of very tall trees. Under the canopy men find extremely dense brush, much of it descending in the form of vines from the trees themselves. To soldiers in the South Pacific, moving in a wildly unfamiliar world, operating far from modern support facilities, and often not knowing where they were, the jungle was treacherous without the presence of an enemy.

Bill Crooks, part of the elite Australian 7th Division, describes the upland jungle they found in several parts of Papua.

> The darkness and dimness of heavy jungle has to be experienced or seen to be believed. The thick matted gigantic staghorn treegrowers and the canopy itself blot out natural daylight. The men became very wary and receded into themselves. They did not talk very much unless the enemy was near. Looking back, I think it was a little psychotic too. We never mentioned our feelings about the jungle among ourselves until long after the war. Most were scared of the strangeness and eerie continual darkness, about what one would find in winter countries about sundown. But worse, we felt hemmed in: the all-pervading closeness of the deep impenetrable forest *green jungle*.
>
> The conditions were nothing we had trained for or had expe-

rienced in England or the Middle East. In the jungle, we were enveloped by a matted tangled tree canopy, 200 feet or so up. Thorn vines descended. Beneath us on the track was a slimy ooze of stinking death. The smell of bodies from both sides decaying just below fungus level. Buried just to the side of the track, they leaked their filth into the mash of mud and the millions-of-years-old root systems that covered the ground. It drove some of our less strong soldiers to total nervous breakdown and weeping frustration.

Infantryman Robert Kennington describes a similar vista on Guadalcanal:

Jungle was really rough. We were hit by the heat, mosquitoes, leeches, and a little bit of everything else. Guadalcanal was about ninety-six miles long by thirty-five miles wide. Except along the beach and the top of the ridges there was nothing but jungle. The jungle had big trees that grew about 100 feet high. Vines grew out of them and dropped to the ground. Some vines grew as wide as your leg. We called them "Wait-a-Minute Vines." They had big hooks on them like a rooster spur. When you tried to get through on patrol and ran into one of those vines you either stopped or you were cut up. When tangled you backed out. You learned not to try to bull through them because those hooks were like a razor. I still have scars from them. In the afternoon you'd really notice a kind of dead smell. Probably from all the decaying matter. Mosquitoes were so thick you could wipe them off your arm in handfuls. You wade through the rivers and you'd come out with leeches you didn't even know were there until you felt a sting. You'd look down and there was this creature on your leg full of blood.

James Salafia experienced some of the worst jungle the Solomons could offer while fighting on New Georgia in July 1943. He recalls the sound, a trying experience to men often within a few dozen feet of their enemy:

The mud in the jungle had a distinct and powerful smell. A damp, musty, dank smell. The odor was unpleasant, but we got used to it. You did not grow accustomed to the noise. The sounds were constant. There were always birds and animals making noise. They were at it constantly, day and night. A loud crow-like sound was constantly going. We've all heard something like it in the movies. It's hard to describe. We were always afraid it was the Japs passing signals. Of course when we dug into the dirt that dirt would smell very damp. And there were the land crabs. Sometimes we thought they were Japs trying to sneak into us. They were little guys, about the size of the palm of your hand. You can bet we slept with one eye open.

Another factor made the jungle an ominous place. Obviously distant from any artificial light source, the men fighting in the South Pacific viewed a panoramic sky. The Southern Cross constellation was so prominent it became the emblem of the 1st Marine Division which earned its initial fame on Guadalcanal. Under the canopy, however, things were different. If eerily dim during the day, the night brought blackness. Ernest Gerber, a squad leader with the American 32d Division, was in the middle of the vicious Buna campaign during late 1942. As Gerber relates,

In my area we were in the jungle and there was little fighting at night. Along the coast, outside the canopy, it was different. The reason there wasn't any fighting, was that you couldn't see anything. If you are in the jungle, in the bush, it is as dark as you could imagine. If you get into a closet at home with no lights and shut the door, you imagine what night was like at Buna. Whether the moon is shining or not makes no difference. It's absolutely pitch-dark. In general, anything that moved got shot. No matter who it was.

Gerber's impressions are echoed by Al Careaga of the Marine 1st Raider Battalion who landed on northern New Georgia during the Munda campaign.

The dark nights were so black you can't comprehend it. We'd put an outpost out there and we'd have to relieve them every two hours. The only way to find them was to peel the bark off the trees, because it was actually slightly phosphorescent, and lay a trail. We'd eat our C-rations out of a can. Spoon out the stew or whatever and pitch the cans. That night the damn land crabs would get in these cans and it sounds like the whole damn Japanese Army is approaching. If we didn't have good fire discipline we would have wasted a lot of ammo on tin cans. It was still scary as hell. You never knew if the Japs were coming or not.

In one regard the soldiers had nothing to fear in the South Pacific jungle. Because there was so little grassland suitable for large grazing animals, no large predators lived there. The host of insects supported an extraordinary array of bird life. In some areas large bats flourished. Yet the animal life, from the soldiers' viewpoint, was more conspicuous by its absence. The noise in the jungle was ceaseless, but it was very rare to see what caused it. Bill Crooks, who saw his share of the jungle, recalls:

We almost never saw wildlife. We saw the spoor, we heard them but didn't see them. The millions of cockatoos and sometimes eagles stayed up in the 200-foot-high canopy. I never saw a snake or a rat: only a giant centipede and a monstrous, hand-sized poisonous spider. The thing that worried the men was the giant four-inch-long land beetle peculiar to Papua. They would eat the insides out of a cadaver and you would not know about it until you pushed a corpse with a stick and it fell apart.

Near the coast soldiers entered the worst terrain found in the South Pacific, the tidal swamps. Depending upon local conditions, the swamp might be covered with marsh or thick brush. Most likely, however, the jungle was there too. Ernest Gerber describes the area around Buna, a place loathed by the soldiers of three armies:

The terrain varied according to the tide. The water could be up to your ankles, or up to your neck. In the area where we were, the famous "Triangle," our only dry ground was the trail which was built up, maybe two or three feet higher than the surrounding terrain. That was the only dry land we were on for a period of three or four weeks. Anything to the right, left, front, or rear was swamp. There were trees that seemed two or three hundred feet high. You couldn't see the sun during the day or the stars at night. The underbrush was such that you could maybe see two or three feet ahead of you. If you were lucky, you might see occasionally twenty feet.

Just up the coast from Buna the Mambare River meets the sea at a place destined to become part of the Gona-Sanananda-Buna battlefield in the winter of 1942. Commander Eric Feldt, one of the first of the famous Australian coast watchers, delegated a small team to observe a Japanese landing at the mouth of the Mambare in December 1942. The Australian official history cites Feldt's description of a Papuan mangrove swamp:

> The Mambare debouches into the sea between low, muddy banks along which nipa palms stand crowded knee-deep in the water. Behind the nipa palms, mangroves grow, their foliage a darker green dado above the nipa fronds. Here and there a creek mouth shows, the creek a tunnel in the mangroves with dark tree trunks for sides, supported on a maze of gnarled, twisted, obscene roots standing in the oozy mud. Branches and leaves are overhead, through which the sun never penetrates to the black water, the haunt of coldly evil crocodiles.

As Feldt points out, the marsh, if not the jungle proper, is home to an extremely dangerous animal. Both freshwater and saltwater crocodiles proliferate in the area. Although every sailor and airman lived with a very realistic fear of sharks, soldiers faced the more remote but equally terrifying possibility of crocodile attack. Carl Weber, an American officer of the 41st Division in the bitter Salamaua campaign during the summer of 1943, watched a comrade perish in the Papuan marsh:

> We went from Nassau Bau up to Salas. A few hundred yards inland meant hacking your way forward yard by yard through the brush. Some went right up the coast. Occasionally the men had a little time for a swim. While we were there one soldier was caught and killed by a crocodile. The guards couldn't fire at the crock because it was mostly under water. It was over in the blink

of an eye anyhow. The crock struck, spun, thrashed about and was gone, leaving a blood stain in the water. No more bathing.

Troops had to confront more than mud, foul smell, and noxious water in the swamps. All tidal swamps were home to trees with aerial root systems. This natural mechanism allows the tree to obtain its nutrients from the water that covers the saturated ground. It makes the root systems, as we shall see, excellent havens for machine guns. It also creates a wicked obstacle for a soldier moving through the area, as Marine Al Careaga discovered on New Georgia:

New Georgia was so thick with jungle and swamp it was incredible. You had to cut your way through the "Wait-a-Minute Vines." Hack away at them with your machete to get loose. The banyan trees were miserable. They have a very odd root structure, very thin and long. The roots start maybe five feet from the level of the water which covers the ground and they branch out. They're not round: they start two or three feet high, and they're solid all the way down to the ground and they project down like a triangle and out until they disappear into the swamp. That's the problem. They're not under the ground, they're under the water but you can't see them. So you trudge through the mush and smash one of those roots with your foot or shin. You fall face down and gurgle some swamp water in your mouth, ears, and nose. The jungle has a deathly, moldy, wet smell. It tastes the same way.

A man-made variation on the jungle played a major role in the war. Coconut trees grow in tremendous profusion through the area. Coconut oil was widely used in soap and some foods. Consequently, the large British firm of Lever Brothers owned coconut plantations in the Solomons, New Guinea, and other parts of Asia. Horticulturalists planted the trees in rows and partially drained the ground to make it easier to harvest the crop. Furthermore, because the crop had to get to market, plantations were near beaches. A coconut plantation was one of the distinguishing features on Guadalcanal and served as a place of shelter for American troops. As Ernest Gerber describes, American soldiers at Buna were not so lucky.

Along the coast they had coconut groves. There it was very different from the swamps so near. It was almost like a garden. The coconut trees were planted in straight rows, the underbrush had been controlled up to a point. You had a much better view. But this strip of land along the coast was only 100–300 yards wide. Therefore, when you were on the coast the Japs could see you much better, and knew exactly what you were doing. I'm not sure it was an advantage or a disadvantage.

Another terrain feature associated with the fringe of swamps were patches of tall, sharp kunai grass. In some places small patches interspersed the ugly marsh landscape. Where the terrain began to rise toward the inevitable hills and mountains, acres of kunai grass served as a boundary between the swamps and highlands. Because it could grow in almost any lowland area where the ground was damp but not inundated, kunai grass was present at all of the South Pacific battlefields. Again Ernest Gerber describes the terrain:

When you start getting into the lowlands and away from the swamps there were some open spaces of kunai grass. Kunai is a tall grass that grows from five to eight feet tall. It is very thick, almost like a lawn except for the height. As you learn when you walk through it, the blades are razor sharp. Growing on the edge of a swamp, or somewhere where it's fairly dry, the ground is generally firm. It is not hard, but soft soil. It is like a damp prairie. There are patches of this all over the Buna area. Immediately after the kunai grass you enter the Owen Stanley foothills.

Gerber did not mention a characteristic of kunai grass that turned the Papuan campaign on its head. Kunai grows near the swamp. It also grows along the rivers and on ancient alluvial plains. A very small percentage of this ground, although it may feel slightly soft, is actually very solid. The grass was wretched to pass through, but it covers, and hides, a topographical feature valuable enough to expend the lives of hundreds of men: ground where a major airfield can easily be built. The ability of Australian and American engineers to spot these few "diamonds in the rough," and the inability of their

Japanese counterparts to do so, proved a tremendous advantage for the Allies.

The kunai grass signaled the move upland. This was the case in every major island in the South Pacific. Although for centuries sailors have reveled in the great beauty of a sunset on a tranquil evening in the South Pacific, underneath the earth's crust chaos reigns. New Guinea and the large islands in the Solomons are volcanic. A large eruption near Rabaul in 1943 frightened the Japanese, and the men stationed there all recalled the sulfurous odor of volcanic activity. More to the point, geologically young volcanic terrain has typical features. On islands, a volcanic mountain dominates the terrain. Rugged ridges fan out from the most volcanically active area. Typically, a highland spine drops precipitously to the sea on one side while, on the other, the decline is more gentle over foothills to the sea.

Each of the major islands in the Solomons is dominated by one or more major peaks. Some of the mountains are quite high. Mount Balbi on Bougainville, for example, is over 10,000 feet. Peaks of approximately 3,000 feet, however, are far more common. In the Solomons, the major mountains rarely had any military significance. All the fighting was done very near the coast. Jungle-covered peaks were left to the birds and the indigenous peoples. The ridges, however, were a very different matter. Rugged, lacking in water, and usually having precipitous slopes, ridgelines figured in almost all the fighting throughout the South Pacific.

The most famous ridgeline in the Solomons was the rugged complex of hills that lay between the Marine beachhead at Lunga Point and Mount Austen on Guadalcanal. As the U.S. Army official history makes plain, the Mount Austen area was a hellish complex of tactical barriers:

Mount Austen, where the Japanese were to make their strongest defensive effort of the campaign, is not a single peak, but the apex of a confusing series of steep, rocky, jungled ridges. The main ridge forming the summit rises abruptly out of the foothills about two miles south of the shore, and east of the Matanikau

River. Aerial photographs do not always give a clear picture of Mount Austen, for a dense forest covers the summit and much of the foothill area is covered by grass. The bare, grassy spaces are not separate hills, though for identification purposes they were assigned numbers. The actual summit appears to be lower than the open grassy areas. Hill 27, a separate rocky mound, 920 feet high lies southwest of the summit. The crest rises just above the surrounding treetops and is barely visible. Hill 31, a grassy area about 750 yards north of Hill 27 overlooks Lunga Point.

Fifteen hundred yards northwest of Mount Austen, across a deep gorge cut by the Matanikau, lies another hill mass. A third hill mass, about 900 feet high, lies just north of the first and is clearly visible from Mount Austen.

The description above points out a geographical feature duplicated on other parts of the Solomons and New Guinea. Along the top of the ridgelines there was frequently grass. On the slopes and in the valleys, however, was jungle. This created a strange situation. The high ground did not have the value it traditionally holds in battle. One could observe an objective like an airfield, but movement through the jungle below would be quite invisible. The Japanese put this feature to very good use, launching their attacks from extremely close range.

Marine Donald Moss saw some of the worst of things at Guadalcanal. A generation later he returned and was struck anew by the challenging terrain.

When I went back I couldn't believe that we went up some of the ridges we did, or that the Japanese hauled their artillery to some of the places they occupied. The ridges are really rugged and extremely steep. And I didn't recall the mountains being as high as they were. Guadalcanal was like a bald-headed guy. There might be hair on the side of the head, but the top was bare. The ridges were bare, but below was dense vegetation, a deep gorge and the jungle.

Typically, the forces of nature carried things to an extreme on New Guinea. A series of large volcanic mountain ranges cuts down the middle of the island. The ranges dominate the Huon Peninsula and the long, tapering southeastern portion of the island. There are no ranges like them in North America. Some of the peaks are over 13,000 feet, but it is ruggedness, not height, that makes them so difficult to traverse. Ridgelines rise and plummet, creating a dizzying array of obstacles.

Probably the most daunting, if not most malignant, military terrain in the South Pacific is situated in a quadrant enclosed by an imaginary line running from the coastal village of Salamaua westward to the inland mining settlement of Wau, and then northwest to the harbor town of Madang. This area includes the Huon Peninsula and the mountains surrounding Wau. Along the coast is the forbidding Finisterre Range. One Australian report provides a good sketch of the area:

> The country in the Finisterre Range is rugged, steep, precipitous and covered with dense rain forest. It rains heavily almost every day thus making living conditions uncomfortable. By day it is hot, by night three blankets are necessary. [It would have been a fortunate Australian infantryman who carried three blankets. One or one-half was typical.—EB] There is, therefore, a constant battle with mud, slush, rain, and cold.

Inland is a complex of mountain ranges that makes up a broad central cordillera that starts at Milne Bay and runs northwesterly across all of New Guinea. In the Wau-Huon area, the major branches are the Bismarck (which includes Mount Wilhelm, the highest peak on the island at 14,800 feet), Rawlinson, and Kuper ranges. Between the coastal ranges and the central cordillera inland run the Ramu and Markham rivers. Nothing, it appears, is consistent in New Guinea. The Ramu runs from the inland mountains in a northerly direction, entering the Bismarck Sea north of Madang. The Markham and Wau rivers run to the south and enter the sea at Lae at the base of the Huon Peninsula. Along these twin rivers runs a valley that resembles a giant trough between the mountain ranges. Between five and twenty-five miles wide, the Markham-Ramu Valley is a grassy, upland plateau. The valley itself is grassy, flat, cool, and holds numerous sites for airfields. It is the most benign terrain in the South Pacific.

Throughout 1943 a large, sustained ground campaign took place in this area. However, from the Japanese point of view, the valley itself was death. There the Allies could use their increasingly superior airpower and artillery to deadly effect. Consequently, the Japanese attacked Wau early in the year through rough terrain. After the Australians crushed them at Wau, the Japanese chose the mountains to fight a hard, and ultimately futile, campaign to defend their bases along the coast. Mountain fighting in New Guinea, however, had little resemblance to what took place in Italy at the same time. The men slugging it out up the Italian boot knew heat, cold, mud, and ridges. They did not know jungle. In New Guinea, the upland jungle covered the mountains except up the sheer cliffs and jagged ridgelines that crisscrossed the area. The combination of jungle and cliff made overland movement, always extremely difficult, almost impossible. Men and supplies moved up trails—"track" is the local term—developed over the centuries by the native peoples. Fighting took place along ridgelines. It was very much like Guadalcanal on a larger scale.

The tracks played an extremely important role in all the campaigns in the South Pacific. As we shall investigate later, the area was home to a large indigenous population. The checkerboard nature of the rough terrain subdivided New Guinea and the larger islands in the Solomons into a patchwork of tribal territories. Although frequently isolated from the outside, they communicated, traded, and made war with their neighbors. Unlike some other technologically undeveloped areas, tracks were not made by animals and used by humans. The South Pacific tracks resulted from long and persistent use by people. Some were no doubt of great age because they followed natural lines of least resistance, but an abandoned track would be reclaimed by the jungle quickly. Only a handful of the largest tracks were charted before the war. When Australian units moved through an area they could gain some assistance from the remnants of their local administration, guerrilla units, and coast watchers. However, tracks frequently lay hidden, impossible to see from the air, until found by infantry. One virtue of both Japanese and Australian operations was vigorous patrolling. Although reconnaissance patrols sought enemy positions above all, they were always on the alert for a new track that might provide the key to a tactical quandary. It was bushcraft at its finest and became an Australian specialty. Eventually, however, American troops also grew adept.

In February 1943 a small group of Australian engineers supported by a team of native bearers was seeking out a series of theretofore unknown tracks that could be upgraded into a jeep road from the secure airfield of Bulldog, on the Port Moresby side of the central range, to Wau. Although the road was not an engineering success, the expedition report provides a glimpse of the land encountered:

> It is almost certain that the country between Ecclestone and Fox Saddles had not been traversed previously by white men, and it was avoided by the Kukukukus, the nomadic race of pygmy cannibals that are found more to the south and southwest. During the journey the natives showed remarkable courage and endurance and, at times, carried heavy loads down cliffs ranging to 1,000 feet in height. The canyon of the Eloa River is awe-inspiring, about 50 feet in width at the bottom, with towering cliffs on either side and waterfalls jutting out on to the stream. It is a barrier that has to be seen to be believed. The stream was waded and steep detours were made up the precipitous sides to provide portage around waterfalls and rapids.

In these mountains of the Huon Peninsula fighting raged with little respite for a year. It was a battlefield where rolling hand grenades down sheer cliffs, instead of throwing them, was a common defensive technique. On the highest ridgelines soldiers were known to stumble from their foxholes and tumble through a cloud layer to their death 5,000 feet below. Sharp, unexpected firefights erupted when patrols unexpectedly collided at point-blank range. One unit might besiege another for days at a distance under fifty yards. It was a place where bloodletting occurred at locations to which the soldiers gave strange and ominous-sounding names: Green Snipers Pimple,

Jap Track, or Shaggy Ridge. We shall look at this battlefield again in greater detail.

However, it is important to realize that, when the war moved into the Huon Peninsula and the Ramu Valley, the Allies were far better prepared to fight and survive than they had been months before. The medical apparatus was better, and the supply situation had improved greatly. Air support was more effective and far more plentiful. Artillery, which was very rare and so badly needed in 1942, was present in substantial quantity. Even the Japanese, until Australian and American advances unhinged their position, were better prepared and supplied than they had been in the summer of 1942. At that time the Allies were building a position on a shoestring. Equipment available was pitifully inadequate. The knowledge and experience that would have made the situation more manageable had yet not been learned. For all of the armies concerned, the 1942 campaign in Papua was a desperate leap in the dark.

All of this brings us to the Kokoda Trail over the Owen Stanley Mountains. (Australian veterans have argued for fifty years over the proper term. The Australian official history employs the term "Kokoda Track." Most soldiers favor "Kokoda Trail" to distinguish it from the multitude of much smaller "tracks" found in the area. The advocates of "Kokoda Trail" seem to have the better argument, and I have used the term. The Australians take military history very seriously.) The Kokoda Trail is not well known to Americans. The epic at Guadalcanal has defined the South Pacific war in the United States. In a similar vein, Guadalcanal for Australians is usually looked upon as a most welcome diversion of Japanese resources away from Papua, Port Moresby, and Australia itself. Kokoda, on the other hand, ranks with Gallipoli for Australians as a trial that in a real way defined the worth of the nation. Japanese accounts of the war perhaps interpret this period most clearly. Imperial forces were deeply and simultaneously involved on both fronts. In east and west they came very close to victory, only to suffer twin calamities at the same moment. The Japanese correctly regard Kokoda and Guadalcanal as two parts of a whole. They were the two fronts of the same remarkable campaign that, in the truest sense of the word, turned the tide of the Pacific war. Just as its German ally saw dreams of empire turn to ash between July and December 1942, so too did Japan's strategic position dissolve in the same fleeting months.

The Kokoda Trail was both a battlefield and a blood-drenched highway between two vicious campaigns on both coasts of Papua. Along the northern coast of Papua are the small settlements of Buna and Gona. For approximately thirty miles southwest of Buna, the land rises gently into the foothills of the Owen Stanley Mountains. The first point of importance along the trail is Wairopi, a wire-rope bridge (Wairopi is pidgin for "wire rope") spanning the steep banks of the fast-running, dangerous, and unpredictable Kumusi River. (American aircraft attacked the bridge many times. Airmen often described it as spanning a deep gorge. In reality, the banks were approximately six feet deep. It was risky but possible to swim the river at this point.) Once over the wire bridge, the terrain becomes steep and rocky as New Guinea shows its ominous face. A small settlement on a plateau with a small air strip, Kokoda is approximately twenty miles from Wairopi. At Kokoda, the trail begins in earnest, moving south along the western edge of a huge chasm called the Eora Creek Gorge. Along the Eora Creek the trail climbs 6,000 feet in less than twenty miles to a point called Templeton's Crossing. Peaks rise to 8,000 feet, and valleys with slopes up to sixty degrees descend to 1,000 feet. The Australian official history describes a short, but savage, portion of the track approaching Templeton's Crossing northward from the nearby village of Kagi:

> After crossing the crest of the range [the Owen Stanleys—EB] the track dropped easily enough through the bush and over the moss for an hour or two. But then its downward trend grew quickly steeper and steeper. The ground fell away precipitously on either side, dense bush pressed in, the track seemed almost to plunge headlong so that a walker slid and fell and clutched at hanging branches for support. In the silence of the bush and moss there first welled and then rushed the roar of a torrent far below. High on the moss-covered logs the track edged across a number of feeder streams, and then, suddenly broke on to the brink of rushing twisting water thick with white and yellow

spume, boiling in whirlpools round grey stones as big as small houses and disfigured with moss and pallid fungus.

Near Templeton's Crossing the trail goes through what Australians in 1942 called "the Gap," an area they thought narrowed to an easily defended, pencil-thin trail. In reality, the trail was thin, but the Gap was several miles wide and was a military barrier of no importance. As the trail begins its general descent at the village of Myola, the terrain becomes less erratic. Yet nothing is simple in the Owen Stanleys. The gorges are less frequent but deeper. The undergrowth becomes more dense. The trail crosses several ridgelines, one of which near Ioribaiwa proved to be the point at which the Japanese offensive finally stalled. Near the village of Uberi, which served as a major Australian supply depot during the climactic battles in September 1942, exists one of the trail's most famous landmarks: the golden stairs. The stairs are logs embedded into the trail to aid indigenous peoples going up or down one of the steepest portions of the journey. The area covered by the stairs rises 1,200 feet the first three miles, drops 1,600 feet almost straight down, and then rises another 2,000 feet in the last four miles. The Australian history describes them:

The golden stairs consisted of steps varying from ten to eighteen inches in height. The front edge of the step was a small log held by stakes. Behind the log was a puddle of mud and water. Some of the stakes had worked loose, leaving the logs slightly tilted. Anyone who stood on one of these skidded and fell with a whack in the mud, probably banging his head against a tree or being hit on the head with his own rifle. Those who had no sticks soon acquired them, not only to prevent falls, but to allow the arms to help the legs, especially with the higher steps. After the first half dozen steps, it became a matter of sheer determination forcing the body to achieve the impossible. It was probably the weight more than the climb, though the climb would have been enough to tire even a lightly loaded man. The rear companies, where the going is always hardest, took twelve hours to complete the nine miles.

Geoffrey Lyon was a young officer with the 7th Australian Division, and already a veteran of the war in the Mideast. His battalion was one of the first to climb the golden stairs to face the advancing Japanese. As Lyon points out, the journey was made more difficult because, when traveling a distance, each soldier had to carry a heavier load. The precarious supply apparatus demanded it:

> We were dependent upon porters. Like all forms of transport, there is never enough. That meant of course that our own men had to carry a great deal. At this time there were many "expert opinions" that proved to be rubbish. One of these was that no white man could carry more than twenty-five pounds. Our troops had about sixty. Take a fellow: he has a haversack on his back with the necessities of life, he might have a Bren gun, a light weapon, magazines of ammunition: parts of automatic weapons. So thirty pounds was just not on. Don't tell me about the golden stairs. We started in the morning and I finished about 9:00 at night on my hands and knees. I wasn't worth a bumper. But we made it.

Corpses of men killed in battle were so numerous that they became part of the terrain. The term "carnage" has become a cliché in a world that looks askance at war. Yet people should never use the term metaphorically when writing about war. The dead are always part of a battlefield. People approaching a large battlefield will almost always smell it before they see it. The grisly sights and smells resulting from putrification made a deep impression on the soldiers involved and were the subject of much retrospective comment. This hideous reality was greatly amplified in the South Pacific. In both Papua and the Solomons much combat was at point-blank range. As we shall examine later, both sides attempted orderly recovery of the dead. Yet battle often made this task impossible. The climate accelerated putrification greatly. Unless confronted by apocalyptic sights, most soldiers, after initial horror, simply grew accustomed to the presence of corpses, both friendly and enemy.

Veteran Marine Ore Marion was with the 1st Marine Division on

Guadalcanal. He provides a vivid description of what thousands of soldiers encountered on a daily basis:

> Jungle smells in a combat situation are also almost impossible to describe. First it was a sweet-sour smell of rotting vegetation. After a short while it was compounded with the stink of decaying bodies. All I can say about decaying bodies in the jungle is that the stink sticks to your body, to everything; your eyebrows, your gum line and the balls of your feet. The stench is unbelievable.

> In the jungle when a man is killed the flies attack him by the millions right away. The maggots are there three or four hours later, moving so that the body moves slightly. It's a horrible sight: the maggots are in and out of the mouth, nose, ears, eyes. Day two and three the body starts to swell. The gases that make it swell stink like hell. In some cases the corpse bursts through the uniform, penis sticking up like a huge erection. On day four or five the swollen body, full of maggots, and oily-like, bursts and, Jesus, what a horrible stench. If you try to pick up the body by taking an arm or leg, you end up with an arm or leg in your hand. You haven't lived until you go to retrieve a friend's body that has been lying in the jungle rotting and have one of those great rats come slipping out of him where it has been eating tender parts.

Ian Page flew a New Zealand Air Force Hudson bomber out of Henderson Field on Guadalcanal. Like many veterans of that battle he recalls the deathly flotsam of war:

> Having been raised on a large dairy farm in New Zealand I knew the sight and smell of dead things. On Guadalcanal there were partial skeletons and bones lying about everywhere, some covered by parts of uniforms. They were Japanese, of course, as ours had been collected in all the rear areas. One afternoon the daily deluge continued into the evening and by dark the bottom of our gully was covered by four to five feet of water. It continued to rise until it entered our tent, which was pitched on rising ground. We slept on canvas stretchers with wooden supports. Mine was slightly higher at the rear of the tent. Each of the four crewmen got out of bed as water contacted their canvas while at the same

time a terrible stench arose. By that time the water had stopped rising, leaving my bed untouched. The others went up to the ridge overlooking our camp to spend the night in the open. I put on my gas mask and stayed in bed. In the morning the cause of the smell was found to be the top half of a corpse which the heavy rain had released from the hillside, and it had become lodged in bushes outside our tent.

New Guinea's numerous battlefields were likewise littered with the remains of those who perished. American GIs called the beach at Buna "Maggot Beach" for obvious reasons. Carl Weber, serving with the 41st Division during the Salamaua campaign in the summer of 1943, recalls the dead becoming part of the landscape:

You rarely saw live Japs during a fight, but we saw dead ones lying around. They were sort of like sign boards, landmarks. No one had good maps of course. They helped us get around. "You know the fat one that's swelling up? Turn left there."

On occasion the presence of the dead provided a needed dose of realism for very young men. In October 1942, troops of the Australian 25th Brigade were advancing rapidly up the Kokoda Trail. The mood was jovial until they entered a battlefield fought over by their comrades a few weeks before. The sight that quieted the men was recorded by the unit diary:

Along the route were skeletons, picked clean by ants and other insects, and in the dark recesses of the forest came to our nostrils the stench of the dead, hastily buried, or perhaps not buried at all.

Robert Ballantine arrived on Guadalcanal in December 1942 with the 25th Division. He describes a macabre scene that serves as a reminder that not all of the dead had come from ground fighting:

We had beach duty when we first arrived, and then again later. Shortly before we arrived there had been fierce naval battles not far off shore. There were smaller shootouts with Jap barges. Every time a tide came in it would bring bodies in with it. You couldn't usually tell which side they were from. I watched a landing craft move off the beach once. It churned up the water pretty good, and sure enough a couple of bodies came to the surface. We assumed they were sailors but, Lord, they could have been fliers, soldiers on the beach, anyone. But we were used to that kind of thing. Guys used to put skulls on the hoods of their jeeps. Guadalcanal was a tough place.

Conditions were so vile that normality could come as a shock. As Ore Marion's Marines were leaving Guadalcanal in December 1942, he overheard a most illuminating exchange:

We went topside for air and a look-see. Guadalcanal was fading in the distance and from the ship it looked like a beautiful tropical island instead of the hell hole that it actually was. Someone said, "What's that strange smell?" The man was dead serious. Someone else answered, "That's fresh, clean air, you dumb bastard."

One of the great paradoxes of the war in the South Pacific is that many of the men who fought there were able to look beyond their own dangerous and miserable circumstances and find beauty in the world that threatened them. They were, after all, making war in the South Seas. All of the factors that made the area hellish to fight in also made it a place of beauty. Marine Donald Moss, after the war a very successful graphic artist, recalls his youthful impression of Guadalcanal:

Lord, Guadalcanal was beautiful. My gosh, the dichotomy, the contrasts of the situation were extraordinary. I was already interested in illustration and painting. A friend and I used to share a foxhole and discuss how we'd render one feature or another on canvas. The ridgelines were abrupt, the plant life so many different shades of green and brown. The light was different somehow than ours at home. The sunsets were beautiful, the colors undescribable. Of course you might be admiring the surroundings and get the shit bombed out of you the next minute.

On occasion infantryman Robert Ballantine and his friends went to the Tenaru River on Guadalcanal to swim in "the most beautiful spot on earth." Ian Page flew his Hudson bomber on long-range patrol throughout the Solomons, frequently at low level. Page had the perfect vantage point for viewing the South Seas:

> The islands were just idyllic. Simply idyllic. The water had a lovely deep blue color. All of the trees and undergrowth, especially the trees on the coconut plantations, the smaller were all different hues of green. The mountains and active volcanoes rise to perhaps 4,000 feet. It was beautiful. The bigger islands had more open space and perhaps were less striking. But the smaller coral atolls were exactly what you would think a tropical island should look like. It was an astounding vista.

If anyone has written about the beauty of tidal swamps in New Guinea I have missed it. However, the mountains of New Guinea, along with the upland jungles and the tracks that passed through them, had an eerie beauty that Australians frequently comment on. In late July 1942 a small Australian force met the swiftly advancing Japanese spearhead at Kokoda village. After a sharp battle the Japanese forced the Australians out of their positions. As recorded in a contemporary report from an Australian officer, as his men retreated from Kokoda they were surrounded by

> the thick white mist dimming the moonlight; the mysterious veiling of trees, houses and men, the drip of moisture from the foliage, and at the last, the almost complete silence, as if the rubber groves of Kokoda were sleeping as usual in the depths of the night, and the men had not brought disturbance.

N. R. Grinyer, who was one of the crack Australian infantrymen returning from the Mideast to salvage the situation on Papua in the fall of 1942, later recounted the mixture of awe and dread created by that land during war:

> Memories stir of the time. There were no carnivorous animals in the jungle. Instead I saw one rare cassowary, an ostrich-type bird, and other flying birds and marveled at their brilliant coloring. Our campsite was at an empty site at the end of the airstrip. Kit

under a tree and this was home. Nothing was prepared, no la-
trines, facilities, nothing. Then we put up our tents, rows of
white tents on a slope. A group of us talking at sunset, then suddenly all was dark as though someone had turned off the light.
Dark, no other lights anywhere, no streetlights, nor house lights,
just deep black dark. If there was a moon, "Tojo's Moon," Japanese bombers would come. Three rifle shots warned of a raid. An
antiaircraft gun opened up nearby, causing more danger from
falling AA debris than from the raiders. Worse yet, the Nip was
only forty miles away and advance parties had been sighted
closer. We were told *not to go out at night alone*. There was no escape from the immediate surroundings. No amenities and no opportunity to get away. You sleep with your rifle. Pretty rough,
and we were only on the coastal plains!

The harsh climate and terrain in the South Pacific was guarantee
that the men cast there to fight faced a grueling task. Yet it was not
the terrain and climate alone that made the South Pacific the most
wretched battlefield of World War II. It was also the breeding
ground for diseases so numerous, pernicious, and debilitating that
they pushed three armies to the breaking point.

Disease

Disease has always been the worst enemy of armies. Until the twentieth century, it was the primary killer during war. Beginning in the
late nineteenth century, the growing understanding of microorgan-
isms and steady advances in the realm of hygiene greatly lowered the
death rates in war due to disease. However, in both world wars disease remained the major cause of casualties, if the term is loosely defined to encompass soldiers incapacitated regardless of cause for a
short or long period. Realizing this, all of the major armies fighting
in World War II had a major medical apparatus and allocated substantial resources to educate officers and men in methods easily taken
to reduce disease. Behind the lines were increasingly complex aid sta-

tions and hospitals ready to treat those fallen ill. While the number of men lost to duty remained very high in World War II, a very high percentage returned to duty after a brief convalescence.

Like most components of the warring armies in the Pacific, the medical establishments of the combatants were caught very poorly prepared for extended operations in the South Pacific. This was a serious problem, because the climate that allowed the jungle to flourish was also home to a bewildering host of microrganisms capable of harming humans. Tropical diseases were the subject of much research in this period. All soldiers, for instance, were inoculated against yellow fever. But, as was soon apparent, a vicious circle developed. The environment that allowed the diseases to flourish in the first place made prevention and treatment all the more difficult. A cycle of illness, consequently, fed on itself. Unless this cycle could be dealt with, moreover, it crippled armies.

Above all, the defense against disease was intimately connected with an adequate supply line. If a military unit suffered shortages of decent rations or safe water, the health of the men deteriorated, making them more vulnerable to disease. A loss of energy led quickly to a decline in hygienic measures, which made matters worse yet. If the supply of malarial suppressants and other basic medicines was cut off, entire units, eventually entire armies, began a downward spiral leading to destruction. As it was, disease, from the beginning of fighting in the South Pacific until the end, was the major cause of serious casualties in all armies. It killed many men fighting for the Allies and caused serious illness to far more. The Japanese eventually suffered much worse. Even though Australian and American forces grew very good at wielding the weapons of war, the worst damage done by the Allied military effort was to deny Japanese forces the ability to sustain themselves. Once deprived of their bases, Japanese units were crippled by the jungle as effectively as by Allied firepower.

The worst medical problem throughout the South Pacific was malaria. Malaria means "bad air" in Italian, reflecting the age-old belief that the disease was caused by rank-smelling air found in swamps. Since the late nineteenth century physicians have known it is not the swamp air that causes the malady but what flies in it. A protozoal disease, malaria infects numerous creatures. Most peoples living in tropical regions have developed genetic defenses against malaria. Humans from temperate climates, which included almost everyone making war in the South Pacific, are genetically defenseless and easy prey to the disease.

Malaria has a pernicious cycle that makes it extremely difficult to combat. It is caused by a tiny parasite transmitted through the bite of the female anopheles mosquito. Once in the blood, the parasites travel to the liver and reproduce asexually. The cells that have reproduced burst, releasing both asexual and potential sexual forms of the parasite. When a female anopheles feeds on the infected blood, the sexual form of the parasite infects the mosquito, completing the life cycle. For reasons that are not understood well, the parasite either remains persistent in the liver or infected red blood cells circulate for a very long time. In either case, malaria usually recurs several times. An infected individual can suffer a recurrence years after initially contracting the disease.

The anopheles thrives in the tidal swamps of the South Pacific. Guadalcanal, New Georgia, and Bougainville in the Solomons, as well as the Milne Bay and Buna areas of Papua, are among the most malarial places on earth. It is present in lesser degrees throughout the area's low-lying terrain.

Malaria can kill, but more commonly it causes a high and prolonged fever. Donald Fall describes the symptoms:

> I had malaria. You get a fever. You shake like you're going to rattle the teeth right out of your head. You're freezing. Then you're roasting. All of a sudden, bingo, it's gone. And you're hungry. But the minute you look at the food, you're not hungry anymore. You feel like you have to defecate. You try, but all you do is dribble some water. It took seven years for that bug to burn out entirely.

Like many veterans of the New Guinea campaign, Bill Crooks had the disease many times during and after the war. As Crooks knew too well, there was no cure for malaria and there was no alternative to enduring the attacks:

I had it for about six years three to four attacks per year. One just lay in bed and rigored or sweated it out because it left one like a wet dishcloth with the gutsy threads gone out of it!

At the time there was no treatment for the disease. There were, however, two suppressant drugs. Quinine, an alkaloid extracted from the bark of the cinchona tree, is one of the oldest useful drugs known. Discovered first by Spanish missionaries in the seventeenth century, it is a moderately effective suppressant. Just as aspirin relieves the symptoms of a minor malady without affecting the problem at its source, quinine masks the effects of malaria but does nothing to cure it. In addition, some people taking quinine experience blurred vision and a loud rushing sound in the ear as side effects. Worse, from the Allied point of view, in the twentieth century quinine had become a sole source commodity, grown only on the island of Java.

Ironically, it was Germany's concern over the same problem that allowed the Allies to fight in the South Pacific. After its experience with blockade during World War I, the German government encouraged its formidable chemical industry to create synthetic substitutes for numerous substances. Quinine was high on the list. The result was the drug Atabrine. More effective than quinine, Atabrine had obvious value. In 1931 the Winthrop Company licensed it for American production using German chemicals. In 1939, as Europe headed for war, a crash program was started to make America independent of foreign sources. Initially Winthrop was able to meet demand with a new plant. It was fortunate for the Allies that they did, because Java fell to the Japanese in January 1942. Beyond stockpiles already on hand, no more quinine would be available for the duration of the conflict. During 1942, therefore, the Army bought 150 million tablets of Atabrine. Demand increased greatly and six other companies licensed Winthrop's process. In 1943 production was 100 million tablets per month. In 1944 the output rose to 400 million per month. As malaria is found in many parts of the world, much of this production went to Lend-Lease aid programs for American allies. Australia, for obvious reasons, received some of the first supplies.

Not widely known outside veterans' circles, Atabrine was one of the most important drugs created in a time of numerous ground-breaking developments in pharmacology. Its military significance rivaled, and perhaps surpassed, the better known "miracle drugs" of the period, the sulfonamides and penicillin. Nevertheless, the soldiers resisted Atabrine at the outset. It had an unpleasant taste. Also, someone taking Atabrine developed a yellowish hue to the skin. Worse yet, rumor had it that it caused infertility. Infantryman Marshall Chaney was on Guadalcanal and describes the attitudes of the men:

Quinine affected our eyesight and our hearing, it sounded like a thunderstorm. Then they put us on Atabrine. But the rumor was out that it made us sterile. That concerned a lot of the boys because they wanted to have families when they got back home. And some of them wanted to get home any way they could. Malaria might be a ticket out of the war zone and back to the States. As it worked out, a lot of guys did get malaria so bad they had to be shipped out. Most of them, however, didn't catch it on purpose. You sure didn't have to try to catch it. I had it several times. In Samoa they took me to the hospital and they had rubber sheets under me packed with ice. The corpsman was asking me questions: I remember that distinctly. I thought I was answering them fine. The corpsman said, "He's crazier than hell." I have no idea what I was saying to him. The fever rose at night. Every now and then in the hospital ward they would come in and quietly take someone away that had died of fever.

On Guadalcanal they had us line up, handed us a pill and gave us some water. Soon the ground was covered with Atabrine, the guys just dropped it. The brass got onto that quick, and they had a commissioned officer see that everyone took it. You stood there, opened your mouth, and the officer would flip the tablet right in. Then you'd swallow. We all turned yellow, but I guess the rumors were wrong about having kids: look at the baby boom after the war!

Despite Atabrine, malaria was a serious challenge in the South Pacific for several reasons. First, the lack of time to embark on a massive insecticide and swamp-drainage program meant there was nothing that could be done to prevent the disease. Mosquitoes came in clouds during the tropical night. The military tried to restrict short-sleeve shirts and short pants, but that was a wasted effort on land. Every person in the theater was bitten several times by infected mosquitoes within days of arrival. Consequently, barring the small percentage of men who carried a genetic defense, almost everyone came down with the disease. The military studied this issue closely during the war and concluded that the infection rate in most units stationed in malarial areas was 85–95 percent. After Guadalcanal, for instance, some Army units were rotated to nonmalarial stations and the men taken off malarial suppressants. Over 90 percent of the men involved came down with active cases of the disease in a very short time.

Furthermore, Atabrine was only partially effective. During the struggle at Guadalcanal and Buna-Gona the American and Australian forces were fighting in extremely malarial areas. The supply of suppressants was erratic, the dosage too small, and the importance of Atabrine not fully understood. Manpower was also in very short supply. Consequently, infantrymen carried on unless their bout with malaria became serious. Marines, GIs, and Australian infantrymen continued to serve at the front unless their fever went over 102 degrees. If a serious case ensued, the doctors authorized evacuation. During the later stages of the Guadalcanal campaign air evacuation was a simple affair, and ill soldiers were moved out readily. On New Guinea, evacuation from the front meant a team of native stretcher-bearers had to carry out the victim at least fifteen miles to an airfield. Consequently, soldiers there were more likely to be sent to the nearby unit aid station where they were allowed to rest and get through their present bout and rejoin their unit.

Losses from malaria were extremely serious even if most of those stricken eventually recovered. For example, the Australian 7th Cavalry Regiment, a battalion-sized armored unit that was forced to fight in New Guinea as standard infantry because of the rough terrain, sent 420 men to the vicious fight along the Sanananda Track in late December 1942. A month later they were relieved. Their losses were: 55 KIA (killed in action); 67 WIA (wounded in action); 3 dead from scrub typhus; and 243 evacuated because of malaria. Having suffered 365 casualties out of 420 men deployed, the 7th required months to reorganize into a new unit, the 2/7th Commando Battalion. Bill Crook's unit, the 2/33 Battalion, pursued the Japanese across the Kokoda Trail and then fought at Gona until relieved on Christmas Day 1942. At the start of the campaign the 2/33d fielded over 500 officers and men. (It is worth noting that there are no mosquitoes above 3,000 feet. The men of the 2/33d, consequently, picked up malaria at Port Moresby prior to the fight, or at Gona at the end.) Crooks emphasizes the long-term chaos that malaria played with the makeup of combat units:

> We came out sixty-nine men strong. Back to Moresby and met our recovered sick and wounded. After a leave we went to our training area in North Queensland. [Queensland is a state in northeastern Australia.—EB] It was 4,000 feet up and had no mosquitoes. From the old unit we had about 250 men and we met up with 400 replacements. It wasn't until July 1943 that we were ready to return to Moresby in preparation for the attack on Lae. While training around Moresby and acclimatizing the unit to the heat we lost 100 experienced men due to relapses of malaria in a month. Long after the war—up to five or seven years—one would front to the Vets Hospitals and get one's Atabrine tabs.

Some units faced a more dangerous situation. At the early stage of the war, the supply apparatus was not functioning properly. Consequently, many units ran out of both quinine and Atabrine. Some Marine units fought briefly without it on Guadalcanal. Australian platoon leader E. J. Randall's unit was one of the unlucky ones:

> Quinine was available at Milne Bay only, and we fought for weeks afterwards with no malaria tablets. At the termination of Sanananda all troops in my unit were infected with malaria. It is interesting to note that we fought on with body temperatures of 102 degrees Fahrenheit. I remember the doctor telling me he didn't even have an aspirin to give me. Atabrine was a godsend.

The tablets were administered by officers and were actually placed in the soldier's mouth as the importance of this tablet was considered paramount.

In general U.S. medical support in the Solomons was somewhat better than that afforded the Australians and Americans in Papua. Nevertheless, losses due to malaria were staggering. The 1st Marine Division suffered 10,635 casualties on Guadalcanal. Of these 774 were killed in action and 1,962 wounded. Malaria put out of action 5,749 Marines. (Some duplication took place in all casualty accounting. Some men, for instance, were wounded and suffered a malaria attack.) In Papua, out of 14,500 American troops committed, most from the 32d Division, 8,600 cases of malaria were reported. According to U.S. estimates, Australian forces during the entire Papuan campaign (June 1942–January 1943) suffered 2,037 killed, 3,533 wounded, and 9,250 casualties from malaria. As we shall see, the Japanese, often fighting without medical supplies, suffered far worse.

An indirect result of malaria attacked the morale of soldiers. Malaria had cycles that moved fast. It was not always easy to detect in battlefield conditions, and could be misinterpreted as battle fatigue. (Later we shall look at the wider ramifications of stress-related breakdown in more detail.) A unit that gained the reputation of suffering more than its share of battle fatigue received unwelcome command attention, often leading to the removal of officers, and led officers higher up the chain to sometimes misinterpret the situation in two ways. Commanders might think that battle fatigue reflected a loss of will or bad combat leadership when it was in fact caused by a genuinely impossible tactical situation. A commander might also think that a unit was cracking, when in fact it was suffering from a serious outbreak of malaria. Henry Dearchs was at Buna and describes exactly this situation:

I had malaria at Buna several times. I went back to the rear to have them look me over. Unfortunately, unless you were having a "chill" they might not diagnose malaria. Instead, they diagnosed the infamous FUO (fever of undetermined origin). Lord knows, there were plenty of fevers in New Guinea. But FUO was also taken as a sign of battle fatigue. There were also plenty of cases of real battle fatigue in New Guinea. But if you couldn't tell one from the other it caused pressure in the unit. My first case of FUO was malaria, of course. Soon I was in the battalion hospital, and not for the first time. When you kicked your bout of malaria, back you went to the swamp.

Malaria unfortunately was only one of a long list of ugly and dangerous diseases that plagued the armies in the South Pacific. A particularly nasty variety was called breakbone or dengue fever. Dengue was rarely fatal, nor did it recur. While it lasted, however, the fever was extremely debilitating and accompanied by throbbing pains in joints or sometimes the teeth. A man suffering from dengue did not go on patrol. Like malaria, the fever was caused by mosquito-borne infection. The species of insect, however, was different. Unlike the anopheles mosquito, which breeds in large open bodies of water like swamps, the dengue-carrying aedes mosquito (the same breed that causes yellow fever) prefers small, stagnant pools. Military camps with their rain barrels, cisterns, bottles, and junk were perfect breeding grounds. On occasion dengue came in local epidemics, impairing the effectiveness of units and causing suffering to thousands.

Another insect-borne disease was scrub typhus. Fortunately it was rare, because its attacks were very severe and sometimes fatal. The culprit was a tiny mite similar to the common chigger. If a soldier was close to an evacuation point or proper care he was probably only in for a high fever and bouts of delirium. If the soldier was on some isolated battlefield like Buna, scrub typhus was something to be feared. Frank Koltun of the 32d Division came down with malaria so severely at Buna that he required a year of rehabilitation in Australia. In early 1944 he returned to his unit and participated in the landing at Aitape on the northern coast of New Guinea. Within weeks Koltun had scrub typhus:

I was doing patrols and picked up a fever that wouldn't go down. I thought it was malaria, but I couldn't shake it. I went to base camp and went to the medic. There was no field hospital in that area and no doctor. There was a dentist with a foot-powered drill, but no doctor. The fever got worse and Atabrine didn't help. When a jeep ambulance came I was on a cot, couldn't move. They had to help me on. When I got to the doctor, he told me not to move, not to try to get up. He didn't tell me what it was but asked if I had seen a bite. He took me into a tent. I took my own temp; it was 108. Body temperatures run high in the tropics, but even there that was a whopper of a fever. I lost consciousness. They put me on oxygen. This went on ten days but I came out of it. I lost a lot of weight. But after my bout with malaria, I guess they figured I was bad luck. That was the end of World War II for me.

Less severe but far more common than typhus was dysentery. Caused by the miserable hygienic conditions inherent in a malignant physical environment, it was extremely common among all the armies. As dimensions of the problem grew more clear, Allied forces took greater precautions against it as the war went on. Yet under all circumstances dysentery is always one of the worst medical problems to plague an army. It causes serious weight loss. Fatigue in a war zone is severe at the best of times, but someone suffering from dysentery is weakened to the point of breakdown. Poor nutrition contributes to the problem. Soldiers lose their appetite and grow weaker and lighter as time progresses.

Clifford Fox of the 1st Marine Division recalls a bad case of dysentery contracted late in his tour on Guadalcanal:

Once we were on an intelligence patrol toward the Matanikau River. On the way back, I passed out, it was so hot. I was brought to the sick bay, it was just a tent. I had dysentery so bad I was passing blood. And wouldn't you know we got these doggone air raids. I'd be out there over a slit trench, passing blood and these damn bombs were coming down. We lost a lot of weight, our shoes were rotted off. We looked a mess. We were very bad off and needed to be relieved. Dysentery and lack of decent food weakened us.

Fox did not mention the matter, but soldiers with dysentery faced another problem. After dark, anyone moving about was in danger of being shot. Soldiers attempting to relieve themselves might easily be targets for trigger-happy comrades. Marine Dallas Bennet spent part of the Guadalcanal campaign on Tulagi. As he recalls, even the most mundane matters caused problems when dysentery struck:

> Military historians of the Army tell of their discovery that cover-alls were not a good jungle uniform when dysentery struck. The Marines had already made the change to belted trousers. These were too time-consuming when a hurried "nature call" was imminent. We called those nature calls the "Tulagi Trots." Our speedy solution was to use a razor blade to remove the thread from the crotch, skivvy drawers (shorts) having been discarded after the first attack. This too had failures when we, under night-time shelling, stumbled, tripped, or fell and found that it was just too late.

Occasionally food poisoning would break out, and an epidemic of dysentery would flatten a unit for a time. As recounted by Carl Weber, serving in New Guinea during the 1943 Salamaua operation, the Army might try to make the best out of a bad situation:

> The neighboring battalion had suffered an outbreak of dysentery. They couldn't dig latrines because it was swamp. We had barrels. You can imagine getting yourself on top of a barrel with dysentery. They had so much dysentery that they got some of these people on the barrel at night to sit up there and relieve the guard. You'd take your rifle and act as guard. Double duty. They all had hemorrhoids: and people say they'd poke them back with a long handled spoon. Dysentery was a terrible problem. Soldiers would get so weak.

Weber's point concerning weakness has been affirmed over and again throughout military history. The broken-down appearance of soldiers too long on the line is usually due to an all out physical assault on their health. What the Marines called the "bulkhead stare" so often observed on the faces of the combat weary reflects something beyond fatigue. Young soldiers during World War II normally entered battle quite fit. Weight loss among young men of nineteen already through the rigors of military training means tissue loss, not shedding fat. It is a sure sign that the combination of fatigue and dysentery has done its work. Soldiers in this condition must be relieved, or they will sink into a nightmare world of mental breakdown, starvation, and death. Commanders knew this and relieved tired units whenever possible. The 1st Marine Division, for example, fought the Japanese and the jungle for four solid months on Guadalcanal. As Clifford Fox relates, in December the Marines were ready to leave:

We were a mess by December. Dysentery, malaria, you name it all took its toll. I went on board ship at 135 lbs. There were Marines that couldn't make it up the rope ladders. Swabbies would climb down the cargo nets and help them up they were so weak. Only 40 percent of the division was fit to fight. But at least when we left we knew the U.S. was staying. A lot of soldiers were coming over. And we knew that the Japanese were in worse shape than we were. The battle was won. I'm still not exactly sure how, but we won.

One more malady requires mention because it afflicted almost every soldier in the theater, and was in its way the best commentary on the malignant character of the South Pacific battlefield: jungle rot—the myriad infections that attacked the skin. Chafing or the smallest open wound served as entry point for germs. Soldiers consequently picked up rot on any part of the body. If a man scratched one of the insect bites he was covered with, infection often resulted. Once a sore started to fester, the man was in trouble. Soldiers were almost never clean or dry, so the problem normally worsened. Skin problems are hard to treat under the best circumstances, but all that was available to American and Australian forces was a blue-colored antibacterial liquid. This concoction might help limit the spread of rot but did not clear it up. In rare instances, rot became so severe that the military evacuated soldiers to the United States for a lengthy stay in the hospital. Evacuation, however, was very rare, and unless a very serious case ensued, soldiers went about their duty and "toughed it out."

Marine Bud DeVere came down with a good, solid case of jungle rot on Guadalcanal. As DeVere points out, one hardship led to another:

Fatigue was extraordinary. I don't recall sleeping a night through on any island that was under fire. If there wasn't some kind of incoming fire, you'd have guard duty. Or torrential downpours. There was more rain there than anywhere I've ever seen. Constant rain. Everything was mud. I had an extraordinary case of trench foot. It was caused from being constantly in water. There was water in all of the foxholes or dugouts. Some of the nights when they had all-night bombardments or attacks you'd sit in a foxhole with just your head out of the water. In a dugout, you might find out if you had a case of claustrophobia. There might be a foot of space between the water and the top of the dugout. So there you sit, completely immersed in water.

So I got this rot between the toes. There were places between my toes I could see bone. The corpsman put a purple ointment on it and wrapped it up. Hell, I couldn't walk. I wrote a letter to my mother and she sent a couple of tubes of something called Fungi-RX. I used that and got rid of the stuff. I think my mother saved my toes.

Ore Marion was with Fox on Guadalcanal. One of the rare Marines who did not come down with malaria, Marion was compensated by an ugly case of jungle rot at a time in the campaign when supplies of all sorts were almost nonexistent:

I went to see the battalion surgeon about getting bandages to cover the tropical ulcers on my back. I would wake each morning with maggots eating away at the ulcer holes. The company corpsman didn't have bandages to spare for that type of a problem. They didn't have any medicine either. The surgeon asked me if I was going on patrol. I said yes. He replied, "If I give you bandages to cover those holes now and then you get wounded on patrol, I won't have any bandages for your wounds." How anyone survived a wound I will never know.

Along with malaria, dengue, and scrub typhus went a host of tropical diseases. In addition, other diseases that commonly afflicted soldiers were also found in the South Pacific. Interestingly, there was an exception. Venereal diseases are commonly near the top of the list of "lost man-hours" during modern war. So it was with American units while training in the United States or stationed in Australia and New Zealand during World War II. When the U.S. Army invaded the Philippines, the rate skyrocketed. However, in the South Pacific contact with indigenous civilians was so circumscribed that venereal diseases were of little consequence.

The terrible physical environment also magnified the grave problem of accidental death and injury. Anyone who studies war carefully has to be struck by the large numbers of lives lost or damaged due to negligence or ugly circumstance. The situation is inevitable. The military at war has tens of thousands of young men, never perfectly trained, dealing daily with weapons, explosives, gasoline, motor vehicles, and dangerous terrain. (I shall examine the related issue of "friendly fire" casualties in a later chapter.) It is impossible to compile all the ways young men found to kill and maim themselves in the South Pacific. Men from every unit tell of some freak death or maiming. For instance, several men unloading supplies were crushed. Huge trees in the jungle, weakened by artillery, came down easily in a rainstorm, sometimes on top of a foxhole. Lightning that accompanied the storms killed several soldiers. Gas stoves blew up killing cooks. Sharks and crocodiles attacked soldiers out for a swim. A slip along a jungle track often led to oblivion.

Stanley Larsen led a group of men of the 25th Division on an orientation patrol shortly after their arrival on Guadalcanal. While crossing the Lunga River, the group suffered a small but all too typical tragedy:

One of the soldiers was sitting on a great big log over the river along with two or three others. This man slipped and fell into the river. The tip of his rifle struck his head severely and he never came up. We held hands and walked up the river. Sure enough the body had stayed under water and we found him after fifteen minutes. We tried for over an hour to bring him back, but his lungs were full of water. I was administering first aid and it was the first time I ever had to pass judgment on whether a man was dead or alive. When the body started to stiffen, I had to make the decision that this man was dead. We carried the body back to the camp. We got back about eight or nine at night. We could tell by the red glow of the cigarettes coming from the regular guard unit that we were finally back to safety.

On a few horrid occasions massive accidents happened that claimed the lives of dozens. Armies do not like to publicize these incidents, but they are as much a part of war as an enemy bomb making a direct hit on a bunker. The worst case I know of in the South Pacific was kept secret for several years after the war. At 4:00 A.M. on September 7, 1943, five trucks containing the men and equipment for Company D of the crack 2/33d Australian Infantry Battalion were waiting to load onto transport aircraft at the end of a runway outside Port Moresby. An American B-24 heavy bomber, loaded with 500-pound bombs and 2,800 gallons of fuel, lost control on takeoff and crashed directly into the trucks. Fred Caldwell, a soldier from another unit awaiting transport, witnessed the event:

> Bombs exploded, flaming high-octane fuel sprayed the vehicles, men became blazing torches and their own bullets, grenades and mortar bombs went off, rescuers also becoming victims. There were dreadful screams. Men charging around with clothes on fire would suddenly disappear as the grenades and mortar bombs they were carrying went off. Others, rolling on the ground, would give a quick jerk as their bandoliers exploded. We did our pitiful best, all the time with one eye on an unexploded 500-lb bomb, while horribly burnt men pleaded to be shot; and, as a doctor told me long after the war, it would have been better so, rather than letting some of them die after weeks of excruciating pain.

Fifteen men were killed outright, forty-four died of injuries, and ninety-two were injured but survived. The eleven-man bomber crew perished. Ironically, because of skill and good fortune the 2/33d throughout the war had avoided the large calamities that brought ruinous losses in a single battle. Bill Crooks was in one of the trucks and describes the scene:

The men had their ammo and their grenades including white phosphorus and explosives to distribute on the plane. Three of the 500-pound bombs exploded and the fourth was red hot. I was blown into a tree with my kit on fire. I knifed the waist belt off and dropped to the ground and ran under a truck chassis. I knew what went up had to come down. I lay there and saw flaming petrol running down the track toward me. Then I saw one of my men stuck to this red-hot bomb and noticed his right leg partially gone. So I'm struggling and cutting, not even thinking about the bomb. I didn't realize it was a bomb until later. Anyway I got him off and then we were inundated by very brave U.S. airmen putting men on stretchers and giving morphine needles. I walked to the control tent to report to the adjutant that D Company was no more.

Therefore we can add sadistic caprice to disease, a fierce climate, and wretched terrain. Yet around the soldiers in this hostile world were thousands of people who over the centuries had made it home and made peace with its fierce nature.

The Peoples of the South Pacific

Although a fierce and terrible place to fight a war, the South Pacific was home for a population that was quite large considering the level of economic development and lack of towns. The numbers are imprecise, particularly for New Guinea. In 1942, as previously noted, very little was known of much of the land. Large areas of the inland mountains of New Guinea had no organized contact with the Western world whatsoever. There were perhaps 2.5 million people living in New Guinea and the Solomons during World War II. Surprisingly, although colonized for centuries, much of the Solomons was a concealed world. In general, if an area possessed something of value, such as a plantation, the colonial presence was substantial. If it did not, the control of white outsiders was lightly exercised or nonexistent. In addition, areas on the coast had far deeper and long-standing relationships with the outside world than most areas inland. This meant, naturally, that the size of the land mass involved was extremely important. A small island in the Solomons might have a colonial outpost, a small port, and almost certainly a mission. Local police or paramilitary forces existed in small numbers in many places. A big island like Bougainville, on the other hand, was administered by Australia in name only once inland from the shore.

When considering the role played by the peoples of the South Pacific during the war, several things must be kept in mind. First, generalization is very tricky. The population consisted of scores of linguistic and ethnic groups that possessed markedly different cultures in many ways. A technologically primitive, intensely warlike people in New Guinea would have had little in common with coastal villagers in the Solomons who followed the Christian faith and were quite familiar with the sleepy Westernized economy shaped by a nearby plantation. A coastal villager from the Solomons might well speak English, read the Bible, and periodically work at a nearby coconut plantation. A hill tribesman in the Stirling Mountains might carry a shrunken head, practice cannibalism, or engage in periodic genocidal wars against neighbors.

Second, the war came without warning or invitation to the people of the South Pacific and concerned issues that few understood in the least. With some very notable exceptions, few in the area had a personal stake in the war or the outcome. It was not a national or ideological crusade. For the most part "control" from the outside was extremely tenuous regardless of which side occupied a given geographic zone. A person's life might change very little if the Japanese came, the Australians left, the Japanese left, and the Australians came again. One must remember how small the battle zone was in the South Pacific relative to the size of the area. Although the region was huge, fighting was very localized. Guadalcanal was a very good example. To an individual who lived on the northern coast of the island between Cape Esperance to a point twenty miles east of Lunga Point, the war would have been an extraordinary event. If that individual, as so many did, fled ten miles inland, it would have been very possible to have lived through the entire campaign without seeing anything related to war beyond a few aircraft. There were areas within a hundred miles of Wau in New Guinea where, it is very safe to say, people were barely aware that war was taking place.

Third, the impact of the war on the local peoples grew greatly as the war progressed. In the period we are looking at, the war was a major part of the life of a small minority of the population of the region. As time went on, this changed dramatically. The rear service buildup throughout the area greatly increased the numbers of Allied servicemen and the scope of their activities. It also created a far greater demand for labor and goods. The rear was also much safer. Many of the thousands of people who originally "went bush" when fighting was nearby returned when the Allies ejected the Japanese. Whereas in 1942 the combatants sought the most basic services from islanders, by 1945 local inhabitants were tending military farms, operating heavy machinery, or employed at the local workshop. From the point of view of thousands of people, the war was a mysterious, perhaps savage experience in 1942. By 1945, for many it was turning the world upside down.

Although the early stage of the war touched a small percentage of the indigenous population, those who were swept up in the conflict played a very important role in events. From the point of view of the combatants, the native peoples were a vital supply of manual labor. In many ways the ground war in the South Pacific ran counter to patterns found in other theaters of conflict. For example, in most other theaters the buildup of combat and service troops went hand in hand. Matters of supply, logistics, and maintenance were an essential component of industrial warfare, and every side found that the need for these elements grew with time. An army simply could not move or fight unless someone was there to keep its insatiable appetite for ammunition and supplies fed, and its machines working. As both the Germans and Russians found out, one ignored these matters at great peril. The American buildup in England prior to D-Day, started with service personnel. This was also true concerning air-base construction in northern Australia.

Yet on the battlefronts of the South Pacific until mid-1943, rear service troops were in very short supply. This reflected a scanty allocation of resources to the area, and was amplified by the great distances involved. It also reflected the type of war being fought and, in its turn, shaped the type of war fought. As always, the jungle was there compounding all problems. Difficulties in one key area, such as a lack of medical supplies, became catastrophic in the jungle. Consequently, there was a tremendous demand for labor to construct basic facilities and keep them intact in the face of the fierce climate. Lacking their full complement of mechanized equipment, all the armies employed manual labor to a great extent. No soldier likes physical labor. Many will accept combat assignments to avoid it. In the South Pacific no one avoided beastly hard, exhausting physical labor. But there were never enough men to both fight and keep things running. The demand for native labor was never satisfied.

Labor in quantity was not easy to find or organize. Consequently, the Allies, able to rely on what existed of the prewar colonial administrations, had a tremendous advantage. This was particularly true in New Guinea, where the need for manpower was most compelling. The Australians divided the portions of New Guinea they controlled into districts and hired a small number of agents to establish a presence, halt the fierce tribal wars, and arrange native labor contracts with local chiefs. Geoff Waters was with Australian intelligence in 1943, and describes the prewar system:

> Each district had a district officer and a staff. Patrol officers covered all the tribes in that area, and in each principal village the hereditary chief was appointed as the Luluai or leader. He wore an official cap, and a medal. A government-appointed man was the tultul, he kept the population records and was responsible for relaying the government instructions to the villages. There was a medical appointment, called the doctor boy, who administered first aid, and was responsible for village hygiene. When a patrol neared a village, the information had been sent ahead by garamuts (native drums) and a new carrying party would come out to meet the patrol officer. The other carrying party would return to their village, and the patrol officer and his assistants would be quartered in a rest house. The patrol officer would hear all of the

problems of the villagers, administer justice, and collect a small head tax. Tracks had to be maintained, and disputes settled despite long-standing feuds between neighboring tribes.

The imperial hand lay lightly on the South Pacific. In New Guinea the civil administration was run by a few dozen individuals. In 1939, for instance, the Australian government claimed "control" of less than half of the Mandated Territory of New Guinea. In point of fact there was little economic activity. There were a few rubber plantations in Papua, but production was small-scale. There were dozens of coconut plantations along the coast, but their administration was largely in the hands of the companies operating them. There also existed the new and thriving gold-mining region near Wau. Supplied entirely by a motley fleet of aircraft, Wau was a New Guinea version of a Klondike boom town, and a very odd place.

In some ways this changed after Pearl Harbor. The Japanese blitz, which swept up the major islands of New Britain and Bougainville, shook government prestige. Quickly, the Australian government instituted what was, in essence, military rule in New Guinea. It drafted European residents and organized many into irregular military units. This heralded the collapse of civilian administration in New Guinea. In its place, the Australians created the Australian New Guinea Administrative Unit (ANGAU). ANGAU was given the closely related missions of maintaining order, ensuring Australian physical presence in the hinterlands, and supplying native labor. ANGAU inherited a system of indentured labor. Although temporary agreements for porterage were common, normally employers worked through local officials and native chieftains and agreed to labor contracts regulated, in theory, by the government. In most cases the contracts were for a short term, and guaranteed the workers' return to their home village at the end of a period lasting several months. Although cared for and given small items, workers were paid through local chieftains. A worker usually fulfilled his term of employment. In theory, the government could fine or imprison the worker for failing to fulfil his end of the contract. In practice, it was a very lucrative enterprise for the village elites, and villagers were most reluctant to anger them. In early 1942, various employers had arranged for the services of 35,000 indentured laborers.

With war and ANGAU came labor conscription. The goods available from Australians were certainly desired by many indigenous inhabitants. The discipline and strenuous labor involved with porterage were not. Consequently, many workers willingly gave their services for a time, while others were dragooned into the war effort. Fortunately for the Australians, when the Japanese landed at Buna, bringing with them over a thousand laborers from New Britain, a small number of Japanese personnel and military police foolishly mistreated local inhabitants. As put by Geoffrey Lyon, a young Australian officer, "The Japanese blotted their copybooks the moment they arrived with improper treatment of native women. That turned the natives against them, which was most fortunate for our side." When the Japanese understood the supply nightmare they had entered, they reacted with harsh labor-conscription measures that made villagers more fearful of them. To make matters worse, when the Japanese retreated, they murdered scores of laborers who might have gathered important military information. They feared that some natives might tell all to ANGAU when the Japanese retreated. Hundreds of Japanese soldiers paid for this policy with their lives in New Guinea and dozens of other islands. Many small Japanese units that became lost or were forced into the bush simply disappeared.

The need for native labor was immediately obvious during the struggle for the Kokoda Trail. As Geoffrey Lyon correctly observed, "Porters were a form of transport. In war there is never enough transport. Never." The problem facing the Australians has vexed every logistics officer since the beginning of armed conflict. Regardless of how supplies are carried, it takes supplies to move supplies. Furthermore, the farther an army advances, the more supplies are required to move supplies. Just as the American trucks supplying gasoline to tank spearheads in Europe consumed more and more gas the farther the tanks moved ahead, so too was it necessary to recruit more and more porters to support the Australians as they moved up the Kokoda Trail. For instance, to supply a relatively small force up the line, 3,000 carriers, each hauling forty pounds of supplies, required an eight-day trip. The Australian command wanted to increase the size of the force and build up a reserve. They found that to build up reserve supplies required twenty days' labor of an additional 2,000 laborers. This would do nothing to increase the size of the force. Problems like this plagued Australian and Japanese operations on the Kokoda Trail. All too often, soldiers were called upon to pick up the slack, which weakened the military power of the units. As we shall see, Allied operations in New Guinea would have been impossible without a massive use of air transport. As it was, thousands of native carriers served throughout the campaign.

The rigors of porterage, particularly under conscription, created an uneasy situation. The indigenous peoples might be willing to tote forty pounds of weight over some of the worst terrain on the planet. They were not, however, prepared for industrial warfare. If combat was near, porters left quickly if possible. ANGAU officials realized that laborers were not soldiers and did not allow them to intentionally get near the front. Australian officers were not happy with ANGAU's attitude, and believed, no doubt with justification, that ANGAU was reluctant to disrupt the long-term relationships that were necessary for the region's economy.

Nevertheless, very simply, the porters were not combat soldiers. The Australians were very fortunate that the Japanese could not spare the aircraft required to attack the Kokoda supply line, or there would have been a crisis with local laborers. Many porters working for the South Seas Detachment fled into the jungle because of the relentless Allied air strikes on Japanese supply lines. This flight contributed to the cruel and often violent measures the Japanese employed to keep discipline. The Allies too had trouble if combat was near. Henry Dearchs was with the 41st Division in New Guinea in late 1943 and recalls a representative incident:

We were moving some supplies to a small perimeter up the ridgelines. I was helping to guard a column of a few dozen native porters. They were nice people and we liked them a lot. We gave them cigarettes and they would give us delicious wild bananas. As luck would have it the Japs must have heard something and opened up in our direction. No one was hurt, but the machine-gun fire was landing close by, and whistling through the trees. Everyone hits the dirt quick when that happens. The natives were terrified, just terrified. Sure can't blame them. We were afraid they were going to bolt for the bush. We just tried to act calm. We gave everybody cigarettes and joked with them. We knew it was probably only harassing fire, although we couldn't be sure. I was afraid myself. After a while everyone settled down, and off we went. Thank God there was no more firing.

Medical evacuation was one form of labor crucial in New Guinea and very important in the Solomons. Reliable air evacuation of sick and wounded did not start in New Guinea until Dobodura airstrip near Buna became operational in early December 1942. Dobodura, however, was still twenty miles from the Buna front through rough terrain. The U.S. 32d Division evacuated some men on coastal craft, but they too had to be loaded many miles south of the fighting. (For this reason, all combatants reserved evacuation for seriously wounded or very ill. Standard cases of malaria, jungle rot, or small wounds were "treated" on the spot.) It took four bearers to carry one stretcher. Ideally, four teams accompanied one stretcher. It was a task the native peoples performed with skill and compassion. Fred Johnson was a medic with the 32d Division. He served at the battalion aid station a few hundred yards behind the front, the position where the wounded and ill were taken for initial care. He dealt with stretcher-bearers on a daily basis:

We were dependent upon our stretcher-bearers for evacuation. I don't know what we could have done without them. I remember they had this characteristic smell of coconut oil and smoke. They used the oil for some kind of insect repellent, I think, and they had smudge pots in their dwellings to keep the mosquitoes away at night. They treated the wounded with tenderness. And they were good at it. When Americans carried stretchers, they carried them with their hands, low to the ground. It made for a bumpy ride, and it was very easy for one person to drop a corner and dump the patient on the ground. I did it myself. The natives, however, carried stretchers on their shoulders. It was more stable and faster. It was amazing to watch them walk. Most were barefoot, and when they would step on a tree root or something, it was like their foot kind of gripped it. They were great.

The treks were not as far in the Solomons, but the terrain was extremely rough. As the months went by American engineers improved jeep access on the islands. Yet there was always need for labor. The early days on Guadalcanal, like the early campaigns on New Guinea, were marked by shortages of everything. As it was, combat soldiers were doing a great deal of manual labor, such as unloading ships or bringing fresh water forward. Naturally, this tired out already ill soldiers and kept many off the line. (If the situation was obviously dangerous, the line filled rapidly.) Yet the few miles between the beach and the perimeter required continual transport of goods over exhausting terrain. (The Marines experimented, unsuccessfully, with pack mules.) Solomon islanders, by and large no friends of the Japanese, were a great asset.

The war was long, unremitting, and costly. Inevitably thousands of local people became involved in the military effort. Both sides based their use of indigenous males in ground forces on political arrangements developed before the war. This was inevitable and a great handicap for Japan. On islands like Saipan, which had been administered by Tokyo since 1918, the Japanese built paramilitary forces on the rudimentary militia and police apparatus that existed. In New Guinea and the Solomons, the Japanese were interlopers, whereas the Allies could expand upon prewar developments.

The Australians and British were the first to mobilize local peoples for war. In 1940 the Australians established the Pacific Islands Regiment of 3,500 men made up of three battalions recruited in Papua and New Guinea. Some of these men bore the brunt of the initial Japanese landing at Buna in July 1942 and were very involved with the early fighting along the Kokoda Trail. At the same time, men who before the war served with the Australian constabulary became part of irregular battalions that harassed and raided Japanese positions. Kanga Force, the most famous, suffered its share of failures, but on many days made life miserable for the Japanese near Lae. They also engaged the Japanese during the fighting near Wau in early 1943.

The British and New Zealanders organized Fijian battalions that Americans eagerly employed in the Solomons. Fiji, a British colony, possessed a deeper connection with the West than found in the Solomons. The local chiefs, through whom the British ruled, supported the war effort. Many did so expecting independence after the war. The units that came out of the effort, which eventually included men from several islands, were far better trained than other native paramilitary units. The Americans quickly found that indigenous peoples in the Solomons were quick to "go bush" when the fighting got near. Fijian volunteers took to war in the jungle with considerable vigor. Although the Fijians were from far away and did not know the local area any better than did the average GI, they were familiar with the jungle and could orient themselves quickly. Many American units became very dependent upon the Fijians helping them.

The Fijian reputation for fierceness was based on fact. Trained in the use of modern small arms, Fijians were scouts and infantry. They were volunteers, extremely well paid for people of the region, and they came from an intensely martial society. Unfortunately, the techniques of traditional jungle war as fought on Fiji did not always suit the operational conditions of the South Pacific. Army researchers at Bougainville, where there were hundreds of Fijians, found a very large number of friendly-fire deaths among them. Less careful about basic security and more active at night than Americans, dozens of Fijians were shot by Fijian or American sentries.

The Fijians, like a small number of other indigenous units, also took part in occasional long-range patrols deep in the bush and behind Japanese lines, to the extent that lines existed. Mark Durley was a lieutenant with the Americal Division on Bougainville in early 1944. He commanded an epic patrol that crossed the entire island in search of a prisoner-of-war camp holding Indian captives from the fall of Singapore.

I led some Fijian Scouts on a patrol across Bougainville. We were ordered to scout Japanese positions, and, if possible, locate a prisoner-of-war camp. We were ordered to avoid combat, which, when you think of where we were, was a very good idea. The Scouts were excellent soldiers in that environment. They were strong and handsome people. Their bushcraft was outstanding. While on the patrol one of the Fijians motioned for us to stop. They stripped down to their shorts and went off into the jungle barefoot. Sometime later they returned. Soon we saw that they had wiped out a Japanese patrol without making a sound. We estimated that they killed seventy Japanese on our trek.

Native guides were a fixture of the war in the South Pacific. Both sides used them widely. In a world without reliable maps, traveling a very short distance was a problem. Longer-range patrols inland were a march in the dark without the aid of the people that knew the land. In general, most Solomon islanders viewed the war fearfully and were not eager to be involved. Those who did, however, sided with the Allies almost exclusively. Once again, the heavy hand of Japanese occupation offended and frightened many. Christian missionaries, who were very common in the Solomons, and their congregations were watched closely by Japan's feared military police. In addition, the British had a local police force before the war and in 1937 began recruitment of a battalion of Solomon islanders to serve as a paramilitary defense force.

Many of the guides were either part of the local police or the small defense force or related to men who were. Personal relationships were crucial in island culture, and an act of cruelty could turn an entire village against an army. (Unless, that is, the force involved was quick to make amends. When Allied aircraft destroyed native fishing boats or mistakenly bombed villages, Allied authorities were careful to make restitution. The amounts of goods or money seem low to a Westerner, but at the time achieved the desired purpose.) As the war proceeded, native guides were used more and more. When the supply situation eased in mid-1943, American GIs showed great generosity toward villagers, gaining tremendous goodwill. Australian soldiers, although never having the means available to GIs through the American supply juggernaut, did much the same in New Guinea. This fact did not always sit well with British and Australian authorities who feared, correctly, that it would corrode colonial authority. In the short run, however, Americans and Australians benefited greatly by being able to reconnoiter and move with natives in areas that otherwise would have been difficult or impossible.

After the 25th Division secured a large perimeter on the island of Vella Lavella in August 1943, Robert Kennington led a good example of the type of mission that would have been impossible without the help of local guides:

I took two Navy officers on a patrol across the island. They were looking for a place to establish a PT-boat base. Their commander was Byron White, later a Supreme Court justice. We had three native guides, the best I'd ever worked with. There was a village near the mountaintop there. A French woman pretty much ran things. Before the war she and her husband operated a plantation. When the Japs came they killed the woman's husband, so she and her son fled to this village. They turned the villagers against the Japanese. The Navy guys weren't up to the trek, and we had to carry their rifles and packs. They slowed us up badly. We took five days' rations and were gone eight, so we were running very low on food. We saw a couple of groups of Japanese, but slipped by them, not looking for trouble. One morning the natives took off, promising to return in about an hour. They came back carrying some giant mussels they gathered on the ocean and had about three wild pineapples and a bunch of wild oranges. They dug a hole in the ground, filled it with a certain type of wood that gave off very little smoke, piled rocks all over the fire. When it got good and hot, the mussels opened up like poached oysters. It tasted as good as a T-bone steak. We had plenty of bananas, papayas, and taro roots that tasted like a sweet potato. When we made it to the shoreline, we borrowed a big native war-type canoe in the lagoon. We left the Navy folks there and PT boats picked them up.

By far the most important military role played by indigenous peoples was connected with the crucial intelligence apparatus that became world-famous under the rubric of "coast watchers." Throughout New Guinea and the Solomons before the war the Australian and British governments had a handful of colonial authorities manning their distant and obscure outposts. Some of them, particularly those involved with the local police or running the efforts to recruit native troops, stayed in place when the Japanese occupied portions of the South Pacific. The Westerners who remained behind had friends and associates among the native peoples, who assisted them in the war effort. Together, they created a formidable military asset for the Allies. Given radios and supplied by coastal craft, amphibious aircraft, or submarines, the coast watchers provided priceless military intelligence for the Allies. It was extremely difficult for the Japanese to launch a major air attack or fleet movement without its being reported immediately by coast watchers or someone working for them. In addition, coast watchers also infiltrated their comrades into Japanese work gangs and often picked up useful, if somewhat unreliable, information. Jacob Vouza of the Solomon Islands constabulary became a legend on Guadalcanal for the help he gave the Marines, suffering torture at the hands of the Japanese in the process. Knighted after the war, Vouza was probably the most illustrious individual in the Solomons at the time of his death in 1986. Also on Guadalcanal was Walter Clemens, an English administrator who became one of the most famous of the coast watchers.

Some of the coast watchers played a much more active role than observation. Control of any territory in the South Pacific was always tenuous. The Japanese garrisons on most islands confined themselves to guarding the most important facilities. In the early part of the war, many local Japanese officers tried to establish good relationships with the indigenous peoples and sometimes succeeded. For the most part, however, they were mysterious interlopers. Japanese patrol boats went along the shorelines, aircraft flew overhead, and occasionally a patrol passed through a settlement. But, for the most part, several dozen miles of fierce jungle separated the Japanese from the villagers. This allowed coast watchers when supplied from the outside to establish little armed bands. Their primary purpose was to protect the coast watchers themselves. Japanese intelligence picked

up the radio transmissions and knew they were under constant observation. A punitive mission against an area that the coast watchers
worked in, however, was risky business. The Japanese learned
quickly that the terror tactics they sometimes employed in New
Guinea were useless. They only made the situation worse. For the
most part, the Japanese could do nothing. In some cases they ceded
control of large portions of some of the islands to the coast watchers
and their allies.

The most celebrated coast-watcher domain was in the eastern
portion of New Georgia. British official Donald Kennedy organized
a little army of former policemen and others sympathetic to the Allies. Japanese patrols that came into the area did so at tremendous
risk. Kennedy and his comrades were so well organized that long before the Allies invaded New Georgia, American advanced reconnaissance units were in place. Kennedy's men helped them reconnoiter
Munda Point and discovered the beach chosen to serve as the landing zone. All of this went undetected, and Admiral Halsey's landing
came as a great shock to the Japanese. They expected an invasion,
but did not think it would come as soon as it did. Nor did the Japanese realize that the beach found by Kennedy and the Americans was
suitable for a major operation. Except for fierce air attack, Americans
landed at New Georgia without opposition.

The Allies received another benefit from the coast watchers. Although distances are large in the Pacific, because the Solomons are
laid out in a long, thin oval, much of the military action took place in
the corridor between the various islands called the Slot by Americans. Consequently, fliers and sailors were never very far from an island. Often this did no good. Hundreds of men from downed aircraft
or sunken ships drowned quickly or were swept to the open sea. Nevertheless, all aircraft had life rafts of some sort. A small one was attached to the flier's parachute. Furthermore it was possible on
occasion to ditch near an island, or perhaps set down on the beach itself. The stories of rescue by natives are a staple among Allied airmen. At least 200 fliers were rescued by local peoples and delivered
to the coast watchers. Some Japanese fliers were likewise rescued if
they went down in a Japanese-held area. (Kennedy's men captured

five downed Japanese fliers and delivered them to the Americans.)
Likewise scores of sailors from both sides were given help by natives
when air and sea search failed. Rescue of airmen and sailors facing
death could earn small rewards for the natives involved. Nevertheless, judging from episodic accounts of many men who owed their
lives to the islanders, human compassion seems also to have motivated the inhabitants.

New Guinea was a very different story. Along the coast, many
Allies received life-saving assistance. Inland, however, the jungle
swallowed fliers. Many no doubt perished because of the elements.
Nevertheless, some of the peoples in New Guinea were intensely
warlike and loathed outsiders. They killed Allied and Japanese servicemen alike. The Japanese, forced by the Australians to move inland in late 1943, suffered serious losses. Likewise on the island of
Bougainville, the Japanese Army and many indigenous peoples were
at war with each other late in the conflict. One can imagine, in the
jungle, who had the upper hand.

The war in the South Pacific was a struggle between outsiders.
To those from the outside, the South Pacific was a wretched battlefield, one of the worst in history. Into this savage world three governments sent their young men to fight each other. It is time to become
acquainted with the participants in this fateful collision.

Chapter 2

The Armies

The outward trappings of military forces in the modern world resemble each other greatly. Uniforms, marching, hierarchy, and discipline are the surface manifestation of very deep currents that make the military unique among human organizations. The same currents create fundamental similarities in military establishments.

The primary reason why armies are so alike is that they make war. Even during peacetime, their ethos and structure are aimed at battle. At the center of battle are killing, dying, and fear. When combat begins, the natural instinct for most is flight. To be effective, an army must make its soldiers fight and win an internal battle with the instinct for self-preservation. The primary way to make a soldier act in a way contrary to instinct and "common sense" is through discipline born of hierarchy and passed on through training. When soldiers do parade drill, group calisthenics, or kitchen police, the military's primary interest is to teach them to follow orders. If the drill instructor says "Jump," the soldier jumps. There may be no reason to jump at all, but it is imperative that the man follow instructions quickly and without question.

Hierarchy has more than one function. The soldier must know to whom to listen. When military professionals talk about "leadership" they use the word in a different way than would the directors of a civilian organization. A military leader, whether he is a sergeant or a major general, is physically or figuratively leading his soldiers into battle. In practice, it is a little more complex, but the image of a junior officer, pistol in hand, leading his men forward is based on real circumstance. Armies know better than anyone that if risk lies down the road, there is great reluctance for soldiers to move forward. They must be urged, cajoled, or ordered. A good leader will have the respect of his men. They will also be somewhat afraid of him. If push comes to shove, it is risky to disobey an order. More to the point, in a well-trained army the question does not come up. The orders are given, and they are carried out. In a very good army these orders will be appropriate to the task. Soldiers are very keen critics of military leadership.

Beyond controlling fear, however, hierarchy and training also allow a military to move with purpose. Military operations are very complex, even if engagements are chaotic, small, and over in an instant. Suppose for a moment that one commands an untrained mob of armed men that is very eager to fight. Imagine also that discipline is unnecessary to conquer fear. If the men, however brave and well motivated, surge forward without formation, timing, or order, a well-trained opponent will slaughter them. Leaders, therefore, are also required to coordinate the movement of an advancing army, or give it coherence in defense. The better a military organization is led, the better it will accomplish its mission. Military establishments spare little effort to convince their soldiers that the more efficient and disciplined the army is, the better the chance it will accomplish its objective with the smallest possible number of men killed and maimed. A good army will demonstrate to its soldiers that it is in their self-interest to train well and follow orders. It is extremely important that the soldiers believe that it is more dangerous to flee than to fight. Bad leadership, naturally, turns the chemistry on its head. An incompetent leader kills his men and fails. Good officers know this very well. Combat soldiers on the line know it better yet.

To accomplish missions with acceptable cost in blood in the modern world has become increasingly complex. One must deal with supply, fire support, weapon maintenance, communications, intelligence, and the care of sick and wounded. No wonder that the practice of purchasing officer commissions in the eighteenth century had given way by World War II to armies run by a professional officer corps that was well educated in the myriad levels of their craft. It is no accident that every army has privates, sergeants, and generals. Questions of organization, balance, and efficiency are also paramount because they bear immediately on allocation of military resources and the ability to control men. Depending upon the situation, a mission might require the concentrated efforts of an entire division of 15,000 men or a twelve-man squad. To meet either eventuality, military organizations must be able to be built up or broken down depending upon the need. Moving from one scale of operation to another is difficult, but flexibility is invaluable in battle. Dispersing or concentrating forces quickly as the situation changes is the sign of a well-trained force. It is thus also no accident that armies all have divisions, battalions, and squads.

Armies also stress tradition and group conditioning of mind and body. It is crucial that soldiers feel some sort of kinship with their comrades. Military men know that a coherent unit will look after its own. Soldiers will take risks to guard their friends. All officers try to convince soldiers that the most dangerous thing to do under fire is to flee. On most occasions this is correct. A unit that breaks and flees disintegrates and loses its ability to defend itself effectively. However, sometimes the safest thing for an individual to do is run. A good military will create the atmosphere that such an act is almost unthinkable. Running, after all, might save the individual but kill his comrade. Maintaining the respect of the group is very important to most soldiers. Peer pressure and the desire for approval are particularly crucial to young soldiers and are two of the most important reasons that war is fought by the young. Thus it is no accident that all military organizations have uniforms, emblems, and heraldry. By such measures armies try to convince their soldiers of two things that do not fit well together. On one hand, they want their soldiers to think they are all in the same boat, face common hardship, and need each other to survive. On the other hand they also want the men in a group to feel they are special, unique, better than their enemies, and better than other units in their own armed forces.

Lastly, because soldiers both kill and die in battle, it is crucial that the military convince them that they are carrying out a special, unique, and transcendental mission. In war, human morality and behavior are turned on their heads. Men must stay when fired upon, knowing in their heart that some of them will die. They also must kill other men they have never met. In civilian life, killing another is murder. In war, the deep group ethos of the warrior replaces standard morality, and killing becomes a task that is honored. Much of this job is not undertaken consciously by the military, but rather comes from the self-preservation mechanism of society itself. Soldiers must believe that what they are doing has a great purpose, that taking lives or giving them is done for a transcendent reason. It is no accident that all armies give medals for bravery and venerate national symbols.

Military organizations have a unique structure with a unique terminology. Fortunately for the civilian reader, with minor modifications, the basic organization of World War II infantry in the Japanese, Australian, and American militaries was the same. This was due to the fact that during World War I a certain military structure proved most efficient. In the late 1930s, following the example of the highly professional German Wehrmacht, armies standardized on what the Americans called the "triangular" division.

The division, simply defined, is the lowest-level military unit that includes all supporting arms under one command. It is the basic administrative unit in all armies. It is the primary constituent of larger groupings such as the corps (two or more divisions) or army (two or more corps). Unlike the corps, the division is permanent. In Europe during both world wars, and during Japan's war with China, the division also served as an important combat unit with all its units coordinated toward accomplishing an objective. In the South Pacific, as we shall see, this was almost never the case. Yet in all theaters the fighting units drew their support and based their command structure on the division. For the fighting soldier the company or platoon was home, the division was hometown.

Divisions varied in approximate organizational strength from between 15,000 to 20,000 men. As implied by the term "triangular," all of the fighting units came in groups of three. Consequently a division had three regiments. (The Australians called their regiments "brigades.") Regiments, like divisions, were permanent units possessing unique numbers not duplicated in the respective army. Historically, the regiment had played the role of the division, and many of the regiments in World War II had very old pedigrees. Consequently, there was only one 35th Regiment in the U.S. Army, and it was one of three belonging to the 25th Division. (To befuddle readers and historians, regiments often had nicknames that matched a unique emblem or crest. The 35th was known as the Cacti.) Likewise the Australian 25th Brigade was part of the 7th Division. The Japanese had the same system. Their 228th Regiment was part of the 38th Division. Regiments had three battalions, numbered 1st, 2d, and 3d. (Australians had unique numbers for battalions as well as brigades. Their battalions had four rather than three companies.) Each battalion was made up of three companies, designated by letter; each company had three platoons, and each platoon had three squads. In addition to the regiments, divisions also had individual units under divisional control that provided either combat or support services. These divisional units included artillery, engineer, medical, signal, and reconnaissance formations.

Every man in a combat division in the South Pacific was at considerable risk. All were vulnerable to air attack and artillery bombardment. Everyone in the theater was prey to the diseases described earlier. Nevertheless, the men who did most of the fighting were combat infantrymen. There were fewer of these men than a cursory look at a divisional structure would lead one to believe. An American infantry division had an authorized strength of 14,253. A full-strength regiment had 3,257 men. Therefore only 9,771 men were assigned to regiments. A battalion strength was 871 soldiers, so 2,613 men in a regiment were assigned to battalions. A rifle company had 192 men, which meant that 576 men of a battalion were assigned to a rifle company. Looked at another way, the division's twenty-seven rifle companies, in Army lore the "heart" of the division, consisted of 5,184 men out of 14,253 assigned. Several thousand soldiers were manning machine guns, mortars, and artillery pieces. Nevertheless, armies found that large numbers of individuals inside the division were required to keep the men fed and supplied and to care for them when sick or wounded.

Beyond the general factors found in modern armies, great differences existed. Although the function of war making imposes a certain level of commonality on the contending forces, armies also reflect societies. They also reflect different military histories, a very important factor in institutions so inherently conservative. These differences concern us here not because they are interesting commentary on the societies involved. Instead, the unique characteristics of the armies had very identifiable and very important ramifications on the battlefield and the course of the war in the South Pacific. Therefore, I will examine the internal structure of three armies. To show how the unique nature of each army was reflected in battle, I shall also analyze their first major engagement in the South Pacific.

The Sword of the Empire

The histories of Japan and Europe have some striking parallels. Both societies showed for centuries an unusual affinity for war. European feudalism and its Japanese equivalent were based upon a set of interdependent relationships among military aristocracies. In many European countries the aristocracy maintained a special relationship with the military until World War II. Remnants of chivalry and the medieval code of military honor are easily seen today. When European nations combined their prodigious martial skills with their advanced technology, a relative handful of soldiers, sailors, and administrators ruled most of the world. The only country in Asia that escaped direct or indirect European rule was Japan.

Japanese feudalism lasted far longer than did the European variety. The policy of isolation instituted by the Shogunate intentionally prevented the importation of European machines and European ways (including Christianity). Firearms were at the top of the list of forbidden technology. During the great civil war that led to the creation of the Shogunate at the beginning of the seventeenth century, the contending forces employed firearms procured from the Portuguese. However, Japanese military aristocrats saw clearly that rifles and cannon were a mortal threat to their special position, which rested much on martial skills and exclusive access to weapons. Consequently, for 250 years the samurai who buttressed the power of the ruling clans remained masters of the sword and developed an intense warrior ethos.

When faced with unmistakable signs of Western power in the second quarter of the nineteenth century, best exemplified by China's shocking humiliation by Britain during the Opium Wars, the first cracks in Japan's isolation policy came with the importing and building of European weapons. When the United States forced the issue with Commodore Matthew Perry's naval expedition to Tokyo Bay in 1854, many far-seeing Japanese scholars and warriors grabbed the opportunity to strike against the Shogunate and create a society based upon "Western techniques, Japanese spirit." Within a generation the Japanese had created an Army based upon the Western model. They drew upon the military expertise of France, Britain, and later Germany as their military increased in power and importance. Soon they added a modern Navy. At the end of the nineteenth century Japan was a player in the great imperial game, carving out a sphere of influence in Korea and China. In 1905 it waged war against Russia, and stunned the world by winning.

By 1941 Japan was the most intensely militarized nation in the world. Military service or training was a part of life from cradle to grave. Elementary-school teachers gave boys a dose of paramilitary training. Male students who went on to middle school, high school, or college all received rudimentary military training by Army officers. Those not going on in school received similar military training in government-run apprenticeship programs. The time spent in these programs in any given year was not great—a few hours a week of instruction, and a few days during the summer for maneuvers. Yet indoctrination and discipline were stressed, as were the twin notions of self-sacrifice for the nation and obedience to the emperor.

In the famous Imperial Rescript to Soldiers and Sailors promulgated by the Emperor Meiji in 1882 (and carried by every Japanese soldier in World War II), a set of virtues similar to the traditional samurai code of bushido was enumerated to serve as a guide for the Japanese soldier. The Rescript stressed the traditional samurai virtues of obedience, truthfulness, and bravery. The paramount duty was loyalty, even at the cost of one's life: "Duty is weightier than a mountain, while death is lighter than a feather." In the same period the emperor dedicated the Yasukuni shrine in Tokyo, a place where the Meiji and his successors came to pray for the spirits of those who died in the service of the emperor. Thus a connection was made between the Army, the people, and the emperor. Over the years, this connection took on an increasingly mystical quality, initially generated by pride, eventually by desperation.

The transition into the Army for some began very early. The Army had technical apprenticeship programs for sixteen-year-old boys. These were two-year courses of a technical nature to prepare graduates to be noncommissioned officers in the technical fields such as communications and aviation that grew ever more important. A smaller number of youths in the same age bracket began the road toward the Ichigaya Military Academy. Originally modeled on the French academy at St. Cry, Ichigaya, like West Point, was necessary if an ambitious young man wished to rise high in the Army. In many ways a student from West Point would have been at home at Ichigaya. The same stress on obedience, physical strength, and rigorous, if not imaginative, course work was present. The American cadet would have found incomprehensible the stress on spirit, on the "will which knows no defeat," which bordered on a cult of death. The Japanese military increased its spiritual indoctrination of the officer corps over time because its social makeup was changing. In the Meiji time, most officers had been young samurai. By the time of war with China in 1936, fewer than 20 percent had that distinction. Mostly the sons of the new middle class or prosperous farmers, the officers had to learn an ethos that a traditional samurai was born with.

All Japanese males between the ages of seventeen and forty were liable for conscription. Conscription had been one of the first of the Meiji reforms, and over time its web was widened and its apparatus became more elaborate. Although one could volunteer for service at a younger age, twenty-year-old men were called each December for physical examination. If over four feet eleven inches in height and in good physical condition, the man was classified as available for active service. Men with physical defects were given lower classifications and put in the reserves. Only men with serious physical problems were classified as unfit for service. Reservists received a short period of training and were required to stand for a yearly muster. If necessary, they might be called into active service. At age thirty-seven men who had been in service or the reserves entered the First National Army and were liable for recall until age fifty. Men who had not received training, plus all untrained youths aged seventeen to twenty, entered the Second National Army, where they received no training but were subject to call-up in an emergency. Barring criminal conviction or serious disability, there were no deferments to service, although a one-year postponement might be possible.

Most young men were classified eligible for service. Unless they enlisted in the Army or Navy, they were called to active service. In peacetime, they did not have far to go. The Japanese Army, drawing on the German model, recruited and trained on a territorial basis. Japan was divided into four Army districts. More important were the fourteen divisional recruiting districts. Each divisional district was subdivided into regimental districts. In peacetime, active divisions were drawn from these various areas and were backed up by depot divisions ready to refit active divisions or create new ones. In other words, more than one division might come from the same divisional district. (The 2d Division faced by the Marines on Guadalcanal was from the Sendai district on the eastern coast of Japan just north of Tokyo. The 42d Division came from the same area.)

A territorial system of some kind was used throughout the world. Few were as sophisticated and all-encompassing as those found in Germany or Japan. The system had two principal advantages. Because training facilities were close to home, it was economical, always a major consideration for the Japanese military. In addition, military leaders believed that young men who knew each other and shared common customs would bond together more readily than total strangers and create units with superior morale. Localism was stronger in the world before World War II than it is today. Thus the recruitment structure was a technique to bind the nation and the locality.

During peacetime, training in the Japanese Army was excellent in most regards. Japanese drill instructors had half of their job already done for them, working with young men who had grown up in a society where obedience and loyalty to the family were among the most treasured virtues. Training lasted a year, progressing from the lowest-level squad training through complex maneuvers involving larger units. By 1941 this system was already starting to break down. The manpower demands for the new Pacific war, in addition to the conflict with China and the reserves held along the Soviet border, required units to complete much of their training in the field. It would not have been unusual for a young Japanese soldier to have boarded a ship with ninety days' training. Unless there was an emergency, further training took place in the field. In this regard, his situation would have been very much like that faced by an American draftee of the same period.

Training stressed fitness, endurance, and small-unit tactics. The world that a young soldier entered does not quite fit the stereotype of the robot-like Japanese soldier that the Allies tried to project. It is true that obedience was expected and received. It is also true that endurance was emphasized and, if the soldier was healthy, likewise achieved. Japanese officers and noncommissioned officers (NCOs) frequently kicked or slapped recruits to make a point, more often than their U.S. or Australian counterparts. Physical abuse, however, was very rare. On the contrary, the Japanese stressed the notion of a special brotherhood in the rifle company that included all regardless of rank. Officers made a point to live the same lifestyle as their men. Indeed, an unusual number of high-ranking Japanese were killed in action in the South Pacific. The Japanese Army was almost cocky about its sloppy appearance. It marched out of step, uniforms were torn and dusty, officers and men alike had stubble on their faces. But if the Army marched badly on parade, it also marched very swiftly in battle, as the Allies found out on several occasions.

Japanese officers had two great advantages by 1942. Because Japan was already at war, the men took training very seriously, knowing it would be put to use. Second, Japan had been at war for over five years. The officers and NCOs either had combat experience or had been instructed by those who had. On one level this gave them an edge. Basic small-unit tactics and company-level communications were very well honed. The Japanese had found out the value of night attack and spent much time studying and refining this extremely difficult maneuver. They had learned to use light mortars and light artillery very effectively. They were expert field engineers.

On another level, however, their experience was counterproductive. It is a cliché that generals prepare for the last war. The Japanese Army, when it engaged the Allies, was prepared for the war it was fighting in China, combined with some new techniques proven during their conquest of Malaya. Unfortunately for Japan, these lessons were not all applicable in the odd and malignant environment found in the South Pacific.

Thoughtful Japanese officers realized that their Army had a very serious defect. Because Japan was a poor country, and because the air arm and the Imperial Navy took so many of the scarce industrial resources available to the country, it could not hope to match the firepower of a Western army. This had been illustrated dramatically in 1939 when Soviet forces, relying on massed artillery and tanks, pounded Japanese infantry at Nomonhan on the Mongolian border. The Japanese therefore were forced to make the best of a bad situation. They did so by trying to develop extremely advanced infantry tactics, and by increasing indoctrination through personal example and spiritual training classes.

The Japanese concept of "spirit" is essential to understand. It was a major reason why the war in the South Pacific was fought the way it was. Much of the indoctrination was negative in the early stage of the Pacific war. Educators, following government guidance, taught Japanese youth that they belonged to a special race that was culturally and morally superior to the decadent and materialistic West. Officers and nationalist educators passed on their contempt for American and European soldiers to recruits, despite the drubbing received at Russian hands. (The details of the battles against the Red

Army were a closely kept secret, of course.) The spectacular campaign in Malaya was living confirmation that the lessons learned in school and training camp were true. A numerically inferior Japanese force skillfully ran a large British Army into the ground.

But the notion of spirit had a deeper connotation. It included the belief that the human will could surmount physical circumstance. Japanese officers taught their men, and believed themselves, that they could do things no other army could simply because Japanese troops would not be denied. Much of Japanese education and military indoctrination dealt with mythological renderings of great acts of heroism in both the distant and recent past. All had one thing in common: the hero died in battle. Death in battle was portrayed as an honor to the family and a transcendent act on the part of the individual. Surrender was a disgrace to the soldier and to his family. No doubt an element of coercion was present on occasion. Soldiers were told that the enemy would butcher them if they were captured. It is impossible to say how many believed that. However, for the most part, there can be no doubt that the astounding physical courage showed by Japanese soldiers came from the inside. It was, in a manner of speaking, voluntary.

The most remarkable behavior shown by Japanese soldiers was their willingness to accept orders that meant certain death and their refusal to surrender. Loyalty to the feudal lord and an unquestioning willingness to die pursuing duty were deep and genuine parts of the traditional samurai ethic. However, feudal Japan had not been a nation in modern terms. A peasant and a samurai were separated by a yawning gulf of power and prestige. A necessary goal of the modernization campaign was to create a nation to match an already unitary culture. Passing on the outward trappings of bushido to the entire population was central to Japanese education and political propaganda for seventy-five years before Pearl Harbor.

As previously noted, every Japanese soldier met by Americans and Australians in battle in 1942 possessed a copy of the Emperor Meiji's Imperial Rescript of 1882. It contains a striking image. The cherry blossom, beloved of the Japanese, falls to earth in perfect form. The Rescript counsels, "If someone should enquire of you concerning the spirit of the Japanese, point to the wild cherry blossom shining in the sun." Thus the Japanese honored the sanctity of the death of the young in battle.

The death of the young is one face of war. All societies know this. The ancient Greek historian Herodotus wrote that war is unnatural because fathers bury their sons. Unfortunately for all concerned, the extreme veneration of death of the Japanese was unique and came dangerously close to becoming a cult of oblivion. It struck at the very nature of the warrior code as understood in the West. In the West, death in war had value only if it had purpose. Soldiers were asked to risk their lives in battle, not commit suicide. An officer intentionally putting his men in a position where they had no reasonable chance of survival would not be obeyed in a Western army. If conditions showed that further resistance was futile, surrender was honorable. It prevented not only the needless squandering of one's own men but also the needless squandering of the enemy's. It was a mutual agreement, manifested over centuries of history, that served as a brake on the worst excesses of war in Europe. The Japanese took this attitude as a sign of weakness. If Japanese officers did not value the lives of their own soldiers in fighting to the death, they likewise showed contempt for the lives of their foe.

The Japanese Army did nothing blatantly suicidal on the strategic level in the South Pacific. As we shall see, it went to great lengths to evacuate isolated units and retreated when conditions demanded it. Tactically, the situation was very different. Time after time, Japanese soldiers fought when circumstances for the unit involved were hopeless. The slight delay caused to the Allies almost never had genuine purpose. It was an exercise, rather, in mutual bloodletting that had no reason beyond fulfilling the requirements of soldierly honor as the Japanese saw it. Thousands of men perished, consequently, for no reason. It was a form of political murder, most of the victims wearing Japanese uniforms. By breaking down the fragile restraint afforded by honorable surrender, the Japanese opened the floodgates for war without mercy. As we shall examine later, their Australian and American opponents proved rather good at the new rules.

One could argue that all wars are wars of attrition and that a Japanese soldier fighting on in an isolated bunker, killing or wounding the enemy, was carrying out a legitimate purpose of war. In this context, the Japanese soldiers who accepted nearly certain death represented a pinnacle of courage, best represented by the suicide pilots later in the war.

However, such an argument misses a central point of war in our time. Wars of attrition fly in the face of the warrior ethos. Bombing cities, starving whole populations, wrecking economies were justified in World War II on specifically unique political grounds. Hitler and the Japanese government, the Allies argued, had started a war of shameless and grandiose aggression, and fought it in a vicious manner. Unconditional surrender, consequently, was the only acceptable outcome of the war for the Allies. Note, however, that surrender would end the killing. (Because the Jews could not surrender, Hitler's policy toward them was not in any way an act of war but murder on a massive scale.) The measures taken to fight the war were so extreme, and ran so deeply against human decency, that modern nations have never remotely duplicated them. The ethics behind nuclear arms proved this point. They existed specifically to make war of extermination impossible because it would be mutual. Neither side during the cold war seriously considered using them for a first strike on the other nation's population. Lest one think we are off on a tangent, recall that the only atomic weapons ever used were dropped on Japan. The American government justified dropping the two bombs by claiming that the invasion of Japan, because the Japanese would fight a purposeless battle to the end, would become a blood-soaked apocalypse. I have not talked to a single Allied combat veteran of World War II who has any regrets concerning this decision. The road from the Emperor's Rescript of 1882 to Hiroshima was sadly direct.

The Japanese Army of 1942 had great élan, excellent troops, and good light-infantry weapons. Judging from the first battles after Pearl Harbor, its leaders were also exceptional. Like so much of the Japanese war effort, however, Japanese ground forces were wildly out of balance. Where they were good, such as in the area of small-unit tactics, they were very good. The extraordinary spirit of the troops proved real and astounded the Allies. Yet in every other area of modern land war—planning, interservice coordination, logistics, and intelligence—the Army was second-rate. Fortunately for the Japanese, they were entering a phase of the war where tactical skill was extremely valuable, thus hiding some of their other weaknesses. Within a year, however, the Allies learned that defeating Japanese ground forces was costly but simple. In an era when "fire kills," Japanese forces proved themselves intrepid victims, but victims nevertheless.

In addition, before the Japanese Army engaged the Allies in the South Pacific, it existed under a self-created cloud of illusion, what Japanese admirals later called "victory disease." (The Navy suffered the same malady before the defeat at Midway.) The self-adulation and contempt for their enemies that had been drilled into officers and men before hostilities were based on fact, judging from Japan's spectacular victories. Like many of their counterparts in Nazi Germany during the spring of 1941, the Japanese believed that because they had not suffered defeat they could not lose. At a time when the most realistic and circumspect analysis was essential, the Japanese Army mentally drifted in a wave of self-congratulation. Interesting testimony on this topic came after the war from Vice Admiral Otto Weneker, German naval attaché in Tokyo throughout the war:

> Early in the war I made a trip through the South Seas and up through the Marianas to see conditions with my own eyes. I was astounded in the South Seas. The Japanese were thoroughly enjoying the lush life. They had parties continually and were drinking all the liquor they captured. I asked them why they did not prepare fortifications and make the places stronger. They said the Americans would never come, that they could not fight in the jungle and they were not the kind of people who could stand warfare in the south. As far as I know all those people in those places, both Army and Navy, once they had got into a place where there was no fighting, would do nothing more about the war.

The Japanese Army first appeared in the South Pacific struggle in the summer of 1942, still supremely confident after its great victories in Malaya and the East Indies just weeks before. Japan's strategic situation, however, had taken a very ugly turn at this early date with the U.S. Navy's great victory at Midway. As noted in the Introduction, Tokyo was forced to examine its strategic priorities in the Pacific in light of a new military balance. Plans to strike directly at the United States–Australia supply line were postponed, as was a thrust into the Indian Ocean.

Although the Imperial Army and Navy quarreled continuously, both agreed that Port Moresby should be taken. They realized that Port Moresby was the key to both Papua and northern Australia. Its seizure would offer several advantages. If the Navy gained revenge for Midway by defeating the U.S. fleet at a future date, Port Moresby was the perfect place to stage an attack on sparsely populated northern Australia. If, however, growing Allied resources forced Japan onto the strategic defensive, controlling Port Moresby would buttress its strategic hub at Rabaul greatly. Tokyo was already worried about sporadic Allied bombing attacks on Rabaul, and realized they would intensify over time. Furthermore, the small Allied presence on the northeastern shore of Papua in the Buna area was a serious potential threat. Officially, the Army was cool toward invading Australia. However, had it succeeded in taking Port Moresby quickly, the Navy's arguments might have been reexamined. Regardless of potential plans for the future, both Japanese services agreed that, with Port Moresby in hand, the Allied position would be weakened greatly.

In light of Midway, Tokyo ceased planning for a second amphibious invasion of Port Moresby. Instead, it ordered the Japanese Seventeenth Army at Rabaul and the Combined Fleet at Truk to seize Buna and then investigate the possibility of using it as a base for an attack over the Owen Stanley Mountains. Naval aircraft immediately began a photo survey of the Owen Stanleys. Before a single Japanese soldier had landed, however, self-delusion had entered the process of military planning. In the preliminary plan for the operation, an elite Japanese Army force was to make a reconnaissance of the area and report on the feasibility of an all-out attack. However, armed with photographs gathered by the Navy and little else, the Imperial General Headquarters in Tokyo, the Army's high command, deleted the reconnaissance phase and ordered the immediate seizure of Port Moresby and the rest of Papua. The Navy independently decided that Port Moresby would have little value unless heavy engineering equipment and artillery, transportable only by sea, could be made available. Thus, it decided that it needed to seize Milne Bay at the eastern tip of Papua to establish a sea supply system. These twin decisions set the stage for the incredible battle for Papua that raged from July 1942 until January 1943.

On July 21, 3,600 Japanese troops of the South Seas Detachment landed at Buna. Although morale was extremely high, the Japanese had already committed dreadful blunders. Most important, they were operating in the dark. Tokyo knew less about New Guinea than did Canberra or MacArthur's headquarters in Brisbane, and that proved very little. The Japanese had no maps or geographic surveys· and were naively ignorant about the medical problems they would face. In a shocking display of ignorance and wishful thinking, they assumed that the Kokoda Trail across the Owen Stanleys included some roads. Consequently, the Imperial Army ordered its engineers to make these roads ready for vehicles on the north slope of the mountains and pack animals on the south slope. (Today it is still impossible to drive across the Kokoda Trail.)

In addition, the dismal relations that existed between the Japanese Army and Navy crippled operations immediately. The Port Moresby operation was an Army "show." The Imperial General Headquarters involved the Navy only as far as required. Tokyo ordered the 100 Navy aircraft based at Rabaul to lend support. A small flotilla of surface warships was to protect the landing. In retrospect we can see that the Japanese were not preparing for any unforeseen circumstances. In July 1942, Japanese naval forces were extremely formidable. Four aircraft carriers and dozens of warships were at Truk, and Rabaul's air wings could have been greatly reinforced. At this time, when Japan dominated the theater, it would have been possible to build up reserves at Rabaul to a much higher level. Likewise there was nothing to prevent Tokyo from moving troops stationed in

Southeast Asia or Manchuria into the South Pacific. The Japanese, in other words, were beginning an important offensive without sufficient reserves in the area. Soon the Japanese paid dearly for this oversight. However, at the time the South Seas Detachment did not need massive naval support for the landing itself. Japanese assault forces landed on July 21 and easily pushed away a handful of Australian defenders.

Allied air attacks from Australia and Port Moresby were a different matter. Japan suffered from a miserable allocation of its inadequate supply of transport vessels. Tokyo, like Berlin, or Washington for that matter, did not want the civilian population to feel the full weight of deprivation that the military situation demanded. "Total war" for the Axis started very late in the day. Far too many vessels were employed keeping the civilian consumer economy moving along. In the distant reaches of the South Seas, transports were like ·gold for the Japanese. (They were like silver to the Allies.) This was the type of planning that Tokyo did poorly. Consequently, when Allied aircraft attacked the invasion fleet, they crippled the enterprise at the start. American B-17 heavy bombers proved to be very poor weapons for attacking swift warships. Lumbering transports, however, were very much more vulnerable. On the journey to Buna, American bombers damaged one transport. Another transport and a destroyer were hit at Buna. The men the ship carried disembarked, but it left before they could unload supplies. (Unloading supplies, as the Marines found out at Guadalcanal, is a difficult proposition. It was another detail ignored by Tokyo.) In the days following, another transport was sunk while a second was damaged and forced to return to Rabaul. The Japanese vanguard was short of supplies before it started. Fortunately for Tokyo, the weather worsened, greatly hindering Allied air attacks. The main body of the South Seas Detachment was able to deploy in the weeks that followed. By mid-August 14,000 Japanese were either in or had passed through Buna.

The Japanese Army stressed speed in offensive operations. The tactical techniques involved were simple in concept but required extremely good men to put into action. Advance forces would march at breakneck speed. When Japanese troops found the enemy, they would deploy along the front, probing the line and hopefully pinning the opponent in place. Simultaneously, Japanese units coming up would go overland, find the flank, and either assault the enemy or surround him. When moving overland, Japanese infantry carried its own rations and supplies, allowing temporary freedom of movement. This system had smashed the British in Malaya. It had failed in the Philippines because the American line on Bataan was continuous, allowing no flanking movement. There the Japanese never penetrated the American front, and required a lengthy siege to prevail. Typically, when planning the New Guinea operations, the Imperial General Headquarters remembered Malaya but forgot Bataan.

Initially, the Japanese thrust up the Kokoda Trail resembled Malaya. The advance party moved swiftly up to Kokoda itself. On July 29 it launched a fierce night attack that hurled back Australian defenders. In the weeks that followed, there was a race to the front between the main body of the South Seas Detachment moving up from Buna and units of the newly arrived Australian Imperial Forces (AIF) 7th Division moving up from Port Moresby. The 7th Division, with two years of combat experience in the Mideast, were the toughest opponents the Japanese had met. New Guinea, however, presented unique challenges that no army of the time properly could prepare for. Geoffrey Lyon was a young officer in the headquarters of the 21st Brigade of the 7th Division, the first veteran unit sent forward. He recalls that the Australians, like the Japanese, were making a leap into the dark:

When we raised the three divisions of Australian Imperial Forces in 1940, we all assumed we would be going to Europe or the Mediterranean. No one gave any thought to fighting in New Guinea. When we returned from the desert in early 1941, the 7th Division went to Queensland supposedly to learn lessons derived from Malaya and Singapore. I thought the lessons were a lot of rubbish. There was one book written about jungle fighting. In it there was a diagram of a jungle track, kind of a single wobbly line running down the page, with defensive positions marked. Well, that was a load of rubbish because, looked at from the left or right flank, there was absolutely no depth in it at all. The author obviously hadn't assimilated jungle fighting at all.

We did not know what was entailed. There were no proper maps. There was one fellow who had a plantation near Kokoda. I was present when he was being questioned about what we called "the Gap," a bottleneck we though existed in the Owen Stanleys. We wanted to know how wide it was. He illustrated it by holding up two fingers, meaning two men abreast could go through. That was absolute rubbish, it was about eight miles across. The Gap really referred to the route that aircraft took to get through the Owen Stanleys. It had a very different meaning to foot soldiers. It didn't represent any sort of defensive bastion. It didn't exist. There were tracks all over the place. The Gap was not a place to block an advance, it could be outflanked very easily. This fellow was giving us the impression that you could hold it up with a couple of machine guns. He was miles from the truth. When I was sent up the track, my parting words from General Allen [7th Division commander—EB] were "You tell Pottsy [Brigadier Potts, 21st Brigade commander—EB] to do what we did in the last war. Dominate no-man's-land, and resume the advance." First World War talk. When I got up there I realized how stupid the message was.

Lyon also believes that at this stage in the war, with the supply situation a shambles and the Australians not ready for what was ahead, the Japanese soldier was the best in the world:

It was a war of shadows. I can distinctly remember before I went up the track a chap came down who was wounded. He said, "I haven't even seen a Japanese yet." That's how it was. The nefarious war of shadows. The Japanese, you see, were so well trained and clever. They had a much lower ration scale than ours. They had two or three days' ration in a mess tin and their weapons weighed a lot less. Their clothing was well seasoned. Traveling so light gave them an ability to outflank that came as a great shock. That took us some time to get over. They had superior training and a more profound understanding of jungle warfare. The experience they had in previous campaigns was a great advantage also.

When they outflanked us we would tell HQ they were across our line of communication. The stock answer was that in that case we were across theirs. The fallacy of this thinking, of course, was the Japanese ability to carry more supplies with them. We relied on day-by-day supply. There were also more of them at that stage. At headquarters, MacArthur's and ours, we underestimated the size of their force.

Yet as the advance continued the Japanese learned some bitter lessons. Supply was a terrible problem for everyone concerned. The Australians had a small airstrip at Myola suitable for airdrops, but the Japanese lacked even that limited capability. Vehicles were useless. Australians later found the Kokoda Trail littered with the bicycles the Japanese had made famous in Malaya. Nor were there any "Churchill supplies," enemy supplies captured as they fled. Unlike the supply depots the British used in Malaya, the Australians had very little to abandon. Furthermore, the Australians fell back but were never routed. This meant that Japanese supplies had to be carried forward by people. The Japanese brought with them 1,000 porters from Rabaul. Unlike the Australians, however, they had no connections with tribal authorities in Papua. Sporadic mistreatment of native women hurt the Japanese cause seriously. Japanese engineers, engaged in a futile attempt to create a road up to Kokoda, could not be used as bearers. Ultimately, the Japanese soldiers themselves had to serve this role. This represented a waste of combat troops, but Japanese officers should have immediately seen that the waste was unavoidable. However, the South Seas Detachment failed to face reality and employ adequate numbers of men as beasts of burden. Naturally, because the men carrying supplies also consumed supplies, this problem became worse the farther the Japanese advanced. Astoundingly, the Japanese Army did not call upon the Navy for supply airdrops until the situation neared collapse. Even as the troops shed equipment and began to suffer from malnutrition, they urged themselves onward. Spirit would prevail.

The Australians sought to find what they called a "firm base" on which to establish a solid defense. They came close to finding one at one of the most rugged places on the track, the village of Isurava.

There the Japanese vanguard was stopped cold. Japanese units made several attacks, but Australian units held firm. A Japanese officer recorded in his diary on August 10:

> Commenced a night attack at 10:20. Advanced stealthily on hands and knees and gradually moved in closer to the enemy. Suddenly encountered enemy guards in the shadow of the larger rubber trees. Corporal Hamada killed one of them with the bayonet and engaged the others, but the enemy's fire forced us to withdraw. The platoon was scattered and it was impossible to repeat our charge. The night attack ended in failure. Every day I am losing my men. I could not repress tears of bitterness. Rested waiting for tomorrow, and struggle against cold and hunger.

At the end of August reinforcements arrived, including 1,000 more men from Rabaul. The South Seas Detachment, now led personally by its commander, General Horii, launched an all-out attack. It succeeded in dislodging the Australians from Isurava. The pattern of flanking and retreat began again. The spirit, the magic of Malaya, it seemed to the Japanese, would triumph.

In reality the Japanese were defeated at this point. The American landing at Guadalcanal on August 7 befuddled a command structure that was not good at facing unexpected turns. It also struck directly at the fierce rivalry between the Army and Navy. In 1942 the Japanese Navy provided almost all the airpower present in the South Pacific. Naval officers quickly turned their attention to the fierce air and naval battles that surrounded Guadalcanal. Soon the Army too was sending troops in that direction. The Imperial General Headquarters was caught between two stools and could not decide which to sit on. Had they turned everything they had against either Guadalcanal or Port Moresby, a victory at either would have been very possible. As it was, they stumbled from one half-measure to another. The defeat at Milne Bay, which we shall examine later, resulted directly from this confusion.

As the Japanese continued onward, into the worst part of the track, Allied aircraft relentlessly attacked the Japanese lines of supply. Therefore, supply columns found it very dangerous to move by day along those portions of the trail not completely covered by jungle canopy. To make matters worse, the pack horses the Japanese had counted upon died like flies. A Japanese soldier recorded the dissipation of strength:

> The road gets gradually steeper. Bushes cover the countryside. Cicadas and birds are singing. We are in a jungle area. The sun is fierce here. One part of the troops crawled up and scaled the mountains and continued its advance. Troops are covered with dirt and sweat so much that it is difficult to tell one man from another. We make our way through a jungle where there are no roads. The jungle is beyond description. Thirsty for water, stomach empty. The pack on the back is heavy. My arm is numb like a stick. My neck and back hurt when I wipe them with a cloth. No matter how much I wipe, the sweat still pours out and falls down like crystals. Even when all the water in your body has evaporated, the sun of the southern country has no mercy on you. The soldiers grit their teeth and continue advancing, quiet as mummies. No one says anything unnecessary. They do not even think but just keep on advancing toward—the front.
>
> "Water, water!" all the soldiers are muttering to themselves. We reach for canteens at our hips from force of habit, but they do not contain a drop of water. Yet the men still believe in miracles. The fierce sun makes them sleepy. The weeds and trees are snatching a peaceful sleep under the burning sun. The sound of the enemy planes and our marching seem to lull us to sleep. The men sleep while they walk and sometimes bump into trees. Enemy planes fly over the jungle and repeatedly attack.

During the last days of August and the first two weeks of September, the Japanese war machine put on an extraordinary performance. The South Seas Detachment, using a series of outflanking maneuvers and relentless attacks, shattered the 21st Brigade of the AIF 7th Division. In Japan's last great land victory in the Pacific war, it prevented the Australians from establishing a solid front and pushed them back to the Imita Ridge less than forty miles from Port Moresby.

On September 16 the South Seas Detachment entered the village of Ioribaiwa after another fierce battle. At night the Japanese troops could see the searchlights from one of Port Moresby's airstrips. However, they were exhausted, and between them and Moresby lay the Imita Ridge, where Australian units were dug in. The Australians had found their "firm base" and for the first time outnumbered the Japanese. Near ruin from the exhausting march, malaria, and very serious battle losses during their victories of late August, the South Seas Detachment was ordered to halt. The men would rest, bring supplies forward, and wait until conditions allowed reinforcement for the final drive toward Moresby. They were waiting for reinforcements from the 2d Division deploying toward Rabaul. But Tokyo, instead of dispatching the 2d Division to Papua, sent it instead to Guadalcanal. General Horii was also waiting for his men to shuttle supplies forward, but between rain and Allied air attacks this proved much slower than anticipated. Lastly, Japanese intelligence correctly ascertained that MacArthur was building up forces in Milne Bay and Port Moresby in preparation for a move against Buna, then almost undefended. For all of these reasons, Rabaul forwarded to General Horii the bitter order to retreat back to Kokoda.

The Australians allowed the exhausted Japanese contingent to slip away. Soon, however, they began a pursuit, this time with a sizable portion of the 7th Division. Pressured from the rear, but terribly reluctant to give up ground, Horii did not handle the retreat well. He assigned one unit the job of rear guard in the rough terrain near the village of Eora. At that position Australian pursuit caught up with the Japanese. The rear guard fought hard, but the Australians gained the upper hand in short order. Throwing good money after bad, Horii advanced to Eora days after he had left it. He arrived too late to change the situation. Forced to retreat again, Horii gave Australian pursuit a much more lucrative target. Horii passed through Kokoda and established a position between the villages of Oivi and Gorari. He hoped to be able to hold the Australians there and, if necessary, retreat to Buna if an American attack took place.

Japan did not lose the ground war in the South Pacific in any single place. There was no equivalent of Waterloo or Stalingrad. Military historians often use the phrase "turn of the tide" to describe a decisive clash of arms that fundamentally alters the direction a war is taking. Yet, in the natural world, the Pacific tide turns slowly, sometimes almost imperceptibly. There is a subtle difference in the appearance of the surface water, and after an hour or so, one can notice the tide line receding. The tide turns, in other words, before a person can see the results. So it was with the war. By November 1942 the Japanese had suffered a number of reverses, and the cumulative effect was producing something resembling panic in Tokyo. Yet, if I were to pick one place where the war turned irrevocably against the Japanese Army, it was at Oivi-Gorari on November 5, 1942.

The Australians approached the Japanese at Oivi and split into two groups. One advanced forward and pinned the Japanese main body. The other moved south, searching for the Japanese flank. On November 5 the attack was under way. The Japanese fought fiercely, but the Australian flanking element continued to move south. Realizing that his entire force was in dire danger, Horii attempted to redeploy. However, the Australians in the south wheeled to the north, to the extent that one "wheels" in the jungle, and attacked the Japanese rear, severing their position. General Horii ordered a retreat that turned swiftly into a rout. Forced inland and off the trail, half the Japanese force, including Horii and his headquarters, abandoned all equipment and headed for the jungle. Australian pursuit forced them into headlong flight up the bank of the torrential Kumusi River into the trackless interior. On November 19, hearing gunfire from the direction of Buna, Horii decided to risk a crossing with his aides in a canoe. All drowned.

It proved impossible to encircle an enemy unit in the jungle. It is a difficult maneuver under any circumstances. In this way, Malaya, or later the Philippines, were far different from the South Pacific jungle. The tracks were too many, too ill-defined, and communication was too crude to enable the attacker to close a noose. Consequently, although it lost more men in this battle than in any single engagement in Papua, much of the South Seas Detachment at Oivi straggled back to the Buna area. The men Horii left before his death showed typical Japanese tenacity when, soon after Horii's demise, they fashioned rafts and crossed the Kumusi. Most arrived in the

Buna area only a few days before the Allied attack on that bridgehead began.

At Oivi-Gorari the Australians had used in the fierce New Guinea jungle the techniques pioneered by the Japanese in Malaya. The AIF inflicted a massive defeat on crack Japanese troops at small cost to themselves. Rarely would the Japanese fight Australian troops in open battle in the future. When they did, the result was defeat. The Japanese tried one more small offensive in New Guinea toward Wau in January 1943 and were thrown back once again. For the remainder of the war in the South Pacific the Japanese Army's operational technique shifted from lightning advance to delay and retreat. Japanese commanders looked for positions where they could hold the Allies and hurt them. When Allied strength grew too great, the Japanese tried to extricate the survivors if possible. Initially in the Buna area, as we shall see, this change of direction caused a nightmare for the Allies. Ultimately, however, when Allied skills and firepower built up, the operations sank into the realm of futility.

Despite defeat, the spirit of the Japanese, however destructive and malignant its long-term ramifications, revealed an individual courage that has no equal in modern war. After the Allies finally crushed the remains of the South Seas Detachment in the Buna area in January, an Australian unit came across a handful of stragglers. The Japanese by this time had lost all cohesion and the Australians and Americans were shooting them down at will. Lieutenant Colonel A. S. Arnold, an Australian battalion commander, and a party of his men stumbled upon two Japanese officers walking aimlessly in a creek. The Australians and the Japanese officers were very close. An extraordinary drama played out in a tiny corner of a horrid place:

> With no stomach left for useless killing, Arnold called on them to surrender, and called again. They gave no sign of understanding or even of hearing. One leisurely turned away. The other washed himself in brackish water and drank some. Then, quite regardless of the silent watchers, he bowed very low three times into the sun. As he then stood erect and faced the Australians, Arnold called, "I'll give you until I count to ten to surrender." With no word the other took a small Japanese flag and tied one

end onto his upraised sword and held the other end in his left hand so that it covered his breast. And so he faced his enemies still silent. Arnold counted deliberately. As he reached "Nine" the Japanese shouted in a loud, clear voice "Out!" Then the Australians riddled him. The other they found hanging by the neck, dead.

These men declined honorable captivity in January 1943. At the same time, Japanese fortunes at Guadalcanal were sinking as fast as they had on Papua. Across the world, the German Army was dying in the snows of Russia. In America, the *Essex*, the first of the new fast carriers, was commissioned. The awesome American task forces were on the way. It is obvious in retrospect that despite the spirit and courage of Japanese fighting men, Japan was far closer to Italy than to Germany in its ability to fight an industrial war. The numerical base that was turning against them could only get worse. Furthermore, Japan had no hope of following the Allies into the dawn of modern electronic warfare.

The men who died in that muddy creek died for nothing. If the blind fools in Tokyo had cared about their country and its people, rather than a feudal cult of death, they would have been looking for a way out of the war in 1943. It would have meant the end of the Japanese military and the Japanese Empire. Yet, considering the terms they received in 1945, their nation would have endured. Armies are to defend nations. After Oivi-Gorari, after Buna, and after Guadalcanal, the Japanese Army was defending itself and its honor. When facing death, many Japanese soldiers found comfort by telling each other they would meet again at the Yasukuni shrine. Rather than meeting at Yasukuni, it would have been better for those splendid men in the creek to have met on the streets of Tokyo. General Hideki Tojo and the men who surrounded him at the top of the Japanese government deserve the contempt of history.

Leathernecks and GIs

Americans growing up in the years before World War II lived in a patriotic time. One of the most enduring images Americans had of their past was that of the minuteman, the citizen soldier. Although the notion is odd in the present day, until 1941 the myth and military reality corresponded very closely. American ground forces during peacetime were always far smaller than the country could have afforded. The military academies produced professional officers in case of need, but federal forces were insignificant. If war came, teachers told generations of Americans, the citizenry would rally around the flag and crush the enemy. Free men did not need great armies, because the armed citizenry was there if tyranny showed its face.

Considering the geography of the United States, it was good policy. Cities, small towns, and rural areas did have local militias. Firearms were widely owned. More important, no external enemies appeared after the War of 1812. What is surprising is how long this policy persisted. At the time of the Spanish-American War in 1898, the United States was the greatest industrial power in the world. Realizing that arming merchant ships in the era of steam warships would not provide an instant Navy, Congress had authorized a modern fleet. The Army, however, was ludicrously small, approximately 25,000 men. Fortunately for Washington, it picked a feeble enemy, because the resultant land war was marked by inefficiency and incompetence at every level.

Stung by the disorganization and muddle of the expedition to Cuba, Congress authorized a larger army and the beginning of a modern staff system. Yet when the United Sates entered World War I, it had to raise an army from scratch. In France, events turned out well, but the experience was unsettling and embarrassing. After the Great War, Congress naturally disbanded the mass army it had raised. Congress, however, did authorize a larger standing army and measures to increase the effectiveness of the Army Reserves and National Guard. Yet disillusionment with involvement in the war also reinforced historic isolationism. The Congress, therefore, never funded the force levels authorized.

Perhaps in the world of the 1920s the American government's inattention to land forces was understandable. In the 1930s, however, the world sank into political insanity. At the beginning of this ugly period the United States had a standing Army of 130,000 men armed with World War I weapons. Many World War I officers joined the Reserves, and the Great Depression saw to it that a dollar a week would fill the musters of the National Guard. Hobbled by the Depression, the government did nothing to strengthen American standing forces.

One must sympathize with the U.S. government as it dealt with economic collapse. Nevertheless, considering the world situation, it was taking an amazing risk after 1936 as events throughout the world grew more violent and menacing. In particular, the government's response to the outbreak of war in Europe was irresponsible, considering later events. Hamstrung by isolationism, and holding an inflated faith in the French Army, President Roosevelt authorized a limited increase of strength of the Regular Army to 227,000 and of the National Guard to 235,000. The Army had wisely husbanded some of its pitiful funds during the 1930s to design modern infantry weapons and keep abreast of more elaborate technology such as tanks and radar. In April 1940 the Army carried out the first large-scale peacetime maneuvers in U.S. history, involving 70,000 men. Considering the scale of the conflict that came so soon, these efforts were pathetic.

The fall of France in May 1940 shook the U.S. government badly. In the summer of 1940 many, perhaps most, military and diplomatic experts in Washington feared that Britain would collapse. The United States, in that eventuality, would face a triumphant Hitler. Because relations with Japan were also worsening rapidly, a two-front war was an obvious threat. A single supplementary military budget passed in October 1940 gave more money to the Army than it had received in total since World War I. Congress authorized a 1.2-million-man Army and weapons to equip it. A massive fleet-building plan went through at the same time. In August, Congress, at the urging of President Roosevelt, activated the National Guard and the Army Reserve. (In the parlance of the time, the Guard and Reserves were "called to the colors.") Shortly thereafter Congress passed, by a very close vote, the first peacetime conscription act in American history. Simultaneously, the Army began establishing a command structure appropriate for war. In all of this the government was five years too late, and still irresponsibly naive about what would be required if the nation went to war. Events allowed the government to escape from the worst consequences of its negligence. Britain, aided by its Commonwealth, survived. Hitler turned east and attacked the Soviet Union in June 1941. When Japan struck at Pearl Harbor, American domestic disputes concerning isolationism were resolved overnight. Nevertheless, few nations had been as fortunate as the United States. Ignorance and foolishness as monumental as that showed by the U.S. government in the years before World War II are normally rewarded with calamity. As it was, our stupidity only cost us military reverses, unnecessary casualties, and no doubt a longer war than required.

To one degree or another, the American ground forces that went to the South Pacific were poorly prepared for what they had to face. We were most fortunate to have in Australia an ally already wise in the ways of war. Furthermore, in an odd way, just as the hideous conditions of the South Pacific initially hid some weaknesses in the Japanese Army, they also hid some of ours. America's first land battlefield in World War II had no rules, because no one really knew how to fight there. The soldiers, although extremely enthusiastic, were very young and very poorly trained. Americans, luckily, proved exceedingly adaptable and repeatedly displayed great ingenuity. Just as important, inside the deficient land forces funded by the U.S. government before Pearl Harbor, there were just enough savvy professionals to hold together and guide to victory what was, in essence, a children's crusade in 1942.

Today the U.S. Marine Corps is one of the most famous fighting organizations in the world. The Corps can point to a long history: its nickname "leatherneck" comes from the leather guard worn by eighteenth-century Marines to ward off saber blows in hand-to-hand combat. Although the long legacy of the Corps is part of its mystique and no doubt contributes to its excellent morale, the Marine Corps played an insignificant role in American military history until the twentieth century.

Although the Marines sent a large contingent to France in World War I, where it saw brief but distinguished service, the Marines began their road to the South Pacific serving as the armed representatives of what passed for an American empire after the war with Spain. While the Philippines was an Army responsibility, various presidents sent small Marine contingents to Haiti, Central America, and China. Along the way, they fought small battles with several exotic enemies on two continents. The remainder of the Corps served as a police force on U.S. warships and guarded dignitaries. Although better educated than the popular stereotype allowed, the famous "Old Breed" of hard-drinking professional warriors was a tough bunch. They were skilled in small-unit tactics and infantry weapons. Under the Navy, but not really in it, and traditionally loathing the Army, Marines lived in a military world apart, rather like a tough Coast Guard.

By the twentieth century, boarding ships in battle was an archaic art. Therefore, after the Spanish-American War, the Marines in theory became the Navy's specialists in amphibious warfare. (A Marine unit landed at Vera Cruz, Mexico, in 1914.) In the 1920s units conducted small exercises, and officers did some very insightful theoretical planning on the subject. While the grizzled "Old Breed" were drinking and fighting their way through Central America, a small number of Marine and Army officers foresaw a future conflict in which the Marines would not participate in extended land operations, the Army's traditional sphere, but would become specialists in seizing beachheads and establishing initial perimeters under fire. The Gallipoli operation of 1915, a British-led landing in Turkey that developed into a catastrophe, had shown the need for that mission very clearly. Furthermore, when this little group was looking forward, they assumed their targets would be Japanese-held islands in the Pacific. (One of these men, Major Earl Ellis, died in 1923 under very mysterious circumstances in the Central Pacific while on a "health leave." It is very likely he was spying on Japanese positions and executed.)

In practice, very little was done beyond planning. In 1933 the Navy formed the Fleet Marine Force. This was to serve as the command structure for a large Marine amphibious force if the need arose. A team of officers led by Holland Smith from the Marines and Ernest J. King from the Navy, both major figures in World War II, developed a tactical manual that outlined the operational basis of amphibious landings used throughout the Pacific war. Undoubtedly, the Navy's sudden interest in the subject reflected its desire to have an independent ground force, ensuring itself a dominant role in a potential Pacific war years in advance. With small modifications, the Army accepted the same manual. The Corps had a new book but no money, as shown by its meager force level. In 1939 the Corps had 19,000 men, including 700 pilots, and was scattered across the globe.

The shock waves of 1940 were felt strongly in the Corps. Washington called up Marine reservists, providing the Corps with much-needed officers and men to help with expansion. The government authorized the creation of two Marine divisions. The 1st Division, formed in Cuba in early 1941, was built around existing units that became the 5th and 7th regiments. Added to these was the 1st Regiment, a skeletal unit built from the ground up. Building the divisions was no easy matter. Manpower management and logistics were never the Navy's specialty, and the Corps' buildup suffered because of this. Ironically, because the Army's peacetime strength was so small, Army officers had given much thought to the problem of rapid and orderly manpower buildup. However, the Navy jealously guarded the development of the Marine Corps and made no use of Army expertise. The rivalry between services, which bedeviled Japan's war effort, likewise hindered America's from the start. In any case, the 2d Marine Division was really only on paper until late 1942. At the time of Pearl Harbor the Corps had approximately 70,000 men, including 10,000 in air units.

They were miserably equipped. Somehow the Corps persuaded the Navy to buy a few specialized shallow-draft landing craft while admirals were placing orders for more capital ships than there were stars in the sky. Naturally, items such as modern infantry weapons and new artillery would have to wait. The Corps would go to Guadalcanal with the weapons it had used against the Kaiser. Somehow Marines came to believe these deficiencies were the Army's fault. Admiral King was very good at his job.

Organizational muddle in the first months of the war added greatly to the inevitable problems of training and expansion. One problem was beyond the Corps' control. Shocked by the Japanese juggernaut that swept forward after Pearl Harbor, Washington's first priority was building up defensive positions in Hawaii and along the island corridor leading toward Australia. Archer Vandegrift, 1st Marine Division commander, working furiously to ready his troops, received orders to dispatch his best regiment to Samoa immediately. Vandegrift chose his most experienced unit, the 7th Regiment, and stripped other units of men and weapons to support it. It was a reasonable decision in the circumstances, and had Midway not stopped the Japanese Navy, Samoa was on Tokyo's list. Ironically, however, because of this, the best Marine regiment was in a lovely part of the South Seas when the remainder of the division went on its adventure to Guadalcanal. (The 7th Marines joined the division on Guadalcanal in late September. Elements of the 2d Division arrived on Guadalcanal and Tulagi piecemeal. At the end of the campaign, most of the 2d Marine Division was deployed there.)

The other organizational difficulties were more complex. President Roosevelt and his son James were interested in the development of units similar to the British commandos. The idea of sending lightly equipped, very mobile expert warriors to raid positions deep behind the enemy's lines had great appeal to some men within the military and more outside of it. The famous "Wild Bill" Donovan, a Roosevelt friend and first head of the Office of Strategic Services (OSS), supported the idea. Consequently, the Corps authorized the first two of four Raider battalions. A small expedition journeyed to Ireland to learn from the British themselves. The commander of the 1st Raiders, the cool and intelligent Lieutenant Colonel Merritt Edson, was authorized to take the pick of the 7th Regiment to form his unit, much to Vandegrift's horror. Lieutenant Colonel Evans

Carlson formed the 2d Raiders. Carlson was a "China Marine" and a brilliant eccentric. He admired the Chinese communists and adopted their term "gung ho" (working together) as his unit's motto. Ironically, the Corps picked it up also. As one officer put it, "Carlson may have been a Red, but he wasn't yellow." Carlson's executive officer was James Roosevelt. Carlson's Raiders were sent on a raid on the Japanese-held island of Makin as Guadalcanal started, hoping to divert Japanese forces. There was little diversion in the short run, but James Roosevelt almost ended up in a Japanese prisoner-of-war camp. Later two more battalions were created. On Guadalcanal the Raiders went on a small number of long-range patrols that proved very valuable. Most of the time, however, they served as standard Marine infantry and delivered splendid service. Ultimately the Raiders were combined and made part of the 4th Marine Division. In retrospect Vandegrift may have been correct to oppose the project, which brought about a major organizational headache at a very unwelcome time.

The Marines also decided, against Vandegrift's advice, to create several defense battalions. They were more or less the opposite of the Raiders, and harked back to the early days of the Corps when it guarded coaling stations. Defense battalions were more heavily armed than a standard Marine unit. Like Army artillery battalions, they had medium and heavy artillery. They had tanks and armored cars. They also had heavy antiaircraft guns. Intended for static use, they would, Vandegrift argued, be a logistic drag, and would duplicate tasks intended for the Army. Ultimately the South Pacific proved to have more static warfare than raiding, and the heavy punch provided by the defense battalions came in very handy at the fierce battle of New Georgia. Nevertheless, the defense battalions also joined the Raiders in the 4th Marine Regiment in 1944.

In short, in early 1942, just months before their fierce and awful trial would start at Guadalcanal, the Marines were small, badly equipped, inappropriately deployed, and in organizational chaos. A betting man might well have demanded very long odds to wager on an American success during their first outing in the Solomons. And yet a deeper look reveals hidden assets of tremendous importance.

The turmoil of 1940 had important consequences for all the armed forces, particularly the Marines. Young Americans of that era were not keen students of international politics. Yet the unmistakable smell of war was in the air, a situation quite obvious to those who would have to fight it. Furthermore, because of the draft, young adults and teenagers knew they were headed soon for the service. Many of them, sensibly enough, waited for events to unfold and for the draft notice to arrive by mail. Hundreds of thousands, however, wanted to control some portion of their fate and enlisted in the regular services, the Reserves, or the National Guard. The Marine Corps, largely because of its mystique, received an extremely good crop of young soldiers.

The generation of young that fought World War II was extremely well suited to the task. The formative event of their time was the Great Depression. Although a dreary period of history in almost every respect, the Depression helped mold a generation of youth uniquely qualified for war. Most were very familiar with physical labor. Whether a young man worked on a farm or hustled for dollars at the local warehouse, it was a generation that got its hands dirty. It was also a time when skills had value. The Depression had not driven the nation out of the industrial age. Millions of teenagers were clever with tools and machinery. Old cars were dirt cheap, but the owner had to keep them running. Tractors and farm machinery required upkeep. It was not a time to pay someone else for doing something if you could do it yourself. That fact alone was a great inspiration to learn a myriad of skills. Furthermore, despite the Depression, young Americans in the 1930s were the best-educated generation in world history up to that time. Schools were very well attended and classes rigorous. All the boys building model airplanes, fiddling with chemistry sets, or making crystal radios in the 1930s were cultivating skills most useful in war.

The generation that fought World War II was unique in another way. The Civil War was much closer in time to them than to us. Many had grandfathers who had fought in that war, or, more likely, were caught up in the war with Spain. Also, the U.S. Army had raised 4 million men and sent 2 million of them to France during World

War I. There was powerful incentive to emulate the head of the family. This same impulse was present in other nations, but in the United States it was not tempered by the dread of mass losses. War, and the traditional military notions of loyalty and bravery, were very much a part of a young man's world in 1942. While the war was a dreadful thing for many young men, disrupting futures and mangling the start of their own families, for others there was an unquestionable element of adventure involved. The "youth culture" we know today did not exist. The options for those coming into adulthood were far more limited than in our time. Coming of age meant working on the farm or getting a job in a factory or the local bank. The military offered a startling, almost exotic vista.

The Corps had good raw material. Its recruits were healthy, hardworking, skilled in countless ways, and lacking in guile. Bud DeVere, who began his long military career with the 1st Marine Division, talks about his comrades:

People were gullible. A lot of them were very young. Right off the farm. From small towns or ethnic neighborhoods. They hadn't seen TV and hadn't traveled. They weren't streetwise. They led a simple way of life. All of a sudden their life got an element of excitement from out of the blue. It was a good time for a few con men too. A whole new lifestyle. A lot of those boys who had never been away from home had very memorable experiences. You can still see it today. I ran into some old-timers last week who served in the Corps three or four years during World War II. You'd think that was all they did in their life. They talked about the Corps like it belonged to them. There I was. I spent twenty-six years on active duty in the Marines and worked another twenty years for them as a civilian. But I didn't have any deeper feelings toward the Corps than they did. Once a Marine, always a Marine.

People from outside the Corps who saw the Marines on Guadalcanal were struck by their youth. There was good reason for that. As Marine veteran Frank Chadwick relates, they were very young:

I joined up when I was sixteen. I changed my birth certificate. I went down to the cigar store, the guy was a bookie and all. I told him what I wanted, gave him five bucks. He fixed it up and away I went. In boot camp the DI [drill instructor—EB] said he didn't think I was seventeen and if I didn't get a letter he'd throw my ass in the brig. I wrote my mother, told her where I was and asked her to write soon. Not wanting to see me in the brig, she did. In our platoon in boot camp we had sixty-two men: I would bet that at least ten of them were under seventeen. One guy's mother found him when we were in Cuba. The colonel threw him in the brig until he was seventeen, then he swore the kid back into the Marine Corps. You know the NCOs and officers really had the whip hand. If we didn't like something, they'd say, "Quit bitching, you volunteered for this." What could you say to that?

Young Marines had first to go through basic training. Most were from the East Coast and went to Parris Island, South Carolina. Training was rough in all the services. There is no indication that Marine basic was any tougher. Of course, the nature of that experience was largely dependent upon the personality of the drill instructor, as Frank Chadwick comments:

In boot camp there were sixty-four man platoons, run by a corporal. They called him, the DI, the little colonel. One DI per platoon. That little son of a bitch had more authority than the colonel that ran the place. Of course today a three-star general would run the place at Parris Island.

Basic training, originally twelve weeks, was later shortened to eight. Then, if the young Marine was fortunate, he would go to boot camp for what passed as advanced training. The problem was, there was no boot camp. Donald Fall saw the beginning of what was later named Camp Lejeune, one of the largest military bases in the country:

I joined the Marine Reserve when I was seventeen and was called up soon in 1940. First we were sent to Quantico and then sent to Guantánamo Bay, where they made the 1st Marine Division.

Our nickname was the "Raggedy Ass Marines." Then we were sent to "Tent City" in North Carolina. They bulldozed some roads, dropped off pyramid tents, and threw up a few concrete buildings. They gave us some tents and said start building. The local farmers were not happy about us building up tent city. Some turned to arson and we spent a lot of time fighting forest fires. There was a big service tent for movies and stuff. Officers would take over front rows with their wives. Marines didn't like this. One of the projectionists put in a sex-education strip with a diagram of a penis on it. That cleared out the wives permanently. It was the coldest winter of my life. On the night of December 7 everyone was oiling weapons, figured we take off right away.

In the frantic days at the beginning of the war, most men received a level of training that was shockingly deficient. Under the best of circumstances, military training in World War II did not have the complexity facing a recruit in a contemporary army. The early Marines, however, cut things thin even for the standards of the time. As Roger Park of the 1st Marine Division recalled:

We had basic rifle training, but I didn't know how to throw a hand grenade until I was aboard ship. They taught us throwing grenades, launching grenades, and other fine points of the art of war on the way to the Pacific. Surprising any of us lived.

His comrade, Donald Moss, echoes Park:

We were all young green kids. We all wanted to fight Japanese because of what they'd done. But all we'd been trained to do was fire our rifle, scream, and run at straw dummies.

Perhaps in a way this first wave was fortunate. A few months later the situation had settled down somewhat. Adam DiGenaro was a veteran Marine who since 1938 did the sort of thing commonly done by men in the Corps. After cursory training, he served as a guard for the *Constitution* at the Boston Navy Yard. Then he served on the cruiser *Brooklyn* in early 1939. When war broke out he was a guard at the summer White House in Georgia. Because of a stint in Brazil,

DiGenaro missed becoming a part of the 1st or 2d Marine divisions. Instead, he was part of the nucleus that formed the distinguished 3d Marine Division. As DiGenaro recalls, some of the training he received would have been better dispensed with:

> We did a lot of crazy things. There was "wrap-sailing." You're up on a cliff. You wrap a rope around your body. They drop the rope down the side of the cliff. You take a poncho and put it through your crotch to keep the friction from busting yourself in half. Then you'd lower yourself down, maybe fifty feet. It started to burn. I got about ten feet from the bottom and was carrying a forty-pound pack, and flipped over. Luckily I landed on my shoulder. We sure never used that maneuver in the war. It was mostly jumping through rubber tires, climbing walls. It wasn't dangerous. It was good, I suppose, but a little foolish. However, beyond a few maneuvers, we were not trained extensively in amphibious warfare. That was not part of our preparation.

Some Marine units in the Caribbean practiced amphibious assault. Several intelligent officers in the 1930s had given the problem serious thought. Ultimately, the Corps was as well prepared for this perilous type of operation as the technology of the time allowed. In 1942, however, there was still much to learn and the equipment was crude. The South Pacific proved a splendid laboratory for this type of war. The Corps made major landings at Guadalcanal, New Georgia, Bougainville, and Cape Gloucester. The Army made many more on New Guinea. Fortunately for both Marine and soldier, the islands in the South Pacific were large. American commanders sought places where they anticipated little immediate opposition. Therefore, in contrast to the landings in the Central Pacific and Normandy where opposition was unavoidable, it was never necessary to put soldiers ashore under heavy Japanese fire.

Although shielded from bloodbaths on the beachhead, Marines still had to master the treacherous techniques required for "hitting the beach." Tony Balsa of the 3d Marine Division describes what was entailed:

I made several landings. On the day of the assault, the Navy gave us a good breakfast: potatoes, bacon, eggs. Might be the last food you had all day. This was about 4:30 or 5:00 A.M. You might not eat until dark. Then you get your equipment ready. You unbuckled your ammo belt so if you fell into the water you'd just shrug off your pack, the rifle, and the whole bit. Otherwise you would sink straight down. About 6:00 A.M. we lined up on a rail, and each guy in charge gave the order to go down. About three or four of us went down the same time. You went over the rail and climbed down a rope ladder that was wide enough for maybe four or five guys. Each ship had four or five nets on each side. In the water below you the landing craft waited, bobbing up and down. When you got to the bottom of the ladder you had to do it right. Some men died making a mistake here. If the swells were high, it was possible to simply fall into the water or get caught between the landing craft and the side of the ship. So as the boat rose with the swell, the coxswain would yell "Now!" and you'd step off. If you time it right, the boat rises to meet you. People are there to help you if you stumble. If the landing craft is sinking before you step off, you might take a nasty tumble into the bottom of the boat. And then you're off. The boat circles as the formation forms and after an hour, in you go. The men do a lot of thinking on the way in.

Although their training lacked complexity, at camp new Marines met the veterans, the "old-timers." They learned much from these men. Donald Fall describes one of the veterans:

One of the unit legends was an old Marine named Lou Diamond, a mortar man. He was a fantastic mortar man: he could put it right down the stovepipe. He went through a case of beer a night when I knew him in Cuba. Every now and then you'd hear an empty can hit the street. He was back from Haiti. To be a salty Marine you had to have served in Haiti. He had a white goatee. In the morning you'd hear his gruff voice: "All right, B Company, outside, clean up, clean up, fore and aft." That meant clean up all his beer cans. After Guadalcanal, at his age, he sort of disappeared. After we left the Canal [widely used slang for Guadalcanal—EB], we were in a formation in Australia one day and here comes Lou walking up the road. I don't know what happened. He hitched a ride on one ship to another until he made it back to the division.

Probably the most famous was Colonel Lewis B. "Chesty" Puller. One of the most highly decorated combat officers in American history, Puller became part of Marine Corps lore. As Frank Chadwick notes, "Puller was colonel longer than anyone in Marine Corps history, he was always in trouble. But he was a good man to be with during a firefight." Gus Merrigan knew Puller well on Guadalcanal, and expresses an affection toward him not held by many of Puller's fellow officers:

Puller was something. I was on leave at my mother's house on December 7. I got back down to Camp Lejeune fast. They were throwing civilians off the trains so servicemen could move quickly. We'd stop for a minute at little towns in the South and people would give us pies. They thought we were off to fight somebody that very day. When I got back two days later, Puller had our battalion fall out in the morning and said, "OK, boys, this is what we wanted." Later, on Guadalcanal, the Army arrived in October. An Army colonel came up to the ridge we occupied on the perimeter. He asked, "Where's the defensive line?" Chesty spit and said, "The ocean."

The Marine veterans contributed some splendid officers to the American war effort. The senior leaders proved unusually good tacticians. The younger veterans who were fit enough for the coming nightmare served as the cadre for junior officers and senior NCOs. They knew each other personally, and were a tight-knit unit. On Fiji and on Guadalcanal before the major struggle began, they did their best to make their young men competent soldiers. All were going into combat, after all, and those training the men had a vested interest in creating decent soldiers. As Ore Marion, one of these veterans, points out, "We were going into combat together, so we made damn sure we wouldn't die because some yahoo didn't know what he was doing."

No doubt much of the skill with weapons developed by the "Old Breed" was passed on to their young charges. As events developed, however, the role of many of them in the war was fleeting. The jungle demolished those not fit. Many fearless old fighters could not bear the vicious combination of fatigue and disease they found on Guadalcanal. But before they left the scene, they gave the young Marines, already an exceptional bunch, a mental strength more important than the finer points of training. First, the Marines had a very keen sense of self-reliance and a respect for the skills needed in ground warfare. Tony Balsa of the 3d Marine Division puts it well:

Every Marine was expected to fight if the situation called for it. Rank and duty did not alter that. And we always had a chain of command. We had the lieutenants, or sergeants: they watched the section or the patrol. The corporals knew each squad. Each squad member knew that if everybody else got killed, he was in command. Somebody was always in command.

More important, as described by Frank Chadwick, the veterans passed along the famous and very real Marine esprit de corps:

Morale was always good. The Marine Corps was like a brotherhood, you looked out for each other. It's hard to describe. You'd be playing cards: you'd get into an argument, get up, slug each other, and then get down and start playing cards again. We were told over and over that we were the best, nobody was better. You took care of your buddies. It was something that seemed to click. In boot camp they instilled the esprit de corps. And then you'd get in with the old-timers, and they'd treat you like an equal. The veterans always drove into you: You're a Marine, you will not let down your buddy, you will not let down the Corps. We had a saying that "it takes more guts to get up in the front line and run then it does to stay there." Because you're afraid if you let them down that every one of your buddies is going to be right on your ass.

Although Marines showed great courage and tenacity in combat, and possessed an undeniable esprit, they did not exist outside the mainstream of European and American military thought and practice. Discipline, bravery, and devotion to comrades was expected and largely received from Marines. However, there was also a great emphasis on sound tactical techniques. In particular, everything was done to maximize the effectiveness of any firepower available. Americans, like the Europeans, had learned deeply in World War I the lesson that "fire kills." In addition, the United States never had a military aristocracy that defined social values as did Europe or Japan. Consequently, American armed forces have traditionally taken a very pragmatic view of their craft. There was certainly no cult of honorable death in the U.S. military. Suffering high numbers of casualties, which was expected and even honored during World War II in highly militarized societies such as Japan, Nazi Germany, or the Soviet Union, was a fast way for an American officer to be relieved. (In this regard, the armed forces of civilian-governed democracies such as Britain and Australia were very like those of the United States.) The sort of massed shock assault that was at the core of Japanese doctrine would have been considered an act of desperation by a Marine officer. Marines were systematic in battle. They took their objectives piece by piece and wore down the enemy in the process. Marine officers knew the Japanese would be a formidable opponent. The "China Marines" had watched the Japanese fight for years. Nevertheless, there was no doubt among them that if good Marines had fire superiority, and fought with "smarts," they would defeat the Japanese. The Marines knew well that death of comrades was inevitable in battle, but the men were trained to kill, not to die.

The Marine Corps was put to the test in the South Pacific far sooner than their officers wished. Minus his best regiment, sent to Samoa, and combed over for the Raider battalions, Vandegrift took his 1st Marine Division to Fiji. Vandegrift knew better than anyone that his unit was far from ready and told this to his superiors. Marine Corps commandant General Thomas Holcomb passed on to Vandegrift assurances he had received from Admiral King that the 1st Marine Division would not go into action until January 1943.

A word about King is in order. General MacArthur has become the major figure of controversy in the Pacific war, but King played a more important role in shaping the direction of American policy in that theater. Although extremely intelligent, he was blinded by his total dedication to the Navy and his hatred for anyone he perceived as an enemy of the Navy. In my opinion, King did serious damage to a rational allocation of resources during the war. By hook or crook, King procured large numbers of landing craft originally intended for use in Europe for his Central Pacific drive, which started in late 1943. Because the landing craft were in the Pacific, an entire Allied Army in the Mediterranean was unable to open a second front in southern France on D-Day. (The invasion of southern France took place in August, far too late to have strategic impact.) Had the Allies launched a powerful drive from the south in June 1944, the German position in Normandy would have been untenable, the bloody six-week stalemate that followed D-Day might have been avoided, and the Germans pushed out of France much faster. This priceless opportunity to put Germany in a strategic vise was sacrificed so King could get an early start on his bloody drive through the coral atolls of the Central Pacific. As further evidence of King's parochialism, when the commanders of Army Air Force units were screaming for modern aircraft for use in the Pacific, King did nothing to aid them. Instead, he built up a naval force so muscle-bound that it stretched his admirals' imaginations to figure out a sensible use for all the warships.

Nevertheless, Guadalcanal was largely the doing of Ernest J. King. In retrospect, we can see that it was one of the great strategic master strokes of World War II. It deflected the Japanese from a more valuable target in New Guinea, unhinged their command structure, and led them into a battle of attrition that the United States ultimately won. Guadalcanal was a victory for the United States, but, more to the point, it was a catastrophe for Japan. To pull off his gamble, however, King had to throw into action the 1st Marine Division (without its veteran 7th Regiment) whether it was ready or not. The Marines found out how ready they were in very short order when they had their first battle on Guadalcanal against an elite Japanese strike force along the Tenaru River.

In some respects, events favored the Corps. In the first few hours of the campaign, the Marines had a tremendous margin of error. On August 7, 1942, shielded by some bad weather, the U.S. armada, which was a very large one for that period of the war, approached undetected. The Marines, therefore, caught the Japanese completely by surprise. Japanese troops on the small atoll of Tulagi put up stiff resistance but the 1st Raiders and a small contingent from the 2d Division swept them away. The 1st Division faced no organized opposition on Guadalcanal. Despite a logistic debacle, which we shall look at later, the Marines quickly seized the airfield the Japanese were building near Lunga Point.

The Marines, however, were hindered by a lack of basic intelligence. Like the Japanese and Australians in Papua, they had no maps and no real idea of the hammer blows all would face soon from the terrain, the elements, and disease. (Guadalcanal is one of the most malarial spots on earth.) The Marines also "shot themselves in the foot." Not realizing how difficult it was to unload supplies from transports under severe time constraints, a job done largely by hand in the early part of the war, sailors assigned the task pleaded for help from the Marines wandering around near the beach. Few of the young soldiers helped in the backbreaking physical labor the job entailed. Therefore, supplies were stacked up on the beach only to wash away when the tide rose. This youthful mistake, not widely acknowledged by the Marines involved, did not have catastrophic consequences, but it did contribute greatly to the malnutrition suffered by the Marines for several weeks. The entire experience at Guadalcanal mortified logistics personnel. They learned much from mistakes and made great improvements in later operations.

Fortunately for the Marines, in striking contrast to the Japanese at Buna a few weeks before, Vandegrift realized the potential weakness of his situation and the inexperience of his men. Rather than trying to occupy meaningless geographic points, such as Mount Austen, he wisely constructed a small perimeter around the captured airfield. Marines and naval engineers, using Japanese construction equipment, started the job of finishing the airstrip immediately. To paraphrase Mao Tse-tung, Vandegrift knew he would win if he did not lose, and deployed his men conservatively. The entire American beachhead covered less than four square miles.

In two days the American operation, which had started so smoothly, appeared in danger of collapse. The Japanese naval victory at the Battle of Savo Island on the night of August 9 smashed the Allied cruiser shield protecting the supply transports. The American transports withdrew the next day, carrying much of the supplies and some combat soldiers with them. The Japanese at Savo Island showed dramatically that they controlled the local waters around Guadalcanal. At the same time, Japanese aircraft started a drumbeat of air attacks hindered only by the weather. The Marines were alone and they knew it. Many Marines sardonically observed that the Navy knew it could draft Marines faster than it could replace warships. Ore Marion recalls the feelings of the men:

> We were surrounded and abandoned all the way down the line. We know now Vandegrift had been told he could surrender. When talk of "easing off" in the jungle was brought up, we little snuffies who fought the war, not those assholes in Washington, Pearl, or Australia, let it be known that "the goddamn Navy brought us here and when those bastards are ready to take us off this island—that's when we'll go." That's how we, just kids, felt: and that's what we did.

War, however, is filled with quirks and odd turns. Although the Marines were in a genuinely perilous position, they had some advantages no one could appreciate at the time. First, two weeks went by before the Marines suffered attack on the ground. In that period the men were able to become acclimated to the area and to scout the terrain around the perimeter. Marines were firm believers in the military adage that "if you dig in, it's hard to dig out." Consequently, they were not good field engineers and never constructed the sophisticated defensive systems the Japanese frequently built. Yet the Marines, as events showed several times, knew how to use terrain very well. Second, the young Marines sparred with small Japanese units outside their perimeter. The Japanese Navy also bombarded them by air and sea. Fortunately, the Japanese did not know the area well either, and their efforts were not as effective as otherwise might have been the case. The Japanese, however, were "blooding" the Marines on Guadalcanal. No training of any type can substitute for being under fire. Bombs and shells did that job very nicely. The Marines, in other words, were able to gradually acclimate themselves to a savage battlefield. As we shall see later, some inexperienced Army units were thrown to the lions without any such preparation and orientation.

The third advantage was crucial. The chaos surrounding the landing, and the rapid withdrawal of the transports, completely misled Japanese intelligence. Some reports from the Japanese Navy correctly estimated the presence of a Marine division. Other reports indicated that American forces were smaller, and that possibly the transports had taken troops with them when they withdrew. As was so often the case when faced with an uncertain situation, the Japanese chose to believe the interpretation most favorable to their situation. The Japanese command estimated that the Marines had landed approximately 2,000 men on Guadalcanal. Misinterpreting information from the survivors of the Japanese garrisons on Tulagi and Guadalcanal, and receiving confirmation from, of all places, their embassy in Moscow, they also believed the Marines had suffered serious losses, were out of supplies, and suffered from crippled morale. In reality, there were 11,000 men on Guadalcanal, well dug in, and determined to stick it out.

Japanese haste at Guadalcanal was strongly influenced by Imperial headquarters's burning desire to push forward at Kokoda. Consequently, it ordered Colonel Kiyono Ichiki to land on Guadalcanal. Ichiki was the type of officer who had brought Japan victory in the past but would lay the groundwork for its defeat in the South Pacific. In 1937 he had commanded troops at the Marco Polo Bridge, in the incident that precipitated open war between Japan and China. In 1942 Ichiki commanded a detachment of 2,000 crack assault troops that had been slated to land on Midway. Turned away from Midway, Ichiki's detachment deployed to Guam, but remained ready for rapid action. Ichiki himself was a noted tactician with a great belief in the effectiveness of massed assault at night. He had also expressed contempt for American troops. Specifically, his orders from superiors were vague in the best Japanese style. He was to rush half of his force immediately to Guadalcanal, land, and if possible seize the then-unfinished airfield. If, on the other hand, the Marine presence was stronger than believed, he was to await the arrival of the remainder of his force and, if necessary, larger reinforcements.

Ichiki and 900 men embarked on fast destroyers, modified to accommodate landing forces. One pessimist was Rear Admiral Raizo Tanaka, commanding the destroyer contingent transporting Ichiki. It was the first trip of many taken by Tanaka to Guadalcanal, where he would bedevil American naval forces for months. Tanaka was a brilliant leader, and urged caution and proper reconnaissance. Ichiki, however, was an author of the Army's doctrine of shock tactics. One value of lightning attack, officers like Ichiki argued with good reason, was the danger that could develop if an enemy was given time to dig in and solidify a position. It would take much to prevent such an officer, given open-ended orders, from attacking at first opportunity. Tanaka, showing his usual efficiency, landed Ichiki precisely at the desired position twenty miles east of the Marine perimeter in the early hours of August 18.

Ichiki landed at night twenty miles from Henderson Field for a reason. Surprise was a vital element to Japanese shock assault. Along the shore of Guadalcanal there was a beach. Ichiki planned to advance up the beach at night, and duck into the jungle during the day. His advance thus hidden, Ichiki planned a lightning blow at night. Had he been dealing with a small, demoralized force of inadequate soldiers, his plan would have been sound. In reality, however, Ichiki was in trouble from the start. American technical superiority was already silently in operation. American intelligence at Pearl Harbor, due to a close and laborious analysis of radio traffic, deduced that the Japanese were going to land an assault force on Guadalcanal on approximately August 20. Vandegrift received the message on August 17, but still did not know the size of the force or its plans.

RIGHT: These men, wounded on New Georgia in July 1943, are being put on a landing craft prior to being taken to a hospital ship. *(National Archives)*

BELOW: Marines wade through the surf to land at Cape Gloucester in December 1943. *(National Archives)*

RIGHT: American gunners fire a 105mm howitzer on Bougainville in November 1943. The 105mm was the mainstay of American artillery in the South Pacific. *(U.S. Army)*

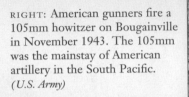

LEFT: Soldiers of the Americal Division mop up on Hill 260 at the end of the Japanese assault of the Torokina perimeter on Bougainville in March 1944. The largest and last land battle in the South Pacific was a debacle for the Japanese. *(U.S. Army)*

RIGHT: An American patrol inches forward during the struggle for Buna. Jungle and malarial swamp made the terrain in the Buna area among the worst confronted in any war. *(U.S. Army)*

RIGHT: Wariness and fatigue are evident on the faces of these GIs moving through the dense jungle of New Georgia in July 1943. Although little known, the New Georgia campaign was a violent nightmare that cost the Americans almost as many men as the longer and more famous struggle
for Guadalcanal.

LEFT: Troops of the American 32d Division sailed to Buna on a motley collection of coastal craft. These pitiful boats were very vulnerable to air attack. Worse, civilian small craft would not carry artillery, tanks, or heavy equipment. (*Australian War Memorial*)

RIGHT: Tobacco was the drug of choice in the South Pacific. These Australian soldiers, sheltered by kunai grass, share a smoke. They are in a "rest" position 100 yards from the Japanese. The front line was within "grenade distance" of the Japanese, less than 50 yards. (*Australian War Memorial*)

Pointless violence was commonplace during battles in the South Pacific. Near Buna the Australians cornered four Japanese soldiers, who vainly tried to swim to freedom. The Australians shot three. The first picture shows an Australian attempting to get the fourth Japanese to surrender. As shown in the second picture, the Japanese soldier puts a grenade to his head. A split second later, the grenade detonated. (*Australian War Memorial*)

Milne Bay in 1942. Note how close the dense jungle comes to the shoreline. The area contained some of the worst terrain in the South Pacific. (*Australian War Memorial*)

RIGHT: The "golden stairs" at the start of the Kokoda Trail near Port Moresby. The Australians loathed this part of the trail. *(Australian War Memorial)*

BELOW: Tough soldiers of the AIF pursuing the Japanese up the Kokoda Trail in October 1942. *(Australian War Memorial)*

RIGHT: Native carriers on the Kokoda Trail played an indispensable role in the crucial struggle. Each load weighs about seventy pounds. *(Australian War Memorial)*

BELOW: An Australian "fighting pit" in the rugged terrain south of Salamaua, New Guinea, in July 1943. From left to right, the soldiers carry a "Tommy" (Thompson submachine gun), a Bren light machine gun, and a Lee Enfield rifle. *(Australian War Memorial)*

Commanders in the South Pacific. General Douglas MacArthur (*center*), commander of all Allied forces in Australia and New Guinea, confers with General Sir Thomas Blamey (*right*) in October 1942. Blamey commanded the Australian Army and controlled Allied ground forces in the theater. Australian Minister for the Army F. M. Forde is to the left. (*Australian War Memorial*)

Admiral William Halsey (*left*) talks with reporters on Bougainville in late 1943. Although under the "strategic direction" of MacArthur, Halsey commanded Allied forces in the Solomons. Fortunately for the Allies, Halsey and MacArthur got along very well. (*U.S. Marine Corps*)

Military "spit and polish" disappeared quickly in the battle zone. These men served with the 25th Division. The stubble and beards disguise the youth of many. *(Courtesy of Ted Blahnik)*

The Japanese garrison on Tulagi shortly before the American invasion on August 7, 1942. These men belonged to a crack Special Naval Landing Force. A grim portent of what was to come, they fought to the last man on invasion day. *(Courtesy of Ted Blahnik)*

RIGHT: Marines render aid to a wounded Japanese soldier after the battle of the Tenaru. Japanese dead lie all around. (*Courtesy of Ted Blahnik*)

LEFT: In 1982 this group of Japanese veterans returned to Guadalcanal to recover and cremate the remains of their slain comrades. American vets helped them find the grave sites. (*Courtesy of Ted Blahnik*)

RIGHT: A Marine camp in a coconut grove near Henderson Field on Guadalcanal. The heavy rain and mud created an environment where malaria and other tropical diseases flourished. Throughout the South Pacific, serious disease caused far more casualties than battle. (*National Archives*)

LEFT: A jeep on Guadalcanal grimly ornamented with enemy bones. Although both sides recovered the bodies of their own slain soldiers when possible, the remains of the dead from both sides were a common feature in every battle zone of the South Pacific. (*Courtesy of Ted Blahnik*)

Some of the pieces of the puzzle fit together quickly largely by chance. The Marines found they had some valuable friends on Guadalcanal. Walter Clemens, a British official there, had cultivated good relations with a number of the native population. When the Japanese landed initially, Clemens retreated to the bush and became part of the famous apparatus of coast watchers. He quickly made contact with the Marines when they landed, and his scouts passed on much useful information. Up the coast from the Marine perimeter was a Catholic mission. The parishioners were no friends of the Japanese and also passed on intelligence. Information from both these sources led the Marines to believe that the Japanese had a radio station on the coast, east of Lunga Point. Vandegrift, already alerted by Pearl Harbor that danger was approaching, ordered a sixty-man patrol to destroy the Japanese position. They left early on August 19. At the same time Ichiki sent a patrol forward to establish a communications post on the Tenaru River, near the eastern boundary of the Marine perimeter.

At noon the two patrols stumbled into each other approximately five miles from American lines. The Marines were extremely well commanded by Captain Charles H. Brush. Alerted at the last minute by native guides that Japanese soldiers were very close, Brush split his forces. He ordered a charge forward with the bulk of the patrol, but sent another to find the Japanese left flank. Situations like this occurred hundreds of times in the South Pacific. They were a staple during Australian patrols in New Guinea. However, in the chaos of a firefight at point-blank range, it proved almost impossible to surround an enemy unit. When men scattered in the bush, normally it was not possible to keep them in the "sack." In this case, however, Brush pulled off a textbook maneuver that had great consequences. Caught by surprise, the Japanese patrol was not able to deploy before it was hit in the flank. John Jackym, a young second lieutenant, led the flanking force and describes the encounter:

We came across the Japanese quite suddenly; they were all cleverly camouflaged and hard to see until they all seemed to pop up out of the bush only yards away. It was horribly frightening, uncertain and confused: they seemed to be all around. I just fired furiously whenever one of them came into view.

Within minutes twenty-seven men out of the thirty-three-man Japanese patrol were dead. Three Marines had died and three were wounded. One of their first serious ground engagements on Guadalcanal was a superbly led firefight that resulted in a lopsided victory. The Marines searched the officers' bodies and found extremely detailed maps of the Marine perimeter. How the Japanese learned these details is still unclear. Regardless, Brush and his patrol returned immediately to the perimeter with their startling information. Although they did not know it, Ichiki was on their heels.

Ichiki had good reason to hurry. Because of the patrol encounter, the Marines knew he was there. (Naturally, the Japanese did not know of intelligence reports sent to Vandegrift by Pearl Harbor.) But they did not know his strength, nor his point of attack. Shock doctrine relies on the assumption that enemy command decisions will take time, and that striking before the opposition has decided a course of action will create confusion. Victory in Malaya had come largely because the British could not keep up with the pace of Japanese movement. Therefore, charging on was a rational decision. Another powerful incentive to hit immediately appeared. On August 20, just as Ichiki's vanguard was closing on the Marine positions, the first Marine fighters and dive bombers landed at Henderson Field.

The Japanese, because of the debacle that followed, have been criticized from all quarters for the attack across the Tenaru River. Perhaps Colonel Ichiki would have made different decisions had he known the Marines' strength. Yet Ichiki's actions were completely in line with a doctrine that had proven successful time and again in the past. Seeing aircraft landing at Henderson could only have strengthened his desire to roll the dice. In retrospect, we know the Marines were tough, brave, and competent. Ichiki believed that they were badly trained, inexperienced, and not ready for an all-out assault aimed at a small point on their line. In a very real sense, Ichiki was acting on assumptions that had to be true if Japan was to prevail in

the war. If the enemy was their equal in skill, if spirit could not overcome material, if night attack could not neutralize firepower, Japan
would lose at Guadalcanal. Japan would also lose in the South Pacific. The Tenaru battle was far more than a single assault. It was a
clash of doctrine and of assumptions concerning the enemy. The
stakes were very high.

The Marine perimeter Ichiki planned to attack was not an impenetrable position. Because of the American defeat at Savo,
Vandegrift believed an enemy attack would most likely be an amphibious assault on the beachhead. Therefore, most of his machine
guns and many of his men were dug in on the beach itself. In retrospect Vandegrift was very wise. Had the Japanese concentrated everything they had as soon as possible on a major attack directly on
Lunga Point, supported by sustained and massive naval artillery, the
Marines would have been in trouble.

The Marine position had an odd look to it in August. The western flank of the Marine position stretched approximately 1,500 yards
west of Lunga Point where it went inland a few hundred feet before
meeting the edge of the jungle. From that point there was a gap of
nearly 2,000 yards running southeast to the Lunga River that was defended by the rough terrain and jungle but by only a handful of Marines. Along the east bank of the Lunga River from the sea to a
position approximately one mile inland there were Marine outposts
guarding the back door to Henderson Field. This outpost line ran
due east for another 2,000 yards until it met the Ilu River, which the
Marines called Alligator Creek after its dangerous inhabitants. The
entire arc from the western hinge of Vandegrift's line to Alligator
Creek was primarily defended by the jungle. The Marine outpost
line in late August was for reconnaissance, not serious defense. Marine doctrine stressed the importance of patrolling. It sometimes got
them in trouble. Normally, however, it was a good policy. Marine patrols were out in this area during the day. The terrain was miserable,
but the area small. Vandegrift believed he could allocate his strength
facing the most likely direction of attack and leave his southwest
flank dangling in the air. The obvious line of attack was from up the
beach from the east. Consequently, the eastern flank running from

the sea up Alligator Creek to the beginning of the outpost line was well defended. From the start, the Marines showed an uncanny professionalism for a unit that was, in truth, undertrained, underage, undersupplied, and inexperienced.

There are other reasons not to view the Tenaru attack as the sole result of tactical insanity on the part of Ichiki. First, the Marine situation was far more precarious than a cursory look would have it. It is true that Ichiki's vanguard was outnumbered greatly by the Marines on Guadalcanal. It is vital to remember that while Vandegrift knew something was going to happen, he did not know where and in what strength. Radio traffic in Truk and Rabaul was extremely heavy. An obvious possibility existed that Ichiki's men were going to close on the perimeter and assault in conjunction with an amphibious assault. Perhaps they were going to deploy along the Tenaru and harass the Marine lines on the east, the way small Japanese units were doing in the west, weakening the position for a larger assault later. Nor could Vandegrift dismiss the possibility that Ichiki would move inland, and try to slip through the back door. All Vandegrift knew was that a Japanese force of undetermined size was moving his way. He had no choice, therefore, but to leave his line strung out. Because of the maps captured, however, Vandegrift did strengthen his eastern defenses along Alligator Creek and extend the line a few hundred yards north. Nevertheless, only a small portion, approximately 100 men, of Vandegrift's force was at the exact point of attack.

In addition, the attacker has the advantage of picking the time and place of assault. Unlike every Japanese unit subsequently undertaking a massed attack in the South Pacific, Ichiki's men were in good health. They had been on the island for only three days and were in better condition than the Marines, who were already feeling the sting of malaria and rot. Ichiki picked the point where Alligator Creek hit the sea. (As noted, the formal name of Alligator Creek was the Ilu River. In later reports, Marine officers mistook it for the larger Tenaru River. The battle, consequently, was misnamed twice.) Alligator Creek did not open cleanly into the ocean except after particularly heavy rain. Consequently, there was a shallow tidal lagoon, 100 feet wide at the maximum, toward the beach. At the end of the creek was a sandbar that was a few feet higher than the surrounding terrain and jutted out to the west. Hitting the sandbar, with the sea as his right flank, Ichiki's men need not fear fire from the sea. The Marines placed machine guns that could fire directly south into the sandbar, and also placed a 37mm antitank gun across the sandbar with a supply of canister shells. In their turn, however, Marine gun emplacements were vulnerable to Japanese machine gun and mortar fire once their flashes gave away their position. Artillery was a mixed blessing. The Marines had taken the precaution of registering defensive fire before the battle. However, when combat is yards apart, artillery is a weapon of desperation, and in fact was not used until the first stage of the assault was over. The Japanese had no such disadvantage. They had light artillery, very similar to the beloved Marine 75mm pack howitzers. They could fire on Marine positions west of the sandbar with little danger of hitting their own men.

Lastly, the Marines, despite all the preparations, were caught by surprise. Advance listening posts to the east of Alligator Creek heard movement and retreated. There were a few shots fired. None of this was unusual along the perimeter. The Japanese shock troops, however, were magnificently trained at silent approach. The attack on the sandbar was not like the Somme River in 1916. "No-man's-land" during a pitch-black night on Guadalcanal was a few hundred feet.

Ichiki was not ready for one obstacle. Perhaps he put too much faith in his maps, because what he encountered should not have come as a surprise: barbed wire. Barbed wire is one of the most effective and cheapest barriers to ground assault in existence. It is widely used today. When Japanese intelligence prepared Ichiki's maps, however, there was none to record. Wire was a commodity that had sailed off in Turner's transports. Fortunately for Vandegrift, an unknown Marine dismantled a small fence on a coconut plantation near the beach and removed some barbed wire. The day of Ichiki's attack, the Marines strung a single strand of wire on the west side of the sandbar. No doubt, at some point, Ichiki's move would have failed. The numbers were much against him. However, the astounding debacle that took place was to some degree because of that one strand of wire. Timing in a Japanese night assault was everything. Nothing could be

allowed to break its momentum. With surprise gone, the shock value
would lessen. It was crucial to get forward with lightning speed and
get into the enemy's position where the battle could turn on hand-to-
hand combat. Ichiki's men were not, however, ready for the wire.

The Japanese closed on Alligator Creek about midnight. They
approached very close without being heard. At about 2:00 A.M.
Ichiki's shock troops charged the sandbar. Donald Moss was there,
and recalls the situation:

> The Tenaru sector of attack was very small. Most of our line was
> nearly at a right angle to the beach. The sand spit on the beach
> was maybe twenty-five yards wide, maybe forty. The night be-
> fore, we had strung a single strand of barbed wire. We were up
> on a slight rise. Not that much. Twelve or fifteen feet at most.
> We were in foxholes. The point of contact was at most three or
> four hundred yards. I didn't hear a thing before the fighting. It
> was pitch black. There we were sitting with machine guns plus
> two 37mm guns placed right across the sand spit. When they
> started forward, they hit the wire right away. They started jab-
> bering like a bunch of monkeys: that's one of the first things I re-
> member. Everybody all along the line heard it. The next thing
> you know our whole line opened up. All hell broke loose. The
> machine guns started going. The 37mms were shooting point-
> blank. I started firing at shadows. And then the Japanese set up
> the flares which lit them up, saying here we are. They seemed so
> invincible. They just couldn't believe they could die. It was a
> crack unit.
>
> The fellow next to me was killed. I picked up his Tommy gun.
> I was firing a bolt-action rifle, like a lot of us were, which was like
> firing a pop gun. We were picking them off in the river and later
> on in the morning some were trying to swim around us, in the
> ocean to the north, and we picked them off there. I know I did.

With Ichiki's first assault stopped cold, a very dangerous hour began. Some of the Japanese got through the wire, as they were trained
to do. Others swam through the surf and got around the Marine line.
Others survived the fire and got into the American foxholes. Hand-
to-hand combat is extraordinarily rare in modern war, but in the

South Pacific it happened with unusual frequency. Japanese machine guns and artillery started laying down covering fire against Marine positions across from the sandbar. At some point, however, Ichiki's position began to unravel. Marine artillery started coming in at approximately 4:00 A.M. with deadly impact. It was very likely that a barrage directly behind Japanese lines caught another attack assembling for a move forward. As the Americans won the heavy-weapons duel, the Marines counterattacked the few positions lost to the Japanese. As dawn approached, Ichiki's detachment was in serious trouble.

At this point, the Marines had won a fine defensive victory. In other instances in the South Pacific, the Japanese would have retreated to face the jungle, and the Americans would have been content to have them leave. (Japanese rear guards, as Americans already knew from skirmishes west of the airfield, were deadly.) Instead, at the Tenaru, a solid victory developed into a stunning massacre. Part of the reason for this was a strange inability on the part of the Japanese to react. At dawn the Japanese, not the inexperienced Marines, acted like green troops. Story has it, Ichiki, seeing his regiment was doomed, had the colors burned and killed himself. It is possible, however, as one survivor claimed, that Ichiki was simply killed in battle. If his other officers were also casualties, perhaps the chain of command broke down. In any case, the Japanese did not conduct a general retreat. Some men stayed on the sandbar. Others moved into the coconut trees. Yet in all likelihood they still could have extricated themselves, except for the fact that Vandegrift and his officers launched a model envelopment of the Japanese position.

At dawn Vandegrift sent his only reserve battalion, which included Captain Brush's company, outside the perimeter on a flanking move. The handful of Marine tanks were also moved up. The flanking infantry marched east into the coconut grove, then moved north, and finally circled back to the west. Ichiki's detachment was in coconut groves, not jungle. The terrain was not as dense, and escape not as easy. All the while Marines were shooting at the Japanese with everything available. There were stories, very possibly true, that some veteran Marines, wearing shoulder padded shooting jackets, were sit-

ting in target-shooting position, firing at Japanese infantry. When
the Marines started coming through the coconut grove from the
north and west, a melee began. One of Brush's men, Andy Poliny,
later described the confusing encounter:

All these young, spunky Marines were firing at a living target for
the first time in their lives. They thought they were at a turkey
shoot, until they started to see some of their own men shot down
dead. Then they started the grim job of fighting. From the edge
of the jungle, through the coconut grove to the beach, was about
five hundred yards. A squad of Japs broke off and started running
east up the beach. Commander Brush shouted, "Line 'em up,
and squeeze 'em off." The Japs never made more than fifty feet
before they were killed.

Our battalion commander, Lieutenant Colonel Cresswell, was
all over the place, darting from one coconut tree to another. It
was frustrating fighting. The high velocity .25-caliber Jap bullets
were real trouble: you'd hear them when they fired ahead of you,
but also when they struck behind you. So you were never sure if
you were taking fire from front or rear. We came to a little depression covered with lime bushes. Inside there were over a hundred Japs. They held their fire until we closed and then hell
broke lose. One Marine saw his best pal killed. He went completely berserk and started picking up Japanese rifles and smashing them against coconut trees. We had to subdue him. Colonel
Cresswell, without telling us, called in artillery support. The
shells started to drop so close you could smell the burnt cordite
after they burst.

The nutcracker was now slowly closing and we could see the
opposite bank of the river in the distance. All of a sudden we saw
two of our light tanks spring across the sand spit. As they moved
forward there was gunfire and human flesh everywhere. The Japs
disabled one of the tanks and tried to swarm on it. The other
came up and both fired together. The Japs were mowed down
like flies. What really surprised me as we approached was the
sight of a single dead mule, already bloating in the red-hot heat
of the day. Where it came from is beyond me. As we approached
closer, some of the Japs ran down the beach. Back and forth

along the beach flew a Marine pilot in a Wildcat just gunning them down.

The Ichiki detachment was annihilated. Eight hundred crack shock troops died in a few hours. The Marine losses were thirty-four killed. The Japanese, in this one engagement, lost approximately the same number of men as the Americans did at Omaha Beach on D-Day. Although larger Japanese contingents assaulted the Marines on Guadalcanal in the weeks following, they rarely had losses this bad in a single battle. Not even the Australians pulled off a victory as lopsided as this. What is striking about the engagement is how well the Marines controlled the flow of battle. The Marines took advantage of every Japanese mistake. The men did not panic, nor did the officers. The Marines pushed hard where prudent, but avoided rash moves throughout. It was a performance that an elite, veteran unit would have been most proud of.

The Tenaru, then, was a double dose of bad news for the Japanese. Like the failed offensive at Kokoda, it showed that courage and will would not triumph over fire and skill. The Marines and the Australians, in other words, proved that the heart of Japanese ground tactics was based on delusion. But it also showed that American Marines were the equal of the best Japanese ground forces in skill and courage. In adaptability they proved superior. In addition, the Tenaru was their first battle, fought without the aid of their most experienced regiment. Vandegrift, as much as the prospect would have amazed him in Fiji three months earlier, had created some of the finest infantry the United States has ever sent to war.

The splendid performance of the Marines on Guadalcanal has been canonized by writers and movie makers. As much as the Marines can be justly proud of their debut in World War II, it has had one unfortunate side effect on the way the South Pacific has been remembered by the American public. The 1st Marine Division, exhausted by the jungle and fierce battle, left Guadalcanal in December 1942, when there was still much fighting to come. More important, Guadalcanal itself has so dominated the history of the period in the United States that it has distorted greatly the memory of what actually took place. The struggle on Guadalcanal did not end anything. Instead, it was the beginning of a year-and-a-half military campaign that raged throughout the South Pacific and New Guinea. Although the 1st and 3d Marine Divisions each had one more operation in the theater in late 1943, at Cape Gloucester and Bougainville respectively, both divisions fought the jungle more than the Japanese. The Marines, in fact, were interlopers in the South Pacific. After the epic at Guadalcanal, they moved on to face their horrid trial in the Central Pacific. The bulk of the land war in the South Pacific was fought by the Australians and the U.S. Army.

The U.S. Army that fought World War II was formed in the months after World War I. Congress and the American people drew two contradictory lessons from World War I. On one hand, Americans believed that "Mr. Wilson's War" had been a mistake. George Washington, it appeared, was right to warn the nation against entangling alliances and European wars. Because Germany was defeated, war with France or Britain unthinkable, and Russia had disappeared from world politics, there were no enemies on the horizon. The Navy could protect the security of the United States in case some nation, such as Japan, was foolish enough to become a threat. Moneys directed toward the Army, it seemed, were wasted.

On the other hand, the war had served as a chilling introduction to modern warfare. Mobilization in the United States had run poorly. The country had been dependent upon its allies for sophisticated armaments. The very dramatic introduction of new weapons systems such as tanks, aircraft, and submarines encouraged congressmen across the spectrum to avoid a similar situation in the future. The Army, most agreed, must improve its capability to mobilize a large civilian-based land force in case the need arose. In consequence, in January 1920 Congress passed the National Defense Act, which configured the Army's basic structure until superseded in 1940 by the draft.

The National Defense Act established a three-tiered organization for the U.S. Army: a small professional Regular Army, a civilian

National Guard, and a civilian Organized Reserves. A much-less-organized structure similar to this one had existed for decades. There were major differences after 1920, however. Previously the various civilian components of the military had been left largely to the states. Under the new system, the Regular Army took over the responsibility of supervising training and providing officers.

To cope with the new duties, the staff system of the Regular Army was overhauled. The Army General Staff took on a modern structure that included the War Plans Division, which prepared military contingency plans and was to serve as the nucleus for a wartime General Headquarters. In 1926 the Air Corps was made an equal combat arm, and much preparation was done for potential expansion. (Six months before Pearl Harbor the Army Air Corps, expanding tremendously, was renamed the Army Air Force.) The National Defense Act authorized a major enlargement of military education. West Point and Annapolis expanded. So did the ROTC programs already present in colleges across the country. In addition, the Army started thirty-one special branch schools to train both Reserve and Regular NCOs and junior officers in various technical specialties. At the top of the new educational structure were the three institutions meant to guide the brains of the Army: the Command and General Staff School at Fort Leavenworth and the Army War College and Army Industrial College in Washington. The last is of interest because it illustrates the great importance the Army placed on matters of logistics and supply in modern war.

Whether this system was a good one or not depends upon what it is compared to. It was a major advance over the Army that existed in 1914. When compared to other nations in the 1920s it probably was a decent system, reflecting political realities and American history. When compared to the armed forces fashioned by potential foes in the mid-1930s, the American system was very weak. The structure of a new mass Army was well thought out. Considering the financial realities, the Army did a respectable job of keeping the Air Corps up-to-date. With small sums of money it developed and procured some excellent weapons. However, when everything is considered, the system was deficient because it was far too small to cope with the challenge of a war on the scale of World War II.

The numbers were pitiful. Although the National Defense Act called for a force of twice the size, Congress authorized funds for an Army of 12,000 officers and 120,000 enlisted men. Half of these men were involved with the National Guard and Reserves. On paper the United States boasted the mighty strength of nine infantry divisions. In practice there were only three, the others existing in skeletal form only. The National Guard added another 180,000 citizen soldiers. The Reserves were smaller yet. Bear in mind that during World War II the U.S. Army raised 100 divisions, a number that we can see now was barely adequate. At this time, military planners contemplating a "worst-case scenario" projected armed forces totaling 4 million men. During the war, the Army was much larger, but, more to the point, was just one component of a 12-million-man military apparatus.

The military was not lacking for vision at the top. All the men who led the Army between the wars, and most top commanders during World War II, had been in France in 1918. The slaughter they saw appalled them as it did every intelligent military man in Europe. The American Army lost nearly 50,000 men killed in about twelve weeks at the end of 1918. General MacArthur, when Army chief of staff in the mid-1930s, did everything he could to advance the doctrine and organizational framework for a highly mechanized Army. (It was for this reason that the United States developed the best and most sophisticated organization for armored divisions in the world during a period when it lacked tanks.) MacArthur, and many other officers, believed that armor and mobility would prevent another bout of trench warfare. American infantry divisions would move with trucks, not horses. Anything of importance, MacArthur believed, should be mobile. As we shall see, the stress laid on mobility and firepower had the ironic effect of ensuring that the Army would not train new units suitable for fighting in the South Pacific, where, of course, MacArthur commanded them.

The American Army then was not the intellectual wasteland it was sometimes pictured to be. There were excellent officers with innovative ideas. Their work, however, was on paper, because the force levels remained so puny until 1940. Nor was the Regular Army as withdrawn from civilian society as it had been in the past. Three quarters of its officers were working with the Guard, the Reserves, or doing civilian-related work. Their problem was a simple one of numbers. Without appropriate force levels, realistic training was impossible. In turn, this made it even more difficult to pick out the rare young officers who had the unusual gift of leadership during war.

In retrospect, weakness had one large advantage. Because American officers were trained to look ahead at a massive mobilization of all types of units, they gave great stress to matters of supply and logistics. After all, unless troops were going to starve to death in basic training or go to war with broomsticks, these matters required thought. American officers shared the pragmatic character of their countrymen and were not hindered by any irrational cult of the warrior. This has often been criticized. The Army approached its task in a very businesslike way. It wanted mobility, firepower, and staying power. That meant it planned an Army built around mechanization, artillery, and aircraft backed by a massive supply base. In many armies, Japan was a prime example, matters of supply were looked upon as the realm of second-rate officers. If Hitler had chosen an American officer to lead the Wehrmacht into Russia, the Führer would have received lengthy memos concerning trucks, mud, high-viscosity motor oil, and dozens of other subjects of weighty boredom. The sort of officer who studied railway timetables before World War I was discredited in Germany, Japan, and Russia. This was not the case in the United States. Over time such an attitude paid off handsomely. Although the Army proved far too weak to create good infantry at the start of the war, when the machine finally began to roll in mid-1943, the results were impressive. When well led, U.S. Army divisions had punch, staying power, and smarts.

As noted earlier, the government's response to the European crisis was inadequate. At the time of Pearl Harbor, although the numbers were going up fast, the American Army was not remotely ready for war. The Japanese juggernaut did not allow anyone to wait for the force level and supply curves to reach the desired levels. Yet

Washington did have resources to expend. Despite the decision to prepare for war against Hitler first, the Japanese push forced the Army to use resources in the Pacific that it needed elsewhere. The quality and nature of these resources varied greatly. So did the time and manner of their employment.

The American Army units that fought in the South Pacific were either Regulars of the 25th Division, hybrid Reserve–National Guard units assembled from independent regiments, or National Guard divisions. As the war progressed the various divisions tended to homogenize. Training and weapons were better, and the replacements from the draft evened out the personnel base. In 1942, however, the differences in quality were significant. These differences also reflected quite different military cultures.

At the start of the war there were very few Regular Army divisions. Two were in the Pacific, the Philippine Division and the Hawaiian Division. In October 1941, as part of the divisional reorganization program, the old style "square" Hawaiian Division of four regiments was split into two new divisions, the 24th and the 25th. The 24th remained in Hawaii until early 1944 and need not concern us. The 25th Division, however, was very active in the South Pacific.

The heart of the division was its two Regular Army regiments, the 27th and 35th. In 1941 these old regiments were building up to authorized strength with reserves. Nevertheless, there were a large number of professional soldiers in each. There was a certain resemblance between the Army Regulars and the Marine "Old Breed." Both were extremely good at weapons and basic tactics. Both were tough crowds in a tough atmosphere. Yet there were differences that reflected the differences between the Army and the Marines. The Hawaiian Regulars were garrison troops. They had an insulated but more routine existence than the Marines in China or the Caribbean. Their lives revolved around Schofield Barracks. It was a world that featured large numbers of bars and bordellos that catered to the soldiers. The Army had permanent facilities and decent quarters. Athletics were an important part of life. Competitions between the various units or teams from the Navy contingent at Pearl Harbor filled many a weekend. The social status of a Regular Army soldier had never been high in the United States, and this was certainly true in Oahu. Scott Wilson came to the 25th as part of the 161st Washington National Guard Regiment in early 1942. He recalls,

> At home in Washington Regular soldiers were kind of looked down upon by civilians. It was always implied that a man joined the Regular Army because he didn't have a good place in normal life. In Hawaii, I think, they were third-class citizens because Oahu was overrun by men from the Army and the Navy. No self-respecting girl would go out with a soldier or sailor on Oahu. I suppose some of the guys were a little rough around the edges. In Hawaii you couldn't get a pass unless you signed out for a "pro kit," short for prophylactic. It consisted of a condom and some medication you were supposed to spread on your genitals. It didn't matter whether you were going to use it or not. You took it.

Robert Kennington of the soon-to-be-famous 35th Regiment gives a bit of the flavor of Army life right before the war:

> It wasn't too tough to get into the Army unless you had a medical problem like bad teeth. They gave you an IQ test. When we arrived in Hawaii in January 1941 a bunch of officers met us. They asked us about our education, could we type, how much we weighed, etc. They asked certain people to step forward. I had to step out. I was chosen for military police. I didn't go for that: I was more interested in sports. I finally got transferred to K company 35th. I was put on class A special duty: football and baseball. I did no fatigue or guard duty. I finished my training like everybody else, but every day after lunch I went off to practice.

The Army had its share of eccentrics, but their stage was much more limited than that found by old Marines. The Army's world was very stratified by rank. Prewar career officers lived a very different life than did their men. Yet garrison duty had its advantages. Unlike the Marines, Army Regulars had more experience with field artillery, communications, and mechanized transport. Like the Marines, they knew their rifles and basic weapons. The hectic transition to divisional-level operations that bedeviled the Marines was much easier for the Regular Army. The Army did not have the esprit or the mystique of the Corps. However, when it came to the finer points of military operations, a good Army unit was more professional.

The Army's concept of professionalism is worth noting. It was almost a mirror image of the Japanese military's stress on spirit and will. The U.S. Army was certainly more reluctant to lead with its chin than were the Marines or the Australians. The Army was careful, and put great stress on probing flanks and using artillery. An Army unit was very quick to call off an attack that ran into opposition. This tendency befuddled friend and foe alike. It could be a symptom of a nonaggressive, poorly trained and poorly led unit. It could also be the sign of men who knew what they were doing, and were willing to spend an extra day at the job and let the artillery have a go at the enemy. An Army unit was never proud of taking casualties. If it could block an opponent and let indirect fire cut them up, an Army unit was glad to do so. A good U.S. Army unit showed great attention to detail. It used engineers intelligently. It is no coincidence that the Army used tanks more effectively than did the Marines.

The 25th Division was the Army at its best. To begin with, the professionals of the 25th entered the war more abruptly than any other American troops. Schofield Barracks is on Oahu. Robert Kennington describes the end of the football season in 1941:

On Sunday afternoon of December 7 we had a football game scheduled. We had won the local championship six years running. It was a big game. Four of us were having breakfast, talking about the football game that morning, when the first bomb hit. We stumbled out of breakfast, and met a Zero flying so low that if I would have had a baseball, I could have hit him. He didn't look right or left and didn't strafe us. He was headed for the Army planes at Hickham Field. Well, they canceled the game on account of war.

Later in the day I was shot in the chest by friendly fire. Everyone was edgy. I was close to dying, but they saved me, and I recovered pretty quickly. But I had a score to settle. A lot of us did. We didn't get beat up like the Navy and the Air Force, but we lost many men in the attack. We all kind of knew something was up, but getting hit hard out of the blue, made us all full of rage.

The 25th was filling its units to full strength. Although field commissions of NCOs added to the officer ranks, the 25th, like all Army units, relied heavily upon Officers Candidate School (OCS) for its second lieutenants. Louis Kidhardt, a Boston College graduate, took a typical path:

I was drafted in early 1941. After basic I was assigned as a medic. While I was on maneuvers in North Carolina, my CO asked me if I wanted to try OCS. I was pretty happy where I was. I was lazy enough, I was driving a truck. Life was okay. He said, "You're a college graduate and we need officers. I agreed. I went through the division board, the corps board, the Army board, and finally was accepted. It was fairly selective at this period. But they were running out of junior officers and they knew they'd be expendable. A second lieutenant or a company commander are the hardest jobs in the Army and I was both. On the way back from maneuvers we were going back through North Carolina in December. There was all kinds of commotion. People were lining the streets in Rocky Mount, North Carolina. It was December 7. The people didn't know who we were. The people thought we were on our way to the coast to fight the Japs. They came out with pies and chocolate bars, cigarettes: it was really a big deal.

I graduated from OCS on May 8. We were not allowed to go home. We were sent directly to Angel Island in California. Boarded the *President Jackson*, the largest merchant Marine transport. My first command was aboard ship, over a bunch of recruits headed to Oahu. By the end of May I was sitting on the beach at Oahu with fifty other brand-new second lieutenants. Odd things happened at that time of history.

When Kidhardt arrived in Hawaii, the 25th had just been taken over by Major General J. Lawton Collins. Collins was one of the finest officers who ever served in the U.S. Army. He was a crack corps commander in Europe and later served a distinguished tour as Army Chief of Staff. He was a protégé of General George Marshall, and

the 25th Division was to serve as a test of his ability to command
higher units.

At the time Collins and Kidhardt arrived in May, the 25th and
other Army units were in a flurry of activity on Oahu. Washington
dreaded the possibility that the Japanese might return to Hawaii with
an invasion fleet, and, along with Panama, it was the first place to receive troops and material.

Stanley Larsen started his distinguished Army career with the
25th and became very close to Collins. Like many, Larsen had a very
high regard for Collins and the men around him:

> First, Collins was an optimistic leader, an aggressive leader. He
> was a great student of maneuver. He was a prime leader in com-
> bat wherever he was. However, he was a sweet man. I use the
> word because he was genteel, and happy. Later when he was
> Army Chief of Staff, he was delighted to see one of his old junior
> officers. He supported us.
>
> General Collins pushed us when he knew we were going to
> Guadalcanal. He pushed training very strongly. Oahu had a lot of
> jungle, not quite like the ones we faced in Guadalcanal, but they
> were jungles. Of course, we had some ridiculous training. One of
> the battalion commanders took his unit out to learn how to dig
> foxholes and to sleep on the ground. Well, the foxhole side was
> good, but I don't think the soldiers felt they had to *train* to learn
> how to sleep on the ground. When we were getting ready to es-
> tablish how we would operate in combat, I had been promoted to
> Major and was the executive officer of the battalion I had been
> serving since 1939. Colonel McClure, our regimental CO, chose
> me to be regimental operations officer. Colonel McClure was
> obviously a good CO. He spoke to soldiers like he would speak
> to anyone that he liked, and the soldiers liked him. He was a
> strong soldier.

Louis Kidhardt, as a newly arrived second lieutenant, had a different perspective, but came to the same conclusion held by Larsen:

> Most of the men I soldiered with were Regular Army: pre–Pearl
> Harbor boys. It was a challenge, but I accepted it. Being a pla-

toon leader with these Regular Army boys made the job much easier because in essence they were training me. We all knew what was happening and accepted it.

Every regiment had a reconnaissance platoon. Colonel McClure assigned me to head the regimental I&R [Intelligence and Reconnaissance—EB] and gave me the pick of the regiment. I chose about thirty to forty men. I looked at all their service records so I knew quite a bit about them. I was McClure's aide also. I admired him, he was very capable. Collins thought so too. I was in Collins' HQ. Later he went on a couple of maneuvers with our I&R. He was a good soldier but very tough. He was very knowledgeable about weapons. He could field strip every weapon in the infantry blindfolded and put it back again.

We were a hot outfit. The boys had been punished at Pearl Harbor and had lost a lot of friends. They had something to fight for. They had a reason to go to Guadalcanal and we had all the experience possessed by the regulars. And they were the ones that lost their friends.

Robert Kennington was chosen by Kidhardt to be in the I&R platoon. He saw things from yet a different vantage point:

I had a score to settle. So I volunteered for the I&R platoon. We went right into training. I've been through a lot of it, and this was some of the toughest I've had. Lieutenant Kidhardt had been an all-conference tackle at Boston College and he was in charge of putting us into shape. Boy, did he do it. When I was done I weighed 188 pounds solid. We trained at night, all hours. They'd wake us up at midnight for maneuvers. We'd go way up in the mountains, as far as the trucks would take us, and we'd have to walk the rest of the way up the mountain. You could almost touch the sky. We had to go through the culverts on the way down in a couple of feet of water. The trucks would take us back to the barracks about 3:30 A.M. At 5:00 A.M. we'd hear the message to hit the deck again. That went on for five and a half months before we went to Guadalcanal. No one was seriously hurt in training. Most made it, but a few couldn't put up with the rules or the training itself. We did judo, karate. Learned some basic Japanese. Without that training, I don't think I would have made it back. In August we shipped out. Of course we didn't know where we were going.

When the 161st Washington National Guard Regiment arrived, it was fortunate for both units. The 161st had been on active service for over a year. It had not received the type of preparation required for the South Pacific, but being grafted onto the 25th helped solve that problem. The commander, James Dalton, became a legend in the Pacific, and was one of the Army's youngest general officers when he was killed in the Philippines. Scott Wilson describes the transformation between Guard and 25th:

The 161st Regiment had been on active duty for fourteen months. We had spent more times on active maneuvers than in barracks. We were originally part of the 41st Guard Division. The whole division went to Fort Hunter Ligget in California. We had maneuvers down there with referees. We'd go charging up a hill, and some referee would come out waving his arms, saying, You can't go up there, you've already been shot. Then he'd tell the lieutenant to go back. It was funny. We learned basic tactics, weapons, and maneuvers. It was an advantage.

During the Hunter Ligget maneuvers there were a lot of prostitutes in trailers. Word was that these were girls from Tacoma that followed the troops down. Our troops were their best patrons, as I understand it. We always remained as a unit. We had a lot of confidence in our leaders and in ourselves. We had a lot of confidence in our leader, James Dalton. He was such a young man, but he looked older, and oozed command. His father and grandfather had been generals and he figured he'd be one too.

It does not take any military background to see that the preparation going to men like Kennington was superior to Scott Wilson's. This was particularly true when considering the extreme youth of so many of his comrades:

Most of our company commanders were National Guard or ROTC. They probably started out in the ranks and took what they called the ten series [a series of standardized exams taken by

enlisted men trying to gain entrance into officer training—EB].
One fellow was a sergeant when we mobilized. Soon he was
promoted to second lieutenant. When he was killed in the Philippines he was a major. When we mobilized, approximately half
our people were seventeen. We had plenty of eighteen-year-old
soldiers on Guadalcanal: one of our squad leaders was eighteen.

We were basically civilians, and did not have a rigidity of
thought drilled into us by years of military training. The Guard
was a good investment. You get a soldier at a cut-rate price, but
you also get a smart one. When we first arrived the Regulars referred to us as Boy Scouts. In reality they weren't far off. After
Guadalcanal the Regular boys had a lot more respect for us.
They treated us like equals after that. Of course on New Georgia
we were into it. I remember going up those roads, and other soldiers would say there are guys from the 161st, they're pretty
tough. I remember trying to look tough for the audience. It's
funny looking back.

Many of the men that Wilson joined in Hawaii, even though
they wore the patch of the 25th Division Regulars, were far less
trained than he and his friends were. William Schumacher was an
ROTC second lieutenant assigned to the 25th shortly after Pearl
Harbor:

My first duty was on maneuvers in Carolina and Georgia in the
spring of 1940. In these we had trucks with the sign "tank" on
them and a piece of stovepipe that said "mortar."

In January 1942 I was called in for active duty and ended up in
Hawaii. I joined the unit on the beach positions west of Pearl
Harbor on June 2, 1942. The company CO gave me a staff sergeant, a corporal, a pfc and fifty-eight draftees who had three
weeks in the Army including boat time to Hawaii. We had seven
81mm mortars and the CO said "You train them." So we started.
Half each day was spent clearing beach positions: cutting down
those tough Hawaiian trees, the other half was training. Four
days after I got this platoon, the Battle of Midway popped and we
were supposed to man the beaches with our mortars and repel an
invasion.

On the beach positions we were living in tents or in little shacks. This went on with maneuvers: we had a live firing exercise. My mortars took a position and we were supposed to fire on a line of simulated enemy. General J. Lawton Collins popped into my foxhole where I was observing. He said, "Lieutenant, do you think you can hit those targets?" I said, "Yes sir, we'll try." He said, "Go ahead, you've got two minutes before the artillery barrage." I called the order back and my platoon sergeant was manning the one gun we were going to use to zero in on the target. He fired, and I heard him cuss over the sound power phone. I didn't tell the general why. That shell fell on top of one of the stakes marking the enemy position. So Collins said, "Fine, you're all set." What I didn't tell him was that the shell had gone through some trees, clipped some branches. The shell was armed and the mortar crew could have been blown to bits. Our training was very good but it did not duplicate the jungle we found at Guadalcanal.

The full story concerning unit deployment to Guadalcanal is tangled. Shipping was scarce and support troops that proved essential in the South Pacific also competed for transport. More important matters were in play, however. There can be no doubt that King wanted Guadalcanal to remain a Navy and Marine operation. The great feud that later erupted between MacArthur and Nimitz over which route to follow during a Pacific advance was already in its initial stage. MacArthur had agreed to leave the first stage of South Pacific operations in Navy hands. King, therefore, wanted to keep his Marines together as far as possible from MacArthur's clutches. King does not appear to have worried as much as either MacArthur or Ghormley, U.S. Navy commander in the South Pacific until November 1942, about a fierce Japanese reaction to Guadalcanal. When the pessimists were proved correct and Guadalcanal became the focus of a massive campaign, Ghormley had no choice but to ask for Army support. The first Army ground units that arrived came from the newly formed Americal Division in October. A new problem, also unexpected, arose. King had underestimated the duration of the

Guadalcanal operation. The 1st Marine Division and supporting units smashed the Japanese in a series of ugly encounters during September and October. However, they were being wrecked by the jungle and were wasting away. Consequently, the situation demanded both more troops for Guadalcanal and the withdrawal of the 1st Marine Division.

Events in North Africa also entered into the equation. Soon after Pearl Harbor, the Australian government demanded the return of its crack divisions from the Middle East. Two of them returned in short order. The third, the Australian 9th Division, remained temporarily, awaiting transport. The situation in the desert, however, reached a point of decision in the summer of 1942. British General Bernard Montgomery did not want to give up the Australians until after he had dealt with the German Africa Corps under Erwin Rommel. An elaborate exchange was worked out. In addition to the two National Guard divisions already in Australia, the Americans agreed to send another division if the return of the 9th Australian could be delayed. Reluctantly the Australians agreed.

Initially, Washington decided to send the 25th to Australia as its part of the agreement. Marshall had his eye on Collins and wanted to see him in action. However, Guadalcanal still appeared to be under threat. Consequently, King and Marshall made another trade. Washington dispatched the 25th to Guadalcanal. When it arrived, the 1st Marines were to proceed to Australia. Because of initial reverses suffered by the U.S. 32d Division in Papua in November, the Australian government did not think highly of U.S. Army troops. The Marines, they believed, were a different matter. Consequently, in return for an emaciated and crippled Marine division whose stay in the theater proved short, the Australians willingly dispensed with the services of arguably the best division in the U.S. Army.

Therefore, after months of wrangling inside Washington and among three Allied capitals, the 25th started to arrive on Guadalcanal in mid-December. Naturally, the men of the 25th Division knew nothing about these matters. Louis Kidhardt recalls the initial confusion involved:

When we shipped out of Oahu we were destined for Australia because the Japs were offering a threat to the continent. Our ship was not combat-loaded when we left Oahu. [A ship that is "combat-loaded" has its cargo arranged for rapid removal. It is less efficient than normal loading because it sacrifices space for speed. A combat-loaded ship is a sure sign that battle approaches.—EB] We got to Noumea and the orders were changed. They combat-loaded us aboard the *President Johnson* and took off after the ten days or so that it required. No one told us where we were going, but Guadalcanal was in all the newspapers. In a couple of days Collins informed us of our destination. We all got a little more serious about being in the Army. Serious about our training. I had the I&R platoon and conducted all my training aboard ship. We started thinking very seriously about our weapons, assignments, morale. We were going into combat. We weren't playing.

The 25th arrived piecemeal at Guadalcanal in mid-December. Most of the division was not combat-loaded, so desperate seemed to be the need for men. The transports, therefore, spent several dangerous days unloading men and supplies. Fortunately for them, Marine pilots had weakened the Japanese air arm at Rabaul sufficiently that the 25th suffered no losses disembarking. The remainder of the Americal Division and the 2d Marine Division and several attached units also arrived in this period.

General Collins was very careful to orient his troops. Orientation and training are not the same. Success or failure in a military operation often depends upon coordination, communication, and matters of detail. Errors are inherent in war, but good officers try to minimize them by learning the terrain and getting the "kinks" worked out of the system before the shooting starts. (Training exercises by battle-hardened troops near the combat zone were a hallmark of General Montgomery's command style in World War II. Modern armies all follow this practice.) Stanley Larsen describes one of the first operations run by the 25th. It shows the unmistakable touch of professionalism:

In the first real action we had I commanded a representative group including one platoon from each rifle company in the regiment. We had twelve companies, so multiply forty men by twelve. So roughly what we had was a composite battalion. There were two rivers, the Matanikau and the Lunga, in the general area where the Marines had fought. The rivers parallel each other up into the hills but a quarter to a half mile apart. We went up the Matanikau River, west of the Lunga River, and spent two nights. On the third day we went over to the Lunga and walked down the river. On the return, we crossed the two rivers dozens of times. The purpose was to acclimate a representative group from each company of what the jungle was like. At night we dug foxholes, set up perimeter defense, and placed our machine guns for protective cross fire.

When we completed our trek up the Matanikau and first crossed over to the Lunga, we went through a Marine battlefield. A lot of the Marine equipment was left there and a lot of the Japanese equipment was left there. There were skeletons in Japanese uniforms. It gave us a good look at the aftermath of a battle. We did not have any combat. We all knew it was a quiet area. But it was excellent training for about forty men from each company in the entire regiment.

Major General Alexander Patch, commander of the Army's Americal Division, relieved Vandegrift as ground commander on Guadalcanal in December. General Marshall later reassigned Patch to Europe, where, like Collins, he rendered exceptional service. As the 25th deployed, Patch decided to break out of the Henderson perimeter and clear the Japanese from Guadalcanal. (Although Patch did not realize it, the Imperial Headquarters concluded at about the same time that they must evacuate Guadalcanal.) When the 25th was ready in early January, Patch's offensive was under way. The Japanese were pushed back to the west toward their final point of embarkation at Cape Esperance on the northwestern tip of the island. The Japanese, however, tried to hold on to Mount Austen. Patch naturally assumed this was done so the Japanese could continue to observe Henderson. Patch, like all American commanders, was most fearful of one more big Japanese offensive, a move Tokyo seriously considered in December. By January, however, the Japanese were attempting to withdraw as much of their garrison as possible. Consequently, the Japanese held a valuable observation post at Mount Austen, but they were also bait for Patch's attack forces. The more Americans sent south toward Mount Austen, the fewer that could push west.

The Americal units that attacked to the south succeeded in partially isolating the Japanese defenders. They also received a dose of terrible medicine. The Marines had won defensive battles on Guadalcanal. They had never fully confronted a large Japanese unit that was well dug in and determined to stay. When the Americal pushed into prepared Japanese defenses they suffered stinging casualties. In addition, some of the Americal units were very tired. Its men had fought very well since October, but the jungle had done its work. Wisely, Patch ordered Collins to send a reinforced battalion toward Mount Austen, relieve some of the Americal units in the area, and eliminate the Japanese position. The remainder of the 25th joined the drive to the west.

The 25th's operations from the start were well planned and more complex than those previously launched by American ground troops. The most notable characteristic was the heavy use of massed artillery. On the first day of the push to the west, the 27th Regiment was supported by artillery fire from every division on Guadalcanal, controlled by the 25th's fire-direction center. They employed a complex technique beloved by good artillerymen called a "TOT (time-on-target) shoot." Normally, when an artillery attack is launched, individual shots from batteries are fired. Observers see where the shots land and adjust the fire onto the target. When the ranging fire is on target, the bombardment starts. This way, the artillery hits its position and the chance of a "short round" falling onto a friendly unit is greatly reduced. The problem is that when ranging fire begins, the enemy takes cover before the main barrage. A "time on target" barrage employs maximum fire from all batteries at a prearranged time with no aiming fire. If the barrage finds its target immediately, the enemy cannot take cover and suffers much worse damage. After a short concentrated attack, the batteries fire en masse at irregular intervals, hoping that the enemy will think the barrage over and expose themselves to deploy for ground attack. If the technique is bungled, however, all the batteries miss together. If they hit friendly positions, calamity can result.

The barrage controlled by the 25th was the first division-level American TOT attack of the war. (It was not the last.) In thirty minutes six field-artillery battalions fired nearly 6,000 rounds into a small area known to have strong Japanese defenses. After the barrage, ground units swept through with little opposition. In engagements of the next few days the 25th also employed close air support, the trickiest technique in ground war, with considerable success and no friendly losses. The infantry showed its skill at assault by storming a key hill on a Japanese position nicknamed the "Galloping Horse" from its appearance on aerial photos. During this engagement Collins personally directed mortar fire on the Japanese. The 27th Regiment of the 25th Division took another Japanese position called the "Sea Horse." Many of the Japanese positions destroyed by the 25th were manned by freshly landed rear-guard troops. Not all of the enemy was starving. Therefore, the advance was methodical to keep casualties low. The 27th lost only seventy-four men killed during the advance, which finally ended when the Japanese abandoned the island at the end of January 1943.

The 25th Division's most difficult problem was at Mount Austen. Mount Austen was not a mountain in the normal sense. Instead, it was a collection of steep ridges, punctuated by some hills. As noted before, a geographic oddity of Guadalcanal was that many ridgelines and hilltops were sparsely vegetated, while the jungle directly below was as dense as any in the South Pacific. On a battlefield in most parts of the world, holding a ridgeline with the enemy only a few hundred yards below you would ensure a rapid and easy victory. In the jungle, everything was different. The Japanese in the valley near Mount Austen were obscured by cover better than any engineer could provide. In addition, over a period of months, they had built a series of bunkers and fortifications that posed a frightful tactical problem to the attacker.

The Japanese position near Mount Austen was called the "Gifu Strong Point." It was manned by the remnants of two Japanese regiments. Both had been part of the ferocious ground assaults launched against Marine positions earlier. Many of the men were from Gifu prefecture on Honshu, and so named their position in its honor. The position was held by between 400 and 600 men. Many were sick. All were malnourished. They consumed their last rations just days before the 25th wiped out the position. Although the matter is not clear, it appears that after the men in the Gifu had stopped the American attack, they were ordered to retreat toward Cape Esperance. The Japanese infantry, however, led by a brave and experienced officer, Major Inagaki, refused to leave their wounded and agreed among themselves to stay and fight.

Stanley Larsen describes the Gifu Strong Point:

> Mount Austen was a 1,500-foot mountaintop that overlooked Henderson Field. The remnants of two Japanese regiments were there ready to fight to the death. I think they had visions of harassing us with one or two artillery pieces and preventing our aircraft from using Henderson Field. It was important to them to hinder our airpower because we were attacking the Japanese ships and other Japanese-held islands. The Gifu Strong Point when our battalion took over had, I would guess, about 400 enemy soldiers. They had constructed a circular fortified zone about 300 yards in diameter. Perhaps a bit more. They had forty-two pillboxes made of dirt. They had built them long enough before so that the weeds had grown over them. You could get to about fifteen feet of them and not see what was there. They were mutually supporting. The American never really knew the size and shape of the strong point.

William Schumacher was a junior officer at the Gifu. As he points out, the positions, as was so typical of combat in the South Pacific, were extremely close:

> Our position was pretty much along a trail. Our foxholes were dug on one side of the trail and the hills were right behind us. The enemy was just a few yards in front of us: I imagine they

could see us from their position. They had beautifully dug-in positions. But the only time we really heard from them was when our guys stepped off the trail toward them. Then they'd shoot up a storm. But they wouldn't shoot when we were on the trail. A couple of days later they called my mortar platoon to move up to the neighboring battalion. We got up there and found a rather interesting situation. There was a trail leading off to the southwest and a couple of the rifle companies were off along that trail. There were a bunch of tall trees along the trail and there were Jap snipers in those trees. If you walked along that trail they'd shoot at you, but if you stepped five feet sideways and walked off the trail, they wouldn't shoot at you. I don't know if their weapons were zeroed in down the trail or what.

The American battalion around the Gifu was up on hills and ridges. Basic supply shortages were a fact of life. By this time Guadalcanal had no shortage of anything the infantry needed. Yet delivering things in the jungle was always hard. There was a jeep road that went close to the Gifu. Nearby units received supplies via rafts pushed up the Matanikau River. (The GIs called these rafts the "Push-Push Maru.") Getting the supplies up the ridges, however, was a serious difficulty, as Schumacher relates:

Some of the food was hand-carried by native bearers. The stuff was brought up the river, to the foot of the hill, and then the natives would practically climb from root to root, grabbing them with their hands, to get up the hill with it. The problem of getting supplies close to our unit was a little better because there was a road that jeeps could traverse. A lot of our supplies on nearby hills on the west of the Gifu came in by airdrop. They tried dropping stuff from B-17s, using shelter halves as makeshift parachutes. Every water can split. Almost all the .30-caliber ammo got bent and wasn't usable. The 81mm mortar rounds were thrown out in three- or six-round clusters and we were very careful taking them out of these cases. I still used well over 80 percent of those rounds with no misfires or stray rounds. Evacuation was a real problem too. The people had to be carried down

that steep hill, then floated down the river until they could get to
the trucks.

With positions so close, the Japanese periodically attempted infiltration attacks at night directed at individual American positions.
These engagements were short, but could be very hazardous. Robert
Kennington's company was on top of Hill 27, the single most important American position surrounding the Gifu. One night his company received a visit from the Japanese:

About seven to eight Japanese tried to come through the lines
early one morning. I was on perimeter guard with a .30-caliber
light machine gun, unlocked so it would pivot freely. All of a sudden on my right someone started screaming, "Japs are coming
through." Everybody cut loose. I just laid down fire with the machine gun. Someone was shooting from behind. Bullets were
coming by my head, hitting the sandbags. I told the two guys in
the hole with me: "Get your butt out of the hole, one take my
shotgun, the other take a rifle. Go to the holes on each side and
turn around. Someone is shooting from the rear." They finally
got out of the hole after I threatened to knock them out.

When it was daylight we found seven Japanese dead that had
tried to get through the lines. One was above my machine gun.
He had been killed by one of the guys in my company. Our guy
saw someone, but didn't know who he was. He was afraid he was
one of us, so he gave the halt signal three times. The guy in the
shadows just stood there. When my buddy received no password
he shot the other guy five times in the chest and killed him. He
was a Jap, okay.

After we checked all of the bodies to make sure they were
dead, I checked the one above me that had been firing on my machine gun, the one my friend had killed. He had a hand grenade
in his hand so no one wanted to touch him. I was young and
crazy enough to take a chance, so I took my knife, cut his pack
off, took his cap and glasses and rolled him over the side of the
mountain with his grenade.

In war the rush and pressure of events increases the always-
present chance of a mistake. Mistakes in combat cost lives. All units,

regardless of how good, experience tragic moments brought on by faulty assessment of the situation. Unfortunately, commanders frequently believe what they want to believe. The line between aggressiveness and self-delusion is very thin. The 25th Division's units besieging the Gifu found this out when they launched an ill-advised assault. Stanley Larsen was with the company involved:

> The battalion commander was told by the 25th assistant division commander that the enemy was exhausted and would not respond with any strength. The battalion commander felt that he should have more time to find out what was in front of him. He had requested three tanks. We did not have any tanks ourselves, but the Marines that were leaving did. But the battalion was told there was no enemy worth a darn and when our forces hit them they would give way. Then our battalion would be able to practically walk through and join the other two battalions a good half mile beyond. The battalion commander was upset, but held his reserve and said, "OK, sir, if that's what you want, that's what we'll do." The attack went off and the battalion lost about twenty-five or thirty men killed within the first twenty minutes and at least as many wounded. By dark the line was the same as that held when they jumped off in the morning.

The unfortunate battalion commander was punished for being correct, as often happens. Relieved and demoted, he was sent back to the United States and eventually on to Europe. Collins remembered the man involved and he was given another battalion under Collins in Europe. Late in the war, Collins personally awarded him a Silver Star. At the Gifu, Stanley Larsen took over the battalion.

Slowly, however, the Gifu was beginning to break apart. American companies enveloped the entire position and discovered several pillboxes. Once discovered, the emplacements were easily destroyed. Nevertheless, as the Americans tightened the siege, positions became even closer. Robert Kennington recalls a brush with his Japanese neighbors:

> We were very close to the Gifu. I could talk to them really, right down the slope. One day we were sent out to repair a break in the

telephone line. We climbed right on the edge of the ridge. If we'd have slipped, we'd have tumbled right into the Jap positions. We found the break in the wire, but they spotted us and began firing with machine guns and rifles. We did the fastest splice in history, and took off like rabbits.

By mid-January the Gifu had been plaguing the Army for over a month. The real solution to this problem, however, was sitting back at the beach. Larsen recalls the destruction of the Gifu:

When I took over the battalion I requested the same thing as my predecessor. I requested three tanks and they delivered them. They started up the hill, but only one succeeded in getting up the steep path. But that tank went in one morning and hit the line of pillboxes. Accompanied by infantry, it knocked out three pillboxes on the right-hand side where we went in. After lunch, it went in again, turned left, and knocked out three more pillboxes. It left an opening of nearly a hundred yards on the circumference and that broke the back of the Japanese resistance. But we had thrown mortar round after round in there and had an artillery barrage the day before. As a result, they had very few men left.

We gave them a chance to surrender but they wouldn't. That night after the tank attack, the enemy made a banzai attack against a company that was overlooking their water hole. It was a steep slope. I've only been in two banzai charges, and they are terrifying. In this one eighty-five Japanese were killed. Twenty-one were officers and the rest enlisted. F Company did not lose a single man. We had a bulldozer up there and we bulldozed a mass grave and all were buried there. That was the end of the Gifu Strong Point. About three days later we were pulled off the hill and sent back toward the water.

The Gifu siege cost the 25th Division sixty-four men killed, half during the abortive assault. The American battalion reported the deaths of 518 Japanese soldiers. The capture of forty machine guns, twelve mortars, and hundreds of small arms supports the estimate. Japanese losses in the general area were at least double that. During their six weeks on Guadalcanal, elements of the 25th fought or moved forward without stop. Considering the amount of fighting involved, the losses of 216 men killed was very modest. It was a very well conducted campaign. Keep in mind that the Americans on Guadalcanal in January 1943 were far better supplied than the Marines had been five months before. They also confronted a weaker enemy. Yet the 25th dismantled the Japanese wherever it faced them. A mountain of supplies and great firepower are not worth much if a unit does not know how to use them. The 25th knew the craft of war very well.

The Gifu episode has an unusual footnote. Decades after the war, one of Larsen's former soldiers was helping some Japanese locate the mass grave at the Gifu. Larsen, then a retired major general, assisted and the search succeeded. In 1992 Larsen returned with many others for the fiftieth anniversary of the landing at Guadalcanal. With some difficulty, he found the Gifu, and there was a monument to the men put up by the inhabitants of their prefecture in Japan. Larsen describes the artifact:

> About a quarter of a mile from Gifu was a Japanese monument to their dead. It was impressive. It had a pedestal with nothing on top of it. Over on the side was an almost life-size statue of a young Japanese fisherman holding his net ready to throw out to the water to catch fish. It had been donated by a small Japanese fishing village that had furnished many of the soldiers who were killed at Gifu. There was a small sign in English that didn't really refer to combat, but said it was dedicated to Japanese who had given their lives for their country.
>
> In retrospect I must admit that these men held out to the last man. Only one got back alive. This doesn't include the ten or so prisoners we took. The monument was very peaceful, and it is far up the hill. I take some pleasure in saying it was a marked area for them. If the situation had been reversed, and we had fought to the last man, I would have wanted to dedicate a monument in such a place to our soldiers.

The 25th Division's stay in the South Pacific was just beginning at Guadalcanal. During the bloodbath on New Georgia, Halsey sent in most of the 25th to serve as a "fire brigade" when the Japanese proved too strong for the invading divisions to handle. Collins's men accomplished all their missions there with skill, speed, and low cost. After New Georgia, Collins left for bigger things in Europe. However, the 25th maintained its high standards. It led one of the first "island hopping" operations on Vella Lavella. Landing almost unopposed behind the Japanese remaining on the New Georgia group of islands, it forced the Japanese rapidly to evacuate the central Solomons. In the Philippines, the 25th was one of MacArthur's finest fighting divisions.

Some large American units did not fit neatly into the categories of Regular Army, National Guard, or Reserves established by the National Defense Act. This resulted from the aforementioned "triangularization" of American divisions. Every time a "square" division of four regiments was reorganized into triangular form with three regiments, an orphan regiment was left over. The Army planned to combine the excess regiments into new divisions. However, when war started, the immediate need for troops outweighed organizational tidiness, and Washington deployed four independent regiments to the South Pacific.

All were National Guard units originally. (No Reserve units served in the South Pacific.) We shall look at the Guard presently. At the moment, it is enough to point out that because these regiments were removed from their parent divisions, they lost their Guard identity more rapidly than would otherwise have been the case. Because many functions normally performed by divisional headquarters had to be carried out inside the independent regiments, a large number of new officers were needed. ROTC graduates or Regular Army officers filled the new slots. Consequently, they did not suffer from the great variation in quality found among the National Guard officer corps. More important, the independent regiments all went through the tremendously valuable period of orientation into combat alongside more experienced units. None was initially asked to achieve missions beyond its capability, and thus all were allowed to develop into good units.

Three regiments, the 132d, 164th, and 182d, hurriedly left the

East Coast in April 1942 bound for the strategically vital island of New Caledonia. New Caledonia proved an important base for the U.S. Navy and was very high on Tokyo's list of potential targets before Midway. Originally, the 132d was part of the Illinois National Guard, the 164th from North Dakota, and the 182d from Massachusetts. In May 1942 the Army created a new division from the three. For reasons not altogether clear to posterity, the new unit never received a number. Instead, Washington named it the Americal Division, a contraction of "America" and "New Caledonia." Ably commanded by Major General Alexander Patch, the Americal was the first Army unit sent to Guadalcanal. It arrived gradually, and at times served very closely with the 1st Marine Division. The 164th Regiment played a key role in demolishing Japan's largest offensive during October. Although relationships between Army and Marine units were always strained, there is no doubt that the Americal benefited much from entering the war in a realm already well understood. In general the Americal performed well on Guadalcanal, considerably better than any of the Guard Divisions. We shall meet the Americal again.

A fourth regiment, the 147th of the Ohio National Guard, was likewise dispatched with great haste to the Pacific. It landed on Fiji before the Marines arrived there. In November 1942, the insatiable demand for manpower at Guadalcanal swept up the 147th. While on Guadalcanal it worked closely with the Marines and served well during the January offensive. After Guadalcanal, like many other Army units, the 147th served in many locales as garrison troops.

Most of the Army's combat strength in the South Pacific and New Guinea came from the four National Guard divisions deployed there. The prewar National Guard was an extremely interesting institution. In one form or another, the Guard was as old as the country. Many of the Guard regiments traced their ancestry to colonial militia. Many others traced their origins to the war in Mexico or the Civil War. Some had served in the trenches during World War I.

Local recruitment was a part of most of the armies in World War II. The Guard had parallels in other countries, but no duplicates. The Guard was unusual simply because very few countries had entities resembling American states. Two factors set the Guard apart. First was the local recruitment base of Guard units. The generation that came of age in the Great Depression still lived in a world where regional differences were very pronounced in the United States. They also lived in a country where rural or small-town life was greatly different from that found in the big industrial cities. If a young man joined the Guard, he trained and served with people he was acquainted with. Often best friends served together. Officers too were local, normally the "upstanding citizens" of the community.

James S. Salafia joined the Connecticut National Guard in 1939, part of the 43d Division. He gives us a good description of the Guard before the war:

I joined the Guard in 1939, a senior in high school. The first sergeant was my scoutmaster, and he dragged me into it. I heard recruiters were getting two dollars a man. A big roundup. My chemistry teacher in high school was company commander. He also said, "Join or I'll flunk you." At that time we just spent time on summer maneuvers at Plattsburg. Our regiment was made up of units from all the towns surrounding Hartford, the state capital. Hartford had headquarters company, the military police, and the service companies. The surrounding towns had rifle companies. I was from Middletown, nine miles away, and was in a rifle company.

We had light machine guns and some artillery attached on paper. But when I joined we had absolutely nothing. No joke: we had trucks with logs on them for cannon, and broomsticks for rifles. The Army was at its lowest point. The Guard was bolstered up soon thereafter because of that. The war clouds were gathering. We wore the wrapped legging, World War I helmets, and used Springfield rifles from the Great War. Ultimately the division encompassed the New England area.

Our general and colonels were citizen soldiers. The general worked in a big insurance company. When war broke out he brought his staff from the company with him. He inducted them into the regiment. Guys made second lieutenant without training. So a guy is a college graduate, works for the general in civilian life, but has no training, and he leads us into battle. That's trouble. Us little guys had just finished high school. We had a year and a half of military training since induction in 1940. The smart officers respected that and learned a lot from us.

Dick Randles joined a Wisconsin Guard unit that was part of the 32d Division. He echoes Salafia:

There was a very strong local identity in the Guard units. The officers were businessmen in town. It was a local affair. Company A came from the surrounding area, towns and the farm communities. People had grown up together. Most were local Menomonie people, the folks I went to high school with. I'm going back to a high-school reunion and I'll see half a dozen of my Army buddies. Our captain was Harry Olson, the banker in town; I delivered papers to him. Another officer ran a gas station. We were called to the colors on October 14, 1940.

Ivers L. Funk from rural Ohio joined a unit that became part of the 37th Division. His description is a vivid reminder that some components of the military were a century behind others. The local armory, one of which Funk describes, was a fixture in medium-sized towns and cities throughout the country.

My earliest recollection of F Battery, 134th Field Artillery, Ohio National Guard, comes from when I was about twelve years old. My mother's uncle took us to the armory in Dresden, Ohio. It consisted of a large barn where they stabled about thirty horses and had supply rooms for uniforms, equipment, harness, and saddles. My brother John enlisted sometime after. I would accompany him to Monday-night drills, watching and yearning for the time when I could join. When the captain saw my interest and asked if I would like to join, I said yes, but that I was only fifteen. He suggested that as I looked old enough, I could just give my birth date as September 15, 1909. I was floating on air just to be in. It was January 17, 1927, four months before Charles Lindbergh flew across the Atlantic.

Most of the battery were city boys and feared the horses. I loved horses and rode them on weekends with my brother, so I was assigned as driver. The driver rode the near (left) horse and handled both the near and off (other) horse, in their harnesses. We were particularly proud of the white draft horses our battery had. Other batteries had horses of various colors but all of our draft pairs were white. The battery always participated in civic events, especially patriotic parades.

Scott Wilson joined the Washington National Guard before the war. Later his Guard regiment joined the 25th Division. Wilson points out the scanty training given. He also reminds us that the Guard played a role in an unhappy political time in the United States:

It's true that before mobilization we didn't really have basic training in the National Guard. Before going to the colors we had a little weapons training, but it was mostly on the job within the unit. It is true we learned how to operate a machine gun, or what the term "primary position" meant. But we also learned how to use clubs to break up crowds. We were used as strikebreakers. This was a sore subject. Some of the guys in our outfit had fathers who were union men or pro-union. They weren't happy when their sons joined the Guard because of this.

When the Guard was mobilized in 1940, a transformation began. Like all Army units, regardless of type, peacetime Guard formations were much smaller than planned for during war. In contrast to many nations, including Japan and Germany, the United States intentionally dispensed with a large conscript standing army that would be supplemented with trained reserves when the time arrived. Instead, standing American forces were skeletal units designed to be brought up to strength with conscripts and enlistees who had no previous military training at all. Note also that the Guard was called up in late 1940, slightly more than a year before Pearl Harbor. A year was plenty of time to dispense with old faces and see new ones. Ernest Gerber of the 32d Division, based upon the Wisconsin National Guard, describes the transformation:

When we were first inducted into federal service, everyone was neighbors, acquaintances, and many personal friends. They were all from Madison and surrounding towns. At one time myself and two brothers were in the same company. Seven brothers were in service during World War II. Thank heaven all of us made it home. As we trained and by the time we went into action many new people were added, and many of the older men were reassigned. In my unit, I would estimate that about 25 percent, maybe a little more, were the people that served before mobilization, my neighbors and friends and so forth. Many of our good people went to OCS and became officers elsewhere. The rest came in from all over hell. We got a beautiful bunch of draftees from Milwaukee. Smart, intelligent, A-1 people. When we left Madison all the officers were Guard from hometowns. At Buna we had two Guard officers remaining in my company. The others were Reserve or ROTC. Some were from the ranks through OCS. You must realize that when we went into service we only had about eighty-five people in a rifle company. All of our units were consequently seriously understrength and had to be built up. It was planned that way. Full strength was 140, and even more under the triangular division. When we shipped over, our companies were 160 to 180. The extras were mostly inductees.

There is an apparent paradox at work concerning the Guard in the South Pacific. Between call-up and the time the first Guard division went into action in November 1942, almost two years had gone by. Throughout this time, all the Guard divisions were training and preparing for war. Guard divisions had more formal training at the division level than did the 1st Marine Division. Yet all the Guard divisions had trouble in their first engagements in the South Pacific. There were several reasons for this situation. Some pertain to the unique character of the Guard units early in the war. Some problems arose from general difficulties caused by an inadequate and overloaded mobilization system. Others dealt with poor command decisions at the top.

As pointed out by Ernest Gerber, Guard units received large

numbers of new men and officers to fill the ranks. The older Guard
officers who had "held the fort" honorably since World War I were
almost all reassigned. Nevertheless, the local core remained in the
Guard divisions, and many Guard officers were highly placed. Carl
Weber was a battalion executive officer in the 41st Division in the
summer of 1943 during the bitter battles near Salamaua in New
Guinea. The battalion commander was Archie Roosevelt, President
Theodore Roosevelt's son. Weber discusses some of the extra difficulties faced because of local ties in Guard units:

> I was Archie Roosevelt's executive officer. We'd laugh about
> a couple of Easterners leading this Western battalion. [The
> 41st Division was made up of units from the Northwestern
> states.—EB] They accepted Archie, he had charisma, and they'd
> do anything for him. I was an outsider. A National Guard orga-
> nization is very local-oriented. You always confronted local and
> family matters. When I was exec and adjutant, we had to be very
> careful when we gave assignments and made promotions. We
> had to watch out that no favoritism came in. Often the person
> who was the most anxious for someone to be promoted was a rel-
> ative. We had to be very careful. Negative family connections
> could be a real problem too. The strong friendships made for
> good morale in some ways, but if someone believed someone else
> was being favored, it led to morale problems.
>
> The Guard had another problem that surfaced in World
> War I, or the Civil War for that matter. If a company or battalion
> was chopped up, an unusual number of casualties could come
> from a single town. There were relatives killed or wounded in
> the same battle. This was an issue before the war, and people
> were touchy about this. Some units felt like they were taking
> more difficult and dangerous assignments. One company com-
> mander was very irate, thought we were picking on his unit. I re-
> member we had to tell him that we picked the best for that job
> and he was it: that helped. So you had to be a diplomat.

Training in a new American division, whether Guard, draftee, or
Reserve, was very poor before the war. The high command had its
hands full organizing the flood of new units and equipment. Men

were being assigned and reassigned. The Army churned out young and inexperienced officers and sent them to the new units. What passed for training consisted of a tough boot camp and much wasted time later.

Walter Johnson joined the 43d Division during this period. His description of basic training would be echoed by millions of soldiers:

I joined the Army at sixteen. I lied to them. I knew several people in my division that were under age. Some were younger than me. For some reason, as I understand it, the Army was more strict in Europe. I was seventeen when I went overseas. I can't remember anyone asking me anything about my records. Some of them were much older, in their thirties. 'Course, anyone seemed old to greenhorns. At first no one wants to deal with you. But after a while I got along fine. I was a replacement. I was from the South, but most of the guys were from New England: Rhode Island and Maine. They figured I was from the South, so I'd do anything. Funny thing is that now we have a Sunbelt chapter of the 43d Division Association. Over the years a lot of men became "snow birds," taking their vacations in Florida. Gradually a whole bunch of them moved down there. So I don't have far to go for reunions.

Our basic training was a lot tougher than what they have today. Thanks to Vietnam they've become mama's boys. Don't shave my little boy's head, don't slap my little boy. That attitude in World War II would get you slapped right on your butt. When that sergeant spoke, you listened. I thought I was doing pretty good in basic, but I had a DI tell me, "Johnson, if you don't get those feet in step, I'm going to jump your butt and get a handful." If you wanted to fight him, the DI would take you at night to a boxing ring. And he'd lay you out. We got the correct training. It wasn't complicated. Kill or be killed. You had to keep your poise. At first we didn't have enough guns to pass around, and we'd use wooden guns.

When the new divisions did more complex training it reflected Army doctrine. American units depended upon firepower, mechanization, and a solid base. During this era the Army went through its

famous multidivision maneuvers in Louisiana, where armored cars
played the role of tanks, World War I light artillery served as medium artillery, etc. Perhaps these were useful staff exercises. But
sophisticated multidivision training of the sort that was championed
by Montgomery did not exist in the American Army before Pearl
Harbor.

The new divisions did what they could in some areas. Gunners
practiced with their field artillery. Infantrymen learned to be very
competent with their M1 rifles. Mortarmen learned to use their weapons. Yet what was lacking in the new divisions were the experienced
professional soldiers that one found at every level in the Marines or
the Regular Army. Paul Sponaugle, who served with the 37th Division, recalls, "Our training before going overseas was the one-eyed
leading the blind. One person who didn't know what they were doing,
followed another person who didn't know what they were doing."

I believe that every soldier who was trained in this period has stories of purposeless exercises and what soldiers even then called
"Mickey Mouse." One must remember that peacetime itself was an
enemy. Intelligent young soldiers knew perfectly well that the
United States was bound for war. And yet until the deed was done,
the Army could not prevent an atmosphere of lassitude from settling
over the entire apparatus. The military was overwhelmed with administration and could not conjure up the greater motivation that
comes when training during war. Much valuable time was wasted.

Another very subtle factor was at work. From the outside, the
National Guard divisions at Pearl Harbor looked good. They
learned to march and shine their buttons. Generals inspecting the
units liked what they saw. On paper, the divisions appeared up to
strength. There were naturally deficits, but those could be made up.
Advanced field training could take place before battle. It was not, unfortunately, obvious that these divisions had to be treated as having
great potential but possessing great weaknesses. For instance, there
was little in the way of the internal self-defense mechanism that operated in the Marines or the 25th. If a Reserve officer came into the
1st Marine Division and was obviously inadequate, one of the professionals would see it fast. There were far fewer people to see this type

of situation in the Guard. The local ties, in this instance, could complicate things. But inexperience was the real culprit. The upshot was that inside the Guard divisions there were some very bad officers. We shall examine the subject at length later, but note the obvious at present: in battle, bad company- or battalion-level officers kill infantry very quickly. Paul Sponaugle, who fought with the 37th across the Pacific, describes a situation on New Georgia, the division's first battle, that is substantiated by contemporary records:

The 37th trained on Fiji, but never received proper jungle training. We went into New Georgia in the dark. Our Guard officers were very poorly trained for that duty. In my opinion one of our major commanders had a yellow streak running all the way up his back. He surrounded his HQ on New Georgia with his companies. They were protecting him in a static position. We took a heck of a beating from mortar fire. Why we were sitting there I don't know. We were cut off. I was in my foxhole with a back full of splinters and a leg full of shrapnel, but no one could get back to the hospital. So I just went on. We lost twenty-nine men on stretchers when we were surrounded: the Japs infiltrated and killed them all. This same colonel had made us do an eighty-mile march in Fiji: it broke many soldiers and was a stupid thing to do.

James Salafia of the 43d Division also fought his way across the Pacific, and he also was introduced to combat on New Georgia. The sad picture he portrays was repeated many times during that battle:

Some of our Guard officers, the old colonels and majors, were too old for jungle warfare. An incident happened to me illustrating this. We were patrolling the edge of a swamp looking for the enemy. I saw a motion off in the jungle in the swamp. Here comes a guy. I dropped and put a bead on him with my M1. He started waving his hands and yelling, "Don't shoot, don't shoot." It was one of our officers, in charge of battalion intelligence. He was completely lost. He was wet up to his neck. He'd been going through swamps and was disoriented totally. He thought I was a Jap putting a bead on him. After I got back he never forgot me. He was so happy to see me, the happiest guy in the world.

The captains had maps, but in the jungle none of them knew where their units were. One got so lost he called the artillery in to drop a smoke shell to verify his position. We ran like hell to get away from that officer. I heard a briefing. The colonel asks, "Where's B Company?" Someone answers, "I don't know." The colonel asks, "Where's D Company?" and hears "I don't know." He went through all the companies like that. Tell me, how the hell can our leaders find the Japs if they don't know where their own men are?

As I have pointed out previously, several American combat units, like the 1st Marine Divisions or the Americal, had the benefit of easing into their combat environment. This did not happen with the Guard divisions. Washington deployed two, the 37th and 43d, to garrison duty until combat assignment. The 43d Division had the misfortune of losing much of its supplies when the transport carrying an entire regiment struck an American mine and sank in the harbor of the American base at Espiritu Santo. Washington dispatched the other two Guard divisions, the 41st and 32d, directly to Australia.

Unless a unit has a high degree of professionalism, garrison duty is notoriously bad for training. Officers kept their men busy building fortifications, installations, and other projects. Periodically, officers led their soldiers off on long hikes. In this regard, however, they were probably doing the wrong thing. All the commanders should have been working on strenuous, well-planned physical conditioning, of the sort found in the 25th. But physical conditioning must be gradually built up and sustained. Otherwise you merely weaken the men involved, and learn nothing.

Furthermore, by this time it was most obvious that all these divisions were bound for the jungle. Nevertheless, none of them received the sort of specialized training required. Nor did their superiors make a serious effort to acclimate them to the tropical pit they would soon enter. Homer Wright was a young officer with the 32d Division, and points out this fact:

The closest we had come to jungle training was a 100-mile march across a part of northern Australia. People came through that with raw feet, sore muscles, and hungry. We needed much more of that. When we got to New Guinea the men were not in very good physical condition.

The Guard divisions were hiding serious defects. Unfortunately, no one knew it. MacArthur had misgivings but hoped for the best. Admiral Halsey in the Solomons seems to have accepted optimistic assessments of his new divisions. Perhaps worst of all, the division commanders did not realize how badly prepared they were. Ironically, had any of them landed in Algeria in November 1942 and fought in Europe, they probably would have served well. By the time serious fighting in that theater began in February 1943, American units had learned much. But instead of going up against Vichy France in North Africa, or serving initially with a veteran unit like the 1st Marines in the Pacific, three of these divisions were thrown alone to the dogs and the fourth escaped by a matter of timing.

The unit that suffered the worst was the 32d Division, originally constituted from the Wisconsin and Michigan National Guards. Although many Guard regiments had long and distinguished histories, few of the divisions had served in war. The 32d Division, however, had served in France during World War I and fought well during its short stay in the trenches. Consequently, war was very much part of the division's institutional memory. Many of the officers who kept it together during the interwar period were combat veterans. So was its commander, Major General Edwin Harding. Harding was a West Point graduate who took over the division in February 1942. In the interwar period, Harding was one of the intelligent officers who had worked on avoiding trench warfare in the future. One of the author's of the Army's infantry manual, Harding believed strongly in "fire and maneuver." It was his fate to be sent to a tropical Verdun without artillery. As Harding wrote later, he knew when he took command that he had his hands full to get the 32d ready for war:

I have no quarrel with the general thesis that the 32d was by no means adequately trained for combat—particularly jungle combat. On the other hand I found the division well disciplined, well behaved, and well grounded in certain elements of training. My estimate when I took over is that it was about on a par with other National Guard Divisions at the time. Unfortunately, we had no opportunity to work through a systematic program for correcting deficiencies. From February, when I took over, until November, when we went into battle, we were always getting ready to move, on the move, or getting settled after a move. No sooner would we get a systematic training program started than orders for a move came along to interrupt it. You can't set up a realistic program in a couple of days.

Harding's description is accurate enough. Like all American divisions forming in 1941, it trained in preparation for European warfare. In prewar planning, the U.S. military had decided to send only air and service troops to Australia. Consequently, in February 1942, Harding expected to take his men to Ireland. Only at the last minute did Washington direct the 32d and the 41st to Australia in response to the shocking Japanese blitzkrieg. On its way to Australia, the divisions stopped in San Francisco and picked up 3,000 almost-untrained reinforcements. In May it landed in Adelaide, Australia. The training it embarked on was similar to that being done in the United States. At this period, General MacArthur and the Australian government faced the prospect of fighting a land campaign in Australia itself. Ironically, the Guard divisions probably would have performed competently in a land battle on the Australian coast: it was precisely the type of war everyone had prepared for since 1918. When the naval battles of the Coral Sea and Midway took off some of the pressure, MacArthur moved the division north to Brisbane in August. Its training program outside Brisbane was just starting when the 32d received orders to proceed to Port Moresby.

All these moves hurt the division. Most of the men were fit in the United States, but months of sea and rail transport eroded conditioning. As often happens in war, one defect led to another. The chaos inherent in the scattered journey taken by the 32d left its supply and support apparatus in a shambles. At the very end of a long logistics train and in a theater that interested Washington the least, the 32d, and its comrades in the 41st Division also in the area, received little of the new equipment that proved so helpful elsewhere. There were no light M1 carbines, no flamethrowers, and no jungle clothing. Radios were very unreliable. The medical supply system collapsed. Quinine supplies were adequate only to give doses to men who were suffering active cases, not on a daily basis. Atabrine did not make it to the 32d until late in the campaign. There was even a serious shortage of machetes, no laughing matter in the Papuan coastal jungle.

MacArthur, one of the most meticulous generals in history, knew of these shortcomings. However, events flowed in such a way that he believed he was forced to deploy his first American divisions before it was ready. Generals often talk of the military "initiative." It is a simple concept but critical. Simply put, the side with the initiative "moves" and the enemy "responds." Freedom of action lies on the side with the initiative. In late 1942, the initiative was in a state of flux in Papua. On one hand, the Japanese had driven across the Kokoda Trail. On the other, the Australians had blunted the immediate threat to Port Moresby. MacArthur, however, feared that the Japanese might triumph at Guadalcanal. If they did so, and they still controlled Buna, a much larger attack on Papua would come quickly. This led to an extremely complicated equation. MacArthur could gather the 32d Division, minus its artillery, tanks, and engineering equipment, and send it around the coast of Papua toward Buna and strike the Japanese from the rear. (This potential frightened Imperial headquarters very much.) However, if he moved too quickly, before the Australians were over the Kokoda Trail in force, the very real possibility existed that the Japanese might throw everything they had into Buna and crush the 32d. The Australians, too, feared Japanese reinforcement and wanted to push the Japanese out of Buna. But they also agreed that the Americans should not move until the Australians were in striking distance.

Therefore, the 32d Division faced the worst of all possible worlds. It was deployed too soon to New Guinea, before MacArthur's staff had decided what to do with it. Most of the division ended up via air and sea movement near the Papuan costal village of

Pongani (a native term meaning "fever ridge"). Here many of the men vegetated for a month, growing sick, bored, and disoriented. In addition, the supply situation at Pongani, as later was the case at Buna, was miserable. Nature had another trick to play in this part of the South Pacific. The miserably charted Papuan coastline from Milne Bay to Buna was thick with coral reefs. No ship, even a small one, would go near it until it was properly charted. (This explains why the troops at Buna were both badly supplied and had no naval artillery support. One American destroyer off the Papuan coastline delivering periodic bombardments might have shortened the campaign by weeks. A massed bombardment would have flattened much of the Japanese positions. Because of the high water table, most Japanese pillboxes were above ground and very vulnerable to the terrific punch of naval artillery.) At the time there were no shallow-draft landing craft in Papua, so the Americans had to rely on a ridiculous little navy purchased from local fishermen and merchants. To add salt to the wounds already accumulating on the 32d, an American South Seas explorer was commissioned to lead the motley fleet: he was killed along with several others, including a *New York Times* correspondent, on his first voyage when his boats were bombed by a U.S. B-25. One sophisticated landing craft of the type that was already in the pipeline heading toward the South Pacific would have transformed operations for the 32d. As it was, MacArthur's headquarters would not allow Harding to bring up artillery. They doubted it could be manhandled near Buna, and also doubted that it could be supplied. Harding managed to dig up two miserable pack howitzers and was promised four Australian field pieces. Engineers, who would be sorely needed in the Buna swamps, advanced without shovels, picks, or a single block and tackle. This was very bad news for an Army that depended upon artillery for punch and engineers for a multitude of tasks. When the men finally moved forward, already sick and hungry, they had poorer arms than those their fathers had carried to France.

The 32d also suffered from a self-inflicted wound. Australian and American intelligence were uncertain about Japanese strength in the Buna area. They knew that the remnants of the Japanese South Seas

Detachment were in very bad shape. However, MacArthur's head-quarters correctly believed that the Japanese had slipped in rein-forcements to the Buna area. Harding had established his own sources. Relying far too much on air photos and, even worse, on native reports, Harding concluded that the Japanese had evacuated troops. Division intelligence estimated that there might be as few as 500 Japanese in the entire area. Harding openly talked about a forty-eight-hour campaign. In fact, the Japanese had built up substantially. All the Japanese engineers who had failed to build a road to Kokoda had instead turned the Buna area into a honeycomb of field fortifica-tions. In addition, Japanese engineers and service troops were fully combat trained. They were joined in the Buna area by Army rein-forcements and by Japanese naval troops. (Japanese naval troops are frequently referred to as Japanese marines. The parallel is inappro-priate. They were good troops, whose specialty was defense. There were a small number of elite assault units, but most shock units be-longed to the Army. Their closest equivalent in the U.S. military were the Marine defense battalions.) Days before the 32d began their attack, remnants of the South Seas Detachment also straggled in. In all, Japanese strength was approximately 6,500–7,500 men. Half were fresh reinforcements, and more arrived during the battle.

The Japanese constructed some of the finest field fortifications in World War II at Gona-Buna. The coastal sector covered was approx-imately eleven miles. On the extreme right was Gona. On the extreme left was Cape Endaiadere. In between these points the Jap-anese held coastal positions at Sanananda, Giruwa, and Buna. The Japanese line snaked along the coast, but extended out approximately four miles in the middle and curved back to the coast. Except along the coastline itself, all this terrain was jungle swamp, the worst fight-ing terrain on earth. The swamp was intersected by several tracks heading toward the costal positions from Kokoda. These were obvi-ous, in some cases essential, lines of approach. In military terms, the Allied advance was "channeled" into very predictable directions. The Australians, and one regiment of the 32d under their com-mand, marched down from Kokoda toward Gona and Sanananda. Other elements of the 32d approached Buna from the same direction. The remainder of the division moved up the coast toward Buna. It all looked good on paper. Waiting for them, however, were scores of snipers, well-placed artillery, and hidden machine-gun nests with prepared fields of fire.

The advance of the 32d Division began with a debacle. Their lead elements in the coast drive moved up by boat and schooner to a point close to Buna where they would off-load and march to battle. Dick Randles describes their boat trip:

> We were in those little trawlers going up the coast. As soon as our fighter escort left us, the Zeros came in. They were so close you could see their faces in the airplanes. They sank all the boats with cannon fire and bombs. Then they started strafing the men in the water. Amazingly, there were very few killed. A lot of luck was involved. It's actually pretty hard to hit someone in the water. You see them diving at you, and you duck under the water. It sounds like someone is pounding a typewriter right over you. Then you come up. I lived, but they sank all the boats, and all the supplies on them. There were no lifeboats, so I swam to shore. I landed in New Guinea naked with no weapon or anything. Fortunately, I was under a thatched hut; raised on stilts. A colonel had his HQ there. He didn't like me being there naked, so I got some pants. Later I found out that my mother knew the colonel quite well in the American Legion auxiliary. If I'd known that, I'd probably got a shirt and who knows what else. Maybe a better job too. At least a cup of coffee. The next morning I was issued a combat blouse, some shoes, and a weapon, and sent to my unit on the front. We were close enough to walk.

The boats sunk by Zeros had many of the 32d's basic supplies, which were short to begin with. At least the inland assault did not have to swim to Buna. Ernest Gerber's men were marching down from the landing strip near the Kokoda Trail to assault the Japanese from the west. He describes the opening days:

> My company walked down a trail toward the Triangle [one of the most difficult Japanese strong points—EB]. We were feeling easy about the whole thing. We had run into one or two Japs along

the way and had killed them. We thought this was going to be a snap, you know. When we hit the Triangle, where the Japanese were solidly entrenched, we immediately had two or three soldiers killed. We were going up the trail when this happened. We weren't thinking about going into the swamp. We were just going to walk up the trail and take things over. We backtracked, thinking maybe it would be a little tougher. The next day we started out again and the same thing happened. This kept up for three or four days. Then we moved into the swamps. We found out that was a losing game. It was all water, and wherever there was any high land, that's where the Japanese were dug in in their pillboxes.

In retrospect Gerber could see that many elements contributed to the wretched debacle:

I have read quite a bit of military history and I don't think anyone ever picked a worse place to fight a war than the coast of Papua. Maybe there were places as bad, but the people were probably better prepared for it.

We had been told this was going to be a pushover. It was generally believed that the Japanese there were sick, half dead, and not numerous. This was what we were told. Hell, we were whistling on the approach march. It wasn't until the end of the first week that we realized that we had a bear by the tail and no one knew what was going on. Either our intelligence was absolutely inadequate, or they were not telling us the truth. One or the other. It was true that the Japanese troops that had advanced to Port Moresby and then had retreated were in bad shape. It may be that intelligence concluded that all of the Japanese units were in the same condition. They were wrong.

The logistics broke down. All of the horror stories told about Buna were true. Mortars did not fire because they were improperly packed: they were totally saturated with water, and the ammunition was damp. The round would fire, plop out twenty feet in front of the mortar, and that was it. My brother was a machine gunner. At the time we had our ammo stored in the old World War I–style wooden boxes. Hell, they were falling apart. The rounds were encased in web links instead of metal links, and because they were so wet the extractor couldn't pull the damn things out of a belt. So you couldn't fire your machine guns. Things like that mount up.

The only way they could resupply us was by airdrop. They had no parachutes suited to the task, so they dropped them free-fall. They would fly as low as possible, and kick things out of the plane. We got M1 ammo in 120-pound boxes; they dropped the damn things free-fall, we'd unpack them and we'd find the ammunition was squashed: it wouldn't fit into the chamber of the rifle. It was worthless. You wouldn't believe it, but it was true.

We didn't understand jungle warfare either. Worse yet, we didn't understand the Japanese. We thought the war would be fought by gentlemen. When a guy had enough, he'd give up and that was it. That's not how it was. We found that out very quickly.

MacArthur was very disappointed in the Buna operation. Headquarters officers, knowing little of the local conditions, came back with reports of units unwilling to press the advance. In war, this normally results in a command change. MacArthur replaced Harding, and put Lieutenant General Robert L. Eichelberger in his place. (On paper, Eichelberger commanded an American corps that included the 32d and 41st divisions. The 41st was still deploying, so his position was ambiguous at MacArthur's headquarters. Under normal circumstances, a new major general would have been brought in to relieve Harding. MacArthur trusted Eichelberger, however, and time was of the essence. Eichelberger, therefore, took over direct control of operations. In the long run he proved an excellent commander.) Anxious to show that a new spirit existed, Eichelberger ordered a major new attack in early December that was shot to ribbons. The failure had one unexpected result. One platoon wisely neglected the target Eichelberger gave them and probed for a line through Japanese positions. Led by a Sergeant Herman Bottcher, a veteran of the Abraham Lincoln Brigade during the Spanish Civil War, the platoon broke through to the beach and set up a position. Japanese counterattacks failed, and Buna village, a good portion of the Japanese position in the south, was isolated. Eichelberger learned fast. He decided against any more frontal attacks. Australian reinforcements were coming with some tanks. In the meantime, the Americans would try to patrol, probe, and wear down the enemy. The question, of course, was who would wear down first.

The Allies were fortunate in one way. Close air support at Buna was a miserable failure. Even the famous Australian Wirraway (an American training aircraft modified for light attack missions by the Australians) could do little near Sanananda. The terrain was far too dense, and the sides too close for effective attack. This gave ground forces the very mistaken opinion that the U.S. Fifth Air Force was not assisting. In reality, Air Force bombers hit coastal positions day in and day out. As the jungle foliage was slowly blown away, heavy mortars became much more useful. They also made resupply extremely difficult for the Japanese. Medium and heavy bombers attacking day and night dispersed three Japanese supply convoys bound for Gona with fresh troops. The troops that got through landed to the north of the battlefield, and were smashed by the Australians when they tried to lift the siege.

The Allies were winning the battle, but the men on the spot could hardly know it. Henry Dearchs served with a platoon near the Japanese strong point, enclosed between two creeks, called the Triangle. He describes approximately a month of dangerous, and usually futile, activity:

> Eichelberger's attack was a massacre. The orders went out to attack today at 8:00. A lot of us ignored the orders. I knew a captain, a company commander, who shot himself through both hands because he couldn't send his men forward, boys he had trained for years, out to die.
>
> We resorted to what we called "Indian fighting." A lot of us were hunters, which was a very good background for this kind of fighting. The town guys would get lost and were scared to death. Patrols were the main business of my intelligence section. On single tracks we were staggered and never bunched up. In the open, we would stagger sideways. We quickly found that if there was an opening in the jungle, the Japs didn't shoot at the first

guy. They'd let you all come in before firing. But realistically, we found bunkers by losing men. A lot of guys "almost made it" to drop a grenade in a bunker, but they stayed there. You had to be careful. There was one particular clearing that was extremely dangerous: several guys that stepped into it dropped right there, with a bullet in the forehead.

When the 127th [the last fresh unit of the 32d Division—EB] came up they were told not to talk to us. The officers told them we were goof-offs. We'd tell them that they were in a big hurry to get killed. They didn't know then what we did. You had to be cautious. But it is true that some of the men were breaking down. The older men were not good as soldiers, they weren't strong or daring enough.

Of course we weren't quite as anxious to take chances as when we first went up there. Boys were sitting around trees crying. Their buddies had fallen on both sides right and left. Let me tell you, there is such a thing as combat fatigue. Even back at headquarters, you'd wonder if you'd wake up alive or not. At night you couldn't see or move. You feared the Japanese and you feared our own troops. It was easy to get shot at night by one of your own. So we were always tense, always tired. We used to say that "we're driving the Japs nuts: they're trying to figure out what we're doing and we don't know ourselves."

Ernest Gerber, who was also at the Triangle, recalls another condition at Buna that strains credulity in retrospect. The entire 32d Division was supported by *one* 105mm howitzer. The handful of Australian "twenty-five-pounders" were low-trajectory weapons meant for antitank or direct fire. (Some Australian gunners proved very good at targeting individual Japanese artillery positions. In general, however, the twenty-five was not well suited to the conditions at Buna.) Plunging artillery fire, which could have obliterated a coconut-log emplacement, was there only in comic quantities:

We had no real artillery besides our mortars. There was a battery of Australian equivalents of our 75mms. The problem was supply. Their guns were airdropped. But supplying them with ammunition was another problem altogether. In North Africa or Europe, during artillery preparation before an attack, they would drop tons and tons of explosive on one mile of line. If we got a salvo of five or six rounds, that was about it. That's about enough to find the proper range. By the time you got zeroed in, you were out of ammo. The terrain made it less valuable too. How do you adjust artillery fire if you can't see where the rounds are landing? It was almost useless.

Dick Randles was along the coast. Although the terrain differed, the tactical situation was equally painful and frustrating:

On the coast, there was nothing you could really call a front. There were people in little slit trenches. When you walked up there, they told you to get down. The snipers were shooting at you. This was on the coast. Just south of the Duropa plantation. The ground was level, a swamp to the left. It was down on the plain. This was a coconut plantation. The snipers were up in the coconut trees. You can't see the snipers. You shoot at the trees, but you've only got so much ammunition, so you can't just blindly shoot. We didn't have the slightest idea of what was in front of us: not the slightest idea. Our unit was acting in the dark. We were hung up for days and days. You'd get up in the morning, do a little patrol, and look around. Once in a while you'd get a shot at someone going to the chow line in the Japanese communication trenches. You'd look for that, but you still didn't know what they were doing. The front did not move. It was stagnant within fifty to a hundred feet for weeks. There was no way to move. We were not equipped to do it. We couldn't get artillery fire. We were too close to the Jap line. We could get mortar fire in on them, but that didn't do much good. You couldn't see the Japanese positions, but they had their fire lanes cleared. They knew what we were doing all the time. Funny thing, though, I saw live Japanese often. Some guy walking along the trenches. Going from bunker to bunker. If the Japs got down on all fours, we couldn't see them, but they'd be in the water. It was that close to sea level. They'd get lazy and walk around. As soon as you'd see one, you'd blast away. They'd fall right away, but you never

knew if you'd hit him or not. All this time we were taking
casualties.

Randles also expresses bitterness at one of the biggest failings
made by the American high command: the failure to bring in tanks.
MacArthur's headquarters did not believe that the 32d could bring in
artillery, much less tanks. American ingenuity and engineering skills,
which paid off so often, were absent on this occasion. The Australians, known more for their fighting skills than logistics magic, believed it could be done and events proved them right. Slowly a
motley collection of barges shipped a dozen American-built light
tanks to a point near the 32d Division's position on the coast. Randall
describes the result:

> All we needed were some tanks. The tanks had a little 37mm
> cannon and that's all it took. If we could have gotten some more
> cannon up there ourselves, maybe we could have done it without
> tanks. But the tanks could move. Eventually that's all it took.
> Four little tanks broke the position.
>   The Australians brought up some light tanks. We pulled back
> and they went right through our position. We left our holes and
> pulled back about 100 yards right before daylight. The Austra-
> lians laid down an artillery barrage, it was really the first artillery
> barrage those Japs had felt on those positions. After we fell back
> we followed the Aussie tanks through. I don't think the fighting
> lasted more than two hours. They went through those pillboxes
> in almost no time. That's all it took. Then we were able to see
> what we had been facing.

Randles simplifies somewhat. The tank assault on December 15
was a tough fight that included twelve tanks. It is very possible that
Randles saw only a portion of it. The tanks had difficulties, and Australian infantry casualties were heavy. Yet, as indicated by Randles, it
was doom for the Japanese at Buna. General Eichelberger described
the attack soon after the war:

> It was a spectacular and dramatic assault, and a brave one. Amer-
> ican troops wheeled to the west in support, and other Americans

were assigned to mopping-up duties. But behind the tanks went the fresh and jaunty Aussie veterans, tall, mustached, erect, with their blazing Tommy-guns swinging before them. Concealed Japanese positions—which were even more formidable than our patrols had indicated—burst into flame. There was the greasy smell of tracer fire and heavy machine-gun fire from barricades and entrenchments. Steadily tanks and infantrymen advanced through the spare, high coconut trees, seemingly impervious to the heavy opposition.

The Australians had to husband their armor and use it wisely, but the December 15 assault was only the first. It was dangerous duty, and the Australians, like the Americans, had not yet developed proper jungle tactics for armor. Some assaults failed. But in subsequent attacks Australian tanks dealt more heavy blows to the Japanese.

As the battle for Buna-Gona wound down, the 41st Division got its baptism of fire. The 41st was deployed near Sanananda, the scene of the worst fighting in the Buna area. It relieved a regiment of the 32d that had been under Australian command. The major position it took over resulted from one of the best moves made by men of the 32d Division. As often happened in that sector, the small coup resulted from an accident. The Sanananda Track ran through the worst swamp in the area. The Japanese, simply enough, defended the position by blocking the track. When the 32d arrived, the Australians, already tired from Kokoda, and battered at the Sanananda Track, encouraged the Americans to try their luck. Due to both luck and tenacity, an American patrol under Meredith Huggins got behind the Japanese position and established a roadblock. Huggins Roadblock, as the position was soon called, became a key position on the bizarre battlefield of the Sanananda Track. Later we shall look at that corner of New Guinea in more detail.

In an area so ugly that not even tanks could penetrate, it took all the formidable skills of the Australian infantry to chip away at the Japanese positions. Americans lacked their experience and battle technique. They also had a more measured and less aggressive style of combat, which frustrated Australian commanders. Australians fought harder, but often paid the price for it. (I shall examine this subject later.) When a unit from the 41st took over the Huggins Roadblock, the Australians pressed them hard to attack out of it. The Japanese position was beginning to come unglued, but the enemy along the Sanananda Track had one more battle left. Because of Australian concerns, Eichelberger and Major General George Vasey, the excellent commander of the Australian 7th Division, went forward to Huggins to call on Major General Jens Doe, commander of the 41st Division, who was at Huggins. Eichelberger's description of the meeting illustrates that New Guinea was not a safe place for generals:

> We went up the Sanananda Trail. American soldiers were lying across the road and firing; there was also American and Japanese firing behind us. Vasey and I crawled down into a trench. This was Doe's command post. It had a roof of sorts and revetments to protect it. I said, "Where are the Japs?" Doe answered, "Right over there. See that bunker?" I saw it and Vasey saw it and it was only fifty yards away. Doe was in the front line and so were we. He gave us some hot tea and then went on with the attack. Vasey was satisfied with Doe's determination and so was I.

The next day, as we shall examine later, Doe's men pushed through the Japanese position and participated in the violent task of "mopping up" that miserable place.

In all, the men serving in the 32d National Guard Division did a very good job. They were not ready for what was to take place and paid dearly. Yet they were the victims of events well out of their control. Only on the matter of intelligence estimates did the 32d command do badly. The division was shattered by the jungle. It suffered 680 men killed, which was bad enough, but also had one of the worst disease-related casualty rates in modern American military history. For instance, the regiment at Huggins that angered the Australians started the campaign with 3,100 men. In late January, there were 600 effective.

It is very hard to judge the military performance of the division because of the extraordinary difficulties it faced without the tools of modern war. Buna was the last location in the South Pacific where a commander would have wanted to fight it out with the Japanese using light-infantry weapons. Nevertheless, the soldiers of the 32d kept up the pressure and weakened the Japanese position on the coast and at Huggins. The Japanese lost hundreds of soldiers fighting the 32d, men who could have been deployed against the Australians.

More important, the 32d did not cave in. No American division in the South Pacific faced a worse military situation. Despite the tactical nightmare, the 32d showed more tenacity than did the other two Guard divisions that faced their first battle in the Solomons six months after Buna. No doubt this is a credit to the men and officers of the 32d. Although the men of the 32d resented MacArthur's treatment of them, General Eichelberger played his role well. However, it is also clear that the presence of the Australians was critical, not just for the campaign, which was mostly theirs, but for the well-being of the 32d. Just as the Marines helped the American, the Australians helped orient the 32d Division into the nightmare world of jungle warfare. It is no accident that the 32d served with great distinction in its many other battles.

MacArthur was mortified by Buna. He was determined never again to assault an enemy position directly. Within months, American forces were strong enough that he did not have to. Remarkably, however, the lessons of Buna did not circulate into the Solomons. Despite the obvious defects revealed in the 32d Division's preparations for jungle fighting, the Navy launched two untested Guard divisions against New Georgia, a loathsome place that proved very nearly as difficult as Gona-Buna. In the process, they lost almost as many men as the Marines and Army had on Guadalcanal and more than the 32d lost at Buna.

One culprit was Admiral Halsey. On balance, Halsey was one of the finest admirals in modern history. As shown on Guadalcanal, Halsey had an unusual combination of aggressiveness, operation competence, and ability to inspire those under him. Ironically, caution got the better of Halsey and his staff after Guadalcanal. This is understandable. Halsey was an admiral, and much of the American fleet was at the bottom of the ocean off Guadalcanal. When he was planning future actions in the first weeks of 1943, the Japanese Navy and Naval Air Force remained in fact very strong and appeared stronger yet. In addition, as Americans moved up the Solomons, they moved toward the enemy's bases at Truk-Rabaul and away from their own. Locations for air bases in the Solomons were very limited and it was most reasonable to seize a good one to support further operations toward Rabaul. Bombers could attack Rabaul and Bougainville from Guadalcanal. Fighters, however, had less range and were far more effective if closer to the objective. The only suitable place, or so it seemed, for a major air base between Guadalcanal and Bougainville was the Japanese landing strip at Munda Point on the island of New Georgia.

At the same time that Halsey's staff argued the importance of seizing another air base, they also underestimated Japanese strength on New Georgia, which they put at approximately 4,000 men. Ignorance of the basic geography was not the problem on New Georgia that it had been on Guadalcanal. New Georgia and the smaller islands nearby covered much territory, and the Japanese controlled only a small portion. As noted in Chapter 1, a New Zealand coast watcher operated openly at one tip of the island. Consequently, American intelligence sent reconnaissance groups to New Georgia that traveled throughout the island. This was how they found the landing beach. Two weeks before the landing, patrols went ashore secretly to chart Japanese positions near Munda Point.

What Halsey's planners did not appreciate was Tokyo's determination to hold New Georgia. After their defeats on Guadalcanal and Papua, the Japanese became very fearful about the theater. Some officers in Tokyo argued that the Allies would not launch a major offensive in the Solomons. The Japanese anticipated that the Americans would make their major thrust through the Central Pacific because it was the most direct route to Japan. In the spring of 1943, however, Tokyo realized that the Allies were going to move forward in the South Pacific. They also knew that if the Allies pushed past Rabaul, the Japanese empire in Southeast Asia, upon which their war economy depended, was finished. The Japanese, therefore, decided to defend every possible position. Their only hope was to delay the American advance to allow them time to rebuild Japanese naval and air forces for a great "decisive battle" in the future. As it proved, Japanese infantry was ideal for defensive battle.

Therefore, the American estimate of approximately 4,000 troops on New Georgia, most of them near Munda, was correct when originally made. However, the Japanese brought reinforcements in from Bougainville. It was very hard for American intelligence to track this concentration. During the reinforcement phase of the Guadalcanal campaign, the Japanese had strengthened some of the small outposts they had established throughout the Solomons in the spring of 1942. After the defeat at Guadalcanal, the Japanese reinforced several of these positions further. Consequently, the Japanese had a network of small bases that they could use to shuttle small vessels and barges at night through the Solomons. The Japanese garrison on New Georgia, therefore, was closer to 8,000. To make things worse, the Japanese commander on the spot, Major General Noboru Sasaki, proved the finest field commander faced by the Americans in the South Pacific.

The disaster that followed may not have been necessary. Both MacArthur and Nimitz had argued that Halsey could bypass New Georgia and attack Bougainville directly. Munda itself was no threat. As events proved, it was simple enough to land American heavy artillery on neighboring Rendova Island and put Munda under heavy artillery fire. Furthermore, the Americans seized a small fighter strip at Segi Point, on the southeastern end of the island, with no opposition. They grabbed another on Vella Lavella with little fighting. Part of the objective, therefore, was obtainable with small loss. Just as important, much changed in the South Pacific between the end of the Guadalcanal campaign in January 1943 and July when the Americans attacked New Georgia. American support units were flooding in. One of the biggest problems in the South Pacific was the supply logjam that took place at Espiritu Santo, New Caledonia, and Guadalcanal. American units would not have to fight on a shoestring again in the Solomons. The Japanese Navy suffered serious losses in late 1942, and they continued in the following year. The Americans, on the other hand, began replacing the ships sunk off Guadalcanal. Washington finally authorized large number of modern planes for American fighter squadrons in the South Pacific. The strategic balance was shifting against the Japanese rapidly. The pace was so quick, however, that Halsey's staff could not properly keep up with it. Halsey underestimated the power at his disposal and played it safe. So the attack went forward.

When Halsey began the offensive against New Georgia in early July, he intended to use the inexperienced 43d Infantry Division supported by two Marine Raider battalions and a Marine defense battalion. Powerful air support came from Guadalcanal, and warships pummeled the shore. After picking off the airstrip at Segi Point, the Raiders landed in the north, bogged down, and never captured a concentration of Japanese coastal artillery that was their objective. The 43d Division, despite powerful support from Marine artillery, stopped cold within hours of landing. The terrain they faced was extremely vile, as bad or worse than that on Guadalcanal. As they inched forward toward Munda Point the men of the 43d confronted cunning defensive positions and sniper patrols in the daylight. At night, small but sharp Japanese counterattacks drove some of the units to a state of paralysis. Although many companies and platoons fought well, others were confused and helpless. The severe confusion that afflicted much of the division reflected inadequate leadership layered from top to bottom. Halsey decided to bring in the 37th Division, another Guard unit without experience. The 37th performed better, but likewise found the advance painfully slow. Although American troops heavily outnumbered the Japanese, and had far better support than U.S. ground forces earlier had on Guadalcanal, they still could not break through to Munda. The jungle, which had been an ally on Guadalcanal, was an enemy on New Georgia. Nevertheless, slowly the weight of numbers began to tell and the 43d moved closer to Munda Point, seven miles from their original landing. Yet Halsey wasn't taking any chances and deployed part of the 25th Division.

The 25th Division had a very tough time on New Georgia. If a defender is willing to fight in tough terrain, there are never easy answers. Nevertheless, Collins's troops steadily achieved their objectives one after another with limited cost. Toward the end of the campaign, the veteran 27th Regiment broke out of the Munda area and made contact with the Marine Raider battalions still bogged down in the north. The 161st Regiment, the least experienced in the 25th, fought next to the 37th. Where possible, the 25th used some of the small number of Marine tanks available, and would have been glad for more. The 25th also employed the combination of flame-throwers and massed heavy-weapons fire against Japanese dugouts with deadly effect. Late in the campaign, the 25th had a nasty battle with the Japanese on the little island of Arundel. Its seizure put the large Japanese garrison on Kolombangara within range of the Marine 155mm "Long Tom" artillery pieces. Lastly, Halsey used the 35th Regiment, the 25th's most experienced unit, to bypass the New Georgia position completely by landing on the island of Vella Lavella. Because it was lightly defended, the Americans and New Zealand assault forces had little trouble taking the island. Strategically, however, it ended the campaign. Fearing that the Americans might isolate all Japanese troops in the central Solomons, the Japanese Navy embarked on a hurried, skillful, and ultimately successful operation to withdraw most of its troops.

On August 5 the 43d Division finally captured Munda Point. In light of the 25th's successes with armor on New Georgia, some of the later attacks against Japanese pillboxes were made with the support of Marine light tanks. Although the techniques involved were very tricky, tank attacks frequently yielded tremendous results. Like the single tank that cracked the Gifu Strong Point on Guadalcanal, and the Australian tanks at Buna, a handful of the same vehicles proved priceless on New Georgia. The Army finally learned the lesson. After New Georgia, armor accompanied the Army and Marines whenever possible. Within months the first medium tanks, M4 Shermans, arrived in the theater. Far harder to destroy than the light tanks used by the Australians and Marines, Shermans found plenty of work in the Pacific war. Nevertheless, during the New Georgia campaign, the military's mistaken insistence that tanks could not be widely employed in the jungle cost the infantry dearly once again.

So too did Halsey's decision not to use the 25th Division at the outset. Every American unit had a tough time on New Georgia, but the combat edge possessed by the 25th was far superior to other Army units. The experience on Guadalcanal had shown the great importance of orientation to battle conditions. It had also shown the value of having an experienced unit and excellent leadership in the extremely difficult early days on the battlefield faced by all green units. This lesson was ignored totally on New Georgia. Halsey gave the 43d Division an extremely hard objective on one of the worst pieces of real estate in the South Pacific. It was one of the last places on earth to send a unit for initiation into the World War II charnel house. After reconstruction and leave, the 43d and 37th both returned to action in the South Pacific. The Army replaced many of the officers and men who could not face the wretched world of combat in the jungle. The core that remained were those who could. They passed on their lessons to the replacements. When the two divisions went back into action they served very well.

New Georgia was a tactical victory for the United States, but a strategic failure. The operation took two months, cost more than 1,000 men killed in action, and inevitably flattened the three divisions employed simply because they had to fight in the jungle. Japanese losses were somewhat higher, but that was irrelevant. They evacuated most of their troops from the New Georgia area successfully. Some fought another day. They also caused Halsey to deploy and damage the 37th and 25th, two divisions he did not want to use, and thus slowed the next move to Bougainville.

After the great victory at Guadalcanal, the shaky outings at Buna and New Georgia served as clear reminders that not all American ground forces had the edge to survive in the South Pacific. New Georgia, unlike Guadalcanal or Buna, was well supported by artillery, naval bombardment, and air attack. No doubt shortages of everything still existed. The hideous terrain in the South Pacific always created a new surprise. The 25th Division at New Georgia, for instance, had found itself in great need of small boats for supply and casualty evacuation. Yet the American supply coffers were filling. What the Americans needed, and to a large extent received the hard way, was combat experience, battle orientation, and better command. They required the skills, in other words, already possessed in surplus by the magnificent Australian infantry.

The Aussies

On April 25 the Australians celebrate ANZAC Day. It commemorates the initial landing made by Australian troops at Gallipoli in 1915. Despite astounding bravery on the part of Australian troops, the Gallipoli expedition failed. The blood shed there stunned the small population of Australia and united the country in grief. Consequently, every year in towns and cities veterans of military service put on their ribbons and parade. Bands play military music, but there are no floats or old cars, the sorts of things that give a July 4th parade in the United States an irreverent and festive air. As I write, pride of place on ANZAC Day goes to the veterans of World War II. If a veteran has passed on, a descendant may wear the service ribbons or decorations. The large and vigorous veterans' organizations in Australia take particular pains to make the day special. The Australians are one of the few people in the world that celebrate a defeat. It is a country that takes war very seriously.

The passage of time compresses events in the perception of present observers. While people are most aware of what might be considered the recent past of their own time, it is easy to forget that previous generations had the same concept. The end of the Vietnam War, to many Americans, is not "history" as much as "current events" in the past tense. Issues concerning Vietnam still raise their head with regularity in American domestic and foreign politics.

To understand the generation that fought World War II, one must begin with the realization that World War I had ended only twenty years before Hitler invaded Poland. The Great War had been the Western world's greatest calamity until that time and it cast a long and very dark shadow over the nations that went to war in 1939.

Memories were fresh of the Marne, Verdun, and the Somme. The wisest and most sensitive individuals in the Western world realized that the second round would prove more violent, destructive, and painful than the first. They were right.

Searing memory of national trauma likewise shaped the political response to the coming of World War II in Australia. Australia had sent a large expeditionary force to Europe during World War I. It was an unusual encounter. Australia's military structure and tradition resembled that of nineteenth-century America with its hallowed local militias far more than it did any found in Europe. Unlike the European combatants, Australia had no large standing army or powerful navy. Nor did it have any experience in land war on a massive scale. Although Australian history has had more than its share of discord and regional disputes, there was no Australian equivalent of the American Civil War.

Despite these factors, the Australians raised a large force that fought with valor and skill. The Australians lacked the stoic courage of the English or French, and certainly never developed Prussian discipline. The qualities of the Australian Imperial Forces (AIF), the term used for the expeditionary army in both world wars, came from an individually generated sense of bravery coupled with great individual initiative. From a technical point of view, lack of institutional experience proved in many ways a great advantage. The soldiers in the trenches were writing their own book, just as their sons did in the jungles of New Guinea. It is no accident that Sir John Monash, arguably the finest Allied general on the Western Front, was Australian. Thrown into this brew was an intense loyalty and identification with the unit. Loyalty to one's "mates" was deep and the perfect counterpoint to the Australian's famous individualism. In this regard, perhaps, Australia showed its kinship with England. The locally recruited units that made up the backbone of the British Army closely resembled those found in the Australian. When push came to shove, Australian troops fought with ingenuity and an unusual ferocity. No wonder they were so coveted by British generals. In 1918 the Australians arguably were the best infantry in Europe.

There was, however, a unique component in Australia's experience during World War I. Australia entered the war willingly to fulfill what it believed to be its obligation to the British Empire, of which it still felt a part. It is true that the Germans had a colony in New Guinea, which a later generation of Australian infantry learned to know well, but Australia was under no threat. Japan was a British ally, the United States friendly, and Germany very far away. A victory on the part of Berlin would have raised no immediate danger to Australia. Only the total devastation of Britain itself might have been construed as threatening in the long run, but that was not a realistic outcome of the war.

In short, there was no compelling reason of state, or national insult similar to the German submarine campaign that drew the United States into the conflict, to explain Australia's large contribution to the British war effort. Australian honor and commitments could have been upheld by a force far smaller. Instead, Australia became a significant belligerent despite its small population. There was little to gain for the country in the trenches. There was, as Australians found out, much to lose. Although the AIF fought extremely well, military skill could not nullify the central reality of the Great War: the trenches meant death. Australia, like Britain and France, lost a generation of young men in Turkey and France. At the time, Australia's population was approximately 5 million. Out of a force of 330,000 men that left for Europe, 60,000 were killed in battle and 165,000 wounded. It was one of the highest casualty rates suffered on the Western Front.

Whether or not the vigorous effort was worth the frightful cost was a burning issue within Australia during the war. It was intimately connected with the larger, and also emotional, issue of Australia's relationships with Britain and the outside world. The AIF was volunteer. Attempts to push through a conscription law failed. (Membership in the local Militia was compulsory.) It is commonly said that Australia's participation in the Great War strengthened its identity as a nation. Perhaps this is true. Yet war is almost always destructive to political institutions. Australians after the Armistice had to ponder the question of whether they had thrown away the lives of tens of thousands of their young men to save the British Empire. It is, I think, noteworthy that Australians made April 25, the start of the Gallipoli debacle, and not November 11, the end of the war, the day to honor. By doing so, they commemorated the pain rather than the victory that resulted from it.

As Australia proceeded into the political mire that engulfed most of the world between the world wars, the nation was greatly confused. Understandably, Australians were intensely proud of their men's military achievements. They were also very reluctant to go through the act again. Strains of isolationism from both left and right in the political spectrum were deeply held. The Australian government during the political crisis of the late 1930s gave strong support to British prime minister Neville Chamberlain's policy of appeasement. When war came, Australia, like Canada, declared war on Germany. Yet, in marked contrast to the war enthusiasm of 1914, the country looked at the prospect of more bloodletting with little enthusiasm. Indeed, because there was no equivalent of Pearl Harbor for Australia, the country remained deeply divided on what it should do. Many believed, like their isolationist counterparts in America, that Australian soldiers would once again be fodder for British interests.

Sadly and without enthusiasm, the Australian government prepared for war. The Australian military was divided into two parts. As in World War I, Canberra recruited a new AIF. Enlistments were initially tepid. The fall of France and the Battle of Britain, however, shocked Australia profoundly. The notion of the swastika flying over Westminster was noxious and enlistments in the AIF soared. Soon three full divisions were on their way to Europe. Many other Australians and New Zealanders also served directly in the Royal Navy and Royal Air Force.

Nevertheless, most Australians served in the Militia. Locally recruited and indifferently trained during peacetime, the Militia invites comparison with the peacetime U.S. National Guard. The job of the Militia was the defense of Australia. This was an issue that had never arisen previously. Geography and the British fleet had kept Australia free of invasion throughout its history. However, people wishing to look down the road had serious qualms about Japan. Japan was no longer an ally, as it had been in 1914. The imposing U.S. Pacific Fleet was a comforting presence, but this time Australia had a potential enemy in Asia. Others in Canberra were sanguine about Japan. Distances are large in Asia. Japan was fighting in China thousands of miles away. The British Empire was intact. World War II, at the beginning, was not a war of national existence. The Militia served to defuse active political opposition to the war effort. Service in the Militia was not particularly onerous, one did not go far from home, and exemptions to service abounded. Units that were called up for more or less permanent duty were allowed long-term leave during harvest. Most important, Militia units were not to serve outside Australia or territory administered by Australia. As long as the war remained isolated to Europe, participation was strictly voluntary.

This changed rapidly after Pearl Harbor. Worried about the influx of the best young men to the AIF, the government forbade the enlistment of Militia soldiers in the expeditionary force. They also recalled dozens of experienced officers from the Mideast to take command of Militia units. For their part, Militia battalions began exercising in large groups, eventually leading to the creation of divisions. The production and provision of basic weapons increased greatly and by mid-1942 the Militia was a ground force to be reckoned with.

Militia units, however, still could not serve outside Australia. An exception was made, however, for battalions that consisted of a majority of men who had attempted to join the AIF. This implied a willingness to serve overseas. Fortunately, for military purposes the Australian government defined Papua as part of an Australian military district. Therefore, Militia units were there very early in the war. In May 1943 a law was passed allowing the free deployment of the Militia in New Guinea and a portion of the East Indies.

It is fashionable at present in Australia to praise the Militia. As we shall see presently, the presence of a small number of Militia units in Papua was most opportune at a dangerous hour in Australian history. Nevertheless, Australia shouldered a very large portion of the land war against Japan in 1942–43, and Australia's war in this period was fought largely by the AIF, the best infantry in the Pacific.

The AIF did not have an equivalent in the American military. In structure, it resembled a tough and highly professional National Guard. In spirit and fighting style, it was more like the U.S. Marines. More experienced, however, it had a better feel for complex operations. If there were any structural failings they are hard to identify. Perhaps, like the Marines, there were times when the AIF pushed when it should have pulled. Logistics and engineering were good, but not up to the standards of the U.S. Army. Unlike the Marines and their leaders in the U.S. Navy, the Australians were smart enough to use eagerly U.S. Army support in many ways. It is one of the curiosities of war that the AIF and the U.S. Army, if one looks below the controversies that continually revolved around MacArthur, cooperated better than did the U.S. Army and the Marines.

Although Australia's experience in large wars started in World War I, there was a deep reservoir of excellent raw material to draw on. Spaces were large in Australia, and outdoor living in one form or another was very common. Several cavalry units antedated by generations the creation of the Commonwealth in 1901. The ingenuity required on the frontier, which Australians sometimes call the "convict mentality," was very real. There was also a genuine ruggedness to the national character. Physical courage was highly prized. A broken nose was easy enough to come by in prewar Australia. In spite of the country's reputation for possessing a rough edge, or perhaps because of it, educational standards were high. Furthermore, Australia was a well-established outpost of the industrial world. Technical and mechanical skills existed in great abundance. It is, I think, safe to say that somewhere along the line the "Protestant work ethic" lost some of its intensity in Australia. An Australian infantryman who served at Milne Bay told me that they were glad to hear of the Japanese attack because that freed them from an ugly road-building detail in the mud. Soldiers who would rather fight crack Japanese assault troops than build roads win wars.

The AIF had two qualities that contributed greatly to its superiority in the Pacific. First, as much as the weight of the Great War acted to confuse and paralyze civilized governments in the interwar period, it had a very different effect on many individuals. As bad as casualties were in the trenches, most of the Australian infantry survived and returned home. The children they had were of military age in 1939. Although many Australians viewed the war as a tragedy, veterans were honored sincerely by almost everyone. An entire generation of young Australian men grew up hearing about the great Australian offensive on August 8, 1918, when General Monash's infantry, supported by machine-gun fire so densely packed it was louder than artillery fire, ripped a gaping hole through the German front. Whether they were fathers, uncles, or schoolteachers, war veterans were heroes in the eyes of many. It should not surprise us that many of the young wished to emulate the deeds of their fathers. Those that did not have a personal connection to the war were also drawn to the guns. The Australians, like everyone else, suffered from the Depression, and the future was not a limitless vista to young men. The pull of war to those of tender age was still strong in 1939. Bill Crooks served with the AIF throughout the war, and describes a bit of the milieu:

> I schooled average but loved the Army. I do *not* know why. None of our family were ever in it. My father was in for a short time in 1918, but did not get to France. I enlisted in the field artillery locally when I was thirteen, by putting up my age. I later joined the Army cadets Militia. We had horses and pretty, colorful uniforms. And the girls liked us. But for little purpose, I can tell you. I was two years in the AIF at war and was eighteen years old in the desert. I was a master marksman on the Bren machine gun, and a low-flying German bomber pulled out of a dive, with his naked underbelly showing only 300 feet away. I shot him down and killed my first seven men. The plane carried a crew of five, so two of them must have gone along for what turned into their final look-see. At the time I still thought babies came by stork or under a cabbage patch. That is a fact. God, boys are so innocent.

Like the U.S. Marine Corps, the AIF was exclusively volunteer. Because of patriotism, memories of the Great War, and the undeniable attraction of war to the young, the AIF received outstanding recruits. They also were strongly motivated young men. Australia did not have a Pearl Harbor, and the early stage of World War II did not sit well with many. Indeed, enlistments in the AIF at the outset were very modest. As noted before, the direct threat to Britain caused by the fall of France heightened enlistments. Hitler's victories in 1940 also stirred the Japanese. After Pearl Harbor, the circle was complete. The Japanese not only attacked Oahu on December 7, they also assaulted the British Empire. Among the defeated in the early Japanese offensive was the 8th AIF Division, which was part of the force that surrendered at Singapore.

As the Japanese juggernaut moved closer to Australia, the men who had joined the AIF to fight Hitler were fighting uncomfortably close to their homeland. Indeed, the Japanese drive was the reason the AIF had returned to Australia to begin with. The 6th and 7th divisions were brought back from the Mideast in early 1942, after Churchill, in a fit of madness, tried unsuccessfully to get one diverted to Burma. As noted earlier, Churchill did succeed in persuading the Australian government to allow the AIF 9th Division to stay in the Mideast temporarily. In November 1942, at the same time that AIF units in Papua were engaged in their epic struggle on the Kokoda Trail, the 9th Division played a vital role in Britain's smashing victory over the Germans at El Alamein in Egypt. In February 1943, the 9th Division left the Mideast for home and war in the South Pacific.

Although, like the Marines, a volunteer force, the AIF was also locally recruited. During World War I, the various battalions that made up the AIF divisions came from individual Australian states. The paper connection between these units and their home areas was never broken. Consequently, when recruitment began again, the same units came from the same places. This caused a unique nomenclature in Australian units. To begin with, the divisions were raised in a sequence that followed the original AIF. In World War I, the AIF raised five divisions, therefore the first AIF division raised in World War II was the 6th. (Four were raised: the 6th, 7th, 8th, and 9th. The 8th was lost at Singapore. After May 1943, the distinction between the AIF and other Australian units blurred somewhat.) Also, every battalion in the Australian military, because it was locally recruited, had an individual number. (American battalions were generic: there was a 1st, 2d, and 3d in every regiment. The regiments were unique.) All battalions of the AIF were preceded by the number "2" to designate it as belonging to the second AIF. Consequently, if one sees reference to the 2/9 Battalion, the unit in question was a crack battalion, recruited from Queensland, of the 18th Brigade, a part of the 7th Division of the AIF.

The local recruitment of AIF units had tremendous advantages for morale. Like an American Marine, an Australian infantryman was not forced by the government to serve. That fact alone is always good for discipline. (One Marine recalls that on Guadalcanal they had a sergeant who liked to preface orders with the phrase, "Up and at 'em. President Roosevelt didn't send you a personal invitation to join the Corps. You signed the line. Up and at 'em." It is an easy bet that many AIF NCOs used a similar line.) Unlike American Marines, Australian soldiers served with men from the same town or area. Frequently, friends enlisted together. Soldiers who became friends in the service often met each other's families when on leave. Every army tries to develop a deep cohesion within its fighting groups. Many Japanese units, also locally recruited, were likewise very close. However, there were few large armies that possessed the advantage of both volunteer and local recruitment. All of this contributed greatly to what one Australian I interviewed called "mateship." No nation had at its spearpoint combat units more closely tied together than did Australia. Bill Crooks describes the astounding combat morale shown by the AIF in 1942:

I never *ever* saw the Oz morale low. I never heard of it being so. When out of action, if the promised beer or smokes didn't show up, they would storm the CO's office. But *never in the field*. There was in my experience never a suggestion of "Oh, let's not go there and then say we did and dodge it." Mind you, we had our small share of shirkers. But the men and the CO soon found them out, mostly before action, and *out*: "Services no longer required." Back to a Docks Operating Company. But those that stayed you could stake your life on. And we did. It was an honor and a privilege to have served with such men.

Crooks also gives an extraordinary description of the fear and self-hatred that threatened someone who, despite his best efforts, let down the most important group in his life:

The filth, mud, exhaustion, and dread found in the jungle as we went over the Kokoda Trail drove some of our less strong soldiers, many medal winners in the desert, to total nervous breakdown. A man could be driven to weeping frustration knowing that he could not keep going. Knowing that his comrades at the time (they would not now) would be looking at him in disgust and abject pity. And they would also feel hate, knowing that there would be one less to help take a turn carrying the section machine gun and ammo, and one less to take a turn on the patrols and less time to sleep because more would have to remain on sentry. In other words the evacuee meant more work for the others, and we were never sent replacements during the Owen Stanley campaign. The World War I veterans, found in every platoon, had a particularly bad time. Many had shaped up well in Libya. But in the jungle *all* fell out. Weak and diseased men, these World War I men eager for appreciation by their fellow soldiers crumbled to collapsed crying and heartbreaking frustration because they *had to fall out*. To an infantryman this was the final insult, to lose control and be a burden requiring the services of up to sixteen native stretcher-bearers to return him to the rear.

The AIF was also an experienced force. It had left for Europe during 1940 and served first in Britain and then in the Mideast. While there, the Australians were very fortunate. First, because they were going to fight, the men received and accepted a very strenuous training program. Australian culture in this period prized physical fitness highly, so the men were prepared, if not ready for the ordeal. The Australian command was also wise enough to keep its forces on a steady training schedule while in the general battle zone. Bill Crooks casts his keen eye on this subject. Note the contrast he finds between the desert and New Guinea:

Discipline in the Aussie Army when well led and morale good never broke down in battle. Our structure was efficient and our training rigorous. When out of battle we trained far harder than the physical conditions we expected to face warranted. We kept at exercises day and night over the hardest terrain we could find. Exercises were never preplanned and we used live ammo. This hardened the men up and gave them some idea of what to expect. In battle—less the Kokoda Trail—we simply never had the continuous exhaustion we experienced in training. In other campaigns—apart from death and wounds—men would remember some terrible exercise, talk about, and say the battle is a "piece of cake." Battle was a type of anticlimax. There was fear and stress, and a well-hidden worry from newcomers that they would crack up. But all knew, and took great pride, that they were as fit and prepared as possible. We were up-to-the-minute battle-trained and able to use the correct weapon when the time came. The Owen Stanleys was a *shocker for all*.

The AIF, as was expected by everyone, the Germans included, served with distinction in North Africa. Yet it was not in combat so sustained or violent that its spirit was damaged. Battle experience is priceless up to a point. If a division is pushed too far, its efficiency and spirit drop. The Australians were in the perfect position: bloodied but not bludgeoned.

This situation aided the Australian officer corps. The standing Army in Australia was minute in 1939. The cadre remaining was excellent. They and the new officers that entered the AIF naturally learned much from the British who had in turn learned harsh lessons in France during 1940. The Australians did, however, have at their disposal thousands of men who had served as young officers in World War I. This was the norm in European armies also. Field-grade officers in the U.S. Army were likewise veterans of the trenches. However, the situation in Australia was particularly favorable. During World War I, social position was no protection for a bad officer. If a leader did not make it, he was "out the door" very quickly. Consequently, many of the men who returned to very senior positions in the AIF or the Militia not only had served in World War I as lieutenants, but had also done so with great distinction. This was a tremendous advantage when rebuilding the officer corps for the AIF.

Unlike the U.S. National Guard units, there were far more Australian officers who knew what it took to lead in combat. (Of course, they never knew until the battle started. But they could make a very educated guess.) More important, they were able to identify men who might be well suited to duties in the rear but would have been poor combat leaders. If so, they had those men sent to the rear where they could serve best. This was vital, because it is axiomatic in battle that a bad officer will do more harm to a unit than a good one will help it. In other words, it is more important to keep the fools out than get the budding geniuses in. A solid army will always find a steady supply of competent leaders if the system encourages promotion of the skilled and rapid expulsion of the incompetent. No army was more dangerous for the career of a military fool than the Australian. Few allowed good ones to rise more quickly. General Thomas Blamey, overall commander of Australian ground forces, was a partisan but competent officer. Most Australian division commanders such as Vasey of the 7th Division, and brigade commanders such as thirty-five-year-old Brigadier General Ivan Dougherty, were excellent.

The AIF was very good and they knew it. E. J. Randall served his country nearly six years in World War II, first as a comrade of Crooks in the 7th Division and later as a junior officer with a Militia unit on Bougainville. Randall puts it simply:

The original 2/9th Battalion was arguably the toughest in the AIF. In four years as a private soldier I never heard a man say he would not go forward. In those days one knew that "Bill" on your right and "Tom" on your left would also be going forward. After our serious losses at Milne Bay and Buna, reinforcements outnumbered the originals and it took some time to get the old unit feeling back. It was back by the time we moved up the Ramu Valley.

The Americans knew it too. Homer Wright, an officer with the 32d Division, flew into Port Moresby while the Japanese were still near the town. He remembers a short but telling encounter with Australian infantry:

A group of Aussies came off the track. They looked ragged but tough. Now they were beat as hell, and here we were in more or less clean uniforms going off to the front somewhere. To show off in front of the Americans they swung into a real sharp British-style march, and marched by us, eyes right. It was a hell of a gesture.

U.S. Marines and Australian infantry developed an odd affinity. They never fought on the same battlefield, but a mutual respect developed across theaters. When the U.S. 1st Marine Division was sent to recuperate in Australia after Guadalcanal, and later set up training camp there, Marines and Aussies frequently crossed paths, with a brawl or two punctuating the mutual admiration society. Marine Donald Fall expresses a common sentiment:

I fought with the 1st Marine Division from Guadalcanal until I got too close to Japanese mortar fire on Peleliu. I'm not bragging, but I think we were the best. Period. Except for maybe the Aussies. If anyone could fight as well as the Corps it was Aussies. If it was up to me they would have all been inducted into the Marines then and there.

Ernest Gerber went through the Buna campaign from start to finish with the 32d Division. As we shall see, there was an element of professional disagreement between the two armies, but Gerber's reaction is simple, to the point, and very representative: "Australian soldiers were kind and good people. The Aussies knew more than we did. Australians were the best."

Although the Australians fought with uncommon skill in the South Pacific, their battle techniques were very similar to those found in the best American units. Both armies were heavily influenced by World War I. The American Army and the Marines tried hard to keep abreast of developments in European combat after 1939 that the Australians knew firsthand. No doubt Australian tactical execution was superior to that of most American units, but the difference was a matter of degree. Like all Western armies, both the Australians and Americans put much faith in firepower. Both avoided massed assault against fortified positions whenever possible. The

Australians had somewhat less firepower in their divisions than did their American counterparts, and consequently put more stress on aggressive patrolling. Nevertheless, if they had the equipment, the Australians were quick to use all the firepower they could muster. Whatever the differences between Australian and American ground forces, they were small when compared to the yawning gap that divided the tactical doctrine used by the Allies on one hand and the Japanese on the other.

Although the military situation appeared most bleak in mid-1942 when the AIF was deploying to Australia, much had been done since Pearl Harbor to prepare for its outstanding campaigns. Many Australians would dispute the fact, but much of this preparation was the work of Douglas MacArthur, commander in chief, Southwest Pacific Theater.

MacArthur's psychology in this period of war is very interesting. On one hand, he was stung and humiliated by Japan's victory in the Philippines. He had seen firsthand the panic that had overtaken the Philippine government and could do nothing to prevent the Japanese from systematically crushing his forces on Bataan. More than anyone in the Pacific he understood the paralysis caused by the Japanese war machine as it swept through Malaya, Burma, and the Indies. It was imperative, MacArthur believed, to resist strongly at the first logical spot. Japan's designs on Port Moresby and Papua were obvious. Therefore, defending the area was a natural course of action. MacArthur personally paid much attention to the buildup of base areas in the theater. In retrospect, his attention to this type of detail was one of his greatest strengths. American engineers were among the first American troops to arrive in Australia. When the Japanese made Rabaul a major base, American and Australian engineers and Militia labor troops furiously worked to build air bases and support facilities in northern Australia. MacArthur also allocated scarce engineers and heavy equipment to building up the facilities at Port Moresby. Recall that prior to 1942 there was not a single major airfield in Papua or the Solomons, nor was there a true port.

Much controversy erupted during the war concerning the Australian government's plans during the dark days before Midway.

MacArthur later claimed, in one of the public-relations disasters that plagued his career, that the Australians were prepared to give up northern Australia and Papua if need be, and that he had changed the plan when he arrived. The Australian government denied MacArthur's charge and claimed it intended to defend every inch of Australian soil as soon as forces were available to do so. A look at the force dispositions made in Australia before the return of the AIF, however, shows northern Australia and Papua very poorly defended. MacArthur badly wanted to shift the emphasis to the north. Regardless of protestations to the contrary by Australian commanders after the fact, in the spring of 1942 there was an undeniable whiff of panic in the air. Prodding the government to spend more time developing bases in the north, and less preparing for a scorched-earth defense of Sydney, was a good policy. Naturally, there was a great deal of self-interest involved. Another battle lost, and MacArthur, who had abandoned an Army in the field, was finished.

Regardless, the man understood strategy. The allocation of resources to northern Australia and Papua greatly encouraged the rapid development of a forward defense. American engineering troops played a key role briefly in northern Australia, but were soon shifted to Papua. They were hectored continually by MacArthur. Under daily pressure from headquarters, U.S. engineers developed "no frills" air bases and installations. They used the famous steel matting that became a fixture throughout the Pacific instead of pavement. Pilots slept in tents. Australian engineers were there, too. Everyone was short of heavy equipment, but troops and contract labor with local inhabitants filled part of the void. By July 1942 northern Australia had several airfields that could accommodate bombers and large reconnaissance aircraft. Port Moresby, with three major airstrips, hosted fighters, bombers, and American transport aircraft, which were essential for ground operations on the Kokoda Trail and later Buna. A fighter base and radar station also appeared, fortunately as events proved, at Milne Bay.

By July 1942, the AIF on its way to Port Moresby would find a much better base to operate from than existed six months previously. It was also a base with a back door. Even if Papua could not be held, the stronger it was the longer it could hold out. Anything that could delay the Japanese, in the early stage of the war, was beneficial. This is why the Americans threw everything they had into northern Australia. Bases there supported Papua, but also would be invaluable in case the Japanese attacked northern Australia itself. Aircraft in northern Australia could also cover an evacuation of Papua if that was necessary. MacArthur had gone through Bataan, and the AIF had lost a division at Singapore. Although the commanders did not often talk in such terms, no one wanted to operate again without a line of retreat.

Australian commanders complained in this period to their government and each other, complaints picked up by the Australian official histories after the war, that MacArthur and his headquarters had no experience at war. They were probably venting personal displeasure with MacArthur and did not deeply hold an attitude so foolish and arrogant. The truth was precisely the opposite, and that was the point. Unlike any Australian commander, barring the men in Japanese POW camps, MacArthur and the "Bataan gang" (the uncomplimentary nickname used to describe his personal staff, in particular Generals Sutherland and Willoughby) had fought an extended campaign against the Japanese. Furthermore, MacArthur, unlike the British in Malaya, had been badly outnumbered. Also, unlike Malaya, MacArthur, after a debacle on the beachhead, had led a masterful retreat to Bataan. For weeks the Americans caused serious problems for the Japanese invaders. Had an unexpected horde of Philippine refugees not consumed the basic supplies of MacArthur's fighting units, the Americans, and the small number of steady Filipino units remaining, might have held out much longer. As it was, they inflicted several local defeats upon the Japanese Army. It was the only difficult campaign the Japanese had in their early offensive.

It was because MacArthur had seen the Japanese at work that he exercised a dose of operational caution while at the same time preparing for a major offensive. MacArthur, for instance, was in no hurry to deploy the AIF to New Guinea until the base was established and it could be supported or withdrawn if required. The returning divisions also needed time for leave and reorganization. In addition, even if the Japanese succeeded in capturing Moresby, a strong base in northern Australia would have caused them unending trouble. Heavy bombers were limited weapons in the Pacific, but an installation like Moresby could have been pounded from Townsville and Darwin. So even if victorious, the Japanese inevitably were being drawn into an area where they had nothing to gain beyond fleeting strategic advantage.

Conversely, the line between offense and defense in the South Pacific was never clear. Bases in northern Australia and Papua would also make it possible for MacArthur to take offensive actions at an early date. Indeed, it was during this period that MacArthur, Nimitz, King, and Marshall developed the "three task" offensive to guide operations in the South Pacific. As mentioned, MacArthur dispatched a small Allied expedition to Buna that discovered the location for the great Dobodura air base. Its primary mission, however, was to reconnoiter a good position to base Australian land forces that MacArthur wanted sent to the area. As it happened, the Japanese got there first, but plans for the later drive up the coast of New Guinea were already in draft at MacArthur's headquarters before the Japanese landed at Buna or the Americans landed at Guadalcanal. (MacArthur often advocated an attack on Rabaul. It is difficult to ascertain whether he was serious or whether it was a device to get more American resources from Washington, where "Europe first" was official policy. Whenever someone in Washington suggested an attack on Rabaul, MacArthur insisted on reinforcements. When the Joint Chiefs decided to bypass Rabaul and move on the Philippines, MacArthur did not utter the slightest protest.)

In Canberra, a good political base was also laid. Australian prime minister John Curtin was a most unlikely war leader. Representing the Labor Party, Curtin became Australia's leader due to the fall of the Liberal government led by Arthur Fadden instead of by election. (Britain's defeat in Greece, which led to many AIF casualties, precipitated Fadden's downfall in October 1941.) Very weak in parliament, Curtin had to struggle against the suspicions many had of the Labor Party and its trade-union associations. The ambivalent attitude Labor had toward the British Commonwealth also complicated the situation. Nevertheless, Curtin played his cards very well throughout this period. Australia formally entered the war in 1939 under the auspices of the British declaration. In sharp contrast, Australia made a separate declaration of war against Japan in December 1941 and openly appealed to the United States, not Great Britain, for aid. Curtin also insisted on the return of two crack Australian divisions from Europe, and parlayed leaving the third in the desert into sizable commitments of men and resources from the United States. At the same time, by giving MacArthur command of all forces in the theater, he was able to combat the serious danger of the Australian states seeking to keep their Militia units close to home. In addition, under MacArthur's overall command, General Blamey was appointed commander of Allied ground forces in the theater. Curtin also handled the divisive issue of overseas service well. Despite Midway, the Australian Militia divisions remained concentrated in the south, even though the chances of a massive Japanese invasion over open water without carrier support was, to put it mildly, unlikely. However, the Militia divisions were strengthened and Australia was politically prepared for their wider use. In 1943 Curtin stood for election and won easily.

By necessity, Australia had cast its lot with the United States. Problems would arise only if MacArthur asked the Australian military to do things it did not want to do. MacArthur did manage to slight Australian pride on numerous occasions. Whenever a communiqué came from MacArthur's headquarters it was prefaced with "American and Allied Forces..." even if there were only a dozen Americans involved. If there were *no* Americans involved, the communiqué would begin with the phrase "Allied Forces...." No doubt this reflected MacArthur's monumental ego. It also reflected his consistent battle with Washington for more resources. Nevertheless, pride and public opinion are extremely important components of a war effort, and many Australians bitterly resented MacArthur's glorification of himself and American forces. No doubt it came as no small comfort that hatred for MacArthur was easily found in American circles also.

Australians also resented MacArthur's performance during September 1942 when, because of the continued Japanese drive over Kokoda, he expressed anxieties concerning the fighting spirit of Australian troops to both Curtin and Marshall. The upshot was a shake-up in command that led to a greater role in operational matters by General Blamey, commander of all Australian land forces, and the promotion of Lieutenant General Edmund Herring to command of forces in New Guinea. Major General Vasey also received command of the AIF's 7th Division. No doubt MacArthur did not, as many in the Australian military believed, understand conditions in Papua. No doubt he handled things badly. However, beyond matters of wounded pride, the command arrangement that resulted was superior to the one it replaced. Blamey, Herring, and Vasey all performed very well in their respective roles. The AIF's splendid fighting qualities were fully matched by extremely competent leadership at the top. During the helter-skelter bush war along the Kokoda Trail, generalship was not a pressing requirement. During the 1943 campaign, however, the Australian command showed itself expert at large land operations in the Ramu-Markham Valley and amphibious operations near Lae.

MacArthur was also criticized at the time and later for not establishing a joint command arrangements for the Southwest Pacific similar to SHAEF in Europe. Australians, after all, provided the bulk of the land forces in New Guinea until 1944 and a large portion of the U.S. Fifth Air Force. Despite these facts, MacArthur was almost certainly correct in keeping sole command. MacArthur was often criticized for keeping his headquarters in Australia. Yet he was able to see very clearly how closely every facet of the war effort touched Australian domestic politics. (Although Australia was a major recipient of Lend-Lease aid, American engineers moved out of Australia to New Guinea as soon as possible. Construction projects in Australia inevitably got them involved in sticky matters of local politics.) He also knew that Australia was, when all was said and done, a small country. In 1942 and 1943 Australia's war effort was central to Allied success. When the American war machine appeared in strength in 1944 and the war moved into the Central Pacific and Philippines, this ceased to be so. Furthermore, SHAEF was to develop into a continuing partnership between two great powers in the postwar world. It is very unclear that Australia and the United States would have wanted the same thing after the Japanese were pushed out of New Guinea. For instance, would Australian public opinion have supported shedding Australian blood in the Philippines? As a nation in Asia, did it not make more sense for Australia to direct its energies toward Indonesia under its own command?

MacArthur, furthermore, never wanted the role of operational commander in New Guinea that Eisenhower tried to play in France. Every military decision of consequence involving Australian forces was made by Australian commanders. Orders to Australian fighting men came from Australian commanders. Conversely, MacArthur frequently allowed Australians to command American ground troops. The U.S. Fifth Air Force, with its large Australian contingent, supported Australian operations fully. The U.S. fleet in 1943 participated in some of the most sophisticated and successful operations undertaken by the AIF. It is difficult to find a single instance where MacArthur asked the Australians to do something that they themselves did not want to do. When one considers the continual war that raged among the services, nations, and individual egos at SHAEF, it is difficult to fault the command arrangements in the Southwest Pacific. Whatever MacArthur's faults, he did much to allow the AIF to fight with adequate support under good commanders.

Nevertheless, war in the South Pacific was not a general's war. The essence of combat in the theater was found at a much lower level of command. We know now that Australia had the best Army in the South Pacific. Yet, when the AIF first arrived in the summer of 1942, this was not at all clear. As indicated previously, the AIF had one thing in common with the Japanese and Americans: they knew almost nothing about fighting in the swamps and jungle of New Guinea.

Some elements of the AIF became deeply involved in the confused retreat down the Kokoda Trail. At the same time, the AIF received a twin baptism of fire in the South Pacific at Milne Bay, one of the most wretched locales in Papua. In late August 1942 it was also one of the most important. Before Pearl Harbor, Milne Bay was noteworthy only for its large coconut plantation owned by the Lever Brothers soap company, its incredible rainfall averaging 200 inches a year, and the astronomical malaria rate. During the struggle for Port Moresby, Milne Bay, for a short time, was a central point in the Pacific War.

Milne Bay lies at the extreme southeast tip of New Guinea. About twenty miles long, it is likewise twenty miles wide at the mouth but quickly tapers to a uniform width of four miles until it reaches the western shoreline. Ships can enter the bay and stand by very close to off-load troops. (This was why Lever Brothers picked it for its plantation.) A crude jetty existed at the western edge, but was not suitable for large-scale use in 1942. Along both the north and south shores of Milne Bay there is beach that is between 100 yards and one mile wide. A trail traverses the beach on both sides of the bay, providing something resembling a line of communication. Beyond the beach, one is immediately in dense jungle and swamp. The Stirling Mountains, an extension of the Owen Stanleys, rise abruptly from the north shore. Rugged hills also descend rapidly toward the south shore. During the rainy season, which begins in late August, sustained two-inch rains at night are common. When that happens, in a few days the mud from the swamps oozes across the coral, turning the entire area into a quagmire. Milne Bay in 1942, in other words, was like an open-ended oblong bowl, a lovely South Seas inlet, surrounded by some of the most obscene terrain on the planet.

Milne Bay was greatly desired by both sides. From the Allied point of view, air bases at Milne Bay served as a major protection against a Japanese amphibious strike at Port Moresby. When the situation improved, Milne Bay was the obvious place to start a supply line for Allied operations on the northern coast of Papua. (In the end, despite the vile terrain, Milne Bay served as a large rear base.) It was for these reasons that Allied commanders dispatched some of the first Australian infantry units serving in New Guinea and some of the first U.S. engineers to arrive in Australia to Milne Bay.

Japan's desire for Milne Bay was a natural part of the land offensive over the Kokoda Trail. The Imperial Army jealously guarded operational control of its advance. To support the Port Moresby drive, however, Tokyo ordered the Combined Fleet in mid-August to prepare a pair of amphibious operations. This was done despite the American landing at Guadalcanal. The major one was directed at a point east of Port Moresby and was to aid the South Seas Detachment when it made its final attack. (This operation was naturally canceled when the South Seas Detachment received the order to withdraw in September.) The Imperial Navy also authorized a preliminary landing at Milne Bay. Port Moresby's air strength had held through months of Japanese air attacks, and Tokyo believed it important to gain a strip near enough to cover the landings near Port Moresby. In addition, as the Navy also pointed out, Port Moresby was worthless unless heavy equipment and heavy weapons could be shipped there. They could not come over Kokoda. A direct convoy route from Buna to Moresby had to run the gauntlet of Allied air bases in northern Australia. Far better to have a coastal supply route based at Milne Bay that could move supplies up in small vessels and barges. The Imperial Navy, in other words, wanted to do at Milne Bay exactly what the Allies were doing.

The Japanese decision to move against Milne Bay was sound in all respects on paper. Nevertheless, the Japanese crippled their enterprise with the same mistakes made at Kokoda and Guadalcanal. First, their strategic reconnaissance was very poor. The Japanese had good geographic reconnaissance. It is not possible to prove, but it is not unreasonable to assume that, in the years after World War I when Japan was awarded Truk and other forward bases, Japanese intelligence services made quiet surveys of potential battlefields throughout the South Pacific. They had twenty years to do so, and cover would have been simple. (Whatever was done was not infallible. As noted previously, the conditions on the Kokoda Trail past Kokoda itself came as a rude shock.) Maps recovered by Allied soldiers after a battle were beautifully made and often included great detail. Strategic reconnaissance was another matter. Milne Bay was a distant point from Rabaul and had very heavy cloud cover. The Imperial Navy estimated Australian forces there at approximately two battalions. The Japanese missed entirely the major reinforcement of the area that took place in early summer 1942. In addition, in what was becoming a hallmark of Japanese operations, commanders proved unable to coordinate multiple operations. Although Milne Bay was exclusively a Navy show, while it took place Admiral Yamamoto at Combined Fleet was throwing the naval air arm and most of his fleet against Guadalcanal. Both the South Seas Detachment going over the Owen Stanleys and the expedition to Milne Bay would have to make do with little air cover and scant naval support.

Inevitably, the Japanese drive over the Kokoda Trail created problems for the move on Milne Bay because it caused the Australians to greatly accelerate the reinforcement of Papua. At the start of the war there were only 1,000 Militia troops in Papua, part of Australia's 8th Military District, most in Moresby. By July, there were 25,000 men. Developments at Milne Bay were a part of this expansion. In June, at the same time that American and Australian engineers were exploring Dobodura, another party was at Milne Bay looking for an airfield site. A suitable one was found at Gili Gili at the far western shore of the bay, on ground made suitable by the operators of the coconut plantation. At the end of the month American engineers landed there. Shortly after, three battalions of Australian Militia troops also arrived along with Australian engineers and service troops. Although the Militia forces began patrolling the area, which was virtually unknown to the Allies, their commanders delegated many men to help build the airstrip. It was ugly work with little heavy equipment available, but it was complete by the end of the month.

Although intended for only one fighter squadron, two Australian squadrons set up operations there in late July. Officially named Gurney Field after a Royal Australian Air Force (RAAF) hero, most knew it as Strip One. Australian communications specialists installed one of their light but effective radar sites, and Milne Bay had air defense in an amazingly short period of time. Immediately, the engineers began the construction of a larger Strip Two to the west capable of handling bombers. In the meantime, needing more space for fighters, engineers and troops began the laborious process of clearing land for

Strip Three right on the bay. Although not finished, Strip Three played an important role in the drama soon to come.

The Australian pilots assigned were extremely good. In a parallel to the return of the AIF, dozens of veteran Australian pilots returned from England or the Mediterranean to Australia. Milne Bay must have come as a rude shock to men accustomed to the well-developed air apparatus present in Europe. Although strategically well positioned, Strip One was a horrid place for fighter operations. William Garing, at the time the commander of all air forces at Milne Bay, later described operational conditions:

It was dreadful country with only a tiny airstrip between coast and Stirling Mountains. We had very heavy rain every night. And the mud was almost indescribable. There was no pavement or proper drainage. There was steel matting to provide strength, but it was covered with a layer of liquidy mud. We had two squadrons there instead of the one the strip was built for, so it was crowded with our Kitty Hawks [the name given by the British and Australians to the Curtis P-40 fighters—EB]. When they took off you could hardly see the plane. A cascade of mud came up the sides and to the rear. Landing was the same, just a spray of mud. It got into everything. It would get into the guns and within a few days the gun barrels were a millimeter above size. [Keeping machine guns and artillery clean was crucial. If mud or dust got into them, firing the weapon would cause abrasion, which increased the diameter of the barrel. The increased diameter of the barrel lowered the velocity of the bullet and lessened its spin, causing potentially serious loss in both range and accuracy. As it was, under good circumstances, barrels were changed at intervals.—EB]
Flying on mud amplified a nasty habit of the P-40. It was a terrific fighter-bomber but had a tendency to do a ground loop. [a spin when an aircraft is taking off or landing; it is somewhat similar to having a spin in an automobile on ice or rain and can be very dangerous—EB]. If a pilot did one, he never did another, and you had to be very cautious on use of rudder. That was the secret. A new pilot in a Beaufighter [Britain's excellent fighter-

bomber, much beloved by Australian pilots—EB] came in and didn't understand this. He went into circles and ran into a Hudson. You hated to see things like this, because at the time aircraft were far shorter than pilots.

The budding base at Milne made the site even more important for the Allies. Conversely, it made it a more tempting target for the Japanese. Allied intelligence began picking up numerous signs of a major Japanese amphibious move in the second week in August. It was unclear whether it was going toward Guadalcanal or toward Milne Bay. Guessing correctly that Milne Bay was the likely target, the Australians reinforced it substantially. On August 19 the 25th Brigade of the AIF 7th Division began arriving in Milne Bay. It was a wise move. AIF units were already going up the Kokoda Trail, and more supplies could not be moved up the trail at the time. Port Moresby was close enough that the brigade could have shifted back had the need arisen. The Militia commander at Milne Bay had informed Port Moresby that AIF reinforcement would be required if the Japanese attacked. His units could secure the base, but would be hard pressed to fight off a determined assault. When the AIF arrived there were 8,750 Allied troops, including 1,300 U.S. engineers. Only about half of these were fighting infantry and none had met the Japanese in the jungle.

The Japanese moved on August 20. Despite the destruction of the Ichiki Detachment on Guadalcanal, Vice Admiral Gunichi Mikawa at Rabaul ordered an immediate attack on Milne Bay with 1,550 men under his personal command. The men involved were from the near legendary Special Naval Landing Forces. As mentioned previously, most Japanese Navy troops were defensive specialists, intended to guard installations or beachheads. Assault units were mostly from the Army. The Navy did, however, have a small group of elite assault troops ready to move at short notice. They were some of the best troops fighting for the Empire. The Japanese Navy, like its American counterpart, cherished the ability to move by itself if the need arose.

The Japanese were coming in two contingents. Japanese commanders at Rabaul ordered the major force of 1,200 troops to attack at the village of Rabi on the north shore of Milne Bay, three miles from Gili Gili. Mikawa ordered another 350 men to land on the northern coast of Papua and march south, attacking the Australians overland. The idea may have been a good one. The Stirling Mountains were very rugged but not as high as the Owen Stanleys. More important, the distance was much shorter, under ten miles. Had they been able to make the landing, however, the Japanese would have encountered local inhabitants who were intensely warlike and had no love for interlopers. As it developed, both armies had an uncomfortable number of missing from units that became scattered into the Stirlings.

The fortunes of war initially favored the Australians. The Japanese expedition sailed on August 24 protected by dense cloud cover. The smaller force ordered to attack over the Stirlings was on seven barges and headed down the coast. The next day they stopped briefly on Goodenough Island in the afternoon, where they were spotted by a coast watcher. Several fighters from Milne found a hole in the bad weather that day and destroyed all the barges. The troops on Goodenough were stranded. Ultimately, efforts to rescue them turned into a costly burden for the Japanese Navy. In one air attack, an important part of the Japanese plan was dismantled.

The rest of the convoy, however, remained protected by bad weather. They were sighted and every aircraft in northern Australia and Milne Bay was eager to strike, but the clouds and rain kept the Japanese safe. After dark, the Japanese fleet entered the bay sailing west. Two cruisers and two destroyers shelled what they believed to be Rabi, doing no damage because there were no Australians within two miles. The Japanese troops disembarked with no opposition and started to unload supplies. Although they did not know it in the dark, they had landed five miles east of Rabi, putting them eight miles instead of three from their destination. In the jungle, an extra five miles is a long way. While the Japanese landed, the Australians suffered a minor debacle. A Militia company was stationed toward the mouth of the bay. The Australian commander dispatched two small vessels to the isolated company. On the return the boats ran into the Japanese warships and the landing party. One evaded the enemy in the confusion, but the Japanese ran the other ashore. Several men were killed or missing.

The Australian commander was Major General Cyril A. Clowes, an experienced AIF officer. Although he had a sizable force, he was operating in a state of serious confusion and uncertainty. An Australian patrol had reported a clash with some Japanese near a mission on the northern coast. The patrol leader believed that the force was small. Clowes knew there were ships in the bay, but he had little idea how many and no idea of what they carried. Soon, however, survivors from the isolated company arrived. These men had seen the Japanese landing party more closely than they had desired, and estimated the force to be at least 2,000. Clowes also faced the very real possibility that another Japanese landing might come and hit a different position. For these reasons he sat tight for the night, and hoped the morning would allow a more accurate assessment of the situation.

August 26 was a bad day for both sides. The cloud cover over Milne Bay went up to 1,500 feet. That was sufficient to guard ships from most long-range bombardment because the bombers could not find their targets. However, the low cloud cover was perfect for the Kitty Hawks at Milne Bay. Protected from fighter attack from above, they could fly along the beach and pummel targets of opportunity. Like the Marines on Guadalcanal, the Japanese found that getting supplies off the beach and inland was a formidable task. The Australian pilots strafed and bombed supply clusters on the beach and destroyed many. An American B-17 found a way through the clouds and bombed and damaged the single transport that was still in the bay unloading supplies. The Japanese lost much of the material they would need in the coming week.

On the other hand, the situation was still shrouded for the Australians. The Japanese troops had moved into the jungle swamps. The Australians still did not know what they were facing. Contacts were very light. Recall, also, that the Australian Army knew almost nothing about the area beyond what their patrols had discovered in the past few weeks. For their part, the Japanese were moving into the most brutal terrain the jungle had to offer. The Australians later would have to fight them there. The American official history of the

battle gives a good description of the narrow corridor between the
foothills and the beach where both sides did battle a few hundred
yards or less from the water:

> It had rained steadily during the preceding few weeks, and the
> heavy tropical downpour continued. The mountain streams had
> become roaring torrents, and the spongy soil of the corridor a
> quagmire. The single coastal track that skirted the corridor had
> in places completely washed away, and the level of the many
> fords that cut across it had risen to almost three feet. Except for
> a few abandoned plantations and mission stations, the corridor
> was a sodden welter of jungle and swamp, an utter nightmare
> for any force operating in it.

An Australian Militia company moved up the beach from an
abandoned mission (sometimes called the K.B. Mission), trying to
find the Japanese. They had sporadic contact that grew as night came
closer. A Militia patrol rejoining its company at the mission received a dose of Japanese infiltration tactics. Despite artillery fire
from Gili Gili, the Australian infantry was pinned by Japanese fire.
Men on the inland flank could hear and sometimes see Japanese infantry infiltrating through the jungle morass. Seaward, Japanese soldiers were moving through water up to their necks round the other
flank. The Japanese commonly heckled Allied infantry at night.
Some bright Japanese infantrymen started "ordering" the Australians in English to withdraw. Later, Australians were accustomed to
and even found humor in the often-jangled grammar. More than one
soldier heard something like "You die! Good morning!" In this case,
however, some of the inexperienced Militia were fooled by the ruse
and left. (English was compulsory at the Japanese Naval Academy
and an elective at the Military Academy. It was widely taught in civilian schools. American soldiers heard many stories about American-
educated Japanese officers using their fluency in the language to trick
unwary GIs. Although there were Japanese students at American
universities, these stories should be viewed skeptically.) The Militia
commander wisely ordered a retreat to the Gama River a mile to
the west.

The next morning the beach was empty. The Japanese had broken off the attack and were in the swamps. Australian patrols that went as far as the mission encountered only sporadic firing. The weather cleared and the Japanese Naval Air Force launched one of its few raids on Strip One, doing little damage thanks to Australian radar. The Militia, however, was starting to show the strain. Conditions were so miserable in the rain and mud, and fatigue so severe, that Militia commanders began sending some of their men to the rear. In terrain as wet as Milne Bay, jungle rot attacked the feet almost immediately and caused a week of pain for hundreds of soldiers on both sides. Only two days into the fighting malaria was already taking a serious toll. Immediately after dark the Militia company was ordered to Gili Gili for rest. The remaining two officers and thirty-two men trudged eastward during the rain, up to their knees in mud, holding on to each other's equipment to keep from getting lost. Arguably no battle in the Pacific war attacked the soldiers' health as rapidly as did Milne Bay.

The Australians continued to act without reliable intelligence. Forty men of the isolated company at the east end of the bay had trekked around Japanese lines through the Stirlings and returned late afternoon of August 26. They confirmed the earlier estimate of 5,000 Japanese invaders. If he was facing a force that size, and did not know where it was, Clowes was in trouble. Group Commander Garing arrived on the 27th. He describes the chaos at headquarters:

We won that battle at Milne Bay by a whisker. If the Japanese had had the brains to reinforce their landing there, we couldn't have beaten them. When I arrived, the whole area was a battle zone. The place was in chaos and everybody was scared stiff. It was appalling. The morale was awful. Soon we were operating right next to the enemy. Right alongside him. At one point Clowes didn't think he could hold the airdrome. We couldn't afford to lose the airplanes, so they were sent up to Moresby overnight. No one wanted a repeat of the Philippine Islands. I stayed at Milne with ground services. I stayed there so our ground crews wouldn't take off over the hills and come home. Nothing deflates morale more rapidly than seeing an officer leave in haste.

Clowes was most reluctant to deploy his sizable AIF reserve until the Japanese had tipped their hand. Yet events prodded him in that direction. He needed information badly. In addition, the Militia unit near the mission that he had relieved needed to be replaced. Consequently, for the first time, he ordered a battalion of the AIF, the 2/10th, up the beach.

The AIF battalion commander knew no more than anyone else in the Allied camp. Lacking decent maps, he relied heavily on secondhand information. Moving out on the morning of the 27th, he made a serious error. Fearing that he might encounter a much superior force, he "stripped" his companies of most of their heavy infantry weapons and took only his essential personnel. For instance, he had two companies leave their Bren light machine guns and replace them with extra Thompson submachine guns. Although the Militia had encountered a Japanese tank on the first night, the AIF battalions' Boyes antitank rifles were left behind. Instead, the commander decided to rely upon "sticky grenades," a large grenade with a magnet attached, Australia's variant of a weapon that failed in every army during World War II. (Few infantrymen in battle wanted to mount enemy tanks. Those who did frequently found the grenades did not "stick.") The AIF commander was thinking in conventional terms. Traveling light under normal conditions would allow a rapid retreat. At Milne Bay, however, nothing could be done rapidly. Furthermore, the fatigue inherent in movement further crippled maneuver. In addition, the Japanese normally launched assaults at night. If the 2/10th was going to receive an attack, it would be when they were "dug in" (to the extent that was possible at Milne Bay) at night. In the future, necessity required AIF units, like all combatants, to travel lightly over ugly terrain and uncertain supply lines. It was rare in the Pacific, however, to intentionally take less firepower than possible into action. As the 2/10th marched down the beach, there was no chance of their simply retracing their steps. It was a very bad start.

The 2/10th marched up the beach and reached the K.B. Mission as night was falling. The men were tired to start with, and trudging several miles through the mud rendered them prostrate. They had left their entrenching tools, and consequently settled into likely looking little positions in the mud and waited for the night. The 2/10th was arranged in a perimeter. As we shall see later, "lines" rarely existed in the South Pacific. Because the enemy could often flank a position, and because positions often became intermingled, units deployed in a manner that allowed them to guard all directions. It was a South Pacific equivalent of circling the wagons on the American prairie.

What followed was a solid defeat for the AIF. It was also one of the most unusual battles of the war. Soon after dark, rain pouring down, the Australians heard the noise of an engine starting. Out of the darkness a tank moved slowly, its spotlight and headlights shining brightly. Minutes later an astounding interlude took place, recorded by the historian of the 2/10th:

> At 1950 hours the silence was again broken, this time by a high-pitched voice chanting in Japanese from the depths of the jungle. The one voice (and a beautiful voice it was) would recite for about one minute, after which the chant would be taken up by a number of other voices, rather nearer to where the 2/10th lay quietly waiting. Upon the second group completing their recitation, a third group, obviously comprising some hundreds of the enemy, and closer again, would sing in sonorous unison. This procedure was repeated three times. Whether it was some form of religious rite, or merely a boasting recital calculated to inspire courage in the chanters and despair in the hearts of the listeners, is not known, nor did the battalion ever again hear this type of musical performance.

Minutes later the Japanese attacked. The tank moved forward and was joined by another. The tanks moved into Australian positions accompanied by infantry, shining their blinding lights in all directions. For three hours the tanks cut through Australian positions, fortunately never attacking the two companies holding the rear of the perimeter. Mold had grown inside the "sticky" grenades, rendering them useless. The tanks were impervious to small-arms fire. The Boyes antitank rifle, so feeble in the desert, was probably powerful enough to damage Japanese light tanks, and the Australians paid for the oversight of leaving theirs behind. By picking the K.B. Mission for defense, they were in one of the few areas where the ground was well enough drained for the tanks to move. Yet the Australians stood their ground and directed withering fire against the infantry. In close fighting, the Australian hand grenade, the best in the Pacific, proved deadly.

By midnight the battle was lost. The Japanese infantry was inside the Australian perimeter at numerous points The Japanese killed the Australian artillery observation officers, stopping Australian artillery support and severing communications with the rear. One experienced platoon leader who had led several counterattacks commented that another one was pointless, because there did not seem to be a position to restore. Some of the companies began to break up. The commander ordered a general retreat, but the withdrawal had started without sanction. Company commanders wisely rallied their remaining men and retreated as best they could. The Japanese had broken the 2/10th in half. Portions of it moved into the jungle and finally returned to Gili Gili on August 30. The remainder moved along the beach. The Japanese continued their pursuit, driving more of the 2/10th into the hills and capturing a roadblock established by a Militia company. By morning they were very close to Strip Three, an area that was cleared of jungle but not yet usable for aircraft.

The Japanese, too, were learning a lesson. In the jungle, especially at night, it was extremely difficult to annihilate a unit. The lines were too porous and breakout (or "sneakout") was done time and again. Because the 2/10th had kept its head and fought it out, losses of forty-three killed and twenty-six wounded were lighter than might have been expected. On the other hand, the Japanese had shoved aside the Militia, and they had shoved aside the AIF. Nor did the Australians believe, after the battle was over, that Japanese forces greatly outnumbered the defenders. The tanks and Japanese night-fighting skills had done the deed. The attackers received reinforcements the next night from another convoy. The question was simple: Who was going to stop them?

After the advance, the Japanese had to bring forward supplies and reinforcements. Movement in the open, thanks to the RAAF fighters, was impossible during the day, so the job was slow. In the meantime Clowes stuck with his policy of keeping his reserves back until he was sure of the enemy's intentions. This caused concern at AIF headquarters in Port Moresby, Canberra, and MacArthur's headquarters. Australian reverses at Milne Bay unfortunately coincided with difficult times on the Kokoda Trail. It was all well and good for commanders on the spot to claim that everything was under control, that the enemy was growing weaker as he proceeded toward the defending base, and that ultimately a counterpunch would throw him back. To those on the outside, in the summer of 1942, all of this looked too much like Singapore or the Philippines for comfort.

With the situation momentarily quiet, Australian Militia patrols up the beach had the satisfaction of finding the two Japanese tanks hopelessly bogged in the Gama River. What the AIF could not do, the jungle did. (This was not unusual. The jungle was an excellent tank killer.) The jungle was attacking the Japanese in every way. They were running short of supplies, and were miles in front of their supply dump. The mud, rain, and malaria were sweeping through the attackers. Furthermore, the battle losses were likewise hurtful. It was in the nature of Japanese infantry attacks that the real firebrands died first. Their loss made it more difficult to keep the forward momentum. Like the Japanese later outside Moresby, or Ichiki's men on the sand spit at Guadalcanal, the naval shock troops at Milne Bay had only a short distance to go. If they could get past the open terrain of Strip Three, they would move into the only area where maneuver was possible. Strip One was nearby, and a breakthrough offered the opportunity of crushing the Militia against the shore.

Although the Japanese were a few hundred yards from breakthrough, the tide was turning. Clowes decided to send the AIF forward. Because of the timing, it would be advancing toward Strip Three as the Japanese attacked it. If the Japanese broke through, a battle of encounter would ensue. If the Japanese failed, they were vulnerable to immediate counterattack.

The latter eventually took place. The Japanese troops, fighting over the relatively open terrain of Strip Three, perhaps underestimated the size of the Australian defensive forces. It is important to remember that Imperial Headquarters believed Milne Bay was lightly held. The attackers had rolled up three units. Perhaps they hoped the Australians would crack. In any case, instead of trying to move around Strip Three through the jungle, they attacked along the beach. During massed assault men have an instinct to bunch. This took place at the Tenaru River on Guadalcanal and also at Strip Three. During a dreadful downpour the Japanese ran into dug-in Militia positions supported by artillery. Although they attacked three times, they were thrown back each time. At dawn, the Japanese pulled back.

An AIF counterattack commenced immediately. What followed was a series of sharp engagements between AIF patrols and Japanese rear guards. Larger fights interspersed the continual skirmishing along the Gama River and at the mission. A Japanese night attack cost them dearly. Very quickly the AIF showed its mastery of the art of patrolling in dense cover. This was where sheer professionalism came into play. Quick reactions, excellent fire discipline, and team-work were all required. So was simple aggressiveness, a quality that the Australians had in surplus. No Australian unit would have obeyed a mad order of the type followed by the Japanese. On the other hand, the Australians fought smarter. It was a dangerous way to fight and high casualties went along with Australian methods. But the impor-tant thing was to keep going, to keep up the pressure. Over time the enemy lost its edge and got sloppy from fatigue. Incidents accumu-lated of Australian patrols shooting the ribbons out of confused and surprised Japanese. As the AIF leaders knew from the many bodies they saw, as badly hurt as their own men were, the Japanese were suf-fering even worse. The Japanese were in a downward spiral and could not get out of it.

E. J. Randall was with the 2/9th Battalion at Milne Bay during the counterattack up the coast. The nightmare world he describes is fully corroborated:

> Our troops were committed to the battle. The road to the front was not trafficable, so everyone was knee keep in mud and the

rain teemed down. We were moved to a tented area near the sea where we would spend the night before being shipped a short distance up the coast to a place where we would take the van of the attack. It was a dreadful night. The ground in the tents was covered in tarpaulins and investigation of movement under the tarps revealed a mass of snakes. I remember quite a few of us slept out in the rain. We attacked the Jap by day. Once making contact, we were expected to push on at all costs. There was no rest. We lay in the water and fended off his attacks by night. After a week our feet were raw, lack of food and the constant rain were sapping our strength. However, the Jap was worse off than we were as the results of the battle showed.

Officers came in to put us in the picture. The Japs were not taking prisoners, therefore we must avoid capture at all costs. "Keep the last grenade for yourself," they said. We moved to the front and the sight of Jap atrocities was unfathomable. We found our blokes who had been captured early tied to trees where they had been used for bayonet practice. I personally saw a dead native girl who had been mutilated and obviously raped. Going through a group of dead Japanese required caution, because one might be feigning death and try to kill you. We were quick to make sure they stayed dead. From that moment we had a hatred of Japs. For many of us that went through those major battles, the hatred persists.

As the AIF advanced, the RAAF fighters pursued the Japanese without letup. Close air support was difficult and friendly-fire casualties took place. Nevertheless, fighters dealt death from the skies. No doubt the psychological shock of air attack often made the job of AIF infantryman easier. William Garing describes the activities of his pilots during this time:

The maps at Milne Bay were almost nonexistent. The Army had to draw their own as they went forward. We got Army officers of rank of major and they became ALO (Army liaison officers). They kept pilots briefed on exactly where the front line was. Marking the front line under the peacetime system failed at

Milne Bay. So we had smoke fired from our gunners and would work from the markers east. East of the marker, everything was fair game. It was a very short distance, don't forget.

Kitty Hawks flew under cloud base of 1,500–2,000 feet. You could see the entire coast. You could often see the Japanese running for cover. Our planes would turn and spray them with their six heavy machine guns. As one Army bloke said, when the strafers came over the coconut trees firing, the palm leaves and the Jap snipers just "fell out of the sky." But the weather was so appalling. The strip was so close to the front that a pilot might fly six sorties a day. The pilots were exhausted.

With their ground forces being chewed up, the Japanese faced a hard decision. The contingent at Milne Bay was in danger of going the way of Ichiki's force. The commander of the expedition and all of his staff were dead, as were numerous other officers. Some reinforcements had landed on the third day of the battle, but their commander was wounded. Originally Rabaul offered to send an Army contingent. It was not at all certain, however, that it would arrive in time. Turned down by the Navy at Milne Bay, the reinforcements (the so-called Aoba Detachment) sailed to meet their fate on Guadalcanal. Instead, the Japanese decided to withdraw from Milne Bay. Over two nights they evacuated first their wounded and then the combat troops still available.

An odd incident took place on the night of September 6, the night of the first withdrawal. Japanese warships entered the bay. As they took on men, a destroyer sailed toward the western shore. At the small pier at Gili Gili a small vessel was unloading and an Australian hospital ship, the *Manunda*, clearly marked in white and green as to its purpose, stood close by. Japanese searchlights quickly found the small freighter, the destroyer opened fire, and the ship sank immediately. Searchlights also bathed the *Manunda*, but the Japanese did not fire. They started bombarding Australian shore positions and did damage. Once again the Japanese destroyer shone lights on the hospital ship, but sailed off. It was a strange end to an unusual encounter.

The figures for Japanese losses at Milne Bay vary. It seems that they evacuated approximately 1,300 of the 1,900 men they landed ten days before. Half of those men were wounded. All were sent to Japan upon return, considered worthless for further operations. In return the entire defense of Milne Bay had cost the Australians 373 battle casualties, including 160 killed and missing. Something over 100 of the killed were AIF.

Milne Bay was an extremely important engagement. Had the Japanese pulled it off the morale impact would have been incalculable on both sides. However, after the Japanese defeat at Milne Bay, the South Seas Detachment coming off the Kokoda Trail near Moresby was on its own. Within weeks it was flirting with doom. As it was, the AIF suffered a sharp defeat in its first fight. What is striking, however, is how quickly it reacted and recovered. Although the air support was most helpful, the AIF counterattack was done with two battalions and did not greatly outnumber the Japanese. Yet it pushed forward and ground down some of the best soldiers Japan possessed. Hundreds of officers, including the fine brigade commander, Brigadier General George Wooten, gained valuable experience fighting in the savage new environment they would have to face.

However, it was not so much what was accomplished but what was proved at Milne Bay that was important in retrospect. What the AIf illustrated at Milne Bay was similar to what the Marines showed at the Tenaru River, except on a larger scale. Japanese spirit would not triumph over bullets. Furthermore, Japan's enemies were starting to win because they were quickly becoming acclimated and oriented to the war they had to fight. The AIF, as shown at Milne Bay, was equal or superior to the best the Japanese had. They were considerably superior to the average Japanese unit. The difference between the AIF and the Marines in late 1942 was that the AIF was larger, and it was situated in a much more dangerous place from Japan's point of view.

Harsh and bloody battles were ahead for the AIF. The Kokoda Trail was an epic of endurance. The battles of Gona-Sanananda-Buna were the most violent it faced in the Pacific. Setbacks are a part of war, and the AIF had many. Yet it never lost a battle after the Japanese withdrew first from Milne Bay and soon after from positions near the Imita Ridge outside Port Moresby. When brought up to strength, and given the flexibility and firepower that modern sea and airpower provided, the invincible Australian killing machine of 1943 developed smoothly from the AIF of late 1942. Few armies in modern times have combined steadiness, savvy, and ferocity the way the Australians did. It was an extraordinary performance.

Understanding the terrain and the composition of the armies, it is now time to examine the nature and tempo of battle in the South Pacific. By looking at the world of combat experienced by fighting soldiers in the South Pacific, it is possible to understand in some measure why the war was fought the way it was, and how the fighting men coped with the world that surrounded them. If these matters can be dealt with, through a glass dimmed by half a century, we can see still the essence of the most violent war of modern times.

PART II

FIGHTING MEAN: COMBAT IN THE SOUTH PACIFIC

The soldiers who fought the ground war in the South Pacific faced a combat environment very unlike those faced by the millions of other fighting men who participated in World War II. There were some similarities between jungle combat and fighting in other theaters, and they grew with time as large numbers of modern weapons entered the Pacific arena. Yet because the South Pacific battlefield was so unusual, combat there developed a tempo unique in World War II. Because of the terrain, geography, and battle ethos of the fighting men, some aspects of the ground war were innovative and sophisticated, while others were crude and technologically primitive. Out of this military hodgepodge came the most vicious light-infantry war ever fought by industrial nations.

To understand the unique flow of battle in the South Pacific, it is necessary to first examine some of the characteristics that defined warfare in the twentieth century. The first factor that shaped combat in the two world wars was the great expansion of the killing zone. Until the twentieth century, even the largest wars were marked by maneuvers by opposing forces culminating in either a siege or a battle. It was very rare for a single battle or series of battles to end hostilities. For centuries, wars between nation-states, if the stakes were high, have been wars of attrition. Nevertheless, prior to 1914 wars were characterized by very definite high points of violence lasting a few days to a few weeks. Low-level killing accompanied these battles on a daily basis wherever armies were close, but it was incidental or subordinate to the big battles. Also, the geographic stage for war has changed little over time. Certain parts of Europe are studded with battlefields from wars of every era. It is the same elsewhere. It is not coincidence that the most climactic battles of both the nineteenth and twentieth centuries happened along the Moscow road. Northern China has likewise seen countless battles. The corridor between Washington, D.C., and Richmond, Virginia, was a military hotbed in two wars. Other parts of the world have likewise been the sites of dozens of battles taking place over centuries. What changed, of course, was the population of the nations involved, the level of technological development, and the weapons used.

Although the percentage of men under arms has remained remarkably stable for a long time (a nation can sustain a war and put approximately 10 percent of its population in uniform for an extended period), two factors worked together to change war in the twentieth century. First was the sheer increase in the size of the nations. The population of the United States in the Civil War was approximately 35 million. It was nearly four times that during World War II. Napoleonic France had perhaps 24 million. At the time of the Marne, the French population had doubled. Yet the numbers do not tell the whole tale. Indeed, the population increase among nations was much more rapid early in the nineteenth century than in the twentieth. Germany's population in 1914 was not much larger than in 1870, nor was that of France or Britain. (Other parts of the world saw continued increase in population, but they were not important areas militarily.) Indeed, the early part of World War I resembled the Franco-Prussian War remarkably. The armies were larger, but there were maneuver and battles. Soon, however, it was obvious that the rules of the game had changed forever.

Machine guns and artillery kill men in modern war. This trend had been going on for some time. Breech-loading rifles used in the Franco-Prussian War allowed infantrymen to kill from long range while lying down. Breech-loading artillery used by Moltke's Germans in 1870 blew holes in French lines because of its power and speed of firing. Nevertheless, the weapons of a generation later were a quantum leap ahead. Machine guns were so much more powerful than rifles that they transformed utterly the role of the infantryman.

Ground armies were still the arm of decision, but riflemen went from the primary element of ground combat to a support element. In World War I and World War II, a leg infantryman had two primary tasks in battle. One, he had to guard machine guns and artillery batteries from infiltration by enemy infantry. Two, he had to patrol the killing zone to locate the enemy's machine guns. Infantry still did much of the dying, but they did far less of the killing. Modern artillery was the machine gun's complement. The greatest difference between the artillery of the world wars and previous times was that modern fieldpieces fire "indirectly." Because communications and weaponry improved greatly in the early twentieth century, it became possible for gunners to fire with great accuracy at targets they could not see. And they could fire fast. An American 105mm howitzer of World War II could fire four to six shells a minute for a surprisingly long time. The high-explosive shells fired could kill and wound dozens of men in the open. Artillery, furthermore, was normally concentrated. Dozens of fieldpieces often fired from a small area. Generals deployed thousands of artillery pieces on a large front. Much of what I have just described concerning the world wars remains true today.

The Battle of Gettysburg took place in 1863, just fifty years before World War I. It is hard to imagine how far Pickett's Charge would have gotten had it been opposed by a dozen heavy machine guns, supported by four howitzers and half a dozen mortars, common weapons in trench warfare. What took 50,000 Union infantry firing shoulder to shoulder to do could have been done by a few hundred men. As best put by Henri Pétain, Marshal of France during World War I, "Fire kills." The power of artillery and machine guns is so great that they spurred warring nations to develop extremely expensive countermeasures to them. The British developed tanks to kill the men firing machine guns, and that remains one of their primary roles today. Tactical airpower, far more expensive than artillery, was developed over the years to either kill artillery directly or, more likely, cut off the supplies required to allow the guns to fire. In World War II the infantry itself increasingly obtained smaller types of machine guns and artillery. On one side was the submachine gun, and on the other was the proliferation of mortars; the infantry's personal artillery. This increased the fire coming from land armies even more, and quickened all the secondary results.

The most obvious result of the quantum leap in firepower was the creation of the linear battlefield. By the outbreak of World War II, a battle dynamic very different from that found in earlier generations was very well developed. An examination of this dynamic illustrates well the tactical principles of land war in the twentieth century. First, if a well-concealed small force armed with powerful machine guns and protected by friendly artillery could hold off a much larger group of men, there was no reason to put large numbers of defenders in a very small area. A position like Cemetery Ridge at Gettysburg, where 50,000 Union infantry were packed together, would have been obliterated by massed artillery fifty years later. Therefore densely packed defensive positions became not only unnecessary but also military idiocy. The principle of "concentration of force" was still taught in all military manuals. In every tactical training course, however, troops were taught to disperse, not to bunch up. It was far better to have a web of positions that could support each other cover a large area in depth than to have a densely packed front. It was also essential to conceal defensive positions. An unseen enemy is not at all unique to a guerrilla war. On the contrary, a revealed defensive position in World War II immediately became the target of withering fire of all types from the attacker.

If it was wise to rely on firepower for coverage and to disperse the defense, then the attacker also had to disperse. Except in very rare circumstances, a massed attack, which on a map might have resembled Pickett's Charge, was in truth a general advance over a several-mile front on the part of dozens of small units. Depending on the terrain, they might have seen their neighbors or not. No one could have observed the battlefield as a whole, even in a reconnaissance aircraft. Dispersing the attacking force might have been interpreted as a fundamental breach of military logic. It was the attacker's greatest advantage that he could pick the time and place of assault, thus assuring a superiority of force at the outset. In fact, attackers still exercised that advantage if their assessment of the defensive positions was correct, because the defense was more dispersed than they were. Yet defensive firepower worked to moderate the ability to concentrate. Bunched infantry and tanks could be massacred by artillery and machine guns. An attack, therefore, was like a giant probe. Artillery fired first at all known or suspected targets. Air strikes came in also. Tanks and infantry advanced in small groups, darting from one bit of covering terrain to the next, always on the lookout for the defensive fire that was sure to come. Units did not advance together. Instead, one unit advanced while another covered it, searching for the location of defensive positions. After a short time the advancing unit took cover, and the covering unit leaped over it, reversing the roles. In military parlance, this was called "fire and movement." (The term "fire and maneuver" is preferred today.)

Ultimately, unless the attacker was extremely lucky, the defensive fire would start. In most cases, attackers knew they were near the unseen defender when soldiers started to die or fall wounded. At this point the attacking units would either halt and call in extra artillery or attempt to storm the position with fire-and-movement tactics. If tanks were present, the attacker was much more likely to try the latter, supported by the accompanying infantry's mortar fire. If ground forces were alone, they would call on artillery if at all possible. Direct assault offered the opportunity of rapid breakthrough. This was particularly so if the attackers had both identified the defensive position and simultaneously infiltrated a part of it. While a major attack was proceeding, light supporting patrols also were going forward all along the battlefront. They tried to weave inside the defensive positions and attack the defenders in the rear or flank. These patrols frequently discovered defensive positions the hard way. If infiltration failed, direct assault on defensive positions was terribly risky. The potential gain was substantial, but the possibility for a brutal disaster also existed. Against modern weapons, an ill-timed assault could bring ruin to a unit in the blink of an eye. One can see that attack in World War II was not a game for amateurs.

There was a further reason that attackers must disperse. No major battle was exclusively defensive or offensive. Defenders, unless in desperate straits, had reserves close to the front. The defending commanders knew which positions were key to their line. If the enemy captured or imperiled one of them, the defender would either retreat, reshape the line, or counterattack. A well-placed counterattack was often a deadly blow. Attackers knew this and could not leave gaps in their own lines. Much of the attacker's strength, therefore, had to be allocated to guarding the flanks of the main point of assault. If this was not done, a counterassault could take the attacker in the flank or, worse, in the rear.

Furthermore, because modern weapons were so powerful in defense, it was very hard to crack a position. Battles took days or weeks. If the attacker was strong enough, eventually attrition and exhaustion took its toll, and the line started to crack. If the attacker had air superiority and could limit the supplies reaching defenders, the process took place much faster. A smart defender realized when the game was up and retreated to a fresh position where the process began again. Ultimately, however, unless heavy losses sapped the attacking units' will to advance, the defense would simply run out of men and supplies. At that point, the defender either had to make a strategic withdrawal or face the prospect of the most feared event in war: a double envelopment. Either prospect was unappealing. This was the position the Germans found themselves in during the fall of 1918. It was also the position they found themselves in during the summer of 1944. In 1918 they withdrew. In 1944 Hitler ordered them to stand, and they were smashed in both East and West. That is why the pace of World War II was so odd. A huge battle would rage for weeks, little movement along the line would take place, and then a breakout occurred. Before the defenders were able to establish a new line, the front might have moved several hundred miles in a matter of days. Usually these huge advances accompanied the wholesale destruction of large defending formations through encirclement. One sure sign of a major defeat in either world war was a large number of prisoners.

From this picture we can draw two conclusions. First, in land war as it developed during the world wars, timing and coordination were extremely important. In Europe, on both Eastern and Western fronts, communication and visibility was good enough to allow operations to be managed on a mammoth scale. It was a war for army-group or army commanders like Montgomery, Zhukov, Rommel, or Patton. Corps and divisional commanders were likewise extremely important. To support these titanic forces, a massive rear apparatus appeared. It is important to realize that land operations as large as those that took place in Europe would have been possible only in Europe. Europe had countless roads and a complex rail network. This allowed trains, vehicles, and horse-drawn transport to move and supply masses of men. Very little terrain in Europe is impassable. Both sides could move their forces forward on the roads, but at the point of fire they could move off-road in almost every case. A related factor appeared. The same terrain that allowed movement allowed observation. Strategically, it was very difficult, although not impossible, to hide the movements of large units entirely. Tactical surprise was frequent, but strategic surprise took place rarely. A defender, therefore, might not know exactly when or where an assault would fall, but he almost always knew that one was coming. On the tactical level, defenders could see attackers, however fleetingly, at a distance. Battles were fought at increasingly long range. Conversely, once defenders fired, they revealed their position. This also could be seen from a distance. Fighting at extremely close range was rare. By the time an attacking force was a few hundred yards away, the issue was normally decided. If a close-range slugfest did ensue, it was usually short and extremely violent. The power of modern infantry weapons saw to that.

Because of the mobility possible, the power of weapons, and the great distances that fighting took place, we can see a second crucial factor in infantry combat: the battlefield was a very lonely place. Even though a soldier might have been in an engagement that included several hundred thousand men, it would have been very likely that he and his company saw little beyond their own little horizon. Even companies broke down. The lines of both sides were principally constituted by thousands of foxholes with sentries on duty and small field fortifications where both cover from artillery and small comforts were available. It is striking in an engagement like the Battle of the Bulge how many vital contacts were between very small numbers of infantry fighting over a roadblock. The violence along the front lines was extreme. Artillery fire was like a steady drumbeat. If the enemy knew where the opponent was, mortar attack could come at any time. Patrols went forth every day down the roads and into the hinterlands. Often events were stopped cold by the instantaneous outburst of machine-gun fire. Men rarely saw the enemy, and when they did it was not for long. Defenders had to stay concealed or die. Attackers had to show themselves to move, but, as mentioned, they would use concealment as they advanced. Tanks did the same thing if possible. It was surprisingly difficult to hit a tank with an antitank gun unless it was at quite close range. Every battle involving tanks had moments of truth: tanks in World War II had to stop to fire. If they did so, it meant they had a target. As the turret moved toward the target, and the gun traversed up or down, the defenders either fired first or prayed the tank would miss. If they had no weapon to fight the tank, they ran. In either case, the climax happened very quickly.

There was an exception that proved the rule in Europe. If fighting in an extremely wooded area, or, more likely, inside a town or city, the factors that led to fluid fighting at long range disappeared. If attackers or defenders could not be seen at a distance, it was possible to get very close. (Frequently infantry did not desire this, but were thrust into the situation.) This was ideal defensive terrain. Riflemen, particularly if carrying submachine guns or carbines, could deal devastating blows from concealed positions. With a little luck and a lot of courage, they could kill tanks. Hand grenades went from useless weight to killing weapons. Single buildings, like the famous tractor factory in Stalingrad, could become major points of battle. The hedgerow country of Normandy, where the Germans bottled up the Allied advance weeks after D-Day, was similar. Yet in either a city or dense European terrain, a unit could still move. Perhaps it could not move forward, but it could move laterally or to the rear. The paths and streets were there. Enterprising infantry in towns found "roads" across rooftops. Furthermore, except for the brutal cold that confronted some unprepared armies, the terrain in Europe did not kill. It allowed killing on a massive scale, but it did not assault the heart of the army by itself.

It is in the bizarre and helter-skelter world confronted by the Soviet troops in the tractor factory, or the GIs in Normandy, that we can get a hint of the pulse of the Pacific war. Whereas in Europe the land allowed movement and supported massive forces, in the South Pacific the land brought operations to a crawl and limited their size. No European commander of the most humble army would have faced battle, like the men of the 32d Division, with one artillery piece. In Europe the land required dispersal. Supplies were channeled by a huge communications net, but men and the machines on the front lines could move overland off the roads surprisingly well. In the South Pacific, the land channeled everything. Objectives were obvious and thus tactical surprise on land lost much of its value. The huge armies in Europe required direction and allowed great commanders to exercise their craft. In contrast, officers commanding units above a company had little opportunity to maneuver in the South Pacific. Their skills were more mundane, although frequently just as important. They kept the supplies coming and saw to the basic deployment of their troops. Battles in the South Pacific were run by captains, lieutenants, or sergeants. The ability to observe the battlefield and thus wield effectively the weapons of mass destruction rarely existed in the South Pacific. There, enemy units could and often did confront each other for days at a time only yards apart. A moment of courage in France might very well have involved trying to get a Sherman's turret into firing position more quickly than could the Panther tank 150 yards away that was also moving its gun. In the South Pacific, the moment of truth might well have been found in a submachine-gun battle at ten yards, followed by a bayonet attack.

The one thing that all battlefields shared was isolation. All were small worlds. The men had to depend upon each other's skill and courage. They also had to depend upon their comrades for the company, the talk, and the humor required to stay sane in a savage environment. But in the South Pacific, it was not just the death and injury coming from the war that made the environment savage. Always there was the jungle, and the jungle killed. It was infantry war at its most basic. Consequently, let us start our examination with the basics, and look at the weapons used by the soldiers in the jungle.

Chapter 3

Weapons for a Harsh War

Although machine guns and artillery have ruled most battle-fields in the twentieth century, the South Pacific jungle robbed the machine gunners and artillerymen of the visibility necessary to make their machines work at full effectiveness. Instead, in the half-blind world of the jungle, the infantry regained its traditional role as the arm of decision in South Pacific land combat. The results were striking. At one level, because fighting was so close, it was extremely vicious. Ground combat had an undeniably hard edge fueled by mutual hatred. Yet, at the same time, the "green fog," as one soldier put it, of the jungle also greatly limited the massive, almost impersonal violence that spewed forth from machine guns and artillery.

Infantrymen in a modern army have a variety of weapons at their disposal. Some basic information might be useful: Infantry weapons are differentiated by type, for instance rifles and machine guns, and also by size and type of ammunition. For production purposes it is obviously helpful to standardize on as few types of ammunition as possible. Ammunition is identified by "caliber" (the diameter of the bullet) and sometimes the length of the shell. Americans and Australians measured caliber in inches. The Japanese, like the Europeans, used millimeters. (For convenience' sake, we will use inches for Japanese weapons also. For reasons known only to the Army, mortars and artillery were measured in millimeters.)

A round for a small arm was made up of a bullet and a case. Normally the metal case was larger, and filled with gunpowder. The thinner, tapering bullet was the projectile that left the barrel of the rifle.

The inside of the weapon's barrel was grooved, the term is "rifled," causing the bullet to spin. The spin made the bullet bore its way through the air, allowing it to fly straight for a great range. (In truth, the bullet followed a curved arc. At long range, sights adjusted for this. At very short range, the arc was very slight.) The bullet itself was usually made up of a hard metal covering which gripped the grooves solidly and increased the range and velocity. Inside the metal, the bullet was filled with any of a variety of substances, usually lead.

Different types of weapons might fire the same ammunition. For instance, the Thompson submachine gun fired the same round as the Colt .45-caliber automatic pistol. The ammunition fired by the Lee Enfield rifle used by the Australians was the same as that used by their Bren light machine gun. There were many other examples. In addition, the use and power of a bullet differs radically upon the size of the shell and the amount of propellent it carries. For instance, the excellent Japanese Nambu 8mm (.31-caliber) pistol carried a bullet that was wider than that of the Springfield rifle. Yet the Springfield's shell was so much larger and barrel so much longer that it could fire much farther and hit much harder. A good shot with a rifle could hit a target at 500 yards. A machine gun, firing the same ammunition, because it fired more rounds, had a somewhat greater effective range.

The men who made weapons were very concerned with the amount of power that a bullet possessed when it struck its target. Hitting power is a function of the weight of the bullet and the speed at which it travels. Rifles and machine guns, which commonly used the same ammunition, had a muzzle velocity of approximately 2,800 feet per second when the round left the barrel. The length of the barrel would also increase velocity, but this was limited by the need to make a weapon manageable. There was a further complication. A heavy bullet, like the .45 caliber fired from the Thompson, had a lower muzzle velocity, but at close range still delivered a very good punch. The problem was that the power of a heavy, low-velocity round dissipated quickly with range.

These technicalities were of interest to the soldiers, whether they were mechanically inclined or not. It is important to realize that infantrymen were surrounded by weapons day and night. People slept with their rifles and carried them everywhere they went in the battle zone. Obviously, a decent weapon could spell the difference between life and death. But they were also a part of the soldier's world, a physical artifact that separated the battle zone from the rear.

It is also important to make a final distinction concerning weapons. In the jumbled world of jungle combat, as we shall examine soon, small squad-level engagements were extremely common. The military assigned the most basic and most portable weapons to all standard infantry squads. These weapons, consequently, would have been present in almost every engagement fought in the South Pacific. Officers placed larger and more powerful weapons higher up the organizational chart. Depending upon the circumstances, therefore, artillery, mortars, or medium machine guns might or might not be used. Direct air or naval bombardment support were at the top of the pyramid and used sparingly. In other words, a large battle might include every weapon the division could bring to bear. In a lightning-fast firefight, the most powerful weapons often remained mute because they were either out of range, out of sight, or there was not enough time to bring them to bear. It is vital to realize that even large encounters often broke down into a very poorly coordinated collection of squad actions. Some squads might be fighting with powerful support while others, a hundred yards away, were back to basics.

Small but Lethal Tools

The twelve men (in battle the number was usually lower) of an infantry squad carried several types of weapons, all extremely deadly in their place. Yet all armies started their weapons training with the rifle. All had made a cult of the weapon. It was a tie to the past, a symbol of the infantry. Pity the poor American recruit who referred to a rifle as a "gun," for he would feel the full wrath of the DI. Tony Balsa, who led a mortar platoon in the Marines, can speak for soldiers of all armies:

If you were a Marine, you were always a rifleman. If you were a radioman, a cook, or anything, you always were expected to be a rifleman. From the first day you started training, the Corps taught you to love your rifle like your mother.

The rifle was also a major part of his combat load. The weapon itself weighed approximately nine pounds. In addition there was the ammunition. Soldiers were issued six to eight clips for the M1. However, almost all combat infantry carried extra ammunition if possible. This was one area where soldiers chose what they wanted as long as the supplies were adequate. Tony Balsa continues:

They gave us an ammo belt with six clips or so. We'd put all sorts of things in them, cigarettes or fish hooks. Who knows. But in our pockets we always carried extra clips, six or eight usually. I carried an extra eighty rounds. I never knew a combat infantryman that didn't carry more than the assigned load of ammunition. You could get separated from your unit on the front line, and then there would be no way to get ammunition. Usually you didn't use what they gave you, but what if you did get into a long fight? Just the thought of running out of ammunition made you feel uneasy: you'd have an empty rifle. Actually, a problem for some of the new guys was carrying too much. Too many clips, or grenades. You had to balance the needs of fighting with getting overloaded.

Marines on Guadalcanal, and Australian riflemen throughout the war, used very similar weapons, the Model 1903 Springfield and the Lee Enfield Mark III respectively. Both were developed in their original form before World War I, both were extremely rugged, and both were very accurate in the hands of a good marksman. Like most rifles used in both world wars, the Springfield and Enfield were breech-loading repeaters. The soldier fired one round at a time, after which he both loaded another round and cocked the rifle by retracting a bolt. The Enfield was probably the best rifle of its type ever built. The Springfield, like most weapons of this type, had a five-round magazine, the Enfield a ten. The Enfield had a smoother action and

could be fired more rapidly. The bullet fired from the Enfield was a
.303 caliber, the Springfield's a slightly smaller .30 caliber.

The Springfield's long service ended at Guadalcanal with the
Marines. The American Army, and later the Marines, used the best
rifle of World War II, the M1 Garand. Unlike the Enfield, the M1
was a semiautomatic weapon. In other words, it was not necessary to
cock the weapon once it was armed. As the soldier fired, the recoil
caused by the propellent operated a mechanism that ejected the old
shell casing and loaded a new one. The magazine held eight rounds.
The rifle was slightly heavier than the Springfield or Enfield, 9.6
pounds versus 8.7. Yet the higher rate of fire and somewhat greater
muzzle velocity more than made up for that one disadvantage. Tony
Balsa expresses his appreciation for the M1:

> The Springfield .30 was a good rifle for its time. The M1 was
> better. It was semiautomatic and fired as fast as you pulled the
> trigger. It was steady. Unlike some rifles, it didn't kick up real
> high. You'd hold it on a target and pump one bullet after another.
> And the M1 had more punch and better velocity. When you hit
> somebody with it, it knocked them down. Someone hit with the
> Springfield might fight back. If the M1 hit you in the arm or leg,
> that was it, you'd stay down.

Balsa was right about the hitting power of the rifle, although the
ballistic difference between any of the models was not great. During
the war the Army sent medical research teams to various theaters
around the world during or immediately after a campaign. Their
purpose was to find out what weapons killed and wounded soldiers,
and, to the degree it was possible, to also ascertain what the soldiers
were doing when struck. The teams sent to the South Pacific were at
New Georgia and on Bougainville during the heavy fighting in early
1944. Although the samples were smaller than ideal, and conclusions
on a few subjects tentative, some findings were very clear and coin-
cide precisely with a mass of observations coming from the participants in battle. One finding was very striking. Although mortars and
grenades caused nearly half the overall casualties, a very high percentage of victims lived and returned to their units after treatment.

Many of these men continued to fight until a lull in the action allowed a medic or corpsman to tend to their wounds. Rifles and machine guns, however, both of which fired the same high-velocity ammunition, killed a much higher percentage of the men they struck. The force caused by a high-velocity bullet at close range (over half the men were hit within twenty-five yards, nearly 85 percent within fifty yards) created a very serious wound. Helmets offered protection from mortar and grenade fragments, but almost none against a bullet. Therefore, a soldier struck by a rifle bullet frequently suffered broken bones and massive hemorrhaging. The most common killing wound came from a rifle bullet striking the head.

The Japanese philosophy toward infantry weapons, as one might expect, stressed lightness and mobility. To a certain extent the Japanese made a virtue out of necessity. The Japanese military had to watch its expenditures closely, particularly prior to 1940 when budgets were tight and a fierce competition for funds went on with the Navy. A light-infantry Army, which suited the military philosophy of the country so well, was also much more economical. Expensive weapons that required massive backup like tanks and heavy artillery were rare in the Japanese military. In many cases this caused serious trouble for Japanese commanders. Ironically, it also led them to develop weapons that were unsuitable for most battlefields, but very good for the jungle.

The Arisaka Model 38 rifle, the most common Japanese infantry weapon in the South Pacific, is one of the best examples of a bad weapon fitting well the freakish circumstances of jungle warfare. A bolt-action repeater like the Springfield, the Arisaka Model 38 was developed early in the century like most weapons of the type: "38" refers to the thirty-eighth year in the Emperor Meiji's rule, 1905. Although the firing mechanism was based on the famous German Mauser, the Arisaka was a unique weapon from the start. Because production techniques were poor in Japan, and the Japanese Army was determined to build its own weapon, it made many compromises. The sights were poor, as was the "fit and finish" of the weapon. More important, Japanese industry was unable to produce a .30-caliber rifle that was strong enough to stand up to the stress caused by repeated firing of a large shell without making the barrel thicker, and the rifle much heavier, than others of its type. Out of necessity they created a rifle like no other. First, it was 50.25 inches in length, six inches longer and a pound heavier than the Springfield. When a bayonet was added, common practice in the Japanese Army, the rifle was longer than many Japanese soldiers were tall. Japanese infantry, shorter than their Western counterparts, had a comic look on parade that may have contributed to many misjudging their prowess. In theory the Japanese should have built a shorter rifle than average for their men instead of the world's longest. As one might expect, the Model 38 was hard to aim, difficult to handle, and tougher on the soldiers because of its extra weight.

The Arisaka also fired a .25-caliber bullet, considerably smaller than the .30 or .303 caliber used elsewhere. (A small increase in caliber means a much larger round. A .50-caliber heavy-machine-gun bullet is five times heavier than a .30-caliber round fired by a medium machine gun or rifle.) The ammunition was less expensive to produce and lighter to carry. But this small advantage could not hide the fact that a modern armament industry would have created a lighter weapon had the Japanese chosen a lighter round. The Arisaka, as noted, was the heaviest weapon in the world. The extra weight came from the extra length. In its turn, the Arisaka was so long because it was the only way that Japanese engineers of the time could give the weapon the muzzle velocity needed for the range and accuracy required of a military rifle.

Infantry weapons last a long time. Although many "old" Marines claimed they preferred the Springfield to the M1 (they were few: the M1 was unquestionably superior), the reason the Corps carried it to Guadalcanal was because there were a lot of them sitting in armories and the Navy had chosen to build ships, not buy M1s. The Japanese military realized that the Model 38 Arisaka was a poor weapon, but did not replace it because they had made so many. In 1939 they started to produce the Model 99 Arisaka, which was shorter, lighter, and fired a .303 round. Notwithstanding the superiority of the Model 99, thousands of the Model 38 existed. As the Model 38 fired the same round as the standard Japanese light machine gun,

switching rifles would have caused serious supply problems. Therefore, the Army made no attempt to replace the Model 38 as its standard rifle during the war. (Most Model 99s went to troops stationed
on the plains of Manchuria, where superior range was important.
Some units in the South Pacific had 99s later in the war.) Although
there was a shorter version of the Model 38 also produced, most Japanese infantry in the South Pacific carried the standard "long"
Model 38.

Japanese infantry, for all the wrong reasons, had an excellent
weapon for jungle use. First, Japanese chemists worked diligently
and produced a very good "smokeless" powder. Combined with the
long barrel and smaller round of the Model 38, it produced a very
small flash with almost no smoke. In the jungle this was crucial. Because a soldier rarely had a clear visual target, a puff of smoke in daylight, or an inch of flame at night coming from the barrel, identified
the location of the enemy. Some GIs called the M1 "old smoke pole"
because of the emission of gas and flame when it fired. U.S. Army
doctors could not understand why there were so many head wounds
suffered by U.S. troops. It is very likely that Japanese infantry during
an exchange of fire aimed at smoke or flame. As long as soldiers held
the stock of a rifle against their shoulder and sighted down the barrel,
this condition would attract rounds toward the skull. (U.S. soldiers in
Vietnam also suffered a large number of catastrophic wounds to the
head and upper body. Both sides had rifles with a large flash and used
tracer bullets. Both sides rarely had visual targets and therefore fired
at the flash.)

Furthermore, because of the small shell, the Model 38 had a very
mild recoil. This was also important. Although it was ungainly to aim
because of its length, a respectable marksman who was firing prone,
or supporting his rifle on some object, could get off a second round
very quickly. Marines trained their marksmen to prepare for the sizable recoil of the Springfield, bringing the barrel down for a second
shot. Those not skilled with the weapon were likely to commit an infantry sin as old as rifles: firing high.

In addition, the .25-caliber bullet gave Japanese infantry two
other advantages that, paradoxically, derived from defects. Neither

the Model 38 nor the light machine gun that fired the same round possessed the fine tolerances required to gain the very high muzzle velocity theoretically possible from the light round. (Rifles firing light rounds at very high velocity, like the American M16 or the Israeli Galil, are the best available today.) Indeed, the bullet wobbled slightly in flight, a condition called "yaw" in ballistics. This gave the round a characteristic "crack" when it passed overhead or struck nearby. Not as loud as larger shells, and possessing an odd noise, it was very difficult to tell from which direction the round was coming. Obviously, the lack of flash or smoke amplified this problem. Allied infantry either had to fire blind or, if they were smart, not fire until they saw something move. Japanese infantry were normally concealed during the day, and if a branch or large leaf moved, GIs would pummel the area with fire. Ernest Gerber was a platoon leader at the "Triangle," a Japanese position at Buna with very dense cover. He describes the effect of Japanese small arms:

Japanese weapons, and especially their rifles, were generally smokeless. We couldn't see where the gun was firing from. Noise is very deceptive. You hear something. One guy yells, "It's over there!" Another guy yells the same thing but points in the opposite direction. This is where you need fire discipline. It's so easy to just start blasting away at anything. That gives away your position and, if you're firing blind, the chances of your hitting one of your own men is pretty high. So you had to look, watch, be patient. In retrospect the situation was very interesting. At the time it was hopeless from the military point of view.

Scott Wilson was an infantryman with the 25th Division on Guadalcanal and had a similar experience:

The positions were so well camouflaged that the only way we found them often was when they opened fire. The density of the growth of the jungle absorbed sound, distorted it. It was very hard to tell from which direction the bullets were coming. You would have to see leaves or something move. It was almost impossible to tell where it was coming from. When I was on Guadalcanal, the division was advancing. Attacking is always harder: they know where you are, you don't know where they are. It's pretty simple.

Louis Kidhardt, a company commander with the 25th Division, also believed that the Japanese derived considerable benefit from their small arms, which, on paper, were poorly designed and poorly made:

You reacted to sounds more than sights during combat. We both used smokeless powder. Except our smokeless powder was very easy to see: they could spot us much easier than we could spot them. Their smokeless powder was smokeless: I do not remember seeing a flash or smoke from a Japanese rifle. We could tell where the Japs were by the crack of the bullet going through a leaf or something in front of them: it snapped like a firecracker. It was a big advantage in detection for the Japanese.

Al Careaga of the 1st Marine Raiders speaks for many American and Australian soldiers when he describes the characteristic sound of the Japanese rifle:

I remember the sound of the Japanese .25-caliber rifles like it was yesterday. It's said that you don't hear the bullet that hits you, and I guess that's true because most bullets travel faster than the speed of sound. But you hear the ones that miss. A round of any kind going over your head makes a kind of hissing whistle. That little bullet is moving a lot of air traveling so fast. You also hear a kind of cracking, pinging sound if the enemy is close. If it landed a few inches from your ear in the jungle, there'd be some kind of impact sound. A thunk, or a splash or ricochet. Plenty of times a bullet hit close by. It would kick up dirt, or rocks or mud. I heard that sound more often than I wanted to in several battles, but I never saw any burst of fire. It was so hard to tell where they were shooting from.

Lastly, the "yaw" from the small round caused a very ugly wound, in many cases more than compensating for its lack of weight. The .25 round, because of its slight wobble, commonly struck at a slight angle causing the round to tumble. An Army medical report described the result:

> The 0.256 bullet, especially one made with a gliding metal (an alloy of copper and zinc) jacket, when it hit a target had an explosive effect which tended to separate, leaving the entire jacket in the wound while the bullet went on through. Small globules of lead scattered through the wound and embedded themselves elsewhere in the flesh. This condition was the result of the fact that the rear-section of the walls of the bullet jacket, which was filled with a lead core, were thinner than the forward walls. The sudden stoppage of the high-velocity bullet when it hit an object produced a tendency to burst the rear walls causing an "explosion." The lead core, which had a greater specific gravity, penetrated, leaving behind the relatively lighter jacket from which it had been discharged . . . The unusually large exit wound openings often found with this caliber of bullet were due to the natural instability of the bullet and the possibility of its being fired from inferior weapons. Similarly, there were elliptic entry wounds, a result of the "keyholing" effect of bullets hitting with their sides.

All riflemen carried a bayonet. It was a good utility tool, but its military usefulness by World War II was very limited. Bill Crooks's description of how the bayonet fit into the scheme of things in the AIF is valid for American forces also. Note, however, that Crooks's observation concerning Japanese infantry is very accurate:

> The bayonet was indispensable for opening your tin of bully beef or hanging an empty tin over the fire to boil your tea. If you stood up at night to take a pee you would fix your bayonet on your rifle and poke the ground around your foxhole. It was usually raining and you couldn't see a bloody thing. Every now and then someone would poke a trip wire the Japs laid. If you heard a squeak, you knew you'd stuck an infiltrator. That was rare. However, we often fixed bayonets before an attack. It was a morale booster for us rather than a weapon. The soldier would let out a yell and charge forward with his bayonet. But the killing

and wounding was done with bullets. Men were killed with bayonets but it was very uncommon. This was true with American
forces also.

The Jap always had a bayonet on the end of his rifle. It was
part of their system of indoctrination. You'd see films of them
marching. Men, fingers stiff, marching with their rifles and bayonets. You add eight and a half inches to a rifle that was already
too long and nine times out of ten it's taller than the bloke carrying it. The knife and sword tied into bushido and the indoctrination the Jap soldiers received. When he was approaching our
lines at night he'd take it off because it would make too much
bloody noise if it got caught in the vines. But we ambushed some
Japs on our way back up the Kokoda Trail. We were lying in
some kunai grass and they were marching down a track, jabbering away, with their rifles slung over their shoulders. They
had their bayonets fixed. Some of the Japanese that were hit tried
to get the rifle off their shoulder and charge us with their bayonet. We killed them first. It must have been reflex for the Japanese, a product of training. It was not our way.

No doubt the rifle had a place in the jungle due to its ruggedness
and power. In a theoretical twelve-man squad, approximately ten soldiers would carry rifles. In the Japanese Army, this percentage was
probably closely adhered to because they had fewer alternatives. Not
so in the Allied armies. The major reason that so many rifles were
employed in the South Pacific was because there were so many rifles
issued. In the close-range fights that often broke out, rifles were in
many respects poor weapons. They were too large, but, more important, they lacked sheer firepower. Consequently, many soldiers
greatly preferred submachine guns.

The submachine gun was developed independently by the Americans and Germans during World War I. It is a fully automatic
weapon that fires pistol rounds. It is meant for close-range combat,
so barrel length and muzzle velocity are sacrificed for mobility and
rate of fire. In the initial stage of the Pacific war, the only submachine
gun available was the Thompson .45 caliber, made famous by Holly-
wood gangster movies.

The Thompson was invented during World War I. The U.S. Army did not purchase it after the war, although some armies bought small quantities. American gun laws were lax, however, and the weapon was sold privately. It was popular not only with criminals and police but also with career soldiers. Many Marines bought them for use on their far-flung postings. When the buildup for war began, a huge demand for the "Tommy" appeared from the U.S. and British forces. By Pearl Harbor it was a standard part of the infantryman's toolbox in the U.S. military. Still wedded to the rifle cult, Army commanders made no place for submachine guns in American infantry battalions. Instead, they became part of a pool of weapons held by the division headquarters and dispensed upon request. (They were issued to mechanized infantry, rangers, and armored units.)

The Thompson was a very controversial weapon. Much more expensive than rifles, they were initially distributed in relatively small numbers. In an American squad, one man might carry a Tommy. It was complex, required constant cleaning, and the barrel overheated in battle, causing a bulge and destroying the weapon's effectiveness. Furthermore, weighing in at over twelve pounds, the Tommy was very heavy. American soldiers in the Solomons did not use the Thompson often because, in their opinion, despite radically different ammunition, it made a sound similar to the Japanese .25-caliber light machine gun. Some used it anyway, but most stuck with their M1s. Marshall Chaney, an infantryman on Guadalcanal explains the view of the majority:

We didn't like the .45-caliber Thompson. In heavy cover it sounded too much like the Japanese .25-caliber rifle. The Japanese also had a poorly made but very serviceable .25 light machine gun like our BAR. They weren't precision-made and I guess were more like the English Bren gun. Our Thompson sounded just like it. Many times when you were on patrol in dense underbrush one of your own men could be a few feet away and you couldn't see him. Well, the Japanese might be a few feet away too. These were crazy affairs, over in the blink of an eye sometimes. There was danger enough of hitting your own people. But if an American opened up with a Thompson, he might draw fire from our own troops.

It is one of the little mysteries of World War II that the opinions of many soldiers and Marines in the Solomons concerning the Thompson were not shared by their American and Australian comrades in New Guinea. In New Guinea, the Tommy was extremely popular. One can see why. Although very heavy and a problem to maintain, the Thompson had important redeeming features. It fired the .45-caliber round used by the standard Army Colt sidearm. Naturally, the Tommy had a much longer barrel than a pistol, yet the muzzle velocity was less than half that of a rifle. This made the weapon both inaccurate and deficient in punch at long range. At point-blank range, however, it was a very different story. The .45 bullet was all lead and heavy. At very close range the weight of the heavy lead bullet compensated for the lack of velocity. The Tommy, in other words, stopped an enemy unfortunate to be hit with one. Although the largest submachine gun in the world, it was still ten inches shorter than an M1 and consequently easier to wield in close quarters. It possessed a larger recoil than other weapons of its type, but soldiers could still fire it from the hip. Also, like all submachine guns, the Tommy was capable of fully automatic fire at the very fast rate of 700 rounds per minute. Military versions carried a 20- or 30-round box magazine, although 50- and 100-shell drum magazines were available. For all these reasons, the Thompson had its advocates in the Pacific and Europe long after lighter, smaller, and more durable makes appeared.

Australians liked the Tommy a great deal. They did so much fighting at close quarters that submachine guns were very valuable. During the dozens of engagements along the Kokoda Trail, Australian and Japanese patrols collided in daylight unexpectedly. When that happened, it was impossible to have too many Thompsons. Originally, submachine guns were not organic to the Australian infantry squad. Instead, infantry battalions had 200 that could be allocated according to the tactical situation. Many AIF units that in

Europe dealt with mechanized equipment or very heavy weapons had no function in the jungle. Given more appropriate tasks in New Guinea, these units drew on the supply of submachine guns whether they were on the spearpoint or not.

In practice the Thompson soon became an integral part of the Australian squad, which was called a section. Although assigned strength was nine, sections often went out with fewer men. This phenomenon was not unusual and was found in all the armies. As noted earlier, the noncombat or semicombat personnel constituted a sizable percentage of men down the line in a fighting division. An Australian division, with a paper strength of approximately 14,000, had thirty-six sections in a battalion (three each for the four line companies). There were nine battalions in the division, three in each brigade, making 324 infantry sections doing most of the fighting. Many of the other units, like mortars and artillery, had important combat roles. Everyone was at risk. Yet, in the jungle, the infantry section was at the point of contact in almost every case. If one allows ten per section, 3,200 men were the cutting edge of the division. In practice, the number was 2,500 or less as combat losses mounted.

There was an obvious practical result from this fact. Infantrymen wanted as much firepower as possible within the limits of weight carried and supplies available. Bill Crooks was a platoon sergeant in the elite AIF 7th Division and describes how all of this worked out:

> You never go into action with nine men. The normal movement of people through the system means you invariably have seven or eight men per section. Usually long-range patrols were led by an officer, a sergeant, or a corporal carrying a submachine gun. It was *sacrosanct* that point scouts carried a rifle, as they often were knocked off and we did not want to lose a submachine gun. But it was also *sacrosanct* that he was always *covered* by a body with a submachine gun, unusually the patrol or section commander, so that he could blast the area or surroundings with lead. The covering section of the squad was led by the second in charge, usually a lance corporal. He also carried a submachine gun. He was also in charge of the Bren light machine gun. So the covering element supported the assault element led by the section leader

and rest of the riflemen. This is "fire and movement" and you could see it operate all the way up the line. Assault section covered by cover section. Now in theory the men carried many extras in addition to their own weapons and ammunition. Some were supposed to lug an extra magazine for the Bren gun, one or two bombs for the platoon mortar, other specialized grenades, entrenching tools, periscopes, and the list goes on. (Ye Gods, I'm having a heart attack thinking about it.) But you see in the desert all of that came up in trucks. In the Ramu Valley we had little two-wheeled trailers where we could dump the extras. In the Owen Stanleys, away went the pick and shovel, away went the mortar bombs, away went the periscopes, away went the wire cutters. Because in the jungle, actions were usually fast and furious: mostly Bren, Tommy and grenades.

The Tommy fitted nicely into the scheme of things:

Even in World War I everybody had long found a need for close-up automatic, blast them, firepower. The rifle was too slow, the grenade too dangerous in close. And the enemy had this habit of coming at you with leg, arm, even head and body wounds, several of them, and they would keep coming. All terribly traumatic and certainly hairy.

The Tommy was a bitch of a thing to keep clean and difficult to maintain. The solid-lead bullet [which had a thin zinc covering that was dispersed by the time it left the barrel, leaving a lead round in flight—EB] did funny things to the barrels and was inclined to jam. But I can assure you that when the chips were down and you were likely to use it to save your or your mates' lives and remove the opposition, *you could guarantee the men kept them scrupulously clean*, with oily rags wrapped around when action was not imminent.

Remember, the basic aim was to quickly blast 'em, but above all to *stop them in their tracks and make sure they stayed hit*. Thus the unjacketed lead .45 caliber. It achieved the same stopping power, even with its low muzzle velocity, of a present-day rifle. In the hands of resolute and experienced citizens of the World War II infantry, and a section leader to add bonus, and a second in charge to add an additional bonus, no one in his right mind

would ever consider stepping down to a smaller weapon that did
not stop anybody if he is primed up on Jap saki or bushido banzai. The experience of the AIF was simply that if you blast 'em
with a solid-lead Tommy bullet, usually in a burst of three to five
rounds, you can lay Custer to the OK Corral, and the target
would have no further interest in proceeding.

Crooks describes how this worked out in practice:

In the real jungle of the South Pacific things happen instantly.
You are all strung out in single file on a native track two feet wide
and you have a dead point scout up front. You do not know
where the shot came from, but you have some general idea: remember, ranges are about ten or twenty feet. At that time *nothing*
can replace a half magazine of solid lead .45 bullets for scaring
the hell out of you the firer, not to mention the Jap (whether he
is hit or not), plus all the wildlife. It was deafening all around
you. The Tommy was the best foliage remover this side of a lawn
mower. This is why you will find all experienced AIF men plug-
ging for the Tommy.

In 1943 the AIF lost its Thompsons. The Australian government
began producing a lighter submachine gun made by the Owen Company. The Owen was lighter, more reliable, and smaller than the
Thompson. It fired a lighter round. It was very similar to the famous
British Sten submachine gun (which the Australian Army recom-
mended adopting) and had two vital advantages. It was "stamped
out" and consequently easy and inexpensive to produce. It was also
an Australian weapon, an attractive idea to a nation that had magnificent fighting forces but used British and American weapons almost
exclusively. On the other hand, the Owen was known for "accidental
discharge," even when the safety was on. Old AIF veterans like
Crooks did not like the new weapon at first, but soon the soldiers
grew accustomed to it and appreciated its many advantages. Australian forces used the Owen until the beginning of the Vietnam War.

In late 1943, Thompson lovers in the American Army also began
losing their weapon. Before the war the Army developed a carbine
version of the M1 to replace pistols for combat commanders and rear

service personnel. ("Carbine" is a very old term referring to a short and light rifle designed for cavalry use.) Although the mechanism was the same as the M1, it had no interchangeable parts and fired a smaller shell of the same caliber. The weapon lost range and punch, but was only twenty-five inches long and weighed less than seven pounds. A late version was capable of fully automatic fire. Designed originally as a specialty weapon, 7 million carbines were produced, making it the most common American rifle in the military at war's end.

The carbine's success was predictable. It represented another step in a long-term trend away from stressing accuracy in a rifle in favor of rate of fire. Soldiers found, in other words, that they rarely had the opportunity to take careful aim at a target. Instead, it was usually wise to put as much lead in the air as possible. Sacrificing range, which was inevitable with light, short-barreled weapons like the carbine or submachine guns, was worth the trade-off. On the European battlefield, the long-range weapons were machine guns, mortars, and artillery. The M1 or British Enfield were less important unless the terrain allowed for close combat. Because it was sent to Europe first, the carbine arrived late in the Pacific, where, of course, it was needed far more. M1 carbines remain in use around the world. The only real defect to the original model was, as with the Owen, related to the safety. The button releasing the safety and the button releasing the clip were close. (Only a fool in a line unit carried a weapon that did not have the safety mechanism engaged. Disengaging the safety meant it was time to fight.) More than one soldier, when reaching to disengage the safety in preparation for firing, pushed the wrong button and watched the magazine drop to the ground. The Japanese had a carbine version of the Arisaka Model 38, but Americans did not encounter it often. The Japanese did not have a submachine gun in common use.

Despite the understandable desire of supply personnel to standardize military equipment, large wars feature a menagerie of weapons. The jungle with its bizarre combat environment invited the use of unusual weapons. Although it was banned by the Geneva Convention, so obviously not standard issue, the American military slipped

powerful Springfield 12-gauge shotguns into the arsenal in the South
Pacific. Some men used their own. The rules banning the use of the
shotgun were an incredible anachronism by the time of World
War II. The wounds delivered by high-velocity bullets and high explosives had made a mockery of the attempt early in the century to
create wars where wounds would be "clean." Many American infantrymen liked shotguns for patrolling. Like the Thompson, it was
loud. Unlike the Thompson, it was an excellent weapon to fire half-
blind because its limited range greatly reduced the chances of
friendly-fire casualties. (All hunters get a bit anxious when they hear
a deer rifle fire nearby. They are far less concerned if another hunting party is using shotguns.)

Robert Kennington walked "point" on patrols. Originally issued
a Thompson, he requested a shotgun instead. He describes his
motivation:

> I picked a shotgun. Originally there was big trouble with the
> cardboard shell casings. In the humidity they'd swell up and jam
> the gun. Metal shell casings solved that. I used it for snipers. The
> snipers tied themselves to the trees. If you hit one with the
> twelve-gauge firing double-aught buckshot, you knew right away
> whether he was dead or playing hooky. If you shot at snipers with
> a rifle, you never knew if you'd hit him. You see, they tied them-
> selves in the tree, so even if he was wounded or dead he wouldn't
> fall. And you couldn't see. The shotgun would make a hole
> through the leaves and a hole through the sniper.
>
> It would tear a sniper up real good at fifty yards. I was on pa-
> trol and saw movement in a limb of one of the big trees. This was
> off Hill 27 at the Gifu Strong Point. I nudged the lieutenant and
> pointed. The sniper sat down on his limb and looked at us, like
> "Who are you: what are you doing here?" I whispered, "Do you
> want me to take him," and brought my gun up. The lieutenant
> nodded, and I shot him off the limb. Before he hit the ground
> one of the other guys shot him. Another Jap jumped out from be-
> hind the tree, and one of the other men shot him down. The
> lieutenant was smart. He decided they'd spotted us now, and we

were risking ambush. We turned around and went back up the hill on the double.

Kennington was not alone in his choice of weapon. Infantryman Marshall Chaney recalls seeing the famous General Alexander Patch, Vandegrift's successor on Guadalcanal, and later Army leader in Europe, on the front lines carrying a shotgun. Chaney recalls, "I never saw a man with a harder face." (While in Europe, Patch's son was killed in combat. Patch remarked, "At least he's not cold, wet, and hungry.")

Every combat infantryman carried hand grenades. The number varied with personal preference, the circumstances, and weight. One of the oldest infantry weapons, the grenade, within its limits, was very valuable. In principle, all hand grenades are the same. The American MK2 hand grenade, called the "pineapple" by the millions of men who carried one, was typical of the breed. It weighed about a pound and a half, and most soldiers could lob one about 100 feet. Inside the pineapple were two ounces of TNT. Surrounding the charge was a cast-iron casing that was serrated, defining the size of fragments emitted after the explosion. World War II hand grenades, unlike many modern varieties, relied upon fragments of metal, instead of the explosive shock itself, to kill and wound. The military call this type a "defensive grenade," because some fragments travel farther than the throwing range, making it most advisable to throw a grenade prone or behind cover. In other words, a soldier who while standing threw a pineapple 100 feet could be killed by a fragment from his own grenade.

When the weapon exploded, its fragments dispersed very rapidly. In particular, fragments that flew at an upward or downward angle become ineffective quickly. Consequently, the military determined a "casualty radius" for such weapons. In the case of the pineapple, a fragment would probably hit a Japanese soldier standing within eight or nine yards of the explosion. The fuze on the pineapple was crude but safe. Immediately before throwing the pineapple, the soldier pulled out a pin safety device, and then squeezed a curved lever.

When thrown, the lever flew off, igniting a five-second time fuze. Sometimes soldiers would remove the lever prior to throwing, thus shortening the time before explosion. If they did so, they eliminated the small risk of the victim's throwing the grenade out of harm's way. The technique also allowed the grenade to explode before it hit the ground, greatly increasing the power of the weapon. The risks of this technique are obvious.

The grenades used by each army differed in detail. We have looked at the pineapple in a generic form, but it is worth noting that early supplies of U.S. hand grenades were notorious for unreliability. The fuzes did not stand up to the humidity, many were too old, and many GIs lobbed a dud in time of danger. This situation improved greatly as new stocks moved forward. The Australians used the British-designed #36 Mills hand grenade. (The pineapple was an improvement on the original Mills introduced in World War I.) It was heavier and more powerful than its American counterpart and much more reliable. Therefore, it amplified both the advantages and disadvantages of the weapon. The Japanese design went in the opposite direction. The Japanese had many small firms building infantry weapons and possessed a multitude of types. Their Type 97 standard grenade was light, weighing about one pound, and emitted very large numbers of very small fragments that were, in the words of one American victim of a Japanese grenade, "almost like pepper." It possessed an extremely odd fuze. A Japanese infantryman held the weapon pointed at the ground, pulled a safety pin, and struck the grenade against any hard surface, igniting the fuze. The fuze itself was noted for its poor quality. A wise Japanese soldier threw it immediately, as the delay might be considerably less than expected.

All grenades had serious defects. First, grenades in the open were good wounding weapons, but not very good at killing, the Japanese and American models particularly so. Tens of thousands of men still walk around with tiny Japanese grenade fragments embedded in their bodies. A more serious difficulty accompanied the grenade's greatest strength. By definition, hand grenades are designed for short-range fighting. Because a soldier can lob a grenade, he can strike at an enemy in a foxhole close by when heavier weapons would be as likely to kill him or his comrades. On the surface, one would think the grenade would have been perfect for the jungle because combat was frequently at close range. Sometimes this was the case. In many circumstances, however, the range was so close that the grenade became very dangerous to use. A jungle firefight, whether day or night, was characterized by a lack of visibility. Time was measured in seconds or minutes, and it was very rare that a soldier could see his comrades, much less the enemy. It was a dangerous environment in which to throw hand grenades. This was particularly true because dense foliage created a serious danger that the grenade would hit a branch or other object on the way to the target and bounce backward. All armies had launching devices that they could attach to their rifles to propel a grenade 100 yards or so. Although useful in places, they were clumsy. Because everyone had superior alternatives for most occasions, rifle grenade launchers were not a vital weapon. Lastly, like many other weapons, American grenades at the beginning of the war did not stand up to the jungle well, and had a high percentage of "duds."

Frank Hurray was a young officer in early 1944 in New Guinea. At this stage of the war, combat was beginning to "open up," with larger units and more firepower involved. Still, the jungle remained. Hurray discusses his mixed feelings toward grenades.

We always carried hand grenades, and we used them. But they were not that important. I personally carried them for months and never used one. They could be very useful at night. If you heard a noise at night and wanted to throw a grenade, you could do it. But it was very tricky. You can't throw one very far. You have people around you and you're not sure of their position. You sure don't want to throw one into another guy's foxhole. So a lot of self-discipline was required. They would get your attention at night. They were very loud exploding so close. But you never saw the results during combat because it was so dark and you had your head down. The next morning there might be a dead enemy nearby.

As Hurray indicates, the grenade, despite its dangers, had its place in the jungle. At night, the Japanese frequently probed Allied positions. Major Japanese attacks invariably were launched during the night. In either case, grenades were very valuable. Bill Crooks recalls an Australian technique of countering infiltration:

Sometimes when we tripped over the Japanese and had a shoot-out at point-blank range, grenades were too dangerous for yourself and your own men. But if the situation allowed it, the Mills fragmentation hand grenade was the most lethal close-quarter weapon at the infantry's disposal. The Jap grenade was a poor tin thing but lethal if it hit the body. The Yank model was too thin and did not have the violent explosive charge ours did. At night, part of the bedding-down procedure included running a line of vine between two empty bully-beef cans containing some stones. They would rattle if a Nip tried to sneak in. Normally, the light machine gun did not fire if we were infiltrated, that would give away the position. But the senior night sentry would bellow "Grenades!" and out would go two or three. And that was the end of that.

I experienced this once. One night a Jap managed to get a lasso around my ankle. He and a mate were trying to drag me out of the perimeter line. I had the presence of mind (*long training*) to fit my bayonet on my rifle, stretch out, and stab him in the eye and cut the vine rope. I got back to my hole and rolled a grenade at them, bellowing our required drill, "Bill Crooks—grenade!" to give your mates a chance to take cover.

Soldiers also used grenades for assaulting bunkers. As we shall see, this was one of the most dangerous tasks in a savage war. Because bunkers normally had a log roof, the blast effect of a grenade inside one was tremendous. E. J. Randall of the AIF comments:

Each soldier carried a couple of Mills hand grenades—a bonny weapon especially in dealing with pillboxes. It was very hazardous closing in on one and required teamwork. Also, the Japs had a habit of throwing our grenades back so we had to hold a four-second grenade for two or three seconds before hurling it through the slits (*courage, don't fail me now*).

The last squad weapon universally used in the South Pacific was the light machine gun, often referred to as an LMG. Machine guns were deadly in World War I, but they were heavy and required a crew of specialists. Therefore, all armies tried to create weapons that were light enough to be carried and fired by one man, and still possessed some of the advantages of a true machine gun. Unlike the submachine gun, which was actually a big fully automatic pistol, a light machine gun fired standard rifle ammunition. Every squad encountered situations where there was no substitute for punch, lead in the air, and accuracy. Only the LMG had all of these virtues.

The American Army pioneered in this field. During World War I an American officer developed the Browning automatic rifle, commonly referred to by its acronym BAR. In its time the BAR was a groundbreaking weapon. Called an "automatic rifle" because it could be fired, in theory, from the shoulder, the BAR was a light machine gun. The World War II version weighed twenty pounds, and fired .30-caliber rifle ammunition out of a detachable twenty-round magazine. The BAR defined the advantages of all light machine guns. It was fully automatic and possessed a very high muzzle velocity, making it very powerful and capable of striking at long range. It also defined their disadvantages. A twenty-pound weapon is not something a combat soldier enjoys carrying. Ammunition must be lugged along too. A light machine gun makes little sense unless there are several magazines available. The squad leader doled out BAR magazines to other men, adding to their already heavy loads. Also, all machine guns are complex. The BAR was very well built, but it required diligent maintenance and cleaning or it would jam. The BAR was the standard American squad machine gun through the Korean War, and a few appeared in Vietnam. It was built in such large numbers that it is still found today in small armies operating on tight budgets.

Australian and Japanese squads also carried light machine guns. An Australian squad carried the British designed Bren light machine gun, which was the best LMG used in World War II and one of the most successful infantry weapons of the century. Slightly heavier than the BAR, the Bren accepted a basic thirty-round magazine, but larger ones were available. Equaling or surpassing its American counterpart in performance, the Bren was more reliable. It also had a detachable barrel. This was a desirable feature, because a worn barrel cost the weapon power and accuracy. In theory, a squad was supposed to bring spares, but in the jungle these were often left behind.

Because weapons procurement was so haphazard before the war, the Japanese Army often employed far too many models of the same weapon type. This was true concerning light machine guns. The Japanese had two poor copies of the Bren (both were based on a Czech design) firing .303- or .256-caliber ammunition. But more commonly employed was the older Model 11 Nambu light machine gun. The Nambu was an inferior weapon in almost every category, and was used because the Japanese Army lacked the funds to replace it. Heavy and very unreliable, the Nambu required constant attention. The structural integrity of the Nambu was so poor that it fired a less powerful version of the .256-caliber rifle bullet. However, like the Arisaka rifle, some of its defects were strengths in the jungle. As previously mentioned, the .256 bullet left an ugly wound. Because the Nambu had an even smaller charge than the Arisaka, it emitted less flash and smoke. In an open battlefield, an Allied officer would have had contempt for the Nambu. In the jungle, when placed in one of the ingenious Japanese field fortifications, an almost invisible machine gun was a deadly weapon.

Every weapon is a product of design trade-offs. Light machine guns were very heavy to carry and the least wieldy weapon in the squad. However, if the situation was right they were irreplaceable. Squad combat was unthinkable without them. Although very useful for covering fire, the LMG was most valuable when the squad came under assault by a superior enemy.

A very good example took place in late September 1942 on Guadalcanal during one of the very few botched battles fought by the 1st Marine Division. On September 14, Marine defenders crushed a large Japanese attack on Henderson. A few days later Vandegrift received a major reinforcement in the form of his 7th Regiment. Consequently, Vandegrift decided that his forces were strong enough to extend the Marine perimeter west to the Matanikau River. Two battalions moved up to the east bank of the river in short order, but ran

into fierce Japanese resistance at the river's mouth. Three companies
of the famous Lieutenant Colonel Lewis B. "Chesty" Puller's battalion were ordered to flank the Japanese by landing a few hundred
yards up the coast. They would then move inland and toward the
Matanikau, attacking the Japanese from the rear. Everything went
wrong. The Japanese were stronger than thought. The Marines
landed in a place the Japanese were reinforcing. A large Japanese air
raid disrupted 1st Division communications. Tactical commanders
misunderstood or did not receive important messages. It was the sort
of bad day on the battlefield that took place thousands of times during World War II in every army in every theater. In this case, the Marines flirted with catastrophe, but managed to escape with a slap to
the face.

When Puller's three companies landed, the Japanese resistance,
initially fierce, ceased temporarily. As the Marines moved slowly inland, the Japanese assembled forces, attacked, and quickly surrounded the Marines. A mortar round killed the mission commander
immediately, and communications with the outside ceased. Incredibly, the Marines took off their white T-shirts and spelled-out
"Help" on the grass, and the message was spotted by a Marine aircraft. It was obvious something was wrong in any case, so Colonel
Puller boarded a destroyer and escorted a small flotilla of landing
craft up the beach. (Coast Guard petty officer Douglas Munro received a posthumous Congressional Medal of Honor for heroism
during the desperate fighting near the beach.) When Puller and the
destroyer arrived, Marine fire-control officers assisted Navy gunners
with signal flags. Puller ordered his companies to fight through Japanese lines toward the beach. Aided by powerful naval artillery, the
trapped companies fought their way toward safety. Gus Merrigan recalls how his squad escaped:

> Chesty Puller was our battalion commander. Three companies
> were detailed to go down the beach and land at Point Cruz. The
> whole thing was fouled up. Although we didn't know it, we
> landed at a major Japanese bivouac area. We were supposed to
> push the Japs up the side of a hill, into the hands of other Marine

battalions attacking across the Matanikau. So much for the plan. Instead, the Japs let us go through an opening, let us up on that hill, and then cut off our retreat to the beach. The Japs knew what they were doing. They thought they would get us in the sack and knock us off. It was Sunday afternoon at 1:00. The Japs started throwing mortars at us, and killed Major Rodgers, our commander. We were surrounded. We couldn't get back, we couldn't go forward. We were in big trouble, isolated. The radio-man was killed. They were throwing mortars and firing machine guns at us. A friend near me had both legs shot by a machine gun. Puller got on the *Ballard* and directed fire at the Jap line near our beachhead. We could all see the *Ballard*, and the fire belching out of the guns. They knocked enough holes in the Jap position that we could move. We were under Japanese fire the entire time, or it seemed so. As we retreated, our BAR man covered us until he was killed. Then the platoon leader picked up the BAR and started shooting standing up. This kept the Jap heads down and we moved to the beach while the platoon leader shot away with the Bar. He was killed too, but we were able to make the beach. The whole thing lasted about two hours. It was a fiasco from start fo finish.

Fire Kills

Above squad level, the infantry possessed more devastating weapons. The more complex and powerful the weapon, the higher up the chain it was placed. In jungle warfare, however, quantity and avail-ability were frequently more important than theoretical killing power. This put a premium on the company-level support weapons that were few in type but large in numbers. Although the details var-ied depending upon the force involved, the outline of the arrange-ment was similar in all the armies. Within battalions there were heavy-weapon companies (or platoons). Unlike artillery, which was controlled at the regimental or division level, battalion weapons were intended to support only the companies within the battalion. (Natu-rally, if an ad hoc situation presented itself, friendly units supported each other regardless of affiliation. In combat, enemy moves often made decisions painfully obvious.) Assigning weapons directly to the battalion was a flexible arrangement that cut out an entire command level.

The heavy-weapons company was divided into a machine-gun platoon and a mortar platoon. In addition, many battalions had a cannon company that had four 75mm pack howitzers to supplement the other heavy weapons. These units were not tied to any particular unit. Instead, they were assigned to the rifle companies within the battalion as the need arose. Frequently, geography had much to do with it. All of these weapons are heavy and not easily moved any distance. When on the defensive, this did not present a great problem. But moving crew-served weapons forward in the jungle for an attack was difficult and required serious preparation. In general, these weapons excelled at defense or during a preplanned attack. Their value declined greatly during small-unit slugfests.

A Marine machine-gun platoon was typical enough. It had a paper strength of forty-eight men who operated four water-cooled and four air-cooled medium .30-caliber machine guns. Although medium machine guns fired the same ammunition as the BAR, there were very significant differences. Medium machine guns were much heavier and had crews of two or three. The weight was required for the heavy tripod and very rugged construction needed for sustained fire. Unlike LMGs, which were loaded with a magazine, a true machine gun fired ammunition attached to a belt made of various materials. A single belt typically carried 250 rounds of ammunition. If the supply situation allowed it, a machine-gun position would have several belts. A well-maintained machine gun could continue firing in bursts for a very long time. What resulted, very simply, was a wall of lead. This was the killing mechanism that made the world wars charnel houses for infantry.

Marine Sergeant Mitchell Paige was a "China Marine," a prewar veteran who served in the small Marine contingent stationed in China before the war. Early in his Marine career, Paige was involved with machine guns, commanding a machine-gun platoon on Guadalcanal. He was not alone among professional soldiers. Machine guns were complex weapons. They had to be operated, maintained, and deployed properly to gain the full benefit of their great power. As Paige describes, veteran gunners were skilled practitioners of their craft. Also, as so often happened, the men who used the weapons felt free to alter them according to choice:

I just loved machine guns; I had always served with machine guns. In my company in Tientsin, China, I was in machine guns. When we first shipped overseas, they put us in an early Liberty Ship that was built like a beer can. The poor young sailors were unprepared, just hopeless. They didn't know the bow from the stern. My sergeants and myself ended up running the security on the ship all the way to Samoa. Naturally, that included the machine guns for antiaircraft. When the division was forming in Cuba, I had a company commander named Mahoney. He was the type who would pick your brain: How can we increase rate of fire and accuracy at long range? Here's the barrel and here's the target at 1,000 yards. Now your machine gun vibrates even when on a tripod and supported by sandbags. If it vibrates one millimeter, at 1,000 yards you miss by three feet. Usually the gun vibrated five to six mils. That puts you nine feet off. No soldier in the world is that tall. Now a faster rate of fire actually lessens vibration. The explosions kind of balance each other. So we drilled holes in the bolt, put in double springs, and put in a much more powerful spring in the bolt itself. We scrounged all of this from a machine shop or anywhere else. We improvised. All of this was done in my tent, no laboratory. I had the platoon machine guns in there anyway, and there were machine-gun parts all over. Captain Mahoney, another sergeant, and myself spent hours there. I had beer under my cot. We drink beer and talk machine guns. It worked, too. Mahoney was sharp. The faster we got the thing to fire, the vibration almost ceased. I had all my guns done this way: I called it the Mahoney system. Out on the firing range my platoon was knocking the black out of all the bull's-eyes at 1,000 yards.

The U.S. .30-caliber machine gun came in air-cooled and water-cooled varieties. The air-cooled was lighter at thirty pounds. The water-cooled weighed slightly more, but required, in theory, an apparatus to keep the barrel soaked in water at all time. The tripod and ammunition added a considerable amount of extra weight to either. Ideally, a machine-gun crew had three men, one gunner and two to handle the loading. The second loader was not necessary but, if the other was killed or wounded, the second loader kept the gun operating. In addition, three men could pick the gun up by the tripod and move its position quite quickly. One man was sorely put to move to a fully equipped machine gun.

Despite the bulk, machine guns were ruthless weapons when in their element. The movies of World War I showing machine guns mowing down helpless infantry at short range greatly distort their normal use. In Europe, machine guns exploited their long range. On occasion this was the case in the Pacific also. If a crew was good, it could even master "indirect fire" techniques, shooting at targets, with the aid of a forward observer, that the gunners could not see. Paige describes how this was done:

> I got indirect-fire problems. While we were on Samoa, I challenged Lou Diamond, one of our great mortar men, saying that I could hit anything with my machine guns that he could with his mortars. We were behind a hill. Lou and I started running a problem. I figured a solution about the same time Lou did. We just cut those targets down like that. Lou lobs his mortar and it hits the same place. Lou was mad as hell, and said he'd hit the target on the nose. So I told him, "All I said was that I could hit anything you can."
>
> Months later we were ready to move across the Matanikau River on Guadalcanal. It was our November 1 attack. We were offering fire support from a ridgeline along the river. To the east we could see the Japanese down in the gullies. But it was the far hills we were after. We fired at 2,000 yards and more. We chased a lot of Japs off that hill. That machine-gun bullet was heavy, powerful.

Although the air-cooled version was more popular and stayed in service far longer, Paige and many others preferred the more reliable

water-cooled type. He would have had many supporters in the Australian Army. The Australians relied more on their versatile Bren
than the Americans did on the BAR. However, for serious machine-
gun support they used the extraordinary British Vickers MkI medium machine gun. Water-cooled, the Vickers was little changed
from the original model deployed in the World War I trenches. It
weighed in at a whopping eighty-nine pounds. The World War II
version, however, had an improved sight allowing for very-long-
range fire. Like the water-cooled Browning, the Vickers could fire
indefinitely as long as the ammunition held out. (Air-cooled machine
guns, if allowed to overheat, lost much long-range effectiveness.)
The Bren was the killer with the AIF, but the Vickers was found at
many critical points. Later in the war, the AIF reintroduced special
machine-gun battalions that had been used with deadly effect in
World War I. Capable of indirect fire, they were used to saturate a
given zone with lead. Bill Crooks saw one in action in the Markham
Valley in the summer of 1943:

> We always had Vickers with us in reserve. In the Ramu we
> started toting them around in a little two-wheeled trailer that
> two to four men pulled with a rope. Corps also introduced
> machine-gun battalions that cumulatively had ninety-six Vickers.
> They fired special ammunition. The Japs hated them because
> you could fire for hours and cover an area of half an acre with a
> bullet per square foot. The mass blast noise was worse than all
> the divisional field artillery, and it shimmered as a noise wave in
> the atmosphere. My God, it was incredibly loud and fearful. The
> whole ground shook and vibrated.

But it was not long-range fire that made machine guns valuable
weapons in the jungle. Allied tactics frowned on mass assault, but the
Japanese used the technique all too often. On a coal-black night on
a jungle perimeter, machine guns often stood between victory and
oblivion. Paige describes his theories on perimeter defense:

> A lot of so-called experts talk about burning out barrels. I've fired
> them till they were so hot they burned the skin off my arm. All

the heat does is wear down the grooves in the barrel. It doesn't prevent the bullet from going out. My theory was as long as the gun functions and everything else is set to fire you're set. I fired all night long and never changed them. A lot of guys were changing barrels for no reason. I would have been dead. The water-cooled gun was the most effective basic weapon for protection against attack. I rarely had water in mine. It would evaporate, get red hot, and still fire. We had a flash hider on our machine guns but they were worthless. You see, a night assault was at such close range it didn't make any difference. I told my machine gunners the ideal firefight is twenty yards. When the Japanese get that close, just pull the trigger and use search and traverse [move the gun side to side and up and down—EB]. Close your eyes if you want to. With eight guns firing, a mosquito couldn't get through.

Paige was given the opportunity to put his ideas to the test in a most dramatic way. In late October 1942 the Japanese made their largest and what proved to be their last attempt to seize Henderson Field and destroy the American position on Guadalcanal. For two nights large Japanese units assaulted several points of the Marine perimeter. Although there were many anxious moments, the Marine and Army defenders prevailed. At 2:00 A.M. on October 26, the Japanese made their last attempt. They struck a western section of the line occupied by Americans only days before—one battalion of Marines on a steep ridge, separated by 400 yards of jungle ravine from its neighbors on the left. Because the terrain was so thick, the ravine was not a gap in the line. However, the distance largely protected the attackers from flanking fire. It was a weak position, and fortunately the Japanese did not strike it earlier with larger forces. As it was, the last act of the battle was one of the most tense.

Paige's machine-gun platoon was attached to the rifle company holding the unsupported eastern end of the ridge. His version of events tallies nicely with the government histories:

The real battle for Guadalcanal was in October. Both sides built up, and got in the middle of the ring. They wanted the airport and we wanted to hold it at all cost. That was it. They sent in ships, planes, everything. It was the last battle and all-out war.

It was the second night of the battle. There had been heavy action down the line. After all the noise earlier it was so quiet you could hear the men breathing. Everybody was alert. We saw small lights flickering in the jungle at the bottom of the ridge. During the day we had strung wire on the ridge and fixed empty cans with empty cartridges in them to make noise. I moved along our line warning the men not to fire yet but to let the Japs get close and then give them everything. Everyone was straining to see and hear but there was nothing to see. We heard soft mutterings down in the jungle. I thought I saw a shadow approach our position. I grabbed a grenade, pulled the pin, but held on to the lever, waiting. The tin cans rattled, someone shrieked, and all hell let lose. We threw grenades over the ridge and Japanese rifle and machine-gun fire opened up on us.

The first Japanese wave swarmed into our position. It was a confusing struggle lit up by flashes from machine-gun fire, grenades, and mortars. Dark shapes crawled across the ground. Men fought on the ground with bayonets and swords, shouting curses at each other. In the flickering light I saw three Japanese charge our number-two gun. I shot two of them but the third ran through one of my gunners with a bayonet, and actually lifted him into the air. I shot him too. The Japs swarmed into another gun position and killed or wounded four men. It was so confusing that I think the Japs didn't really know I was there. One took a swipe at me with a bayonet, which I warded off with my hand. Someone had shot him that instant and he dropped at my feet dead. About seventy-five of them broke through our position and moved down the other side. The others vanished, just melted away down the slope.

The respite was not long. The situation in fact was serious. The Marine line was thin. Movement was so difficult in that terrain that keeping back a mobile reserve was pointless. Behind the ridge occupied by Paige and others was another ridge with the company command post. Once over that, the Japanese were near the beach road that led straight to Henderson. When the Japanese came up the first ridge again, they had little difficulty pushing aside what remained of the Marine company. Paige describes the chaos:

> I ran from gun position to gun position and found only bodies. I thought I might be the only one left on the ridge. As I ran, I kept bumping into enemy soldiers running around aimlessly in the dark. It seemed they did not know they had almost complete possession of the ridge. I kept going until I reached our neighboring company on the right. I found two men I knew, grabbed some ammunition, and told them to fix bayonets and follow me.

The Japanese had kept going and attacked the company command post on the next ridge toward the sea. Paige and a handful of survivors went from gun position to gun position and fired into the rear of the attacking Japanese infantry. As dawn neared, Paige and his small band would soon be visible. Low on ammunition, three of his men brought fresh belts:

> It was almost daylight and we came under rifle fire. Star got to me first with a belt of ammunition, but almost at once he got his in the stomach. Then Reilly arrived and he got hit in the groin. Joneck had been hit earlier, but when he reached my gun he got hit in the neck. I was looking at him when it happened. A piece of flesh just disappeared from his neck. It was getting too unhealthy, so then I dashed from gun to gun, fired a few bursts, and then moved off before the Jap grenades could get me.

As dawn broke, the company commander organized a scratch force and counterattacked the Japanese who had taken the rear ridge. Shoved off and forced to retreat, the Japanese started back up Paige's ridgeline. Paige took a machine gun off a tripod, and charged down the hill with several other Marines:

> The men followed me, shooting and yelling. At one time I almost ran into a Japanese field officer. He had emptied his revolver and was reaching for his two-handed sword. He was no more than four or five feet away when I cut him down. We went all the way down to the bottom of the ridge to the edge of the jungle where the last of the enemy disappeared. The shooting

and yelling stopped and then there was that strange quiet that always seems to follow.

The Marines found 300 dead Japanese on the ridge and in the ravine. Bloodstained trails led into the jungle. The defenders had killed far more Japanese in other phases of the battle. In all of them, machine guns played a crucial role, proving a devastating weapon in defense. Several Japanese officers committed suicide, realizing the magnitude of the defeat. One of them noted in the final entry of his diary, "We must not overlook firepower," then added, "I am going to return my borrowed life today with little interest." For his part, Mitchell Paige received the Congressional Medal of Honor. Years later Paige returned to Guadalcanal:

> You still can find a lot of stuff on some of the hills we were on. Much remains the same as it was. I tried to find the route the Japanese took to get to my position. They really had to work to get through. I had a rough time carrying no pack or weapon in daylight. They went through very sharp kunai grass, six to eight feet high. It would just cut you up. Then they went down into a swamp, then up those steep hills. All the time the mosquitoes biting, and on low rations of simple rice. I'm amazed with the stamina of the Japanese fighting man.

The other heavy weapon attached to rifle companies was the versatile and deadly mortar. One of the oldest forms of artillery, the mortar is simple in principle. A relatively small shell with a powerful propellent charge is fired at a very steep angle. This allows the round to be fired over objects that otherwise would interfere with the shell either where it was fired or where it landed. Modern mortars have other advantages. They are simple, rugged, and possess a very fast rate of fire. An American mortar crew in the South Pacific could fire eighteen rounds a minute for a sustained period, and nearly double that for shorter times. Although an exhausted infantryman forced to carry one might have a different opinion, mortars were very light. The U.S. 60mm mortar had a thirty-inch-long barrel and weighed forty-two pounds. The 81mm mortar, the other variety widely used by U.S. forces in the Pacific, weighed nearly twice that. The ammunition used looked like a very small bomb with small fins to stabilize the flight. Mortars had excellent range. The 60mm could fire a "mortar bomb," weighing about 2.5 pounds, nearly 2,000 yards. The 81mm fired a 7.5-pound round up to 3,800 yards. Mortar ammunition served many roles. In addition to standard high explosive, there were also rounds that produced smoke to mark a friendly or enemy position and flares that could light up the night sky. The eerie glow that normally accompanied World War II night combat usually came from mortar-fired flares.

Three men usually served on a crew. The weapon was disassembled and carried in pieces by the crew along with some bombs. Other men in the weapons platoon carried bombs also. As can be readily seen, if a mortar was going to see heavy use, some sort of transport was essential. It was invaluable to have a powerful indirect-fire weapon attached to a rifle company, but it would do little good unless there were dozens or hundreds of rounds available for each tube. Several rounds were required just to bracket the target. Probably more than any person in the company, the mortar-platoon leader had to know where the rifle units were. If a call came in for support, the crew fired a round. Someone close to impact would tell the crew over field telephone or "walkie-talkie" which way to adjust the weapon. Once the crew had put a small number of bombs in the right place, they would fire as fast as the situation and ammunition supply warranted. This made mortars excellent weapons on either attack or defense if placed in a prepared position. A good crew could fire with great accuracy, but there was no substitute for the precise preparation possible from a set position. Like machine guns, they were ideal for defense. A crew would prepare firing solutions for a defensive line that would allow them to begin supporting fire very rapidly. Unlike machine guns, mortars were usually indirect-fire weapons and consequently were not on the front line. Under most cases, mortars fired at will. (If the enemy could identify the location of a mortar position, "counter-battery fire" from the enemy's own mortars or artillery would be on the way quickly.) When Paige's machine-gun platoon was cutting down Japanese infantry, his position was supported by Marine mortar fire. It was a problem the Japanese had no good answer for, and added greatly to the task facing any large ground assault against either American or Australian positions.

Louis Lyster served as a forward observer for a heavy (81mm) mortar platoon on New Georgia. He describes a situation where mortars were invaluable:

When we went up trail on New Georgia we usually could not see more than five feet to either side because of extremely dense vegetation. Often there was only room to move single file. We advanced stop and go, our artillery passing over our head, blindly striking at the areas in front of us. It was so hard to move and to see that it was very easy to get bogged down. One time our company wandered a few hundred yards off course and managed to get surrounded by the Japs. That cost us some men killed.

Later when we got near Munda, the rifle company we were supporting got pinned down by the Japs for a whole day. Somewhere in front of them there was a Jap 90mm antiaircraft gun firing with its barrel depressed right at the troops. [Japanese defenders at Buna used the same technique with deadly effect.—EB] There was a machine gun out there too. Shellfire killed and wounded some of the men. The Jap position was very close but you couldn't see it. It was almost suicide to move forward in a situation like that. American artillery was firing barrages into the area all day, but they were afraid to target anything close to the pinned-down company. We set our mortars up behind a hill immediately to the rear of the infantry. The next morning the riflemen were still pinned down. Because I was a forward observer, I was ordered forward to try to find the Jap emplacement. I crawled along through the jungle, laying field-telephone wire behind me. A radioman was helping me, but he did not get far before he was shot in the head and died instantly right next to me. I crawled forward a while longer. Every few yards I slowly stood up to look around. Finally about fifty yards ahead I could see the muzzle of the Jap gun. I got on the field telephone and gave my mortar crew the approximate position. The first shell went beyond the target. I told them to shorten the range by ten yards. The shells got closer. One landed very near but off to the left. I told them to adjust to the right just a hair.

The next shell landed in the gun emplacement and the Jap bodies came flying out of the hole like butterflies. After that the rifle company could move forward again, with us right behind them. But believe me, we moved slowly. It took us over a month to get to Munda.

Nevertheless, there were serious disadvantages to mortars that prevented them from playing the large role they did in Europe or more open parts of the Pacific theater. If it was not possible to plot a target in advance, it was necessary for someone to see it. Very often in jungle combat the enemy was either invisible or far too close to consider asking for mortar fire. Only on the most desperate occasions did squad leaders or officers request supporting fire directed at their own position. In addition, mortars, like grenades, were much better at causing wounds than killing. The rounds were heavier than a grenade and more powerful. But outside of a ten- or fifteen-yard radius, the damage caused dropped off sharply. (It did not cease. Many freakish deaths took place when a soldier was hit by a small shell fragment from a mortar or artillery round that had landed a considerable distance away.) Furthermore, communications in the jungle were often very poor. If a rifle unit was out of touch with supporting fire, it was on its own.

Lastly mortars, like all indirect-fire weapons, were dangerous. As we shall see, "friendly fire" was a very serious problem on jungle battlefields. If a mortar was improperly aimed or the amount of propellant not correct, it was very easy to land a round in a comrade's foxhole. Mortar teams did not receive the training given to artillery because the weapon was less powerful and much simpler. Most crews did very well. Yet so many mortars were used that a small percentage of incompetent crews could cause tragedy. Furthermore, mortars were so simple to operate that if the crew was killed or wounded by enemy fire, infantry who were poorly trained in mortar use might continue to fire. The weapon could also be dangerous to the crew. Jungle canopy was a constant hindrance to mortar crews. Mortar bombs went up at a very steep angle, and could not be used if something was above the mortar tube. Sometimes mortar crews tried to cut things a little close. Frank Hurray led a heavy-weapons platoon in New Guinea in early 1944 and explains the problem and one solution:

> I led a weapons platoon in a rifle company. It had two sections: one had three machine guns and one had three mortars. The 60mm mortar was a very good weapon. The mortar round fits snugly along the tube. That's what gives it the "oomph." It was very tough and reliable. However, on New Guinea the trees made using the mortar difficult. You had too much overhead cover to allow you to fire. Rounds had what we called a point detonating fuze. Any little thing that hit it would set off the fuze. If the round struck a branch above you, it exploded.
>
> Sometimes we would boresight the weapon to get around this problem. You'd take the tripod off, get a pair of gloves, and boresight it through an opening in the trees and fire it. Everyone yelled the first time we tried that: it works. From then on, we did that a lot. We learned a lot of lessons in later years from that. You just manipulated the tube with an observer fifteen to twenty yards ahead. He'd say down a little, you'd move down and be right on the money. If you fired two rounds you could hold it bare-handed. More than that, it got warm fast.

Australian mortars were very similar to their American counterparts in type and used in a similar way. The Japanese, however, marched to an entirely different drummer in this field. In Allied forces, mortars were valuable support weapons but took a backseat to field artillery. The Japanese reversed the order. Japanese mortars played the central fire-support role in all ground operations in the South Pacific. Arguably, mortars were their most important weapon of any type. One model in particular was among the most brilliant infantry weapons of World War II.

This is another case where it is difficult to separate economic and military factors. As noted before, paradoxically both Japan's victories in China and its defeat at the hands of the Red Army in 1939 drove Japanese officers to improve the firepower and mobility of their infantry. The Russians had shown the Japanese the importance of

massed artillery and tanks. Imperial Army officers planned to up-
grade both as soon as it was feasible to do so. Indeed, one reason that
Japanese leaders justified the brutal conquest after Pearl Harbor of
the "Southern Resource Zone" in the East Indies and Malaya was to
allow the Japanese economy to produce a modern, "heavy" war machine. For the time, they had to make do with what they had.

Artillery is expensive, heavy, complex, and requires a huge "supply train" to keep it operating. Mortars, however, are far lighter,
much less expensive to build, and much easier to use. They were
ideal for a light army that stressed mobility and shock tactics above
all else. Consequently, the Japanese Army trained its mortar teams
well. They employed a wide variety of types. Some were much larger
than the American or Australian 81mm, but still much lighter than
an artillery piece. The Japanese also widely employed models that
were equivalent to those used by the Allies. However, as befits the organization and ethos of Japanese ground forces, their best was their
lightest, the famous Model 89 50mm "knee mortar."

The term "knee mortar" was a misnomer but descriptive. The
Model 89 was a grenade launcher. A greatly improved variant of the
World War I "trench mortar," the Model 89 fired a standard Japanese hand grenade fitted with a small propellant charge. Unlike most
mortars that are "smooth bore," the Model 89 had rifled grooves inside the barrel. This allowed the Model 89 to dispense with fins on
the ammunition. The Model 89 weighed only ten pounds and had a
ten-inch barrel. Prior to firing, the soldier attached a curved base
plate at the bottom of the barrel. The shape of the base suggested
that the weapon was fired from the knee. Because the recoil would
break a man's leg, the plate was used to brace the launcher against the
ground or anything solid. Aiming was done by sight, but the Model
89 could fire nearly 700 yards. There was an added bonus. Because it
fired a grenade with a time fuze, the chance of accidentally exploding
a branch over the firing soldier's head was far less than with a contact
fuze. Naturally, if a grenade bounced off an obstacle toward the firer,
it was time to "hit the dirt." A cheap, one-man weapon, the Model 89
was a squad grenade launcher and used in huge numbers.

Army medical studies suggested that half of American casualties came from mortars. Because of the nature of fragmentation wounds, it was not always possible to tell what type of mortar had done the damage. However, owing to the large number of wounded struck with small fragments and the relative percentages of weapons captured, the Army estimated that 80 percent of mortar casualties came from knee mortars. It is important to note that the Japanese normally operated on the tactical defensive. Consequently, they had more visible targets than Allied troops. At two locations, Guadalcanal and Bougainville, Americans constructed strong perimeter defenses around airfields. Unlike the Japanese, who emphasized concealment, Americans stressed firepower. It proved simple enough to locate strong points on American lines. The skills of preparing invisible field positions were not as well developed in American or Australian forces as they were in the Japanese Army. In short, Japanese mortarmen did not lack targets. It was a perfect environment for them to operate in.

Most American or Australian combat infantrymen met the Japanese knee mortar or one of its more conventional brethren. Frank Hurray recalls them from his days in New Guinea:

> The Japanese did not have artillery in our sector. However, they used the knee mortar to very good advantage. They would survey our positions during daylight and make plans. They'd come in at night, and the little bastards would throw the knee mortars at us. That kept us on our toes. It was a formidable weapon, and it shook us up. At the same time they often tried all sorts of shenanigans. They blew bugles, raised hell. They'd get juiced up and start yelling "Banzai!" Lord, they were quite an enemy.

Paul Sponaugle, like thousands of Allied infantry, underwent several mortar attacks. During the fierce battle on New Georgia in 1943, he was caught in the middle of a bombardment from knee mortars:

> It was daylight and I had just returned from a water detail. When I was gone my buddy was killed when a mortar shell hit his hole. My first sergeant called me over to his hole to tell me about my friend. I just got in the hole, took off my helmet, and two knee

mortar shells struck that hole. No doubt the Japs saw me jump in. This hole was better than most and had logs and dirt on top. There were three of us in there and I was on top. The explosions were awful. They were right on top of us. The Japs used a knee mortar: a bigger one would have killed us. The first one caused the splinters and made a hole, the second one showered us with shrapnel. I knew I was hit right away. I was pelted with splinters from the logs on the back and had a leg full of shrapnel. At least I was smart enough to stay where I was. The other two were stupid and ran for another hole. That's really asking for it during a mortar barrage. The chances are pretty slim of getting another direct hit. They were both hit in the open.

The doctor bandaged me and said I'd have to go to the hospital. However, at that time we couldn't retreat, so I proceeded on and the thing healed up. I asked our company CO after the battle if I could still go to the hospital. I sure hadn't thrown away the evacuation ticket the doctor gave me. But the CO just laughed. I guess he was right, it had healed by that time.

Field artillery was at the top of the military pyramid during World War II. In Europe it was the primary dispenser of both death and wounds. In the jungle, field guns, like mortars, were prevented from exercising their full power. Yet even when hampered by an unfriendly topography, the pure killing potential of artillery was always significant. The Allied superiority in this arm, which grew greatly over time, was one of the reasons that Japanese forces fought pitched battles at such a disadvantage.

Artillery is a rich man's weapon. This has been true for 400 years. Wars are connected in the historical memory of nations with infantry and cavalry, whether they carried sword and shield or rifle and saber. Grand and beautiful warships, which are oceangoing artillery platforms, are also there. In modern times, tanks and aircraft have joined them in the public's consciousness. World War I, which was dominated by artillery, is equated in retrospect with machine guns and biplanes. The impersonal power of artillery, firing from a distance, no doubt has made it difficult to visualize. Even military writers rarely look at the grim mechanics of modern artillery. Soldiers, however, know the devastating power of the gun and howitzer. In the past 200 years armies throughout the Western world have spent countless man-hours and great treasure building and refining the complex apparatus that culminates with an artillery barrage.

As we have seen, American ground forces were miserably weak in many areas when Japan attacked Pearl Harbor. Fortunately, during the interwar truce, a small number of brilliant American officers examined the performance of U.S. artillery in France during 1918. The American gunners had performed credibly, but the United States had been forced to use large quantities of French and British equipment. Considering the self-evident importance of field artillery, this was a sobering experience.

An Army review board after World War I prepared recommendations that transformed American artillery from a competent arm into the world's finest. Perhaps because the issue was so obviously important, the major recommendations all became policy. First, the standard American 75mm fieldpiece was replaced by a 105mm model. All future heavy artillery would be 155mm or larger. A new heavy gun of 155mm was also developed. In addition, all American artillery was mobile. Even old French designs that served in the Pacific were altered so they could be towed. Following the doctrine of mobility and firepower, American officers realized it was vital to have superior communications between front lines and the guns. Artillery could be brought to bear quickly in the attack, and used with startling speed to stop an enemy counterattack, without the elaborate preplotted grids beloved by gunners. The new prototypes were developed and techniques polished. It helped that artillery had great prestige in the U.S. Army, and it attracted fine officers. (For instance, Harvard ROTC made artillery a specialty. Many of the young Harvard gunners joined a Massachusetts National Guard cavalry unit that was shifting to artillery. Many ended up operating the batteries of the Americal Division on Guadalcanal.) Some of these measures bore fruit only in Europe. Others were also much in evidence in the Pacific.

Although the details varied, in the Pacific American artillery was assigned to artillery battalions under divisional control and allocated where needed. (As noted earlier, light 75mm pack howitzers were part of battalion heavy-weapon units in some cases.) Divisions had four artillery battalions. Each had three batteries (corresponding to infantry companies) of four "tubes" (military parlance for a gun or howitzer) each. Three of these battalions employed the excellent 105mm howitzer. The fourth had heavier 155mm howitzers. In addition to these weapons, corps headquarters above the division had a small number of extremely powerful 155mm guns. Some basic definitions might help again. A howitzer has a relatively short barrel and fires its round in a high arc toward its target. A gun uses the same shell, but fires with a much more explosive propellant. This allows it to fire at a lower trajectory and faster velocity. On impact, this adds a great deal of kinetic force to the explosion of the shell. In general, howitzers are more useful. Their "plunging fire" deriving from the high arc makes them excellent for attacking open targets and light field fortifications. A stronger target is more vulnerable to the pure velocity of a gun.

The M2 105mm howitzer was the mainstay of American artillery in the Pacific and was widely used in Europe also. Americans classified it as a "light artillery" piece. Only in the world of artillery would the 105mm be considered "light." It weighed 3,750 pounds and fired a thirty-three-pound high-explosive projectile up to 12,000 yards. On paper it had a crew of six men, although gunners often made do with fewer. The round was encased in a brass shell, meaning it could be loaded in one piece, rather like a very large rifle. A good crew could fire ten rounds a minute or faster. American "medium" artillery was provided by 155mm howitzers. In the South Pacific most medium batteries were given improved versions of the M1918 model. It weighed 12,750 pounds and fired a ninety-five-pound projectile up to 12,530 yards. As the model number suggests, this was a U.S.-produced version of the French-designed 155mm howitzer used in World War I. It had rubber tires and could be towed. Yet unlike more modern versions going to Europe, it was necessary to manhandle the howitzer to change left/right deflection.

Serving on a gun crew required skill, teamwork, and physical strength. With the possible exception of engineers, gunners did more physical labor than any other branch of the fighting military. Trucks or tractors towed the weapons, but under normal circumstances crews would prepare some type of position. They had to move and tend to the ammunition, which had great cumulative weight. They often had to prepare a "field of fire," which meant cutting down all or part of trees to allow the projectile to leave the position without striking something. If it was necessary to "fine-tune" the position of the howitzer, which it often was, gunners had to lift its 600-pound trail and move it one way or another.

Firing was hard work and complex. Bill McLaughlin was a section chief for a 155mm howitzer in the American Division on Guadalcanal and later Bougainville. He describes the sequence required to fire his weapon:

Unlike 105mms, which had a single-piece shell, the 155mm had a separate propellant and projectile. Powder bags contained seven increments tied together with close straps. This allowed the charge to be cut to fit the distance we would fire. The straps would be untied and the block of powder bags, similar to a kid's bean bag, would be reduced to the charge called for. The shell, which had either a point-detonating or time-delay fuze depending upon the circumstance, was rammed into the breech and the powder bags seated behind it. The breech was closed and a primer, looking like a blank cartridge, was inserted in the firing-mechanism block and screwed into the face of the breech. The gunner would check his panoramic sight, making sure the two aiming stakes were aligned for deflection, while the section chief would seat his gunner's quadrant on two stainless-steel blocks on top of the breech, after setting it for elevation. The sequence of fire commands beginning with "shell, mark 1, charge 4, etc." could be stopped at any time until the elevation command was given. This was the last in the firing order, and at that command the shell was rammed home and the piece loaded. At the executive officer's command of *Fire!* a crewman pulled the six-foot lanyard, causing a hammer on a pivot to swing up, hit the primer, and send a flame through a vent in the breech block to the base charge that contained highly inflammable black powder. This in turn ignited the slower-burning spaghetti-like powder in the other charges and sent the shell on its way. Standing behind it, you could watch the shell from the point that it left the muzzle to the peak of its climb. When it began to drop, it was lost to sight.

The crew repeated the process McLaughlin describes many times. A good 155mm crew could fire six rounds a minute, double the expected rate. The Army estimated that if one round per tube in a battery landed at the same point, there was a 50 percent chance of striking a standing enemy within a radius of 150 yards. The chances of killing or wounding declined markedly if the enemy was dug in, or simply in a foxhole. Therefore, for artillery to do damage, two things were required. Either a barrage must catch the enemy in the open, in which case devastation occurred instantly, or a battery must fire a very large number of shells. In either, case gunners had to know where their target was.

American artillerymen used indirect fire almost exclusively. Crews manning the much smaller 37mm antitank guns, usually attached to companies, fired their weapons directly at pillboxes, attacking infantry, or very rarely tanks. Howitzers had special "canister" ammunition for direct fire against attacking infantry, making it the world's most powerful shotgun. However, I know of no case of its being used this way in the South Pacific. (Direct fire with standard ammunition did take place on occasion, but not at the extremely close range canister is designed for.) Because the crew does not aim the tube visually with a sight, indirect fire requires accurate data for "fire missions." The first way of acquiring a target was to use preplanned coordinates if firing on a static position. This technique was an old one, but invaluable for perimeter defense. It was also used for what gunners call "interdictory fire." Gunners employed this technique by choosing spots that might logically contain a target, such as a major trail or water hole. Artillery would fire at them blindly, hoping to hit something at random or at least keep the Japanese on edge. It was an expensive technique, but very effective if the ammunition was plentiful and the spots were picked well.

Artillery could support men in the field. Field radios of the time were unreliable in jungle conditions, had a short range, and could be blocked by hills. Nevertheless, on more than one occasion a patrol called in artillery support via radio. In such a case, forward observers on the spot would guide the guns to their targets just as they would for a mortar. Divisions had two or three light Piper Cub aircraft that they used for artillery spotting and reconnaissance. Extremely useful in more open terrain, the spotter planes were badly hampered by dense jungle. Field telephones were set up whenever possible for the same purpose. Artillery battalions also had their own observation posts (OPs) located at high points and connected to the batteries by telephone. In theory, an observer could communicate with semaphore flags, an ancient technique rarely used in World War II. Various aiming instruments were set up at the OP and used along with mathematically plotted firing tables to estimate solutions. To save ammunition, aiming rounds went out, and when the target was found, the barrage started. As mentioned earlier, American gunners pioneered a complex variation of this called time-on-target (TOT), which was used with sometimes spectacular effect. Bill McLaughlin describes an artillery lookout spot used to supplement an OP established on Bougainville. As is obvious, nothing was simple in the jungle:

> On Bougainville, which was jungle from shore to shore, there were 100-foot-plus banyan trees in which platforms were built near the top and which were reached by bosun seats and pulleys. From these perches, we volunteers would watch for Japanese patrols and call in fire. This was hairy in that the OPs were in front of the infantry lines, and ahead of some 100-yards-deep intricately laced and lined barbed wire all booby-trapped and locked up at night.

The Australians used the fine British twenty-five-pounder. Not as good as the 105mm for a standard barrage, the twenty-five-pounder had some advantages. As the name implies, it fired a lighter twenty-five-pound round at slightly less range. It was, in military terms, a "gun cannon," a hybrid howitzer-gun. It could not be elevated to the degree possible for a howitzer, but it could also fire at a lower trajectory. More important, many Australian twenty-five-pounders were lightened and altered so they could be dismantled and carried by air transport, an invaluable quality in the jungle. It was a fine weapon manned by excellent gunners. Australian artillery lacked the numbers and sophistication of its American counterpart but was well suited to its environment and very deadly.

As noted previously, Australian artillery, although few in number, played a very important role during the Buna-Gona campaign. Conversely, the lack of artillery crippled the U.S. 32d Division. Airlifted artillery also was instrumental in saving the strategically important gold-mining center at Wau in early February 1943.

Six months after Buna-Gona when the AIF started its large operations toward Lae, the situation was transformed. Like their American allies, Australian forces went to battle with a far greater supply of support weaponry. In 1942 the small number of tubes were crippled by a chronic shortage of ammunition. In the summer of 1943, hundreds of tubes supported Australian forces with thousands of rounds.

No weapon escaped the effect of the jungle. Artillery put a huge strain on weak Allied supply lines early in the war. Moving artillery was always difficult, and the gunners had to tote the ammunition with them, besides. Like all supporting fire, howitzers were of little value in a jungle shootout. The possibility of friendly-fire casualties was always present. Well-operated artillery was very accurate. Yet gunners made mistakes and defects existed in some rounds of ammunition. Unfortunately, the impact of a "short round" from a howitzer was far worse than that of a mortar. Another problem presented itself. Tall trees, when struck by high-explosive shells, created their own deadly, wooden shrapnel in addition to the shell fragments. A shell hurtling to earth, on target, might hit these trees and cause a shower of splinters traveling several hundred miles an hour into a friendly position. The shell, however, was actually heading where it was aimed. It was a difficult problem with no real solution. Clifford Smith, who served with the 25th Division on Guadalcanal, comments on the situation:

We had a lot of artillery. Officers allowed for 10 percent of casualties for fire coming from our side. I couldn't believe so many people died accidently in my division. Of course you didn't always know if someone died because of Japanese fire or American. Some of the dead were very badly shot up. We also called in a lot of aircraft. We might be awfully close to the enemy when the planes came in. At Vella Lavella we had 105 air raids in one month. A few were from our own side, I think. I also think we shot at and shot down some of our own planes.

Despite the dangers, artillery was an invaluable weapon. A simple but extremely effective application of massed firepower was used by Marine gunners during the Battle of Bloody Ridge on the night of September 12–13, 1942. Although the enemy force of approximately 3,000 was not as large as the one that struck in October, it came closer than any Japanese assault to taking Henderson Field. Leaving forces to attack both the eastern and western flanks of the Marine perimeter, the main force of Japanese infantry moved overland through the jungle. The Marines knew the Japanese were preparing for an attack, but the location was a mystery. Fortunately a Marine Raider battalion commanded by the tough and brilliant Lieutenant Colonel Merritt "Red Mike" Edson stood in their way. Edson, who guessed early in the evening that an attack was coming, had made sure that artillery was ready. It was good that he did. The Japanese infantry penetrated Marine lines and one of the fiercest battles of the campaign ensued. For hours Marine artillery fired onto "Bloody Ridge." Fred Heidt was part of a Marine battery that did much to turn back the Japanese a few hundred yards from Henderson:

> The battery fired all night. Infantry projectiles bounced through our position all night and snipers fired at our steady gunners. Sergeant Hancock shouted orders to sweep the hill. A bedlam of noise and odors filled the night, as well as Jap shrieks and battle cries. Next day a part of a Japanese regiment lay dead on the knoll.

Damaged but not crushed, the Japanese tried again the next night. On the Japanese side, a combat correspondent named Gen

Nishino had accompanied the Japanese commander, Major General Kiyotake Kawaguchi, on the march across Guadalcanal. Kawaguchi had doubted his mission from the start, maintaining that the Americans were stronger than believed in Tokyo. Immediately before the assault, he told Nishino, "No matter what the War College says, it is extremely difficult to take an enemy position by night assault. If we succeed here it will be a wonder in the military history of the world." Although Marine machine-gun fire was fierce during the assault, artillery broke the attack and saved Henderson. Nishino recalled, "The artillery fire seemed to be a never-ending earthquake. Trees toppled over and red-hot shrapnel whistled through the air."

The Allied artillery arsenal buildup caused an insoluble dilemma for the Japanese. Whereas Americans and Australians learned to cope with fierce Japanese night assaults, the Japanese attackers increasingly became the target of withering, devastating barrages that crippled assaults before they reached the defenders' lines. If the Japanese decided to stand on the defensive, the Allied artillery was a prime method of "nibbling to death" defensive redoubts.

The logical way through this problem for the Japanese Army was to employ its own artillery. However, this was one area where it was extremely weak. In their arsenal, the Japanese possessed some modern artillery types closely corresponding to Allied tubes. If anything, they had more types of guns and howitzers than did the Allies. However, in yet another case of either faulty doctrine or lack of funds, the Japanese organized their artillery in a very deficient manner. They used their more powerful types in small numbers to support ground troops but deployed most larger weapons in a purely defensive role, firing from elaborately prepared positions. When well dug in, they were very effective, as American troops found out on Iwo Jima and Okinawa. The base at Rabaul had dozens of large artillery batteries ready for an invasion that never came.

However, Japanese infantry divisions on the move relied upon 70mm howitzers and 75mm guns for most of their support. Whereas the Allies used howitzers in most cases, guns were much more popular with Japanese forces. Imperial doctrine stressed forward employment of artillery in direct-fire mode. Guns, with their low trajectory, were ideal for this. The tactic yielded a certain advantage. Because their tubes were placed up front, the Japanese could afford to sacrifice range. Consequently, designers made as many compromises as possible to lighten their artillery. Japanese divisions had less vehicle transport under the best of circumstances. Consequently, the Japanese could not keep the costly and elaborate supply train required for sustained artillery fire. Japanese guns were shock weapons, used for a brief period to soften up a point on the line in preparation for assault. They did not have the support required to make them mass producers of death and injury.

Not having the elaborate communication and fire-control systems developed by the Americans before World War II, Japanese guns and howitzers had to be registered slowly to find their targets. If Allied air forces were present, this made them very vulnerable to attack. It almost made them desperately vulnerable to Allied "counterbattery fire," barrages aimed at firing artillery. There were no large artillery duels in the South Pacific. As a rule, the Japanese fired several rounds and then moved their position. This worked to conceal their guns, but prevented them from starting a slugging match with enemy artillery, much less winning it. Also, the lighter guns, which were very convenient in rough terrain, had very little killing power for artillery. Their light 70mm howitzer fired an 8.5-pound round 3,000 yards. The 75mm gun had a fine range of 12,000 yards but fired a 12-pound round, half the size of the round fired by the Australian twenty-five-pounder and one-third that of the U.S. 105mm howitzer.

The story of the famous "Pistol Pete" of Guadalcanal illustrates the futility of Japanese artillery. During October the Imperial Army was able to land a small and mixed batch of what in Japanese terms was heavy field artillery. (Most pieces were either 105mm howitzers or 105mm guns.) The gunners' mission was to cripple Henderson Field. The Japanese 105mm howitzers did very little damage to anyone or anything on the Marine perimeter. Concealed approximately three miles from Henderson, the crews spent most of their time avoiding the deadly American Airacobra fighters that roamed the skies of Guadalcanal looking for targets to strafe. A battery of 105mm guns was a somewhat different story. In place by mid-October, the battery commander decided to sacrifice reliability for range. Employing the maximum amount of powder possible, the artillery could strike Henderson ten miles away. Eventually this policy of loading the maximum amount of powder demolished the guns, but the Japanese had little ammunition in any case. When the Japanese guns began firing at Henderson, the Marines nicknamed them "Pistol Pete," personalizing their tormentor. In the world of artillery, an airfield is considered a "soft target," an objective not fortified and easy to damage. At this stage, the Americans lacked revetments for their aircraft, and the planes were out in the open. A good artillery unit could have stopped Henderson from operating. As it was, Pete was able only to harass the Americans. The Japanese guns occasionally found a target, but it was a nuisance, not a threat. The battery the Marines called Pete fired only 800 rounds during the campaign. Some American batteries fired that many during a single battle. Pete also had to move constantly to avoid destruction from the air or U.S. artillery.

The tactics employed by Pistol Pete stand in dramatic contrast with those used by Marine defense battalions in the New Georgia campaign. The Japanese did not often dare use the airstrip at Munda Point, the main objective of the invasion, because they feared air attack from Guadalcanal. When the land battle started, Munda's fate was sealed in an instant when a battery of Marine 155mm guns, the excellent piece nicknamed "Long Tom," set up on the island of Rendova within range of the strip. The Marine gunners pummeled infantry positions defending the Munda strip for days on end. Had any aircraft been there, they would have been blown to oblivion in a moment.

To make matters worse for the Japanese, Allied commanders had little respect for Japanese artillery or gunners and were emboldened to attack or move freely when they might otherwise have hesitated. Their attitude reflected a shortage of Japanese artillery pieces. The Japanese were extraordinarily tenacious and managed to drag their light field artillery across almost any terrain. Yet when they did so, the gunners had so little ammunition with so little punch, and used such crude techniques, that Japanese artillery was not a factor in any significant engagement in the South Pacific. American artilleryman Bill McLaughlin gives his opinion of his opponents' skill:

> Their artillery was erratic. They used it little on Guadalcanal, but it was erratic during later battles. I have been in a spot where they established a bracket on our position and as we waited for the barrage to come, found the next shot some distance away and off to the side. Whether they had no spotters or what, we never knew.

I have already discussed the U.S. military's foolish attitude early in the Pacific war toward tanks. Tanks, probably better than any weapon used in the South Pacific, illustrate the fact that the more specialized the weapon, the more difficult it is to use. However, because a weapon is specialized, assuming it is a good one, its impact is tremendous when the circumstances allow its proper use. In other words, tanks were severely limited in the South Pacific, but when they could be used they were devastating.

Both U.S. and Australian troops employed the American-made M3 Stuart light tank. The Stuart was one of the ugliest examples of an ugly breed of weapons. Tall for its width and boxy, the Stuart looked like it belonged in World War I. Yet it was the best light tank of the war. Designed for lightning raids and reconnaissance, the aptly named Stuart (J.E.B. Stuart was a famous Confederate cavalry commander) could travel at thirty-five miles per hour on a road or clear terrain. In the jungle, this attribute was worthless. Tanks, as we shall see, could move only at walking speed. The Stuart 37mm gun was hopelessly inadequate for use against most German tanks. In the jungle, however, it was deadly when the targets were bunkers or pillboxes. Like all guns, the 37mm could fire armor-piercing or high-explosive ammunition. Both were useful against targets in the jungle. It could also fire canister rounds, which emitted a horde of small fragments from the barrel like a shotgun, for use against infantry in the open. The Stuart also carried two .30-caliber machine guns, one in the hull, and one mounted on top of the turret that could be used by the commander. Like most American tanks, whatever their other failings, the Stuart was very reliable.

Many problems confronted a tank in the jungle in 1942. The most obvious obstacle was the terrain. There were ridges too steep or swamps too soft for a tank to move across. Although tanks are built to confront it, mud is an enemy for tanks as it is for any vehicle. The Stuart weighed fourteen tons, light in the world of tanks. Yet one can imagine the problems facing the crew if one got bogged in the mud. Fallen trees and stumps, which were very common in battle zones, could also stop or damage tanks. Specialized tank-recovery vehicles were absent in the South Pacific until very late, and it was not unheard of to abandon a damaged tank "stuck in the mud." Their carcasses are still there today on old battlefields throughout the South Pacific. Furthermore, tanks are a maintenance nightmare. The tracks that propel the tank and the suspension system necessary to support its weight required constant attention. Fortunately for the Allies, thousands of their soldiers had experience with bulldozers or heavy farm machinery and served as a pool for crewmen who, in addition to serving and risking their lives in a very hazardous duty, did the general maintenance on the vehicle. Yet the Stuart was a well-designed tank and could move across terrain that would stop any other vehicle. It could run through jungle underbrush and knock down small trees. (A favorite technique for destroying pillboxes was simply to drive over them.) Often some work by American engineers could gain entry for tanks into areas thought unreachable. Considering the prodigious skills of their engineers, American commanders' inability to find a way to get Stuarts to the battlefield is even more inexplicable.

A tank crewman lived a rough and dangerous life in the jungle. Tanks of that era were not well ventilated. A crewman therefore had to put up with infernal heat to accompany the very loud cacophony of noises a tank makes on the move. The interior of a tank traveling over ten miles per hour was so loud that internal speaker phones were necessary for the crew to hear each other. In battle, this problem got worse. Under normal circumstances, the tank commander and the driver rode with their hatches open and their heads in the open air. This cooled the interior somewhat, but, more important, greatly aided visibility. When under fire, the tank crew "buttoned up" and closed the hatches. They were more secure, but were nearly blind, seeing only through small observation slits. (Many brave commanders tried staying in the open for this reason: it was a mistake made only once. Not only was the commander in obvious danger, but an open hatch invited enemy grenades.)

It took tankers some experience to realize how vulnerable their vehicles were in the jungle. The Stuart's armor could stop small-arms fire or shell fragments. No army yet had bazookas. Yet the Stuart could fall prey to the small antitank guns commonly found inside major Japanese perimeters. In the dense jungle, infantrymen also were a serious threat. The Japanese, like other armies, had explosive devices attached to magnets. In addition, soldiers are extremely clever at preparing their own weapons, and the Japanese had their version of the famed "Molotov cocktail." The Japanese also found that if they stuck a rifle barrel in the suspension they cold stop a tank cold. (American tankers countered by improvising better guards for the wheel mechanism.) Unless it was protected, Japanese soldiers would swarm over a tank and destroy it. Sometimes the tank crew could escape out the tank's hatches, but all too often they died along with their vehicle. Many were burned alive.

The perils of tank warfare were well illustrated on September 15, 1942, on Guadalcanal. On the previous two nights the Marines had defeated a fierce Japanese assault at the Battle of Bloody Ridge. Japanese soldiers of a second contingent advancing along a different axis toward the Tenaru River became entangled in Marine wire and were forced to retreat. The next morning the Marine commander, fearing that Japanese were still very close by in the kunai grass and thick shrub outside the wire, sent four tanks to patrol unsupported. Blinded by the terrain, the tanks passed a Japanese gun that destroyed them in short order. Fred Balester served with a Marine reconnaissance unit and arrived an hour or so later:

> By the time we arrived it was too late. Fortunately for us, the Japs had already left, and all we found was a pile of Japanese 37mm

shell casings neatly piled, four shot-up tanks, and one survivor. In looking over the scene we had to admire the courage and skill of what must have been a very small Japanese unit. They had provoked an attack by a much larger force and with one antitank gun wiped out four tanks and got away scot-free. Three of our tanks had been drilled nearly through the turret before they got close to the gun. One tank had made it to the river but was upside down in the water, so we could not see how it had been hit. One man was left in shock. He said he was the only survivor. He had somehow managed to get out of a burning tank. He didn't have a shirt on and was blackened with smoke and grit. The poor fellow was nearly incoherent. To be honest, we escorted him almost like a prisoner, although he didn't know it. We knew that many Japanese spoke English, and this fellow was so beat up we couldn't honestly tell whether or not he was a Marine. He was one of ours, of course, but you didn't take chances in those days. He was able to walk back, and we heard he was able to come out of it OK.

In short, tanks were dependent upon infantry for protection. As tanks crawled forward, troops followed immediately behind, ready to shoot Japanese infantry that crawled onto the tank. They also acted as the tank's eyes. If a target or potential danger appeared, a friendly infantryman would literally pound on the hatch and relay the information. All of this required cool heads and good leadership. Eventually the tank-infantry team was a fixture of combat in the Pacific. Later in the war, the Stuarts were joined by medium Sherman tanks that could withstand many blows fatal to light armor.

The Japanese Army had a large number of tanks by 1941. Technical authors have pointed out their many failings. Not having the production facilities to create a modern variety able to stand up to Russian armor, the Japanese settled on creating tanks that were fast and carried decent armament for their size but were very lightly armored. The widely employed M2598 carried the same 37mm gun as the Stuart but weighed only 4.5 tons (Americans, having nothing remotely that small, classified it as a "tankette"). The somewhat heavier Model 95 carried the same gun, but offered enough armor to stop heavy-machine-gun fire. The Model 97 medium was also common and was their best variety. It weighed the same as the Stuart but carried a 57mm gun. In armored combat, sacrificing protection for striking power is a prescription for disaster. When Japanese tanks met Shermans in the Philippines, the American armor demolished them. Excellent Soviet tanks in Manchuria brushed Japanese armored opposition aside in 1945. Considering the expense and industrial sophistication that were required to produce a good tank in World War II, the Japanese were in a weak position and knew it.

Nevertheless, in the jungle the important factor was not the tank's technical quality, but its presence in the first place. There was no tank-to-tank combat in the South Pacific, and armor served exclusively for infantry support. In war, the old adage that "in the land of the blind, the one-eyed rules" describes many tactical situations. Like the Americans, the Japanese doubted the usefulness of armor in the jungle. Unlike the Americans, their shipping was so scarce and other equipment so desperately needed that they had a better excuse for leaving their tanks behind. They did have serviceable antitank guns that were present in fortified zones, and that would suffice in Japanese eyes.

Both the potential and peril of using tanks were dramatically illustrated the only two times the Japanese employed them in the South Pacific. At Milne Bay, described earlier, two tanks played a central role in handing the AIF one of its few clear defeats. Weeks after Milne Bay, the Japanese landed a dozen tanks on Guadalcanal. Their purpose was to spearhead an assault across the mouth of the Matanikau River that was intended to draw Marine defenders toward the west flank. The next night, a larger force, which had marched overland, would strike the center of the Marine perimeter and take Henderson. As it turned out, the march through the jungle was slow and confused. The Japanese commander tried to postpone the Matanikau attack by a day, but the message did not get through.

The Japanese attack came as no surprise. Indeed, it was part of the Japanese plan that the Marines knew a threat existed on the Matanikau. On October 20, the evening preceding the Matanikau assault, a Japanese patrol accompanied by a pair of tanks approached the Marine position. As one Marine in a foxhole later put it, "We got the shock of our lives because no one had any idea the Japs had tanks." The Marines knocked out one tank and drove off the patrol. The next evening a larger patrol advanced, but the Marines stopped it also. The main feint attack on October 23, mistimed in any event, was a catastrophe. After an artillery barrage very large by Japanese standards, nine tanks, a mixed group of Model 97s and tankettes, lumbered toward the Matanikau at sunset. Behind the tanks massed infantry advanced. The Marines opened fire with their 37mm anti-tank guns. At the same time, a blistering artillery barrage was coming down on the following infantry. Eight tanks were destroyed very quickly and only one actually penetrated the Marine line. After it had destroyed a foxhole, a quick-acting Marine disabled its steering mechanism with a grenade. Turning wildly, the tank headed into the surf. Minutes later, one of a handful of Marine half-tracks used for beach defense hit the crippled tank with its 75mm gun, destroying it. The following infantry were crushed by artillery in a scene reminiscent of World War I. Marine losses were minimal. The Marines estimated the corpses found the next day at 600. They also found an additional three tanks probably destroyed by artillery. The Japanese often failed trying to do the impossible. In this instance, they failed through gross incompetence.

Gooney Birds

The infantryman's world was a small one. In the South Pacific, where no strategic objective had inherent value, every ground battle took place to seize or protect an air base. A large and furious air war accompanied the crude struggle in the jungle. Likewise, great fleets maneuvered continually and frequently fought each other in some of the most dramatic engagements in military history. The air and naval fighting, as thoughtful infantrymen knew well, was central to the outcome of land battles. If one side established a significant air and naval superiority in an area, it severed supply lines to enemy ground forces. As shown many times, an isolated force in the jungle was either doomed or forced to flee toward a new source of supply.

As we shall see, infantrymen were sometimes the target of air and naval bombardment. On occasion they also were fascinated but passive observers of large aerial dogfights or naval battles close to shore. Nevertheless, for the most part, the war fought by aviators and sailors remained unseen by men on the ground.

This situation was not entirely planned. Before the war, the American military, like many others around the world, believed aircraft would be found on the front lines providing "close support" to infantry. In practice, however, the techniques required proved more complex than anticipated and were not well developed until 1944. It was always difficult to coordinate air attack and a quickly moving infantry engagement. Also the potential for "friendly fire" casualties always existed. In the jungle, where observation was so difficult, the problem was worse. Behind enemy lines, however, the situation was very different. Aircraft supported the ground war by hindering enemy supply and movement, what the military calls "interdiction." They also attacked anything resembling an artillery position. On both Guadalcanal and Kokoda, for instance, U.S. and Australian aircraft pounded Japanese lines of communication relentlessly. In both places, and many others, Allied pilots played a key role in successful ground campaigns. Japanese pilots played a similar role during their early victories in the Pacific war.

Although critical to the outcome of operations, both air and naval power impacted the men in foxholes only indirectly. Most action took place out of sight. Furthermore, with very few exceptions, soldiers were told little about military operations. Few Marines on Guadalcanal, although they often heard naval gunfire in the distance at night, had any idea of the horrible price paid by the U.S. Navy to win the campaign. Nor did AIF infantry in the 1943 campaigns in New Guinea fully realize that it operated under an umbrella of air superiority that was hard won by American and Australian pilots pummeling Japanese airpower in both the Solomons and New Guinea. It is only in retrospect that we can see how closely all the components of the struggle interacted on the far-flung battlefield of the South Pacific.

In the crucial area of combat air transport, however, the connection between Allied ground and air units was direct and obvious for all to see. Ground operations in the South Pacific, hamstrung in so many ways by the forbidding terrain, were the first in history to depend heavily on air transport for the movement of men and supplies. It is important to note that armies in the South Pacific traveled light by necessity. Transport ships were small in number until 1943, and severely limited in their ability to move by Japanese bombers. Inland, supply networks were crude without exception. Therefore, commanders dispensed with many of the accoutrements of modern combat routinely found in Europe. They never possessed the huge numbers of vehicles, tanks, and artillery pieces that put such a burden on logistics in other places. Aircraft, therefore, could carry a much higher percentage of supply. Consequently, because the theater was so primitive, it became the birthplace of military techniques that transformed land warfare after 1945. Today, military operations large or small would be unthinkable without the use of a vast fleet of transport aircraft. The road from Kokoda to the Berlin Airlift, to Vietnam and finally to Desert Storm was a straight one.

Like so many aspects of the war in the South Pacific, the importance of combat air transport was not anticipated and techniques were developed on the spot. Before World War II, all armies procured transport aircraft, usually variations of civilian airliners. The original role given them, however, was far more limited than the one that evolved. Transports, military leaders believed, would be useful for moving officers and select groups of men from one place to another. Also, all armies experimented with paratroops. Moving and supplying an army, however, appeared out of the question. The staggering tonnages required for the task necessitated sea and rail transport. (For this reason, most armies, relying on railroads, failed to procure enough trucks. Such an oversight cost Hitler dearly in Russia. This mistake was not made by the United States.) Consequently the number of air transports was small and little thought was given to their best use. The U.S. Army did not buy its first DC-3 until 1940, five years after the plane's civilian debut. Ironically, when the U.S. Army ordered its first DC-3, the Japanese Army already had built approximately 400 DC-3s under license from Douglas.

In the foul environment of the South Pacific, however, combat air transport played a central role from the start. Although many types of aircraft were involved, the Americans were fortunate to have at their disposal the DC-3, one of the greatest designs in aviation history. The military version of the DC-3 was designated the C-47 Skytrain. (As was often the case with aircraft, the official designation of the aircraft was used less than an informal nickname awarded by servicemen. It is safe to say that the C-47 was more often called the "Gooney Bird" than the "Skytrain." In addition, each individual Army aircraft had its own nickname given by the pilots and ground crew. Like most Army planes, C-47s also sported elaborate nose art. For reasons known only to admirals, the Navy frowned on such displays of individuality and officially did not permit nose art or aircraft nicknames.) The C-47 possessed splendid lines, a rugged airframe, and a pair of excellent engines. In theory it could carry 8,000 pounds of cargo or twenty-eight fully loaded men. In practice, far heavier loads were common. Forgiving to young pilots, and extremely rugged, the C-47 remained in service through the Vietnam War, and hundreds fly today. It was the perfect plane for the South Pacific.

Although the C-47 served admirably in the Solomons in many roles, particularly at Guadalcanal, naval transport carried most supply in the islands once a suitable air umbrella existed. New Guinea was very different. Until late 1943, the only decent Allied harbor in New Guinea was Port Moresby. (Nearby Milne Bay was a valuable supplement.) Ships could bring men and supplies to Moresby. However, at that point the problems began. As previously mentioned, there were no true roads, and both Japanese and Australian infantry had to rely on porters and their own labor to haul supplies over the fierce terrain. From the start, the Australians depended upon a handful of American transport aircraft to establish supply dumps along the Kokoda Trail. In the summer of 1942, C-47s and other transports were the most valuable aircraft in the theater and were treated like gold by the Australians.

When the Allies began their siege of the Gona-Buna area in November 1942 the C-47s grew in importance. Fortunately for the Allies, they also began arriving in larger numbers. Although every Allied command fought for more C-47s, enough were coming off the assembly lines to equip several new squadrons for service in New Guinea. The need was very pressing. Because the waters near Buna were uncharted and infested with coral reefs, the Navy would not risk oceangoing transports or warships in the area. Modern shallow-draft landing craft, like the LST (landing ship, tank) had not yet arrived in the theater. The U.S. 32d Division was dependent upon a motley little fleet of small craft for supply. So inadequate was this fleet, much of which was sunk during November, that the 32d was the only American division during the war to fight a major campaign without artillery. The Australians, completing their drive over the Kokoda Trail, remained uncomfortably dependent upon native porters.

American C-47s filled the breach and kept the Buna campaign going. It was very hazardous duty. None of the airfields would have passed inspection in the United States. The steel matting used instead of pavement provided support for the aircraft, but it was often covered by mud, making any landing a potential adventure. The need for the transports was so great that planes flew that the Army Air Force would have scrapped in a moment during peacetime. The weather in the Owen Stanley Mountains is unpredictable and ugly. Dense fog or fierce storms come up quickly. To make matters worse, pilots, like generals, had miserable charts and navigational aids. Meteorological services were unreliable at best. If a pilot became lost, he flirted with doom. The New Guinea landscape has few landmarks and few places to put down. Most transports that were lost simply disappeared. To make matters worse, marauding Zeros often appeared near Dobodura searching for transports and shot down several. Lastly, good transport pilots were at a premium. Although the men were very young, and not well trained prior to deployment, many of the pilots quickly showed maturity and good judgment. As commanders knew well, the transports were more valuable than any combat plane, and their cargoes frequently consisted of forty infantrymen. It was not a good place for a hothead or someone who lacked caution. Good pilots consequently racked up extraordinary numbers of missions and hours flown, far greater than found among other branches of the combat air arm.

Until the airbase at Dobodura near Buna opened in late November, Allied forces depended upon airdropped supplies. Airdrops continued after Dobodura was built. If a unit needed something in a hurry, pilots employed airdrops even if air bases were in the proximity. (If a transport landed men or supplies at Dobodura, it might take two or three days for them to arrive at the front. Frequently, there was no time.) Amazingly, the Army Air Force had given no thought to dropping supplies from the air. Specialized parachutes did not appear until 1943, so the pilots and ground crew had to develop suitable techniques on the spot. David Vaughter was a young C-47 pilot in New Guinea and describes the problems posed:

When we first went in to drop supplies we didn't have any training. I'd never dropped anything in the States. We had dropped some paratroopers but never supplies. Frankly, we didn't have a clue as to what to do. There was no book on the subject, so we wrote our own. At first, we and some of the other early-arrived squadrons went at it wrong. Until Buna we dropped Australian supplies. The Aussies packed it up, and wrapped it in beautiful wool blankets covered with burlap. We dropped everything from ammunition to canned fruit.

The first crews given this duty told us to go in as low as possible, and make sure we had enough speed to go over the trees: approximately 150 knots. This was for safety, because we might have to turn to do it again. If you went too slow, you could stall the airplane, which is a bad idea at low altitude. Well, we were actually in there "skip bombing" supplies at ten to twenty feet elevation at 130 to 150 miles an hour. We'd kick the stuff out the door and it hit the ground like shrapnel, almost blowing apart. Sometimes the supplies would ricochet off the ground and fly down the hills. We often averaged only 20 percent recovery. If everything was demolished, we'd have to do it again.

Gradually we learned that logic was leading us astray. It made sense to drop low. However, we learned that the optimum altitude for supply drop was around 300 feet. We flew higher, and also as slow as we could, maybe eighty or ninety miles per hour. The supplies then had the opportunity to lose forward momentum and fell almost straight down. This more than compensated for greater height, and lost material dropped considerably. When they requisitioned parachutes for this duty, there were times when we had 100 percent recovery.

The AIF had found that the Kokoda Trail was a miserable land route across the Owen Stanley Mountains. As soon as possible, C-47s were given the task of moving men as well as supplies. Thousands of Australian troops and several units of the U.S. 32d Division flew through what pilots called "the Gap," a small corridor between the highest peaks of the Owen Stanleys. After unloading men, the transports often returned with wounded on board. David Vaughter describes the sad round trip:

Buna was a tough place, a real mudhole. In the early stage of the battle we brought in a lot of men from the 32d Division. There was always a wise guy or two on board telling us what he was going to do to the Japanese when he got there. It was so strange. A few days later we would often recognize the same guys. This time they were wounded and heading back to Moresby. On several occasions I had wounded GIs ask me if I was the one who flew them over. Many of the men who were conscious told us they were happy to have been wounded. They were going back to hospital and would live because they picked up the "million-dollar wound." The men they left behind might not be so lucky. What a miserable battle.

The Australians did much fighting inland from the New Guinea coast and therefore made the most extensive use of transport aircraft. The most spectacular example of the value of combat transport took place during the battle at Wau in late January 1943. Inland from the

Japanese base at Salamaua, Wau was a gold-mining settlement, the only outpost of Western "civilization" in the interior of New Guinea. Because the mines needed supplies, Wau possessed a serviceable airstrip. When war broke out, Wau served as a base for a small band of Australian irregulars designated Kanga Force. Kanga Force had made a series of raids, varying greatly in success, against Japanese positions at Salamaua and Lae. In January, with the Buna campaign developing into a major defeat, the Japanese attempted to salvage something by seizing Wau.

It was a very shrewd move by the Japanese. If they could hold Wau, they could forestall an Australian thrust up the river valleys leading into the Huon Peninsula. Wau also sat astride a series of tracks and trails leading to any point of significance in the area. One route led to Port Moresby. Although longer than the Kokoda Trail, it was easier to traverse. Still optimistic in this stage of the war, the Japanese Army entertained hopes of starting another drive on Moresby. Even if an offensive proved impossible, a position at Wau would either delay further Allied moves in New Guinea or force the Australians to retake Wau. The latter prospect would have been extremely unappealing immediately after the savagery at Gona-Buna.

The Japanese received help from an unlikely source. One of the miners who knew the area best was a German citizen who had been under surveillance by Australian authorities before Pearl Harbor. The German had discovered an unknown track that allowed a Japanese strike force from Salamaua to move on Wau without being detected. A Japanese force of 3,000 moved inland on January 14. Although Kanga Force had some sporadic contacts, the Japanese were six miles outside of Wau before the Australians realized that a major assault was under way. A race began immediately. The Japanese attempted to push through rugged terrain and take the Wau airfield. The Australians had only 500 defenders at the outset. For their part they had to hold the airfield and fly in reinforcements as fast as possible.

In 1942 there were obscure and primitive airfields in every corner of the globe. The airstrip at Wau, however, had to be the strangest on the planet. In the 1930s engineers could locate only one place near Wau suitable to handle the multiengine aircraft required to bring in supplies. The location chosen was at the base of a crescent of mountains. The strip was 1,100 feet long and possessed an incredible twelve-degree gradient. The upper end at the base of the mountain, in other words, was nearly 300 feet higher than the lower end. Ernie Ford flew 364 missions in New Guinea, many of them into Wau:

> Landing at Wau required some novel flying. As you approached the strip you flew over a river, descending slowly at ninety miles per hour with your flaps down. As soon as you crossed the river you raised flaps and gave it full power. In the middle of the strip the Aussies set out some barrels. That's what you aimed at. When you landed you pulled up, almost like you were taking off. It was a controlled crash, really. Believe me, you had no trouble stopping the aircraft going up that incline. It was crude flying, but finesse got you into trouble at Wau. There was plenty of testimony to that. You were surrounded by wrecks. There were a couple old Junkers transports from the mining days. There were a couple C-47s, a B-17, a fighter or two, and a B-24. Some of these planes could never have landed there, but the pilots must have thought it was better to crash-land at Wau than take their chances in the New Guinea jungle. I've never seen anything like it.

Difficult under the best of circumstances, Wau was a very uninviting stop in the middle of a battle. Ford continues:

> At the end of January 1943 things got hot at Wau. The Japanese had infiltrated a large force and reached the edge of the airfield. Aussie defenders were desperate for reinforcement. I think almost every transport in New Guinea was involved. But we had to wait for the weather. Weather was always tough in the Owen Stanleys, and Wau was surrounded by hills and mountains. It was often fogged in. We had Aussie troops ready to go at Moresby, and they wanted to get in bad. Luckily, the weather broke just as the Japanese were closing in on the field, and off we went. Planes came in every few minutes. Sometimes we had to circle so the

Aussies could clear Japanese troops from the edge of the runway. When we got down, the Aussie troops got out on the double. During the first days, they went right into battle. Of course, they didn't have far to go. There were mortar rounds and small-arms fire coming in. I can tell you we got out as fast as we could. But as long as the weather held, there was another load waiting. After a week or so, the Aussies threw the Japs back.

At the height of the battle on January 31, forty transports made seventy-one flights into Wau. Within two weeks Australian troops outnumbered the Japanese and smashed the attack. Kokoda, Buna, and Wau, however, were just the beginning. During 1943 Australian troops fought a major offensive in the Ramu Valley depending largely on air supply. It was one of the most successful employments of airpower in World War II.

In stark contrast to the crucial role played by Allied combat transport, the Japanese never developed a serious air-transport system. In retrospect, their failure to do so is almost inexplicable. They had several aircraft that could have served well, including, as mentioned, the C-47. Both the Japanese Army and Navy trained thousands of pilots to fly twin-engined bombers. By late 1942, however, Japanese bombers were increasingly vulnerable to Allied fighters and antiaircraft fire. At the same time, the sea-lanes became ever more hazardous to Japanese merchant shipping. It would have been far better to have employed some of their multiengined aircraft to supply their malnourished troops in the field than to sacrifice them in futile bombing raids. This is another example where the Japanese cult of the offensive crippled rational tactical doctrine.

A last word on weaponry is in order. As in all wars, armies during World War II were far better at designing weapons than they were at using them. Something that worked well on the proving ground, or in the orderly world of the peacetime military, did not necessary function as planned in battle. Combat assaulted machines as well as men. The elements, especially in the jungle, took a constant toll. Maintenance was rarely at peacetime standards. Weapons from the most simple to the most complex malfunctioned often. The complex supply apparatus required to support weaponry was not always up to the challenge. A shortage of spare parts often stopped the employment of expensive weapons as effectively as enemy action.

More important, on the battlefield violence and confusion reign. No matter how brave, experienced, and well trained the soldier, battles are imprecise. Statistically, most weapons missed the target a vast majority of the times fired. It is surprisingly hard to kill a man unless the target can be clearly seen, in which case killing often becomes a simple act. Estimates vary, but U.S. ground forces spent tons of ammunition to kill a single Japanese soldier. The ground war in the South Pacific was fought between opposing soldiers who held a frightening hatred for each other. It was a cruel irony that the jungle, so malignant in almost every way, acted so often to shelter men from those who wished them dead. Only in the jungle could you be close enough to hear the enemy breathe and not be able to strike him. It is time to look at combat.

Chapter 4

The Squad War

T he ground war in the South Pacific was a war of perimeters in-stead of lines. The size of the perimeters varied from a small group of infantry huddled in their foxholes to a large prepared fortified zone like the Marines built on Guadalcanal, the Army cre-ated on Bougainville, or the Japanese constructed in the Buna area. This situation was caused by the jungle terrain. It also reflected the fact that forces were relatively small considering the large size of the battle zone. The jungle crippled visibility so severely that it was im-possible for a single machine gun to control several hundred yards of front. The jungle and swamp, because of mud and foliage, were al-ways difficult to move through. In some cases, they were effectively impenetrable. Soldiers might try to hack their way through dense brush, but they found that an exhausting and agonizingly slow pro-cess. They also found that a trail hacked out Monday was overgrown the following week.

Yet the jungle was porous. There were various tracks, trails, streambeds, and ridgelines that allowed slow, cautious movement. Infiltration was always possible. The Japanese were particularly good at it. Consequently, a unit had to guard not just its front, but its rear. An accurate battle map of engagements in the South Pacific does not show lines as often as it shows a series of circles, myriad well-armed wagon trains ready for blows from any direction. Dick Randles, a ser-geant with the 32d Division at Buna, puts it nicely:

All through the Pacific war there was no such thing as a front line. There were isolated perimeters. You covered all sides. One company would be in one place and another off a way. In the morning, you'd go back and forth to check each other out. *Never* was there a front. We were facing the Japanese, and they were behind us. All around us. The terrain burdened and shaped everything.

E. J. Randall of the AIF describes the same situation:

Because of the lack of vision in the jungle, our defensive patterns were changed. While the unit as a whole would be mutually supportive, each platoon was responsible for its defense. So came into being the perimeter defense system: a system where the platoon dug in in a tight circle with the platoon headquarters in the middle.

Furthermore, there were very few points of value in a South Pacific battle zone. This fact imposed a certain simplicity to operations. There were a small number of places a side wished to attack or defend. The other side knew this too. As a result, the areas actually contested were relatively small. All the fighting and movement on Guadalcanal took place in a relatively small quadrant on the northwest portion of the island. It was a rare day during the Kokoda campaign that an AIF or Japanese unit went more than a few miles off the main trail. Most of New Georgia was untouched. Fighting on Bougainville was likewise confined until late in the war to a small corner of the island.

Consequently, each side knew the general area held by the enemy. What it did not know were the specifics. As long as it was impossible to reliably ascertain the enemy's position, continual ground patrols were necessary. As long as it was possible for the enemy to get around a position, it was necessary to form perimeters. Accordingly, the flow of operations at the squad level had two simple but dangerous phases: patrolling and guarding the perimeter.

The Patrol

To operate effectively, it was essential to have some conception of
where the other side was and in what strength. Furthermore, the
lines of communication were so poor that moving large units in uni-
son was extremely difficult. It was much more feasible to move in
small groups, gingerly advancing, alert for enemy machine guns.
Similarly, even in large perimeters as at Buna or Guadalcanal, there
were more conceivable lines of advance than there were troops to
cover them. Therefore, the defensive lines in the most powerfully
protected perimeters were made up of relatively small numbers of
men in mini-perimeters who hoped the jungle and daily patrols
would keep the enemy at bay. (The Japanese, as we shall see, put
more faith in the jungle and brilliantly designed field fortifications.
The units involved, however, were still small.) There was no choice
in the matter. Unless one had time to clear miles of jungle terrain,
men in foxholes had very limited visibility. There was no Maginot
Line in the jungle.

In addition, there was a tremendous difference between the attack doctrines of the two sides. Previously, we have examined several
of the large and savage encounters that punctuated the fighting in the
South Pacific. With few exceptions, large engagements were night
attacks launched by the Japanese. These assaults, often described in-
correctly as "banzai charges," were at the center of Japanese shock
doctrine. Although the Allies on occasion launched multiunit assaults
against Japanese lines, this was done in daylight, usually with heavy
fire support, with the aim of unhinging a Japanese position rather
than crushing it. Both American and Australian units probed Japanese positions and attacked systematically, trying to chew up the position one piece at a time. Australians certainly took bigger bites than
Americans, but the principle was the same. No Allied commander
would have thrown whole regiments into one assault against a heavily defended Japanese perimeter. The Allied approach was more patient and slower. It was also far less costly. On three different
occasions on Guadalcanal, the Japanese lost more men in one night

than the 1st Marine Division lost in the campaign. Even during their victory over the AIF 21st Brigade on the Kokoda Trail, Japanese losses in those two weeks of successful battles probably approached those suffered by the AIF in the entire Papuan campaign, including Kokoda and Buna-Gona-Sanananda.

Major consequences flowed from this situation. The most obvious is that the war in the South Pacific was a small-unit war. Corps and division headquarters were there and played a role, but on the spearpoint were squads, platoons, and companies. The importance of small units was greatly increased by the crude communications available. Marine squad leader Ore Marion describes the situation on Guadalcanal:

> Communication on land in 1942 was a joke. We had been taught semaphore signaling with flags. Not very effective in the jungle. In stationary positions we had the hand-cranked field telephones between company and the rifle platoons and back to a battalion switchboard. When on the offense, we had nothing— *nada*. Sometimes when moving forward the regiment would send two men with a hand-cranked radio to supply communication between the company headquarters and regiment. But between platoons and company we had to depend on runners, who were frequently shot or wounded. So most times when the firefight started we had to depend on luck, common sense, and our skills honed in training.

Brigade Major Geoffrey Lyon was with the first AIF units that moved up the Kokoda Trail to try to stop the Japanese. Lyon, serving with headquarters, was in an excellent position to comment on the communications problem. According to Lyon, the AIF was in no better position than were the Marines on Guadalcanal:

> We had almost no ability to communicate with other units. The radio was useless. There was a single strand signal wire that went up the track, but that was all that was available from front to rear. Along that had to go all of the basic information concerning casualties, ration requirements, everything. Communications consequently were extremely poor.

It is a cliché in the military world that all battles are small-unit battles. There is much truth in this, but the communications used in 1942 put the armies fighting in the South Pacific with one foot in the sophisticated military apparatus that developed quickly during World War II and one foot in the American Civil War. One of the primary reasons armies of the past were concentrated was that it was impossible to control them otherwise. The weapons that forced dispersal of forces were accompanied by the development of the telegraph, field telephones, and finally radio. In the South Pacific, both weapons and terrain forced dispersal while at the same time communications were miserable.

Shrewd generals realized this and made plans accordingly. In no other theater did subordinate commanders receive the autonomy routinely delegated in the South Pacific. A division headquarters could usually communicate with a regimental headquarters. Anywhere down the line from that point, however, problems could occur. It is safe to say that unless he was manning a larger perimeter, a company commander would have been most fortunate to know the exact location of his platoons. A good company commander would do his best to see that the phone lines were laid, the radios working, and the platoon leaders oriented. Attention to detail in command is often as crucial as courage. It is important to note that no unit of any army had acceptable maps of the South Pacific. Much fighting, in other words, was done in the dark. In this situation, the squad leader was king of the hill. Ore Marion expresses well the feelings of many of those who ran the squad war:

> The squad leader, a corporal or sergeant, is the man who sees that the assault orders are executed. Reams and reams of paper are used to write orders from the highest authority down telling everyone what to do and how to do it. They have predictable phrases: "take and occupy," "assault and capture," "operation orders," "annexes to the operational orders," etc. The squad leader never sees the reams of paper consisting of brilliant orders written by officers who have attended every war college in the world. The annexes to the orders cover everything from the battery

voltage in hand-held radios to the rolls of toilet paper that will be available. These orders and annexes are sent to the war colleges, the archives, and the "Big File in the Sky." But the snuffy squad leader doesn't care a tinker's damn about them.

When push comes to pull, the lieutenant or platoon leader tells his squad leaders, "When I give you the word, first squad move out in that direction, second squad keep contact with first squad's right flank and move out. Third squad will be reserve for now. Got any questions?" Everyone is thinking to themselves, "Yeah, can I go home now?" So the lieutenant says, "Move out." The squad leader tells his twelve or so men, "So-and-so move out, number two is . . ." and so on. An enemy machine gun is pounding like hell at you. One of your snuffies says, "Jesus Christ, Sarge, you're going to kill every one of us." You yell back, "That's right: move out and get killed or I'll have to kill you." And so it goes.

All of those assholes (or most of them) who wrote all of those brilliant operations orders never were squad leaders. It's actually simple for them. They just wrote that on such-and-such a day and time *we* will do this and that. When the battle is over (they are often thousands of miles away, of course) they congratulate each other on a job well done; get a medal and a promotion and a better desk.

When the squad gets to the objective, the corporal or sergeant is dead. The assistant squad leader, the senior PFC has taken over. There are four or maybe five men left of the original twelve. The original squad leader doesn't get promoted because he is deader than hell. He can't be decorated because there was no officer present to witness his bravery. And of course enlisted men are not mentally qualified to determine if a man has performed a heroic deed. The pompous ass who wrote the order is decorated and the body of the squad leader who carried it out is rotting in the jungle.

After my first combat experience I had a hell of a time trying to control my mind over the fact that I had been responsible for the death of a lot of my men by ordering them forward in the face of heavy enemy fire. That is one hell of a burden for a half-intelligent young (eighteen- or-twenty-year-old) man to have to carry for the rest of his life. You either make a mental block or you end up with a problem.

Obviously, Marion's thoughts were shared by his Australian counterparts. Bill Crooks, a platoon sergeant in the AIF, describes the heart of the Australian Army:

The rifle company was God's own band. It was the "queen of battles" and the "salt of the earth," to give you a couple of clichés. It was the home of the Digger: the people who found the enemy, were found by the enemy, killed and were killed, and wounded, some of them horribly. The stuff of nightmares and the subject of millions of words and thousands of books and countless films. The *men* of the rifle company. *Everything else* in the Army was back there supporting that rifle-company man, seventeen in the rear to keep one Digger at the front. Each company had three platoons and each platoon had three sections. The section [the Australian term for squad—EB] leaders were special men with special attributes. Yet outside some technical literature there was only *one* military textbook dealing with leading a section. Just think of it. Only *one* book about the a man holding that position. God, to become a section leader for a Digger was the next best thing to becoming a prime minister or a fighter pilot or a university professor.

You must understand that generals didn't make a bit of difference during the Owen Stanley campaign. There were a few exceptions, like the battle of Oivi. But for the most part, it wouldn't have mattered who the generals were. Don't misunderstand me. We had some good people. Later I worked with many of them on exercises and got to watch them. Vasey, Allen, Wooten, Potts,— all had strengths and weaknesses. In the Lae operations they were much more important. But Kokoda was a straight-out corporal's war.

Company commanders did not go out on patrols. Tactical decisions were initiated by lieutenants, sergeants, or corporals. If they survived they were good. Section leaders would simply ignore an inappropriate order. They simply wouldn't move. It wasn't a mutiny. They'd say, "Let's have another look." The section leaders conferred with each other frequently. Out in the field, if the section leaders said no, a company commander would not dare overrule them. The rosters were set, and the patrols went out. If they found anything, the platoon would hear about it first, then the company. The company would ask us what they could do to support. There really wasn't any other way.

Ernest Gerber was a squad leader in the swamps at Buna and echoes Marion and Crooks. He also points out the lack of cohesion typical of jungle operations:

It was a small-unit war. The division didn't know where their people were. Even regiments were split up. In our regiment, a piece was here, a piece there. One of our battalions was under Australian control. We operated at company level at the highest. An attack was at the company level. Everything was done at the company level or less. There was nothing like "OK fellas: at 0500 the whole regiment jumps off and makes for the ridge. And let's roll them up." You waited until the sun came up, and you sent your squads out or platoons or at most the company, and you hoped for the best.

The squad war alternated between patrols and guarding the perimeter. Patrols varied greatly in size and scope. For the most part, however, single squads patrolled almost always in daylight. The purpose of patrols, whether based on a static perimeter like that at Guadalcanal or serving as the eyes of an army on the move like the Japanese or Australians on the Kokoda Trail, was simply to find the enemy. It is important to emphasize the huge number of patrols that took place. Because perimeters were half blind, patrols went forth in all directions every day. Larger units moving single file down a track would have sent patrols forward and, if possible, along the flanks. Along the way, the men on patrol faced a set of obstacles that made their job extremely hazardous.

One of the most common and serious dangers faced on a patrol was contact with a similar enemy patrol. These contacts took place in two forms. Most common was an encounter with snipers. The sniper

war was not always well understood at the time by all the men involved, and is rarely handled correctly in print. The Japanese sniper
of lore tied himself in a tree and fired down at unsuspecting GIs. In
most circumstances, however, it is very unlikely that snipers in the
jungle were firing from above. John Miller, Jr., wrote the volumes in
the U.S. Army's official history of World War II dealing with
Guadalcanal and the Solomons. Miller, in addition to being a fine
historian, was also a Marine on Guadalcanal. His observations about
Japanese snipers are perceptive:

> One of the great bugaboos of the Guadalcanal campaign which
> slowed nearly all advances by infantry was the belief, firmly held
> by nearly all troops, that Japanese "snipers" operated from tree-
> tops. But this belief, which the Japanese curiously entertained
> about American "snipers," was seldom supported by facts. The
> Japanese rifleman was not especially equipped for sniping, nor
> did he usually climb trees to shoot.

In another volume Miller elaborated on the subject:

> Whereas the Japanese, like the Allies, used trees whenever possi-
> ble for observation posts, it is doubtful that snipers used many
> trees in the jungle. Anyone who has ever climbed a tree in the
> jungle can testify to the difficulties a man with a rifle would
> encounter—lack of visibility, tree limbs in the way, and the innu-
> merable little red ants whose bite is like the prick of needles.

Miller noted that many Japanese soldiers scanned the trees looking for American snipers who were not there. He also argued that
most snipers were either outpost guards or members of a small ambush patrol. Robert Kennington of the 25th Division, who did shoot
a sniper in a tree, describes what was more typical:

> They would dig holes under the roots of those big trees. The
> roots came out like a fan. The Japs would dig a hole straight
> down like a well. Then have someone camouflage it on top, put
> a man in there with a rifle or machine gun. As soon as some GIs
> came by, the Jap would rise out of the hole and cut some Amer-
> icans down. I had two friends killed that way. One was shot to

pieces from the rear. A doctor was near by chance and we took my friend to him. But he was shot through the throat and chest and died right away.

E. J. Randall endured the sort of anguish inflicted by the many snipers in the Buna campaign. Randall's infantry unit participated in the spectacular Australian tank assault near the coast. During a lull, Randall and some fellow Australians rested behind some coconut trees:

> A long shot rang out. Lyle Hicks was a few yards ahead of me. I asked him if he had picked up the sniper's position. He said, "No, but that shot was close." As soon as he had uttered the words, the next shot took him in the temple. He slumped forward, killed instantly. Ted Rollo jumped up and ran toward the shelter of a bomb crater. He was shot in the throat before he got there. The next bullet grazed my back and burrowed into the buttocks of my mate Les Judd. We moved quickly and took shelter behind a tank. The tank's commander knocked down many nearby trees trying to dislodge the sniper. But the next morning we found that the sniper was firing from a raised position off the ground shielded by young coconut palms.

If a field of fire existed, however, the Japanese did climb trees. This was often the case in coconut groves or on a ridge that overlooked a major trail. Bill Crooks was on a patrol that observed the Japanese creating a position. Note that Crooks's patrol just avoided a collision with another patrol. In this case, it was fortunate for Crooks and his mates that they did:

> Our unit was not bothered by snipers in the Owen Stanleys or the fighting around Lae. There were a few near Gona, but we dealt with them simply enough. We would use our Brens or Vickers and blow the tops of the trees off. But I saw them on my first combat patrol. We were on a patrol out of Iorobaiwa in September. This was a time of great confusion with three of our battalions trying to retreat and our brigade trying to move into position. The Japs were attacking full blast. We were a platoon and ordered not to engage until our brigade occupied a ridgeline.

We saw the Japs advancing through the jungle and up the right flank of the ridge our brigade was assembling on. There were hundreds of them, green-uniformed and covered in branch-vine camouflage, moving in two or three single files. It was our first sight of the Japs. Naturally we were anxious to get back and warn our battalion what was coming up the hill. We guessed this was their main attack, that they had been waiting for us and knew we were trying to get into position. But temporary confusion and disorientation reigned. We lay doggo. I recall stopping breathing! I could hear my heart pounding away and saw visions of the Japs filling us full of holes like rag dolls. But then sanity came back and we knew they wouldn't do that if they were involved in a surprise flank attack.

Then, we noticed that one or two sniper observers were roping up special trees. It took three or four men to leg them up. Anyway, the Jap companies passed us by and to this day I cannot understand why they didn't trip over us. They were just twenty paces away from their nearest new enemy. After they had gone, the platoon leader and myself, the platoon sergeant, conferred on whether we should bring down the snipers with our Bren. We did not and we both regret it now. But we were afraid we would alert the other Japs and we had been ordered not to engage.

Whatever their position, Japanese snipers were a plague in the Solomons. Adam DiGenaro was a squad leader with the 3d Marine Division on Bougainville in late 1943, and recalls the fear they caused:

Snipers were the worst. We dreaded them. You didn't know where that fire was coming from. If you could hear the direction of the sound, you could spray the tree. I never saw a sniper killed. I'm sure most got away. You tend to spread out and try to get out of the way of the sniper. Ordinarily we wouldn't try to approach them, but would rather change our line of approach. We would bypass them. It might sound cruel to bypass an ambush, but the troops behind you had more time to deal with them slowly. You had to move on. The reason they were there was to slow us down. And of course they didn't think anything of giving up their lives. They were like kamikazes. It was the reason for a lot of their success.

Snipers operated in small numbers. Less common but potentially more dangerous and always more chaotic was a collision of patrols. Sometimes these were ambushes, on other occasions they were a matter of two small units, doing the same thing, stumbling into each other.

Specific instances of collisions of this type were almost never recorded simply because they were so frequent. As noted, both sides patrolled continually. It was the only possible way to get some idea of what the enemy was doing in the local area. Patrols by the dozens issued forth from the Marine perimeter on Guadalcanal. Clifford Fox was on many:

> I was on quite a few reconnaissance patrols. There were set times of the day, usually in the morning and evening, when the perimeter knew people were going out. The artillery knocked off interdictory fire, and our guys in the foxholes were less likely to pull the trigger. We went out as far as told and would scout out the area. Normally nothing happened. Sometimes you'd see some Japs or signs that they were around. Then you'd report back as soon as possible. Sometimes you ran into each other. When a skirmish took place you fought until someone was wiped out or someone took off. Usually someone took off. Fights like that were usually quick. Sometimes you'd exchange fire with some Japanese along a ridgeline. That might be a little way off. But in the jungle, it was always close, very close. It was face-to-face sometimes. Lord, sometimes men fought with bayonets.

Patrolling was intense when large units moved forward. William Schumacher was with the 25th Division when it moved out of the Guadalcanal perimeter and toward Mount Austen. His description of jungle firefights is a good one:

> A lot of fighting resulted from our daylight patrols. I was in several firefights, and they were very frightening. You would learn to stay very alert and strain the senses. But you would still get

caught by surprise. It happened so fast that you were never really ready. They were very short. Someone would open fire. Then, at the same time, everybody would shoot and dive for cover. After blasting away for a few seconds the shooting would stop. You didn't usually see the Japs at all.

Robert Kennington was part of a battalion reconnaissance patrol with the 25th Division. Like Schumacher he recalls that patrolling picked up significantly after his regiment moved toward Mount Austen and the Gifu Strong Point:

Combat on Guadalcanal was constant for the three months the 25th Division was there, especially near the Gifu. With all of the casualties from disease and battle, and all the guys dragging stuff from the beach to the fighting front, we became short of men right away. We had a lot of fill-ins. Cooks, mechanics, band members became riflemen. Everyone was a rifleman. Fighting was short, quick, with small exchanges. At the Gifu it was in-and-out, hit-and-run patrols. We wanted to keep them penned in.

Fred Balester was also on Guadalcanal. One afternoon his squad was walking point for one of the large company-sized patrols that the Marines sometimes mounted. From his description one can visualize how rapidly the "green fog" could descend on a jungle firefight:

After working slowly through thick kunai grass I finally got to the top of the hill and turned to see how the troops were coming along. Spread out below I could see a couple of hundred Marines threading their way through the grassy maze. As I watched a shot rang out. In less than a wink of an eye they all completely disappeared into that long grass. I knew from the direction of the sound that it was an accidental discharge, but they could not tell and were taking no chances. All I could think of was all the times in training when the noncoms had to holler and swear to persuade the men to get down and out of sight when commanded to hit the deck. When that shot rang out there was no need to urge the men to comply: there were no slowpokes. Everyone just vanished.

Richard Loucks fought with the 43d Division on New Georgia. He describes patrolling in some of the most difficult terrain that existed in the South Pacific. Note Loucks's description of how the terrain channeled the movement and combat in the jungle:

Patrols were usually linear, that is, in a single-file column. The principal characteristic of the jungle is its density. There are no landmarks. There are trails, and in many places we could move only on them because of the impassibility of vines, underbrush, tree roots. Mangrove swamps, for example, were totally impenetrable. We were, therefore, in great danger because the Japanese knew where we had to go and prepared for us. Parallel columns sometimes were successful, but they frequently veered out of eye contact. The scouts out front were particularly vulnerable because they had no instantaneous support from the troops behind them. Often the scouts were on top of the enemy before either side realized what was happening. Since they were moving they were at terrible risk and took many casualties. Combat was close, though we seldom engaged in hand-to-hand fighting. The range was from zero to fifty yards. Concealment, as you would surmise, was very easy. Often, in fact, one merely stood still. If the Japanese were not fortified, and we were too strong, they just melted away in the jungle. We knew we'd meet them another day.

Constant and aggressive patrolling characterized AIF operations in New Guinea. They had learned its importance the hard way, during the harsh battles in August and September of 1942 when the South Seas Detachment outflanked one Australian position after another. Once Australian sections adjusted their tactics for jungle warfare, they became the most lethal small fighting units of the Pacific War. Australian fighting techniques upped the ante of ground combat. When near an Australian force, the Japanese suffered probes, ambushes, attacks on isolated strong points, and anything else possible to cause anguish. In return, however, not even crack Australian units could avoid a central reality of combat: contact and casualties are directly related.

As a platoon sergeant, Bill Crooks was in an excellent position to observe combat on the move, Australian-style.

> We did most of our fighting and suffered most of our casualties patrolling. Our fighting in the Pacific was a squad or platoon war, most of it on patrol. People would go out, there would be short vicious firefights, grenades thrown, and people screaming like mad. It was over fast. And then the men would get going again or stay there dead. Fire had to be controlled. A seven-man section could expend all its ammunition in three minutes if you went all out. So it was rare indeed that *rapid fire* was ordered. That's why we used three-round bursts from the Brens and Tommies and two magazines per minute from the rifles, unless you could see the *whites of their eyes*. I can remember only two or three occasions like that with small groups: furious, split-second action.

As Crooks states, most combat was small-scale and over fast. He did experience, however, a collision between two large patrols soon after his battalion first moved up to face the South Seas Detachment in September 1942:

> We, D Company, actually walked into an ambush just below a rock face too steep to climb. It was matted in bamboo and lawyer vine. Suddenly all hell opened up from the vines, a blast of massed fire. At the time we thought we had bumped head-on into a battalion. But experience after leads me to believe it was probably two companies. They were advancing around the cliff in probably four single-file columns. That is, one of their companies in two single files, four or five yards apart and ten yards out, and their other company the same. We were strung out in single file and we must have walked into the middle of the head of their column. It was the loudest noise of a massed firefight I ever heard. We had in a minute the platoon commander and a section leader killed and ten or twelve wounded. *And bloody* confusion. Nobody said a word. I remember moans and groans later in the night. Terrible screams of the wounded. It must have been theirs because we recovered all of ours straightaway and sent them back. But you could never tell with the Jap. They used to talk and

scream, hoping one of us would come looking and bang! Later we passed the same place and recovered our two dead.

It was all over in say ten minutes. We must have fired half our ammo and they half theirs. Bushes and light trees disappeared as if cut by a scythe. Grenades were bursting. Our Brens and their light machine guns were blasting away. The bullets were zinging and zipping all around us. The noise was absolutely deafening. It was all extraordinary: the sound of it, the number of men involved and the closeness. We were in the center of them and they in the center of us. Do not have a clue how many Nips we hit. Probably the same ratio as they hit of ours. We never found a body later, but they dragged their dead away and hid them for burial later by night or burnt them.

Australian patrols were also extremely active in the campaign in northern New Guinea in the summer and fall of 1943. Operations took place in some of the most loathsome terrain New Guinea had to offer. High mountains with very tall and extremely steep ridges interspersed with gullies of kunai grass made the war in this theater both fierce and bizarre. The enemy was numerous in the theater, but did not have the quality of the elite South Seas Detachment faced in 1942. Fortunately for the AIF, like the Americans in New Georgia, they were far better supported than they had been six months before. For a portion of this campaign elements of the U.S. 41st Division served under Australian command. Charles Crary was with the 41st near Salamaua in July 1943, and describes the conditions faced by patrols:

For the most part the terrain near Salamaua was straight up and down. If one wished to go from one ridge to another there usually wasn't a high-ground connecting link. In general, it seems that one always had to descend into a valley to get on top of an adjacent ridge or mountain. It was covered by rain-forest vegetation, which grew out of wet red clay that turned into grease with the passage of a few feet. The vegetation on the ground was not sufficient to provide a buffer for the surface. If one cut a trail through virgin jungle for a squad patrol of ten men, the last man in the column was ankle-deep in mud. Crawling up a slope was very hard because the footing was so slick. You had to keep a hand free to grasp something. Many men took a tumble.

The terrain was so steep that it could, on some fortunate occasions, protect men advancing up a ridge. In October an AIF platoon assaulted a group of Japanese infantry dug in near a major Japanese stronghold on Shaggy Ridge in the high foothills of the Finisterre Mountain Range. The Australians were strongly supported by mortars and artillery, which chewed up the ground and made climbing easier. Japanese defenders rolled grenades over the ridge but they bounced beyond the attackers. The attackers had suffered few losses before they hurled themselves over the ridge and on top of the Japanese foxholes. What ensued, as described in the Australian official history, could have only happened in New Guinea:

> We could see them now and opened fire on their heads as they bobbed up above their foxholes. Their fire began to slacken off. One of our chaps gave a shrill bloodcurdling yell that startled even us, and was partly responsible for some of the Japs running headlong down the hill in panic. Unable to stop at the edge of the cliff, they plunged to their doom hundreds of feet below.

The fierce battle described by Crooks and the action near Shaggy River were exceptions. The small, short encounter was very much the norm. After years of study and reflection, Bill Crooks describes perfectly the pulse of the ground war in the South Pacific:

> As time went on I grew more experienced and was promoted. I talked to others and there was reading, reading, reading. I studied both our training and theirs. I have concluded that had the sort of fighting we encountered in New Guinea taken place in Borneo or the Middle East there would have been mass slaughter. That did not happen in the jungle. This was true because we were *too close to cause more damage to one another.* Nobody could see anything. We were all flat on the ground and the boles of the trees and massed timber over a short distance made protective walls.

Human nature and self-preservation being what is, *nobody* is going to keep on attacking in the *face of point-blank small-arms fire once it breaks out*. They, as us, will *go to ground*. And you will never get them up again until the mass fire is neutralized. It all balances out.

Our war was not like World War I. There it was up and over the top, your men were shot down, and you suffered 50 percent casualties in one day. In the Pacific it was a nibbling war. But nevertheless from August 1942 to the end in Papua we had nearly 10,000 casualties.

The Australian fighting techniques produced results. After their early setbacks at Milne Bay and along Kokoda in early September 1942, they never suffered a major defeat. Yet the strain on the best and most intrepid of their men was immense. The Australian official history, discussing the summer 1943 campaign in the rugged ridgelines near Salamaua, pointed out that aggressive tactics were accompanied by a grim mechanism that afflicted every good unit in every army in the war:

At this stage most companies were about half strength. Platoons with good men in them and with good leaders got results. Average patrols produced casualties but often no worthwhile results. An experienced company commander who had led many patrols in this fight later described a regrettable but necessary method of achieving patrol results. "All of our patrols which were likely to run into trouble were made up time and time again with the few really good men at patrolling. As these men were killed, wounded, or evacuated sick, the numbers of men available became less and less and the 'pitcher' went to the well again and again."

Squads on patrol faced another dreadful danger: enemy field fortifications. Both sides entrenched, but the Japanese made a military art form out of creating sophisticated field positions. Lacking the support, technology, and expertise of American engineers, the Japanese relied upon long study and sheer cleverness when creating their fortified zones. The Japanese Army had learned much about trench warfare in its war against Russia in 1905. The Japanese lines in China were never solid, but rather loosely connected fortified zones. Also, in the Japanese Army, soldiers expected to be put to work. No doubt Japanese soldiers hated digging as much as their Allied counterparts, but they were far better at it. The group ethos and strict discipline of Japanese infantry were valuable assets.

Another point must be considered. Because basic facilities were so crude, and airfield construction at such a premium, the Japanese, like the Allies, always had engineer units with them. Although American and Australian infantry ran into Japanese strong points in every campaign of the war, the two toughest and most elaborate fortified zones were at Buna-Gona and on New Georgia. In both cases, Japanese engineers had been in the area for several months. In addition, they had excellent materials with which to work. The ubiquitous coconut trees had an unusually tough and fibrous texture. Very hard to cut down, they were equally hard to blow up. Consequently, the Japanese could build rugged emplacements aboveground in areas where the water table prohibited digging. Pillboxes were the perfect place to put the Nambu light machine gun. In some cases heavier weapons, such as antitank guns, were also concealed. At Buna the Japanese emplaced some powerful naval antiaircraft guns, very similar to the famous German 88 that was dreaded by all who faced it. To make matters worse, from the Allied point of view, the massive root systems of certain trees created ready-made machine-gun nests. So did the very dense underbrush. To approach a Japanese strong point it was often necessary to destroy or force retreat of these smaller, lighter positions.

In short, Japanese field positions were numerous, well designed, and tough. They also were almost invisible. Ernest Gerber saw many of them at Buna and describes their construction:

Japanese positions were extremely formidable. In our area the water table was so high that they did not usually dig down. Instead they built their pillboxes out of coconut logs, maybe three or four logs deep and on top. Coconut logs were very strong because of their fibrous nature. Around them might be fifty-gallon gasoline drums filled with sand. They were practically impenetrable to our fire. Mortar rounds bounced off them. Australian twenty-five-pounders had a hard time too. Their trajectory was too low for high explosives. So they had to land a direct hit, preferably with armor-piercing shells.

Of course you had to find them first before you could do anything. On top of the pillboxes the Japanese piled dirt and planted grass and shrubs. Vegetation grows incredibly fast in the jungle. In American terms they kind of looked like a really dense large shrub you might see in a garden. You could look right at one and it looked like the jungle. People don't believe it now and our officers didn't understand it at the time. You had to be right on top of one of those things, you almost had to touch it to see it. And then you knew where it was. No doubt there were times we stumbled upon a Japanese position without them seeing us either. The terrain could work both ways.

However, in all cases where they had these pillboxes or fortifications they cut out a field of fire. It was done in a deceptive way. They had a forward vision of twenty-five or maybe even fifty yards in front of them. It depended on where they were. They of course had the biggest advantage: they were sitting and waiting, while we were moving. If we were fortunate we might recognize one of those fields of fire and then we would be on our guard. Normally, however, you did not see it and someone was shot.

Gerber's last point is very important. The Japanese were quick to dig in in any position, but in areas that received special attention, they built a web of mutually supporting positions with what the military calls "interlocking zones of fire." A pillbox under attack by Allied infantry, in other words, could be supported by a neighboring position, probably unseen. The result was a tactical nightmare.

Tanks, as described earlier, were the best answer if the terrain allowed. Plunging artillery fire from howitzers was sometimes effective if the fire was sustained and the ammunition very plentiful. On New Georgia, American gunners fired thousands of shells into areas they thought might harbor Japanese positions near Munda. According to Paul Sponaugle, who was there with the 37th Division, "We had a saying that the Australians were the best jungle fighters, and the Japanese second. Nobody knew about the Americans, because they knocked the jungle down and then fought." Although Allied artillery was scarce at Buna, American bombers were not. Munda was likewise pounded from the air. The losses from bombardment were painful to the Japanese, as reports from the front to Rabaul testify. Nevertheless, as illustrated on a much larger scale during battles in Central Pacific islands like Iwo Jima and Okinawa, it was extremely difficult to knock out fortified zones with indirect fire. The simplest foxhole, as the Marines found out on Guadalcanal, afforded excellent protection from air attack and naval artillery. The strong bunkers and pillboxes built by Japanese engineers were nearly as difficult to neutralize as the trench positions had been in World War I. This meant, of course, that the infantry had to do it.

The only way infantry could destroy Japanese positions was to first find them and then assault them. Both tasks were done with small units. It is very hard to distinguish between attacks and patrols in the South Pacific. The fortified areas had no obvious point to attack. Furthermore, because the Japanese frequently held on to isolated positions, cutting off positions from their supply did not mean they were knocked out. Instead, what developed was a very slow, violent, giant patrol lasting weeks. Yard by yard, small groups of Allied troops would slip through the seams of the fortifications. Along the way they destroyed some positions and forced the Japanese to abandon others. Soon perimeters became incredibly intermingled. The Allies inevitably would win under these conditions because their supply line to the rear was solid, while the Japanese were cut off. Whatever the Allies could not accomplish with weapons, starvation and disease would finish.

The fiercest fighting of the Papuan campaign took place in December 1942 along the track leading to the coastal village of Sanananda, between Gona and Buna. The terrain in this area was swamp, jungle, and kunai grass, very much like the "triangle" at nearby Buna. After the December battles at Buna, E. J. Randall was sent to the Sanananda front. He describes a frightful scene:

The Jap had his defenses in a swamp: I can still smell its stink. Each defense position was a mud-hardened shell almost like a bird's nest. They were linked by a boardwalk of logs. Because of the high casualty rate, the Japs threw their dead into some of these "bird's nests" and left them to rot. We were dug in near a place called Soputa. We were twenty yards from the Jap for days.

Although most of the U.S. 32d division was at Buna, General Eichelberger consented to putting two battalions under Australian command. Instead of marching toward Buna, they headed down the Sanananda track. Meredith Huggins was a young officer and recalls his battalion's entry into the savage world of war in the swamp:

The situation was utter chaos. Nobody knew what was going on. We were green kids more scared of the jungle than of the Japanese. My unit was under Australian command. They ordered us to attack. My battalion commander didn't know what was in front of us and wanted to do a recon. The Aussies assured as they knew the enemy dispositions. We were slaughtered, two companies cut to ribbons. We withdrew about 100 yards, which in the jungle is the equivalent of about forty-five miles in the U.S.A. As luck would have it, my company found ourselves behind the Japanese on the main track. The commander was killed and I took over. We had a ration party with us, so I ordered the establishment of a double perimeter, two men to a foxhole. This became Huggins Roadblock. The Japanese came up behind and established another one behind us. And so it went. I was shot in the head by a sniper. Luckily, I didn't have any brains, so I wasn't badly hurt. We were surrounded at the time. Aussies were a few hundred yards away but so were the Japs. You measured things in inches. I laid wounded in a hole for five days I think, until a relief party came through and moved me out.

Huggins Roadblock was the first of several. Wise enough to take advantage of a stroke of luck, Huggins's men were behind the main Japanese position on the track. The Japanese counterattacked fiercely and were mauled. Consequently, they moved a roadblock of their own behind Huggins. The Australians, in their turn, established one farther down the line called James Roadblock. Soon the Japanese moved behind James. The position looked like a beaded necklace, and was one of the most freakish dispositions of forces in military history. From the rear and flanks, and out of the road-blocks themselves, came patrols and supply columns. The lines stayed essentially stagnant for close to a month. During this period, everyone at the front was within 100 yards of the enemy, most at considerably less.

AIF infantryman Ben Love served through most of the Sana-nanda campaign, and kept a diary, which he edited after the war. When his battalion arrived fresh, the commander was ordered to push forward and get his men "home for Christmas." Ordered to Huggins, Love's section had to move through a 200-yard zone of ku-nai grass and marsh infamous for sniper activity before reaching the American roadblock:

My God! I'll say it was no-man's-land. Twice I tripped and went headfirst into about four feet of "choice" mud and slush. It was tedious going. Just after finishing the pleasant 200-yard crawl through the danger zone, we met some of our chaps who had come up the day before. They were patrolling the track and had struck a Jap patrol—killed two and lost two. One Nip was lying in the mud near path, large pool of blood spread into muddy wa-ter which we must splash. Nearing Huggins, we came to a clear-ing where Yank and Jap patrols had clashed—dozens of Jap bodies about, only the bones with all the clothing on them. Reached Huggins at six P.M. The Yanks in this perimeter have been here twenty-one days—lost about 200 men since leaving Soputa—220 left. It has been terrible experience for these chaps—they look "all in." As I sit in my one-man trench writing, I just notice a small cross of two sticks in the ground a yard to my left. Yes, there was a small metal identity disc tied to the "cross"—Jack Deveraux, son of Mrs. J. Deveraux, Minneapolis—lies there.

The next day we leave Huggins to lay phone line. The scheme is to take cable through to James roadblock. Two of our platoons will make small perimeters along the track to patrol the supply path and maintain the cable. Leaving Huggins we passed through the Jap camp our Yankee friends had cleaned up twenty-three days ago. They caught the Nips asleep—killed over 100 of them. From the number of skeletons and high stench they certainly made a slaughterhouse of it.

Love's men set up position, waiting for the command to decide a course of action. Patrolling, as always, went on daily. Throughout this period it rained every night:

Here we are, twenty of us in our small circle—we shall live, sleep, and eat in these six-by-three-by-two-foot dugouts, except when patrolling. The Nips' long suit is attacking and sniping men in these perimeters, but they are definitely the best all round protection in this God-forsaken jungle country. Dug down only eighteen inches for my home and find myself in three inches of water. Had a good rest until 10:30 P.M., then it poured—wouldn't it! "Visit the tropics and die," they say. My sincere recommendation is to "die" first. Yes we bought a dear fight. It is ten days since our good Colonel Logan [killed the first day—EB] led us from Huggins, planning to reach Sanananda Point that night. Here we are in our own perimeter, roughly 500 yards forward and no hope of further advance against the strong enemy positions in front of us. Our casualties have now passed the 100 mark.

The battalion was initially ordered to "eliminate" the Japanese positions. A series of squad- and platoon-sized Australian attacks was decimated by Japanese fire. As Love put it, "So again we gained nothing and good men were just mowed down." The tactics were changed. Love and his comrades were ordered to send out "fighting patrols" to ambush Japanese supply columns. They were also to probe the Japanese flank, to learn if it was possible to move around the fortified zone. The AIF, in other words, tried to put the Japanese under siege:

Before lunch a small party went out to reconnoiter a track the Japs were supposed to be using. Heard shots soon after. Our men came back later. They had killed two of three Japs who had come up the trail while our men were resting. The man sitting is the man who does the hitting—naturally you hear movement first—take up position and just wait until the other poor devil is practically on top of you—you simply can't miss. As Clive said, he fired the first burst with his Owen submachine gun, it was pure murder. And that is exactly what this jungle warfare amounts to.

Five of us out on patrol. Only covered about forty yards, and we found ourselves fifteen yards or so from the outer edge of a large enemy defensive line. Three Japs happened to be in a group just to their right. One of them spotted Cyril, so knowing further recce was out, he gave them a full magazine of his Owen. Down went those Nips and out came our chaps at the double. The three of us covering them needed no explanation and followed also at double.

The Allies were short of specialized weapons, normally associated with combat engineers, designed to destroy bunkers. They had some flamethrowers, pioneered by the Germans in World War I, and carried by all Japanese combat engineers. Neither the Australians nor Americans had incorporated this grim weapon into their standard arsenal before the war. This situation changed dramatically later, but in 1942–43 the flamethrower was still a novelty in Allied ranks. Joe Salini tested flamethrowers for the Americal Division and describes the appalling device:

I tested flamethrowers when we were on Bougainville. They were frightening weapons. When you use a flamethrower the blast gives off an intense heat that burns off your eyebrows. An arc of flame goes out that is six feet wide and maybe forty feet long. It creams everything it hits. Just destroys it.

Ernest Gerber explains the problems with the device on Buna:

We thought the engineer's flamethrower would be ideal. It was one of the new innovations at the time. We thought it would be the weapon to take out the pillboxes. We finally got hold of a few flamethrowers and engineers to operate them. We immediately ran into two problems. First, you rarely got close enough to use them. The Japanese would shoot you before you were within range. A serious difficulty, to put it mildly. If you did get close enough, half the time they malfunctioned. We were praying for some tanks with flamethrowers. But the tanks couldn't operate in our area because of the swamps.

Frank Chadwick served with the heavily armed 9th Marine Defense Battalion. Toward the end of the New Georgia campaign, Chadwick's unit confronted some Japanese positions and used some improvised weapons backed by heavy fire to crack pillboxes:

When we moved out to Kindu Point after the capture of the airfield, the Japs were beginning to lose their effectiveness. We must have killed sixty or seventy Japs in pillboxes or trenches. We burned them out with forty-pound blocks of TNT. We approached positions like this carefully. We had air-cooled .30-caliber machine guns. We also had a 20mm antiaircraft cannon on a wheeled mount. You'd just lay down a field of fire into those pillboxes, and someone would crawl up with a forty-pound block of TNT with a hand grenade fixed to it. You'd arm the grenade and push the TNT into the gun slot. That blew them to pieces. We didn't have flamethrowers on Georgia. The Japanese had them, and so did the Army. The Marines always got things last.

Combat engineers also had a device called a bangalore torpedo. It was a metal pole with an explosive charge at the end, and was intended to blow holes in barbed wire or demolish small bunkers. These devices were rare in the early stage of war. However, the Australians created a homemade version of the bangalore torpedo, sometimes called a "jungle cocktail," putting several sticks of dynamite on a ten-foot pole. An arming mechanism was fixed, and a soldier would stick the charge through the slit of the bunker, and drop it inside, where it exploded in an instant. Australians also poured gasoline through the slits and ignited it, a task, E. J. Randall assures us, that was not appreciated by those called upon to do it. The 25th Division on New Georgia tried when possible to mass machine-gun or 37mm-cannon fire on pillboxes, covering the way forward for its infantry. The 25th used its flamethrowers carefully and had much success with them. Most pillboxes that were destroyed by infantry, however, were destroyed with grenades.

It was a harrowing experience to locate a bunker precisely. Once found, it was even more harrowing to assault it with a hand grenade or any of the homemade explosive devices. Observation slits were very thin. Consequently, one could not realistically lob grenades in from a distance. However, the dense terrain that guarded the fortification proved a fatal liability to the defenders if an attacking infantry man could get close enough. Then it was he, not the gunners inside, who could see. Infantry able to get this close were skilled and brave. On more than one occasion, these men were no doubt "on the edge." Homer Wright, a young officer with the 32d Division, describes the death of one bunker at Buna:

> It was a case of knocking out the pillboxes one by one. The shrubbery and vegetation in the jungle grew so fast that it was rare for us to detect one before it opened fire. We had a chaplain. They're not supposed to be armed but he was. Chaplains tend to funerals and he had seen a lot of our men die. We found a Japanese fortification. Although it was not his duty, for some reason the chaplain went forward. Somehow he managed to get right next to the thing. He yelled into the bunker, which was inhabited by several enemy, "Come out and be saved." He was met by a hail of rifle fire. He dumped in a couple of hand grenades. Debris came out the slit. Then he took his pistol and fired all six rounds through the slit. Everyone inside was killed. From that point on he was known as "Come out and be saved."

Buna, Sanananda, and New Georgia all ended the same way. Slowly the Japanese were wedged out of their positions. Often they evacuated isolated posts. American and Australian infantry stayed in the field and slugged it out. Although pressed to the limit by the enemy and the elements, the Allies had the invaluable aid of the jungle. Ernest Gerber's description of the 32d's ultimate victory at Buna could apply to smaller but similar fights throughout the South Pacific:

The thing that eventually worked the best was sheer guts. You waited and waited until you knew where the fire was coming from. Then, some brave souls, or a brave squad, would sneak up as well as they could and try to lob a hand grenade into their slot. Usually we tried to get up from the rear. There were openings in the front. In many cases, to be blunt, the Japanese were forced to evacuate. They were getting killed too. And they were dying of disease by the dozens. Once in a while we were fortunate. There was some damned place that we attacked day after day after day, got shot and killed, and just couldn't get at it. Then one morning we'd walk up to it and there wasn't a goddamn soul there. Once in a while that was it. More often, it was slug it out. One by one. Take one, and try another, do this, get a few guys killed and wounded, get the next one. The combination of that and the Japanese just finally getting tired was what made the operation successful.

Victory in one of these prolonged and violent brawls brought little satisfaction, beyond the relief caused by survival and hope of a fast move to the rear. There were no grateful civilians lining the streets throwing flowers. Nor was there any real feeling that the fighting was going to affect the course of the war. Paul Sponaugle describes reaching the airfield at Munda Point near the end of the battle of New Georgia:

The Japs had dug in under a big tree. I thought our captain was moving too fast. We started shooting it out with the Japanese before the other troops could come down and silence the Japs from the rear. One of my guys was shot through both legs. I took my shovel and tried to dig in so the Japs couldn't hit the poor guy again. I got a hole shot through my battle pack from off that hill. I am almost sure we were both shot by our own men. The captain was a glory hunter. He wanted to be the first one from our division at the airport. We were. But so what. We only had fifty-one men left out of our company when we got there.

James Salafia had almost the same feeling when his unit finally reached its objective at the Munda airfield:

The airfield was a big disappointment. We saw it and thought, "This is what all the work was for? What a shitty airfield." It was, too. The field was small, crude. There was nothing there except shell holes. Of course the bulldozers arrived fast and started expanding it. They covered it with coral. But considering the cost, we just wondered if it was worth it. The fighting was almost over. That was more important to us. There were more islands to come though.

Salafia's comment would have been echoed by thousands of veterans from both sides. The "green fog" of jungle war was so dense that it was often difficult to identify something as elementary as victory.

The Perimeter

The world of combat infantry in the South Pacific was divided between patrolling and guarding the perimeter. An unusual division of labor developed between the two sides that reflected their respective fighting techniques. With very few exceptions, Allied infantry did not move at night. The Japanese, however, frequently did. Doctrine and training contributed much to this fact. Japanese shock tactics required tactical surprise. It was vital to get as close as possible to the point of attack before facing machine-gun and artillery fire. Night assault and night movement allowed for both. Consequently, Japanese infantry trained hard at night operations.

The Americans and Australians put strong faith in firepower. The large-unit land warfare found in Europe, which both the American and Australian armies prepared for, required concentration of fire and coordinated movement. The night hindered both. Still, night patrols were part of European-style warfare. Furious battles at night between patrols in no-man's-land were a staple of trench warfare in World War I and were common enough in Europe during World War II. What really kept the GIs and Aussies pinned to their perimeters at night was fear of friendly fire.

Armies have long trained their officers in elaborate techniques designed to limit friendly-fire casualties because it had a devastating effect on morale. Nevertheless, it was not a subject that any military discussed in public during World War II. Civilian morale, in a war against nations, is a critical factor. No government wanted its people to know that a large number of young soldiers were being killed by their own side. (Photos of American dead from any cause were rarely published in the United States during the war. Censorship in most other nations was tighter yet.)

Nevertheless, officers have known for centuries that friendly fire is very common and a major cause of combat casualties. It could hardly have been otherwise. Artillery and machine guns relied on a heavy volume of fire to kill. If soldiers pounded an area with lethal missiles, inevitably some would strike their own men. Death and injury at the hands of one's own comrades could come from every possible direction.

Artillery and mortars were major culprits. Due to small irregularities in the propellant, a certain percentage of artillery rounds did not travel as far as intended. These were the "short rounds" of World War I fame. Artillerymen, for this reason, did not like to fire at targets close to their own men. Unfortunately, frequently this was where the fire was required. The dilemma was made worse by the ballistic effect of artillery. Most World War II artillery rounds exploded on contact. Because they followed an arc through the sky, they struck the ground at an angle. Shell fragments consequently tended to scatter forward in a butterfly-like pattern. (Mortar rounds, because they came down so abruptly, showed this tendency less.) If a round fell directly behind a friendly position, most of the shell fragments not expended skyward headed directly for the soldiers' backs. To make matters worse, defenders under artillery attack take the best cover they can find. Attackers are prone during a friendly artillery barrage but not dug in, and very vulnerable to shellfire. For both these reasons, if a round fell short, it would very likely do more damage to friendly soldiers that it would have to the enemy had the shell found its mark. Furthermore, in the jungle, a perfectly aimed round could strike a tree and scatter wood fragments a very long way. Another problem arose when coordination broke down between artil-

lery spotters and the infantry. This happened often. Field-telephone
wires were very vulnerable and often cut by the Japanese. Maps
were poor. If the men and artillery were in fixed positions, few
problems arose. If on the move, disaster was waiting. Infantryman
Marshall Chaney was on the wrong end of an American barrage on
Guadalcanal:

> On the Bonegi River we had some artillery fire that was falling
> short. We had telephone communications. Our lines were lying
> on the ground and apparently the Jap stragglers had cut the lines.
> We had advanced farther than the artillery thought we had. But
> with the phone out we couldn't get through to them and have
> them cease fire. We took casualties from that. We all knew it was
> the sort of thing that happened in battle. Our first casualty on
> Guadalcanal was shot by one of our own sentries. It really wasn't
> the artillery's fault. But even so, it was the most demoralizing
> thing imaginable to get it from your own side. It just laid us low
> for a time.

Aircraft could also deliver shattering blows to men on their own
side. Airmen know that close air support is one of the most complex
operations possible. Like artillerymen, they much prefer "interdiction" attacks well to the rear of enemy lines. Furthermore, the sort
of coordination that developed later in the war between fighter-
bombers and ground troops was sorely lacking in 1942. Consequently, in the jungle, where vision was so badly obstructed, calling
in air support was a very risky proposition. It did no good that aircraft received large quantities of "friendly fire" in return from antiaircraft on land and on warships. Bud DeVere supported Marine
pilots flying out of Henderson Field on Guadalcanal, and had the sad
occasion to deal with infuriated Marines struck by their own planes:

> Marine pilots really admired our soldiers out on the perimeter.
> They were eager to provide close support to the troops. Unfor-
> tunately, it was a lot more complicated than any of us realized.
> There were a lot of friendly-fire casualties from our strafing at-
> tacks. A Wildcat could lay down a lot of lead. When I went to the
> front lines, which wasn't far to walk, I would hear those ground

pounders just knocking hell out of aviation. They'd tell me, "Don't come up here looking for a little excitement. We're not happy with you guys shooting our people." They were bitter, and made it sound like our pilots had done it on purpose. It was a strange feeling between the ground and aviation troops up there when that kind of thing happened.

Yet most friendly-fire deaths occurred when infantry shot their own comrades. In this regard the jungle war was particularly vile. Friendly fire was a serious problem in other theaters, but there artillery would have had a larger share of the blame. Furthermore, night patrols went out in Europe continually, and men on perimeters were alert to the possibility that someone moving in front of them could be one of their own men. In the jungle, the tendency was to shoot first and at very close range. Bill Crooks gives a good analysis of an inevitable but tragic by-product of war in the jungle:

Combat in the jungle was very ragged, day or night. There were men charging forward, yelling, shooting their Tommies, totally out of their head. You couldn't really see. So often they were shooting their own men. I once saw several men in one of our sections, all with .45-caliber slugs in their legs. You could never tell for sure, but I don't think the Jap fired at all. We had a battle with ourselves. At night, when the Japs made one of those charges of theirs, there could be a new guy in a position. You'd forget he was there and blow his head off. When I helped wounded to the regimental aid post just to the rear, you would see men that you knew had been hit by our stuff. The doctors knew it too. They would shake their heads with a sad look when they pulled a .45 bullet out of a mortally wounded man. Of course his family was told he was killed in action. I am not sure what the percentage of "friendly-fire" casualties was, but it was far higher than we wanted to admit. It would have been too hard to morale to let out the truth.

American data gathered during the war strongly support Crooks's retrospective opinion. As part of the aforementioned U.S. Army studies on New Georgia and Bougainville concerning wounds and "wounding agents," the doctors were very interested in estimating how many men were injured or killed by friendly fire. They were also very interested in how friendly-fire casualties took place. Although the samples were too small to be considered definitive, and could not be used to judge the impact of friendly fire in other theaters, the findings were sobering. On both New Georgia and Bougainville approximately 12 percent of casualties came from friendly fire. The percentage of men killed by their comrades was higher: approximately 16 percent on Bougainville and 24 percent on New Georgia. The reason that a high percentage of killed resulted from friendly fire was simple enough: infantrymen shot infantrymen at close range with rifles or machine guns. Consequently, those wounded had a very high chance of extremely serious injury. (The numbers might be adjusted slightly downward: it is possible a few of the men committed suicide.) Most of these small tragedies took place at night.

What one soldier called the "jungle jitters" caused frequent firefights between friendly units in the pitch-black night. This was particularly true with green troops, such as those found on New Georgia. Several of the victims on Bougainville were Fijian scouts who were known both for their excellent bushcraft and for their very poor fire discipline. To add insult to injury, dysentery, which was endemic, also posed a serious threat. Dick Peterson of the 25th Division outlines a dilemma that cost many lives:

Dysentery was rampant on Guadalcanal. It is a miserable malady. I went from 155 to 128 pounds in about six weeks. They had this "D Ration," a kind of vitamin-filled chocolate bar. It would go through you like a dose of salts. The desire to relieve yourself is just tremendous. At night, what do you do? We had passwords, but the Japs were all over and guys were quick to shoot. So do you stay in the hole or go out for a minute and risk getting shot. Those were the alternatives. Most people stayed in the hole, but I'm afraid many of the men shot after dark had their pants down. It was amazing how many ways you could get hurt in World War II.

Obviously there were very good reasons to keep night action to a minimum from the Allied point of view. There were risks in yielding the night to the Japanese. Yet Allied officers knew from the start that the Japanese troops were better trained to move quietly and kept better unit discipline. Had the Americans or Australians contested control of the night, they would have suffered ugly losses in crazed encounters with the Japanese. More important, however, their own men in the perimeters would have been seriously weakened. Even with the use of passwords, in a world where opposing sides might be only yards distant, scared and tired men in foxholes would need much restraint not to open fire on obvious movement. The danger of shooting when they should not would also have been compounded by the danger of not shooting when they should. In other words, shooting quickly might cost a friend his life. Hesitation, however, could cost one's own life. The problem as it stood was bad enough. Venturing out would have made it worse.

It was far better, from the Allies' point of view, to allow the Japanese to roam the front at night. It simplified matters greatly: anyone outside the perimeter was considered hostile and was shot. The Allies did not give up any great tactical advantage when they yielded the night to the enemy. As shown over and over, the Japanese, despite their training at night maneuver, could not coordinate smoothly large night assaults. Allied soldiers inside their perimeters were willing to take their chances with smaller groups of the enemy. It was no simple matter for the Japanese to get close to a perimeter without raising an alarm. Allied perimeters were surrounded by trip wires with noisemakers attached, and sometimes barbed wire also. Allied soldiers learned to stay awake, peering out directly over the ground. The result was a nerve-racking nighttime war with a resourceful enemy made worse by fatigue and a malignant physical environment.

All units in the battle zone established perimeters and all perimeters were based on field fortifications usually prepared by the soldiers themselves. The most common home for an Allied infantryman was what the Americans called foxholes and the Australians called fighting pits. Under most circumstances these were pretty crude affairs. Depending upon the terrain and how long a unit intended to stay in an area, a foxhole might be two or three feet deep. Australians added width to theirs so soldiers could lie flat. Neither American nor Australian soldiers were famous for their love or skill at digging. In addition, digging was done with the famous infantry entrenching tool. Light enough to carry and foldable, the entrenching tool was a combination shovel and pickax. Yet because the handle was short and the digging surface small, it is stretching the term to call this device a shovel. "Digging in" was hard work.

Experienced men soon learned that it was a very bad idea to have a foxhole that left the body exposed. A man below ground level was almost impervious to, for instance, a Japanese knee mortar. Someone with a leg or a knee dangling out picked up a wound easily. Army medical studies found that men were more likely to be killed on patrol, but were more likely to be wounded guarding the perimeter. No doubt the Japanese knee mortar, frequently aimed at Allied foxholes, accounted for the difference. So did the fact that massed Japanese assaults took place exclusively at night and were accompanied by a volley of grenades, mortars, and light artillery. There was good reason to dig.

Gus Merrigan describes a typical portion of the Marine perimeter on Guadalcanal:

> Normally we had two men to a foxhole. The one next to you might be ten feet away. You had foxholes with riflemen. Then you had foxholes with BARs and foxholes with MGs. They were set up with a prearranged field of fire. A cross fire. If an enemy came toward you, you were protected by the machine guns on the right firing to the left, and the machine guns on the left firing to the right. In the middle were riflemen.

If assigned a position of line for any length of time, units dug in more thoroughly. Deep slit trenches sprouted in the rear, offering nearby shelter from air attack or artillery bombardment. Some sort of protection over the top was ideal. Ore Marion explains the effectiveness of the simple positions used by front-line Marines on Guadalcanal:

On Guadalcanal we dug individual "spiderholes" and because of that type of hole we had very few casualties from air attack or naval bombardment. When we heard the first round or bomb coming in we would dive or jump into our spiderhole and pull a Jap-made reed sandbag over the top. The only way they could get us was with a direct hit—which seldom happened. Our naval gunfire did very little damage to the Japs and their defenses also.

The nerve-racking job of guarding the perimeter was made much worse by fatigue. Fatigue was the reason that the Allies learned to put two men in a foxhole whenever possible. In theory, coverage was better with individual holes. In practice, however, two men could share the watch, share the boredom, and share the tension if the situation turned ugly.

Dick Randles's experience manning the front line along the coastal sector at Buna with the 32d Division was not unique:

We had two to a foxhole. It was two hours on and two hours off. It was very dull at night. You were blessed lucky if you could stay awake. You got so tired. People went to sleep on watch. I suppose I might have done it myself. But it's a different kind of sleep. You kind of jolt yourself awake and you don't know you've been asleep. Sometimes there'd be noises. Someone would panic and throw a grenade, but that was about it. You sure didn't shoot your rifles unless you had to. That's a way to say, Shoot me: the flash is there: here I am.

The Japanese harassed American lines far more often then they attacked them. As Frank Hurray points out, one of the reasons for this Japanese tactic was to compound fatigue and wear down American infantry:

The nighttime was the worst. The Japs were good at infiltration, and knew the avenues of approach. It was very frightening. Our guys were not trained as night fighters. The Japanese were very active at night. They would shriek and yell threats. It shook some guys up to hear "You die tonight!" yelled by someone who was awfully close. It was important not to shoot without a target, or you might get a grenade from close range. One part of their tactics was very simply to keep us awake. That is a very important element of combat over time. It is a very important part of a soldier's life to try to get rest. You needed the strength for the daylight. The foxhole is the soldier's best friend. That's home. Normally we used one-man holes, sometimes we had time to dig two-man. That was a good idea. Maybe twenty-five yards apart.

Skillful soldiers kept their wits about them. Most nights nothing happened. But Japanese night patrols were very real and potentially very dangerous. Donald Fall kept situation maps for Marine intelligence on Guadalcanal. But at night, he did his turn on the perimeter:

On night perimeter you learn to look straight ahead. If you do that, you notice any movement in your area of vision. You learn to sleep with an eye open. That lasted a couple of years after I was out of the service. You're asleep, but you're not. I hated the night. The Japs were good at night infiltration. One guy usually manned a foxhole unless it was a two-man machine-gun position.

James Salafia experienced the same thing on New Georgia. As an experienced squad leader, he took security seriously. Early in the campaign, a Japanese night raid mauled a company and isolated a regimental headquarters, killing many Americans. Fire discipline and security were important:

On Munda we didn't really sleep. There were two or three guys in a foxhole. We slept with one eye open. I shared a foxhole with our medic. He carried a gun and blasted away in battle just like me. He was a friend from my hometown. He saved my life one day. At night we'd stay within earshot. You couldn't dig very far in some places because of the water table. Some places were lucky and we might be able to go down maybe a foot and a half and cut some branches of coconut trees so they couldn't lob a grenade at us.

One night we got a bunch of replacements from who knows where. A few guys were from New York, and they knew everything. Anyway, we dug in that night. I told them, Don't fire. If you hear something, wait until you're sure, because they're going to try to get you to fire so they know where you are from the blast. Use grenades, don't use your rifles. These guys were yakking all night long like they were on a NYC curb. I told them to shut up. They kept talking. So I picked up a piece of coral and zipped it over into the next foxhole. My God, everybody let loose with machine guns and everything. The next morning they said, "We saw Japs out there! They threw a grenade at us." They were quiet the next night. The guys on the perimeter would smoke, but they'd keep it down.

Many men serving behind the front also had perimeter duty because infiltrators and stragglers were common. In an emergency, everyone became an infantryman. Marine Bud DeVere served in Henderson Field's control tower. During the Japanese attack on Bloody Ridge in September 1942, Japanese infantry drove to within a few hundred yards of Henderson. DeVere helped the Marine air crews establish an unusual but potentially very lethal perimeter based upon Dauntless dive bombers. The Dauntless was a two-seat aircraft with a machine gun facing the rear:

There was a land push and they were afraid the front line was going to be breached near Henderson. They got information that there were going to be quite a few Japs coming down that way. Our squadron turned the tails of the planes toward the jungle. We had two men standing on each plane: one man standing in the cockpit with the twin .30-caliber machine guns facing the jungle and the other guy on the ground to feed him ammunition if he needed it. If they broke through the lines they were going to run into another line of .30-caliber machine guns. The hordes they always talked about would have had one more surprise before they had Henderson Field. Fortunately, the situation did not arise. But we spent a couple of long nights in the cockpits waiting for them.

Support troops in a combat zone did not have an easy life. Their world had little resemblance to rear areas far behind the front where thousands of soldiers and sailors lived a relatively comfortable life plagued more by boredom than danger. Men directly behind the lines more than earned their paltry salary. Disease struck them as readily as it did combat infantry. Frequently they did heavy and dangerous physical labor in a beastly climate. Yet everyone knew that infantry, frequently positioned a mile or less away from the "rear," confronted a much tougher and more violent war. Commanders rotated line units when possible to positions in or very near the rear to give the men a little rest. On Guadalcanal, for instance, there were always units defending the beaches against a Japanese landing that fortunately never came. It was much better duty than manning a foxhole on a ridgeline.

However, a unique agony existed for men within large perimeters. Men serving directly behind the perimeter line were more likely than their comrades in the forward foxholes to confront the chilling experience of heavy air attack. The reason for this was simple enough. Men on the front went to great lengths to conceal their position. The jungle itself provided extremely effective cover from aerial observation. Bomber crews on both sides might know the general location of infantry positions, but getting a good visual fix was extremely hard. Air attacks were major military operations and not undertaken lightly. Attacking a perimeter would very likely lead to holes in the jungle or a small loss to dug-in infantry. (At Buna, Allied bombers attacked the Japanese fortified zone continually, believing correctly that if they dropped enough ordnance, some of it would find a target.) In general, it was far better to attack airfields and supply depots, targets that were far more visible, vulnerable, and critical.

The Japanese Naval Air Force based in or near Rabaul had launched a furious air assault against Port Moresby early in 1942. The American landing at Guadalcanal forced the Japanese Navy to shift most of its air effort to the Solomons. In 1943 the Japanese Army belatedly sent a large air contingent to New Guinea. By that time Allied airpower was dominant and Japanese Army pilots spent most of their time defending their own positions. Consequently, Australian and American troops in New Guinea faced sporadic air attack but no sustained air offensives.

The Solomons were very different. During every American landing the Japanese Naval Air Force put in an appearance. Fortunately for the Americans, invasion forces always were protected by large numbers of fighters. Supporting warships bristled with antiaircraft weapons and were perhaps as effective as fighters for keeping bombers at bay. Damage done by Japanese air power to troops "hitting the beach" was consequently slight. (Ironically, the one exception was at Buna where, as previously related, the Japanese shredded the miserable flotilla of coastal vessels that passed for a fleet in those waters.) However, the Japanese airmen were relentless and under the strictest orders to halt or delay the American advance. Furthermore, once troops were ashore, warships left the area. American fighter cover remained, and inflicted dreadful losses on Japanese attackers. Some, however, always made it through.

A characteristic pattern developed first at Guadalcanal and later throughout the campaign in the Solomons. The Japanese would build up their air strength in and near Rabaul and attack American supply dumps and airfields relentlessly. After a time, American fighters, antiaircraft, and accidents weakened the Japanese attackers drastically and the offensive slowed significantly. Tokyo then rebuilt its forces at Rabaul, and renewed the fight as soon as the situation allowed. This ebb and flow continued until Allied bombers crushed Rabaul in late 1943 and early 1944.

The Japanese launched their most sustained air offensive against Guadalcanal. Other areas, like New Georgia and Bougainville, were assaulted by as many or more Japanese aircraft. But at Guadalcanal the defenses were crude and the Japanese pilots excellent. Later this equation reversed. The Japanese attacked the landing furiously and pounded the beachhead for weeks. When Henderson Field became operational in late August, it became the primary target. The Japanese bombed Henderson almost daily during the battle for Guadalcanal. During 1943 the Americans continued to build up their air bases on Guadalcanal; therefore, the Japanese continued to raid the Henderson complex long after the battle for the island was over. Marine Fred Heidt describes a visit by Japanese bombers:

The Japs did everything they could to make life miserable on Guadalcanal. They had some artillery in caves in the mountains

that we called Pistol Pete. They would give you a potshot and retreat. And then they had "Adolph the Sub" who surfaced some
nights and shelled us. Another night visitor was "Washing Machine Charlie." He came in very low, right over the trees, making
this loud noise and dropping a bomb or two to annoy us. You
could see the blue exhaust of his engine. Probably an old seaplane: just to annoy us. But the worst thing were these big flights
of medium bombers we called "Bettys." [The versatile Mitsu-
bishi G4M, called "Betty" by the Allies, was Japan's standard
bomber throughout the war.—EB] They'd usually come about
noon. You could just about set your watch by them. They came
in vee formations. There might be twenty to forty aircraft in a
flight. You could hear them throbbing off in the distance, so
you'd know they were coming. When they came over at about
20,000 feet, you could see the bombs drop very clearly. Everyone
said it looked like the bombs were headed right at you, and that
was the case. If the bombs appeared directly overhead, it meant
they were continuing to travel forward and were going to miss
you. Bombs on the way down made a loud whistling noise. When
they struck the earth the noise was very loud, and shrapnel flew
all over. Everyone who could, was in a shelter. Direct hits killed
and wounded many people. But they did less damage than you
would think when a raid took place. Nevertheless, it was very
frightening.

Marine Bud DeVere worked at Henderson and was at the receiving end of many attacks:

From the day we landed the Japanese had airplanes overhead.
Dive bombers, fighters strafing, Bettys, anything they could
throw at us. We didn't know what to do at first. Japanese bombers looked like a swarm of insects in the distance. It was hard to
determine what they were. But we learned fast that when airplanes approached it was time to take cover. When you realized
that the specks were bombers trying to kill you, you started looking for a hole and stopped looking at the bomber. When you
start hearing the bombs come down you have no interest in what
things look like at all. You just kept your head down. And I mean

down. There was a lot of shrapnel in the air, and any part of your body that was exposed might not be there when the planes left.

Robert Kennington's men received a low-level attack when they landed at Vella Lavella:

Just before we were ready to jump off the boats at Vella Lavella, Japanese fighter planes flying out of Bougainville hit us. We were supposed to get air cover, but it was twenty minutes late. We jumped into the water over our head, carrying our packs and rifles. The jungle was right at the beach so I get my squad under a tree as soon as possible. I laid my squad behind a little tree that seemed about ten inches in diameter. The Japs kept up the attack, dropping bombs and strafing. They came in so close you could shoot them with a slingshot. They flew in, one right after another. Strafing planes cut the limbs and leaves off trees all around us. We huddled down and could see the smoke coming from the guns mounted in the wings and the bombs drop on the beach. We were lucky that day, or maybe the Japs were losing their touch because casualties were light. But it scared the hell out of everybody.

Most men who fought in the Solomons witnessed many air battles large and small. As many men commented, cheering on American fighters almost took on the flavor of a spectator sport. Bud DeVeer's vantage point at the communications center at Henderson Field was unusually good:

I would listen to the Wildcat pilots talking over the radio. They were fascinating to watch. You'd see them fighting above you. And you'd hear what they were saying to each other on the radio. Someone would say something like "Hey Joe, there's one on your tail." And you'd look up and see some fighter on Foss's tail [Joe Foss was the leading American fighter ace at Henderson Field—EB]. They were often quite low during the dogfight and then you could see them very clearly. When they'd shoot one down you'd see the plane go down, go over the horizon, and explode. I remember seeing one Zero get its wing blown off. It spiraled down like one of these maple-leaf helicopter toys. I bet it took ten minutes to hit the ground, trailing smoke all the way. It was a fantastic sight.

As noted by DeVere, action could get very close. On a Guadalcanal ridgeline, Clifford Fox witnessed the sort of extraordinary sight possible only in war:

The Jap fighters would come down and strafe us. I was strafed several times, especially when we were on the ridgelines. They'd come in at treetop level or lower if there weren't any trees. If you looked up you could see the pilot's face. One day in November on Bloody Ridge some Zeros strafed us. It was a bad day for one of them. The Army flew P-39 Airacobras for low-altitude ground attack. They couldn't compete with the Zeros at high altitude. But at ground level, they could get the jump on a Zero. Anyway, this Jap came over and we ducked into our holes and started shooting our rifles at him. That was futile really, but made us feel good. Over the trees a P-39 came in. He caught the Jap plane with his cannon and the Zero disintegrated in the air. It floated right down into this ravine in the jungle in front of us. You could see the pilot and the engine of this Zero coming down together. They were the heaviest objects and going forward the fastest. The rest of the plane was sort of floating earthward, shot to smithereens. We were all cheering. But it didn't always go our way. A few times we saw our own planes coming back from dogfights. Sometimes they couldn't make it to Henderson and we would watch them crash into the jungle.

In early 1943 the Japanese launched some of the largest air attacks of the war against Henderson. One was in March, intended to strike units of the Americal Division that were leaving Guadalcanal on troopships. Artilleryman Bill McLaughlin was one of the men leaving. Lying on the deck of his troopship, he watched what was, by South Pacific standards, a massive air battle:

The sound of approaching bombers filled the air. The sky was turning black with them, coming on in a massive wave of planes. What a sight! From Henderson Field our own came up: Wildcats, Corsairs, and P-38 Lightnings, anything that could fight.

Upwind, downwind, and crosswind, it seemed, they clawed off the strip, fighting upward, circling to gain height. The P-38s, powerful interceptors that they were, simply put their tails down and went straight up after the enemy already dropping their bomb loads on the fleeing ships.

As they gained range, the American planes opened fire on the enemy. Soon planes were smoking down, great streams of black smoke coming from them as they dropped like stones to the bay. Some, miraculously, leveled off and, when the smoke stopped, they turned and zoomed back up to fight some more. It was impossible to tell friend from enemy, all were jumbled together. It was awesome. With all possible speed we exited Iron Bottom Bay forever and headed southwest for Fiji.

Any soldier who suffered through one loathed air attack. Yet for one evening on Guadalcanal, everyone near Henderson Field suffered what is possibly the most terrifying experience of war: naval bombardment. Infantry all detest artillery. Naval guns, however, are extremely large. On land the massive weight of artillery pieces and the difficulty in moving them restricts their size greatly. On sea these limitations are reduced. Furthermore, warships carry guns, not howitzers, that fire with great muzzle velocity and attain great range. A ship's magazine can carry large numbers of rounds, and sophisticated loading devices allow guns to fire quickly. Naval fire direction is accurate, and warships can hit a stationary target from a long distance. When American and Japanese destroyers attacked each other's shore positions, an unpleasant time was in store. On the night of October 13–14, 1942, Admiral Yamamoto dispatched two battleships, *Kongo* and *Haruna*, to Guadalcanal to obliterate Henderson and shield the largest landing of Japanese troops to date. What resulted was what most Marines, sailors, and soldiers who went through it called simply "the Bombardment."

The guns carried by battleships had few equivalents on land. A 155mm howitzer fired a ninety-eight-pound round. An eight-inch naval gun found on a heavy cruiser fired a round weighing 335 pounds. The high-explosive fourteen-inch shells carried by both *Kongo* and *Haruna* were five feet in length and weighed 1,400 pounds

each. (The U.S. sixteen-inch naval gun fired a projectile nearly twice
as heavy.) Fortunately for the Americans, the two Japanese battleships carried only 300 rounds of the high-explosive ammunition that
was ideal for a "soft target" like an airfield or infantry dugouts.
The remaining 600 shells fired were "armor piercing" and designed
for use against other warships. When they struck shore targets,
armor-piercing shells penetrated deeply before they exploded, made
tremendous concussions, left monstrous holes, and terrified men
near them, but spread few killing shell fragments through the air.
Kongo and *Haruna*, however, like all battleships, possessed numerous
smaller quick-firing secondary guns, similar to those carried by destroyers, that they also threw into the attack. Aided by flares dropped
by aircraft, and light-producing "star shells" fired by their own armaments, the battleships concentrated their fire on Henderson and the
surrounding supply-and-command facility. Considering the small
size of the area, it was one of the most intense bombardments of
the war.

Marine Clifford Fox was stationed near Henderson Field and
had a ringside seat at "the Bombardment":

The battleship shelling was the worst moment of the war. I was
there the night of October 13, and I remember it so well because
it was the most frightening time of my life. Two battleships and
several other warships came in about midnight and shelled us for
hours. The battlewagons were throwing huge fourteen-inch
shells. We all had dug little foxholes. Even though my name is
Fox, I didn't dig mine as deep as I should have. As luck would
have it, the Jap Navy showed up the night that the first contingent of the Americal Division arrived on Guadalcanal. The poor
guys had been bombed when they came ashore, and now this.
They linked each Army unit up with a corresponding Marine
unit. They were going to learn about the area from the units they
would relieve. We had a boy from Army intelligence.

About midnight a little floatplane dropped this green flare. It
looked like it came down right on top of me. I made a dive for my
little foxhole. There was no warning. I thought it was Washing
Machine Charlie dropping a bomb. We didn't know about war-

ships coming. My foxhole was just out in the open: like you were camping. Right on top of me came this boy from the Americal. And then came the shells from the sea. We were located less than a thousand yards from Henderson, so some of these shells drifted into our position, landing among us. God, the noise was incredible. Boom. Boom. They sounded like freight trains coming through the sky. The earth shook like it was going to open up and swallow us all. I thought it was the end of the world. I'm Protestant and I was praying. The guy on top of me is reciting all these Catholic prayers. By that time some people were going crazy, some of the older men especially. A sergeant in our unit cracked up. People were trying to get into anyplace where there was cover. One guy dove on top of us, but there was no room in our little foxhole. There was a dugout occupied by our cooks and some of our officers nearby. Several Army boys had sought shelter too. There was a direct hit on it and many were killed. When I got up at sunrise, it looked like some god had swept his giant hand and knocked these palm trees down, leaving jagged stumps in their place. The devastation was amazing. Our Air Force, what little we had left, was really knocked out. That was not the only naval shelling, but it was by far the worst. It's terrifying when you can't fight back. I dug that foxhole a lot deeper the next day.

Marine Fred Heidt was also near the center of the attack:

When the battleship shells went over, it sounded like an express train: a whooshing noise. The explosion from a *Kong* class battleship generated enormous heat. Everyone talks about the noise and concussion, but a nearby explosion causes a hot blast. The shells had these base plates on the bottom. These things exploded and there were big pieces of molten metal flying around everywhere. They stayed hot for a time, and anyone who touched one regretted it. One thing was amazing. The next morning we saw cattle and pigs wandering around the jungle. They were shell-shocked because of the shelling and the bombs. A lot of us were too.

Archer Vandegrift, the Marine commander on Guadalcanal, endured a near hit on his command post and was knocked to the ground. Near the center of the shelling, the normally reserved officer later commented on the experience:

> A man comes close to himself at such times . . . and until someone has experienced naval or artillery shelling or aerial bombardment, he cannot easily grasp a sensation compounded of frustration, helplessness, fear, and, in the case of close hits, shock.

Although the battleship attack did frightful damage, the American recovery was quick. Aircraft were up the next day and did serious damage to the Japanese transports landing supplies. Ironically, a much smaller bombardment on October 17 by the American destroyers *Lardner* and *Aaron Ward* probably did more serious damage when they smashed a major Japanese ammunition dump that was intended to support the large attack on the Marine perimeter the next week.

Americans and Japanese on Guadalcanal also had the unique opportunity to observe a series of violent surface battles that took place during the campaign. Because all of them involved either protecting or attacking transports, they took place very close to Guadalcanal. In all, fifty warships were sunk in the general area, most in the waters between Tulagi and Guadalcanal, the zone American sailors called Ironbottom Sound. All the engagements were at night and were impossible to monitor with any precision from shore. (The confusion implicit in these fierce battles also made them impossible to monitor from the respective flagships.) Yet hundreds onshore heard the rumble of naval guns and watched the flashes, the flares ignited to illuminate the battle, the red-hot shells flying through the air, and stricken ships burning. It was somber and frightening for those on shore because it was impossible to tell the outcome. All knew, however, that if the Japanese prevailed decisively, the American ground forces on Guadalcanal were doomed.

Marine pilot Jake Stub was on the island of Tulagi after being rescued from his downed Wildcat by friendly local inhabitants. On November 15, 1942, Stub had the extraordinary opportunity to watch events on the last night of the three-day naval Battle of

Guadalcanal. The highlight was one of the rarest events in modern naval warfare, a duel between two battleships:

> There was a hill on Tulagi where the Japanese had built an anti-aircraft position. We were using it now. The Japanese had left a pair of high-powered binoculars on a tripod, on top of a wooden tower. Several of us were up there, expecting another round in the naval battles that had been going on the past two nights. Nothing happened for hours and many guys left. But I was positive something would happen. About midnight guns started to fire. I would estimate I was twenty miles away, and I don't recall hearing the guns. But you could see much. Flare shells went up and illuminated portions of the area. You could see the shells clearly. They were red hot when they left the guns and looked like glowing tennis balls almost floating across the sky. The Japanese battleship *Kurishima* started burning, so I could see it very clearly. The U.S.S. *Washington* had shattered it and the Japanese were abandoning ship. You couldn't really tell what the men were doing, but I could see things so well, I could almost imagine it. Unfortunately I couldn't see the *Washington*, it was behind Savo Island.
>
> I did see a huge explosion. I thought a battleship or cruiser exploded. I later found out that it was the American destroyer *Walke* that blew up. At the time I thought everyone was dead, but remarkably there were many survivors. One of them later was my neighbor. I'm a Marine and I hate the Navy. But that night they fought very bravely.

Although terrifying or remarkable to the men directly involved, air and naval attacks on ground targets in 1942 were not very effective. The number of planes and ships was not high enough and the techniques were too crude. Most of the killing and dying was done by infantry.

This was certainly true in New Guinea. Australian units were as serious about perimeter security as they were about patrolling. The Australians had learned much about patrolling when fighting the South Seas Detachment on the Kokoda Trail. Likewise, the men of the AIF learned how vital perimeter security was, because the elite Japanese shock troops were expert at both outflanking Australian positions and penetrating their lines with lightning attack.

During the last days of August and the first two weeks of September 1942, the Japanese war machine put on an extraordinary performance. The South Seas Detachment, using a series of outflanking maneuvers and relentless attacks, shattered the 21st Brigade of the AIF 7th Division. During the last Japanese land victory in the Pacific war, they shoved the already battered 2/14th Battalion out of its place on the Australian line at Ioribaiwa. A large Japanese force moved at night adjacent to the seriously outnumbered Australians and blasted them with concentrated machine-gun and artillery fire. During this fighting one of the AIF platoons was split, and two men left behind in their foxholes. One of them was L. F. "Pappy" Ransome, who later recorded an extraordinary account of a very common occurrence in the South Pacific—being isolated behind Japanese lines:

Len Edwards and I were both behind a couple of rails when Len said, "This is a bad position, Pap." So we made a dash for a hole about three yards away and hopped in, much better there. We stayed for about an hour when Len went to check an adjoining hole fifteen paces off. He got just to the edge of the hole when he stopped a mortar round in the groin. He went over, half in, half out of the hole. Poor Blossom, as we used to call him, never knew what hit him. I did some serious thinking while I hugged the bottom of my hole, expecting a mortar round at any second. I decided to wait until light failed. It was ten in the morning, but anything I did was risky. I never shifted in the hole for an hour and a half when I heard a Jap voice. I peered over the top and, by Gawd, standing fair in the middle of the track was a Jap pointing at Blossom. He was jabbering at others I couldn't see. I thought for two seconds, but he was too good a target to miss. So up with the rifle. After killing him I expected all the hardware they had but nothing happened. By cripes, the stillness was getting on my nerves. I heard voices, chucked a couple of grenades. No idea what happened, but there were no more voices.

After several hours fire suddenly broke out between the Japs and our guys. I couldn't see anything, but just as I was settling back to the bottom of the hole, I saw bushes move on the next rise, and then saw a Jap's head. He seemed quite unconcerned so I slid the rifle over the top and waited. He broke the bush fair in front, and I got a good look before I fired. He gave a hell of a scream as he fell among the bushes. They opened up with machine-gun fire around Blossom's hole. I kept very quiet, thinking my chances of getting out were looking bleak. There was another lull and then more firing. I looked over the top again and noticed a green bush at the foot of a tree on the forward slope of the next rise. I thought, now that wasn't there before. I watched that bush for what seemed like a lifetime. Then it moved, and disappeared behind the tree. He had leafy branches stuck in his helmet and clothing. He started having a good look-see. I waited till he gave me the best target. He spun round and fell at the foot of the tree.

As it worked out, "Pappy" Ransome was only a few hundred yards from the Australian perimeter and managed to sneak to safety late in the afternoon. The battle Ransome was a part of was larger than most that took place on the Kokoda Trail. The Australian pursuit that began soon after quickly became strung out along the trail and the "squad war" moved front and center. The Australian advance up the Kokoda Trail was punctuated by numerous small Japanese night attacks on individual Australian perimeters. Bill Crooks's platoon was engaged in several:

What Americans called foxholes, we officially termed "fighting pits." The men called them "funkholes," a term they picked up from the Germans during World War I. Typical of the dry humor of the Aussie Digger, it was a play on having a funk or scare or "excuse me, I want to go away and have a little cry or a panic." Normally meant for two, they were home for one man as sections shrunk to five or six soldiers. They were four feet deep or so, and round with a tail like a tadpole so you could lay down to sleep.

We did *not* know Japs were near our positions until we tripped

over them. Sometimes a bloodthirsty hand-to-hand would ensue.
The long rifle was useless so close and the grenade too dangerous
for your own men. So most had a knife and sporadically you
would hear grunting, screaming, and groaning.

A Jap attack was always about the same. They'd spend eight or
ten hours to get a few feet forward. You strain to hear and to see.
But it is pitch-black and usually raining. In an instant, the Japs
would get up and go in screaming straight through. Then they'd
keep going and move to right or left. If there was an opportunity,
they'd shoot someone in a pit. They'd be gone in an instant.

Small night attacks and harassment were so common simply because the enemy perimeters were usually so close. Frequently Japanese soldiers got lost, or were in search of food to steal. They might
appear several miles from the nearest Japanese perimeter in the middle of an Allied support unit. After a major assault there were almost
always remnants of Japanese squads intermingled with Americans or
Australians the following day. All of this added a heavy dose of chaos
to the menacing atmosphere that accompanied operations in the
jungle.

So too did verbal taunting and threats shouted by Japanese soldiers at night. Most Allied infantryman heard them. Sometimes these
were unintelligible shrieks, other times threats of death. Often the
yells came from Japanese lurking only yards away from the foxhole.
This form of psychological warfare was premeditated and no doubt
effective in its way. It had several purposes. First, if Japanese infiltrators were trying to get through a line prior to an assault, it was tremendously helpful to know exactly where Allied infantry was dug in.
The best way to do this was to goad someone into firing and reveal-
ing his position, a classic mistake made by inexperienced troops. Like
all harassment tactics it kept men awake and on edge. Only the most
exhausted soldier would sleep knowing Japanese infiltrators might be
fifty feet off shrouded in blackness. Ben Love recalls the night psychological warfare that went on between the two sides at Sanananda:

It is a strain on the old nerves doing the hour "watch" through
the night. One in four we do. Every time a branch shakes or a

leaf falls everyone becomes tense: rifles and Owen-guns are grasped tightly as we crouch down in our holes—you cannot see, only listen—and wait. Then suddenly shots ring out—someone, somewhere in that blackness has started a little game of blind shooting practice. What they see to shoot at, goodness knows, but the Nips evidently think it worthwhile to scare us and keep us awake with this aimless shooting, shouting, and letting off flares over our perimeters. When the Jap goes to reset, our twenty-five-pounders and mortars commence plastering their positions—there seems to be no shortage of shells from the amount of stuff they send over. Yes—we certainly enjoy these nights of tropical splendor.

Japanese harassment tactics lost some of their effectiveness quickly. American and Australian infantry were quick to pick up the spirit of threat and insult. On occasion, shouting matches started between men dug in at very close proximity. Al Careaga was with the Marine Raiders on New Georgia and witnessed a good example of jungle wit:

We holed up for the night. We'd dug in and put up our outposts. And try to get some sleep in the rain and mud. If the Japs attacked at two or three in the morning all hell broke lose. The Japanese were pretty silent in their approach. They were the most fantastic jungle fighters you'd ever want to know. But there comes a time when they get close enough that you can actually hear them breathing. And there was heckling. One night, the Japs closed with us at about 2:00 A.M. Both sides shot away, but the firing died off. One of the Japs yelled "Fuck Roosevelt," and they laughed. One of our guys yelled "Fuck Tojo," and we laughed. One of them yelled "Fuck Eleanor." One of our guys yelled back, "No way, *you* fuck her." Both sides started laughing. I don't know if the Japs knew it, but Jimmy Roosevelt was a Marine Raider.

Robert Kennington relates another example that illustrates the commingling of hatred and black humor that was typical of the South Pacific.

The first guy that was killed in my outfit was on a recon patrol. The Japanese took his body into the Gifu Strong Point. I was on Hill 27 and looked down into it every day. The Japs ripped his body up, tied him to a tree, cut his penis off, and stuck it in his mouth. And dared us to come get him. So I did a little teasing myself. A night or two before, we had killed a Jap officer infiltrating our line. I went through the belongings of the guy we had killed. I took his Japanese flag, his money, his glasses, and his hat. During the morning I stood up in front of my foxhole, put on the Jap's hat and his glasses, and I'd wave the Japanese flag in front of our position. I'd holler, "Tojo eats shit." As soon as I'd say that, I'd hit the dirt and they'd start shooting. My buddy manned a machine gun and fired on the Japs shooting at me. I did that for three days until the lieutenant told me to knock it off.

Although I have already discussed the fierce impact of air attack, it is appropriate here to look at perhaps the most notable weapon used by the Japanese in the war of nerves that made night in the jungle so threatening: Washing Machine Charlie. "Charlie" was the nickname given by Marines on Guadalcanal to the solitary Japanese aircraft that came over their perimeter almost nightly dropping bombs. The Japanese allocated dozens of planes of several different types to this duty. Their engines were put slightly out of tune, so the aircraft made a much louder than normal sound. Although associated with Guadalcanal, the Japanese used Charlie throughout the Solomons and frequently in New Guinea. (Because air operations over Guadalcanal were so fierce, Japanese aircraft made few sorties during the Buna campaign, sparing the Allied infantry in that horrid place one plague.)

Because it was almost impossible to locate combat perimeters at night from the air, Charlie favored supply areas or large targets like airfields, which were plainly visible on a moonlit night. When pitch black, Charlie would drop flares, lighting the area with an eerie greenish glow. Louis Kidhardt, a platoon leader with the 25th Division, recalls Charlie:

You could always look forward to the night bombings from Washing Machine Charlie. Charlie would drop bombs or sake bottles. A sake bottle dropped from a high altitude would whistle coming down: it sounded like a bomb. You couldn't distinguish between bomb or bottle until daylight, when you would see broken sake bottles lying around. It was psychological warfare, trying to keep us from resting. But you couldn't ignore the raids. They used daisy cutters on their night bombings. [A daisy cutter is a bomb with a fuze that causes it to explode just above the ground, creating a large shower of fragments.—EB]. When you heard Charlie you had to get into a hole. You learned not to dive under a truck or something because once a daisy cutter hit the ground it didn't penetrate the ground. The fragments just flew over the surface a couple of feet, and they would cut you to pieces.

Infantryman Robert Ballantine also has fond recollections of Washing Machine Charlie:

You never know where Charlie would drop a bomb. We would get into our big bunkers. After a while we got used to it. You'd sit there and watch him. The searchlight beams from the antiaircraft units would catch the plane. He was not very high, and he would fly in and out of the beam. Of course, they couldn't hit him, but it was quite a sight. Sometimes you could hear the bomb-bay door kind of click open. You sure could hear the bombs coming down. If it makes a kind of swooshing, whirling noise, the bomb is by you and will miss. If it's hissing, it's going to be close, and you might have to change your underwear. Once a Betty bomber came down near our position on the line. We went over to the wreck and checked it out. The crew couldn't get out, I guess, and they were spread out all over. I've never seen so many vertebrae: they looked like hambones.

Normally, night air attacks were almost impossible to stop. Stanley Larsen, a battalion commander with the 25th Division, recalls a rare loss for Charlie:

The Japanese bombers would come over almost every night, even after the fighting was over. There was no way they could accurately find a target. They knew many of us were camped along the shore and on moonlit nights they could see the shoreline. Our searchlights went up after them and we could almost always locate the planes and it was fun watching the searchlights follow them across the shore. We couldn't see them drop the bombs but we could hear them when they came down and exploded. There was only one time when they hit our area. A bomb landed in the artillery headquarters and killed two or three men and wounded several others.

I don't recall our antiaircraft hitting a Japanese bomber when it came over. About May or June 1943 our first night fighters were assigned and they had radar on the planes. They didn't need searchlights because their radar could pick them up. We knew they were going to use these night fighters. One night we stood out there, heard the Japanese plane coming and we knew that our night fighter was going to go up and try to take one down. And sure enough, almost overhead, where we were standing out in the open, we could hear both our planes flying up there, but we couldn't see them. Suddenly we saw a whole splatter of bullets from our plane. Then you could see the Japanese plane suddenly explode on fire. One of the wings came off in flames and we watched it gently float down to earth. From then on Charlie's attacks were much more sporadic.

Rain and mud were enemies that conquered all the armies. Soldiers often tried to erect some kind of defense against the pelting rain that made a night in the foxhole both miserable and a serious health hazard. All sorts of solutions were tried. At best they kept the men out of the rain, but being genuinely dry was a rare luxury. (There were dry intervals in the Solomons and parts of New Guinea. The heat dried the surface soil rapidly. The result was choking dust until the rains came again. The wait was never long.) Trooper Ben Love describes a skirmish with the elements:

It rained cats and dogs last night. Smart little Trooper Love fixed a ground sheet as a roof before it started. I felt very pleased with myself as I lay in my trench, all nice and dry, whilst most of the others hastily prepared any makeshift shelter. But as our leaders tell us, our worst enemy is "complacency." Alas and alack, my ground sheet sagged in center after half an hour of heavy down-pour. Realized something had to be done and tried to tip water carefully over the bottom end of the trench, but tipped it all over my dry little self instead. I was mortified and wet.

As Love's comment illustrates, a combat perimeter was a necessity, and sometimes a place of temporary safety. It was not, however, for combat infantry in any way a home.

A War of Annihilation

The small-unit war of patrolling and watching the perimeter had a brutal pace. During a campaign there was no letup in the activity or the violence. The Japanese landed at Buna and started over the Owen Stanley Mountains in July 1942. Rabaul was bypassed in early 1944. In the time between, significant contact existed between Allied and Japanese ground forces every day. Although punctuated with a small number of massed Japanese assaults, the war in the South Pacific was a war of attrition. Day in and out soldiers were killed, maimed, or stricken with fearful disease.

Many characteristics of the war, such as the immense casualty rates, the poor replacement system, the hideous climate, and malignant terrain all worked to push the armies toward exhaustion. Yet the soldiers fought the land war in the Pacific with a savage and relentless intensity that had no parallel in World War II. Although it is possible to identify incidents of restraint and humanity on both sides, the essence of the conflict was something very close to a war of annihilation. On the surface this situation is difficult to explain. Unlike Hitler's barbaric war aims in the Russo-German war, neither side in the Pacific war overtly threatened the biological existence of the other. Although Japan's occupation policy was crass and frequently brutal, there was no precise parallel to the Holocaust in areas conquered by Imperial forces. Within Japan, and to a far lesser extent without, some people of importance, dupes no doubt, believed that Japanese occupation would lead to a new order in Asia under Tokyo's benign leadership. Furthermore, there was no heritage of conflict. Japan had fought neither the United States nor Australia in the past. During the period examined here, almost all the fighting was between military forces. Air raids on Pearl Harbor, Tokyo, and Darwin killed a handful of civilians, but there was nothing like the London blitz. Nor did the fighting inflict sustained misery on the indigenous population. In this regard, the conflict in the South Pacific resembled the campaign in North Africa's Western Desert between the Germans and Allies where army fought army, plane fought plane, and tank dueled with tank, a struggle Rommel called "war without hate." Unfortunately, the opposite situation existed. Instead of a "clean" war between armed forces, the jungle war was propelled forward by a deep and visceral loathing between the foes.

For fifty years former combatants, writers, and academics have tried to explain why this was so. In our day, when racial and ethnic issues loom so large in academia, deeply ingrained racist attitudes on both sides are emphasized to explain the astounding bitterness of the war. Although Japan receives a share of the blame, deeply ingrained Western racism, as manifested in the United States, is found the prime culprit. Scholars point to the wartime cavalcade of racist propaganda posters, films, cartoons, and articles in the press. The Japanese were systematically portrayed as animals, consequently, so goes the argument, extermination was a natural response to Japan's attack. Many now argue that wartime propaganda campaigns in the West were only one manifestation among many of an old pattern of racist behavior that created the slave trade, underlay colonial empires, and led to the incarceration of thousands of American citizens of Japanese descent in the United States during 1942. Add to this brew various academic discourses concerning the "other" that is inherent in nation-states. The argument is cogent at first glance. It is, however, almost entirely wrong.

No doubt a number of deep currents contributed to the dark and sinister side of combat in the jungle. World War II took place in the waning days of an overtly racist age. Claims of cultural or racial superiority in the West were used to justify imperialism. In the United States during the 1920s there was a brief renaissance for the Ku Klux

Klan and racial-exclusion laws directed at the Japanese. This spirit, when added to corruption and the fear brought forth by Pearl Harbor, led to shameful acts against Japanese-American civilians.

Nevertheless, major changes were taking place in attitudes in the West toward the outside world. Sensitive people could see that, just as slavery had crumbled in the nineteenth century, imperialism and the notions of Western cultural superiority that sustained it were waning in industrial democracies. In the United States, Gandhi was a hero. Pearl Buck was a best-selling author, and the Chinese were treated as a valiant people struggling against the Japanese onslaught. Every major university in the United States had departments dedicated to the study of Chinese and Japanese history and culture. Among the elites who could afford it, travel to Japan was popular. The rapid collapse of imperialism immediately after World War II shows how deep were the currents running against old attitudes concerning race and culture. So too did the burgeoning civil rights movement in the United States.

However, the most important factor to realize is that at the battlefront, the larger cultural currents that were remaking the world went largely unnoticed. Men in the armies sent to fight far from home lived an isolated existence. To the extent that eighteen-year-olds from a largely provincial world, in a self-possessed time of life, shared the attitudes of the larger culture, the soldiers did. Ironically, however, no group of Americans was more insulated from propaganda of any type. A Marine on Guadalcanal or an Aussie on the Kokoda Trail received no formal indoctrination from the military. A propaganda machine arose later in the war, but the soldiers of 1942 were short of food and ammunition. No one was forwarding the latest propaganda leaflets to the front. Yet the soldiers grew to hate with a frightening passion. The hatred of the ground soldier toward the Japanese was on a completely different level from that found among sailors on warships or airmen. It was a hatred born of hard experience, caused by reality seen firsthand and further fueled by rumor. Above all it was a hatred caused by the cult of death that marked the Japanese battle ethos. No doubt, like America's other Asian wars in Korea and Vietnam, the war between the Allies and Japanese would have been very harsh under any circumstances. Yet the American and Australian soldiers who faced the reality of combat against the Japanese did not descend willingly into the hellish world of a merciless war. They were pushed there by the Japanese.

Certainly the overall political object of the war received little scrutiny from American soldiers. The brightest of the young knew war was coming. America's military mobilization began, belatedly, well before Pearl Harbor. The Japanese attack on Pearl Harbor was so powerful in its effect that it eliminated, for the only tine in American military history, overt antiwar sentiment from the political landscape. It is certainly worth mentioning that a very large number of the men who were at Oahu that Sunday morning were fighting in or near Guadalcanal a year later. Many had lost friends and all were angry. Australians, in the dark days of summer 1942, were fighting close to their home. Whether or not they believed the Japanese threatened the existence of Australia, a powerful and fierce enemy that close to home was incentive enough to fight. In addition, a division of the AIF had gone into a brutal captivity after the fall of Singapore, adding a bitter personal element to the struggle.

Nevertheless, when talking with veterans of the combat infantry about warfare in the South Pacific one is struck by how rarely they mention issues such as patriotism, defending the nation, or Pearl Harbor. No one questioned the need for the war itself; its necessity at the time as in retrospect was self-evident to soldiers. The most common attitude held was that there was a job to be done, and the soldiers had to do it. It is testimony to the power of Pearl Harbor that few questioned why the job confronted them, or whether it had merit.

None of this explains the unique ferocity of combat in the jungle. The men that fought the Germans held the same political attitudes. Combat was fierce, casualties were heavy, and passions ran high. Yet a sense of restraint existed in Europe that was absent in the Pacific.

The difference between the theaters derived from the intense fear, coupled with a powerful lust for revenge, that poisoned the battlefield in the South Pacific. Both emotions, so closely linked, arose from a series of local events that were never part of the public's perception of the war at the time or since. Instead, they were the private property of the men at the front or those who have studied the campaigns closely. The incidents in question all created or reinforced a perception that the Japanese soldier was uniquely dangerous and uniquely cruel. Although it mattered little at the time, we can see now that many of the incidents of wanton cruelty on the part of the Japanese were the acts of individuals and not the policy of the Japanese Army. However, the most horrific episodes blurred the distinction between war, suicide, and oblivion. These events took place in large number and, rather than the work of a brutal element within the Imperial Army, went to the heart of the code of behavior expected from and largely followed by every Japanese soldier. Death was not only expected as a matter of duty, but was viewed as a rite of personal and national purification. A war is a very bad place to hold such beliefs.

As the Marines sailed toward Guadalcanal, they were already aware of the beheading of several Marines captured on Wake Island early in the war. (It did not help that some of the Japanese engineers working on the strip at Guadalcanal at the time of the invasion had previously been at Wake. Marines found pictures of dead Marines and personal effects obviously taken as souvenirs amid the huge quantity of material captured the first two days.) Rumors, later confirmed, about the death march on Bataan were also circulating widely. The lesson drawn was simple enough: If you surrender to the Japanese, they will kill or torture you. In addition, based on information about Japanese operations in Malaya and the Philippines, Marine officers told their men that cornered Japanese units would not surrender. This information was given great credence on the first day of fighting on Guadalcanal. Although the Marines landed on the main island without opposition, a nasty fight took place on the small nearby atoll of Tulagi. A small Japanese garrison fought to the last man.

It is important to understand how surrender is handled on the battlefield. The concept of surrender was accepted by every army in the world. Even Imperial forces took prisoners. This reflected tacit recognition that when violence was separated from military purpose it became either murder or suicide. It also stemmed from powerful self-interest. If a soldier knows the enemy will take prisoners, he is far more likely to give up. If he believes he will die regardless, he fights on. Most armies wish to end battles as quickly as possible with minimum losses and welcome surrender. They realize, however, that there is a reciprocal relationship. If one side takes prisoners, so must the other.

In practice, surrender entails great danger on the battlefield. Surrender is much safer if it is done by several people at once, and with some type of prearrangement. It is also very helpful if the enemy is distributing leaflets encouraging men to give up their arms. Once fighting starts, the situation changes drastically. If a machine-gun crew starts a fight, inflicts casualties on the other side, and then decides they wish to surrender, they are facing likely death. If they are powerful enough, the enemy might accept surrender out of simple self-preservation. If not, the code of battle allows men to take retribution. If one side has committed an atrocity, the chances for safe surrender by its soldiers also decline greatly. For instance, during the battle of the Bulge, the Waffen SS murdered several dozen American prisoners. In the weeks that followed, GIs killed hundreds, perhaps thousands, of Germans in retribution. Consequently, surrender should be viewed as a pact. It is done to avoid mutual violence, and breaks down in the midst of bloodshed. This is true in all wars. Killing the helpless was not unique to the Pacific.

What was unique to the Pacific war was the general refusal of Japanese soldiers to surrender when any other army would have considered capitulation the only rational and ethical choice. American soldiers learned this lesson quickly. Two crucial incidents took place early in the Guadalcanal campaign that became part of the informal indoctrination received by every soldier who served on the island.

The first was the tragic Goettge patrol. In the first few days of operations on Guadalcanal, there was very little fighting. Japanese engineers had fled to the bush across the Matanikau River. A few were captured, as were some Korean laborers. One of the prisoners during interrogation suggested that others in his unit might want to surrender. Patrol craft had already spotted what appeared to be a white flag up the beach. Other reports indicated that dozens of Korean laborers were wandering helpless in the area. The 1st Marine Division's intelligence chief, Lieutenant Colonel Frank Goettge, trained to seek information from prisoners and eager to save Korean lives, convinced Vandegrift to authorize a patrol to seek out potential prisoners. Despite many qualms, Vandegrift agreed. Goettge personally led the twenty-five-man patrol, which included a battalion surgeon and the division's interpreter. Incredibly, the interpreter had worked on code-breaking in the United States before requesting a combat posting. Had he been captured and tortured, the Japanese could have pulled off one of the great intelligence coups of the war. As it was, he joined the dead.

The patrol took a landing craft a few miles up the beach and put ashore. Immediately a firefight broke out, killing Goettge. In the next few hours the American patrol was whittled down. Three survivors made it into the surf and swam off. The last one left at dawn and later claimed that as he was swimming off "the Japanese had closed in on those who were left and were hacking them to pieces. I could see their swords glinting in the sun." Vandegrift ordered a large patrol to cross the Matanikau, clean out Japanese positions, and find any survivors of the patrol. Crossing the river several days later, the Marines ran into enough resistance to deter a lengthy stay. On the beach, they found the half-buried bodies of the Goettge patrol. (Because the Marines were not able to recover the bodies, later accounts have stated that the patrol was never found. That is incorrect. One of the survivors of the Goettge patrol was with a later one and identified the position and several corpses.)

Coming on top of Pearl Harbor and Wake Island, one can imagine how the news of the Goettge patrol was received by the Marines on Guadalcanal. The real possibility exists that Goettge's men died because of military incompetence and not perfidy. At the time, however, every man on the island was hearing the lurid details of calamity. Marine Clifford Fox recalls the impact of the Goettge patrol:

I knew a kid in division intelligence. He went on a patrol with Lieutenant Colonel Goettge. Goettge organized it because supposedly there were some Japanese that wanted to surrender up near the Matanikau River. It was August 12. The kid I knew was killed along with almost all of them. A Jap prisoner had told Goettge that the other Japs were ill and wanted to come in. And our people walked right into a big old trap. That settled it: we couldn't trust any Japanese. They were treacherous. They were a cruel race actually. Bataan and Nanking and all of the other things they did showed it. I believed that at the time anyway. There are a lot of things I admire about them, but some of the old feelings remain.

Soldiers at the front have plenty of time for talk, and war and rumor are a natural combination. No doubt the story grew in luridness with the telling. However, to the men involved the truth was obvious. Goettge had gone on a mission of mercy, had been betrayed by the Japanese, and had paid for the mistake with his life. In addition, during the small contacts along the Matanikau, the Marines had already been introduced to the widely practiced Japanese tactic of verbal taunting and harassment. Included was an often-repeated ruse with a Japanese soldier, pretending to be a wounded American, calling out for help in English. The land war in the South Pacific was less than a week old, and the Japanese had developed a reputation among the men fighting them for treachery and cruelty.

In retrospect the Goettge patrol was an ambiguous situation although it was not perceived that way by the Marines. Not so the aftermath of the Tenaru River battle. As already recounted, the Japanese attacked the eastern flank of the Marine perimeter on August 21. Crushed by Marine defenses and a counterattack, 800 Japanese infantry perished. The death throes of the Ichiki detachment took place in daylight and hundreds of Marines watched events unfold. Many wounded Japanese took hand grenades, armed them, and held them to their heads. This type of behavior was incomprehensible to a Marine. But far worse, several of the wounded tried to kill Marines who were attempting to take prisoners. Infantryman Andy Poliny was involved in the closing stage of the battle:

As we approached a pile of Jap bodies, up jumped three Japs. Two of them were in good shape, but the third was wounded. They were carrying him as though they wanted to surrender. But just as they got near us, our sergeant jumped out in front of them and yelled "Cut 'em down, cut 'em down!" He saw something we didn't. As soon as he yelled the two unwounded Japs reached in their shirts for grenades, but they never got to use them.

After two weeks of battle on Guadalcanal, every rumor heard in Marine boot camp about the Japanese was confirmed. The very young and very unworldly soldiers believed they were fighting a fanatical enemy who would do anything to kill, and if thwarted, looked upon death as a duty and honor. The image held by these men were very close to the truth. Furthermore, the Goettge patrol and the aftermath of the Tenaru were just the beginning. Throughout Guadalcanal and every campaign that followed, the Japanese displayed a desperate bravery that was almost incomprehensible to Americans and Australians. Their attitude toward death made every encounter with the Japanese at whatever level fraught with danger. Allied infantry were afraid of the Japanese. Yet it was not a fear that drove men from the battlefield, it was a fear that drove them to kill.

Marine Donald Fall recalls the frame of mind that developed on Guadalcanal at a very early date. Note the clear element of revenge at work:

On the second day on Guadalcanal we captured a big Jap bivouac with all kinds of beer and supplies. Thank goodness for that because we needed the food to make it through those first two weeks or so. But they also found a lot of pictures of Marines that had been cut up and mutilated on Wake Island. The next thing you know there are Marines walking around with Jap ears stuck on their belts with safety pins. They issued an order reminding Marines that mutilation was a court-martial offense. On New Britain a lot of guys who captured Japs tried to pry their mouths open and take the gold teeth out. They did that with dead ones too. You get in a nasty frame of mind in combat. You see what's been done to you. You'd find a dead Marine that the Japs had booby-trapped. We found dead Japs that were booby-trapped.

And they mutilated the dead. We began to get down to their level.

Admiral Halsey captured the mood of his men. In the type of gesture that made him the American leader most respected by soldiers and sailors, he ordered the construction of famous billboards first on Tulagi and later throughout the Solomons. The message was simple enough: "Admiral Halsey says: Kill japs, kill japs, kill more japs. You will help kill the yellow bastards if *you* do your job *well.*"

In this atmosphere it was natural to dehumanize the Japanese. American veterans often use the term "animals" when answering how they viewed the Japanese during the war. They also recognized that the process was a two-way street. Ore Marion describes the harsh impact of battle on the young men involved:

> We learned about savagery from the Japanese. Those bastards had years of on-the-job training on how to be a savage on the Asian mainland. But those sixteen-to-nineteen-year-old kids we had on the Canal were fast learners. Example: On the Matanikau River bank after a day and night of vicious hand-to-hand attacks, a number of Japs and our guys were killed and wounded. At daybreak, a couple of our kids, bearded, dirty, skinny from hunger, slightly wounded by bayonets, clothes worn and torn, wack off three Jap heads and jam them on poles facing the "Jap side" of the river. All of a sudden you look up and those goddamn heads are there.
>
> Shortly after, the regimental commander comes on the scene. He can't believe the scene in that piece of jungle. Dead Japs and Americans on top of each other. Wounded all around, crying and begging. The colonel sees the Jap heads on the poles and says, "Jesus, men, what are you doing? You're acting like animals." A dirty, stinking young kid says, "That's right, Colonel, we are animals. We live like animals, we eat and are treated like animals— what the fuck do you expect?"

Some Americans viewed the vicious state of affairs with a sad detachment. Bewilderment at Japanese tactics was a reaction that accompanied or sometimes substituted for hatred. Almost all Allied infantry had a grudging respect for Japanese bravery and their prodigious skills at night fighting. Yet the result, whether an individual was blinded by hatred or not, was the same: kill the Japanese. Louis Maravelas was a squad leader with the 1st Marine Division and expresses well the sadness and confusion of men who found that the reality of combat in the jungle matched what their training and logic told them to expect:

> I have thought about the Japanese for fifty years. I had a high regard for Japanese soldiers. They were brave, tenacious, sly, and very good at pulling off the unexpected. But in another way, I feel that many of things they did were simply stupid. They sacrificed their own men needlessly, for no purpose at all. During a battle along the Matanikau three or four were straggling toward us as though they were going to surrender. There must have been a dozen of us with a bead on them. Sure enough, one bent over and there was a carbine or submachine gun slung on his back that his comrade tried to grab. We shot them down instantly. Later we were out on a large operation. There were maybe a hundred of us. Suddenly, one Japanese officer comes charging out of the jungle screaming and waving his sword. We riddled him. What did he accomplish? He was only one man, what could he hope to accomplish? They did this type of thing so many times. It got to the point where we took no prisoners. It wasn't a written order, but a way to survive. No one should take a chance to take a guy prisoner who might try to kill him.
>
> I don't know how you can defend this attitude. I feel the military in Japan fooled their people. Somehow they convinced their soldiers that their lives belonged to someone else. So the Japanese was tough and smart but at the end he was finished and had to blow himself up.

Bill Crooks of the AIF echoes Maravelas:

> I don't know that we were indoctrinated with a hate for the Jap. We knew what they had done in Nanking. We knew they had machine-gunned our nurses on Banka Island. We knew they had bayoneted AIF prisoners after they captured Rabaul. We

knew they had bayoneted hospital inmates in their advance down the Malayan Peninsula. But we did not develop a hatred. We just would kill every bastard soul of them the moment we came against them. We knew their bushido banzai code was to take no prisoners in battle and never surrender. So we killed them.

We will never know how deeply Japanese infantry believed in the cult of purity through death. The battlefield experiences of 1942 that greatly influenced the behavior and attitude of Allied soldiers for the remainder of the war were shaped to an unknown degree by unique circumstances. The Japanese troops who fought the Allies in both New Guinea and Guadalcanal were either elite units or riding the crest of a series of astounding victories. The ersatz samurai ethic was very strong in either case. It is possible that the idea of becoming a "guardian spirit of the nation" was more comforting in the flush of victory and in a time when the men believed that the war would end favorably. War weariness, in other words, had not yet set in. When Australian forces engaged two standard infantry divisions in the Ramu Valley in 1943, Allied intelligence picked up signs of declining discipline and falling morale. The pounding from the elements, coupled with the growing realization that the glorious future promised by Tokyo was not going to take place, was taking its toll. There comes a time when military forces begin to doubt the possibility of victory. When that time arrives, it is as though someone turns an hourglass upside down; inexorably, the will to continue drains away. This process started in the German Army in 1944 and culminated in the disintegration of a very large force in early 1945. It is no coincidence that sizable numbers of prisoners appeared for the first time during the Pacific war at the end of the Okinawa campaign.

Interesting testimony on this issue comes from former Marine Frank Chadwick, who, by chance, met up with an old enemy forty years after the war:

In 1988 I returned to New Georgia and made friends with a Japanese fellow living there, operating a seashell-export business. Beautiful shells are all over there, and I remember our men collecting them. He was a Japanese citizen but had lived in the

States. His father came out for a visit and we met him. The old man had been on Guadalcanal. He told us: "You chased me out of Guadalcanal, you chased me out of here, and then you chased me out of Bougainville." And he described their conditions. "You were sick and hungry and had one meal a day. But we would smell your food or see you eating. Sometimes we ate grass." He was bitter toward the fools running the Japanese Army. They would land troops with ammunition. But they only had three days' food supply each. The supporting stuff wasn't there. Medicine ran out. Our Marines had to put up with malaria, jungle rot, and dengue. The Japanese, he told us, faced the same thing, but their medics couldn't do anything to treat problems. It had to be horrible. He was on a 57mm gun crew. I saw those things in New Georgia. He said they had to break that thing down and haul it for miles through the jungle to fight the Marines on the Canal. He also said when they landed they were gung ho, but they got their ass beat. And then they had no food, medicine, or ammunition and had to walk fifty miles through the jungle to get back to the beach. When you got back there, there was nothing to eat anyway. He was evacuated to Munda. The old man told us, "We were given some good food. Then an officer gave us a big speech about our great victories to come. I thought to myself, the son of a bitch is crazy. Most of my crew were killed on Munda by American artillery. It was asinine."

A tragedy took place in the South Pacific that stemmed largely from the grotesque manipulation of the Japanese people by the military government. By successfully convincing their soldiers to find meaning in oblivion, and to accept the frightening idea that spiritual purification comes through purposeful death, the Japanese government created the mental framework for total war. If Japanese soldiers would not surrender, American and Australian troops very simply would not take prisoners. This in turn started a vicious circle. Japanese propaganda picked up the theme of Allied "butchers" and used it to convince soldiers and civilians alike that defeat in the war meant dishonor, humiliation, and death besides. Although impossible to prove, it is very likely that some Japanese soldiers would have surrendered later in the war had they not believed Allied soldiers would kill them. Also, it is very likely that more Japanese soldiers would have surrendered had Allied soldiers given them the chance.

I do not suggest that overall Japanese conduct of the war in the South Pacific was suicidal. Japanese commanders had far less regard for the lives and well-being of their soldiers than did their Australian or American counterparts. The same, however, could be said about Soviet or German officers. That said, their military plans were purposeful and plausible, and when failure loomed the Japanese took great risks to evacuate garrisons. If the situation demanded, divisional commanders could order retreats and cease failed attacks. The desperate actions at locations such as Buna or New Georgia, in Japanese eyes, served the legitimate military purpose of delaying the Allied advance. The Japanese garrison on New Georgia was successfully evacuated, and plans existed for a retreat from Buna that were poorly implemented.

The Japanese cult of death was most prominent when resistance began to fade and the Allies were nearing certain victory. Many campaigns in the South Pacific ended with an apocalyptic collapse. Thousands of Japanese soldiers were sick, starving, wounded, or had failed in an attempt to evacuate. If these nearly helpless men had fought for a civilized government, they would have surrendered with honor. Considering the fact that during this phase of battle American and Australian soldiers cautiously did take prisoners, it is reasonable to assume that they would have accepted far more had the opportunity arisen and the surrender been arranged. Japanese deaths, consequently, served no legitimate purpose. The delay that the final stage of resistance caused was minimal and the damage inflicted by starving Imperial soldiers was grossly out of proportion with the cost of Japanese lives. Had the Japanese just killed themselves, one could wonder at the powerful cultural indoctrination in the hands of a criminal government. Yet they also killed Allied infantrymen for no purpose, and stepped close to the ill-defined zone that separates combat from murder.

In late January 1943 American soldiers and Marines were advancing cautiously toward Cape Esperance on Guadalcanal, the last

Japanese base on the island. At this stage of the campaign, unknown to the Americans, the Japanese were preparing a daring plan to evacuate their ground forces from the island. Some fresh units were assigned rear-guard actions and fighting was sharp along the river lines near the coast. The Japanese achieved their military objective and coolly saved over 10,000 men in early February in the face of furious American air attack.

However, at the same time, the island was littered with small groups of Japanese soldiers who because of sickness and near starvation could not move. Some were simply abandoned. Americans took a small number prisoner. GIs and Marines simply shot many others. It was very common at this time for American patrols to stumble upon these broken men. Marshall Chaney of the 25th Division describes a series of events that was all too typical:

We were maybe 700 yards south of the coastline, traveling west. When we entered the woods we found this row of dugouts with ruined radio sets. Later as we got deeper in the jungle we were following a well-worn path. Most of us were on it. I spied a Jap under a lean-to near the base of the slope, next to a riverbank. He was asleep or pretending to be. Maybe he was ill. He had both hands folded together stuck under his head. His ammo belt was hanging from the pole that was propping up the lean-to. I opened fire and shot him. He was screaming almost like a baby. We spread out, and our sergeant said, "The Jap's still kicking." He fired a couple of shots and that quieted the Jap.

There was a lot of new and serviceable Japanese equipment around. Officers' boots, nicely polished. You could almost smell the enemy: they were close. I saw another one right below a banyan tree. He was crouched, with his head and shoulders between his legs. He was maybe three or four feet in front of me. I shot him twice in the left side of his head near his ear. The bullets were maybe two inches apart. He just went back against the tree. As we started the advance again, one of our men whirled and started to shoot. I couldn't see exactly what he was shooting at. I just surmised he was shooting at the Jap that I'd just shot. I started to say, "Don't shoot that damn Jap again, I've already

killed him." When I turned I saw a half-raised shelter top with
someone sitting almost upright. He gradually was lying down.
Then I realized our guy saw the concealed shelter top raise up,
and had shot into it before the Jap could kill me or one of the
others. While this was happening, the Marine unit to our right
were taking several casualties from pockets of the Japanese who
were fighting on. All of this just delayed us. But they could have
surrendered like the Germans.

Scott Wilson's unit of the 25th Division, also moving west, was
more fortunate and encountered little combat. However, as Wilson points out, the end at Guadalcanal was wretched throughout
the area:

When we are pushing the Japanese off Guadalcanal we would go
up into the hills and through valleys. There were Japanese dead
all over. I remember taking a Pall Mall, breaking it in half, and
sticking it in my nose so the smell didn't gag me. A friend of mine
who couldn't smell was the only person who was not gagging. A
few companies had some serious contacts, but on Guadalcanal
for us it was mostly just mercy killings going up the coast. Killing
the stragglers, the ones who were too sick to be evacuated.

Paul Sponaugle of the 37th Division was present during the
"mopping up" at Munda Point:

There were pillboxes all over the airport built out of rock. When
we crossed it, one Jap came out holding a hand grenade. He
stood there for an instant, armed it, and dropped it at his feet.
Then we had to clean out the holes that contained sick and
wounded. I saw a hole that looked like a good place to sleep. Inside were two live Japs with a hand grenade. Again they refused
to come out. One of our men lobbed a grenade inside. One from
another hole finally surrendered. He spoke English and said he
was from Yokohama. Some went out in the water and tried to
drown themselves. I helped bury eight of the suicides in one
bomb crater. That included one of the Japs who tried to drown
himself: one of our boys had helped him out.

The largest number of these miserable episodes took place in the final days of the battles in and near Buna. Dick Randles went through Buna village immediately after it fell in January 1943:

The battlefield was horrible. All the palm trees had holes in them or were lying on their side. There were shell holes and bomb craters everywhere. The Japanese bunkers were exposed. At the end the Japanese fell apart. There were dead Japanese all over. Wounded Japanese would throw grenades or lie on them to commit suicide. I saw one, very weak, tapping his grenade to arm it so he could blow himself up. He kept tapping it, trying to activate the fuse. He was so weak. Finally he got it going and blew his guts out. That's the way they were. They didn't want to surrender, at least the diehards wouldn't. We took a few prisoners. We put them in jeeps and sent them back to headquarters.

The "endgame" at Gona was equally foul. In the last hours, two AIF battalions, greatly weakened by losses themselves, pushed the last Japanese at Gona into a thin corridor leading to the beach. Australians killed over 100 Japanese who tried to break through their lines. Gona adjoined the sea. On many occasions when collapse was under way on coastal areas, Japanese soldiers fled into the surf, where they either killed themselves, drowned, or were shot by the Allies. The Australian official history describes the fate of Gona's last defenders:

An atmosphere that was strangely macabre even for that ghastly place seemed to well over the battlefield in the darkness that night, stemming from the despairing efforts of the Japanese to escape. A group, trying to steal along the seashore, was mown down by machine-gun fire from men of the 2/27th. Survivors, taking to the water and swimming for the open sea, illuminated themselves in ghostly light as the tropical phosphorescent water boiled up around them and guided the merciless Australian fire. Into one of the 2/27th's company headquarters a Japanese officer burst with flailing sword and fell upon an Australian soldier there, so that, to other Australians close by, there came the sudden sounds of two men fighting for their lives in the black night, of sword blows, shots, panting breaths, and screams.

After the last Japanese had perished, an Australian battalion diarist observed the remains of the Gona garrison:

The afternoon was spent in burying, salvaging, and cleaning up the area. Gona village and beach were in a shambles with dead Japs and Australians everywhere. Apparently the enemy had made no attempt to bury the dead, some of whom had obviously been lying out for days. The stench was terrific. The Japs had put up a very stubborn resistance. They still had plenty of ammunition, medical stores, and rice, although a large quantity of rice was green with mold. In one dugout rice had been stacked on enemy dead. More Japs had died lying on the rice and ammunition had been stacked on them again. 638 Japs were buried in the area.

Six weeks later, men of the U.S. 41st Division fought two of the final skirmishes of the Papuan campaign. One was at "Hospital Lot" near Giruwa, the main Japanese headquarters for the Sanananda front. In the waning hours of a bitter six-month fight, an American company came across a clearing in the jungle that contained several huts, including a military hospital. Taking fire that wounded two men, the Americans attacked the clearing. Sergeant Joe Murphy later recounted events to the 41s⁺ Division's historian:

Company G opened up on the shacks with all possible firepower. A hut collapsed under a stream of bullets. We flanked the shacks and picked off riflemen. From the nearby cemetery the Japanese light mortar fired only three or four times before we killed it. Meanwhile, grenades began exploding among the huts as able-bodied defenders and hospital invalids blew themselves up—or tried to blow up G Company. Some Japs fought in the open, some fought from foxholes and trunks of large trees. Others ran and were cut down. And in the huts our tense riflemen found live Japs under blankets and dead Japs under blankets. And G Company had no chance to check each corpse with a stethoscope— not when a pale hand might reach out to blast a grenade in your face. So G fired first and pulled blankets off corpses later. Some Nips were dead or dying of wounds, malaria, dysentery, and blackwater fever. Some patients held live grenades under blankets and tried to blast us or blow themselves up. I saw one Nip rifleman with an amputated leg—prone and firing from the floor of a hut. We found newly dead grenadiers hiding under blankets beside skeletons.

Twenty patients were killed, not counting the patrol defending the area. Another sixty-seven men in other huts, too weak to protest, went into captivity. The next day the battle for Sanananda came to an end when a battalion of the 41st Division attacked the final Japanese perimeter on the Sanananda Track. This position was strong and had held for weeks. The defenders had killed or wounded hundreds of Americans and Australians trying to destroy the fortifications. Interestingly enough, before the attack a lone Japanese soldier sneaked through American lines, surrendered, and identified a Japanese strong point that the GIs could not see, greatly aiding the American attack.

Probably no incident of the war in the South Pacific better illustrates the cumulative effect of fatigue, malnutrition, and confusion. Although attacked by a force no larger than those beaten off before, the Japanese perimeter, which at this time was deep inside Allied lines, simply fell apart. Allied artillery and mortars pounded the position in the morning. American infantry without the aid of tanks penetrated the perimeter quickly. Perhaps dazed by the bombardment or simply exhausted, Japanese infantry wandered in the open as American soldiers shot them down. In the words of one soldier, "We caught most of the Japs still underground or trying to extricate themselves from shattered bunkers. The garrison panicked and ran up Sanananda Road across our line of fire. We had great killing." At the end of the day the Americans counted 520 dead, the worst loss suffered by the Japanese during the coastal fighting, and one of the bloodiest days endured by the Japanese Army during World War II. American losses were negligible. The same American unit added another 100 Japanese infantry to the butcher bill the next morning when a Japanese relief force, which had wandered lost for several days in the swamp and jungle, finally found the perimeter only to find before they died that it was now held by American soldiers.

The same Japanese infantry that had held off the AIF and the U.S. 32d Division for weeks perished in two hours. What makes this incident so particularly wretched is that a large, well-garrisoned perimeter was exactly the type of position that could have arranged an orderly and relatively safe surrender. Fighting in a hopeless position, well beyond the time when resistance had any meaning, almost as many Japanese soldiers perished in that single spot in a few hours as the 32d Division lost killed in the entire Buna campaign. Instead of honor, the Japanese chose death. In doing so they taught yet another division firsthand that Japanese soldiers would not surrender and added fire to the lethal momentum already building.

If the circumstances were right, military honor and basic humanity on the part of many American and Australian infantry prevented the war from descending into the realm of simple slaughter. It should be emphasized that the Allies took small numbers of Japanese prisoners in all their campaigns. As already mentioned, the 25th Division, and later all divisions, had Japanese-American interpreters in their intelligence sections. Americans distributed leaflets and tried loudspeaker appeals. More of this was done as the war progressed. None caused mass capitulation, but there were always small numbers of men who chose life. One American battalion commander on religious grounds refused an order from a regimental commander to kill several prisoners. Dozens of incidents took place where individuals willingly took risks to take prisoners. Scott Wilson describes capturing a Japanese prisoner during the closing days of the Guadalcanal campaign:

> I was involved in bringing in a couple of prisoners. One Japanese soldier was stuck on this ledge across a river. I was one of four guys that swam over there with a litter. We could see he didn't have a rifle or pistol but we were afraid he had a grenade. They would arm a grenade, put it to their belly and pull the pin, and we feared he would take us with him. The poor guy was in poor physical shape, but he didn't want to come with us. We stuck him onto the litter. The four of us swam him back because it was

a pretty swift stream. The Nisei were part of divisional HQ and they came in and interrogated him. You always hear about the true samurai who would never surrender. We had a lieutenant, a sergeant, and a corporal surrender to us. The officer still had his sword and he could speak some English. He was half-starved, but a handsome man. He kept saying, "American food very good very good." We fed him some C rations. We thought, you're the first one who said that today.

Chuck Ables of the 3d Marine Division expresses a reaction that was very common among Americans when confronting prisoners:

Any rare prisoners were brought back to headquarters. We had the interpreters. We didn't have many prisoners. But there was an odd thing about them. The Japanese captured were usually in such poor physical shape that they looked amazingly harmless. They were tiny. Most of them looked five feet tall and weighed about ninety pounds. It seemed like they shouldn't have been as tough as they were.

As Bill Crooks makes clear, although Australians were as quick to shoot the Japanese as were Americans, many in the AIF took a very dim view of simple murder:

We did not kill sick prisoners. They were as well looked after as our own men. But you had to be careful to guard them. If one of our men had lost a relative or a man's mate had just died horribly in a firefight, then they might take revenge on the prisoners. I can remember only one occasion where we killed men trying to surrender. The battle of Oivi turned into a slaughterhouse affair. Our movement was too swift (we were learning, you see) for the Japanese to escape. Many Japanese tried to cross the Kumusi River. A few succeeded, but most drowned or committed suicide. But some medical corps Japs were captured. They had put up their hands, the only time I ever heard of that happening. And one of our officers shot all of them in cold blood. He was proud of it and boasted of it. He had been decorated, but was quite mad really. His explanation: We would have to supply guards and food for them back to Moresby! Well, this disturbed a lot of men. They no longer trusted him and the padres never spoke to him. Neither did many men, and that included postwar reunions. Headquarters did send an enquiring party to question witnesses but no one would come forward. They were frankly scared of him, and this included the officers. A couple of years later before we invaded Borneo, he stabbed somebody in the officers' club. He was cashiered along with two other officers. Strangely, all three were prewar regular soldiers.

There was also an odd netherworld that developed after campaigns that fit no standard mold in war. Many Japanese units either took to the jungle or were abandoned. Consequently, Japanese infiltrators became a fixture around Allied camps long after a campaign finished. They often came and tried to steal supplies. Rarely did they try to kill Allied soldiers. Sometimes they gave themselves up. Confrontations between them and American patrols took place periodically. Sometimes the Americans killed the hapless Japanese. Other occasions turned out better. Jim Litke of the 41st Division was in the Salamaua campaign on New Guinea in the summer of 1943. New Guinea became the home for hundreds, perhaps thousands of Japanese stragglers. As Allied intelligence knew, many of the average Japanese soldiers in this area were growing sour on the war. Litke recalls a scene that took place in some form many times:

After we took Salamaua, a lot of Japanese took to the bush. There were stragglers around the area until the end of the war. On one patrol we came across a tent. That wasn't unusual, there was a lot of Japanese equipment strewn around. We opened it carefully, and there was this Japanese soldier sitting there with a dazed look in his big brown eyes. Our lieutenant struggled to get his pistol out of his holster. It was comic really, he just couldn't do it. We all had our weapons on the Japanese anyway. He finally drew his pistol. But how could you shoot someone looking at you like that? We just took him away. Not long afterward, we saw this Japanese soldier walking up a trail we used regularly. I remember, his uniform was clean. He was unarmed, though. No one tried to chase him down. We just watched him wander off.

No doubt Litke and the men who watched the Japanese soldier walk down the trail were growing tired of violence. Judging from Litke's further account, there were young men on the other side who felt the same way:

During the siege one of our soldiers on patrol disappeared. That was not unusual in dense terrain. Unfortunately, the Japanese killed this man. We found his grave a few days later. The Japanese had buried him under a crude wooden cross. We removed the body of course. His rings were on his fingers, his dogtags were still there, and we found a letter in his pockets. The Japanese had obviously treated his body with great respect. This was not the action of fanatical killers.

Despite acts of humanity and restraint, the South Pacific was a savage place for the men who fought there. Yet acceptance of the war's necessity and a deep hatred of the enemy were not enough to keep the armies in the field for campaign after campaign. To understand how the momentum of war carried many men from small toeholds in the South Pacific to the gates of Tokyo, we must examine the physical and psychological factors that sustained the armies. It is time to look at the complex subject of morale.

Chapter 5

Day by Day: Morale in
the South Pacific

A ll armies face a difficult problem. Most people do not like risking death, killing people they do not know, or taking orders. In the distant past, the warrior ethos was so powerful that a man's skill at arms helped define his value in society. War was also one of the very few ways to obtain wealth and fame. Those were powerful incentives, and it is no wonder that some type of military aristocracy has run much of the world for several millennia.

In the modern era much changed. Although wars increased in violence, they decreased greatly in number. Ancient codes of conduct that accepted war as inevitable and an acceptable way to show courage and gain things of value gave way. In their place arose the idea that war was an unfortunate necessity. The men who led and served in armies embraced the idea that their sacrifices served the transcendent purpose of defending the homeland and the values held dear by their people.

Yet it was not enough to instill the belief in soldiers that they served so others could live in security. In an increasingly sophisticated and wealthy world, nations found they needed professional soldiers to run mass national armies. Officers and men had to be clothed, fed, and, in the case of career soldiers, arrangements made for their family lives.

Discipline also complicated matters. In the past, combat infantry lived a life regulated by draconian discipline. When Frederick the Great commented that he wanted his men more afraid of their officers than of their enemies, he was describing a state of affairs that had existed since antiquity. Modern weaponry helped change the equation because it caused dispersal on the battlefield. This led to more responsibility put in the hands of men of lower rank. In modern mass armies recruited out of a single population base, the background of young lieutenants, young sergeants, and young enlisted men was often very similar. It was not enough for junior officers and NCOs to simply give orders; they ideally had to lead. At a minimum they had to share the risks faced by enlisted men. In war there is also a strong tendency for a certain informality to show up on the battlefield. In the South Pacific, enlisted men and their immediate superiors were often on a first-name or nickname basis. In addition, the Allied armies could not call upon the sort of ironclad discipline that their enemies, or their Soviet ally, could.

In short, it was crucial to create armies where men would fight more or less willingly. To build an army like this, the officers did what they could to increase the group identification of the men. At the same time, they took great pains to make the day-by-day life of their soldiers tolerable. Neither task was easy. Powerful forces were constantly at work eroding morale and eating at the will to fight. Fear, exhaustion, and war weariness undermined patriotism and comradeship. Eventually, those forces would have brought all the armies to their knees. Fortunately for the Allies, the war was won before a crisis was reached.

Comrades and Leaders

The American military during World War II was the first fighting organization to employ social scientists in large numbers to aid the war effort. Hundreds of psychologists, psychiatrists, and sociologists wrote hundreds of studies dealing with group behavior, morale, and psychological well-being. They particularly wanted to understand how soldiers coped with fear and stress. One finding showed up over and over: a soldier did not fight for "God and country" but rather because the small group of peers he was a part of expected him to do so. Soldiers deeply wanted to gain the respect of their comrades, and knew well that they risked the scorn of the others if they did not do

their part in battle. Young men, to use the vernacular of the time, did
not want to be thought of as "chickenshit." This attitude, which all
armies tried to build up, went beyond the strong desire for peer approval that is so powerful among the young. It was also a very rational view well suited to most situations on the battlefield. In the squad
war, if everyone did his part, the group had a decent chance of making it through the mission with little or no harm. If one man, however, was seriously derelict, he could put the whole unit at risk.

Group cohesion played a critical role in building both morale
and fighting effectiveness at certain junctures during the land war in
the South Pacific. Before units entered battle for the first time, or after a prolonged period of rebuilding in preparation for a new campaign, the men lived and trained together for months. In some cases,
men stayed together for three or four years. During this time the soldiers came to know one another and, to the degree that such a thing
was possible, learned what was expected of them. If the human
chemistry was right, and it usually was, battle initially pushed the
group together. Young men, in addition, often formed deep personal
friendships. The group cohesion that resulted was extremely intense,
but fragile. Marine Frank Chadwick describes the dynamic very well:

Our unit was together for a long time. Everybody was on a first-
name basis. You ate the same, lived the same, shared the same
risks. We lived with the officers. They ate what we ate, they slept
in the holes right beside us. There was no saluting, no calling
anyone sir. No rank. Even the colonel. We called our colonel
Sweet William or Wild Bill depending upon what kind of day he
was having. Our major was named Walter Wells: we called him
Waldo. Waldo was a heavyweight wrestler at Columbia and later
taught hand-to-hand combat. If there was some trouble he'd
come over and see you. He came over to see me one night. I
weighed about 130 at the time, and he was big. He suggested we
go outside and I said no way. He picked me up by the shirt, the
buttons ripped off, and said, "You screw up again, you son of a
bitch, and I'll break your skull." I said, "Don't worry, Waldo, I'm
on the straight and narrow." Everybody liked him. One day he
came down smiling and said, "Hey, I made major." We told him

we didn't know he was a captain. We were well trained. We could do just about anything. It was a good outfit and a very close-knit family. It was a special group, in a special time. Of course, I wouldn't want to go through it again.

Bill Crooks of the AIF describes the importance of unit cohesion in combat:

After having been at war and gone through all the ranks, and studying for nearly sixty years, I have come to the conclusion that man is losing his personal aggressiveness. Sneak attack, yes. But about 50 percent or less of the men will have the will to fight close-up, man-to-man, slashing and hacking. In the AIF the section leader, the lance corporal, and the Bren LMG man were the backbone of the section. Like in all armies, the rifleman, knowing the drawbacks of a rifle in the jungle at close quarters, simply lay flat in the tadpole part of his funkhole and hoped to Christ. They will lag behind, feign being hurt, or simply disappear back to the rear aid post. In the jungle it was worse because of the frightening, strange surroundings where every bush or tree may have a Jap. But that same man, when the eyes of his mates are on him, will let out his bloodcurdling yell to boost his morale (that's why we taught it to them) and will fight like one demented. For a certain type of soldier, however, if his leader is shot down or disappears . . . he is off like a rabbit and one will find him back at the rear area bullshitting about being dazed by a mortar or grenade. He might even bruise himself to not suffer the shame of blame. So the leaders kept things going. Fortunately our leadership was always top. If it wasn't, out!

Bear in mind that Crooks described one of history's best armies. The tension between duty on one hand and fear and exhaustion on the other existed at all times. Because this was true, all good armies allowed for the expulsion of soldiers not steady enough or bright enough to shoulder the burden for an extended period. All too often, accounts of war describe combat infantry as cannon fodder or the dregs of the military. It is true that armies find some use for people with very limited abilities. However, the front line was no place for fools. A near moron might be digging a latrine a few miles back, but on the spearpoint, the men were very able. E. J. Randall of the AIF makes the point:

> All men are afraid. Self-preservation is a very strong instinct. Good training and good mateship help to overcome fear. When it was obvious that someone was not coping too well, his active patrolling role would be substituted for manual tasks around the trenches. Support from mates and a good rest usually got the shaky ones back on their feet. When it was obvious that a man would not perform in battle the platoon leader would direct this soldier to base work. You know, "one bad apple . . ."

Fred Johnson served as a medic in a battalion aid station at Buna. He witnessed firsthand how an American fighting unit handled men unwilling to go on:

> Evacuation was very difficult at Buna. Things got better when the air base at Dobodura got in operation, but it was still reserved for seriously wounded. Malaria patients lay in cots until they could return to their units. Between illness and battle the division was shrinking fast. They were raiding every support unit for replacements. Anyway, three guys came back, threw down weapons, and said they were sick and couldn't fight. We checked them out, and couldn't detect anything obvious. They said they had dysentery and all sorts of things. Well, a hell of an argument ensued. No matter what the doctor said, the men refused to go back. So finally the doctor gave up. In his diagnosis that the men carried to the rear he wrote "scared shitless." Off they went.

In the early stage of the war in the jungle, cruel necessity added great importance to mutual reliance. The replacement "pipeline" was rudimentary or nonexistent. As combat units dwindled in size, they either pulled together or broke. In addition, there was no proper "rear" in jungle warfare. Men behind the lines faced far less risk than those in the foxholes, but if one wished to bolt, there was simply nowhere to go. On Guadalcanal the situation was unusually stark, simply because the men there had very well founded fears that the Japanese would win and they would perish. Marine Donald Moss puts it well:

> Sure we thought we might lose. The 1st Marine Division, we thought, was expendable. Everybody said that it was easier to draft men than to build new ships, so it was very unsettling that we saw so few supply ships in the early months. The Japanese ships and planes, however, seemed everywhere. We would give it all we had and that was it. There really wasn't anyplace to go, was there?

William Schumacher of the 25th Division was also on Guadalcanal. By the time the 25th had arrived, fears of Japanese victory had ebbed, but the isolation was still very real:

> The morale was very good on Guadalcanal. The guys had trained together and were close. Think about it, though. There wasn't anything you could do except fight. It would have been too much to try to evacuate anybody, or try to sneak back. You were stuck with your buddies. You did what the rest of them did: you worked together. There wasn't much choice.

Dick Randles, who led a squad at Buna, describes a similar situation:

> Morale was pretty good at Buna considering the awful situation. All of us were afraid that the Japanese might come in and land in strength south of our position and cut off the division. We had no idea how much Guadalcanal had weakened them. The Army told you nothing. I was an NCO. I had no trouble with the boys. The company commander was kind of one of the boys. A fireman from Eau Claire was our platoon leader. All the officers and NCOs were right there. You sure couldn't be very far away.

As Randles indicates, officers were never very far away. It is difficult to overemphasize the importance of good leadership in combat. Often leadership and comradeship meld. If a small unit had been together for a time, wartime intimacy broke down the barriers that existed during peace between enlisted men on one hand and NCOs and junior officers on the other. The Marine Corps was famous for this and took pride in the fact. The Army largely followed suit at the front. Louis Kidhardt was a lieutenant and platoon leader with the 25th Division on Guadalcanal and describes relationships that developed:

> Junior officers had a very hard job. You had to carry out missions assigned from higher command, but you also had to protect your men. And you knew your men as individuals. You were one of them. No one called me "lieutenant" on Guadalcanal. And I never wore my insignia. It was underneath my collar because the Japs had a tendency to snap off an officer. If someone said "Hey lieutenant," your life was in jeopardy. So I was "Hey Lou." It made it difficult when you went from combat into a rest area. You're one of the Joes during combat, but an officer who demanded respect in a rest area. The superior officers wanted it that way. I think the men did too.

William Shumacher, also with the 25th Division, led a platoon and later a company. He echoes Kidhardt:

> We didn't deal much with high commanders. We were under Navy command. We did get some news about Navy victories and that was fine. MacArthur was in the Southwest Pacific, so he didn't exist for us. But at my level practically all my dealings were with my regiment. Our local and small-unit leadership was excellent. They had to be, they realized it and they did a good job. But our battalion and regimental commanders and staff were young West Pointers and Reservists or from OCS who could work together. We were the same age, all had pretty much the same educational background, we had been together for years and they would do everything to make things a lot easier in spite of some occasional foolishness from the top.

Robert Kennington looked at the situation from an enlisted man's point of view, and has similar recollections:

> Most of the officers and enlisted men got along very well: 90 to 95 percent. My regimental commander and his officers were good people. They didn't pull rank on you. Discipline was very

different in combat than it had been at Schofield Barracks before Pearl Harbor. For a start, in combat, you don't call officers by their rank. Snipers are looking for them. They don't wear their bars or insignias. Also most of the young officers who came in were smart enough to get help from the veteran soldiers.

Senior officers played a different role. At the time, most ground troops did not have deep feelings about their top commanders. In general, Admiral Halsey, who commanded American forces in the Solomons, was popular but extremely distant. MacArthur, as one might expect, stirred up more heated reactions. Many men in the 32d Division disliked him because he had removed many of their officers and said some foolish things about the division. (This type of thing drove the excellent corps commander Robert Eichelberger to distraction.) Those men, however, who got the "MacArthur treatment" firsthand often left in awe. As time went on, many of his troops grew to appreciate deeply his ability, in sharp contrast to the bloodbaths in the Central Pacific, to manage large battles with little cost. Nevertheless, at the time it was a rare soldier who grew attached to a commander the way that sailors did toward some of their great admirals.

Battalion and regimental commanders were in a unique position. During World War II, most battalion and regimental commanders established headquarters quite close to the front. Difficult communications and lack of mobility necessitated it. Consequently, they were in close contact with line soldiers. However, they were older and usually career officers. There was not the level of informality that was found at the platoon level. Yet soldiers respected bravery and demanded competence. If a field-grade officer showed these, it helped the morale greatly. Louis Maravelas of the 1st Marine Division led a squad in the battalion commanded by "Chesty" Puller, the most famous Marine combat leader of the war. Maravelas recalls the importance of Puller's leadership:

When I was called up from the Marine reserves before the war the "China Marines" were special, everyone's hero. Puller was a China Marine. But he had a reputation for being off his rocker.

I think we all thought he was crazy at first. But after a while, we realized he was a genius. His philosophy was to never sit still, go out and give the enemy hell. And he was willing to do it himself. I recall that during the first engagement my squad had on Guadalcanal. There is a terrible feeling being under enemy fire the first time. You think to yourself, "Why is this guy trying to kill me?" Well, the fire wasn't withering, but it was coming in steady. And there was Chesty walking up and down the line in everyone's view. He'd come up and say, "What you aiming at, son? Let's go get the son of a bitch." That really raised our morale.

Marshall Chaney's regimental commander compiled a distinguished record on Guadalcanal. Chaney relates an episode that shows steady leadership at its best:

We were pinned down, under heavy Japanese fire. Our own Brownings were in the rear supporting us and we had been advancing under their arc of fire. So our machine-gun bullets were going one way and the Japanese bullets going the other. But Lieutenant Colonel Hayes was walking upright with his arms spread out and palms down motioning to everyone to get down and take cover. He walked across our positions saying, "Men, take cover, you're going to get hit." It had been raining and then the sun had burst out shining. We could see the mist coming up from the sea. You could see tracer bullets crisscrossing over our heads. And there was Hayes walking about looking after us. It was amazing he didn't get hit. Later I saw him get wounded saving a half-track from destruction. He was a splendid officer.

The same close comradeship that derived from shared experience and shared risk also caused a very intense rivalry among the services. If one's unit was special, after all, it followed that another one was not, particularly if the uniform was different. The emotions ranged from a rivalry reminiscent of athletic competitions to a very real dislike. Ill feeling among the services had nothing to do with the extraordinary infighting that took place among them at the highest level. Typical of the South Pacific, things were more personal. The Marines, frankly, were in the middle of this. They were trained to believe they were special and they believed it. Ian Page, a New Zealand bomber pilot flying from Henderson, was a neutral observer to spats among the servicemen:

> I liked the Marines. They were very generous. In New Zealand their reputation was not always the best. They had a reputation of being obsessed with sex and brawling. The Marines were notably different from the Army. They hated the Army. One fellow's brother was in the Army relief force and he wouldn't go meet him. The Marines were volunteers, they looked at the Army as low-level soldiers because they were draftees. The Army looked at us in the air corps as self-indulgent blighters living on the fat of the land. It was a little immature, of course, but they were all so young. I was twenty-eight and felt like an old man over there.

As Page indicates, the classic rivalry was between Army and Marines. The Marines looked at soldiers as being an inferior breed, and also blamed the Army for any or all supply and equipment deficiencies the Marines suffered. The last point was very misguided, of course. The Navy had much to learn about supplying a large land force, and the Army did the job better. The Marines were supplied by the Navy, so logically the complaints should have gone in that direction. But logic did not always count for much in these matters. The Army resented the Marine publicity machine. For some reason it was true that the press liked the Marines. Soldiers outnumbered Marines in the South Pacific by a wide margin and consequently did far more fighting. Nevertheless, the epic struggle at Guadalcanal, and later Marine operations in the Central Pacific, overshadowed everything the Army did in the theater. Soldiers fighting at Buna were almost forgotten by the media because of Guadalcanal. Ernest Gerber expresses the feelings of many of the soldiers on New Guinea:

> I was never enthusiastic with comparisons between the Marines and the Army. The Marines had a public-relations operation that was outstanding. Everyone knew when all the Marines got out of bed. The 32d Division got very little of that. I ran into some poor Marine units in the Pacific, and some excellent ones. The

same was true with the Army. No matter what they say, being a Marine did not make them two steps ahead of everyone else.

Other soldiers believed, with some reason, that Army operations were more sophisticated and less showy. As Louis Kidhardt of the 25th Division put it, "The Marines were terrific near the beach. Get them 100 yards inland, and they were lost." Many Army officers quietly criticized Vandegrift on Guadalcanal (wrongly, in my opinion) for staying behind his small perimeter. The Navy was not forgotten. Both soldiers and Marines envied Navy rations and creature comforts. Just because the Marines were administratively a part of the Navy did not mean there was any excess of affection between the two. The opposite was often the case. Many Marines on Guadalcanal felt they had been abandoned by the Navy in the first days of the campaign, which was a simplification of a complex situation. Furthermore, there were old grudges. Veteran Marine Ore Marion expresses feelings toward the Navy that were not his alone:

Each time we went aboard ships (I counted fifty-four large ones in my career) we were always made to feel like unwelcome relatives. Usually we were treated like crap—fed crap. I couldn't believe it: time after time. "We have met the enemy, and he is us." It was always a pleasure getting ashore, even under fire.

In Australia, men who joined the AIF and those who enrolled in the Militia frequently expressed contempt for each other that had ugly political overtones. Occasionally sentiments like these spilled over into interservice nose breaking in bars across the Pacific. Although stories concerning the precise coalition involved vary, the epic "Battle of Queen Street" in Auckland, New Zealand, in mid-1943 pitted Marines against men from the U.S. Army, the U.S. Navy, and the New Zealand Army. (Rumor has it that the "Battle of Capetown" between returning AIF troops and South African servicemen in early 1942 was more spirited.) Smaller skirmishes were common affairs.

Comradeship and good leadership constituted the heart of good combat morale and sustained the will to fight. Yet the combination was fragile and susceptible to breakdown from a number of directions. An obvious threat to unit morale and effectiveness was bad combat leadership. If an incompetent officer was wise enough to recognize his limitations, little damage might be done because the men underneath him would run things. Real trouble, however, occurred when a fool tried to exert authority. In every good army, men find ways to defend themselves from military incompetence. Almost as bad as incompetence was favoritism or personal vendetta on the part of an officer or NCO toward an individual. Although very rare, bad officers and NCOs could die because of this type of thing. Marine Fred Balester watched an inadequate officer unknowingly flirt with oblivion on Guadalcanal:

> I was passing a line company when I heard the company commander berating a Marine for walking along the top of the ridge. Because of sniper fire it was against regulations. I knew this captain was a Reserve officer, and stopped to watch. The Marine on the skyline did not immediately come down as ordered. The captain proclaimed that he had one minute or the captain would shoot him on the spot for refusing a direct order. He looked at his watch and placed his right hand on his sidearm, a showy, chrome-plated, ivory-handled, Smith and Wesson revolver. A few yards behind, a Marine was cleaning his rifle and seemed to be paying no attention. He replaced the bolt, loaded the magazine, and put a round in the chamber. Then he cradled the rifle in his arms and gazed off into the distance. I noticed that the piece just happened to be pointed right at the captain's back. The Marine on the ridge ambled down, the captain took his hand off his revolver, the rifleman took the bolt out of his rifle, and I continued on my way.

Paul Sponaugle led squads of the 37th Division on New Georgia and Bougainville and puts things more bluntly than Balester:

> One captain on the front didn't like something I was doing and threatened to court-martial me. I told him if he brought up the subject again, I'd shoot him. He didn't bother me anymore. The front was no place for petty discipline. Some of the leaders didn't

quite get the idea. A few were shot, no question. I saw it almost happen twice. It was nearly insane to come across hardened infantry and give them some petty harassing order. Good soldiers, the ones who made it through all the rotten things, were tough and used to killing. If a leader they didn't respect gave them a foolish order just to show them who was in charge, he was taking his life in his hands. Some people should not lead others in battle, it's that simple.

Fortunately for the Allies, most officers and NCOs were brave and competent. As the level of combat experience grew and material resources increased, leadership of most small units undoubtedly grew better as the war progressed. The extraordinary spirit found in elite U.S. and Australian units in late 1942 may never again have been duplicated in the Pacific war. But there is no question that standard American line units, built from conscripts and reserves, grew better with time. The same was true of units from the National Guard and the Australian Militia.

The armies could do their best to supply good leadership to their combat units. However, they could not avoid a massive turnover of men in the line units. Including men struck by serious diseases, there were extraordinary casualty rates in combat divisions. Casualties can never be reconstructed with absolute precision, but the pattern is clear enough. During the period the 1st Marine Division served on Guadalcanal, August 1942–December 1942, 774 were killed and 1,962 wounded. Another 8,500 received treatment for disease. Just before departure, Marine Corps medical officers estimated that in one of the regiments fully one-third of its remaining strength was unfit for further combat. If one factors in the time spent on the island, the casualties for the other Marine and Army units were very similar to those suffered by the 1st Division. Papua was worse. Approximately 20,000 Australian soldiers served in the campaign from July 1942 to January 1943. In that period 2,165 men were killed, 3,500 wounded, and 15,575 received treatment for disease. Approximately 14,500 Americans, mostly from the 32d Division, served in the Buna phase of the same campaign (November 1942–January 1943). They added another 930 killed, 1,918 wounded, and 8,700 disease victims to the list. Japanese casualties, because of their un-willingness or inability to withdraw endangered forces and poor medical care, were horrifying. Counting naval and air personnel, 30,000 Japanese were killed at Guadalcanal. Imperial forces lost ap-proximately 13,000 killed in Papua. A civilized policy of surrender might have saved half of these men. The 5-to-1 "kill ratio" in favor of the Allies later grew even larger as the American war machine pro-vided both U.S. and Australian forces with more firepower.

The numbers bear a little more scrutiny. In military terms, a 30 percent casualty rate in a combat unit is considered very serious. Af-ter that point is reached, a downward spiral in fighting spirit often begins. If a rate surpasses 50 percent, the unit is flirting with disas-ter. In the twin campaigns during 1942 on Guadalcanal and Papua, many of the wounded and diseased patients returned to their units. Many of the casualties were "double counts," men who were both wounded and stricken with disease. (No doubt many were "tri-ple counts" or more.) On the other hand, fewer than half of the men involved were on the spearpoint with combat infantry. The casualty rates among fighting infantry frequently went to 70 percent. For ex-ample, the reported strength of the 126th Infantry Regiment of the 32d Division at the start of the Buna campaign was 3,171. At the end in January it was 611. Large numbers of replacements never arrived in Papua and only began to appear on Guadalcanal late in the day. Every Allied combat unit, in other words, was shattered.

This led to an unusual pace of war in the South Pacific. Long pe-riods of training and rebuilding were interspersed with relatively short but intensely violent campaigns. The sequence rarely varied. An Allied division went into battle and stayed there until the cam-paign was won. Invariably battered, its units were withdrawn to a se-cure area in the rear and rebuilt. After several months, the division was ready to go again. However, when it started its next campaign, the faces were not the same. The dead were buried. The most seri-ously wounded went back to the United States or Australia to stay. Many victims of disease entered prolonged treatment in hospitals and ultimately were reassigned to other units. In addition, the mili-tary promoted men who showed a cool head under fire and sent oth-

ers to officer training schools. Upon reassignment they usually
moved on to other units. As rear service units grew in size, many men
wangled reassignment there. In Australia, Canberra assigned many
AIF veterans to duty with Militia units to prepare them for overseas
service. The armies involved filled the ranks with the thousands of
replacements that came into the theater with every convoy. As one
can imagine, an infantryman starting a third campaign in the same
unit he started with was very rare.

Frank Marks was one of the exceptions, serving with the famous
35th Regiment of the 25th Division from before Pearl Harbor until
war's end. He describes the process of turnover and renewal:

> On Guadalcanal our losses were great, mostly to malaria and
> dysentery. Most of those who were wounded or came down with
> disease never returned to our company. Near the end of the cam-
> paign we started to get replacements from a replacement depot
> on New Caledonia. We had a complete replacement of our offi-
> cers. Many were promoted and assigned to other units. [An un-
> usual number of 25th Division officers rose to prominence with
> other units. Professional officers with combat experience were
> always at a premium in World War II, and the 25th Division, be-
> ing Regular Army, had the most in the Pacific.—EB] A few of
> our enlisted personnel were promoted and sent to other compa-
> nies. Some replaced the men we had lost. Some of the men pro-
> moted from the ranks should have been left there. They were
> promoted because of their personality rather than their ability to
> lead. Two of our sergeants, both older than most men's fathers,
> should not have been there in the first place and were sent home.
>
> After the New Georgia campaign and some R&R in New
> Zealand, we went to New Caledonia. One of the first changes
> was sending home everyone over thirty-nine years old. We lost
> 20 percent of our company due to this order. Then they sent
> home almost everyone who was in the company prior to the out-
> break of the war. All the while, we got in more and more replace-
> ments. Finally in October 1944 they started the rotation plan,
> sending home men based upon "points" awarded for length of
> service, time in combat, wounds, children at home, and other
> things.

Marks's account points out something very important. The much-studied group identification was very important but extremely ephemeral. No doubt the men who came into Marks's unit formed their own bonds. But they too would see those who were close die or leave. The men who did stay in place, or continued to serve in other units, no doubt formed new friendships and bonds of a sort. But it was rarely the same as it had been for those unique men in 1942 who went to war with friends and comrades, going together on a journey into a violent unknown. Walter Johnson of the 43d Division talks about the change that all combat units underwent with time:

> My best friend was another underage kid. He was killed on New Georgia. After that I didn't get very close to people. There were so many replacements over time. After you're in and have been through combat, it's harder to make new friends for some reason. Guess you don't want them to die and hurt you. I think a lot of guys felt that way. The funny thing is that now because of the reunions over the years I have more friends from the division than I did during the war. We're dying off now too. At least it's natural this way. It's bad for the young to go.

Adam DiGenaro of the 3d Marine Division expresses similar sentiments:

> We weren't that close on the squad level. You're pretty much on your own. People come and go very frequently. The ones that survive have an independence, and initiative. It's nice to have a close friend, but a dependence is there. It can weaken you. If people are close and one gets killed, that's real trouble. I've seen it happen. Some men lose their judgment. A friend dies, his buddy is distraught, does something he shouldn't, and gets killed. In combat you get caught up in doing what you have to do: fighting the enemy. If you want to live, that's your main concentration.

The internal strength of a combat unit is also under constant assault from fear and exhaustion. Ultimately, as all wise commanders know, fear and exhaustion will always win out. That is why it is so essential to relieve line units before their cohesion cracks. The 1st Marine Division on Guadalcanal fought with extraordinary skill and bravery. Yet, as squad leader Louis Maravelas recalls, the Marines were wearing down when they were relieved in December 1942:

> We were so tired and so haggard after months of poor food, poor nutrition, and exhaustion. You couldn't really sleep at night. Everyone was sick. Combat, the aftermath of combat, and the anticipation of combat all wear you down. I was so on edge that I was kind of jumpy for a while after the war. By the time we left Guadalcanal, I think my mind had gone over to the clouds somewhere. You lose some touch with reality, fortunately not for very long.

Clifford Fox, another Marine on Guadalcanal, expresses a similar thought:

> The sights of combat have no equivalent in normal life. That's why some of the memories stay with people who have seen combat. You dread the thought. People were very fatigued. The humidity, the heat, and the torrential rains just wore you down. One time I was up on that ridge in the middle of an artillery duel, in November I think. We were lying in the foxholes. We were soaked and lying in water. All these shells were going over, first one way, then the other. And I went to sleep. But you'd wake up and you didn't really sleep. There's no doubt that by the time we left Guadalcanal we were just dragged out and beat tired. We'd lost a lot of weight. I came over at 160 pounds and left at about 130. That's not normal for a young man. We all got rock happy or island happy: the famous stare. Guys' moods would change from day to day. You never knew when some guy, because of the stress on the island, would just explode in anger about something little. I know I had difficult days when I wasn't as rational about certain things as I should have been.

James Salafia's platoon on New Georgia, like many in that intense battle, almost ceased to exist:

> Before we landed on New Georgia we were on Guadalcanal and the Russell Islands. A lot of the combat veterans told us how

tough the Japanese were, how bad it was going to be. It might have made us more fearful than we should have been. On New Georgia, a lot of my buddies got sick with dysentery and malaria. A lot were killed and wounded. When we went in, I had a platoon of forty-some guys. I was a platoon sergeant. We lost our lieutenant right away and never got another one, so I led the platoon throughout. By the end, I was one of seven. We were ready to quit at any time. We were defeated. But just at that time things broke and the Japs fled. We survived, and that was something on New Georgia.

Dealing with fear and stress was largely an individual matter. Although reactions to combat itself varied greatly, most soldiers had a particular loathing for threats they had to face passively such as mortar attack or snipers. If they were able to fight back, adrenaline provided a powerful but temporary defense. On Guadalcanal and New Georgia, Frank Chadwick's Marine Defense Battalion was in combat of many types. As he notes, most fighting is over quickly:

Air attacks, bombardments, and most combat is over very quickly in most cases. For instance, during a low-level air attack the crews stayed at their antiaircraft guns and nobody headed for their holes. You stand your ground and just keep putting up the lead and try to bring them down. We shot down many aircraft on Rendova. Most guys weren't scared before things took place. We were awfully young, you know. During the chaos, you're so damn busy you don't really think. The training takes over. You're conditioned to act in a certain way. It's the thing to do to save yourself too. Afterward, everyone starts to shake. You break out those cigarettes. You kind of lose it, really.

However, as Chadwick also points out, enduring a moment of truth with no ability for self-defense is a harrowing experience. Being strafed by aircraft was fast, but fits the category nicely:

We were strafed several times. When you're running for a foxhole and you see that trail of bullets heading for you it's terrifying. You don't really know which way they're going and there's shrapnel flying all over. Your mind is totally concentrated on getting the hell out of there. Do you hit the ground or head for a hole? When the plane comes toward you you can see the guns and cannon flash, and see the bombs drop. They're close to you before you hear that loud whistle from the bomb. When it hits the deck you see a shower of sparks and shrapnel whistling by. And a tremendous noise. It's quite an experience. You can't tell what came first or what was making what noise.

Nor did Chadwick and his comrades like being on the other end of an artillery barrage:

Being shelled by artillery was awful. On New Georgia we were setting up to shell the island of Kolombangara. Before we got into action, the Japs started shelling us. You'd be in your hole, look out, and see the flashes and count them: you'd see the smoke, too. And then the artillery would come barreling in like a freight train. I used to peer out and think to myself: there's one, two, three, four: now let's see where they're going to hit. The shelling lasted about half an hour. They never hit us, but shells landed to the left, in front, and behind us.

Despite these perils, Chadwick and most of his comrades were able to continue to serve well through several campaigns. The best defense against fear, it would seem, was youth:

We didn't know any better. We were so young. Most of us felt it will never happen to me. You knew people were killed and wounded all the time, but deep down you thought it would happen to some other guy. So we worried more about our buddies. You made yourself believe that nothing could happen to you, that you had to worry about your friends. It wasn't logical, but it would have been a lot harder to go on brooding about it.

Scott Wilson expresses the same sentiment, but notes that along with combat experience comes a little more maturity:

At age twenty you're invincible. It's never going to be you, it's going to be the other guy. It's not bravery, it's idiotic adolescence. I was a much more cautious soldier as a section sergeant in my third campaign at age twenty-three. Most of the guys were the same. On Guadalcanal the 27th Regiment saw more fighting than we did. I remember them coming back, swaggering, bragging about their first exploits. Believe me, those of us still around after New Georgia didn't act the same way when we headed to the Philippines.

Many men, however, found it impossible not to contemplate the very real possibility of imminent death. Charles Crary served in the Salamaua campaign in 1943, a nasty siege in some of the ugliest terrain New Guinea had to offer. Fear was very much on his mind:

The landing and the ensuing days were filled with dread for me. There was the constant fear that a bullet with my name on it or a stray piece of shrapnel would kill me. I never once thought of the possibility of being just wounded and not killed. To be hit was to be killed. I guess there were times that the fear of death was not in the forefront of my mind; but certainly that oppressive shadow was constantly with me even when the current activity had me so occupied that all conscious thoughts were directed toward that task. As a result, if I slept at all, it was fitfully at best and I was able to come fully awake at the slightest provocation.

The interaction between fear, stress, exhaustion, and illness created a dreadful dynamic that threatened to break the spirit of fighting men. Paul Sponaugle saw it happen several times during the miserable fighting on New Georgia. Like James Salafia, also on New Georgia, quoted above, Sponaugle points out the harmful effect "hazing" by combat veterans had on the new troops:

Before we shipped out, everyone was telling us how bad it was going to be. It was a mistake to instill fear into our soldiers. When you got into combat that fear was ten times greater. I saw many guys get the shakes. If you can get to them in time, you can maybe help. One friend of mine started shaking and crying. I stuck my rifle butt behind his helmet and shoved his face into the rocks. He whirled around, furious at me. I told him if he wanted to fight that the Japs were close enough. That seemed to do it. But others just found a hole, got in, started to shake, maybe cry or whimper, maybe just stare off. Many of those men were worthless from that point. Some came back after rest, others we never saw again. The men needed better leadership.

On New Georgia, where the troops were inexperienced and very badly oriented for what developed into a bitter campaign, there was an unusual number of psychiatric casualties. The problem on New Georgia concerned the Army very much. Consequently it was closely studied during the campaign and immediately after by officers and psychologists. Army psychologists on the spot found that there was a very close correlation between individual cases of breakdown in a unit and officer casualties. In retrospect it is clear that the commander and staff of the 43d Division did a very poor job of removing a large number of National Guard officers who did not belong in a viper pit like New Georgia. The Army was deeply disturbed because so many men broke up very early, and it seemed to have a contagious effect. Infantryman Frank Gilberto of the 43d Division later wrote about his experience:

> We had quite a few more casualties than normal. These men were not wounded. These men seemed to be suffering from both physical and emotional trauma. Their eyes appeared vacant and their skin pale and clammy, and their breathing shallow.

John Huggins, another 43d veteran, recalled that when a psychological casualty was sent to the rear, "they'd put a tag on him and they'd put a stick in his hand and he'd be shaking. His whole body would shake." As the men were evacuated down the trail toward the beach, dozens of men coming up the trail were so unnerved they refused to go on.

Fortunately for the American Army, the problem with the 43d proved very isolated. Three-quarters of the men returned to duty. After the first two miserable weeks of the campaign, the number of psychological casualties dropped off dramatically. The Army gave the malady the name "war neurosis." Never again in the South Pacific did it occur like an outbreak of a contagious disease. As for the 43d, after retraining and an infusion of good officers, it fought very well during the Philippine campaign.

One unfortunate side effect of the sad events on New Georgia was that they drew too much attention to the problems of the 43d Division and tended to overshadow how widespread psychological breakdown was throughout the theater. The problem should not be overstated. Everything considered, morale was good in the South Pacific among American ground troops in 1942–43, and better in the AIF. Furthermore, the military was a little mystified by the problem of breakdown. The physical punishment confronted by men in the theater had no precedent and made it very hard to determine whether an individual was beat into the ground physically or psychologically. The widely encountered "FUO" (fever of undetermined origin) was thought by some doctors to be psychosomatic. Others believed it was misdiagnosed malaria or some other tropical treat.

Furthermore, transient breakdown was extremely common. A death of a friend, an ugly firefight, or a host of other things could trigger momentary loss of will. Sometimes friends helped men through dark hours, sometimes they worked it through themselves. Mark Durley led an extraordinary long-range reconnaissance patrol across the very large and rugged island of Bougainville in early 1944. Durley recalls their return after two weeks in the bush:

All of us were exhausted. For three or four days we were useless. Some of us, myself included, would break out in tears for no specific reason. It is a little hard to remember the period. I tried to stay away from people for a while. After a few days we started to snap out of it.

Good leaders or doctors recognized potential problems and tried to deal with them before they got out of hand. Measures might be as simple as giving someone easier duty for a couple of days. As Robert Kennington recalls, a little cheer came in handy:

When we came off of Hill 27 after the Gifu had been destroyed, I walked by Captain Gordon, the regimental surgeon. He was standing in the doorway of his tent and saw me. He told me to get over there. He said I looked really bad, and had lost weight. He was right there. I came in at 188 solid and left at 155. He went into the tent and came back with a bottle of little white pills: sedatives of some kind, eight or ten. He said, "If you get uptight, take one of these. It will settle you down." He went back to his foot locker, came back with a bottle of gin. He said, "I want you to take this, get some of your buddies, sit down under that tree, and drink it. You need it." He was right. I needed a boost like that to get straightened out.

Progressive breakdown was the most common sort of battle fatigue. Good soldiers very simply gave what they could and could not go on. Adam DiGenaro led his squad into many battles with the 3d Marine division and saw the process several times:

You can't really say how people handled fear. You could see some internalize it. For me, anticipation of battle was the most stressful. Snipers wore at your nerves. Everyone is afraid. But by nature I'm a fatalist, not a worrier. It was my salvation in the war. The tension was there, sure enough. But I can't say I had a fear of dying. I just didn't think of it. I don't think of it now and I'm seventy-four. It doesn't bother me. I know I can't know when I'm going to die, and I sure know I can't prevent it, so why worry about it.

Others internalized fear differently. Some could not cope with it. A number of men under me could not handle it. There were very obvious signs. The man wouldn't move much. He didn't want to do anything, but would just sit and stoop. They might say something like "I don't want to go back, I can't live with it, I can't cope with it." Often they would cry. They couldn't face the fear of death. It was not something that hit right away. I've seen seasoned guys for no reason whatsoever break down, even though they'd gone through many other situations tougher than the one that was doing them in. It just seemed to hit them all at once. Maybe their perceptions changed, and they lost their ability to judge risks. I never thought they were cowards. Their mind and focus was on death and they couldn't face it. Their physical and mental being became disoriented and they couldn't function anymore.

I think the people most likely to crack were the guys who went out on recon patrols, especially the point man. Those were the

guys who suffered the most. They'd come back from missions totally out of it. They were afraid that the next step would be that
sniper. They were the walking warning. The snipers sometimes
waited for the main body to approach so they had more targets,
but point was harrowing. It usually isn't a patrol anyway. Just half
a dozen guys, moving quietly. They're not supposed to fight except to protect themselves. You need the information or you're
flying blind. One way to find the enemy is to get shot at. It was
tough going in the jungle. You couldn't see, and the uncertainty
would feed the fear. War is so stupid. The whole thing is so
wasteful. The waste of life, money, and disruption of normal life,
and usually for little purpose.

Homer Wright was a young officer with the 32d Division at
Buna and later campaigns. He makes the point that the jungle greatly
increased a problem that is universal in war:

The battle fatigue we had was different from the World War I
variety or what you saw in Europe. The climate and disease wore
out good men so fast. We were tired beyond imagination. The
first impact was weight loss. We were skeletons when we went
back to Australia after Buna. You couldn't really sleep. More like
a fitful type of nap. You were often interrupted. We had guards
out, but you had to be on alert at all times.

The people who suffered were evacuated to the portable hospital. From there some went to Australia. In some cases some
went to the U.S. A good friend went through the phases of battle
fatigue. He never fully recovered from his jungle experience. He
was brave and a good officer. But he was just worn out. Beaten
into the ground. We were all tired of the war. The 32d was in
combat through the Philippines. The number of people we saw
massacred, both Japanese and Americans, gave all of us a bellyful
of that particular phase of the war.

The important role played by the physical pounding was under-
scored by the large number of older soldiers who broke down.
Clifford Fox saw many proud Marine veterans crack in the malignant
environment of Guadalcanal:

A lot of the older guys cracked quicker than the younger ones. The old NCOs just couldn't take it as long as the younger fellows. They just got physically ground down: they didn't have the physical strength of the younger guys. And then they got psychologically worn out. They didn't have the reserve to draw on. A lot of them were in their late thirties and early forties. They probably weren't as dumb as some of the nineteen-year-olds. They had families and so forth. They took it harder.

Paul Sponaugle observed the same correlation between age and breakdown that Fox saw:

In the rear we had a "pioneer" platoon that did manual labor. When one of our men or noncoms didn't function correctly, they often assigned him there. A lot of officers and noncoms joined the pioneers. Didn't always help them because a lot of the poor guys were killed too. The Japs hit our rear areas more than once. They were fatigued and some just couldn't hack it. Most were in the later twenties or thirties. Anyone twenty-five years old was considered an old man.

Some men had private demons they could not purge. It is very likely that the unusually severe acts of self-destruction were done by men suffering from preexisting psychosis. The Army quickly recognized that its screening procedure during conscription was inadequate to eliminate young men who were seriously mentally ill. Most were diagnosed during training, but some made it overseas. (In 1944 an average of twenty-two soldiers suffering from very severe psychosis were evacuated every day from the Pacific theater. Note there were at least 2 million men in the theater.) Whatever their mental state, the urge to get out of the front lines drove hundreds of soldiers to self-mutilation. Robert Kennington recalls a failed attempt to get out:

Some guys shot themselves in the foot, or chopped themselves with machetes to get off the front lines. A good friend of mine did that: cut himself with a machete, figuring they'd evacuate him. They sent him to the hospital, healed him up and back he came.

Marine Donald Fall saw much the same thing, but on a more serious level:

When we were in the Russells [a tiny island group in the Solomons near Guadalcanal—EB] in mid-1943 we started getting in a lot of replacements while we were in intensive training for the Cape Gloucester operation. These hard-assed Marines started telling all sorts of combat stories to the new guys. There were a few suicides. In the middle of the night you'd hear a rifle shot, a bunch of flashlights would go on, and they'd find someone dead. When you came off a rifle range, you came off with your bolt open. I remember one guy shot his toe off: he didn't realize he was supposed to have his bolt open so he couldn't say it was accidental. He got out, but he also was up for a court-martial. I remember another guy swear he wasn't going to another battle, so he broke his ankle.

Frank Chadwick relates a sad story of a young man who literally killed himself because of a fear of death:

We were on ship going to Rendova at the start of the New Georgia campaign. There was a guy sitting on gun watch. We'd been through some air raids. It was nighttime. He stood up and said, "I've had enough of this," and he dove overboard and was gone. We didn't even stop. Earlier on Guadalcanal we had a sergeant who had jungle rot. He wouldn't take care of it because he wanted to get the hell out of there. And he did. But before he left everyone understood what he was doing, and they blackballed him. No one had anything to do with him. The major had the choice to put the screws to him or get rid of him. He got rid of him. We had a few cases like that. But the percentages were extremely low.

Although in retrospect most veterans look back with compassion on their comrades who broke down, at the time the reaction was very different. Fred Johnson, a medic at Buna, outlines the problem:

Men on line didn't like the guys who cracked. It was an easy way out. Understand that a lot of guys talked about the "million-dollar wound," one that wouldn't cripple them but would be bad enough to get them out of combat. No question that a lot of guys wanted out. Sometimes it seemed that nobody thought they were going to live. But every less person on the line meant more danger and more risk for those left. It wasn't like later where you got in a supply of replacements during a campaign. On Buna, you just watched the units dwindle. It was the same with the Aussie units.

Many of the men who broke down were aware of the feelings held by their comrades. Guilt made the problem worse. John Augustine was an MP (military police) with the 32d Division at Buna. He recalls an unhappy duty:

> One of our duties was to get the men who broke down back to the rear. They were brought to division headquarters. At that point one of the MPs escorted them to Dobodura airfield and flew with them back to Port Moresby. I did this several times. It was very cold in the aircraft when we flew over the Owen Stanleys. The men we escorted were miserable. If you tried to do anything for them they'd break down and cry. Some cursed themselves for cowardice and called themselves worthless. It was so sad.

As one can see, it was a difficult and unending task to keep units operating physically and psychologically in this violent world.

The Medical Effort

The military did several things to maintain morale or rebuild it when it was shaken. Probably the single most important thing done was to build a massive medical apparatus to care for those overseas. Morale and military effectiveness are closely intertwined in war. This was especially true in the South Pacific, where a very serious disease problem existed alongside high combat casualties. In the jungle the medical effort influenced morale both directly and indirectly. As already noted, physical exhaustion attacks the will to fight. In a disease-infested environment, it was never possible to keep men healthy. It did prove possible to keep them going. It also proved possible to restore their health and spirit when campaigns were over. Keep in mind that every division that fought in the jungle needed months to rebuild before it could be sent to battle again.

Many soldiers, usually the very young, proved able to handle the fear of death by denying its possibility. It was a tenuous solution, but one as old as war. Wounds, however, because they were so much more common, were very different. A soldier might condition himself not to think of the consequences of being hit, but all armies knew that it was a tremendous aid to morale if combat troops realized that there were trained personnel there to help them if they were wounded. It is not surprising that corpsmen and medics who risked their lives to get the wounded out of danger or doctors that treated soldiers near the front are almost universally praised by former soldiers. Also, men were always short in the Pacific. The replacement "pipeline" took many months to get working efficiently. Therefore, it was very important to return as many experienced soldiers as possible to their units. They not only filled the rolls, they were also often the best soldiers. For all these reasons Allied armies developed a large, very expensive and complex medical apparatus that saved tens of thousands of lives and no doubt did much to keep the forces in the field. Japan's inability to do so cost it dearly.

Like much in the South Pacific, the medical support apparatus was extremely crude at the outset of fighting. The American military did a very good job establishing modern hospitals at their major island bases and in Australia in a very short period of time. Supplies, as usual, were short throughout 1942. As luck would have it, a freighter carrying much of the early batch of medical supplies intended for Australia foundered outside Brisbane. Serious problems were averted thanks to skillful salvage work in treacherous waters. As the months passed the facilities grew larger and more complex. The Australians could base their medical establishment on their preexisting civilian hospital network, which was an obvious advantage.

A man who was injured and made it to a proper hospital in 1942 received excellent care even in modern terms. Doctors understood the basics of trauma very well. Surgical techniques and equipment were quite advanced. A high percentage of men entering hospitals in the Pacific returned to duty within several weeks. Those who suffered debilitating wounds returned to the United States for prolonged care. The tropical diseases that plagued every army raised new challenges. Many of the most serious maladies like scrub typhus resisted the treatments known at the time. Penicillin did not appear until late in the war, so infections were always dangerous. Doctors could treat malaria only partially. There was no genuine cure, but a soldier with a severe case was far better off in a hospital than at the front.

The sheer numbers confronting the medical establishment were staggering. The following figures cover losses suffered by the U.S. Army in 1942 and 1943 in the South and Southwest Pacific theaters.

	DISEASE	INJURY	PSYCHIATRIC	WOUNDS
1942	128,295	25,788	6,438	2,887
1943	411,571	61,646	27,070	6,811
Total	539,866	87,434	33,508	9,698

The figures require some explanation. First, they do not include Marine, Navy, and Australian losses, all of which were heavy in late 1942. The 1943 figures also include the concluding phase of both the Buna and Guadalcanal campaigns. More important, a casualty was not necessarily a casualty. On the front lines, particularly early in the war, many wounds that would have sent a civilian to the emergency room today were treated on the spot by the medic and never tabulated. The same is true for many cases of disease. Injuries were nonbattle mishaps. Hundreds were very serious, but the great majority were relatively minor and most commonly reported in rear zones. Lastly, wounds tended to be the worst single problem because many were so dangerous. Minor wounds, conversely, were underreported. An injury in the rear meant a trip to the aid station, where someone made a note on a record. On the front lines men accommodated minor wounds or injuries without formal aid. Furthermore, it is doubtful that keeping records at the front was done with great precision or enthusiasm.

With these exceptions aside, it is plain to see that doctors, medics, corpsmen (naval personnel who served as medics for the Marines), and nurses had their work cut out for them. The medical apparatus that grew increasingly more capable was also a perfect illustration of the "law of diminishing returns" that operates in the realm of manpower allocation in modern war. Thousands of medical personnel and support staff came to the Pacific to keep the armies capable of fighting. In no theater was their role more important. However, the people involved with care also required more personnel to support them. Support personnel, in turn, got sick and injured. This led to more men and women and supplies required in the theater. The cycle had countless parallels. This is one reason why there were so many more victims of injuries and disease in 1943 than 1942. The rear had grown so much in that time that there were more people to treat.

Throughout the war, however, the biggest problem facing medical personnel was getting care to the wounded and seriously ill on the battlefield. A very sick individual in New Caledonia was in a very different world than a very sick soldier in a Papuan swamp. Conceptually, the process was simple enough. On the battlefield someone had to get a stricken soldier to a place of temporary safety and administer emergency first aid. Next, other men had to evacuate the soldier to an aid post that was usually close to the front. If the wounded man was hurt badly, he had to be moved quickly to whatever passed for an emergency hospital. Finally, others had to evacuate the wounded soldier to the rear. Each step had perils and potential for breakdown. This was particularly true in 1942, when, like everyone else in the war, medical people worked in a shockingly crude environment.

Combat soldiers during World War II lived in a world where pain and injury were commonplace. They redefined to an astounding degree standards of acceptable comfort and acceptable health. Infantryman James Salafia remarked, "If you lay at night in your foxhole and were covered with mud and water, you grew pleasantly warm."

In the civilian world a notion like that would not occur to many. It made sense in New Georgia. In addition, nine men out of ten on the front would have been considered unfit to work in civilian life. Most would have been in the hospital. The same was true with injuries. Combat soldiers did hard physical labor. Digging, carrying water up steep slopes, or unloading supplies all promised cuts, bruises, and assorted sprains. Open sores, gashes from knives or vines, bleeding feet were part of life. In this warped world, taking a clean "flesh wound" or having your "bell rung" by concussion from a mortar round was hardly considered cause for comment. A medic on the frontlines might bandage a light shrapnel wound, give the soldier a shot of morphine (if he was lucky), and have him continue on. The men of the Depression generation did not seek medical attention in civilian life as readily as people do today. Yet even considering that factor, soldiers in the jungle accepted and continued to serve after suffering injuries that would have laid flat a civilian. The reasons they would do so were simple enough. Everyone was needed on the front, and the pressure to stay unless necessity intruded was powerful. Also, combat soldiers knew what genuine trauma looked like. So if a soldier said a nasty gash in his arm was "nothing," his frame of reference had nothing to do with civilian life. Instead, he was comparing his injury to a shattered limb, or a massive wound caused by a high-velocity bullet passing through the shoulder. Relative to trauma like that, a gash was "nothing." Only a physician would see injury and death through the same eyes as a combat soldier.

E. J. Randall of the AIF describes the almost offhand manner with which men treated "minor" wounds when surrounded by far more grievous injury:

> I was wounded only once, this at Buna. I was sent from my battalion regimental aid post (RAP) to a casualty clearing station at the rear. The conditions at Buna were bad and any resemblance to a proper casualty clearing station was nil. There were large numbers of casualties from the attack of 18th December. The wounded lay under the palms and waited their turn. The doctors and orderlies attended them and administered liberal doses of sulfa powder, the new wonder drug. From this station casualties

either walked or were carried to the nearest airstrip for transport to Port Moresby and on to Australia. The large gash on the back of my hand plus the possibility of sundry broken bones was not life-threatening, so, armed with a handful of gangrene tablets, I headed back to take over my platoon. Men were scarce. Leaders were very scarce. You just had to get back and get on with the job.

Wounds in combat were extremely common, sudden, and physically traumatic. Allied soldiers were most likely to die from machine-gun or rifle fire and most likely to be wounded by fragmentation coming from grenades, artillery, mortars, or bombs. Frank Chadwick received a representative World War II wound when his gun emplacement was struck by a bomb. Chadwick describes the experience:

Early in the New Georgia operation, the Japs hit Rendova hard with air attacks for several days. They also hit the landing beach just across the channel. Most planes come in at treetop level. You see the firing of the guns on the wings, you see the bombs drop from the plane. You see the pilot with his goggles up. This is taking place very close, maybe fifty, sixty, ninety feet away. You'll even feel the prop wash if the plane passes right overhead. It happens in an instant.

They got me with a bomb. I heard this terrific noise, and felt an intense heat. The concussion bounced me around and I could hear the shrapnel flying all over. And then I was sitting there thinking, "What the hell happened?" You don't think very clearly after a bomb goes off, and I didn't really understand what was going on. I started getting this pain in my leg, reached down to rub it and my hand was all red. I think, "Christ, I've been hit." A numbing effect set in. You start to get the shakes fast unless a wound is very serious. At that moment the second bomb landed and knocked me silly. It blew out a tooth and injured my mouth. The first thing I knew I was spitting out four or five teeth. I looked down and saw my wrist bone sticking through the skin. But it didn't hurt. At first I didn't have any pain. I'm not real clear what happened. They moved me back a little way to an aid station where there was a doctor. The doc set my wrist bone, snapped it back in place, and put a splint on it. Then it hurt like hell. It was strange though. Lying there and being treated seemed like it took forever. It was only one night. That was worth a Purple Heart. Also five weeks in a hospital in the Russells. But then back to my unit. That's where I wanted to be at the time.

Chadwick's Marine Defense Battalion was pounding Japanese positions on Munda Point with heavy artillery when Japanese planes attacked. His comrades took him to the aid station. On the front lines medics and corpsmen were at the point of fire. These young men received training in basic first aid. On paper they were supposed to be unarmed and, by international law, immune from intentional fire. International law does not last long in war, and in the field medics normally carried weapons and almost never displayed any markings on their helmets or uniforms. The Army had a rough attitude toward medics. Officers know that men instinctively stopped to aid wounded friends. Believing that this would slow an attack and endanger other men, officers instructed soldiers to leave the wounded in place and wait for medics to deliver care. This attitude did not make medics happy. The policy was very often ignored. As attested to by the large percentage of decorations given to men who aided wounded comrades, other soldiers were often on the scene first. All had rudimentary first-aid training and in theory carried bandages. Nevertheless, on every battlefield the cry of "Medic!" or "Corpsman!" was one of the quintessential sounds of battle.

Medics were probably the most admired men on the front. They faced harm every time they went forward to aid a wounded man while a firefight was taking place. Medics naturally did not move against massed fire, but they got to men very quickly, often putting themselves at risk doing so. When a medic arrived he was trained to first get the wounded man out of the line of fire. In the jungle, that could usually be accomplished quickly because of the dense terrain. Then the medic administered rudimentary first aid. Corpsmen and medics saved many lives doing so. Blood loss was a serious danger, and medics frequently were able to stop bleeding that was going to kill. If the supply situation was good, a medic would try to sprinkle sulfa powder on the wound and then bandage it. If a man was in serious pain, a medic might inject him with morphine.

The next problem confronted by a wounded soldier was serious. With luck, an aid station might be very close by. But more likely it was not. If the wound was serious someone had to transport the victim to more elaborate facilities in the rear. The mode of transport varied. In some cases jeep ambulances could make it very close to the front and drive wounded strapped on stretchers to aid. Such a ride was slow, treacherous, and extremely bumpy, but it was the fastest way to the rear. On Guadalcanal, inventive Marines and soldiers set up a raft system to float the wounded down the Lunga River to a point where they could be loaded on jeeps. However, at some point, a wounded man who could not walk would have to be carried by stretcher over rough terrain. Stretcher-bearers were in constant demand during battle. Officers stripped rear units to find them. Natives would serve very well but were reluctant to get close to fire. Consequently, members of the divisional band, cooks, or anyone else handy carried their injured comrades. Stretcher-bearing was exhausting work, and a serious drain on manpower. Four men were needed to carry a stretcher. If it was done over long distances, more were required to provide relief.

Charles Crary received a "friendly fire" artillery wound near Salamaua and went through this procedure. Note that Crary met his first doctor very close to the front. Earlier in the war, this might not have happened:

> A shell hit a tree about ten feet above our position, showering us with shrapnel. The shrapnel that hit my leg passed between two men to find me. Our platoon lieutenant a few yards away got a large piece in the abdomen that destroyed his kidneys. He died the next day.
>
> There was no pain, but I knew that I'd been hit and where. I used my belt as a tourniquet. My pant leg had been destroyed and there were a goodly number of pieces of meat the size of my

thumb tip scattered on and around the wound. My leg looked severed. When the medic arrived in a few minutes to clean and bandage the wound I learned that my lower leg was still attached to the rest of me! I was greatly relieved, but I secretly hoped that I had a "home run"! I'd had enough of living in this mud and wanted a change of pace or, if possible, a return to the States.

The medic gave me two ampules of morphine, so I kind of "floated" for the next several hours. The first stop was the battalion aid station, where the doctors stopped the bleeding and prepared me for the trip down the mountain to the portable hospital. At that point my litter was hoisted to the shoulders of the native porters and the trek off the mountain began. At the first slope the agony began, because I was literally hanging from the injured leg that had been lashed to a crossbar. We rigged some shoulder straps to take weight off my leg, and the rest of the trip was in reasonable comfort. However, please recognize that the trail we were taking down Mount Tambu was of red clay the consistency of pudding, just about ankle deep and slippery as grease. This meant that the porters were doing a lot of slipping and sliding on the mountain. Many bearers fell flat, but kept their arm extended to keep me from falling.

Crary arrived at a portable hospital. Earlier in the war he would not have seen anything quite so elaborate. Nevertheless, no one would mistake it for the Mayo Clinic. (One could have met Charles Mayo, however, operating on men near Buna.) Crary continues:

We reached the portable hospital, but I had to wait. I was given plasma. I vaguely remember my arm taped to a board so that I wouldn't disturb the IV. The mosquitoes saw my arm as a "free lunch" counter. It was black with them. Because of the shock and heavy sedation I just lay there and watched them. During this time my clothing was removed and burned. It had been worn unwashed for about three months. Eventually I went into surgery, heavily sedated. An anesthesiologist asked me to start counting backward. I got to ninety-five and out. I woke and discovered my leg was in a cast that let my toes peek out and came two-thirds of the way up my thigh. I really felt great. I'm sure that much of my feeling was euphoria that I was out of immediate danger of being shot at. On the second day a crew of twelve porters was assigned to take me to the airstrip at Wau.

On the way we chattered and joked in pidgin. But around 9:30 A.M. I began to feel sick. It started with a knot in the pit of my stomach, but gradually grew into a pain that restricted my breathing. It wasn't too long before I began to believe I was going to die. My crew began to run with me. We arrived at a way station that had a doctor. He diagnosed my problem as secondary shock and overmedication of morphine. Relieved, all I wanted to do was sleep. Sometime during the night I was awakened by a sharp pain in one of my toes. It felt as though it were being cut with a knife. I couldn't move the leg because of the cast and weakness. I called out and finally someone came. They found a huge jungle rat trying to eat my toes!

Eventually, after enduring an infestation of maggots that appeared under his cast, a lack of crutches requiring him to crawl to the latrine, and a loss of his medical records, Crary made it to a more elaborate hospital at Dobodura and then on to Australia. After a major skin graft and serious physical therapy, Crary was given orders to return to the front. Fortunately for Crary, the Army was learning that reassigning men who had been ill or badly wounded to frontline service was a serious mistake. Because Crary's wound prevented him from wearing combat boots, the Army sent him to the United States, where he spent an unhappy year in American hospitals.

Charles Crary saw the medical apparatus at a high level of efficiency in the summer of 1943. It continued to increase in sophistication until the end of the war. However, the wounded, medics, and doctors in 1942 were much less fortunate. Fred Johnson was a medic at a battalion aid station immediately behind the front at Buna, and describes conditions:

We were usually about 300 yards behind the front line, sometimes right on it. We had pouches of sulfa, morphine, and bandages. The battalion surgeon was a glorified first-aid man. We didn't have any splints. Atabrine hadn't arrived yet, so we administered quinine. It was just a little tent. Sometimes the battle swarmed around us. In early December the Australians got some open-tracked vehicles that were armed with machine guns and carried infantry. They called them Bren carriers. They attacked with those things and the Japanese shot them to pieces. One of their officers came to us with his arm essentially hanging by a tendon. He wanted us to bandage him up so he could get back into battle that instant. Amazing.

About two miles back was the collecting station. It was a few tents, just a spot on the trail. Men with fevers lay in the grass. You had to watch out for rats. They proliferated in the area like crazy because of all the dead, and they weren't particular if someone was dead or alive before taking a bite. If someone's fever was very high, we laid him in a stream. No one with malaria was sent farther to the rear, we just waited for the fever to recede. There were Jap stragglers around. Once a small group of them threw some grenades into the grass and killed some of the wounded. They were shot down going through our rations.

Ironically, the first U.S. portable hospital, constructed so it could be hand-carried in modules by its personnel, was on its way via small boat to Buna when sunk by Japanese planes before the fighting started. (This was the same little convoy Dick Randles was on, as described earlier. The 32d Division had more than its share of bad luck at Buna.)

Beastly conditions also existed on Guadalcanal. Typical of the haste that permeated the operation, very little planning was done about medical support. Although the distances traveled were not far until the December American offensive, the steep ravines made evacuation of the wounded extremely hard. When they arrived behind the lines the wounded went to the 1st Marine Division hospital. Doctor Victor Falk was a flight surgeon with a Marine squadron at Henderson and recalls conditions:

The hospital was a crude wooden shack built by the Japanese that had an electrical generator and an ice maker. Adjacent, Navy Seabees built an underground shelter, where we had to work during bombardments. It was a foul and smelly place. Our sick bay was two-thirds of a Quonset hut built by the Seabees. We had about twenty beds that were always full, mostly with malaria and dysentery patients. The other third was a little mess which prepared the basic triumvirate of Spam, Vienna sausage, and corned beef, accompanied by dried eggs and dehydrated potatoes.

As Dr. Falk relates, physicians near the front faced serious danger. On October 13, 1942, Dr. Falk arrived on Guadalcanal aboard a transport to join his squadron. As already recounted, that night Japanese battleships delivered the most ferocious naval bombardment ever directed at Americans during any war. One of the huge shells dropped short of Henderson, causing a disaster that Dr. Falk describes:

A Japanese plane dropped brilliant green flares. Everyone was accustomed to nightly harassment of "Washing Machine Charlie" but this was different. The flares were followed by shelling from the battleships *Haruna* and *Kongo* and 900 fourteen-inch shells aimed at Henderson Field. Many of the shells fell a bit short, exploding in the coconut trees in our bivouac area. Exploding wood added to the high-explosive blast and shell fragments. The commanding officer of my squadron and his two assistants were killed. Dr. Henry Ringness, flight surgeon of another of our squadrons, was badly wounded. Many planes were destroyed. The precious aviation gasoline went up in great fiery pyres and the ammunition dumps exploded like mammoth fireworks. The ground about the foxholes vibrated like a continuous earthquake.

Despite the shelling a messenger got to our foxhole with an urgent request for help. I picked up Dr. Ringness. He very coolly described the level of his spinal-cord injury but fortunately he was not aware that one buttock had been sheared off by a shell fragment. Although paralyzed in the lower half of his body, Ringness had administered morphine and plasma to four wounded men in his position. I am not sure that he understood how badly he was injured, but three days later he died. The next morning we had one transport capable of flight. We filled it with casualties and flew them back to New Hebrides. The next day I flew back alone wedged in between aviation gasoline and bombs. A week later two more flight surgeons flying toward Henderson on a transport disappeared. Whether it was due to enemy action or something else we will never know. There were seven surgeons in my group and three were dead in a week.

As Dr. Falk mentions, transport aircraft had a crucial role beyond getting men and supplies to the front. Medical evacuation by air, a technique first used in the South Pacific, saved thousands of lives. Airlines had been flying the DC-3 for years, and the military had procured many C-47s (the military version of the DC-3) before the war. Incredibly, there was no formal plan for their use in medical evacuation. In retrospect this was a stunning oversight, and testimony to the chaos that reigned in the American military before World War II.

Because the Marines were starved for supplies early in the Guadalcanal campaign, C-47s started flying into Henderson as soon as possible overloaded with all types of cargo. It did not take Napoleonic insight to understand that it was stupid to fly loaded aircraft forward and fly them back to base empty. (Transports were far too valuable to normally stay at Henderson until Guadalcanal was more secure. They were "in and out" quickly, if at all possible.) Soon enough, doctors began loading wounded and seriously ill onto the aircraft.

When the great air base at Dobodura opened in November a similar process started in New Guinea. During the Guadalcanal campaign, transports evacuated 7,000 men. They flew another 27,000 men to safety during other battles in the Solomons. During the Buna-Gona campaign, 13,000 Americans and Australians flew over the Owen Stanleys to the hospital at Port Moresby by January 1943, almost a third of the ground forces involved. By war's end 250,000 men had flown to hospitals throughout the theater. Ships carried more when the situation was secure, but if a man needed urgent care that could not be provided in the crude frontline facilities, air evacuation was literally a godsend.

As time progressed the evacuation system became very elaborate.

First one and then two corpsmen or medics accompanied flights back. Soon a few flight nurses flew in with the aircraft and accompanied them out. This small number of nurses were the only women near the battlefield during operations in the South Pacific. (Large numbers of women arrived as time went on to help staff the hospitals. Flight nurses became a fixture of the air-evacuation process later in the war.) Surgeons, too, accompanied men in some situations. Ground crews altered the aircraft to hold eighteen wounded on folding stretchers, although more went back if necessary. The C-47 was unpressurized, so a flight over the Owen Stanleys was cold and uncomfortable. Nevertheless, the men got to modern hospitals within hours. As the war progressed, small but modern hospitals sprouted up throughout the South Pacific, bringing aid closer yet. An American or Australian who was wounded in the morning could potentially be in Australia by nightfall. At the same time, medical supplies, which took up little bulk compared to food or ammunition, got to the front in adequate quantities at any time past mid-1943. It is paradoxical that men fighting in the most crude and technically retrograde theater of the war were the first to employ something as innovative as air evacuation. In retrospect, air evacuation was one of the most effective uses of airpower in the war, and has long been an integral part of all modern militaries.

In 1943 the medical system improved tremendously. In addition to more and better points of treatment, the Allies implemented a serious program of preventive medicine. Mosquito-control parties slowly brought malaria levels down in major base areas like Milne Bay. Improved sanitation, nutrition, and water supplies lowered the rate of dysentery. Dentists, equipped often with foot-powered drills, stood ready to help men from a generation largely ignorant of dental care. The South Pacific remained an unhealthy place to serve until the end. Yet the nightmare world faced in 1942 was never reproduced.

In contrast to the Allied medical system that began crudely but quickly improved greatly, the doctors and medics tending Japanese soldiers went in the opposite direction. Basic medicine in the Japanese Army was very good. Doctors were well trained and knowledge of first aid was widely taught. If able to work under good conditions, Japanese doctors could give their soldiers care that was similar to that found in an American or Australian hospital. In 1945 when the Australians occupied Rabaul after Japan's surrender, they were amazed to find a sophisticated hospital and dental clinic operating with surprising efficiency despite appalling handicaps. The skills were there if they could be used.

However, as the Allies slowly but inexorably gained control of the air and sea lanes, the Japanese medical system was one of the first casualties. This situation was not helped by the criminal arrogance on the part of many Japanese officers who committed men to battle despite deficiencies in every important category of supply. Men not given enough to eat are not likely to be well supplied with quinine. In short order, as the Japanese supply apparatus came unraveled, a medical catastrophe built inside the Japanese armed forces. If quinine was in short supply, malaria ran rampant. Public health in Japan was not on Western standards, and dysentery was endemic. Add into this foul brew the other maladies the jungle had to offer and a general shortage of food, and one can see why the health of Japanese infantry often collapsed. Certainly one of the reasons that Japanese ground forces never repeated the impressive victories scored by the South Seas Detachment against the AIF was that they never again had soldiers who were relatively as healthy.

Japanese planners, as so often was the case, reacted slowly to the growing calamity. By the time they realized that the jungle was killing their men faster than the Allies were, they found themselves with few alternatives. Time and again they resorted to pitiful expediencies such as landing small quantities of supplies with submarines or barges at night to beleaguered positions. Consequently, Japanese ground forces that went to battle were broken almost beyond repair whether they were wiped out or not. Frequently, the Japanese Navy was able to evacuate hard-fighting infantry at the last minute. When returned to Japanese lines, however, the men were in such bad condition that they were worthless for further combat. This was yet another example of the lack of depth to Japan's war effort. This particular failing, however, cost the lives of tens of thousands of Imperial troops. Fighting the jungle without an adequate supply of medicine was the equivalent of launching a massed attack against entrenched positions armed with rifles and knee mortars. Only the engine of death changed.

All armies tend to the dead with care. There are few tasks that bear more directly on morale. Although soldiers rarely talk about these things, many men are very fearful of having their remains mutilated or lost. Furthermore, it is a sign of respect, honestly and deeply felt, for an army to honor its dead. It is no accident that military funerals possess a rare dignity, and that taps is perhaps the most melancholy tune in American music.

The problem, of course, is that men get killed in battles, and battles are dangerous places to care for their remains. Few officers asked their men to expose themselves to direct fire to recover a body. Nevertheless, as soon as possible, something was done to recover the dead or mark their location despite the element of risk. Bill Crooks explains how seriously the men of the AIF took this matter:

> The Australians had an unwritten military law/tradition. One *never* left one's mate shot down dead or wounded in the field. Bugger the operation or the officers if they said differently. And volunteers were not lacking to bring in the victim. If alive, he was sent to the rear. The dead were wrapped in their ground sheet and buried beside the track. The site was very diligently marked. The graves-registration people would be there the moment we left the area to mark it by map and cross section. If possible there was a service given in the field.

The procedures in the American Army and Marine Corps were almost identical. Like everything else in the war, in the early part of hostilities things were not well organized and service personnel of all sort were very short. The job of graves-registration personnel sometimes fell to the men on the line. Someone had to recover temporarily buried bodies quickly or they were easily lost. Robert Kennington had to face this grim and sad task on Guadalcanal:

> After we secured Guadalcanal we moved back to the rear. After about five days, my company commander called me in to talk to

him. He asked me to handle the worst thing I had to do in the war. He told me that five men from our company were buried in marked shallow graves in the jungle. He requested a group of volunteers to go up there, dig them up, and bring them to the rear. Because they were men that we all knew, I got five other volunteers. We went up in a two-and-a-half-ton truck. We had buried them in ponchos and marked the graves. We started digging. When we got down to the bodies it was something you can't really visualize, unless you were there to see and smell it. It was very hot and the soil dank. When we got down to the bodies and started to take them out, there was nothing left: it was like soup. They had dissolved. All of us took turns of about three minutes each. That was as long as we could stand it. We had a cloth across our face. We were puking. It was terrible. After a while we got everyone out. The flesh did not adhere to the bones. We could really only get the bones out. Having in your mind what the guys looked like alive, and then seeing this was horrid. But we finished our job and turned them over to graves registration so they could be returned to the States and buried properly. I know the families appreciated that. I know I would have wanted it. But I would never do it again.

Early in the war, services for fallen comrades were sparse at best. Later, memorial services became more common. The military returned most of the dead home. Many, however, stayed in the military cemeteries established on many of the battlefields. The mordant wit of the GI was never inactive for long. The cemetery at Buna was called "Eichelberger Square." Others went to large military cemeteries on Oahu and other locations.

Many men in the jungle became separated from their patrols and were killed. Others were obliterated by a direct hit from a bomb or mortar shell. They entered the rolls of missing and presumed dead. A handful later appeared in Japanese POW camps, but for the most part no one encouraged any false hopes concerning survival.

The Japanese were meticulous in their care of the dead unless battle conditions got out of hand. If that happened, the familiar carnage of the jungle battlefield took on a new dimension and corpses lay in mounds. Because of Japanese shock tactics, it fell on the Americans and Australians to bury the dead when the assault failed (which it almost always did). On Guadalcanal, this was a task given to Japanese prisoners. Normally a bulldozer sufficed. Ironically, years after the war, American veterans groups helped their Japanese counterparts locate some of the burial sites. The mass grave used for much of the Ichiki Detachment was located and the bodies exhumed due to American aid. Likewise Americans helped locate the Japanese dead at the Gifu Strong Point.

Body and Soul

In a world of pain, fear, and death, the military tried to make spiritual support available to its soldiers. A very complex relationship exists between the military and organized religion. On one hand, the military as an institution has historically encouraged religious worship in the ranks and has gone to great pains to identify itself as the protector of traditional values. Although it is difficult to say so in a politically secular society, protecting the nation's values implies protecting the faith. Many professional soldiers think about their craft deeply. Christianity does not glorify war or death in battle. The problem of the "just war" is one of the oldest in Christian theology, and has usually been resolved by arguing that the state has the role of providing the worldly setting for worship to take place in safety. If the state is in peril, particularly from infidels, then war and the killing that accompanies it receive the sanction of God. This goes to the heart of the modern warrior ethos, which justifies war and finds transcendent value in battle through self-sacrifice. The soldier kills and risks death, both inherently bad acts, for a higher purpose, the defense of the nation. Many have joked at phrases such as the "the war to end all wars" or "fighting for peace," but concepts like these are essential in order for modern militaries to fight. War itself is not good, but defeat is worse. Battle alone has no value unless it is connected to a realistic hope of a tolerable peace to follow.

On the other hand, the dynamics of combat, and the training developed to prepare men to face it, require a mode of thought and action far more akin to the warrior ethos of antiquity which found inherent glory in killing and triumph. Soldiers are trained to kill quickly and efficiently. On the battlefield, not everyone has the talent, but those who do are invaluable. The devices of war, and the words used to describe them, are deeply, intensely violent. Unless crushed by fear and fatigue, combat soldiers, even if they have had a bellyful of war, have an undefinable aggressiveness, a kind of swagger about them. Regardless of the uniform worn, a decent infantry squad in the South Pacific was a very tough bunch of men.

Because of these contrary currents, religious practice in the South Pacific developed along a curious line. The American and Australian armies' large combat units included chaplains who held services in extremely unlikely places. However, it does not appear that large numbers of the young soldiers on the battlefield participated. Obviously, this was a matter that varied widely according to individual preference. Some soldiers were most devout and attended services regularly. Yet very young men are not at an age that is well represented in any church. Marine Bud DeVere comments on the subject:

> I never saw a chaplain on Guadalcanal. Of course if I had, I'd have walked the other way. It wasn't the phase of my life I was looking for them. War made me wonder about human nature, though. Before we landed, a buddy of mine and I were up late on ship. He was talking about how he couldn't wait to get at the dirty Japs, and how he was going to kill them all. That night when we got there and underwent all that bombing and shelling I heard this guy lying in a foxhole saying, "Oh please, God, let me live through the night. I'll go to church every Sunday." It made a religious fanatic out of him overnight. I remember being surprised to hear promises like that: what if he was called on them someday? But I did my share of praying in the foxhole. Or on top of the ground when I got caught without one. We all did.

There were many chaplains at Guadalcanal, as there were at all the battles. Al Careaga recalls one who accompanied his Marine

Raider unit on a hideous march through the roughest area of New Georgia:

> A forty-year-old priest named Father Redmond accompanied us. He wasn't fighting, of course, but he was in those jungles, sharing our risks. Many of the men admired him greatly. It was a grueling place to be for men half his age. I remember him saying Mass in the jungle. He'd put vestments on some ammo crates and conduct service. On more than one occasion things were interrupted because of snipers. He was a courageous man and helped many. That's important in battle.

However, as Bud DeVere suggests above, religion was probably more often a private comfort than an organized ritual at the front. E. J. Randall of the AIF was surprised at Buna that so many American soldiers carried and read Bibles. The Americans Randall was fighting alongside were wearing down in December 1942. Although impossible to prove, it is likely that men under extreme pressure might have been unusually receptive to religious comfort. James Salafia's men on New Georgia, also being ripped to shreds, seemed to be:

> So much happened that we could never explain and didn't understand. We always hoped God was looking out for us. We were the most religious and holy guys you would ever want to find. At night we were all praying and shaking in our holes. We had a chaplain whom the men grew to like a lot. He was killed in a mortar attack. It was a little hard to take. The man was up at the front, walking around trying to cheer the guys up. He told us not to be afraid, and then he gets killed. He didn't exactly prove his point. The guys said, "It's OK to believe in God, but you don't need to help him along." The chaplain told us God was with us. We asked ourselves, "How often can he be with you?"

The connection between fear and faith was not lost on the chaplains. F. J. Hartley, a chaplain with the AIF, stayed in the middle of the apocalyptic struggle that took place between the Huggins and James Roadblocks along the Sanananda Track in December 1942 and January 1943 and wrote a memoir of those weeks. While he was there, Hartley's duties included tending to the wounded and burying the dead. In mid-December Hartley's party made one of their many hazardous excursions into isolated James Roadblock. Although the words have a distinct Victorian ring, Hartley's description of his arrival was no doubt accurate enough. Note the implication that, prior to battle, Hartley's message was not closely listened to:

> It was grand to see these besieged men again. Back at Huggins we had faced up to the possibility that we would never see them alive. I was overwhelmed at the welcome they gave me personally. It seemed that the chaplain had become symbolical of many things that these men had thought deeply about during the past few days. They had been face-to-face with death. They had seen their cobbers, a moment before so full of life and strength, snuffed out as a candle. On every hand I was greeted with such remarks as "My word, I'm on your side now, Padre," "I've never prayed so much in my life before as I have these last few days," "I'll never have to be persuaded to go on a church parade again." In this quaint way these men expressed the fundamental truth that they had learned in their peril. In similar circumstances men of all ages have learnt the same lesson. Man is fundamentally religious and in the hour of need he turns to his Maker for succor. In many people religious consciousness has not advanced beyond this stage and it is only in hours of extremity that they give expression of the deep feelings of the heart.

Hartley and a few volunteers toward the end of the battle searched the battlefield for remains. It was the type of job most men avoided if at all possible. Several of the bodies recovered were his close friends, killed in a battle a few days earlier. In words that were undoubtedly sincere, although perhaps not of our world, this very brave man tried to find a Christian meaning in political massacre:

> As I read the burial service over these men I had more time for reflection than previously. The end of the long and grueling task was in sight. I found myself considering with deeper understanding the words of the burial service. I had recited the words of this short service over a hundred times now. It would not have been

strange had they now come mechanically from my tongue. But such was not the case. The words seemed more pregnant with meaning than ever before. As I laid to rest their remains I could not consider them dead. Their living personalities were far too fresh in my memory. In the midst of all that death and destruction my belief in immortality was strengthened. The service was not a mechanical muttering but an expression of faith. With confident conviction I said, "Earth to earth, ashes to ashes, dust to dust; in sure and certain hope of resurrection to eternal life, through our Lord Jesus Christ."

As I made my way back I had a glorious feeling of satisfaction. The job of identification had been long, grueling, and difficult, but I cannot think of anything which has given me a greater sense of accomplishment. I knew how much it would mean to the relatives to receive definite news of the burial of their loved ones. We had done all we could. We had paid our respect and honour to our comrades. We had buried them with the benediction of Christ, now all was in his hands.

Length of service on the part of individual soldiers varied widely within units, but was one of the most important factors shaping morale. Most soldiers, simply put, grew weary of war quickly. As the military knew well, for several reasons this problem grew as the war progressed. At the outset most men had come into the military at about the same time. Pearl Harbor and the early defeats created an urgency about the war that could never be repeated. Going into battle for the first time, although it carried with it the fear of the unknown, was also accompanied by an innocent sense of adventure. The potential length of the war was not considered often by the first wave of soldiers. Stanley Larsen recalls a meeting of 25th Division battalion commanders that took place after victory on Guadalcanal:

After the Japanese left Guadalcanal the division moved to the beach and started to patch things together. General Collins ordered a critique of division operations on Guadalcanal. There was a rampant rumor among the men that we had done so well that we were heading back to the States and would parade down Market Street in San Francisco. At the start of the critique, General Collins said, "I want to assure you of one thing. You are *not* going back to the United States, the war is *not* going to be over by next Christmas, and if you return to the States it will be at the end of the war. We will probably have to circle the world and you will probably come back by way of New York." He disabused us of any feeling that one big fight was sufficient. It settled us down to recognize that we had tough going ahead. It was the right thing to have done. We were tired, glad to be alive, and hopeful that the war would come to an end soon. We didn't realize what an extended period it would be before we ever thought again of coming home.

As Larsen indicates, the situation began looking different to many men in 1943. They knew firsthand the dangers and hardships. But they also knew firsthand the geography of the area. Hostilities on land began in July and August 1942. Six months later, the Allies had secured Guadalcanal and the coast of Papua near Buna. At the end of 1943, they were fighting on Bougainville or farther up the coast of New Guinea. After a year and a half of struggle, Allied soldiers were still a very long way from Japan. Trapped in the military for the duration of the war, many men began to speculate about a war without end. For a while men accommodated themselves to the fact by allowing routine to shape their lives. Marine Frank Chadwick captures well the combat soldier's view of time:

Every day was the same. There was no Sunday or Monday or Friday. A day was a day. The routine was the same. You did the same thing over and over. You ask someone what day it was, or maybe what month it was, they'd say, "How the hell do I know?" No one kept track. What for? There was no end in sight. All the divisions were on their respective islands: Guadalcanal, the Russells. Waiting for the next move. Everyone was in the same boat. By the time we got through in New Georgia we had been there for a year and a half. In the Solomons, I think everyone recognized the basic strategic situation, but we recognized it better than anyone else. If we were going to seize every island all the way to Japan we'd be 100 years old by the time we got to Tokyo.

When they bypassed Rabaul, the strategy was changed and the pace picked up.

The military did what it could to help sustain men for the long haul. Very early in the struggle, both the American and Australian military were getting mail to the front lines with surprising regularity. Along with letters and parcels from home, some soldiers received news magazines. It is likely that many men in the South Pacific learned more about the "big picture" from *Time* than from the military, albeit two or three weeks late. The mail system was also the source of many small luxuries that in a harsh world were most welcome. The military censored outgoing mail. It also did not allow soldiers to keep diaries. Thousands of Americans back home received letters from distant places with little holes made by the censor's diligent scissors. This was taken by most men as typical military idiocy. One might point out, however, that the Allies frequently gained useful order-of-battle intelligence from Japanese letters and diaries that fell into their hands.

Many men feared and some received the infamous "Dear John" letter. Although a motif in many bad movies, it was a very serious matter. It was a generation that took marriage seriously. Many of the young men in the Pacific had wives, many others were engaged. In addition, soldiers in the South Pacific lived in an entirely male world. Relationships with native women were out of the question. Consequently, the "girl back home" was doubly important to many. One of Ore Marion's fellow Marines received the "letter" from his fiancée while the division was rebuilding in Australia:

During World War II, "Dear John" letters caused as much mayhem with some guys as the slopeheads and Tokyo Rose. "Dear John" letters have never received the attention they should have had. After receiving them during the big war, several men I personally knew threw all caution to the wind and shortly after became combat statistics.

In Australia one of our buddies read his letter and slowly rose from his bunk sobbing and growling. He picked up his metal bunk and threw it halfway through the barracks wall. He went staggering down the Balcombe Hill like a drunk, kicking and throwing rocks, pulling up small trees and shrubs and letting out sobs that made his whole body shudder. No one went after him. It was time to leave a man alone, now. When you have been in combat with a man, you get to know his every ache or pain and we knew our friend was in bad pain. All of us hated that faraway woman we had never seen nor knew, but we hated her then for all the hurt she was causing our buddy.

The NCOs start the big cover-up then and there. Our friend is not reported absent even after he is gone for twenty-four hours. About the middle of the second day, word comes that a constable from a small village five or six miles up the coast is detaining an American corporal. There were no charges, but a request that "someone come get the poor bugger."

Gabe Robidart, who was with the Americal Division on Bougainville, addresses the same subject, but illustrates how it tied into the larger question of absence from home:

"Dear John" letters were terrible. One married guy got a letter that his wife had borne a child with a different man. That was extreme, but we saw many of them. They had a devastating effect on the guys who got them. It was quite a contrast. We were out in the middle of the ocean on an island no one had ever heard of. We lived with secondhand supplies. We patrolled the jungle and faced a lot of fear. Yet life went on in the States without us. I was a young semi-farmboy from California and had joined the division recently. Some of the guys had been called up with the Massachusetts National Guard five years before. We stuck it out and did our job. But it was easy to feel abandoned.

After the sullen reception of the Korean conflict and the turmoil that surrounded Vietnam, veterans of the Pacific are grateful that the country supported them and the war effort. The point is clear enough and honest. On the other hand, a subtle but profound rift occurred between the men abroad and those at home that grew substantially over time. Young men do not have long personal histories.

As many grew to adulthood in faraway places in the company of other soldiers, home grew distant. Soldiers at risk were keenly aware that the hardships of battle were very unevenly distributed. There was bitter feeling directed toward men given military deferments. Many soldiers had grown up in households involved with the political divisions of the Great Depression. There were not large numbers of combat infantry from the Ivy League, and many considered themselves supporters of labor unions and the New Deal. Such sentiments, however, did not keep them from loathing John L. Lewis and other union leaders who led or sanctioned walkouts. The millions of servicemen supporting the relatively small number of soldiers, sailors, and aviators fighting the war were sometimes envied, sometimes scorned, sometimes both. The perception that many fellow servicemen were living lives of relative comfort and safety fueled a profound feeling that they had done their job and it was someone else's turn to face the Japanese. Furthermore, many young soldiers realized that their experiences at the spearpoint of the worst war in history separated them from others.

The Australian soldiers underwent something similar as the war progressed. Bill Crooks reflects on some of these matters from an Australian perspective:

> There was no such thing as rotation in the Australian Army. You went on until you dropped dead, sick, or wounded. We had men wounded three and four times and still returned. The usual rackets went on, of course. You might get your employer to claim he needed you because all of his workers had gone into service. Or maybe your mother, wife, or child was dying. Or better yet, maybe the *farm needed you*. By late 1944 when we were winning and the Americans were more involved, the military considered claims like this. But if you were a proven combat soldier the CO would never approve it. We had the Japs on the run. It was push, push: never give the enemy a chance to turn and dig in. So there was no rotation in the Oz Army.
>
> Men did go home on leave. But you must understand the home front was riddled with lies, distortions, strikes, profit goug-

ing, useless politicians, and corruption. And there was an absolute ignorance of what was going on up front. I think some of us
were relieved to come back to our units.

In late 1944 Mark Durley of the Americal Division received an
emergency home leave because of family illness. (Emergency leaves
were rare and given only to soldiers with long service records.)
Durley's interlude at home was unsettling:

You would meet new people or talk to your family and old
friends. Everyone would ask you how things were "out there." It
was always "out there." At first, I would try to answer the question, and describe the part of the war that I knew. But people
didn't really want an answer to the question. They couldn't understand, and for some reason they didn't want to try. Instead I
would hear all sorts of things about the "hardships" at the home
front. Civilians considered gas rationing, for instance, to be a
major sacrifice. It was a little hard to take. So, after a while, I
would tell people that soldiers kept their beer cold by putting it
in a bucket, filling the bucket half full with gasoline, and let the
evaporation cool the brew. I remember one fellow turning red
with anger at the thought that we were wasting their precious
gasoline. When I returned to my unit after a few weeks it was like
coming home. To me and the men with me, the front was reality.

Marine Louis Maravelas also found that the experience of battle
was a type of chasm between combat soldiers and their countrymen:

A buddy of mine couldn't talk about the war to others. I found
that I couldn't either. We talked about this. We realized we'd
only talk about war with other men that had been there. You
didn't want to talk with civilians. They meant well and I didn't
resent anyone. But people had to appreciate what it meant to be
hungry, tired, and afraid. The folks at home could never understand the feeling. So we kept to ourselves. I found this true with
many veterans over the years. My gosh, it was easy to tell a liar
telling war stories in a bar, and there were a lot of them.

From at least one perspective, the situation in Japan was similar.
Artilleryman Akio Tani served on Guadalcanal, and was one of the

Japanese gunners known collectively by Marines as "Pistol Pete." After the war Tani began an extended correspondence with many Marine veterans of the battle. He describes his experience after he was evacuated from Guadalcanal after suffering excruciating hardships:

> I returned to Tokyo in August 1943 and was made an instructor at the heavy-artillery school there. I was an expert and experienced artilleryman, but nobody wished to hear about what we Guadalcanal veterans had been through. They avoided us at school. They wished not to be exposed to "defeatism." Also we had been through horrors they could never imagine. They could not really comprehend our experiences and they did not want to try. I never returned to frontline service. I wanted to go, but my friends urged me not to; they said I had gone through enough. I guess my commanding officers thought the same way. Other officers I knew were chosen to go to Saipan, the Philippines, and Okinawa. None came back. They were all killed.

Combat soldiers in the South Pacific had to cope with their strange and menacing surroundings day by day. As the months and years dragged on, boredom was also a frequent companion. Consequently, small comforts or amusements that in peacetime would not have been noticed took on great importance at the front.

When Napoleon said that an army travels on its stomach he was expressing an idea as old as war. Soldiers in the South Pacific, who had enemies enough, also had to face military rations. On both New Guinea and Guadalcanal in 1942 the most serious problem was simple quantity. Because military necessity outran the logistic support system in this phase of fighting, American and Australian soldiers faced malnutrition. At both Guadalcanal and Kokoda food shortages for a brief period threatened operations. Life in or near a combat zone is extremely strenuous. It did not help soldiers, facing appalling hardships, to live with a dull hunger weeks on end. On Guadalcanal the 1st Marine Division was saved from genuine crisis by the Japanese supplies they captured in the first days of the invasion. Most Marines gave Japanese canned tuna high marks, and many ate rice in quantity for the first time in their lives. Excellent Japanese beer livened up the first few hours, although some unwary men underestimated the strength of sake. Yet like the AIF in New Guinea, most Marines were soon on two-thirds or one-half rations. The situation improved somewhat in a few weeks, although inadequate rations disturbed operations until December. In New Guinea the quantity of basic supplies increased slowly, although full rations were never available for infantry during the Buna-Gona campaign.

For most men at most times, however, the problem was not quantity but the boring monotony of the fare. At a certain level, although I doubt a soldier who served there would agree, the military did a good job feeding its men. By and large, food was safe and the calorie content adequate. (It is a testimony to the severity of the Depression that many soldiers received much better food in the service than they had seen at home.) Dehydration, still not a culinary art form, allowed much easier transport of bulk foods. Furthermore, the military was not able to call upon a developed agricultural base near the battle zones to supplement rations. On many islands the U.S. Army set up farms, run by natives, that served this function, but the effort did not start producing until later in the war.

The soldiers were faced with the reality of battle cuisine, and few enjoyed it. Joe Salini of the Americal describes GI fare:

We had Spam every day for six months. Then the next six months we had Vienna sausage. Then we received what they called "D rations." It was a kind of chocolate brick that you couldn't break with a brick. Nobody had ever heard of this stuff before. And pancakes like you wouldn't believe, every damn day. Flour and water with syrup made of sugar and water. There was some kind of grease involved. Someone got his hands on a mountain of lousy Australian jam that was always around. Out in the field you had canned rations, usually some kind of stew from World War I, or before for all I know. Field soldiers also got hardtack, a kind of dried cracker that had the texture of wood. You would soak it in coffee and it would blow up like a balloon. For those special occasions we got dehydrated mashed potatoes that had the consistency of mud. No breakfast was complete without wretched dehydrated eggs. Later we started getting some Australian "bully beef." For my money that was the worst. You'd open up these big cans and inside was congealed fat with bits of ancient steer mixed in. Incredible. Rumor had it, the Aussies actually liked the stuff. We did have canned fruit that tasted like food. I honestly think the guys spent more time talking and dreaming about good food then they did about good-looking girls. The Army sure took care of you.

Soldiers were always on the lookout for ways of supplementing rations. Packages from home were one source. Infantryman Raymond Hahn recalls Christmas at Buna:

On Christmas Day some commander gave us a real treat. A special effort was made and much of our accumulated mail was brought up to us. There were several packages. Our lieutenant got a box with sardines and Baby Ruth candy bars which we polished off in a hurry. Another got a box of Fanny Farmer candy and a flat iron. One man got two black neckties, a shoeshine kit, and some phonograph records. Another got two dress shirts. It was a joke. But there was more food, the only thing we were interested in. There were dill pickles, Polish sausage, cake, candy, and one package with several cans of Norwegian crab claws: they were the most wonderful seafood I've ever eaten. I also had the happy, if incongruous, experience of eating caviar within 100 yards of the Japs.

Native settlements were abandoned but occasionally soldiers found poultry or livestock. Paul Sponaugle relates an incident on New Georgia that one hopes is true:

A story made the rounds on New Georgia. We hadn't had a fresh meal in weeks. Supposedly a patrol stumbled on a Jap holding a chicken. The Jap dumps the bird and bolts into the jungle. All the guys raise their weapons, and the sergeant yells, "Hell with the Jap, blast the chicken." The guy sure had his priorities straight.

American and Australian youth were fine sportsmen. Some men actually found time to hunt wild boar (probably feral pigs in most cases) that populated many of the areas. More common was fishing with hand grenades. If the men were near a lagoon, it was a simple matter to drop a few pineapples in and pick up stunned fish. If they collaborated with natives in canoes, the take could be very good. When operating near coconut plantations, many men would overdose on the produce grown in short order. Those fortunate enough to work with natives learned to find various wild fruits. A few lucky soldiers ate delicious wild bananas. Sometimes nature lent a hand. Frank Chadwick describes an unusual bounty that came to his unit on Guadalcanal:

> On Guadalcanal the supply situation varied from one day to the next depending upon which ship had come in. One day, during which we were on single rations, a blue marlin got caught up between a coral reef and the shore. We killed it with a machine gun and hand grenades. That afternoon we had fresh food. It was about ten feet long and maybe 500 pounds. The meat was excellent. It didn't last long in that climate. The next day the boat came in and we had Spam and rice again.

Later in the war occasional luxuries appeared from the military itself. Many units began to get a small beer ration. Rear services received ice cream makers that sometimes made their way to the front. On New Georgia a small allotment of beer and ice cream appeared at the same time, with beer drinkers and ice cream lovers trading their small bounties. Although one might think that the beer would have been in much greater demand, this was not apparently the case. Both Australian and Americans grew up in a time when excellent milk was inexpensive and consumed in large quantities. Fresh milk was one of the most longed-for items. Ice cream, even if made from dried ingredients, was close enough.

One item was uniquely Australian. Immediately behind the front lines during every AIF engagement was a representative of the Australian Salvation Army who dispensed tea to soldiers. These extraordinary people, who suffered tremendous hardship and considerable danger to carry out this simple task, earned the respect and appreciation of thousands of Australian soldiers.

Although it seems odd in our day, soldiers of all armies in the South Pacific received cigarettes as part of their rations. The military dispensed huge quantities to combat zones as soon as possible. If primitive canteens (small stores) run by the military were available, the military sold subsidized cigarettes for rock-bottom prices. Cigarette makers did not produce filtered or low-tar brands. In the American Army, World War II was fought on a steady diet of Chesterfields, Lucky Strikes, Camels, and Pall Malls. As James Salafia recounts, even nonsmokers fell under the onslaught:

After New Georgia the 43d Division returned to Guadalcanal for a while. Once there was a typical supply snafu. It was common to need one thing and get a ton of something else. For some reason everybody in my platoon got twenty-seven cartons of cigarettes. See, we were supposed to get one carton per month. Cigarettes also came in K rations. Our allotment got lost somewhere so here comes the tobacco. Pity for me. I was a nonsmoker and here I had twenty-seven cartons under my bunk. Everyone else had them too, so I couldn't trade them or even give them away. Wouldn't you know it, I started smoking, got hooked, and became a heavy smoker for years. It was a good war for the tobacco industry. We got English cigarettes, we got cigarettes in cans, we got them in every way imaginable.

As Bill Crooks relates, cigarettes were a very serious matter in the Australian Army:

The drug, the soother, the "after dinner drink" so important to combat soldiers was the smoke, the cigarette. Men under the constant threat of death or maiming, plus the nerve-racking experience of waiting before an attack or patrol, needed something. We sometimes did without food. We were often short of water, and would mount special patrols down the rivers, sometimes 2,000 feet down, to get it. But we had to have smokes. It was the *only* factor that would lead the Aussie to lay down his tools and refuse to attack. They did not run away of course, but no smokes, no war. Cigarettes were rationed and stolen by rear-service troops, so the soldiers became wise. A man saved his cigarette butts, added them to used tea leaves, and put them in a tin. He would trade with the natives for their version of tobacco. They would carefully mix the various ingredients, roll them into the thinnest "roll your owns" and light up. It was his nerve soother. Remember, in those days there was no Valium, no serapax, and we had never heard of heroin. Soldiers had little access to grog or booze, so smoke was it. It later ruined the health of many with respiratory and heart problems. Cigarettes have crippled and nearly blinded me. But without cigarettes, there would have been no success in the war. In action and awake twenty-four hours on end, men, myself included, would smoke sixty or seventy a day. You would have dreadful dreams about the deaths of your mates . . . mainly the way they died . . . and what you did in revenge. You would wake up screaming and only a smoke calmed one.

As Crooks also points out, there was a real need for another common vice during war:

It was an unwritten rule that an officer had his weekly issue of Johnnie Walker Scotch whiskey. Most troops were not aware of this. But due to the experiences of World War I, duplicated in the Owen Stanleys, we knew that platoon commanders were the first to get knocked off. Young men were out front with too much responsibility and too much stress. They all had the hip flask of medicinal. The secrecy rarely broke down. The frontline soldiers probably knew. But they also knew that if they reached the "end of the tether" or were badly wounded or sick, they would get a snort too.

No doubt Crooks is right that "grog or booze" was hard to come by for infantry fighting either in the fast-moving slugfest along the Kokoda Trail or the nightmare that ensued at Sanananda and Buna. Guadalcanal and the Solomons were equally violent but more slowly paced. In this environment, American soldiers with a taste for drink devoted their famous ingenuity to making it, trading for it, or stealing it.

An American fighting unit had individuals at hand possessing startling arrays of skills. If one includes the extraordinary American military engineers, there was little limit to what could be done. For sheer ingenuity, few if any units matched the illustrious construction battalions (CBs or Seabees) of the U.S. Navy. The Seabees were a unique institution early in the war. Because the Navy did not have the equivalent of the Army Corps of Engineers, it recruited volunteers directly from the ranks of the construction and trades industry. Given little military training, Seabees were allowed to do what they did best: build things. Henderson Field was their most pressing project, but the Seabee net grew very wide as the months went on. Ultimately they made Guadalcanal, against the expressed wishes of Admiral Nimitiz, into a major rear service base.

Seabees, in startling contrast to Marine combat troops, were older men. The Navy recruited men with skills, and did not expect the physical endurance of youth. Consequently, many Seabees were in their thirties, some older yet. Also, many volunteers came from Appalachia and the South. Memories of Prohibition were fresh enough for many, and more had an acquaintance with federal revenue agents of the Depression pursuing the "moonshiners" in the family. Skilled in many ways, with an adult's taste for liquor, Seabees stood at the center of the production and distribution of alcohol of all sorts. Much of it was homemade. Seabee stills sprouted up within days of the landing on Guadalcanal. The best, run by accomplished moonshiners, produced proper distilled "white lightning" out of anything that would ferment. Those less ambitious produced "raisin-jack," which more closely resembled hard cider. Seabee Jim Rothermal describes the process:

> Every Seabee outfit built stills. I made raisin-jack in five- and ten-gallon batches. You would get a gallon can of raisins and put them in a five-gallon can. You would then fill it with still water and add some yeast. Then in goes five pounds of sugar. Put a stopper in with a rubber hose which you stuck in another can of water so it wouldn't smell. You didn't want a nosy CO or master of arms (Navy MP) to find it. We'd hide it in foxholes. In about twenty days it was ready. Sometimes it was pretty strong, sometimes the batch didn't work out. Depended upon the weather or

something. One batch was outstanding. I filled a soup bowl full, drank it down, and in twenty minutes I could barely walk. Good stuff.

Marine Donald Fall recalls that the soldiers pitched in on the effort themselves:

The real drunks would drain Aqua Velva through bread. They learned a trick from the natives. You could take a coconut, punch three holes in it, pour in sugar, and plug it up again until it fermented. There was some Jap medical alcohol around too: you could dilute it with water in your canteen, and put in powdered lemonade. If you were lucky, you could find little vials of ether, crack them against the canteen, and cool it off. It was like drinking a Tom Collins. If you had this torpedo juice, you could inject it into an orange. I wasn't a drinking man myself, but a lot of the fellows enjoyed a nip.

The Navy was the source of all wonders for combat soldiers. The Army Air Force jealously guarded its smaller supply line of alcohol and soft drinks that came in from rear bases and Australia. Ships, however, are large and even small corners could contain wonderful treasures. Liquor and fresh food were the most sought-after items. As any economist will testify, all trade requires a distribution network. On the islands the Seabees and Navy corpsmen were in excellent positions to act as middlemen in a thriving trade. Protecting free enterprise was, after all, an American war aim.

The most simple medium of exchange was cash. Items such as liquor, cigars, and Cokes fetched astronomic prices for the time. Robert Kennington recalls the exchange rate on Guadalcanal:

We bought medical alcohol from the medics. When we hit the Canal, within two weeks all these guys from the South had a moonshine still up. They sold all they could make for $20 a bottle. We'd cut it in half with grapefruit juice. Seabees were bootlegging real whiskey just like they were running a bar downtown. You could buy all you wanted for $40 a fifth. A friend and I spent three weeks attacking the Gifu Strong Point. The lieutenant sent us back for a five-day rest. We ran into a blackjack game in a tent.

I saw some guy drinking bourbon whiskey and they were smoking cigars. They said it was all for sale from the Seabees. So I sat down and won quite a bit of money. We made a trip to the Seabees and bought eight bottles. We spread it out to the other guys. White Owl cigars, $10 a box; $1.50 for a Coca-Cola. That was a lot of money back then. Some guys sent their money home. But most of us didn't really know what to do with it. There weren't any stores. What was money for? Especially if you might be dead after the next air raid. So you didn't think much about it.

Sometimes barter was involved, as Scott Wilson recalls:

I was in the hospital for about a week after the fighting stopped on Guadalcanal. There was a medic who wanted a Japanese flag. I had five of them. They had a certain smell of death to them. The medic had a movie camera with three lenses and several rolls of raw film. I arranged a trade. I later traded another flag to a fighter pilot for a quart of genuine whiskey, which I sold to another guy in our outfit for $50: he split it in two and sold each half for $30 apiece. Of course there wasn't anything to spend money on, but I thought it was a good deal then.

As Wilson indicates, military souvenirs were highly prized by almost everyone. Battlefields were littered with refuse and, as previously noted, corpses were plentiful. Swords were the most prized items but very rare. (Most Japanese officers did not have valuable swords, and those who did almost never carried them to the front. Most were military issue and not the priceless artifacts that have attracted modern collectors for decades. Few Americans would have known the difference at that time.) Men collected large numbers of weapons, but found them hard to get back to the States. The handsome and practical wooden mess kits carried by Japanese soldiers were very popular. However, Japanese battle flags, borne by all Japanese servicemen, proved popular, portable, and did not raise the ire of superiors. Bud DeVere recalls gathering some booty, and counterfeiting what he could not find:

Often if you had a few hours off you'd go up to the front lines and start souvenir hunting. I was a nineteen-year-old kid. I'd

probably give it more serious thought now, there was risk involved after all. But at the time I wanted a good Japanese sword
or bayonet or a .25-caliber rifle, and then take it back to the
States. I've been an artist all my life. I made Japanese flags out of
parachutes and sold them to sailors. I copied the Japanese char-
acters and sold them for $35 apiece. By the same token the folks
that came in later on ships or transport aircraft brought in whiskey and traded it for weapons and stuff like that. Troops on the
line hadn't seen any decent whiskey for a long time, so if you had
a good weapon, you'd trade it for a bottle of booze. I did find a
U.S. Army saber later and sold that to a sailor as a Japanese
sword.

The saber DeVere found was probably one of hundreds sent to
Guadalcanal to substitute for machetes, which were, for some reason,
in very short supply. Also flag counterfeiting was very widely practiced. Because airfields were rarely far away, damaged parachutes
were about. Skilled practitioners of the art buried their wares for a
week or two so they would take on a faded look and musty odor.
Nevertheless, there were very many of the real items around. After
the war a few American soldiers had second thoughts about what
they had picked up. Henry Dearchs of the 32d Division relates an incident that has dozens of counterparts today:

I was pretty beat up at Buna. It took a while to get back together
after the war. Once I was grocery shopping in Iowa and saw a
Japanese war bride, and for an instant I looked for my rifle. I still
wake up now and get nervous. I picked up a battle flag off dead
Japanese soldiers. A lot of us did. There were enough dead to go
around. Anyway, I knew that the writing on the flag was from
family and so forth. A few years ago, I wrote the Japanese embassy, and sent them a photo of the flag. They answered very
quickly, and said it was authentic and helped me get in touch
with the family in Japan. I guess it was kind of an event back
there. It was in their local newspaper. I got a wonderful letter
from the man's daughter. The town sent me a set of beautiful and
expensive dishes in exchange. I felt pretty good.

If something desirable or necessary was not obtainable through normal channels, or not for sale or barter, soldiers would steal it if possible. This was not theft in the normal sense of the word, although petty crooks and con men existed in large numbers in all the armies. Instead, it was a way for a unit to grease the wheels of the supply system. Anything was fair game. Small items like supplies of canned fruits were very vulnerable. Beer shipments were best guarded with tanks. Probably the single most sought-after big item was a jeep. Jeeps were so valuable and versatile that a unit could never have too many. They all looked the same, so a quick paint job was usually enough to transfer the vehicle from one service to another. Equipment used in combat was normally not tampered with, but behind the lines anything was fair. Units preferred to pilfer from another service but, if required, would pick the pocket of a neighbor.

Harry Bronstein was a medic on Bougainville and describes a good night's pickings:

The perimeter at Bougainville was pretty well built up. There were some tough moments, but mostly we were pretty lucky. That meant we had some time on our hands. Receiving supplies was a little like playing cards: you never knew what the hand would be. One day we were sent a huge supply of shoe polish. You grew to expect that sort of thing, so you'd fend for yourself. Someone at our collecting station decided we needed a generator. We had seen a few that probably had belonged to the Marines stored close to the road. There was a rule on Bougainville that the only vehicles allowed out at night were ambulances. Well, what do you know, we had an ambulance. We went down the road, loaded the generator and no one was the wiser.

According to Joe Salini, jeep hunting was also excellent on Bougainville:

We would take jeeps and go see the movies with other units near the airstrip. When we left, we would take out the magnetos so no one would steal our jeep. Of course, if there was one untended, we stole it. We got more than we lost. A lot of them had been left over by the Marines when they left. People didn't really account

for all this stuff. The waste was extraordinary. When we left
Bougainville in early 1945 we had stolen and gathered so much
equipment that it took a hole half the size of a football field to
bury it. Later Congress got mad about that kind of thing, but
they had no idea how much equipment was left rusting, thrown
over a pier, or buried. Who needed jeeps after the war?

The cumulative effect of wholesale theft led to a never-ending
headache for the men handling logistics. (Of course, it was no secret
that logistics personnel had first crack at desirable items. They were
more strongly monitored, but the opportunities for a big score were
greater. It has never hurt to be friendly with a supply sergeant.) No
doubt many of the stories of military idiocy were due to inventive
soldiers rerouting supplies to their own units.

When the crisis at Guadalcanal passed, space on some transports
was freed for items not considered essential for the war effort but
very good for morale. The Navy found room to ship phonographs to
the battle zone. Responding to massive demand, the Navy also
shipped Coca-Cola in industrial quantities, knocking the bottom out
of the black market for that commodity. A little pressure was put on
moonshiners as weak 3.2 percent beer made its appearance. In some
place volleyball nets showed up, as did softballs. The creation of a
genuine rear area, American-style, was well under way by the beginning of 1944 at Guadalcanal and other parts of the South Pacific.

During quiet times at the front, or, more likely, during the long
periods devoted to rebuilding divisions after battle, there was a good
deal of idle time. Some officers made it a point to keep men busy all
the time, fearing the effect that boredom would have on morale.
Others were more lenient. Scott Wilson of the 25th Division recalls
how he and several of his comrades spent many spare hours:

> I did more reading during my five years in the Army than any
> time before or since. I didn't do that much reading in college.
> Books were widely available. When I was on Guadalcanal, I be-
> longed to the Book-of-the-Month Club. I always had a *Reader's
> Digest* in my pocket: lots of guys subscribed to that. The big
> thing out in the field was playing checkers. We had little boxes

with checkers attached to pegs and you'd play away. If the game was in doubt, you'd close the box, put a rubber band around it, and carry on the next time you had spare time. We didn't have any portable chess sets, but lots of guys played that too.

Young men love music. It was not long before banjos, guitars, and harmonicas started showing up across the Pacific. Sometimes entertainment came to the soldiers. Popular comedian Joe E. Brown brought his act to Guadalcanal in December 1942 while fighting was still in progress. Vincent Seminavege of the 25th Division describes how his unit tried to lighten the load:

Between February 1943 and August 1943 we rested and trained on Guadalcanal to be ready for the next campaign. The kitchen started serving hot meals and we started to put some of our weight back on. We still had our foxholes and Jap air raids were common, but it was better than before. Near the beach someone built a bandstand and a canvas canopy. The division band had served as stretcher-bearers during the battle. Later a Navy ship brought in their instruments. They would put on concerts and skits, something we all enjoyed. One of the great moments for me took place when a friend and I were walking toward the Sea-bee area of the beach. We heard this wonderful music playing, so we went to check it out. There was Artie Shaw playing his clarinet with a few of his band members. After they were done they were nice enough to talk with us. He was one of the most famous musicians in the country then, and it was something just to run into him.

Another source of music entertained thousands of Allied soldiers. If they served near a command post or an area that had a radio, men could listen to the music and propaganda broadcast by the Japanese. The radio hostess was the famed Tokyo Rose. Stories of Rose are legion among veterans. Her ability to predict the movement of troops has, perhaps, been exaggerated. Nevertheless, Rose did personalize many messages to specific units, which both amused and unsettled the soldiers involved. Robert Kennington was a fan of Tokyo Rose:

Tokyo Rose played all kinds of popular and sentimental music. She sent messages to us on Guadalcanal and Vella Lavella. She had a soothing voice and told us to lay down our weapons. The first night on Vella Lavella she said hello to our unit. She said as soon as we got into the jungle Japanese troops were coming, so we should surrender right away. A guy got angry and let a shot fly toward the hills, hoping to hit her. Most of the guys would lie back, enjoy it, and just say "Play it pretty, Rose." I never could figure out if the Japanese really thought someone would surrender.

For a small number of men, little corners appeared in their malignant universe in which they found a type of exotic magic. Unlike the other theaters in World War II, or the other American wars of the twentieth century for that matter, it was not feasible for combat soldiers to "go native" in the South Pacific. Yet circumstances would throw individuals or units into places where the level of threat was low, life was comfortable, and the war far away. Some soldiers serving along the New Guinea coast in 1943 became involved with the locals, learned "pidgin," and experienced a bit of the unusual mixture of peoples and technology that characterized life there before the war. Frank Marks, a longtime NCO with the 25th Division, found a bit of paradise on Vella Lavella:

When we landed on Vella Lavella in late July, we were told to watch out for survivors from some Jap troop-carrying barges sunk by our Navy. We went down the shoreline a few thousand yards from where we landed. We met no resistance, but the entire shoreline was covered with the bodies of dead Japanese who had washed ashore from the barges we had sunk. We were at a mission on the shore of a little lagoon which consisted of two or three small tin-roofed buildings. In the weeks that followed we suffered many air raids but not battle. The raids tapered off and the dead washed away. We took canoes and whaling boats to small nearby islands, once looking for shot-down Japanese airmen, another time investigating reports of a "white woman." We never found a thing.

After the combat we experienced on Guadalcanal, being on Vella Lavella was almost like having a vacation. Of all the places we went and territory we saw, Vella Lavella was tops. I would have been satisfied if they had dropped me off and let me live the rest of my life at the lagoon where the mission was located. It was like what most people would envision a tropical paradise to be. If I could afford to, I would like to go back. I would say my vision of the areas we encountered and the way I saw things was a great deal different from the majority of our men. I was "all volunteer" while most of the others were draftees and hated the fact that they were even in the service.

One crucial aspect of morale is impossible to ignore but extremely difficult to describe. American and Australian soldiers both possessed a dry, cynical, and dark sense of humor that is hilarious if one is privileged to hear it firsthand. A shared type of wit was certainly a major reason why American and Australian troops collaborated so well at the front when thrown together on a daily basis. (Their respective commanding officers had less to laugh about, and bickered continually.) This black humor served many purposes. It was an effective, and safe, way of expressing scorn at the sort of idiocy that comes with military life in every war. It was an extremely effective way to get a serious message across to one's fellows or superiors. It was also a genuine and effective defense against fear. Trooper Fredy Beale was one of the AIF veterans reassigned from the Middle East to New Guinea. His description of his introduction into his new battle zone is a choice example of making it through a bizarre and sinister moment:

I will never forget my first day in action in New Guinea. My knees were knocking, my heart was pounding, and I was *frightened* all day. And to make things worse, it was raining like hell. We were in single file following the leader, wading in green sludge and slime. I was nearly buggered, when one of my mates yelled out, "Hey Fredy, step over the log, but watch out because the water is deep on the other side." Unfortunately for me, I was one of the shortest boys and when I stepped over the log I sank right down to my waist in the muddy water, and the so-called log slid under my groin. When I looked down at it, a Jap skull was looking up at me, with no eyes, no nose, and a hole where his mouth was. Well, my hair stood straight up, and my helmet tipped over my forehead. I grabbed a prickly vine for support, and my stomach was coming up to my throat, but I had to keep on walking, or I would have been lost.

When I caught up to my mates and told them, they just laughed, but I was one sick boy. A bit farther along I felt a lot better because of one of my mates at the head of the pack. I saw this clean skull of a Jap, stuck on a stick, with a condom hanging from its nose, a note was also hanging from the stick that read "This will happen to you if you don't take your Atabrine." For a few moments I forgot about the war and my stomach. I just stood there and laughed like hell.

In one lone respect, geography was kind to American soldiers in the South Pacific. Most airmen had some sort of rotation policy that got them back to the States for extended periods. Sailors spent much time at the pleasant bases at New Caledonia or Espiritu Santo, and most found their way to Pearl Harbor or the West Coast of the United States when their ships required major refitting. Soldiers, however, were stuck in the South Pacific. And yet many of them who survived combat at one time or another were granted rest and recreation leave in what many men called the Land of Oz, Australia.

The Land of Oz

Washington based three American divisions (the 1st Marine, 32d, and 41st) in Australia during 1942–43. The divisional camps were near or north of Brisbane and were fairly primitive places to begin with. When the 32d Division returned from Buna it was sent to a camp outside Brisbane that, according to Dick Randles, was a "tent city out in the bush with kangaroos running through it." Compared to Buna or Guadalcanal, however, a spartan camp in Australia was a splendid home. Most important, it meant good food. Beef, lamb, vegetables, butter, and milk were all things soldiers or Marines would have risked injury to obtain at the front, and all were plentiful in Australia. The military allowed the men to rest, put on weight, and treat the diseases most of them carried. (Malaria was not unknown near Brisbane. The Marines were moved to Ballarat, near Melbourne, because of this. Army mosquito-control personnel ultimately reduced the problem to a nuisance level.) The Americans took in replacements and put to use what they had learned in battle in a major retraining program. Slowly the divisions rejuvenated. Both the 32d and 41st were certainly better divisions after this period. The Marines perhaps never regained the unique spirit they carried to Guadalcanal. However, when they finally left Australia they were better trained technically, a sophistication they sorely needed for the nightmare that awaited them in 1944.

Although most of the time spent in Australia was dedicated to soldiering, the men best remember leave. Australia was big steaks, strong drink, real cities, hotels, and girls. And most of the people liked American soldiers. Australian civilians treated the 1st Marines when they came in from Guadalcanal like heroes. When the Marines paraded on ANZAC Day in Sydney, they were the featured attraction. (This attention did not sit well with everyone in the AIF, as one might imagine. They too rebuilt in Australia, but were preparing already for their next offensive.) Marine Donald Fall recalls his days in Melbourne:

> I always found someone during service to call me son. I wasn't a drinking man, with a couple of exceptions. In Melbourne it was a woman who owned the New Yorker Hotel. Even if I didn't have a reservation, she'd know if someone wasn't coming in. I wasn't much of a drinking man, so I was a bit of a loner. I got interested in figure skating. I also liked the ladies. I'd skate all day and then go to the ballroom and dance until one in the morning. You couldn't come out with one girl. You'd have four or five on your arm. The Australian fellows didn't treat women the way we did. We spoiled them. When the Australian division came back from the Mideast all hell could have broken loose. It was tense sometimes. I remember we had a great big beer party on the cricket grounds to soothe the feelings. You'd go out with a girl in

Australia, and she said, "Yank, I know what you're after and you ain't going to get it. You want to go and have a good time?" And you'd go and have a good time. Yet we were there for nine months, and when we left there were plenty of pregnant women waving good-bye on the docks. I tried for fifteen years to talk my wife into moving to Australia. It was kind of like the States twenty years behind, which is good if you ask me.

Many of the younger Marines and soldiers, already introduced to war, were also introduced to liquor and various temptations available in the city. Lou Maravelas went with his young Marines into Melbourne soon after their arrival at Ballarat:

It was overwhelming. We were heroes in Australia and it felt great. At first, you couldn't buy your own drink in an Aussie bar. Aussie beer is stronger than what we were used to. A lot of our soldiers had never really done any drinking. But what the wonderful civilians didn't understand, and I guess we didn't really either, was that we all had malaria. Our systems were still very weak. So we got drunk real fast. There were Marines falling on the ground all over the place. They thought our guys couldn't handle their drink. Probably true of some of the kids, and Australians set high standards when it came to drink. But as our guys gained strength, we put on a respectable showing. They were wonderful people. I'll never forget them.

Dick Randles, after three months at Buna, was on his way to a vacation in Sydney. As he relates, he never made it. Instead he spent some time on what is now Australia's famous Gold Coast:

I got a leave to Sydney. I got on a train. Not far south we had to change trains. For some reasons that only the Australians know, the gauge was different from one state to another. Like Russia and Western Europe. Anyway, during the layover I went to a pub nearby. I never did go on to Sydney. I just stayed there on that beautiful beach that runs for miles and miles. It was gorgeous. I had a fine time. It was wonderful. I got a room right up over the pub. Rested in paradise and drank great Australian beer. Sure beat Buna.

In theory, the 1st Marine Division had gone to join MacArthur's forces in the Southwest Pacific Command. In practice, they had a small but nasty campaign at Cape Gloucester before the Navy reclaimed them for operations in the Central Pacific. The other divisions that served with them in the Solomons for the most part received their R&R in New Zealand. The atmosphere there was somewhat different than in Australia. Because the population was so much smaller and the society largely agrarian, the impact of huge numbers of American servicemen was unsettling to some of the people. Americans who enjoyed the urban attractions of Sydney or Melbourne found New Zealand a bit sleepy. As one pilot put it, "New Zealand during World War II was the world's most beautiful small town." On the other hand, many American servicemen loved the country for that very reason. Scott Wilson's unit of the 25th Division went to New Zealand after the campaign on New Georgia:

> The best three months in the Army were R and R in New Zealand. There was no training, and no real duty. There was a combined mess with the 3d Marines, but I can't remember eating in the mess hall. Because everyone was on pass, some of our mess sergeants had so much food left over they would take it to their girlfriends' families. We ate wonderful food. The men from small towns and farms were right at home. The country was so beautiful. Almost everyone had a horse. It was hard to do, but I know there were several marriages eventually. Most of the people were extremely friendly and many invited soldiers to their houses.
>
> Many of New Zealand's servicemen were in Europe. There was a lot of dating between our guys and the local girls. It caused some friction. One night I was at the movies in Auckland and *Bambi* was playing. There was a part of the film where Bambi's mother is killed and Bambi is saying, "Where's mother?" Some New Zealand sailor yelled out: "Don't worry, kid, she's probably out with some bloody Yank." People collapsed with laughter.

Another common stop for several units or soldiers in need of temporary hospital care was the island of New Caledonia. The capital of the nominally Free French colony was the sleepy coastal town of Noumea. A thousand miles southeast of Guadalcanal, New Caledonia was a lovely island that was drier than the Solomons and malaria-free. Having a long and deeper contact with Europe than the lands in the battle zone, New Caledonia possessed some of the accoutrements of colonial society. Robert Ballantine trained with the 25th Division on New Caledonia in late 1943. To a veteran of the prewar Army, it brought back some memories:

> New Caledonia was a very interesting place. After we left Hawaii and until we reached the Philippines, outside of rest and recreation leave, most of us never saw a young woman. That's two years. New Caledonia was crawling with soldiers and sailors. It was a French colony and you could buy wine and things like that. There were some pretty half-caste girls. But the local cathouse was the main point of interest. It was called the Greenhouse. The MPs used to stand outside making sure that the lines were orderly and that everyone got their turn. They did the same thing at some of the establishments in Hawaii. No one was complaining as long as there was enough to go around.

Yet even in safe, faraway, and beautiful places the war could intrude. In late 1942 the 43d Division was on New Caledonia awaiting movement forward. James Salafia was on beach patrol and first confronted war:

> We were guarding the beach at New Caledonia. One day on guard I saw a speck off in the water. It came closer and it turned out to be a lifeboat filled with fifteen or twenty guys. They were covered with oil and all half dead. The sailors had come from an Australian tanker torpedoed by a Japanese submarine. All of them had jumped into the water. This group survived, but they were in a horrible shape. Many were badly burned. Blistered and covered with oil, it was hard to recognize some as people. All were suffering from thirst. They could barely talk, or barely see, but they were awfully glad to see me. I got them to the aid station immediately and all survived as I understand. It was the sort of thing you see in the movies. Except this was real. It wasn't quite what I expected to find during a nice stroll down the beach.

Despite all the efforts on the part of the military and the men themselves, morale among the fighting troops was subject to intricate fluctuations. In the fall of 1943 the military started detecting things they did not like. More and more of the men were conscripts. Most draftees did their job with dedication and honor, but the "children's crusade" that, in conjunction with the fierce professionalism of the AIF, had stopped the Japanese in their tracks in late 1942 was coming to an end. Tokyo was a very long way away. After New Georgia and Lae, the Allied progress, considering the cost, was painfully slow. The morale of Allied units remained good, but it was unquestionably starting to waver among the men who had gone to the well too often. The war was in the doldrums. All could see that Japan was not going to win. Yet no one could see an Allied victory in the foreseeable future. Had the situation remained like this for an extended period, the momentum of events might have slowed considerably. We shall never know. In a very short time, rather than looking at a war with no end in sight, the Allies smashed the Japanese in the South Pacific and brought the battleground to Japan's doorstep.

Chapter 6

The War Leaves the South Pacific

I n retrospect, we can see that the Japanese were losing their ability to control events very early in the struggle for the South Pacific. When the AIF and the Marines held their ground in the fall of 1942, and later pushed the Japanese back, these were not local reverses but a fundamental shift in the pattern of the war. This was not obvious at the time in Tokyo, Canberra, or Washington. The Japanese worried about the ramifications of the twin defeats at Buna and Guadalcanal, but believed that the major reinforcements they sent to New Guinea and Rabaul could restore the situation. With their fleet intact, they had hopes of rebuilding their carrier forces in preparation for a great "decisive battle" with the Americans. Allied forces were so badly mangled by their "victories" at Guadalcanal and Buna that only a relatively small land campaign near Wau in New Guinea took place in the first half of 1943. Nevertheless, to the shock of leaders in Tokyo, in late 1943 the entire Japanese position in the South Pacific fell apart in a matter of months.

The Japanese Collapse

Had one known where to look in the summer of 1943, the signs of the impending obliteration of Japan's position in the South Pacific were plain enough. Some things were mundane. As Joe Salini observed, "On Guadalcanal we had Spam for Thanksgiving. But on Christmas, and I remember this well, we had a turkey dinner." The logistic apparatus, in other words, was beginning to work. The South

Pacific, compared to Europe, remained a poor relative in terms of support. Yet the Allies did not require the technological power to subdue Japan that was necessary to defeat Germany. No American or Australian force in the Pacific went into battle on a shoestring again.

They also did not have to enter battle blind again. Allied tactical intelligence by mid-1943 was much more sophisticated than it had been a year before. The Allies pooled some of their linguistic resources and created a joint translation and interpreter section that provided invaluable order-of-battle intelligence to the front lines. (This group caused difficulties for MacArthur on several occasions when their findings, usually more pessimistic, clashed with official intelligence estimates. The linguists were rarely wrong.) Also air reconnaissance, combined with proper utilization of information that already existed, allowed Allied cartographers to make and distribute more or less accurate maps.

The Americans started to supply their forces with new weapons in early 1943. Modern fighter aircraft like the P-38 Lightning and the F-4U Corsair established qualitative superiority over the redoubtable Japanese Zero and its poor cousins flown by Japanese Army pilots. The Army's Fifth Air Force in New Guinea developed specialized low-level tactics to destroy shipping and air bases with its B-25 Mitchell medium bombers. In March 1943 Australian and American planes devastated a large Japanese troop convoy in the Bismarck Sea off the coast of New Guinea, serving dramatic notice that the Japanese could reinforce that front only by landing far to the east. Just as important, more C-47 combat transports were on the way, eliminating or alleviating the crippling effect that the jungle had on supply and allowing better advance medical care and better evacuation service. Although the statistics are not clear, there appears to have been a major drop in the killed/wounded ratio between 1942 and 1943 (approximately one to three at Guadalcanal and Kokoda-Buna, approximately one to four and a half thereafter). In turn, as ground units advanced, they built new airfields.

The American Navy too was gradually going through a metamorphosis. The prewar fleet was badly battered in a series of fierce battles off Guadalcanal. The Japanese too took a pounding. But

American shipyards by late 1942 were launching dozens of new capital ships and hundreds of smaller warships. Modern destroyers, carrying improved torpedoes, arrived weekly, joining new cruiser flotillas. The Navy modernized the older ships to such a degree that they were essentially new designs. Powerful 20mm and 40mm anti-aircraft guns sprouted on unoccupied spots on ships. In January 1943 the great light cruiser *Helena* shot down a Japanese plane with a "proximity fuze," a revolutionary weapon that detonated a five-inch shell when it passed near an aircraft. Although not apparent at the moment, American warships were becoming almost invulnerable to conventional Japanese air attack. This was a terrible situation for the Japanese, who placed great importance on the ability of their land-based aircraft to parry American fleet movements.

Worse yet, from the Japanese point of view, was the condition of American aircraft carriers. In the battles of 1942 the American and Japanese navies almost eliminated each other's prewar carrier fleets. After November 1942, when the *Enterprise* played a central role in smashing Japan's last attempt at victory on Guadalcanal, both sides withdrew what little remained of their carrier forces. (The *Saratoga* remained in reserve in the South Pacific throughout 1943, Halsey finding no reason to risk it in battle. For a short time the British carrier *Victorious* also helped keep a vigil for Japanese carriers that never sortied. The Navy sent the *Enterprise* to Seattle in 1943 for a much-needed refitting.) However, steadily during 1943 the Navy commissioned one modern carrier after another. It was only a matter of time before a much larger and much better carrier fleet returned to action.

From the infantry's point of view, the most important addition to the arsenal was the arrival in early 1943 of the first LSTs (landing ship, tank) and LSIs (landing ship, infantry). Along with other large specialized landing craft, and a general increase in merchant shipping, infantry could bring with them heavy supporting arms: proper artillery, large amounts of ammunition, trucks, and tanks. All the engineering weapons—like flamethrowers, so useful against Japanese field fortifications—that before were rare became common. William Schumacher, a junior officer in the 25th Division, discusses the transformation of his unit:

A lot changed after we gathered in New Caledonia after the New Georgia operation. Previously there had been very little tension between fighting men and service troops in the rear. However, the rear was growing greatly, and it was most obvious that they were living a lot better then we were and were a lot safer. A lot of men did not like this, but I guess it was true in every war. On the other hand, the contrast with Guadalcanal was extraordinary as we built up for the Philippines. On New Caledonia, training was intensive. We went into Guadalcanal with 10 percent of our divisional transportation. And they took half of that away. On New Caledonia they brought us nearly up to strength. I wound up with twenty-four jeeps and trailers to carry my mortars. They also issued us M1 carbines and bazookas. [The bazooka was an individually fired rocket launcher used against tanks and bunkers.—EB] Both were useful weapons against Japanese positions.

There was an across-the-board improvement of rear services. Preventive medical care and general hygiene improved. Although many men continued to live in hard conditions, many others had a much more tolerable life. Jack Williamson was one of the C-47 pilots attached to MacArthur's headquarters at Lae. The conditions he describes in early 1944 would have been unimaginable a year earlier:

Our aircraft was one of several for flying VIPs around New Guinea. Several congressmen came out and officials from the State Department and military. Our crew lived pretty well at that time. We had movies most nights. The chemical people would spray the area to keep the mosquitoes away for the evening. They cleared out the wretched anthills that were common. The soldiers did a lot of trading with the natives for souvenirs and food. Nearby a native chief used a downed Japanese bomber as his house. If we could identify them, we'd try to guard wild banana trees. The fruit was delicious but few stalks were fertile. Of course, the natives usually got there first, so we would have to trade with them. It was very interesting duty.

All these factors were incremental. It is very possible that the Allied commanders, planning in the immediate aftermath of the defeats and very hard-fought victories experienced in 1942, realized how much their position had improved. Whether it was apparent or not, in later summer and early fall of 1943 the Allied war effort began to move into high gear. There was a large quantitative increase of forces of all types. Washington provided new Army, Marine, and Navy land-based air groups for the theater, and increased the replacement rates for old ones. The Army's Fifth Air Force in New Guinea nearly doubled in size in this period. Land forces likewise began to redeploy and build. The Australian Militia divisions, well trained and led by veteran AIF officers, became available for overseas service. The AIF 9th Division returned to Australia after its splendid service at El Alamein. Organized into a three-division corps with the 6th and 7th AIF divisions, the Australians had a splendid elite strike force supported by good standard divisions. Washington also reinforced American ground forces. In the space of a few months in the fall of 1943 General MacArthur received the 1st Cavalry and the 6th, 24th, 31st, and 40th divisions. After December he lost the Marines, but the obvious American buildup in the Central Pacific put Tokyo into yet another bind, more than compensating for the Marines' departure.

The flow of battle reflected the steady Allied buildup. As noted previously, Halsey's attack on New Georgia in July 1943, although well supported with air and artillery, was a poorly managed and violent affair that was proof of Japanese skill in defense and the continued weakness of "green" American units. Although a bad hour, much was redeemed by Halsey's brilliant stroke at Vella Lavella, which unhinged the Japanese defense in the Solomons east of Bougainville.

At the same time, MacArthur and the Australians developed a sophisticated plan of operations for New Guinea. In the first phase, Australian infantry, supported by C-47s, advanced out of Wau toward the coast at Salamaua. Elements of the American 41st Division landed on the coast at Nassau Bay, extended their line inland, and linked up with the Australians. A slow, cautious, but well-run campaign followed in some of the worst terrain in New Guinea. Fighting ridgeline by ridgeline, the Allies forced back the Japanese and took Salamaua in early September 1943. The settlement was so foul, and the airstrip there on such poor ground, that the Allies abandoned their plan to use Salamaua as an advanced base. On paper, this might have looked like a another New Georgia, although with far less cost. In fact, the operation was a brilliant ruse designed to draw Japanese defenders south from Lae to defend Salamaua. This part of the operations succeeded well, as 10,000 Japanese infantry took the bait, many of them killed in the process. In September, the Allied avalanche began.

The first blow was a textbook attack on Lae by the AIF. In the first week of September the 9th AIF Division, using MacArthur's new landing craft and naval support, landed twenty miles east of Lae. At the same time American paratroopers seized the undefended airfield at Nadzab a few miles northwest of the objective. A steady stream of C-47s deployed the AIF 7th Division at Nadzab and it began a march through relatively open terrain toward Lae. Caught in a vise, Tokyo decided to abandon Lae. Already battered by disease, malnutrition, and battle losses at Salamaua, the Japanese defenders knew they could not retreat up the Ramu-Markham Valley. The terrain was good and forage was available in the valley, but the Australians would have crushed the Japanese in the open. Consequently, the Japanese began the first of their grueling overland retreats through the fierce New Guinea mountains during which, as one Japanese officer put it, the men survived on "potatoes and grass." (Movement through the mountains on the Huon Peninsula, done by both sides, was more difficult than traversing the Kokada Trail. The terrain was so foul that battle was almost impossible in the worst areas.)

Heavily reinforced with new squadrons and able to use new airstrips farther north, in the fall American and Australian warplanes of the Fifth Air Force began a withering assault. They were supported by Army, Marine, and Navy squadrons operating in the Solomons. The targets were the Japanese Navy Air Force at Rabaul and the Japanese Army Air Force deployed at a network of small bases near Wewak in New Guinea. In December, American carriers briefly joined the attack on Rabaul. By February 1944, Japanese airpower in the South Pacific did not exist.

In theory the advance up the New Guinea coast and the drive up the Solomons were aimed at the capture of Rabaul. In the fall, both sides reassessed their goals. In Tokyo the Japanese were shocked by the sudden collapse at Lae, particularly after suffering a string of defeats elsewhere. They had lost Attu and Kiska in the Aleutians. They also knew that Nimitz was soon going to move into the Central Pacific. Consequently, Tokyo drew a new boundary for the "absolute defense zone" of the Empire. The new line ran through the East Indies, the western quarter of New Guinea, west to Truk, northwest to Saipan, and northeast to Japan. This left Rabaul and most of New Guinea outside the zone. Nevertheless, the Japanese reinforced Rabaul and New Guinea with land forces, ordering them to delay the Allied advance and inflict as much pain as possible. Ships and aircraft were growing scarce, as was the oil to operate them and the technology to service them. Japanese infantry, however, were there to sacrifice if the transport was available.

In August 1943 the American Joint Chiefs could also see that the war was going in their favor. They suggested to MacArthur that he bypass the Japanese stronghold at Rabaul and extend operations farther up the coast of New Guinea. Washington also authorized MacArthur to seize the Admiralty Islands lying northwest of Rabaul, completing the isolation of the Japanese base. When a string of mutually supporting bases was seized on New Guinea, Washington promised MacArthur that he could then move against the Philippines. The Australians would push into the East Indies. These decisions, ironically taken before Tokyo's establishment of the "absolute" defense line, rendered Japanese plans useless. MacArthur did not intend to clear whole areas; instead he was after small strategic points that could serve as bases. In addition, MacArthur had no intention of landing where the Japanese were strong. Consequently, every Japanese soldier sent to Rabaul or New Guinea entered a POW camp, or cemetery, of immense size. This was obvious very quickly.

It was AIF policy to pursue the enemy if at all possible. As soon as Lae was in the sack, two AIF brigades began an overland advance through the Ramu-Markham Valley. Supplied largely by air, the force moved quickly over the open terrain and by October was far behind Japanese positions on the coast. At the same time, other AIF units landed at the key Japanese base of Finschhafen at the easternmost point of the Huon Peninsula. Seeing that their entire position was in danger, the Japanese rushed a new division to the area and attacked the Australian beachhead in early October. After a few tense moments, the AIF crushed the attack and resumed the advance.

The Australian juggernaut was not only rolling, it was doing so with very little cost in Australian lives. Disease preyed upon all soldiers in New Guinea until the end. The Japanese, however, were losing their ability to cause pain to their enemies. Fewer than 1,000 Australian soldiers were killed from February 1, 1943 (the end of the Buna-Gona-Sanananda campaign) until January 1944. During the large Japanese attack on Finschhafen, fifty-two Australian soldiers lost their lives, a minuscule figure in the grim arithmetic of war. In the process, in addition to the 13,000 dead suffered in Kokoda-Buna, the Japanese lost another 30,000 men. We will never know exactly how many died in battle, but the "kill ratio" on New Guinea was mounting to levels rarely seen in modern war. It is worth noting that in none of these battles did the Japanese make a suicidal last stand as they did at Buna or parts of Guadalcanal. The standard troops of the Imperial Army were not as good as the elite forces of 1942. Unable to fight on even terms, their commanders were not as quick as their counterparts in 1942 to throw away the lives of their men. Ultimately perhaps half of the 180,000-man Japanese Army sent to New Guinea returned to Japan, after existing for a year and a half in total isolation.

As the AIF went from victory to victory in the Huon Peninsula, the Americans also pressed forward with an increasing momentum. The long-expected drive in the Central Pacific opened in November 1943 with the attack on Tarawa and Maikin in the Gilbert Islands. (On Tarawa, the 2d Marine Division lost 979 men killed; more than the 1st Marines lost on Guadalcanal and more than the entire AIF lost in the Huon Gulf campaign.) At the same time in the Solomons the 3d Marines seized a small perimeter on the island of Bougainville with little loss. Shortly thereafter, the 1st Marines took another perimeter at Cape Gloucester on the Island of New Britain.

In retrospect all American commanders agreed that the Cape Gloucester landing was unnecessary. Fortunately, Marine losses were small.

Adding to the weight of the great Australian victories, American troops also delivered a heavy blow to Japanese resistance on New Guinea. In January 1944 the 32d Division, finally rebuilt after the Buna debacle, landed at Saidor on the New Guinea coast. By doing so, it broke in two the Japanese Eighteenth Army on New Guinea and isolated the two Japanese divisions opposing the AIF. Once again the Japanese retreated overland and suffered a severe punishment from the jungle and mountains. Meredith Huggins, who had played a prominent role at Sanananda, was at Saidor and recalls the extraordinary contrast between the two campaigns:

> When we landed at Saidor it was an amazing sight. There were dozens of warships bombarding the coast. The sound was like a rolling thunder and the smoke hung along the ground. As we approached the beach, air attacks began. Heavy bombers dropped their load of high explosive from a few thousand feet. Then came in the B-25 strafers shooting everything in sight, clobbering positions. Behind them came fighters to give the Japs a final working over. There was very little opposition when we landed. We found a few Japs wandering around in shell shock. What a contrast from the days at Buna and Sanananda, only a year before, when we were fighting with rifles, grenades, and rocks!

Saidor was a crushing blow to the Japanese, but only the first. In early 1944 the Americans seized the Admiralties, and one perimeter after another on the coast of New Guinea. With few exceptions Japanese resistance was weak and ineffective. Excluding disease and accident, American combat casualties were minute, particularly when compared to the bloodbaths taking place on the Central Pacific islands, which were too small to employ the "hit them where they ain't" tactics that MacArthur and Halsey learned to favor in the South Pacific.

As the Australians and Americans destroyed Rabaul's military value and moved rapidly up the New Guinea coast toward the Phil-

ippines and the East Indies, the war moved steadily out of the South
Pacific. Fiercely contested battlefields such as Guadalcanal and
Milne Bay became major rear-base areas. Others like Munda Point
started to wither, becoming almost irrelevant outposts in a fast-
moving war. Once the area of operations for the finest troops the
warring nations could muster, the South Pacific became a dumping
ground for men suffering from battle fatigue and those earning well-
deserved leaves. The skies and sea-lanes, so fiercely contested as late
as the fall of 1943, were empty of the Japanese by April 1944. The
South Pacific, which for nearly two years was the nexus of a harsh
war, had become the rear.

The Last Banzai

Sadly, the Japanese insisted on one final violent act in the vicious
saga, long after it had any military logic. As noted, in November
1943 the Marines seized a perimeter at Empress Augusta Bay on the
island of Bougainville. Although the terrain and climate were particularly foul, Japanese resistance was light. Seabees and Army Engineers quickly developed three airstrips near the Torokina River to
support the final destruction of Rabaul. Their work complete, the
Marines left for far more brutal operations in Admiral King's blood-
soaked Central Pacific offensive. The Army sent the 37th and Americal divisions to replace the Marines and establish a perimeter around
the air base.

Bougainville was a large island, covered with dense jungle and
dominated by a series of ridgelines, each rising progressively higher
until they reached a mountain range that ran through the center of
the island. One of the largest peaks, Mount Bagana, an active vol-
cano, was close to the American perimeter and created a spectacular
backdrop to events. The indigenous inhabitants had no love of outsiders and killed the unwary of both sides with considerable enthusiasm. There was no plan nor reason to expand the American presence
beyond the vicinity of the Torokina air base. Had the situation been
left up to the men and officers of the American divisions, they would

have guarded their little perimeter for as long as necessary, and the devil could have taken the remainder of the island.

When the Americans landed on November 1, 1943, two full Japanese divisions along with naval personnel were awaiting the attack on the southeastern portion of the island where the Japanese had built the Buin airfield complex and had a good anchorage. By January it was obvious that the Americans were not planning to come to the defenders, and were content to build their own strip and let the Japanese sit in the Buin area until the end of the war. Ironically, the Japanese commander at Bougainville was Lieutenant General Haruyoshi Hyakutake, the commander of Japanese ground operations at Guadalcanal. Unfortunately for all concerned, the local Imperial Army Headquarters at Rabaul ordered Hyakutake to wipe out the Torokina air base. Apparently Hyakutake's intelligence officers played a role in precipitating the catastrophe to come. They estimated that the American perimeter held 30,000 men, 10,000 of whom were there to support the air groups. In truth, the Americans were almost twice that strong. In addition to two full infantry divisions, there was a Marine defense battalion, a tank battalion, and powerful antiaircraft units that were well suited for use against ground troops.

In late January the Japanese began moving slowly toward the American perimeter. Approximately 19,000 infantry, carrying two weeks' rations, started out along both coastlines, converging near Torokina. Having learned much about the perils of moving through the jungle, Japanese engineers created crude roads that enabled trucks and horses to move supplies reasonably close to Torokina. By using barges at night, the Japanese landed four 150mm and two 105mm howitzers, which they laboriously dragged onto a ridgeline overlooking the Americans. These six large pieces had a pitiful 300 rounds of ammunition per tube. The Japanese also had a much larger number of 75mm pack howitzers. According to "paper strength," they could have possessed as many as 168 of these small pieces. American intelligence later estimated the number at closer to fifty. They were better supplied with ammunition than the larger howitzers but, as events proved dramatically, were incapable of standing up to American artillery in a slugging match. Japanese gunners had one small advantage. Because each ridgeline was somewhat higher than the next, the ridges occupied by the Japanese afforded a good look at the American position. It was not enough.

As it stood, Hyakutake gathered the largest Japanese artillery and troop concentration destined to fight in the South Pacific at a single place. The Japanese 6th Division, the main striking force, was a crack division with long experience in China. If Japanese soldiers and equipment had been at Guadalcanal in such numbers at a single time, the Marines would have been in trouble. However, the Allied war effort had made a quantitative and qualitative leap that the Japanese could never follow. On Bougainville, the Japanese force was completely, stupidly, inadequate in every possible way.

The Japanese attack was the worst-kept secret of the war in the South Pacific. The logic of the situation, given the past Japanese record, suggested they would attack. Every branch of Allied intelligence picked up signs of troop movements. In February a series of firefights began near advance Allied outposts. Americans and Fijian Scouts took several prisoners and a few deserters who were willing to tell what they knew. Most important, the Japanese Army, because its field communications were so poor and its attacks so complex, distributed written orders far down the chain of command. Consequently, weeks before the Japanese Army on Bougainville began its death ride, papers collected from corpses gave American commanders a very clear idea of the general Japanese plan of attack.

Knowing what was coming, the Americans built up their perimeter quickly and efficiently. The situation resembled Buna in reverse. At Buna, Japanese engineers had several weeks to prepare fortifications that caused agony to the Allied light-infantry armies that attacked them. As good as Japanese engineers were at constructing field fortifications using simple equipment and materials at hand, American engineers were far better trained and equipped. They spent weeks preparing fixed fortifications of great strength. Furthermore, realizing that a major assault was near, American combat infantry, normally the planet's most unwilling diggers, and support troops alike put their backs into the defense effort.

Along the shoreline the base of the Torokina perimeter was approximately 11,000 yards long. Following the Torokina River on the west, the thumb-shaped salient projected 8,000 yards to the northeast. The northern sectors were based on steep hills. The eastern flank was flat terrain covered by marsh, kunai grass, and jungle. Inside the perimeter the engineers constructed a basic road network that allowed U.S. commanders to shift units from one place to another quickly. This network was the inspiration of Major General Robert Beightler, commander of the 37th Division. The only National Guard commander to stay at his post throughout the war, Beightler was a good general with an eye for detail. Marshall Chaney's unit was originally part of the 37th, and he recalls the general's love of roads:

> General Beightler of the 37th Division was a civil engineer in peacetime and a great believer in keeping troops busy. Before the war he blacktopped every trail in Ohio. When his division was on Guadalcanal waiting for the move to New Georgia, they improved the coastal road on Guadalcanal. On Bougainville they started with basically no roads at all, but doggone, he had some all-weather roads and feeder roads built. He was restless, and couldn't slow down. After the war they kept him happy by putting him in charge of the Ohio Highway Department.

Although Major General Oscar Griswold, the overall commander on Bougainville, placed most of his infantry on the front lines, he had enough men to keep a reserve force and time to prepare defenses in depth. The Army official history of the campaign contains a splendid description of the Torokina perimeter the Japanese attacked:

> All units had been developing and strengthening positions on the main line of resistance which now consisted of rifle pits and earth, log, and sandbag pillboxes, wired in behind double-apron or concertina barbed wire. In front of the wire were minefields. Various devices were employed to give illumination at night: searchlights, either shining directly or reflecting a spread beam off clouds; flares tied to trees and set off by pull wires, flashlights; thermite grenades; and cans full of sand and gasoline. Grenades,

with wires attached, were set up as booby traps along obvious approach routes. Oil drums, each with scrap metal packed around a bangalore torpedo, were wired for electrical detonation. Fields of fire fifty yards or more deep, deep enough to prevent the enemy from throwing hand grenades at the American positions from cover and concealment had been cleared. Almost all infantry regiments possessed extra machine guns, and had issued two BAR's to each rifle squad. All regiments had constructed reserve positions.

Safely inside the perimeter was American artillery. Had the two-division corps at Bougainville been in Europe, it would have had more artillery, but as things stood it was well supported. Griswold could call on six battalions of 105mm howitzers (seventy-two individual howitzers), two battalions of 155mm howitzers (twenty-four pieces), eight powerful 90mm antiaircraft guns put in reserve positions, twenty lethal 40mm quick-firing antiaircraft cannon, and six cannon companies armed with 75mm pack howitzers (twenty-four pieces). Equally important, artillery ammunition was carefully and safely stockpiled in huge quantities. The heavy support weapons accompanied the usual complement of mortars and machine guns. In addition, Griswold was defending an air base in an area where air bases were very common. He could call upon scores of combat aircraft of all types if the need arose. Likewise, American warships could have supported the perimeter with their powerful guns had the situation somehow become serious. There was nothing missing and little left to chance.

Hyakutake and his officers created one of the overly complex Japanese assault plans that required great precision and sophisticated timing to work. According to plan, the troops would approach the perimeter during the night of March 7, cut defensive wires, and prepare for assault. On March 8, Japanese artillery would fire on the airstrip. That night two infantry forces were to attack key hills on the northern sector of the American perimeter, one held by the Americal, the other by the 37th. Assuming that these attacks would succeed, Hyakutake believed they would force the Americans to send their reserves to the north. Three days later, the major attack would take place against 37th Division positions on the flat terrain to the west. Breaking through below the northern front would unhinge the American position and allow the Japanese infantry to occupy the airstrips and encircle the GIs fighting for the hills.

Whether Hyakutake believed that this plan could work no one can say. He was known to be a cautious commander. From the dark days on Guadalcanal in October, he knew what massed American firepower could do. He had also survived the nightmarish aftermath of American assault and was one of the last to leave the island with the shattered, starving remnants of his army. It is possible that his initial reluctance to move against Torokina showed a dose of realism. Apparently Hyakutake's officers were confident, and their army was reasonably healthy. Whatever Hyakutake's thoughts, he urged his men toward doom with the sort of rubbish that was standard fare in the Japanese Army:

> The time has come to manifest our knighthood with the pure brilliance of the sword. It is our duty to erase the mortification of our brothers at Guadalcanal. Attack! Assault! Destroy everything! Cut, slash, and mow them down. May the color of the red emblem of our arms [the 6th Division shoulder patch—EB] be deepened with the blood of the American rascals. Our cry of victory at Torokina Bay will be shouted resoundingly to our native land. We are invincible! Always attack. Security is the greatest enemy. Always be alert. Execute silently.

As ready as it was possible to be, the Americans awaited the assault. On the night of March 7 there were sharp firefights between Japanese wire-cutting parties and advance American outposts. On March 8 the grand artillery barrage, Japanese style, commenced. Stan Coleman was with Americal artillery and describes the beginning of a several-day artillery duel:

> I remember the beginning of the March attack as if I was standing there today. The Japanese had dragged all their artillery and placed them in hills to the north of our perimeter. We had several visual sightings from our forward observers and our scout

planes had also picked out some positions. Everyone knew that they were going to attack because there had been skirmishing all around the perimeter. We were ready. Our howitzers were targeted on the positions identified and loaded. All we had to do was pull the lanyard and off would go the first round.

It was early in the morning. It was dark, almost dawn. Some of our batteries were already firing at a likely position. Shells going over your head are very loud, especially those coming from the Marine 155mm "long Toms" to the rear. It has almost a shriek, the shell is moving so fast. All of a sudden we heard a very different sound. It was a weaker noise, a kind of "whoosh." It was made by a shell at the end of its flight, not the beginning. It was "incoming mail." All hell broke loose. In the rear some fuel dumps went up. Every American artillery piece in the perimeter went into action.

The Japanese barrage did little damage. Relying on direct-fire techniques, the Japanese were unable to target American artillery positions on the reverse slope of the line. Because American positions were dug in, they were difficult to see and target. Japanese troops, in any case, were moving close to the perimeter. Consequently, very little artillery landed on American infantry positions. Instead, the Japanese relied on their effective knee mortars and light support weapons. After the first two days there was a notable slackening of Japanese fire. Americans picked up the location of more and more positions. American "counterbattery" artillery fire was deadly if a Japanese position was discovered. Therefore, the Japanese guns had to move quickly or face destruction. After the first two days, during which it was marginally effective at best, Japanese artillery reverted to the nuisance role of "Pistol Pete" on Guadalcanal. Imperial troops would fight without tanks, aircraft, or effective artillery. The contrast with the power skillfully used by the empire's hated enemy was almost sorrowful.

The major target of the artillery barrage was the air complex. To play it safe, most aircraft relocated to New Georgia. A few stayed to make shuttle attacks on the Japanese ridgelines. New Georgia and other bases were close by, and American aircraft were overhead daily. As illustrated by Mark Durley of the Americal, U.S. aircraft at this stage of the war had learned much about close air support:

> American aircraft attacked Japanese positions all along on the ridgelines. Some targets were quite close to us. One morning, four blue Marine Corsairs came in with rockets. Rockets were a new ground-support weapon and I had never seen them. The planes came in very low over our head, and let loose a volley toward a ridge. The rockets in flight made a fearful display. There was a tremendous concussion when they struck their target. Mount Bagana was directly in the background. I was so transfixed by the sight that I didn't notice that the Corsairs looped after their attack, and came back for a second pass. It was extraordinary.

At sunset the rain came and continued throughout the night. At midnight the Japanese assault began against Hill 700 on the northern sector of the line. Although the hill was very steep and heavily defended, the Japanese again proved themselves skilled at the difficult craft of getting very close to the defenders without raising an alarm. Charging up the steep grade of Hill 700, supported by machine guns and knee mortars, the attackers managed to seize one side of the hill and reach the crest. They did so in the face of fierce American fire and took heavy losses. Unable to push the Americans off the hill, the Japanese dug into captured American field fortifications and a close-quarter slugging match began. The next night there was a virtual replay at Hill 260 on the northwestern corner of the perimeter. The American commander later expressed amazement that the Japanese could approach so quietly and launch a determined surprise assault despite the terrain and the fact that every American soldier expected them to come. Yet on Hill 260 the Japanese likewise took serious losses and were able to hold only part of the real estate.

The fighting on Hills 700 and 260 was fierce. Although frequently hampered by the proximity of American troops, U.S. artillery and mortar fire rained down on both small battlefields. Tanks were not able to reach either position, so close-quarter combat reminiscent of Buna took place for several days. The soldiers of the 37th and Americal divisions, however, were much better trained and far better equipped than their comrades had been on New Guinea. GIs used flamethrowers to deadly effect. They had satchel charges and bangalore torpedoes in sizable numbers. Close-quarter firing with 37mm antitank guns destroyed many Japanese pillboxes. American troops covered the men attacking Japanese positions with withering machine-gun fire. Furthermore, the Americans were fighting in positions they had built. In sharp contrast to Buna, the Americans knew exactly where the Japanese defenders were located. On Hill 260 a 150-foot-tall banyan tree, which the Americans used as a forward observation post, became the visual symbol of the battle. The end of the fighting on Hill 260 took place when American attackers, using flamethrowers and phosphorus grenades, incinerated Japanese defenders who had set up positions in the tree's massive root system. By that time the famous "OP tree" was a colossal, burned-out stump. The Japanese killed 200 American soldiers in these two attacks. The Americans buried nearly 900 Japanese found dead on the immediate battlefield.

The Japanese attack on Torokina entered the realm of murderous folly on the night of March 11, 1944, when the main force struck 37th Division positions on the western side of the American line. The terrain there was mostly flat, but interspersed with small ravines and gullies. The Americans had cut down a fifty-yard strip of jungle in front of their lines and cleared the trees behind them. The first night set the pattern. The Japanese attacked fiercely on a narrow front, and seized a small salient in the American line. The next morning, American artillery pounded the Japanese, keeping them pinned to the ground. Tank and infantry attacks followed, destroying the Japanese salient. For four days the pattern repeated itself as the Japanese made small gains at night, only to be wiped out in the day.

Stopped cold on the hills, Hyakutake ordered a temporary halt. He assembled all his remaining forces and diverted them to the eastern sector. On March 24 they made a final attack. The Americans were waiting. With the pressure off the rest of the perimeter, all U.S. artillery was free to support the threatened sector. When the Japanese attacked, they faced what the soldiers in World War I trenches called a "storm of steel." Although a few attackers got through to seize yet another tiny salient, most of the Japanese were trapped in the ravines, unable to advance. They were slaughtered by artillery. Stan Coleman remembers the last night attack:

> One night 37th was hit with an all out banzai attack. We swung our guns max elevation. Our shells were going way and the hell gone. We fired all night long and into the day. I loaded shell after shell. Every howitzer in the perimeter was firing at the Japanese and it sounded like thunder that lasted for hours. When we ceased fire, smoke lay over the land everywhere. I loved the smell of gunpowder. Still do.

The night of March 25 the Japanese pulled back. The offensive was over. Several Japanese units stayed on their ridgelines for several weeks, harassing American positions and causing some sharp fire-fights. In April, their supply situation growing serious, the Japanese began their retreat back to their corner of Bougainville.

When the smoke literally cleared, the Americans began to realize what had happened. American losses on the eastern flank were seventy-eight killed. Although the Americans counted hundreds of dead Japanese inside the little salients they seized, when they moved into Japanese rear areas they realized what had been taking place. In the gullies and ravines along the eastern sector of the perimeter, the Americans found nearly 3,000 Japanese dead. As other units pushed carefully forward off the hills, they found many more. Altogether Americans counted 5,522 Japanese dead. Most of these men were not killed on the line, but rather they died in the approach. There is almost nothing in the world of battle that is more feared or more catastrophic than being hit by artillery while moving forward. This is precisely what happened several times to the Japanese. One must understand that whole companies were dying in the blink of an eye. Interrogations with several prisoners led American intelligence to believe that artillery had obliterated several rear-service units. Considering the fact that the Japanese made strenuous efforts to retrieve their dead, American intelligence estimated that 8,500 Japanese troops died at Torokina. Between February and April 1944, a period that also included many violent firefights on patrol, the Americans lost 320 men killed. As noted previously, there was an American medical team on Bougainville during this period that was studying wounds and fatalities. Although they wished very much to conduct autopsies on Japanese dead, they found that Japanese bodies had been struck by so many different missiles that the task was futile. The Americans had, quite literally, shot the Japanese attackers to pieces.

Leonard Owczarzak was a young antiaircraft gunner on Bougainville with the Americal and saw the aftermath:

My crew manned a 90mm antiaircraft gun. There weren't any Japanese planes in the area, and in February we got news that the Japanese were coming to hit us hard. They moved most of our guns to a secondary line which protected the fighter strip, just in case. The enemy never was close to breaking through, but if they had, our line was very formidable. Our guns were like big rifles: they fired with almost no trajectory and had a great muzzle velocity. It was very much like the German 88mm gun that caused so much trouble in Europe. For days we heard artillery and small arms and watched bombers come and go. When the Japanese left, I went up to the front. The MPs were already trying to keep the souvenir hunters away. They thought there might be booby traps. They also thought it was unhealthy. I can see why. The sight was frightful. I saw Japanese soldiers stacked up four deep like cordwood. There were hundreds of them. All over there were shattered trees and shell holes. We smashed them. I never saw anything like it in the rest of the war.

Three months after the Americans at Torokina crushed the last Japanese ground attack in the South Pacific, the great "decisive battle" long awaited by the Japanese Navy took place at the Battle of the Philippine Sea (June 18–20, 1944). The Imperial Combined Fleet, employing all the strength it could muster, engaged the vast American task force guarding the invasion of Saipan. The result was what the American pilots called the "Great Marianas Turkey Shoot." The Americans dominated the battle in every possible way and massacred the remnants of the once-proud and powerful Japanese Navy Air Force at almost no cost to themselves. American aircraft and submarines also devastated the warships of the Imperial fleet. What the 37th and the Americal divisions accomplished on the ground with almost no fanfare was reproduced by the Navy's fliers in the skies near Saipan. In both cases the Americans did not defeat the Japanese, they smashed them. The Americans handed to Japan the sort of humiliating defeat that Japan had dealt out two years previously to one enemy after another. The difference, of course, was that Japan had no chance for recovery. All the trends that had brought their ground, naval, and air forces to a hopeless condition were increasing in momentum. World War II in the Pacific as a military contest was over.

The dying was not. Incapable of fighting a meaningful war, the Japanese called upon their servicemen to squander their lives for an unknowable purpose. Aided by a blind and foolish strategy created by Admiral King, the Japanese raised the tactics of military suicide to new levels. Whereas MacArthur's forces cut through Japanese forces with ease because their commander chose battlefields where he could maneuver and employ his firepower, King and Nimitz threw Marines and soldiers into larger equivalents of Buna and New Georgia. Even so, the issue was never in doubt in a single battle. And the result was always the same: nearly total extermination of Japanese forces. Japan lost more men on Okinawa alone than the American armed forces did in the entire Pacific war.

Ironically, the least violent campaign of the period took place against the remnants of the Japanese Empire in the South Pacific. Australian and New Zealand forces relieved American units on New Guinea, New Britain, and Bougainville. On all these islands sizable Japanese forces still existed. However, cut off from all support, the Japanese soldiers had reverted to a semiagrarian existence. Why the Australian and New Zealand governments did not simply leave well enough alone is still a hotly debated question. Yet the campaign was never pressed with great vigor and casualties were low on both sides. In none of the areas were the Japanese pushed to the point of surrender or suicide. After Japan's capitulation, Japanese officials were surprised to find out how many of their men were still alive and still in uniform although serving no military purpose. The once-fierce and awful battlefield upon which Japan's war effort foundered provided a kind of shelter to thousands of Japanese servicemen. Had they been in other locations the Japanese troops left behind in the South Pacific might well have been sacrificed without a thought by their own government.

As for the victors, if there is any satisfaction to come from war they deserved it in full. When young American and Australian infantry did battle with the Japanese in the dark days of 1942, the outcome was unknown to soldiers and commanders alike. They fought an enemy that was ruthless, skilled in light-infantry war, and possessed a fierce courage. After a year and a half of violent, elemental warfare, in terrain so hideous it almost defies description, the Allies prevailed decisively. Their victory greatly hastened the doom of a wicked government that had spread death in Asia since 1931.

World War II was a charnel house, the worst in modern times. However, the agony was unavoidable. The Allied soldiers in the South Pacific fought, in self-defense, one of the most necessary wars in history. If political values can compensate for the death of the young, the men who died to win that vicious war lived lives of great purpose. Their countrymen today continue to owe them gratitude and remembrance.

Epilogue

War, Peacetime, and
Memories of an Old Battle

3d Class Petty Officer Morita, Yokosuka 5th Special Landing Force

During the confused fighting at Milne Bay in late August 1942, small Japanese units were forced into the rugged Stirling Mountains. Some were unable to regain contact with the main Japanese force before it evacuated Milne Bay on September 5. Petty Officer Morita was one of the men left behind. He recorded the ordeal in a diary that was later recovered by Australian forces.

30 August. Beginning of the retreat into the mountains with a grenade splinter through my right hand. Rotting of the feet makes it difficult to walk . . . sleeping in the mountains with the rain falling almost incessantly. It is harder to bear than death.
15 September. Our troops have not arrived for 14 days. I have been waiting patiently, but I am beginning to lose consciousness. . . . potatoes . . . potatoes . . . my wife . . . my mother.
22 September. Engaged a large enemy force. Lost all of our weapons and have only the clothes we wear. Nothing to eat.
25 September. I have fever and am nearly unconscious but holding on.
26 September. Our forces haven't arrived yet. No use waiting . . . I'm mad.
28 September. I detest rain. (This is the last entry.)

Bill Crooks, 7th Division, Australian Imperial Forces (AIF)

In the course of my research, I spoke to and corresponded with scores of combat veterans of the Pacific war. Many discussed the difficulties that faced them upon returning home. Many also spoke of a deep pride in their service, tempered by a melancholy feeling that something had gone wrong in their country since the war. Veterans widely hold the view that their country has forgotten the importance and value of their sacrifice. In addition, there is little love lost toward their former Japanese enemies. All of these emotions were well illustrated in the furor that surrounded the Smithsonian Institution's abortive attempt to stage an exhibit presenting a revisionist view of the atomic bomb. No two veterans view these issues in the same way. Bill Crooks, however, expresses very well the thoughts of thousands of men in Australia and the United States.

> I joined what the government called "Special Force" on September 23, 1939, the day Army recruitment opened. A few months later they changed the name to the AIF. The recruiting depot was only about 150 yards from my home, and I was the first one in line. I was young and keen. Those already in the service had priority. I had joined the Militia when underage, so I was already an old soldier at age seventeen. The Army accepted me straightaway.
>
> During the war we developed what the British called esprit de corps. That wasn't the type of term we liked, but we always wanted to prove to people that we were as good as anybody else: *period*. It was like an athletic team. We wanted to be the best. If you have the best men and the best leaders, nothing is going to stop you. Because the Militia units along the Kokoda Trail had not done well, we shifted many good veteran soldiers from the AIF to the Militia. By about 1944 they were just as good as we were. In the summer of 1944 we probably reached the peak of size and effectiveness in the Australian Army. I think it was true for the U.S. Army too.
>
> This esprit continued until the wherewithal of providing the

soldiery started to weaken. It weakened in World War I, it weakened in World War II. There comes a time when the good are used up and things start to deteriorate. Our commander, General Blamey, knew this would happen. Our population was 7 million and we had limited manpower. In late 1944 Blamey knew we were very good but were losing the ability to reinforce.

Many people, mostly family members, have asked me since the war if my mates and I weren't getting weary of the whole thing. In my unit I don't think this was true as long as the war continued. There were things holding us together. I was a twenty-three-year-old platoon sergeant and knew what was going on. I had refused a commission four times because in the Australian Army you had to leave your unit if you became an officer, and could not return. Leaving my unit was unthinkable. You had more power as a platoon leader than a commissioned officer anyway. You could carry on as a sergeant and be the Supreme Being. You had this authority and you had the respect of the men around you. At the finish of the war there were only thirty-one men in the battalion that had gone through the war from start to finish. I believe all were NCOs at the end. We understood that this was the only time we would get to live with and lead men from all walks of life: academics, artists, butchers, workers, everyone. The blokes liked you, they would do anything for you. We felt that our blokes could not do without us. You see, most of the good officers who led early in the war had been killed, wounded, or promoted. Hundreds were assigned to the Militia. So many of the new ones we were getting near the end were absolutely hopeless. It was hard to even go on leave. I worried that some reinforcement officer would get hold of my platoon and bugger them up or get someone killed. You stayed because of loyalty of man to good men.

When the war was almost over, the people back in Canberra started to realize that our old hands, the blokes we called the "Originals," were getting killed and shot up. The government introduced the "Five and Two" Legislation. Soldiers that had been in the Army five years and overseas for two could elect to take a discharge and come home. We heard about the legislation when we were preparing for our push into the East Indies. Because we were involved in an operation in progress, the commanders decided we would have to wait until its conclusion for our discharge. As planned, the operation would have lasted months. It did not matter to us that much. None of the old hands would have thought of leaving the unit while the war was on.

Our landing at the oil-producing center of Balikpapan on Borneo was the last major Allied operation of the war. Seven of your cruisers and twenty-four destroyers joined our ships on the naval gun line. As I recall, there were several squadrons of Liberators. We wanted to obliterate the Japs to keep the casualties down. That was done.

Soldiers live on rumors. Sometime in the summer we started hearing rumors that the Americans had invented some device and were going to drop it on Japan. We all thought it was gas: none of us could spell the word "atom." The rumor spread like wildfire. Some people said it was planted by the Japanese to make us ease up. Especially after the Five and Two Legislation there were some people who weren't eager to be the last one killed in the war.

While we were at Balikpapan we heard the news about the A-bombs and then the Japanese surrender. The Air Force went mad. Planes were up doing barrel rolls and screaming and diving all over. Young pilots were acting like a bunch of idiots. The Australian and American navies took it quietly. There was no reaction from the frontline units. The soldiers in the funkholes just sat down and cleaned their weapons. There was no exultation and no jumping for joy. There was no champagne around to open. There was some discussion. In the back of our mind there was something of awe. But events like the bomb and the end of the war were things beyond out knowledge: they were not of our world. I don't think things really sank in until we got home. As far as the bomb goes, it wasn't until many months later that we saw movies of the bomb going off and the great mushroom cloud.

After the bombs were dropped, all the officers and NCOs with long-term service had a meeting. Our commanding officer had appealed to us to stay on a bit. There was no telling that the war was really over. The Jap units near Balikpapan didn't come out for six weeks. They had to send officers in from Tokyo to convince them that the surrender was genuine. We had six long years of it and we all elected to leave. It was a hands-up decision. We went back up to the CO and said the consensus was that absolutely we were leaving. We told him that if the rot set in we would come back if he requested after we had a six-month leave. But I don't think any of us would have after getting a taste of home life. That was on August 14. On August 15 the war was over. On August 17 they put us on the first boat back to Australia. Trouble was that it broke down and we sat on some island somewhere for a couple of weeks while they fixed it. So instead of being the first ship home and getting all the girls, we were about the seventh ship home.

All the soldiers had some readjustments to make and it was hard on us and our families. I had married a beautiful girl a few months before the war ended. We just had our fiftieth anniversary. For the first three months I slept on the floor. I couldn't sleep in a bed. I couldn't sleep on a mattress. That disturbed my wife a bit, she thought I had gone around the bend. I was very tense and it was hard to sleep. I would say we were all dog tired for twelve months after the bloody war, absolutely dog tired. When you went to sleep of course you dreamed and you'd wake up fighting the pillow, sometimes screaming and yelling. My wife was going to leave me at one point because she wasn't used to this sort of thing. Your nerves were terribly on edge. If a train or a bus backfired you'd have been about fifteen feet in the air straightaway. If there was some explosion, you were on the ground looking for your tin hat. All of us were seeing the headshrinkers at the Department of Veterans Affairs. They'd give you a needle or a pill or whatever. We were also suffering dreadfully from malaria recurrences, attack after attack. This seemed to happen about once a fortnight. It took about four or five years to wear off. They got less and less severe as time went on. We were all issued Atabrine, and stayed that yellow color until the malaria abated.

My self-treatment for peacetime adjustment was to reenlist in the Civilian Military Force, the new name given the Militia. I worked for a newspaper in Sydney, and they were very understanding about the interruptions that part-time military service caused. I could see being a sergeant during peacetime was no good. People looked at sergeants like they were one of Al Capone's gunmen. Officers made more money too, and my family needed that after the war. So I gained a commission. I ended up a lieutenant colonel commanding a battalion in Sydney. I could go to the officers' club in white tie and tails. And I knew where to put my little finger while holding a coffee cup. Most of my men were former servicemen. We were expected to go anywhere in the world quickly. We never had to fight, but we had some interesting times during the cold war.

When we returned from the war, we could not do without men's companionship. After our ninety-day disembarkation leave was up we held our first smoker and formed our unit association. Our unit was from Sydney. Every Saturday men from the unit met in a pub and almost took it over. It was a terrible thing to do to our wives at the time. Our association grew larger as the years passed. Most of the fellows were seventeen to early twenties when they went into the Army. Many were twenty-one or twenty-two when they were discharged. The first thing they had to do was learn a skill or go back to school. If he was married he would have a family. So soldiers had their responsibilities and no one made a high wage. Many of the younger men showed up for a smoker maybe once a year. Things started to change about twenty-five years later. By that time the man had made whatever way he was going to make for himself. He was a success, a part success, or a failure. As a result, he started to seek companionship. He either needed it because of his failure, or he needed to tell someone about his success. So he went into his unit organizations. Our association, I am proud to say, is still running to this day complete with its own newspaper. It used to meet once a month, but now we meet every third month because people are getting old.

There was also the Returned Serviceman's League (RSL). The RSL started after World War I. It is a vast organization and one of the biggest employers in Australia. When we first stepped on the ship going back to Australia there was an RSL representative on board to recruit us. You paid ten bucks to join, and half went to the local branch where you lived. When we left the boat we had our identity card and the address of our local hall. At present there are something like 7,000 branches. There were many reasons to join. Australia had rationing for years after the war. At the RSL you could buy cigarettes, liquor, and candy for good prices. They had picnics for the children. Veterans could buy insurance for low rates. There were RSL halls all over the country. In the towns that's where they have all the dancing, and the bingo. The government allowed slot machines in, and they make millions off them. The RSL is still big and powerful. But it is not all social. When you go into an RSL hall there is a cross up on the wall. At 9:00 each night the cross lights up and a bugle plays the "Last Post" (your taps). People stand and recite the "Ode to the Dead." It's the same way in Britain, Canada, New Zealand.

Our relationship with the Japanese is a complicated subject. After the war, a series of Australian governments lived beyond our means. Unfortunately, in the early 1980s there was a terrible financial squeeze. We were bailed out by heavy borrowing from international banks, half of them Japanese. The majority of our products are sold to Japan. Japanese have very large holdings in Australia outright. They have built golf club after golf club and planes come in from Japan every day. They used to go to Hawaii, they now come here. Many of our jobs now are in the service industries, low-paying casual jobs. A lot of young blokes are standing behind bar serving the Japanese tourists. On top of this, 5 million of the population are Asian immigrants. Our prime minister has said Australia must become an "Asiatic country." Lee Kuan Yew, the prime minister of Singapore, said not long ago, when Britain was in the lead Australia wanted to be British; when America was in the lead we wanted to be American. Now that Asia and particularly Japan has taken the lead, we want to be Asiatic. Well, Lee Kuan Yew had a point. We ex-servicemen are much the minority because we are old and growing smaller in number. But much of this really gets under our gizzard.

The veterans affairs minister deals with us on these things. They want to call VJ Day VP Day [Victory in the Pacific, as opposed to Victory over Japan—EB]. We have a bigger embassy staff in Japan than we do in America. The Department of Foreign Affairs and Trade is now called the Department of Foreign Affairs and Asiatic Trade. That's how far the government has bent over because of the national debt and because Japan is buying most of our production. They do not want to insult the Japanese people. To many of us who left friends on the Kokoda Trail, this is hard to take.

The Australian soldier who actually fought the Japanese dislikes him intensely. It's not to mean we'd cross the street, slap his face, and call him out to a duel. We would just ignore him. We don't like him because we knew what he was up to, what he did: the torture, the murder. During the war they were vicious and cruel. A lot of our blokes believe you can't change a leopard's spots. But most of our blokes are too old to refute things when professors and journalists go off and rewrite history. They say, Oh hell, I'm going to be dead in five or six years' time, or five or six months' time, or five or six days' time: why bother.

The young people do not come into the RSL club. In our country we have four communities. There is the multiethnic community, and they have their own clubs. The RSL group is still large. You have a small number of wealthy with their own wealthy clubs who don't come into contact with anyone but themselves. And then you have the ordinary Joe who makes up the poor side of society and he's laying bricks, lying on the beach, or in jail. The RSL crowd is losing power and losing numbers. If this keeps up, every young Australian and every multiethnic is going to kiss the bum of every Japanese tourist that walks past them. But we wouldn't trust them as far as we can throw them.

The world may break down with a series of minor civil wars, a major breakdown of civil control, breakdowns in police control and a breakdown in monetary control. Sometimes I fear that it is close to that now: closer than many people think. If the Japanese yen or the Japanese economy collapses, we've had it in Australia. It's as though history is laughing at us.

I do not think the Australians of today, or the people of any industrial society, could do what we did during World War II. Look at the military failures in recent times. Everything from Vietnam to the failure of the rescue attempt at the Iranian embassy. The battle with Iraq was won with technology. But Bush was so terrified of suffering any casualties that he stopped things before the war was won. In our forces there have been recent incidents of serious training accidents resulting from simple negligence. Look at the Red Army! They beat the German Wehrmacht and won World War II. A few years ago they got whipped in Afghanistan and now can't handle the little countries that used to belong to the Soviet Union.

No, we couldn't do what we did before. The Depression hardened people. The First World War hardened people. So did the low standard of living. It is as though you lose if you win. Countries like Australia got richer after the war no doubt. But with the ease came welfare and crime. During the war Americans at Iwo Jima and Okinawa had to stand against mass fire and die by the thousands, and they did because it was necessary. When it was necessary, our blokes did the same. Now, people are better educated, but don't seem to have much to hang on to. I think they would weigh the odds, and say, "I'm liable to get killed. It's better to be around tomorrow." I'm not saying it's a bad thing to be educated or bad to be rich. But I have deep fears. I am glad that I was young when I was.

Ore Marion, 1st Marine Division, U.S. Marine Corps

No one, but no one, has explained, or been able to explain, how bonding between comrades occurs. I can't explain it, and my friends from the war can't either.

On Guadalcanal it was do or die together. We were abandoned. We were sick, hungry, and in a lethargic state. That's when you make mistakes and get killed. We suffered like hell—but together. After Guadalcanal I was in combat with many other men and I cannot remember their names or picture a face. But the names and faces of those guys I was with on the Canal are clear as if we had seen each other two weeks ago instead of fifty-two years.

I went to a reunion three years back. Old men walked up to old men. We weren't seventeen or nineteen years old anymore. Most of the people hadn't seen each other since the war. But we recognized each other right away. "Hi ya, Sark, how's it been?" "Good, Ma-Keck, how about you?" "Good. Have you seen Yogi?" We were talking like we'd all been away for a week. In our subconscious, or whatever, we had always been on Guadalcanal, and always will be. One of the people, talking about someone we knew, said, "He was one of our guys."

About ten years ago I started getting letters and phone calls from a number of "our guys." They call to see how things are. They write about their grandchildren, their health. A year ago I had major surgery. Christ, I got mail and phone calls from all around the country from "our guys." Was everything all right? Did I need help? How come I didn't tell the "guys" that I was ill?

"The guys" are dying off like flies now. But as our group gets smaller we appear to be getting closer, if that's possible. Bonding: I've given it a lot of thought, but there are still some pieces missing.

Notes

Introduction

PAGE

11 *"The artillery in this theater"*: W. F. Craven and J. L. Cate, *The Army Air Forces in World War II*, vol. 4, *The Pacific: Guadalcanal to Saipan, August 1942 to July 1944* (Chicago, 1950), p. 119.

Chapter 1

67 *"As we dug a two-company perimeter"*: Dudley McCarthy, *Australia in the War of 1939–45, Army*, vol. 5, *South-West Pacific Area—First Year: Kokoda to Wau* (Canberra, 1959), p. 284.

68 *"The weather alternated between hot sun and heavy rain"*: Ibid., p. 406.

73 *"The Mambare debouches"*: Ibid., p. 446.

78 *"The country in the Finisterre Range"*: David Dexter, *Australia in the War of 1939–45, Army*, vol. 6, *The New Guinea Offensives* (Canberra, 1959), pp. 771–72.

82 *"After crossing the crest"*: McCarthy, *South-West Pacific Area—First Year: Kokoda to Wau*, p. 109.

83 *"The golden stairs"*: Ibid., pp. 195–96.

86 *"Along the route were skeletons"*: Ibid., p. 281.

88 *"the thick white mist"*: Ibid., p. 129.

92 *Ironically, it was Germany's concern*: Robert Anderson, *Medical Department, United States Army: Medical Supply in World War II* (Washington, D.C., 1968), pp. 73–75.

103 *"Bombs exploded, flaming high-octane fuel"*: Caldwell letter, courtesy N. R. Grinyer. See also Dexter, *New Guinea Offensives*, p. 358.

Chapter 2

167 *"We came across the Japanese"*: Guadalcanal Campaign Veterans, *Guadalcanal, 50th Anniversary* (Paducah, Ky., 1992), p. 38.

174 *"All these young, spunky Marines"*: *Guadalcanal Echoes*, Quarterly Newsletter, Guadalcanal Campaign Veterans, April 1985.

211 *"I have no quarrel"*: Samuel Milner, *U.S. Army in World War II: Victory in Papua* (Washington, D.C., 1957), p. 133.

222 *"It was a spectacular and dramatic"*: McCarthy, *South-West Pacific Area—First Year: Kokoda to Wau*, pp. 456–57.

224 *"We went up the Sanananda Trail"*: Ibid., p. 526.

258 *"It had rained steadily"*: Milner, *Victory in Papua*, p. 82.

261 *"At 1950 hours the silence was again broken"*: McCarthy, *South-West Pacific Area—First Year: Kokoda to Wau*, p. 168.

Chapter 3

290 *"The 0.256 bullet"*: James Coates, *Medical Department, United States Army: Wound Ballistics* (Washington, D.C., 1962), p. 19.

314 *"We must not overlook firepower"*: Richard B. Frank, *Guadalcanal* (New York, 1990), p. 366.

329 *"No matter what . . . whistled through the air"*: *Guadalcanal, 50th Anniversary*, pp. 42–43.

337 *"We got the shock of our lives"*: *Guadalcanal, 50th Anniversary*, p. 53.

Chapter 4

356 *"One of the great bugaboos"*: John Miller, *U.S. Army in World War II: Guadalcanal, The First Offensive* (Washington, D.C., 1949), p. 318.

356 *"Whereas the Japanese"*: John Miller, *U.S. Army in World War II, Cartwheel: The Reduction of Rabaul* (Washington, D.C., 1959), p. 112.

364 *"We could see them now"*: David Dexter, *Australia in the War of 1939–45, Army*, vol. 6, *The New Guinea Offensives* (Canberra, 1959), p. 789.

365 *"At this stage"*: Ibid., p. 187.

370 *"My God! I'll say"*: Diary of Ben Love, courtesy N. R. Grinyer.

394 *"A man comes close"*: Richard B. Frank, *Guadalcanal* (New York, 1990), p. 317.

396 *"Len Edwards and I"*: Diary of "Pappy" Ransome, courtesy James McAllester, 2/14th Battalion Associa-

tion. See also McCarthy, *South-West Pacific Area—First Year: Kokoda to Wau*, p. 231.

409 *"the Japanese had closed"*: *Guadalcanal, 50th Anniversary*, p. 37. See also *Guadalcanal Echoes*, April 1989.

419 *"An atmosphere"*: McCarthy, *South-West Pacific Area—First Year: Kokoda to Wau*, p. 441.

420 *"The afternoon was spent"*: Ibid., p. 442.

420 *"Company G opened up"*: 41st Infantry Division Association, *41st Infantry Division, Fighting Jungleers II* (Paducah, Ky., 1992), p. 37.

421 *"We caught most"*: Ibid., pp. 37–38.

Chapter 5

439 *Every Allied combat unit*: John Bradley, *The West Point Military History Series: The Second World War, Asia and the Pacific* (Wayne, N.J., 1984), pp. 278–85. See also McCarthy, *South-West Pacific Area—First Year: Kokoda to Wau*, p. 531.

446 *"We had quite a few"*: *Hartford Courant*, July 26, 1993, courtesy of Robert J. Conrad.

446 *"they'd put a tag"*: Ibid.

454 *The following figures cover losses*: William Mullins, *Medical Department, United States Army: Neuropsychiatry in World War II*, vol. 2, *Overseas Theaters* (Washington, D.C., 1968), pp. 116–24.

472 *"It was grand"*: F. J. Hartley, *Sanananda Interlude, The 7th Australian Division Cavalry Regiment* (Melbourne, 1949), courtesy N. R. Grinyer.

472 *"As I read the burial service"*: Ibid.

479 *"I returned to Tokyo"*: *Guadalcanal Echoes*, April 1989.

493 *"I will never forget"*: 7th Aus-

tralian Division Cavalry Regiment Association, Bulletin 76, December 1992, courtesy N. R. Grinyer.

Chapter 6

505 *Consequently, the Japanese began:* Japanese Demobilization Bureaux Records. *Reports of General MacArthur,* vol. 2, part 1 (Washington, D.C., 1966), p. 224.

507 *Fewer than 1,000 Australian soldiers:* David Dexter, *Australia in the War of 1939–45, Army,* vol. 6, *The New Guinea Offensives* (Canberra, 1959), p. 817.

512 *"All units had been developing":*

Miller, *Cartwheel: The Reduction of Rabaul,* p. 355.

514 *"The time has come":* Ibid., pp. 357–58.

518 *Considering the fact that the Japanese:* James Coates, *Medical Department, United States Army: Wound Ballistics* (Washington, D.C., 1962), pp. 308–10, 345.

Epilogue

523 Japanese Demobilization Bureaux Records, *Reports of General MacArthur,* vol. 2, part 1 (Washington, D.C., 1966), p. 156.

Sources

This book is based primarily upon the contributions made by American, Australian, and New Zealand veterans of the war in the South Pacific. I interviewed most of the veterans personally. Others corresponded with me or sent audio tapes describing their experiences. Without exception, the men involved were candid, self-effacing, and eloquent. Although describing events of half a century ago, their memories were very clear concerning the dramatic events they witnessed and participated in.

I also relied heavily upon the official histories commissioned by the United States and Australia. The volumes published by the U.S. Army are among the most important books written about World War II. They are cautious, objective, and display excellent scholarship throughout. Although the combat volumes were obviously important to my research, the works concerning logistics, ordnance, and the medical effort contained very valuable information. The Australian official histories are likewise splendid. Although somewhat partisan in approach, they are vigorous, elegant, and accurate. American scholars should make much more use of them than is the case. All of the official histories served to corroborate the essential accuracy of testimony given to me by individual veterans. I have also listed the secondary works that were most important to my research.

Veterans of the South Pacific

Chuck Ables
John W. Augustine
C.L. Baker

Paul H. Baldwin
Fred Balester
Robert Ballantine

Tony Balsa
Arnold Bate
Charles Bayman

Dallas Bennet
Ted Blahnik
Harry Bronstein
John L. Butler
Al Careaga
Frank Chadwick
Marshall Chaney
Stan Coleman
Charles Crary
Bill Crooks
Robert F. Dakin
Henry Dearchs
Edwin Dennis
Bud DeVere
Adam DiGenaro
George Dingledy
Mark Durley
Warren Engstrom
Victor Falk
Donald Fall
Roger Fond
Ernie Ford
Clifford Fox
Ivers Funk
William Garing
Fr. Fred Gehring
Ernest Gerber
Al Glenn
Ed Grajek
N. R. Grinyer
Gene V. Friar
Raymond Hahn
Fred Heidt
Lindsey P.
   Henderson Jr.
Warren R. Hester
Leo H. Hoefler
Wellington
   Homminga
Ralph Honner

Harry Horsmann
Meredith Huggins
Frank Hurray
Louis Hyster
Fred Johnson
Walter Johnson
Robert Kennington
Art Kessenich
Louis Kidhardt
Arthur G. King
Frank Koltun
Stanley Larsen
Jim Litke
Richard Loucks
Geoffrey Lyon
Thomas Lyons
James McAllester
Herchel N.
   McFadden
William McHugh
Bill McLaughlin
Gerald T. McPhillips
Don McRae
Louis Maravelas
Ore Marion
Frank Marks
Sister Mary Theresa
Gus Merrigan
Donald Moss
Robert C. Muehrcke
Noble T. Murray
Lawrence J. O'Boyle
Arthur V. O'Connell
Leonard Owczarzak
Ian Page
Mitchell Paige
Edwards Park
Roger Park
Dick Peterson
Otto Petr

Charles A. Poux
Ray E. Poynter
E. J. Randall
Dick Randles
Albert Re
Gabe Robidart
Jim Rothermal
Nick Russo
Robert D.
   Rutherford
James S. Salafia
Joe Salini
Donald Santee
Harold A. Savides
Harry T. Schnell
William Schumacher
Vincent Seminavege
Al Seton
Stanley Shylanski
Clifford Smith
Paul Sponaugel
Maurice Storck
Jake Stub
Howard Thomas
William G. Ulbricht
William H. Vana
Kenneth
   Vander-Molen
David Vaughter
Boyd W. Vokes
Eric Wadleigh
Jack Warkow
Geoff Waters
Carl Weber
Hargis Westerfield
Jack Williamson
Scott Wilson
George Wray
Homer Wright

Official Histories

Anderson, Robert S., and Charles M. Wiltse. *Medical Department, United States Army: Medical Supply in World War II*. Washington, D.C.: Office of the Surgeon General, Department of the Army, 1968.

Coates, James Boyd, and James C. Beyer, eds. *Medical Department, United States Army: Wound Ballistics*. Washington, D.C.: Office of the Surgeon General, Department of the Army, 1962.

Craven, Wesley, and James Cate, eds. *The Army Air Forces in World War II*. Vol. 1, *Plans and Early Operations, January 1939 to August 1942*. Chicago: University of Chicago Press, 1958.

———. *The Army Air Forces in World War II*. Vol. 4, *The Pacific: Guadalcanal to Saipan, August 1942 to July 1944*. Chicago: University of Chicago Press, 1950.

Dexter, David. *Australia in the War of 1939–45, Army*. Vol. 6, *The New Guinea Offensives*. Canberra: Australian War Memorial, 1959.

Dod, Karl C. *The Corps of Engineers: The War Against Japan*. Washington, D.C.: Office of the Chief of Military History, 1966.

Gillison, Douglas. *Australia in the War of 1939–45, Air*. Vol. 1, *Royal Australian Air Force, 1939–42*. Canberra: Australian War Memorial, 1962.

Greenfield, Kent Roberts, ed. *Command Decisions*. Washington, D.C.: Office of the Chief of Military History, 1960.

Hough, Frank, Verle Ludwig, and Henry Shaw. *History of Marine Corps Operations in World War II*. Vol. 1, *Pearl Harbor and Guadalcanal*. Washington, D.C.: Historical Division, Headquarters, U.S. Marine Corps, 1966.

Leighton, Richard M., and Robert W. Coakley. *The War Department: Global Logistics and Strategy, 1940–1943*. Washington, D.C.: Office of the Chief of Military History, 1955.

Link, Mae Mills, and Hubert A. Coleman. *The Department of the Air Force: Medical Support of the Army Air Forces in World War II*. Washington, D.C.: Office of the Surgeon General, USAF, 1955.

McCarthy, Dudley. *Australia in the War of 1939–45, Army*. Vol. 5,

South-West Pacific Area—First Year: Kokoda to Wau. Canberra: Australian War Memorial, 1959.

Matloff, Maurice. *The War Department: Strategic Planning for Coalition Warfare, 1943–1944.* Washington, D.C.: Office of the Chief of Military History, 1959.

Matloff, Maurice, and Edwin M. Snell. *The War Department: Strategic Planning for Coalition Warfare, 1941–1942.* Washington, D.C.: Office of the Chief of Military History, 1953.

Mayo, Lida. *U.S. Army in World War II, The Technical Services: The Ordnance Department: On Beachhead and Battlefront.* Washington, D.C.: Office of the Chief of Military History, 1968.

Miller, John. *U.S. Army in World War II: Guadalcanal, the First Offensive.* Washington, D.C.: Office of the Chief of Military History, 1949.

———. *U.S. Army in World War II, Cartwheel: The Reduction of Rabaul.* Washington, D.C.: Office of the Chief of Military History, 1959.

Milner, Samuel. *U.S. Army in World War II: Victory in Papua.* Washington, D.C.: Office of the Chief of Military History, 1957.

Morton, Louis. *U.S. Army in World War II: Strategy and Command: The First Two Years.* Washington, D.C.: Office of the Chief of Military History, 1962.

Mullins, William S., and Albert J. Glass, eds. *Medical Department, United States Army: Neuropsychiatry in World War II.* Vol. 2, *Overseas Theaters.* Washington, D.C.: Office of the Surgeon General, Department of the Army, 1968.

Odgers, George. *Australia in the War of 1939–45, Air.* Vol. 2, *Air War Against Japan, 1943–45.* Canberra: Australian War Memorial, 1957.

Wigmore, Lionel. *Australia in the War of 1939–45, Army.* Vol. 4, *The Japanese Thrust.* Canberra: Australian War Memorial, 1957.

Japanese Demobilization Bureau Records. *Reports of General MacArthur.* Vol. 2, Part 1. Washington, D.C.: U.S. Government Printing Office, 1966.

United States Strategic Bombing Survey (Pacific). *The Campaigns of the Pacific War.* Washington, D.C.: U.S. Government Printing Office, 1946.

————.*The Air Campaigns of the Pacific War.* Washington, D.C.: U.S. Government Printing Office, 1947.

————.*The Allied Campaign Against Rabaul.* Washington, D.C.: U.S. Government Printing Office, 1946.

————.*The Fifth Air Force in the War Against Japan.* Washington, D.C.: U.S. Government Printing Office, 1947.

————.*Interrogations of Japanese Officials.* Vol. 1. Washington, D.C.: U.S. Government Printing Office, 1946.

————.*Interrogations of Japanese Officials.* Vol. 2, Washington, D.C.: U.S. Government Printing Office, 1946.

————.*Summary Report.* Washington, D.C.: U.S. Government Printing Office, 1946.

U.S. War Department. *Handbook on Japanese Military Forces.* Introduction by David Isby. Novato, Calif.: Presidio Press, 1991 (Imprint of *War Department Technical Manual TM-E 30-480.* Washington, D.C.: U.S. Government Printing Office, 1944.)

Secondary Works

Bradley, John H. *The West Point Military History Series: The Second World War, Asia and the Pacific.* Wayne, N.J.: Avery Publishing Group, 1984.

Chwialkowski, Paul. *In Caeser's Shadow.* New York: Praeger Publishers, 1993.

Dowever, John W. *War Without Mercy: Race and Power in the Pacific War.* New York: Pantheon Books, 1986.

Dull, Paul S. *A Battle History of the Imperial Japanese Navy (1941–1945).* Annapolis: Naval Institute Press, 1978.

Feuer, A. B., ed. *Coast Watching in the Solomon Islands.* New York: Praeger Publishers, 1992.

Frank, Richard B. *Guadalcanal.* New York: Random House, 1990.

Goldstein, Donald, and Katherine V. Dillon, eds. *Fading Victory: The Diary of Admiral Matome Ugaki, 1941–1945.* Pittsburgh: University of Pittsburgh Press, 1991.

Griffith, Paddy. *Forward into Battle: Fighting Tactics from Waterloo to the Near Future.* Novato, Calif.: Presidio Press, 1990.

Harries, Meirion, and Susie Harries. *Soldiers of the Sun: The Rise and Fall of the Imperial Japanese Army.* New York: Random House, 1991.

Hayashi, Saburo, and Alvin D. Coox. *Kogun: The Japanese Army in the Pacific War.* Westport, Conn.: Greenwood, 1978.

Lindstrom, Lamont, and Geoffrey M. White. *Island Encounters: Black and White Memories of the Pacific War.* Washington, D.C.: Smithsonian Institution Press, 1990.

Mayo, Lida. *Bloody Buna.* New York: Doubleday, 1974.

Overy, R. J. *The Air War, 1939–1945.* Chelsea, Mich.: Scarborough House, 1981.

Spector, Ronald H. *The Eagle Against the Sun: The American War with Japan.* New York: Vintage Books, 1985.

Willmott, H. P. *Empires in the Balance: Japanese and Allied Pacific Strategies to April 1942.* Annapolis: Naval Institute Press, 1982.

———.*The Barrier and the Javelin: Japanese and Allied Pacific Strategies February to June 1942.* Annapolis: Naval Insitute Press, 1983.

Winton, John. *Ultra in the Pacific.* Annapolis, Md.: Naval Institute Press, 1993.

41st Infantry Division Association. *41st Infantry Division, Fighting Jungleers II.* Paducah, Ky.: Turner Publishing Company, 1992.

32nd Division Association. *32nd Division, "Les Terribles."* Paducah, Ky.: Turner Publishing Company, 1992.

Guadalcanal Campaign Veterans. *The Guadalcanal Legacy.* Paducah, Ky.: Turner Publishing Company, 1987.

Guadalcanal Campaign Veterans. *Guadalcanal, 50th Anniversery.* Paducah, Ky.: Turner Publishing Company, 1992.

Chronology of Events

December 7, 1941: Japan attacks Pearl Harbor.

December 1941–April 1942: Japan seizes Southeast Asia and Philippines.

May 3, 1942: Battle of Coral Sea: Carrier battle forces Japan to cancel invasion of Port Moresby.

May 1942: Australian divisions return from Mideast.

June 4, 1942: U.S. Navy wins major victory at Midway.

July 21, 1942: Japanese land at Buna and advance toward Port Moresby.

August 7, 1942: U.S. lands at Guadalcanal.

August 21, 1942: Marines defeat first attack on Guadalcanal perimeter (Battle of Tenaru River).

September 1, 1942: Japanese landing defeated at Milne Bay.

September 12, 1942: Marines defeat second attack at Guadalcanal (Battle of Bloody Ridge).

September 20, 1942: Japanese withdraw from outside Port Moresby.

October 22–25, 1942: Marines defeat main Japanese assault against Henderson Field (Battle of Henderson Field).

November 8, 1942: Australians defeat Japanese at Oivi-Gorari on Kokoda Trail.

November 13–15, 1942: Naval Battle of Guadalcanal: Japanese attempt to land new army fails.

November 18, 1942: Australian and U.S. troops begin siege of Japanese fortified zone at Buna-Gona-Sanananda.

December 18, 1942: U.S. begins offensive on Guadalcanal.

January 23, 1943: Australian and U.S. troops complete destruction of Japanese position at Buna.

February 1, 1943: Australians break siege of Wau.

February 8, 1943: U.S. declares Guadalcanal "secure."

March 2, 1943: Battle of Bismarck Sea: Allied air power destroys Japanese troop convoy heading for New Guinea.

June 30, 1943: U.S. invades New Georgia in Solomons.

June 30, 1943: U.S. and Australians move on Salamaua, north of Buna.

August 15, 1943: U.S. invades Vella Lavella in Solomons.

September 4, 1943: Australians land at Lae and Finschhafen.

November 1, 1943: Americans land at Bougainville.

December 1943: Air offensive destroys Rabaul and Wewak: Japanese air power driven from South Pacific.

January 20, 1944: U.S. landing at Saidor breaks Japanese position in New Guinea.

March 1, 1944: MacArthur invades Admiralty Islands; Rabaul bypassed.

March 8, 1944: Japanese launch futile attack on Torokina air base on Bougainville: last battle in South Pacific.

June 18–19, 1944: Battle of Philippine Sea. U.S. fleet destroys remnants of Japanese carrier strength. U.S. captures Saipan.

October 20, 1944: U.S. lands at Leyte in Philippines. Triggers the naval Battle of Leyte Gulf on October 23. U.S. destroys Japanese surface fleet.

January 9, 1945: U.S. invades Luzon, main island on Philippines.

February 10, 1945: U.S. lands on Iwo Jima. Island secured on March 25 after heavy losses.

April 1, 1945: U.S. lands on Okinawa. The most violent battle of the Pacific War ends on June 21.

July 1, 1945: AIF occupies Balikpapan on Borneo, the last large Allied operation of the war.

August 6, 1945: U.S. drops atomic bomb on Hiroshima. Nagasaki hit on August 9.

August 15, 1945: Japan agrees to accept Allied terms, ending hostilities.

September 1, 1945: Japanese sign surrender on deck of U.S.S. *Missouri* in Tokyo Bay, ending World War II.

Military Terms and Acronyms

ANGAU: Acronym for Australian New Guinea Administrative Unit. ANGAU was a wartime institution run by the Australian military responsible for organizing the native inhabitants of New Guinea in support of the war effort.

BAR: Browning automatic rifle, the light machine gun used by American forces.

Bren: A British-designed light machine gun used by Australian forces.

Digger: A slang term sometimes used for Australian infantrymen in World War II. Originating in the gold- and tin-mining days of late-nineteenth century Australia, its American equivalent would be "prospector" or "forty-niner." The term was much more commonly used in World War I.

Knee mortar: A light, one-man grenade launcher widely used by Japanese infantry.

Imperial Combined Fleet: The combat command of the Imperial Japanese Navy, responsible for implementing naval operations. In much of 1942–43, it was based at Truk in the Central Pacific. Combined Fleet was under the control of the Imperial Navy General Staff. Its American equivalent was the U.S. Pacific Fleet at Pearl Harbor.

Imperial General Headquarters: A standing organization in Tokyo that, when it met with the emperor, included the Army and Navy chiefs of staff. In theory, although rarely in practice, it coordinated the war effort and carried out the wishes of the emperor.

Joint Chiefs of Staff (JCS): A standing committee including Army Chief of Staff General George C. Marshall, Navy Commander Ernest J. King, and General Henry Arnold of the Army Air Force. The JCS was presided over by Admiral William Leahy, President Roosevelt's chief of staff. The JCS was responsible for coordinating American military strategy.

LCI: Landing craft, infantry, a large, seagoing, shallow-draft landing craft. The LCI was 160 feet long and could carry 200 men. LCIs began arriving in the South Pacific in early 1943.

LMG: Abbreviation for light machine gun.

LST: Landing ship, tank, one of the largest shallow-draft landing craft. It was 316 feet long and could carry tanks, men, and large quantities of supplies to the beachhead. LSTs arrived in the South Pacific in early 1943.

MG: Abbreviation for machine gun.

M1: Military designation for the Garand semiautomatic rifle. The M1 was the standard rifle carried by American ground forces.

M3A1 (Stuart) Tank: A light American tank widely used by Australian and American forces in the South Pacific.

Index